Kenneth B. Murdock

ENGLISH PULPIT ORATORY FROM ANDREWES TO TILLOTSON

ENGLISH PULPIT ORATORY

FROM

ANDREWES TO TILLOTSON

A STUDY OF ITS LITERARY ASPECTS

BY

W. FRASER MITCHELL, M.A. (Edin.), B.Litt. (Oxon.)

LECTURER AND TUTOR IN THE UNIVERSITY OF READING

SOCIETY FOR PROMOTING CHRISTIAN KNOWLEDGE

LONDON: NORTHUMBERLAND AVENUE, W.C.2
NEW YORK AND TORONTO: THE MACMILLAN CO.

First published 1932

Printed in Great Britain

TO
MY PARENTS

FOREWORD

BOOKS such as the present are in a peculiar sense testimonies to the kindness and helpfulness of others. They require leisure to produce, and leisure in these days is to an ever-increasing extent intimately connected with money. It is, therefore, my first duty to acknowledge my indebtedness to those who have made possible the pursuance of this particular study.

To the Carnegie Trust for the Universities of Scotland, who in 1924–25, and again in 1925–26, awarded me a Research Scholarship, in order that I might continue my reading in the seventeenth-century divines at Oxford, I take this opportunity of expressing my thanks. I have also to acknowledge the generosity of the University of Reading Research Board, who have made a contribution of £50 towards the subsidy required for the publication of this book, and to record the further kindness of the Carnegie Trust, who have become guarantors for a like sum against loss in publication. These very substantial gifts, and the patience and generosity of my parents over a long stretch of years, alone have made possible the completion and publication of this work.

A second type of kindness, of which I am specially conscious, is the generosity with which several older scholars have been ready to share with me their treasures of knowledge and experience. In particular I would mention the never-failing patience and readily-given help of Professor H. J. C. Grierson, who, along with the late Mr. Gordon Hislop, then Lecturer in English in the University of Edinburgh, first suggested the interest and usefulness of this subject, and who during the intervening nine years has continued to assist me in more ways than I can enumerate. It is to me a matter of extreme regret that Mr. Hislop, after giving so lavishly and for so long of his criticism and advice, should not have lived to see this book in print.

To my former supervisor, the President of Magdalen, Mr. G. S. Gordon, I owe the invaluable suggestion to write a readable book on my chosen subject. If I have failed in making my book readable the fault is entirely my own.

To a whole series of librarians I am indebted for special permissions without which I could not possibly have gained access to such numbers of books in the time at my disposal.

In this connection I should like to thank Mr. N. H. K. A. Coghill, M.A., and the Library Committee of Exeter College, Oxford, for their kindness in allowing me the use of the library for study at practically all hours, and for permitting me to take to Scotland during vacations a number of valuable seventeenth-century books. To Mr. W. H. B. Somerset, M.A., of the Bodleian, I am indebted for many kindnesses, particularly in verifying dates of editions and other details which present so great a difficulty to one working outside of Oxford. To Mr. E. V. Stocks, M.A., Cosin's Librarian, and the Trustees of Bishop Cosin's Library, Durham University, I am deeply obliged for repeated access to the Cosin's Room, and for the loan—entirely without a precedent—of over eighty volumes, which were sent me for use to the Library of Armstrong College, Newcastle-upon-Tyne. At the last-mentioned I have to thank my former chief, Professor W. L. Renwick, for securing such a loan, and Dr. Frederick Bradshaw, the librarian, for arranging for the reception of books, and also putting at my disposal the beautiful Merz room of his library. I have also to thank the Librarian and Trustees of Dr. Williams' Library, Gordon Square, London, for many kindnesses and especially for the loan, in Scotland, of seventeenth- and early eighteenth-century books.

Among those who have shown me particular kindness I would mention Professor Sir Charles Firth, who not only gave me generously of his time and ripe scholarship, permitted me to draw upon his library, and himself suggested books for reading, but kindly consented to my quoting from an unpublished lecture on the divines of the Restoration and Revolution Period.

To the Rt. Rev. Sir David O. Hunter-Blair, Bt., O.S.B., Abbot of Dunfermline, I am indebted for valuable information on the gradual transformation of classical into mediæval Latin—a subject upon which there is still wanting a detailed account. To Dr. J. Vernon Bartlet I owe much information on patristic preaching, and also some useful additions to my bibliography. Professor Morris W. Croll, Ph.D., of Princeton University, and Professor V. de S. Pinto, D.Phil., of Southampton University College, have both assisted me with great readiness in forming a just estimate of particular writers in whose work they are specially interested. From Professor and Mrs. F. M. Stenton, of Reading University, I have received a variety of kindnesses and much practical assistance during the publication of this book.

Also, among acknowledgments, it is pleasant to record the generous way in which several friends have assisted me at various times in reading typed MS. and in correcting proofs. For help of the former kind I would thank my mother and Mr. A. Watkin Jones, M.A., B.Litt., now of Grahamstown University, South Africa. The Rev. W. T. Cairns, M.A., Edinburgh, very kindly read the whole book in proof, and Mr. W. G. Maclagan, M.A., Fellow of Oriel College, Oxford, in addition to sharing in the correction of typescript, most obligingly co-operated in reading a large portion of the proofs. Finally, I would pay tribute to the patience and helpfulness of the late Miss Helen Goalen, Oxford, who undertook the typing of my entire MS.

Apart from acknowledgments the principles governing the Select Bibliography appear to call for a few words of explanation. So far as is possible the bibliography has been framed to fit the threefold structure of the book. It proceeds by way of Theory to Practice and from Practice to Criticism, recording first the different works that fall under these headings, and then books in other categories which supply incidental references.

So far as is possible the lists given have been cut down to a minimum. The editions of classical texts, passages in which can be easily consulted by giving generally used numerical references, have not been cited, nor has the occurrence of the various patristic writers in Migne's edition been noted. The main histories dealing with the seventeenth-century have been left unrecorded, as also, in the main, editions of seventeenth-century authors with which it might be assumed the ordinary educated reader would be acquainted. What has chiefly been aimed at was to supply an adequate intro- duction to the rhetorical background and education of the period, and to assemble as large a body as possible of criti- cism directed at literary style, particularly as it was revealed in the sermons of the period. The whole of this part of the bibliography could not, I venture to think, be considered unwarrantably bulky.

With regard to the recorded list of sermons, after much consideration I have resolved to include the whole of the material examined. For one thing I feel fairly confident that no one is likely, for a considerable period at least, to desire to re-examine it, and I owe it both to my present readers and also to any future student of the subject to give an accurate account of the sermons upon which I have based my general conclusions. While this book deals for the most part with the achievements or shortcomings of the better-known preachers, and does not pretend to have discovered—even in Mark Frank or Peter Sterry—a neglected literary figure deserving of notice, the opinions expressed and the conclusions arrived at have at all times been largely influenced by the bulk of the matter read. There is a general consent about the practice of the age, which, although apparent even to the casual reader, only becomes fully significant to the man who has read his sermons by the hundred. Readers have a right to know upon what acquaintance a writer sees fit to form opinions. Each will have his own idea of how he would have undertaken such a subject. Some will think first of the leading preachers of a sect or theological party, others will call to mind the great men of the age who were also divines ; others still will incline to those divines whom they already know as men of letters. There are theological, historical, and literary approaches to such a subject, and in order to satisfy a variety of readers I believe I may be serving a useful purpose in presenting the list of sermons read without curtailment.

So far as editions of separate or collected sermons are concerned, where possible the first, and in all cases the earliest obtainable, was used. This has secured a uniform spelling in most passages quoted. There is one notable exception, namely South. As no complete edition of the latter's work appeared in the seventeenth century, it appeared advisable to use the Oxford edition of 1823. This has the additional advantage of being the most likely to be procurable for reference by the majority of readers. For a similar reason Baxter's sermons are quoted from Orme's edition.

W. FRASER MITCHELL.

THE UNIVERSITY,
  READING.
   July 9th, 1931.

CONTENTS

INTRODUCTORY

I. Introductory

(i) *Origin and Aim of the Study*

THE present study had its origin in that increased interest in the prose works of John Donne which has been a marked feature of literary criticism during the last decade. In particular it was desired to determine in precisely what relation Donne stood to the other pulpit orators of his day, whether his merits and achievements were to be regarded as the peculiar products of genius, or considered rather as the fine flower of an age indubitably rich in such culture, in which Jeremy Taylor and South and Tillotson are to be thought of less as isolated monuments than as pinnacles on an edifice uniformly massive and more frequently than not singularly impressive. It was felt that a comprehensive study of representative seventeenth-century divines was as likely to prove profitable in determining the place of Donne as a pulpit orator as a study of the lesser seventeenth-century dramatists had proved in throwing into relief the greatness of Shakespeare ; moreover, the seventeenth-century English sermon seemed to have quite unique claims for attention. The seventeenth century in England was *par excellence* an age of sermons. It was a century of violent theological and political upheaval, and the sermons of the period reflect its varying opinions and emotions as no other literary remains of the time can be said to do ; for the sermon, except in a few cases, such as the harangues of Tillinghast and other Fifth Monarchy men, or the addresses of the Jesuits before James II and Mary of Modena, was a public pronouncement of views held by an appreciable number of contemporary Englishmen, and the sermon has come down to us stamped with the sincerity of conviction or urgency of appeal of strong-minded individuals or of the great theological parties which were then struggling for supremacy in England. For the century in question the sermon, besides its strictly religious function, took in large measure the place of the journalistic press at the present day, and enjoyed the enormous influence, reinforced by a tremendous sanctity of authority, of a modern broadcasting company. For one person who witnessed a play or ten who happened

3

to read it, thousands may, without exaggeration, be said to have attended sermons, or afterwards studied them from shorthand notes or in printed copies. While, therefore, the immense amount of labour which has been expended on even the minor dramatists of the Jacobean period has been justified both by the relief into which it has thrown Shakespeare, and by the intrinsic interest of the study, the fact remains that the seventeenth-century sermon has been overmuch neglected.

To the initial interest in Donne and recognition of the possibilities of the seventeenth-century sermon as a literary and social quarry for the period, there was added the conviction, that, in order rightly to understand the theory of prose style in the seventeenth century, it is necessary to examine in detail the vogue of ' metaphysical ' preaching and the critical hostility which that vogue aroused. It is, in a way, remarkable that no such examination has hitherto been attempted, for there is no lack of evidence either of the corruption of clerical taste and the consequent ill-effects on contemporary prose style, or of the criticism which aimed at the reform of so obvious an abuse. Yet although the deliberate simplification of style, effected simultaneously by Dryden and Sprat—which ultimately accomplished not only the reformation of pulpit oratory, but also resulted in the creation of a plain, workmanlike prose suited for all purposes for which prose might be required—is well known, the gradual reaction against ' witty ' writing and the steps by which this simplification proceeded have been left unrecorded.[1]

This particular use to which the study of the neglected sermon may be put combines readily (it will be seen) with any study of the precursors, the contemporaries, and the successors of Donne, as Donne quite definitely, though not most obviously of the Jacobean divines, was a ' metaphysical ' preacher, just as he was a ' metaphysical ' poet, and, in order to carry out such a study, both illustrative and critical, it is absolutely essential to commence with a clear understanding of what ' metaphysical ' preaching stood

---

[1] *Vid.*, however, Professor Spingarn : ' Critical Essays of the Seventeenth Century,' 3 vols., Oxf., 1908, vol. i, p. xxxvii, who there points out this omission. *Ibid.*, pp. xxxvii-xlviii gives a brief account of contemporary European ' metaphysical ' preaching and the attacks it provoked.

for. Only by making such a start can we fully appreciate the attacks of the critics, while, in turn, we shall do less than credit to the ' metaphysical ' preachers, or, indeed, to any of the various types of preachers of the period, unless we go back beyond the sermon as delivered or published to the sermon as conceived by the preacher, and endeavour to appreciate the hermeneutic ideals which underlay its composition.

The sermon, it is clear, is a particularly happy medium in which to study the changing tastes of a period, especially where, as is the case with the English sermon in the seventeenth century, a sufficiently wide range of theological interests is represented, each making a direct contribution to the change and modification of content or structure. While the man of letters writes at rare intervals, and always with a strong spice of individuality to season current fashions, the sermon extends continuously across the century, and, by illustrating the various literary tendencies of different schools of theological thought at different periods during the century, affords a clearer and more connected view of the evolution of English prose style than any examination of the spasmodic creations of literary artists can hope to do. It is like a chain consisting of a series of minute links, and we are able, by observing it carefully, to tell where a change of pattern occurs, and why. In this opportunity for continuous observation lies the importance of the seventeenth-century sermon for literary criticism.

Since, actually, the sermon illustrates the corruption of clerical taste as well as the various stages in the conflict for simplicity, it is consequently in its ' metaphysical ' extravagances that it demands first of all to be considered. In order to make plain, at the outset, what underlies this term ' metaphysical,' which we shall find occasion to use somewhat frequently in the course of this study, it is desirable to give as accurate a definition as possible of both ' witty ' and ' metaphysical ' preaching as conceived of at the period. ' Witty ' preaching of the baser sort, which was closely allied to, and often consisted in, quips and word-play, could boast of a long lineage, but its vogue in England can be definitely traced to the closing years of Elizabeth's reign, when Thomas Playfere, Lady Margaret Professor of Divinity in Cambridge, gave solemn countenance to the fashion, and to the great example set by Lancelot Andrewes, the favourite court preacher of the reign of James I. From his own time to the present day Andrewes has been celebrated as a ' witty ' preacher, and there can be no doubt that during the earlier part of the seventeenth century ' witty ' preaching in the manner of bishop Andrewes was deliberately aimed at by younger preachers. Although a casual acquaintance with the work of the ' witty ' preachers may suggest that word-play was a prominent feature of their sermons, yet so far as Andrewes, Hacket, Brownrig, and the greater exponents of the vogue are concerned, their *wit*, as a rule, is of that " proper, grave and manly " sort, which Glanvill later in the century describes as " a perfection of our Faculties, chiefly in the Understanding and Imagination." [1] " Wit in the understanding," the same writer further describes as

" a Sagacity to find out the Nature, Relations, and Consequences of things ; Wit in the Imagination [as] a quickness in the phancy, to give things proper Images " ;

and adds :

" Without wit of these kinds Preaching is dull and un-edifying . . . but the other [kind of wit] which consists in inversions of Sentences, and playing with Words, and the like is vile and contemptible fooling."

By 1677 when Glanvill wrote, *wit*, it is true, had ceased to be primarily intellectual, and was coming to convey a sense of liveliness mingled with propriety, but the facility in discovering resemblances between the most disparate things, especially where one of these happened to be of a religious character, was of the very nature of ' witty ' preaching as understood by the Jacobean court. Spingarn has summarised the various characteristics of this type of preaching as follows :

" The far-fetched simile, the conceit, the pun, the absurd antithesis formed the basis of the new preaching. A new

[1] ' An Essay Concerning Preaching,' 2nd ed., 1703, p. 71. The original edition was approved by the bishop of London in 1677, published 1678.

manner, peculiarly adapted to the pulpit, was also evolved, as marked and definite as Euphuism itself. This was the *concetto predicabile*, or *conception théologique*. . . . Its function was to inculcate a moral truth by means of a scriptural or physical symbol ; the symbol selected seemed so far from the purpose that the mind received a shock of surprise when the preacher appeared to justify its selection by argument and by sacred authority. Ingenuity overleapt itself in seeking strange symbols and similes, and strange titles for the sermons in which they appeared." [1]

This description, however, while it covers most of the traits of ' metaphysical ' preaching, fails to bring out the unique distinction of the ' metaphysical ' conceit. The word is applied to preaching in the same sense as Dr. Johnson applied it to certain of the seventeenth-century poets, and, as Professor Grierson interprets it,[2] marks the change to " the more intellectual, less verbal, character of their wit compared with the conceits of the Elizabethans." The term is also used to denote " the finer psychology of which their conceits are often the expression ; their learned imagery," and, " above all the peculiar blend of passion and thought, feeling and ratiocination which is their greatest achievement." The definition passes over readily from the poetry to the preaching, taking with it this somewhat multiple meaning ; and if we remember that Donne was at once a ' metaphysical ' preacher and a ' metaphysical ' poet, the transference presents no great difficulty. When, therefore, we speak of preaching as ' metaphysical ' we mean that it is quaint and fantastic, not because it employs unusual or whimsical expressions or images, but that when it does employ such it derives them from a background of remote learning, and adapts them to use by a curious transmutation effected by means of the peculiar temperament or deliberate endeavour of the preacher. In short, ' metaphysical ' defines precisely the form which ' witty ' preaching took in England in the early seventeenth century. Other preachers, not of the Andrewes group, and later in point of time, were to be ' witty '—Fuller, for example, Glanvill in both his earlier and later styles, and South

---

[1] *Op. cit.*, pp. xxxix–xl.
[2] ' Metaphysical Lyrics and Poems,' Oxf., 1921, Introd., pp. xiii–xvi.

—but after a different fashion ; and ' witty ' preaching, in spite of its early association with the more rhetorical or more purely verbal side of the sermon, remains a badge of the first thirty years of the seventeenth century, when the ' witty ' preachers were also ' metaphysical ' preachers. The later preachers, like the contemporary critics, might pursue a Protean conception of *wit*, but never again was learning or passion to play so conspicuous a part ; on the contrary, excess either of the one or of the other came in course of time to be precisely the thing to be avoided.

This change in aim and attitude as the century advanced, partly a direct influence on, partly a direct reflection of, the taste of the time, had, as has already been indicated, its origin in the attacks levelled at the particular type of clerical extravagance which we have defined as ' witty ' or ' metaphysical ' preaching. The attack gathered strength, as time went on, from a variety of sources, due partly to the identification of the ' metaphysicals ' with a particular theological and political party, partly from the fact that this type of preaching, while for a period the prevailing vogue, never completely superseded the other modes of preaching even among the most prominent and influential of the clergy. If bishop Andrewes was a ' witty' preacher, bishop Hall, known to contemporaries as " our English Seneca," was Senecan in style as well as in thought. Archbishop Ussher, according to his biographer Parr,[1] during his sojourn in Oxford, " quite put out of countenance that windy, affected sort of Oratory, which was then much in use, called *floride* preaching on strong lines." Parr, it is true, is writing of the year 1642, but nothing that we know of him would lead us to believe that the innovation of plain preaching which Ussher made at Oxford was an innovation on his usual practice. Again, if the court preachers owed much of their popularity to such characteristics as we have outlined, it was for a very different reason that the City crowded to hear Henry Smith, and that he earned the soubriquet of " the silver-tongued preacher."

As we pass in swift review the great preachers of the century, not flinching when we find ourselves amid the long-winded clamours of Parliamentary preaching, but detecting

[1] ' The Life Of the Most Reverend Father in God, James Usher . . . by Richard Parr, D.D.,' Lon., 1686, fol., pp. 48–9.

even amid them the pitiless logic and the golden periods
that give Baxter and Jeremy Taylor distinction, and move
out beyond to where Barrow, South, and Tillotson, and the
lesser, but yet remarkable, preachers who were to survive
to the age of Queen Anne, present us with our subject in a
new form but with an interesting sense of continuity, a
number of definite facts emerge. The old question that
occurs whenever we pause to consider the work of Donne—
the question as to how large a part temperament, how large
a part culture, has played in producing such a result—begins
to take a new direction. While not losing sight of the individuality of genius, we come to think less in terms of men
than of ' schools '—' schools ' of theological thought and
hermeneutic practice—and to regard men rather as types
than individuals. We begin to see, that although a man of a
peculiar temperament will select particular elements out
of the common stock and turn them to peculiar uses, it is
seldom the material and practically always the artificer we
are to look to for the quality of uniqueness. A man's
theology will determine his reading : with the Anglo-
Catholic the Fathers, with the Puritan Calvin will bulk
large ; in a learned age the rhetorical moralists will serve
to supply quotations to balance the Catholic writers ; when
men, as was the case with the Cambridge Platonists, have a
philosophical bent, Plato, or at least Plotinus, will give a
direction to thought ; nor are protestations against quoting
from one or another source to be taken as literary objections
to this smothering of a freer prose, but they who protest
loudest will often be found to quote the most, so long as
their quarry is the Holy Scriptures. In every case a
preacher's theology will supply a bias not only to thought
but also to expression. Andrewes is ' witty ' at times
because St. Ambrose was ' witty,' and quibbles where he
found St. Bernard quibbling. At times Donne quotes, but
at other times he continues in a terse, crisp manner when he
is no longer quoting Tertullian. Everywhere we are met
with a man's ' school ' and its resultant influences.

Along with a preacher's theology went his general
education, and this latter, to a very great extent, explains
the rhetorical flavour of much seventeenth-century preaching. It explains also the appreciation which preaching
of certain types was able to evoke. More particularly is

this true of the earlier part of the century, although it is always to be remembered that when preaching bears little or no trace of contemporary rhetorical conventions this is almost certainly due to the theological or religious prepossession of the preachers and not to their ignorance of rhetoric.   That some sermons owe less to rhetoric than others, and some appear wholly unacquainted with the art, can generally be accounted for by the choice of the preacher or the conventions of the party to which he belongs.   Practically never, except for a brief interval in the Independent ascendency during the Commonwealth, was the function of ' humane ' learning as a handmaid to religion called in question,[1] and for the first half of the century we may assume that variations in style, whether of form or content, were directly traceable to divergence of ideal as to the design and form of a sermon, while after the inception of the Royal Society it is obvious that divines of all parties, whether within the Established Church or not, had in view the coming stylistic change.   The fact that with a common basis of education such diversity in literary accomplishment should be apparent goes far to prove that the stimulus to variety was of a most vital character, resulting, as it sometimes did, in a very thorough rehandling of traditional manners.

Theological bias, therefore, affecting the use to which men put this cultural preparation appears to account for many of the variations in seventeenth-century preaching, but the criticisms and antagonisms which went to the modification and rehandling of the sermon during this period cannot be attributed wholly to one cause.   If criticism of a pulpit style frequently originated in the ranks of a particular coterie, and was directed against the preaching of their theological opponents, as the outcry against Andrewes for quoting the Fathers or the Apocrypha,[2] or the attacks of the High Church clergy on the Latitudinarians, all criticism was not of this type.   Churchmen within particular parties, as we have seen, were not always in sympathy with particu-

---

[1] E.g. by Sydrach Simpson, in a ' Commencement Sermon ' (1653), replied to by Dell. John Webster's ' Academiarum Examen ' (1654) and bishop Ward's reply—' Vindiciæ Academiarum ' (the same year)—are other pamphlets on the same theme.

[2] Andrewes : ' XCVI Sermons,' 3rd ed., 1635, " Certaine Sermons," p. 31—' Of the Worshipping of Imaginations.'

lar modes—though on the whole the connection between
thought and form is close—and laymen were quite as prone
to condemn absurdities in pulpit fashions as were rival
theologians.   Right at the beginning of the century we find
Bacon [1] complaining that the revival of preaching at the
Reformation had led to " an affectionate studie of eloquence " which had speedily degenerated into a striving
after " the sweet falling of the clauses," and an undue
partiality for tropes and figures, and Dryden's remark,[2]
seventy years later, that corruptions in style tend to find
" benefit of clergy " and survive among preachers, reveals
a similar awareness to a contemporary danger.

All through the century the sermon clearly interested men
from two angles, the religious and the literary or rhetorical,
and men were quick to recognise the enormous influence for
good or evil which a pure or a vicious style of pulpit oratory
could exercise.   The recognition of this fact led to the
second main ground of attack on clerical fashions of taste.

The attacks of the critics had the desired effect ; but
just as men like to know not only *that* Waterloo was won by
the British but also *how* it was won, so the process of this
literary struggle is both interesting and instructive.   To
describe the process is the ultimate aim of the present study.
This it is proposed to do by considering the seventeenth-
century sermon from the three aspects of Theory, Practice,
and Criticism.   By studying the first of these aspects it is
hoped to determine with some precision what in the last
resort the sermon of the period was intended to be ; by
attending to the second it is hoped to make a fairly comprehensive study of the published works of divines of all schools
from Andrewes to South and Tillotson, and thus to throw
into relief the personal or the sectarian factor ; finally, by
reviewing briefly the criticism directed against the sermon
at various periods during the century, it will be possible to
estimate to what extent the alterations and modifications
in pulpit oratory reflected the taste of the period, as also
to what extent the practice of the preachers kept abreast
of the avowed literary canons.

[1] Bacon : ' Works,' Spedding and Ellis' ed., Lon., 1857-9, vol. iii, p. 283—
" The Advancement of Learning," Book I.
[2] Dryden : ' Essays of . . .' Ker's ed., 2 vols., Oxf., 1900 ; vol. i, pp. 173-4
—" Defence of the Epilogue . . ." 1672.

(ii) *Method Proposed*

So far as the theoretical side of seventeenth-century preaching is concerned, our enquiry falls into three main divisions. In the first place, the general rhetorical background of the period is to be considered, supplying as it does the ideals, tastes, and presuppositions of current literature. Secondly, the rhetorical bias of contemporary English education is to be kept in mind and its influence duly pondered ; while, lastly, the definitely avowed purpose of the preachers as set out in their manuals of preaching, or collected from the traditional works on preaching which they recommend, is to be used as a standard, at once explanatory of what they attempted, and legitimately applied in assessing what they achieved. In order to arrive at as clear an understanding as possible of contemporary opinion in these matters, it has been found necessary, not only to pass in review the leading rhetorical manuals and *artes concionandi* of the period (which will be found enumerated in the bibliography), and, treading in the footsteps of Brinsley and Hoole, to explore seventeenth-century education on its rhetorical side, but a large number of diaries, lives, memoirs, collections of letters, and other contemporary works have been carefully sifted, wherever there was any likelihood that further information about the tastes, desires, or ideals of our ancestors might be discovered. From publications of the last-mentioned type a rich profusion of detail relating to the subject of preaching in the seventeenth century has been recovered. The preaching scene, the *extempore* and the histrionic preacher, the note-taker in the pew, or the careful scholar adding his Latin quotations, in text or margin, before his sermon went to the printer—all are brought vividly before us. In the same way we learn what was approved of and what disapproved of, and, occasionally, why.

Coming to the practical side of our task, a comprehensive study has been made of the published works, whether bulky folios or single sermons, of divines of all schools of theological thought, beginning with the more celebrated preachers of the period, whose sermons have been examined in detail, but including also a wide range of obscure men, or sermons not themselves intrinsically remarkable, but rendered

interesting because of the part played in public affairs by
the preachers who delivered them. In this way (as the
bibliography again will show) it has been possible to form
an impression of a greater collection of English sermons
than has ever previously been considered from a literary
standpoint, to analyse their components, and to consider
in how far they may legitimately be regarded as the products
of the rhetorical ideals of the time on their hermeneutic
side, and to what extent they merit the criticism which we
find levelled at them.

The criticism of the sermon is derived from two chief
sources, and, as is natural, quite frequently leads back to
the previously examined works on the theory of preaching.
Coupled with particular preaching ideals are frequently
to be found criticisms of contemporary modes of preaching,
and these, taken along with critical works of the period in
which allusion is made to preaching, provide the more
obvious approach ; but there is another way in which the
comments of the century can be brought to light, and here
again lives and memoirs have been fully called into use.
At times, too, the sermons themselves supply us with
critical material, at times the attacks of obscure preachers
on the popular style of the hour, or, in at least one well-
known case—that of South and Jeremy Taylor—the attack
of one great stylist on another.[1]

From whatever angle we approach our subject there is no
lack of illustrative material, and although no new sermons
by any of the greater divines have been discovered, or
hitherto unknown essays in criticism revealed, it may safely
be claimed that so extensive a collection of passages from
contemporary sources dealing with the composition and the
adaptation of the sermon has not previously been brought
together and related to as comprehensive a survey of preaching, with a view to throwing light on a long-neglected subject. Not only have contemporary sources been largely
tapped, but a general study of preaching in its descent from
classical epideictic oratory has been made, the patristic and
the mediæval sermon has been examined, with at every
period the *artes concionandi* which make explicit the aims of
the preacher, while works on preaching, especially those of
the eighteenth century, which supply much criticism in

[1] South : ' Works,' Oxf. ed., 1823, vol. iv, ser. lix, p. 153.

retrospect, have been freely used. To such a study, so liberally supplied in every sense, from contemporary printed sources or the publications of various learned societies in last century, manuscript sources could hardly be expected to provide material of great value—indeed, to make a point of hunting unpublished sources, as would have been necessary in dealing with the Middle Ages, when so much and so valuable evidence lay to hand in print, would have been foolish—and the material considered, in consequence, has been confined to the published work of English divines, and to the printed rhetorics, secular and sacred, and other books containing criticism of preaching, which belong to our period.

This limitation of our evidence to published works of the period—and to contemporary work subsequently printed— raises, in the case of the sermons, an immediate question as to the nature of the texts with which we are dealing. If the sermons which we are considering as illustrative of the preaching practice of the period are printed sermons, then it is necessary to determine as clearly as possible what the published sermon of those times represented.

(iii) Sermon ' Texts '—how derived

The printed sermon in the seventeenth century, it is fairly obvious, might represent one of six things. It might be a sermon written, delivered, and sent to the printer by the preacher, as were a large number of the sermons in question ; or it might be a sermon written, delivered, and ' pirated,' often by a pious hearer, who would send it to the printer. It might be written, delivered, and edited, often elaborately, before printing by the preacher himself, as was the case with Baxter's ' Reformed Pastor,' which, he tells us,[1] was originally a sermon preached to his brethren at Worcester and printed " with necessary Additions," and with a sermon by John Spencer at Cambridge on the occasion of the Restoration, of which " the Reader " is informed that it is " not presented to the eye with the same brevity it was to the ear." [2] It might be a sermon delivered from notes, never fully written, and ' pirated ' on delivery, as it seems likely was

---

[1] ' Reliquiæ Baxterianæ . . .' 1696, fol., p. 180.
[2] ' The Righteous Ruler. A Sermon preached in St. *Maries* in Cambridge, June 28, 1660 . . .' Camb., 1660, 4to.

the case with a sermon of Donne's published in the volume
' Sapientia Clamitans,' [1] or it might be a sermon written
by the preacher and never delivered, but afterwards
printed, frequently posthumously, though sometimes out
of a kind of vanity as was bishop King's sermon, the ' Vitis
Palatina,' which was " appointed to be preached at White-
hall upon the Tuesday after the mariage [sic] of the Ladie
Elizabeth . . ." but apparently was never delivered.
Lastly, it might be a collection of sermon-notes prepared for
the press, either after the death of their author, as was
Sterry's ' Rise, Race and Royalty of the Kingdom of God
in the Soul of Man,' [2] or by the preacher himself, as was the
case with at least a number of Donne's sermons.[3]

The subject, it will be noticed, is one which involves not
only several possibilities in the nature of texts, but also
depends largely on the prevailing vogue of carefully written
or more or less *extempore* sermons at different periods in the
century. The full-dress sermon, written as planned,
delivered as written, and printable as it stood, the sermon
re-edited for one reason or another before printing, the sermon-notes written up for printing either by preacher,
pious hearer, or ' pirate,' in an age when sermons as well as
plays, and almost certainly even more so than plays, were
profitable stealing—all confront us in the mass of sermon-
material which lies to our hand. Fortunately, there lies
also to our hand a wealth of evidence upon all these matters,
and this evidence when duly considered itself furnishes us
with many interesting sidelights upon our texts and the form
in which they have been transmitted to us.

Naturally, where the question is one of arriving at texts
in as nearly as possible the form in which the sermons were
delivered, the carefully written sermon read by the preacher
must take first place in point of accuracy. The sermon
printed practically *verbatim* from a hearer's shorthand notes,
and the written sermon revised for printing, where revision
did not consist merely in addition of citations and references,
follow. All other types of printed sermons, with the possible exception of the posthumous written sermon, must be

[1] *Vid.* Simpson : ' A Study of the Prose Works of John Donne,' Oxf., 1924,
pp. 260 *seq.*
[2] London, 1683, 4to—described by the publisher, White, as " posthumous,
and not designed for the Press."
[3] *Vid.* Simpson, *op. cit.*, p. 238.

regarded as receding farther and farther from the sermon as delivered. The case of sermon-notes written up by the preacher introduces us rather to the literary sermon for devout reading than to the sermon as originally spoken, although, if the writing up of the notes was undertaken soon after the delivery, we may assume a fairly close resemblance between the spoken and published sermon. In any case, both the sermon as spoken and the various printed versions, whether garbled by a piratical publisher or carefully printed from a preacher's MS., are equally good evidence for the preaching fashions of the time, and were bound to have exercised much influence in their day.

The written sermon, printed after delivery in the author's life-time or after his death, as was the case with Andrewes' 'XCVI Sermons,' from the student's viewpoint, is certainly the most satisfactory. We feel that we know all about it, as we cannot feel that we know about the other forms of sermons. Thus Andrewes wrote, thus Andrewes spoke, thus his editors published his sermons; and whether delivered to the court at Greenwich or Whitehall, or read in the studies of the clergy or by the pious in their closets, it was thus that his style impressed his generation, stimulating in aspirants to pulpit fame immediate imitation or provoking criticism and antagonism. Yet the fact that we cannot have such complete satisfaction in the case of other preachers must not be attributed to less careful preparation or to a relative lack of influence on their part. Some of the most outstanding prelates of the day are the worst represented—archbishop Ussher being a remarkable example—and the determining factor, allowing always for accidental loss, in the authenticity and preservation of texts, appears to have been whether or not the preacher in question delivered his sermon from a written copy, or preached *extempore*, either using notes or trusting entirely to memory. In the latter case, which was the prevailing usage in Scotland not only in the seventeenth, but also throughout the eighteenth century, it is to be noted that the sermon was usually written out beforehand and then memorised, thus supplying a text suitable for subsequent printing.[1] *Extempore* preaching, in the sense of discourses delivered without previous meditation, as a proof

---

[1] *Vid.* "The Life of the Author," appended to Burnet's 'History of His Own Time,' vol. ii, 1734 ed., p. 675.

of direct Inspiration, need not be considered, as they obviously made no claim to literary interest, and seldom reached the printer ; though, in the absence of printed evidence for some of the wilder statements of Eachard and of the 'Scotch Presbyterian Eloquence,' assuming the honesty of the critics, we may refer their examples to the effusions of ranting *extempore* preachers of this kind.[1]

The ideal of the *written* and *read* or the *extempore* sermon (as described above) varied at different periods in the century, and was at all times liable to be ignored by the choice of a particular preacher. In an age of *extempore* preaching, Tillotson, the greatest preacher of the day, read his sermons.[2] As a general rule, however, certain broad facts can be recorded with regard to custom and taste in this matter. The question of practice, moreover, was merely one phase in the long history of preaching in which the *read* and the *extempore* sermon have each played a notable part, the prominence of either at a particular moment being determined by the circumstances of the time. Thus the simple straightforward address, often reminiscent in character, of the apostles and early missionaries, gave place to the patristic sermon modelled on the classical oration, both of these, at least so far as their delivery was concerned, the direct appeals of the speaker to his auditory. With the growth of monasticism came the growth of the written sermon, usually written up from the notes of an auditor, which supplied work to the copyist and edifying reading material for the community. The sermon written before delivery is intimately associated with the Scholastics, the subtlety of whose arguments required accuracy of definition and precision of treatment. On the other hand, the preaching of the Friars was of the vivid *extempore* type. At the Reformation the *read* sermon became all important, partly as affording a record of what a preacher had said, should he be questioned for heresy,[3] partly as providing a body

[1] *Cf.*, however, Nicholl's 'Defensio Ecclesiæ Anglicanæ,' Lon., 1707, p. 331, where the histrionic manner and canting terms of the Nonconformists are described.

[2] Birch : 'The Life of the Most Reverend Dr. John Tillotson . . .' Lon., 1752, 8vo, p. 22.

[3] Southey, in his 'Common-Place Book,' Third Series, ed. Wharton, 1830, pp. 466–7, quoting from Strype's 'Memoirs of Cranmer,' notes that in the latter years of Henry VIII bishop Gardiner advised a namesake to write out all he intended preaching in a book, which he should then give to

2

of Protestant doctrine which might survive through times of persecution. In England the need for sound instruction produced the 'Book of Homilies,' while the doctrinal and ecclesiastical contentions of the Puritans led Queen Elizabeth to endeavour to confine preaching as closely as possible to those homilies contained in the reissue of 1562. In the closing years of Elizabeth's reign, however, the stage began to be set for the various kinds of preaching which greeted the advent of her successor. These sermons, as produced by all schools of theological thought, were elaborately prepared and in many cases written before delivery.

Some idea of the great pains taken by Andrewes in the composition of his sermons may be gathered from a reference in the sermon preached at that prelate's funeral by Buckeridge, bishop of Ely, who assured his hearers that—

"most of his Solemne Sermons he was most carefull of, and exact ; I dare say, few of them, but they passed his hand, and were thrice revised before they were preached." [1]

Of Sanderson's preparation we have evidence in the biography entitled ' Reason *and* Judgment. Or, Special Remarques Of the Life of the *Renowned* Dr. Sanderson . . . ' [2] to which Aubrey adds the information that the bishop " had no great memorie," that when himself a freshman he had heard him " out in the Lord's Prayer," and that he " alwayes read his sermons and lectures." [3] John Lightfoot, also, in his sermon at the funeral of bishop Hall (1656), reported in Barksdale's ' Memorials,' speaking of Hall's diligence in his early cures, mentioned, on the bishop's own authority, that the latter

" never durst clime up into the Pulpit to preach any Sermon, whereof he had not penn'd every word in the same order, wherein he hoped to deliver it : although in his expressions he was no slave to syllables, neither made use of his Notes." [4]

" the chiefest man there " [i.e. present] that can read, and to take care that he said nothing further.

[1] P. 21 of the sermon as appended to the 1635 ed. of Andrewes' ' XCVI Sermons.'

[2] London, 1663, 4to, pp. 20 and 21.

[3] Aubrey : ' Brief Lives,' ed. by Andrew Clark, Oxf., 1898, vol. iii, p. 212.

[4] ' Memorials of Worthy Persons . . .' by Cl. Barksdale, Lon., 1661, 12mo, p. 62.

Here then we have evidence of the *written* sermon read or spoken from memory according to the ability or wish of the preacher. On the other hand, we find bishop Bilson, Andrewes' predecessor at one remove in the see of Winchester, explaining in an address " To the Christian Reader " prefixed to " The effect of certaine Sermons Touching The Full Redemption of mankind," that the book does not profess to give the sermons *verbatim*, for the reason that—

" In setting downe the summe of that which I preached, I neither do, nor can promise . . . the same words which I spake ; I wrote them not."

" Manie proofes and authorities " were added on publication. The date of this volume, however, is to be noted— 1599, and the place of the delivery of the sermons—Paul's Cross, where one would naturally expect *extempore* preaching. However, among the orthodox clergy, we learn from his life by his son, that bishop Bedell was able to, and frequently did preach " upon very little warning," that he prepared himself " only by meditation," but that he always wrote downe his sermons " after he had preached them." [1] There was diversity of practice, therefore, but always with a tendency towards some full-dress printable form sooner or later.

Bedell, like the majority of contemporary bishops, was a Calvinist in theology, and his reading, whatever else it may have included, had been in the literature from which Laud and Andrewes and their disciples were turning away, and which was to become more and more the distinguishing mark of the Puritan's reading. That Bedell bought Perkins' library is significant, [2] for Perkins' own works became one of the standard authorities of the puritanically affected, and his ' Art of Prophecying ' (dedicated " To the Faithfvll Ministers of the Gospell . . . 1592 ") became a notable *ars concionandi* among such. In that manual, Perkins refers to " the received custome for preachers to speak *by heart*," and advises rather a memorising of the

---

[1] William Bedell's " Life " of his Father, p. 8, § 16, in ' Two Biographies of William Bedell. . . . Edited . . . by E. S. Shuckburgh,' Camb., 1902, 8vo.
[2] *Ibid.*, p. 6, § 12.

method of the sermon than a striving after accurate memorisation of the whole.[1]   This supplies us with information
rather about the delivery of the sermon than about its
composition, as clearly Perkins' preparation might consist
of a skeleton or a highly finished discourse.   That it was
very probably the latter may be gathered from Perkins'
allusion to memorising the whole sermon, word for word,
and from what Burnet's son tells us was the practice in Scotland when his father first entered upon the ministry there.
Burnet is writing of the year 1661, but his remarks have a
bearing on the Presbyterian and Calvinistic custom of
preaching.   His father had been particularly attracted to
Nairn, " then the admired Preacher of that Country,"
and, continues the biographer—

" was not a little surprized to find that he always preached
extempore.   For though all sermons in Scotland were delivered without book, yet were they premeditated Discourses,
first written and then learn'd by heart ; which was a loss
of time Mr. *Nairn* could not submit to. . . ." [2]

Nairn, accordingly, gave Burnet similar advice to that
which we find in Perkins.

As the century advanced to the Puritan ascendency under
the Commonwealth, the vogue of the *memoriter* sermon
naturally increased, so that afterwards, when *extempore*
preaching of the recollected method type was in fashion,
the previously written and carefully memorised sermon
became a badge of dissenting preaching.   Thus at the
opening of the eighteenth century we find John Edwards,
son of the sturdy old Presbyterian who wrote ' Gangræna,'
dissuading young preachers from mere reliance upon memory, as from close reading of their sermons, and declaring
that—

" the generality of Dissenting Preachers win upon their
Auditors by this [i.e. memoriter preaching] as much as by
anything." [3]

[1] ' The Workes of . . . Mr. William Perkins. The Second Volume,'
Lon., 1631, fol., p. 670.
[2] " Life of Bishop Burnet," appended to ' History of His Own Time,' vol. ii,
1734 ed., p. 675.
[3] ' The Preacher . . .' 2nd ed., Lon., 1705-9, vol. i, pp. 217, 221, and 223.

But the earlier preachers even of Puritan leanings had at times shaken themselves free of this bugbear, and we are told of John Dod (who died in 1645) that, having found the disadvantage of " binding himself to words and phrases," which resulted in his being " at a *Non-plus* " in a University sermon—

" he resolved afterwards never to pen his sermon *verbatim*, but his usual manner was to write only the *Analysis* of his Text, the proofs of Scripture for the Doctrines, with the Reasons and Uses, and so leaving [sic] the rest to meditation, in which course he never found defect." [1]

It was recognised that—

" a man cannot ordinarily be so much affected himself (and consequently he cannot so much affect others) with things he speaks by rote ; as when he takes some liberty to prosecute a matter according to his own immediate apprehension . . . according to the working of his own affections, and the various alterations that may appear in the Auditory." [2]

The insistence, consequently, of the later Puritans, or Dissenters, on the carefully memorised text must at first sight appear a sheer perversity dictated by sectarian prejudice. But that is not the case. The earlier Puritans had recoiled from the extraneous learning and the ' metaphysical ' ingenuities of men like Andrewes with their thrice-varied MS. sermons, because they felt that such preaching did not speak to men's condition as their own plainer, more purely Scriptural discourses were likely to do ; and their successors, for the same reason, when the pleasant, topical, essay-like sermon of the Restoration period became the vogue, or the Quakers cried down all clerical preaching and cried up their own testimonies, sought by means of the strongly reasoned, stoutly supported, scriptural sermon, to establish

[1] ' A General Martyrologie . . . Whereunto is Added The Lives of Thirty Two English Divines . . .' by Samuel Clarke, Lon., 3rd ed., 1677, fol., p. 169. The first edition appeared in 1659. *Vid. post*, pp. 112–14.
[2] This is an opinion attributed to Dr. Styles, of St. George's, Botolph Lane, London, in the life of Samuel March, D.D., dean of York, in Lloyd's ' Memoires . . . ' Lon., 1668, fol., p. 511.

men in the Faith and supply a body of evidence on religious matters which should be an anchor to men's souls.   When the *extempore* mode of preaching had become that generally received, objections began to be raised to the use even of notes in the pulpit, and we find Cotton Mather defending the custom with an appeal to

" the Words of the most accomplished Mr. *Baxter* with some Gainsayers !   It is not the want of our Abilities, that makes us use our Notes ; but it's a Regard unto our Work, and the good of our Hearers.   I use Notes as much as any Man, when I am lazy, or busie, and have not leisure to prepare. It is easier with us, to preach three Sermons without Notes, than one with them." [1]

Mather then proceeds to draw a distinction between " the *reading* of *Notes*, and the *using* of Notes," and suggests pointedly that the minister should use his notes as the lawyer does his.

   That preaching from notes was still largely the habit after the Restoration may be gathered from Calamy's remark in his autobiography that on the Sunday after the murder of Sir Edmund Berry Godfrey in 1678—

" it grew so dark on a sudden about eleven in the morning, that ministers could not read their notes in their pulpits without the help of candles. . . ." [2]

Bishop Bull, Nelson relates,[3] seldom " composed his Sermon entire and committed it to Writing ; which is the Reason that he hath left so few Discourses behind him."   When he preached " he had only the Scheme of his Sermon before him in Writing."   In the year subsequent to Godfrey's murder, Evelyn notes in his *Diary*, on the 23rd of November, that he went to St. Paul's

" to heare that greate wit Dr. Sprat. . . . His talent was a great memory, never making use of notes, a readinesse of expression in a most pure and plain style of words. . . ."

---

[1] ' Magnalia Christi Americana . . .' Lon., fol., 1702, Book III, p. 121.
[2] ' An Historical Account of My Own Life . . .' by Edmund Calamy, D.D., edited . . . by John Towill Rutt, 2nd ed., Lon., 1830, vol i, p. 83.
[3] ' The Life of Dr. George Bull . . .' by Robt. Nelson, Lon., 1713, 8vo, p. 59.

The suggestion is that the preacher's discarding of notes was still somewhat of a novelty, though Palmer, in his introduction to ' The Nonconformist's Memorial,' defending the *memoriter* preaching of the " outed " clergy of the black Bartholomew-tide, recalls that—

" Whichcote, and other episcopal clergymen, preached without notes, though not without study ; which certainly is no disparagement of any one, but more worthy a christian minister than the mere *reading* a sermon like a school-boy : a custom which in many foreign churches, both popish and protestant, would not be tolerated." [1]

This allusion to " foreign churches " reminds us that the taste of the royalist exiles who returned in 1660 had to a considerable extent been affected by their sojourn abroad, especially in France, where the *memoriter* declamation was the fashion. On the 2nd February, 1679, Evelyn heard Dr. Durell, dean of Windsor, preach at Whitehall, and expresses astonishment that—

" he read the whole sermon out of his notes, which I had never before seene a Frenchman do, he being of Jersey, and bred at Paris."

Up-to-date Anglican preaching, therefore, came to be modelled on the French fashion, and the written sermon fell into desuetude. The substitution of the unwritten for written sermons is one of the changes which Canon Overton notes in the Restoration Church.[2] Elaborate and learned discourses were not to the liking of Charles II, and in 1674 the Duke of Monmouth, as Chancellor of the University of Cambridge, censured " in the king's name " the use of MS. in the pulpit, a course which was also taken by the authorities at Oxford.[3] *Extempore* delivery, it appears, was

[1] *Op. cit.*, 2nd ed., Lon., 1802–3, pref., p. x.
[2] ' Life in the English Church,' pp. 259–60.
[3] The immediate cause of these enactments we learn from Wood (' The Life and Times . . . printed for the Oxford Historical Society,' vol. ii, pp. 297–8), was the appearance of Nathaniel Vincent, of Clare Hall, Cambridge, in the pulpit before Charles II at Newmarket, " with a long perewigge, and Holland sleeves," and, apparently, a written sermon, which he proceeded to read. The King immediately caused Monmouth, as Chancellor of Cambridge University, to send a letter thither, commanding " that they put the statue

thought likely to result in lucid and correct discourses, though Sprat himself, whom we have heard described as a striking *extempore* preacher, probably compelled to revise his ideals by the thin and apparently casual tone of some of the later seventeenth-century sermons, in his ' charge ' of 1695 protested against this style of preaching.   Tillotson, the most celebrated preacher of the period, as has been noted, continued to read his sermons [1] ; but it is to be remembered that he had had his upbringing among the Puritans ; yet Barrow wrote his sermons with the greatest possible care, rewriting some of them as many as four or five times over, according to Abraham Hill, his biographer,[2] and almost certainly read them to his auditories, though hardly perhaps at such length as they extend to in his manuscripts.[3] South and Burnet were definitely *extempore* preachers, the episode retailed by Wood, of the former's discomfiture in an early sermon at court,[4] and the statement of the latter's son, already noticed,[5] being good evidence for the fact.

The Anglican attitude to the question is well summed up by Patrick in his ' Discourse of Profiting By Sermons . . .' published in 1684, who endeavoured to meet the objections of the contemporary Nonconformists that the episcopal clergy read their sermons (meaning apparently their sermon-notes), instead of repeating them *memoriter*, with arguments very similar to those previously quoted from Baxter.

" As for *reading of Sermons* " [Patrick wrote],[6] " it is not universally used : but there are those among us whom God

in execution concerning decency in habit . . . and that they have their sermons *memoriter*.   This being done (Nov. 1674) the like order was put in execution [at Oxford] by the vicechancellor, 24 Nov., 1674, by his programma then stuck up in all colleges and halls."   The chancellor, Ormond, was then in Ireland.   The ' programma ' of the vice-chancellor, Ralph Bathurst, deals first of all with immoderate hair, and then proceeds to direct that all preachers before the University, whether in English or Latin " *concionem, more majorum, a principio ad finem memoriter recitare tenebitur, ita ut vel non omnino vel saltem per-raro nec nisi carptim et strigente oculo librum consulere opus habeat.*"

[1] Birch : ' Life,' p. 22.
[2] Quoted in ' The Theological Works of Isaac Barrow . . .' edited by the Rev. Alex. Napier, Camb., 1859, 8vo, vol. i, p. xvi.
[3] *Vid.*, ' The Theological Works of Isaac Barrow . . .' edited by the Rev. Alex. Napier, Camb., 1859, 8vo, vol. i, p. xv.
[4] ' Athenæ Oxonienses,' 1721 ed., vol. ii, p. 1044.
[5] *Ante*, p. 20.
[6] *Op. cit.*, p. 9.   The objection to the *reading of sermons* is stated on the previous page.

hath blessed with such strength of Memory or readiness of Conception that they need not the help of any Notes at all in the Pulpit.[1] And others do not tye themselves to them, so as never to look off the Book ; but only assist their Memory by them sometimes. Whereby the Auditory is assured that they hear nothing but what hath been beforehand considered and digested. . . ."

If occasionally preachers tied themselves too slavishly to their notes and read all, then Patrick suggested that the auditors might look not at the pulpit but elsewhere, and benefit by hearing. They benefited by hearing the Bible read aloud, why not, he enquired, by hearing sermons, and concluded by remarking that this particular objection would hold against some of their " own preachers of great note who read every word."

The position, therefore, in the last quarter of the century resolves itself as follows : the Anglican sermon for the most part was an *extempore* address, delivered either with or without the assistance of notes taken into the pulpit by the preacher. In no case was it a *memoriter* discourse,[2] such as was affected by the Nonconformists ; consequently, the latter were able to criticise it on two grounds : if it was obviously delivered with the assistance of notes, then it was *read*, but if, as was the case with Burnet's sermons, the preacher retained the method of his address in his memory, and spoke spontaneously at the moment of topics previously thought out, then it was trifling and insufficiently prepared.

---

[1] Patrick himself was not " blessed with such strength of Memory," and, in 1671, when made the King's Chaplain by bishop Blandford, dean of the King's chapel, whether he would or not, " earnestly begged him to be excused that service, finding it very difficult to get a sermon without book."—' The Auto-Biography of Symon Patrick . . . Printed from the Original Manuscript,' Oxf., 1839, 8vo.

[2] Muralt, writing of the year 1694, makes both these points plain. After praising English sermons for their brevity he continues : " ils les lisent au lieu de les réciter par cœur, ou, pour mieux dire, en les prononçant, ils s'aident de leur papier sur lequel ils jettent les yeux de tems en tems." In his opinion this custom set the preachers free " à donner de la force à leurs Sermons, sans en perdre une partie à les aprendre par cœur."—' Lettres sur les Anglois et les François,' no place, 1725, 8vo. I am indebted to Sir Charles Firth both for drawing my attention to this book and for lending me a copy of it in which he had entered a MS. note to the effect that Muralt received a pass to go from England to Holland, 16th December, 1694 (' Cal. S. P. Dom,' 357, 1694–5). References in the text show that the writer's visit occurred before the death of Queen Mary.

To the former the Nonconformist could oppose his *memoriter* discourse, to the latter, ignoring for the moment his objections to *read* sermons, his own carefully written sermons. It was a position from which there was no escape.

So far as we are concerned with the subject in its relation to the nature of printed sermon-texts, the following conclusions may be regarded as more or less definite. Throughout the whole century the Puritans favoured the carefully written sermon, delivered *memoriter*, although some of their number considered notes sufficient, and probably only wrote up their sermons for printing after they had been preached. Where the sermon was written *in extenso* for memorisation naturally a reliable text was available for publication. Anglican practice, on the contrary, varied before and after the civil wars. The earlier Anglicans wrote their sermons before delivery, whereas the Restoration preachers favoured notes and schemes retained by the memory. Yet Donne, as we have seen, probably was an exception to the older custom as Barrow and Tillotson were to the later. Wherever there was a written sermon a good text came to the printers' hands, though it might not represent a *verbatim* report of the sermon as delivered. For literary and critical purposes, however, this uncertainty is not of importance. The second possibility, moreover, leads to the second question with regard to texts, the re-editing of these by their authors previous to publication.

Baxter is one of our best authorities for information about the republishing or alteration of sermons on their publication, and an authority all the more reliable because of his freedom from all personal ostentation or desire to attract by mere literary brilliance. Among records of the printing of particular sermons which we have in the ' Reliquiæ,' we find him saying :

" About that time I had preached a Sermon at *Worcester*, which (though rude and not polished) I thought meet to print, under the Title of the *The True Catholic*, and the *The Catholick Church Described*," [1]

an instance, it would appear, not only of a sermon not carefully written up but of his bare notes for one sermon

[1] ' Reliquiæ,' p. 112.

being made serve for the matter of two. His 'Treatise of Conversion,' he informs us, consisted of

" some plain Sermons on that Subject, which Mr. *Baldwin* (an honest young Minister that had lived in my House, and learnt my proper Characters, or Short-hand, in which I wrote my Sermon Notes) had transcribed out of my Notes. And though I had no leisure, for this or other Writings, to take much care of the stile, nor to add Ornaments, or Citations of Authors, I thought it might better pass as it was, than not at all ; . . ." [1]

The treatise on 'The Divine Life,' prepared for the press at the request of the Countess of Balcarres, was similarly printed without elaborate additions, " being," as he says, " but popular Sermons preached in the midst of diverting Businesses. . . ." [2] On the other hand, an Assize sermon on 'Galatians vi. 16 ' was later enlarged " to a Treatise, entituled, *The Crucifying of the World by the Cross of Christ.*" [3]

On the whole, however, Baxter's evidence is of a negative character (although he establishes one important point— the intimate relationship of the sermon and the treatise, important in the case of a man like Bunyan, whose direct sermons are lacking), and we have to turn to other preachers for examples of the motives which customarily led to the altering of sermons. Playfere, some of whose confidences we have already received, in an epistle dedicatory to Sir Edward Denny,[4] explains that he delivered so much of the matter of his sermon

" as filled up the ordinary time of an houre : but that was scarce halfe the Sermon. I vttered no more, to auoid the Offence of the hearer ; I wrote no lesse, to procure the profit of the reader. . . . I thought good in publishing this Sermon rather to inlarge it to the comprehension I had conceiued and meditated in my minde, then to scant it according to that strict compasse of time which I was tied to in the pulpit."

The sermon in question was deliverd before Prince Henry at Greenwich in 1604. In his dedication of an earlier sermon,

[1] ' Reliquiæ,' p. 114. [2] *Ibid.*, p. 120. [3] *Ibid.*, p. 116.
[4] Of " The Sick-Mans Covch," in ' The Whole Sermons . . .' 1623.

'The Path-Way to Perfection,' preached at St. Mary's Spittal in 1593, the same preacher supplies us with information as to the adding of quotations which was frequently incidental to printing.

" Gentle Reader " (he writes) " the sentences are so framed, as thou maist reade them without any regard of the Marginall notes, . . . Doe therefore herein as thou shalt thinke best. The quotations which are marked without a Parentheses, as thus, a b c, were all uttered when the Sermon was preached. The rest which are marked with a Parentheses, as thus (a) (b) (c), were thought conuenient to bee printed, though not the quotations themselves, but only the matter contained in them was preached."

Here, therefore, we have an example of a sermon expanded in order to increase the serviceableness to the reader, with references added so that support might be given to the particular points made. Edification and conviction supply the motive. Some preachers, however, probably elaborated their discourses with a view to displaying their own learning, and Sherman may have had this fact in mind when dedicating his volume of College Commonplaces, ' A Greek In the Temple,' to the Governors of the Charterhouse School, whom he assured that he did not add to them or polish them for publication,[1] though the fact that he mentions that they were the first commonplaces he made might be construed as implying that he intended to apologise for these early efforts, which he was publishing just as they were delivered. Sherman's discourses were immensely learned college exercises full of Greek quotations and references to secular learning, though the author warns his hearers against " A fastuous affected swelling exercise," and urges " in the dressing of thy notionall matter," modesty and restraint " as in the clothing of thy real matter, thy body." [2] Baxter's remarks, already quoted, obviously imply that a considerable amount of improving of sermons went on, and Bradbury's ' Epistle to the Reader ' before ' God's Empire Over the Wind '—a sermon occasioned by the great storm of 1703—tends to confirm us in the belief.

[1] *Op. cit.*, Camb., 1641, 4to.   [2] *Ibid.*, p. 7.

" This sermon " (Bradbury wrote) " was designed for no
other Sense than the Ear, and no further a spread than
among a single Congregation, and therefore it's easie to observe, with how little Guard either of Accuracy or Language
it comes out. As my own hurry in making it ready for
the Press, allow'd me only Time to transcribe it, so indeed
I durst not be at any New Pains to prepare it for the Publick Tast ; lest it should appear more like a Gaudy jest ;
than a Memorial, or an Improvement of the late Storm." [1]

The written sermon, therefore, sometimes, if the preacher
had " Leisure for Polishing and Exactness, or any Ornament " (to use Baxter's phrase), and was not driven to
publish by " Apprehensions of *Present Usefulness or Necessity*," [2] appeared in print with more literary grace than its
pulpit prototype ; if sermon-notes were used these might
afterwards form the basis of published sermons slightly
different from those delivered orally, as happened in the
case of Donne's sermon preached at The Hague,[3] and to
Baxter's sermons in their enlarged *treatise* form. The publication of the posthumous written sermon was also at times
an occasion for the alteration of the written text. Particularly was this so in Tillotson's edition of Barrow's sermons.
Not only did Tillotson seek to refine upon certain of Barrow's
expressions, and excise the more unusual words which he
found in his manuscripts, but he took considerable liberties
in dividing and rearranging a number of sermons. The
publication by Napier in the last century of an edition of
Barrow's works from the author's own manuscripts, which
can be compared with Tillotson's edition, reveals the extent
of this tinkering, although it is only fair to add that some of
the divergencies to be found are due to passages adopted
by Napier from " second, third, and even fourth drafts "
of particular sermons. But the fact remains that Barrow's
MSS. show clearly " the divisions made in Tillotson's handwriting, as directions to the printer." With regard to two
sermons, the former divided into four, the latter into five,
shorter sermons, and which, reprinted in entirety, extend

---

[1] *Op. cit.*, Lon., 1704, 8vo. The great storm occurred on the 27th November,
1703. *Vid.* Burnet : ' Hist. of His Own Time,' vol. ii, 1734 ed., p. 353.
[2] Baxter : ' Reliquiæ,' 1696, p. 124.
[3] *Vid.* ' LXXX Sermons,' heading to Sermon lxxi.

respectively to seventy-nine and one hundred and twenty-six octavo pages in Napier's edition, there seems reasonable doubt as to their having been delivered at such length,[1] but in at least one other instance, where no fewer than three MS. drafts of a sermon exist, "one the copy used by the printer, and two others, . . . in none of these copies is there any indication of the threefold division adopted by Tillotson."[2]   The extent of Tillotson's editing consequently becomes clear.

Where the posthumous editing was from sermon-notes the difficulties experienced were great, but the divergencies which were bound to occur are more pardonable.   Which-cote, for example, published nothing during his lifetime, and no record of his discourses was available except "hastily written and very imperfect notes," which, according to Salter in his preface to the *Aphorisms*, when strung together make it impossible for critics to do more than judge of the general tenor of his preaching.[3]   A text so composed may serve to confirm a previously formed opinion as to the thought or exegetical method of a particular group of divines.   It can do little else.   It may even possess consider-ably less resemblance to the *spoken* sermon than do those types of text which we have yet to consider, the ' pirated ' sermon printed from shorthand or other notes taken by an auditor, or the sermon from such notes published more or less by consent, and at times after the death of the preacher. It is, however, the last *legitimate* text in a series which, starting with the written sermon printed *verbatim*, embraces the written sermon elaborated from motives of religious usefulness or personal vanity, or altered to suit the whim of an editor, and the sermon which represents in a literary form the main topics found in a preacher's notes, or touched upon in an *extempore* pulpit address. The question of note-taking, shorthand, and the ' pirating ' of sermons opens up fresh interests and calls for separate consideration.

(iv) *Note-taking, Shorthand, and the ' Pirated ' Sermon*

Note-taking " after " preachers (as the phrase was) was characteristic of seventeenth-century religious auditories.

---

[1] Ed. cit. Preface, p. xv.   [2] *Ibid.*
[3] 1753 ed., pp. x and xiv, quoted by J. Bass Mullinger : ' The University of Cambridge,' Camb., 1873–1911, vol. iii, p. 590.

When we find Mrs. Hutchinson writing about the *repetition* of sermons then in vogue :

" By the time I was four years old I read English perfectly, and having a great memory, I was carried to sermons ; and while I was very young could remember and repeat them exact . . ." [1]

we realise that we are dealing with an age in which the sermon was regarded as of great importance ; and Aubrey's statement that ' the matchless Orinda '

" was very religiously devoted when she was young ; prayed by herself an hower together, and tooke sermons *verbatim* when she was but 10 years old," [2]

further emphasises the fact that from their earliest years children of the period were encouraged to memorise carefully or preserve by means of notes the sermons which they heard.[3] That this custom was bound to have considerable effect both on the theory and criticism of the pulpit oratory of the time is obvious, and one of the most important ways in which the sermon influenced the literary taste of the century is revealed. The intention, however, of those who encouraged, and even enforced, note-taking of sermons by children, was not merely pious, nor dictated, as was much sixteenth-century note-taking by adults, by fear of Romanist persecution and a desire to preserve a sound body of Protestant exegesis ; it was rather a distinct feature of the public education of the day on its rhetorical side, and had in view not only the religious welfare of the young note-taker, but

---

[1] ' Memoirs of the Life of Colonel Hutchinson . . . with Additional Notes by C. H. Firth, . . .' Lon., 1906, p. 15.

[2] ' Brief Lives,' ed. Clark, vol. ii, p. 153.

[3] Sir Ralph Verney's advice to his brother-in-law, in a letter of 1650, so far as it relates to shorthand, is quite exceptional : " Let not your girle learne Latin, nor Shorthand ; the difficulty of the first may keepe her from that Vice, for soe I must esteeme it in a woeman ; but the easinesse of the other may bee a prejudice to her ; for the pride of taking Sermon noates hath made multitudes of woemen most unfortunate."—' Memoirs of the Verney Family . . .' 2nd ed., 1904, vol. i, p. 500. A more typical advice is that given thirty years earlier by Lady Hatton to her son, Christopher, then at Jesus College, Cambridge : " Heare sermons ; strive to take notes that you may meditate on them, . . ."—' Correspondence of the Family of Hatton . . . A.D. 1601–1704 . . .' Camden Soc., 2 vols., 1878, vol. i, p. 3.

his worldly welfare also, which was most likely to be ensured by a thorough mastery of the *theme*. And the sermon, as the schoolmaster saw it, was a fine example of the *theme*.

The late Professor Foster Watson, in ' The English Grammar Schools to 1660 : their Curriculum and Practice ' [1] has collected an invaluable amount of information about the education of the seventeenth century, its rhetorical bias, the relation of the latter to the sermon and consequently the purpose of note-taking, and further the relation of this note-taking to the development of shorthand. In many instances Foster Watson found his evidence in John Brinsley's ' Ludus Literarius,' first published in 1612 and reprinted in 1627, and in Charles Hoole's ' New Discovery of the Old Art of Teaching Schoole,' an educational work of 1659, so that we are able to get fairly complete information on the subject over a great part of our century.

Brinsley was born either in 1564 or 1565, took his bachelor's and master's degrees from Christ's, Cambridge, and became a minister and master of the public school at Ashby-de-la-Zouch in Leicestershire. He was " a strict puritan, not conformable wholly to the ceremonies of the Church of England," and about 1619 was prosecuted and " enforced from keeping school." He therefore went to London, where he became a lecturer, and eventually died. His wife was a sister of bishop Hall of Norwich, and the latter contributed ' A Commendatorie Preface ' to the first edition of the ' Ludus Literarius.' [2] The theological outlook of the man is more or less clear from these details.   In chapter xxii of his work, that entitled ' Of knowledge of the grounds of Religion and training of the schoolboys therein,' he advised :

" For the Sabbaths and other dayes when there is any Sermon, cause everyone to learne something at the Sermons. The very lowest [i.e. youngest] to bring some notes."

All who could write, he insisted, must take notes. The monitors were to enforce this, but with care, so as to prevent

[1] Camb., 1908.
[2] Reprint of the ' Ludus Literarius.' Edited with Introduction and Bibliographical Notes by E. T. Campagnac, Liverpool, 1917, Introd., p. xxxiii.

causing a hubbub, and the note-takers were not to stir
" out of their places to seeke of one another." Those who
had had practice in such note-taking were to set down—

" 1. The Text, or a part of it. 2. To marke as neere as
they can, and set downe every doctrine, and what proofes
they can, the reasons and the uses of them."

In the highest forms all the sermon was to be written down.[1]
Next morning the boys could be set to turn it into Latin
by way of an exercise, and a week later " someone of the
higher formes might be appointed in order to make a
repetition of the whole Sermon without book . . ." [2]
Practically half a century later Hoole was quite as earnest
about the attention to be paid to sermons for the same reason,
but he advised the writing of notes, by the younger scholars
of " as much, and in as good order as possibly may be," by
the older ones from memory, rather than from note-taking
in church, which he believed, no doubt with reason, tended
to cause a " stirre." [3]

Brinsley's injunction that the highest form should reproduce the sermon in its entirety reminds us of the close connection between the note-taking of sermons and shorthand.[4]
Attempts at the formation of systems of shorthand for this
purpose naturally came from the adult note-takers whose
labours, as has been hinted, were more than likely inspired
by their Protestant zeal. Several of the early English
manuals on the subject refer expressly to the possibility of
the device for preserving sermons. Thus Peter Bales, who
had published ' The Writing Schoolmaster . . . The first
Booke, Entituled : The Arte of Brachygraphie . . .' in 1590,
in reissuing his manual seven years later, mentioned that
one of the uses which might be made of his system was the
" taking of Sermons and Lectures, or any other Orations
or speeches, worthie the writing," and he adds :

[1] Ed. cit., p. 255.
[2] *Ibid.*, pp. 257 and 258.
[3] ' A New Discovery of the Old Art of Teaching Schoole . . . edited . . .
by E. T. Campagnac,' Liverpool, 1913, pp. 270–71.
[4] Simon Patrick, in his ' Auto-Biography '—first printed at Oxford in 1839
—writes : ' I had an early sense of religion . . . which was much increased
by my attending to sermons : for having, when I was a school boy, learnt
to write in characters, my father required me to take sermons I heard in that
manner, and read them over when I came at home."—*Op. cit.*, p. 5.

" Sermons, Lectures, and Orations of excellent learned men, shall hereby be kept, recorded, and registered, to the generall benefite of all ages and posterities." [1]

Thomas Shelton, the author, in 1630, of ' Short-writing,' in his address " To the Reader " before ' Zeilographia ' in 1650, recalled the fact that the homilies of Chrysostom and others were taken by shorthand,[2] and pointed to its similar employment in his own day by means of which the sermons of Preston, Sibs, and divers others were " taken and published, which else had perished." Should a persecution such as took place in Mary's reign occur again much sound teaching could be preserved in this way. Again, in some commendatory verses prefixed to Job Everardt's ' Epitome of Stenography,' published in 1658, we read :

> " *Letters* and Other *things* may bee
> *Transcribed* with Celeritie :
> And *Sermons* writ, even from the Lip . . ." [3]

The desire to preserve sermons in as entire a form as possible obviously stimulated the improvement of stenographic systems, while the existence of such systems was found to react in turn on the note-taking of sermons. What the boy learned at school as part of his religious as well as rhetorical education piety suggested to the grown man to continue to practise, and the fact that all preachers did not write their sermons *in extenso*, nor make haste to publish readable copies of their discourses, would lead their admirers to endeavour to *take* as much as possible of what they heard. Particularly was this so among the Puritans. It is interesting to note, however, that the system most in use, and especially

---

[1] ' The Arte of Brachygraphie : *that is* To write as fast as a man speaketh treatably . . .' Lon., 1597, 12mo, unnumbered pages, B, B *verso*, and B ii.

[2] Haarhoff : ' Schools of Gaul,' Oxford, 1920, p. 185, mentions that " one of the borrowings from the pagan schools which the Church found most useful was shorthand. The bishops had their ' notarii ' just as much as the officials of the imperial Civil Service. They were employed to take down the proceedings of the Councils, the *acta* of the martyrs, and the speeches and sermons of the prominent clergy." This classical shorthand, however, became in course of time a lost art.

[3] John Phillips, Milton's nephew, in both his satires against the Puritans— ' A Satyr Against Hypocrites,' Lon., 1677, 4to, and ' Speculum Crape-Goworum, The Second Part . . .' Lon., 1682, 4to—makes much of the craze for taking sermons by shorthand.—*Vid.* former, pp. 5 and 8, latter, p. 11.

among the Puritans, was not one of those already mentioned, but that invented by Rich ; so much was this the case that for a person to use Rich's system was held to coincide with the holding of Puritan views in religion, or a definite connection with the Puritan party. The editor of bishop Cartwright's *Diary* alludes to this fact when describing the manuscript from which the diary was printed.

" In some places " (he says) " there are passages which are written in character. The system of short-hand which the Bishop used bespeaks his Puritan origin. It is that of Rich, which appears to have been constructed for the peculiar purpose of taking down the Sermons of Puritan Divines. . . ." [1]

This same system of shorthand, Orton informs us, Doddridge wrote himself, and " one of the first things he expected from his pupils " was to learn it. [2]

Of the habit of writing down sermons as they were preached there is no lack of evidence. In Clarke's ' Lives ' we are told of Hildersham that—

" he was alwaie's a delighted frequenter of the publique Assemblies . . . . . . He used often even in his old age to write Sermons in the Church," [3]

and Manningham's *Diary* in England and Hay of Craignethan's in Scotland afford proof of the extraordinary interest with which sermons were attended and their main doctrines often fairly fully noted down. Hay's *Diary* was not his customary book of sermon-notes, and the fact that we have fuller particulars of certain sermons was apparently due to some mishap like that which occurred at Humbie when he heard Calderwood the historian preach and records—

" becaus [sic] my man had lost my sermon writt book, I resolved to write this dayes sermons on this book. . . ." [4]

[1] ' The Diary of Dr. Thomas Cartwright, bishop of Chester . . .' edited for the Camden Society, 1843, by the Rev. Joseph Hunter, F.S.A., Pref., p. xv.

[2] ' Memoirs of the Life . . . of the late Rev. Philip Doddridge, D.D.,' Lon., 1819, 8vo, p. 65.

[3] 1677 (3rd) ed., p. 122.

[4] ' The Diary of Andrew Hay of Craignethan, 1659–1660,' edited by Alex. George Reid, F.S.A., Scot., Edin. (Scottish Hist. Soc.), 1901, p. 13.

Manningham's *Diary*, which deals with an earlier period, is definitely a diary, a large portion of which is devoted to analyses of the various sermons heard by a lawyer of the period.[1] It is one of the great sources of information for details concerning preaching. Its records of sermons are clearly written up from memory day by day, and probably owe nothing to note-taking at the moment, but the desire to retain the main heads of treatment is one and the same.

Apart from the bearing of note-taking on the theory and criticism of the sermon, to which fuller reference will be made later, the custom reacted interestingly on the procuring of printed texts. Dr. Evelyn Simpson, in her discussion of one of Donne's sermons appearing in ' Sapientia Clamitans,' already alluded to,[2] has illustrated some of the possibilities of the case from different editions, authentic and ' pirated ' of a sermon by Henry Smith, a Puritan lecturer of St. Clement Danes, whose preaching was in great estimation round about 1590. This preacher's popularity invited piracy, and we have in one instance a sermon printed from his manuscript and a ' pirated ' version of the same, which is openly described as a sermon " taken by Characterie," [3] and " published for the benefite of the faithfull." Smith's printed sermons supply us also with an instance of a sermon " taken by Characterie," and published (apparently without the preacher's consent), the same sermon " taken by Characterie and examined after " (presumably by the preacher), and the further version of the same, " newly examined and corrected by the author." [4] This goes to show that the printing of sermons from notes taken by auditors might be of two sorts, either deliberate pirating, for pious or commercial reasons, or printing by connivance, or even with the consent of the preacher. Where sermons were delivered *extempore* it is obvious that considerable variation might exist between the sermon as written up and published from the preacher's notes and the sermon as

[1] ' Diary of John Manningham, of the Middle Temple . . .' 1602–1603,' edited . . . by John Brown Esq., for the Camden Society, 1868, *vid.*, pref., pp. xvi and xvii.

[2] *Vid. ante*, p. 15 : and ' A Study of the Prose Works of John Donne,' pp. 268, 269.

[3] ' True Trial of Spirites,' 1591, was printed from Smith's MS. ; the ' pirated ' version—' A Fruitful Sermon . . . by Henrie Smith &c.' the same year.

[4] This is the ' Benefit of Contentation,' first two versions published in 1590, the third in 1591.

published from the notes of a stenographist. The latter may quite well be the more accurate report of the sermon as delivered ; the former represents the preacher's main intention in approaching his subject, or his later reflections on the same theme. The former, consequently, is likely to be the more literary and the more suitable field for criticism, though, if the latter was based upon fairly full notes, afterwards revised by the preacher, it may not only be considered preferable in point of accuracy, but also tolerably representative of the popular sermon of the time.

That contemporary ' pirating ' at times was carried on with an amount of connivance seems clear from the remarks of certain preachers. Thus, in dedicating ' The Meane in Mourning ' to Lady Carey in 1595, Playfere wrote—

" . . . this Sermon hath beene twice printed already without my procurement or priuitie any manner of way " ;

and Nathaniel Shute, " Rector of the Parish of Saint Mildred *in the Poultry*, London," in his epistle dedicatory to ' Corona Charitatis,' a funeral sermon preached in 1626, alluded to

" the common bridge of Pretence vnder which most Bookes passe, . . . the Abetting of diuers friends to these Publications."

The pretence is a familiar one where secular literature is concerned, and it emphasises the theological bias of the age to note that it was employed to excuse or facilitate the issue of sermons in printed form.

Genuine piracy, however, was easier and probably commoner, Donne's ' Sermon of Valediction,' as printed in ' Sapientia Clamitans,' being a good specimen of the process. That the printed products of such piracy often grossly misrepresented the style and tenor of thought of the preacher was only to be expected, and Outram's editor in publishing ' Twenty Sermons ' in 1682, protested against this fact. Outram, in his lifetime, it appears, could not be prevailed upon to print his sermons, but after his death a bookseller published six sermons purporting to be his, with a prefatory epistle which announced that these were printed from shorthand copies taken many years previously. Even had the statement been true the bookseller had no right to publish the transcripts, and in this instance the shorthand copies were not adequate representatives of typical sermons by this preacher, being in two cases mere portions of larger addresses. The Scots editor of Andrew Gray's *Communion Sermons* was fully alive to the injustice addresses so derived might do to the reputation of a preacher, and was careful to warn his readers that the sermons published were " taken from [Gray's] Mouth by the short Hand : So that what of them may not run so smoothly thro' [sic] the Want of some fit Word, or, Perhaps, Sentence, is not to be imputed to the Author but the Writer." [1] The warning is timely, and recalls us to our immediate interest in the subject. Taken along with our knowledge of how sermons were prepared, delivered, and edited for publication, our evidence as to note-taking, whether by long hand or stenography, with its results, completes the fairly accurate but variegated information it is possible to gather about the published sermon of the seventeenth century. It is clear that the sermon as published represents many possibilities, and that, in criticism especially, one must be keenly alive to these ; we must not censure as abrupt what is merely imperfectly reported, nor regard as over-erudite for an ordinary audience what has been carefully edited in order to give emphasis from many citations. Yet diverse as the sources of the printed texts are, they may be taken on the whole as a fairly true representation of typical sermons of the period—the more so, as many of those derived from impugnable sources tally so well with those whose authenticity is less reliable—and, allowing in particular cases for such facts as have been enumerated, made the basis for a study of the sermon on its literary side.

[1] ' Eleven Communion Sermons,' Edin., 1716, 8vo, " To the Reader."

PART I

THEORY: RHETORICAL AND HOMILETICAL

II. The Approach to Theory : General Rhetorical Background

IN order in any way to form a clear conception of the English sermon in the seventeenth century, it is necessary in the first place to endeavour, as far as is possible, to approach it from the point of view of contemporaries. If at times we are arrested by the passionate declamations of Donne, or suffer ourselves to be borne along on the golden periods of Jeremy Taylor, we must pause and ask ourselves whether it is the strength of the argument or the authority of the ordained preacher, the felicity of the language or the grandeur of the style, which delights us—for it is likely to be one or other of these things to which we react—and, having made up our own minds on the subject, go on to enquire whether it was these same qualities, diversely appreciated by different men, that led to the popularity of these preachers in their own time. Did men go to Henry Smith only for doctrine, because being a *lecturer* he was more likely to satisfy a City auditory than were the surpliced priests, and, if so, why has he been remembered as " the silver-tongued preacher " ? Was Adams merely acceptable as a Calvinist, and, if so, were listeners indifferent to those elements in his work which made Southey call him " the prose Shakespeare of Puritan theologians " ? Was it a kind of frivolity which made others thrill to the *jeux d'esprit* of Andrewes, or a taste for *pastiche* which was gratified by Cosin's sermons on the infancy of the Saviour ; or, in an age when such learning was more in fashion, did men recall the oratory of St. Ambrose and the reflections of St. Bernard, and in a court where the elaboration of the Masque was a main preoccupation, did the patterns of the *schemata* receive an equal welcome ? Why was Tillotson so celebrated in his own day, and why does he seem so comparatively dull in ours ? These are all questions which force themselves on our attention and call for answers. The fact that they do so reminds us that the appreciation of our ancestors differed widely from our own, and suggests at times that behind the apparent reasons for their tastes and estimates, which we might be prone to assign in particular instances, lie other reasons generated by the period in which they lived and their educational outlook.

At the very outset we must shake ourselves free of the
modern conception of the sermon as a somewhat trivial
occasional concomitant to public worship, something more
solemn by virtue of its theme but less impressive in point of
thought or style than an article in a good periodical, and
something much less important and far less calling for public
attention than a University lecture or the address of a prominent scientist. To think thus is entirely to distort our
perspective. To the Englishman of the seventeenth century, whether Puritan, Laudian, Platonist, or whatever we
may choose to call him, the sermon was intimately bound
up with the Oracles of God, whether he believed those to be
derivable from the Scriptures, the Church, or certain philosophers ; it was the explication of these Oracles, a message
promulgated by God Himself, and consequently of the most
infinite importance. But it was something more, unless to
the Vanist, the Quaker, and men of the stamp of Sydrach
Simpson, by whom the peace of Cambridge was disturbed ;
it was the Word of God expounded in a certain manner
consecrated by long tradition and proved effectual through
many centuries. It was not only a message of the utmost
consequence, but the vehicle by which it was conveyed
was of a venerable antiquity, and neither religious Reformation nor ceremonial controversies had resulted in its abo-
lition or called for its discontinuance. That vehicle had
served in turn the sharp invectives of Demosthenes, and
the rolling periods of Isocrates, the model of Cicero, had
been employed by Libanius during the silver age of ' the
Second Sophistic,' and had been converted to its holiest
uses coincident with the conversion of the Greek and Latin
Fathers from their careers as rhetoricians to their careers as
preachers ; across the centuries it had preserved a striking
continuity of form and design, so that it is possible to recognise in the *schemata* of the Scholastics a resemblance to the
classical oratory on the one hand, and, on the other, a resemblance to the devices beloved of the Euphuist and sixteenth-
century English preacher. Even its more curious and apparently capricious features have frequently a long history,
and are explicable by reference to remote causes. It
represented the survival of pagan culture in the midst of
Christianity, vindicated the demand for the ornate often
in the midst of austerity, and imposed upon a conspicuously

internal and esoteric religion the architectural stability of external design. All this the sermon was, and all this, consciously or unconsciously, the auditor of the seventeenth century recognised it to be, by virtue of his own education or as a consequence of patient attention to outstanding sermons which he had heard. The better educated he was the more he appreciated the design of the preacher, but the existence of design at all times he assumed, whatever motive he may have attributed to the preacher who made choice of it ; and the preachers for their part moved solemnly to the business of the pulpit as men act deliberately in pursuance of an act which is dependent on known rules and accepted conventions. In short, the sermon in the seventeenth century was a work of art, and the preacher was an artist, or at least a craftsman, who worked by recognised methods, which were more or less appreciated by his hearers, or readers ; for preacher and hearer alike, or preacher and reader, had in view, to an extent almost unbelievable at the present day, a *theory* of rhetoric which governed all compositions whether oral or literary, to which in the long run the sermon, as an oratorical product, was ultimately referable. In order, therefore, to understand the sermon it is necessary to examine the theory.

Any such examination of the rhetorical and homiletical theory of the period falls naturally into three main divisions. In the first place the general rhetorical background of the subject has to be considered. As has been hinted in the *Introduction*, the seventeenth-century English sermon was merely a phase in the wider development of oratory, secular and sacred, in all ages. It was an organic growth ; there was nothing phenomenal about it. In order to assess it rightly we must remember its heredity as well as its environment. Particularly must we envisage the forces of the past as they became concentrated in certain tendencies which went to its shaping. Closely connected with these is the second approach which can be made to the subject— that which lies through an acquaintance with contemporary rhetorical education. One phase of this has already been touched on in treating of the place of note-taking in the supply of texts, but the habit referred to was only part of an elaborate system, to which boys in the great London schools and in grammar schools in the provinces were subjected, and which went far towards determining the form of the sermon and the reaction of religious auditories. But a third and even more precise ground of information is available in those works which treat of preaching as a branch of rhetoric.   The *artes concionandi* mark the transition from mere rhetoric to sacred oratory ; when they are English *arts of preaching* they tell us fairly adequately what the English preachers were aiming at.   Taken along with the chance remarks of diarists and biographers or the occasional confessions of preachers in their sermons, such manuals reveal to us the last stage in the process by which the epideictic oratory of the Ancients became the much valued sermons of our ancestors.

Bearing in mind, therefore, this threefold background of theory, we can approach the products of the seventeenth-century preachers with considerably more intelligence and appreciation than would be possible did we pass to the sermons direct ; we can realise the inevitability of the *trope* and the *figure* to public pronouncements as we recognise the persistence of the *syllogism* in reasoning ; we can note the particular application of transitional vogues in a special period, and the adaptation of general rules to a specific end ; and, finally, though at times we shall be aware of the incidence of purely theological bias, we shall be able to lay bare the operation of the cultural as distinct from the temperamental or the ecclesiastical elements, which to different degrees are accountable for the work under discussion.

The sermon as it appears in the first great florescence of pulpit oratory in the fourth century of our era was a product of two divergent civilisations.   On the one hand it pointed back to Judaism ; on the other it not only recalled but also perpetuated the classical tradition.

From Judaism, with its monotheistic religion and prophetic theory of history, quite naturally came the religious address.   The pagan religions, as Julian the Apostate afterwards was to realise so clearly, were essentially ceremonial religions without the consistent intellectual content which could form the basis for a reasoned discourse.   Even the official Jewish faith suffered this handicap, and it was in the synagogue and not in the Temple at Jerusalem that preaching as a definite feature of public worship was first established. Simple exposition and exhortation in course of time, under the influence of the heads of the Sanhedrin, became transformed into formal sermons delivered on the sabbaths, the great festivals, or at marriages, deaths, and the ordination of rabbis. Such addresses were based on portions of the Old Testament connected with the occasion, and were developed along the lines of the allegorical exegesis which the followers of Plato had introduced in the handling of the Homeric poems, with the design of rationalising the ancient mythology, and which Philo of Alexandria [1] adopted in his attempt to construe Jewish theology in terms of Greek philosophy.[2] The process was a highly complicated one, and was the source of that interminable allegorising and seeking of multiple meanings in the text of Scripture, which was to become an outstanding feature of Christian preaching. This Origen was to carry to a vicious extent, and this, after fascinating Ambrose and Augustine, was to fascinate through them the whole Middle Ages. At length we find St. Thomas Aquinas, in the thirteenth century, affirming that, as the true author of Scripture is God, acting through the intellects of the nominal authors of particular portions—

" there is no incongruity in holding, as Augustine says, that even according to the literal sense, there may be many meanings in one literal passage of Scripture,"

" the literal sense " being " that which the author intends," and God simultaneously comprehending all things in His intellect.[3] It is, however, certain that this strange avidity for a multiplicity of ' senses,' the chief of which, as recognised by the Middle Ages, were the historical, the literal, the allegorical, the tropological or moral, and the anagogical —the three last being divisions of the ' spiritual sense '— was a legacy of the Synagogue.[4]

---

[1] *Cir.* 20 B.C.–*cir.* A.D. 50.

[2] *Vid.* Hartwig Hirschfeld's article on " Jewish Preaching " in Hastings' ' Encyclopædia of Religion and Ethics.'

[3] Hugh Pope, O.P., ' St. Thomas Aquinas as an Interpreter of Holy Scripture,' Section C, " His Principles of Exegesis," p. 30.

[4] Examples of the Philonic type of exegesis are to be found in the Pauline epistles, where the story of Abraham and his two wives is allegorised (Gal. iv. 21–31), and the humane precept of the Mosaic Law, ' Thou shalt not muzzle the ox when he treadeth out the corn,' is treated (1 Cor. ix. 9) as an assertion of the preacher's right to maintenance.

Very different from the exegesis of the Synagogue was the preaching of Jesus of Nazareth. While not neglecting the Synagogue He resumed the prophetic strain, and it is interesting to note that He employed pithy sayings and interesting fables in precisely the manner which Aristotle recommends in his work on Rhetoric, in advising men to make use of γνῶμαι and παραβολαί. From His injunction to evangelise the world preaching, in the strict sense, was born. During His lifetime the Apostles made at least one missionary journey, and, it may be assumed that, as far as possible, they adopted His manner. After the crucifixion and resurrection the content of their message naturally underwent a change. It consisted thenceforth of a brief account of the life and acts of Jesus,[1] with citations from the Old Testament to prove that He is the Christ. Such ' speeches ' of the Apostles as are reported in ' the Acts ' are of this nature.[2] They abound with ' proof texts '— another ominous influence—and show no recognition of even such simple devices of rhetoric as men of limited education learn gradually from practice.[3]

Such avoidance of all rhetorical devices in early Christian preaching was not entirely due to the ignorance of the first missionaries, for Paul was distinctly a man of culture—a native of Tarsus, which at that very period surpassed even Athens and Alexandria as a seat of learning—but had its origin in the Jewish detestation of rhetoric. This, as Professor Jebb saw,[4] underlies " the popular modern notion that the greatest oratory must be extemporary," which is most strong in " those countries which have been most influenced by the Reformation," and consequently by the writings of the Old and New Testaments. Moreover, this

[1] *Vid.* Peter's address to Cornelius' household, Acts x. 34–43.

[2] Allowing for the fact that ' reported ' speeches in ' the Acts ' cannot be considered as *verbatim,* there seems no good reason to doubt that, as they occur, they represent the type of address given by Christian preachers of the first century.

[3] Paul's speech before the Areopagus, recorded in Acts xvii. 22–31, is no exception to this statement, although his address has sometimes been represented as an appeal to the " enticing words of man's wisdom " aimed at impressing the Athenians. But the method employed was the familiar one of the other Apostles, and Paul merely selected striking verse from the Greek poets, which he used on the analogy of the ' proof-texts ' (which were so effective a weapon in combating Jewish antagonists), to point assent to what he was about to say.

[4] ' Attic Orators,' vol. i, 1886, p. lxxxiii.

conception has definite affinity with a precept reported of
Jesus : " Take no thought what ye shall say, for . . . it
shall be given you," between which and a precept of
Cæsar's (reported by Cicero [1]) *verborum delectum originem esse
eloquentiæ*—' an accurate choice of words is the foundation
of eloquence '—a great gulf lay, a gulf which had to be
bridged by the use of the despised pagan rhetoric, if the
' good news ' was to be conveyed to the world at large.
Admirable as it may sound for Bernard of Clairvaux,
centuries later, to exclaim, as many in the seventeenth
century, and in all centuries, have been ready to exclaim :

" Peter and Andrew and the sons of Zebedee and all the
rest of the disciples were not picked from the school of
rhetoric or philosophy, yet nevertheless the Saviour made
His salvation effective through them throughout the
world," [2]

the statement is a travesty of the facts. Before anything
can be ' effective ' men must be persuaded that it is of vital
interest to them, and if they are to be persuaded the customary means of persuasion must be used. Consequently,
the preachers of the Gospel were compelled to turn their
attention to the study of rhetoric, and, in order to make the
appeal of the Cross in the chief seats of learning and govern-
mental power, to adopt the oratorical devices long familiar
to the Greeks and Romans.
    In taking this step the Christians were to respond in a
manner beyond all expectation to the challenge thrown out
by Antonius in the ' De Oratore,' [3] where he is made to
declare of all oratory :

" By the same power of language the wickedness of
mankind is brought to destruction, and virtue to security.
Who can exhort to virtue more ardently than the orator ?
Who reclaim from vice with greater energy ? Who can
reprove the bad with more asperity, or praise the good
with better grace ? Who can break the force of unlawful
desire by more effective reprehension ? Who can alleviate
grief with more soothing consolation ? "

[1] ' Ad Brutum,' lxxii.   [2] ' Super Cant.,' Sermon xxxvi.   [3] Lib. II, ix.

Thus the religious exposition of the Jew charged with a new and wholly remarkable content became one with the official and paramount culture of the period.

Classical oratory in the early Christian centuries was a term synonymous with higher education. The round of subjects which the intending orator must study made the training it provided the university of the day.

" No man " (Cicero had made Crassus declare) " can be an orator possessed of every praiseworthy accomplishment, unless he has attained the knowledge of everything important, and of all liberal arts, for his language must be ornate and copious from knowledge, since, unless there be beneath the surface matter understood and felt by the speaker, oratory becomes an empty and almost puerile flow of words. . . . [1] The accomplished and complete orator I shall call him who can speak on all subjects with variety and copiousness." [2]

Not unnaturally so many-sided a training, coupled with a carefully cultivated power of persuasive speaking—itself an outstanding advantage in a world in which ordinary business was still largely conducted before massed assemblies in the open air—provided the customary initiation to a public career. It is not wide of the mark to say that the classical rhetorical education supplied its pupils with the advantages of a university education combined with the advantages of active membership of the Oxford Union. That this tradition of rhetorical studies as a preparation for public employment still clung about rhetoric in its more meagre and less liberal days is a noteworthy fact, and goes to some extent to explain the insistence upon the subject, even in its driest and most mechanical aspects, which lingered all through the seventeenth century.

In its origins rhetoric had been something much less ambitious than the encomiums of Cicero indicate. Two main influences had gone to its foundation—Sicilian rhetoric and Ionian dialectic. From the latter as taught by the Sophists, such as Protagoras of Abdera,[3] the Athenians learned ὀρθοέπεια—correctness in speaking or writing ; from the former, as prescribed by the ' rhetors,'

---

[1] ' De Orat.,' Lib. I, vi.   [2] *Idem*, Lib. I, xiii.   [3] *Fl.* 455–415 B.C.

they derived their passion for εὐέπεια—the study of beautiful diction.   The Sicilian rhetoric, which had its origin in the multitude of lawsuits which followed the fall of the Tyrants in the early part of the fifth century B.C., was strictly practical in aim.   Its interest was in ' arrangement,' whereby men might be helped most effectively to present their cases before a judge, and from the Τέχνη or ' Art of Rhetoric ' of Corax of Syracuse is derived the five-fold division into proem, narrative, argument, subsidiary remarks, and peroration, which thenceforward was to be the recognised scheme of division in any address.   But in course of time the more comprehensive Ionian culture united with the simple Sicilian strain ; a third influence, also, was added, that of Gorgias of Leontini, who, while on an embassy to Athens, dazzled and delighted the Athenians by his glowing and almost poetical use of language.   By Gorgias' pupil Isocrates—' the old man eloquent ' of Milton's sonnet—something much more ornate and much more skilfully modulated was achieved than had hitherto been attempted in prose, something, moreover, that could be reproduced with fair success in any language that was sufficiently flexible and polished, and which consequently was able to pass from Greece to Rome and so into modern Europe and become a norm of literary prose.   Well might Cicero exclaim :   " Ex Isocratis ludo, tanquam ex equo Troiano, innumeri principes extiterunt " [1]—from the school of Isocrates, as from the Trojan horse, innumerable great men appeared.   Of these Cicero himself was the greatest.

Although Cicero considered Demosthenes the great example for those whose oratory was confined to the spoken word, whether in judicial or deliberative assemblies,[2] he persistently modelled himself upon Isocrates, and thereby created a type of oratory not only elocutionary but literary. In the productions of those who are mere speakers—

" there is " (to quote De Quincey [3]) " no eddying about their own thoughts ; no motion of fancy self-sustained from its own activities ; no flux and reflux of thought, half meditative, half capricious ; but strains of feeling, genuine

---

[1] ' De Orat.,' Lib. II, xxii, 94.   [2] *Vide* ' Ad Brutum,' ix.
[3] ' Essay on Rhetoric,' Masson's ed., vol. x, p. 121.

or not, supported at every step from the excitement of independent external objects."

The speaker who composes his orations with a view to their being afterwards read, and whose aim is twofold, namely, to produce sufficiently effective arguments to achieve his immediate purpose, and also to employ such amplifications as will not only momentarily delight his hearers but also create in them the wish to possess his speech in written form, is not only a rhetorician, but also a literary artist. Such was Cicero, and such, in the noblest periods of pulpit oratory, have been the greatest preachers—conveying at the moment a distinct and urgent message (calming an excited populace, as Chrysostom in his discourses ' on the Statues,' or insisting, as Barrow, on the duty of providing for the poor), but stimulating by the very fecundity of their thought, or the felicity of their illustrations, the desire to obtain their sermons in a more permanent form. No wonder, then, that the Isocratean prose, as developed and modified by Cicero, became the great model of patristic preaching.

Between the unadorned narratives of the Apostles and the great products of patristic oratory, however, several stages intervened. To the apostolic addresses, such as those recorded in ' the Acts,' succeeded homiletical epistles, modelled upon those of St. Paul. There circulated among the churches short admonitory treatises like that known as the ' Second Epistle of Clement,' but these were without literary interest. Neither do the Apologists (of whom the greatest were Justin Martyr and Tertullian), who succeeded the apostolic preachers, furnish us with any direct specimens of the religious address of the time. Their writings, which are of a polemical nature, reveal more culture and intellectual power than those of the Apostolic Fathers, and furnish evidence of wide reading and considerable acquaintance with literature and philosophy—Tertullian in particular shows distinct acquaintance with the devices of rhetoric [1]— but in their time the religious address was still of a purely

---

[1] *Vid.* J. Wight Duff : ' A Literary History of Rome in the Silver Age,' Lon., 1927, p. 231, who, speaking of Seneca's influence on Christian writers, notes the peroration of Tertullian's 'Apologeticum,' with its " antitheses, exclamations, historical instances, and short crisp utterances " as an intellectual echo of Seneca's style.

informal nature.   As Broadus reminds us,[1] the Greek word
ὁμιλία signified a conversation, or mutual talk, as did also
the Latin *sermo*.   The early Christians did not use the terms
applied to the orations of Demosthenes and Cicero ; neither
were they forced to apply the Aristotelian ' persuasives '
in the endeavour to convince a pubic auditory.
   Nevertheless, as another writer tells us :

" The application of rhetoric to the pulpit began early.
From the time of Origen (A.D. 185–254) indications multiply
that the Greek schools were beginning to influence the
preaching of the Church." [2]

The conversational style no longer sufficed.   During the
third century A.D. the greater publicity allowed Christian
worship, and the fact that strangers were frequently present,
created the demand for a fuller exposition of Scripture.
Origen adopted the method of verse by verse commentary.
But greater things lay ahead.   After the conversion of
Constantine, attending church and hearing preachers
became a social function, and we find Chrysostom complaining [3] that the people behaved in church like spectators,
not as disciples, and sided with the doctrines of the different
preachers as they did with the combatants in the arena.
Their approval or disapproval was readily shown, as
applause was permitted to the worshippers.   " The force
of eloquence," Chrysostom also declared, " is more
demanded in a church than in a school of rhetoric."
   Then, as in the Paris of Louis XIV, fashionable people
in Constantinople, Alexandria, and Antioch flocked to
hear the preachers, and talked of them, as Chrysostom
intimates, almost as enthusiastically as they spoke of the
favourite horse in the races, or the reigning actor in the
theatre.   Men of culture, trained in the universities of
Greece, were advanced to the chief sees, and eloquent
bishops swayed the passions of the citizens and influenced
politics ; the homily developed into the oration, not always
free, it must be confessed, from the faults of the pagan

[1] J. A. Broadus : ' A Treatise on the Preparation and Delivery of Sermons,'
Lon., 1898, p. 15.
[2] J. Oswald Dykes : ' The Christian Minister and his Duties,' Edin., 1908,
p. 239.
[3] ' On the Priesthood,' Book V, i.

sophists of that age of decadence. "From Augustine to Melanchthon," states one writer,[1] "homiletics were treated almost exclusively as an application of classical rhetoric " ; and the Christian preachers disregarded one of the most vital things in Augustine's ' De Doctrina,' namely, wherein the Christian orator ought to differ from the pagan rhetorician. It is necessary that the preacher should *teach*, *delight*, and *move*, " *ut doceat, ut delectet, ut flectat*," says Augustine,[2] discarding the more superficial *prove* (*ut probet*) of Cicero as inadequately conveying this idea ; for, valuable as the power of pleasing and moving is, the one thing the preacher must do, first and last, is to *teach*. More than a thousand years after, Hyperius of Marburg, writing of the application of rhetoric to preaching, stresses the same fact, and proceeds to enumerate some of the additional ways by which this may be done.

" Whatsoever thinge " (he urges) " is profitable to teach perspicuously, or also to moue and perswade withall, all that shall the Preacher purchase to himselfe as most requisite and necessary furniture. Therefore let him know, that argumentations tripartite, quinquepartite, Euthymemata : also Schemes and Tropes : further the crafte of amplifying and mouing of affections, and finally whatsoever else of this order is taught of the Rhetoritians, masters of well speakinge, also appertayne and belonge unto him." [3]

When Hyperius wrote, devout men had begun seriously to doubt whether the use of rhetorical devices was consonant with the spirit of Christian preaching. The Fathers had no such scruples.

" When Symmachus, as deputy of the Senate, appealed to the Emperor to restore to their house of assembly the altar of Victory, the most venerable symbol of the pagan Empire, S. Ambrose resisted the proposal with all the arts of a rhetoric, trained, like that of his opponent, in the ancient schools."

[1] Oswald Dykes, *op. cit.*, p. 240.
[2] *Ibid.*, p. 241 ; ' De Doct.,' Lib. IV, 12.
[3] ' The Practise of Preaching . . . Conteyning an excellent Method how to frame Divine Sermons ; . . . First written in Latin by . . . Andreas Hyperius . . . Englished by John Ludham . . .' Lon., 1577, chap. xv.

Nor is this instance, recorded by Dill,[1] a unique example of contemporary practice. When highly cultured men embraced Christianity they proceeded to urge the claims of the new faith with the same Pisteis, Taxis, and Lexis—the same "persuasives," the same orderly arrangement, the same careful attention to style and diction—which they had previously employed on secular and often imaginary subjects. This is not to be wondered at, when we remember that Basil and Gregory of Nyssa were the sons of a rhetorician of Neocæsarea in Pontus, that the latter, even after he had become an ' agnostes,' or reader in the Church, was seduced by the charms of a worldly career, and himself embraced for a time the calling of a rhetorician, while the former, along with Gregory of Nazianzus, was educated in the schools of Cæsarea and Athens. At Athens these Fathers were the pupils of Proæresius and Himerius, two of the leading rhetoricians of the day, and Basil had also visited the schools of Constantinople. Chrysostom was the pupil of Andragatus and of Libanius, the most celebrated rhetorician of the period, who afterwards so greatly admired his pupil's eloquence, that it is related, being asked on his death-bed which of his pupils he desired should succeed him, he replied : " John, if the Christians had not stolen him."

The Christians, however, stole not only the young rhetoricians, but also the rhetorical methods. Whether in the East or the West, events ran the same course. " *Per illius os potissimum me Dominus ab errore liberavit*," Augustine writes of Ambrose—" God chiefliest by means of that man's mouth delivered me from error " [2]—and in the ' Confessions,' [3] he tells, how as a young teacher of rhetoric at Milan he went to hear the latter, not that he might benefit by his teaching, but that he might criticise his eloquence, and was so enthralled by what he heard that he hung eagerly upon his words, and was delighted by the agreeable style of his sermons.[4] Yet to represent the appropriation of rhetorical devices to the service of religion as a theft is hardly an adequate metaphor. The fact is, that the

---

[1] Samuel Dill : ' Roman Society in the Last Century of the Western Empire,' 2nd ed., Lon., 1905, p. 22.

[2] Ep. 147. 23.

[3] Lib. V, xiii.

[4] *Loc. cit.* : " Verbis eius suspendebar intentus . . . et delectabar suavitate sermonis."

education of the day was being adapted so as to give effective expression to what was becoming more and more a dominant fact—namely, the promulgation of the Christian view of the Universe.   We must not be led too easily by the glamour of great names or the example of influential writings to conclude that the rhetorical tincture imparted to the sermon at this period, and never wholly lost to it at its greatest moments since, is to be entirely explained by the practice of the great patristic preachers. If a modern should adopt methods obviously traceable to Chrysostom or Augustine, we might well conclude that his practice is conditioned by his models. The conclusion would not hold in an age when rhetoric was still a living force.   Andrewes and Donne and Barrow derived much from the Fathers—weird allegorisation, curious economy in wringing the utmost meaning from words, and even grammatical constructions, and richer and more poetical imagery than is habitual to Englishmen—but they did not derive their rhetoric from them.   When they turned to the Fathers with any rhetorical intention it was to seek in them consummate examples of rhetorical devices with which they were themselves familiar.   It was not to learn they went so much as to admire ; and what was true in so late a period as the seventeenth century was much more definitely the case in the patristic period. The discourses of the Fathers were delivered to a world which was predominantly a *rhetorical* world—meaning by that a world whose cultured classes had received the rhetorical type of education—just as at the present day the sermon is directed to an audience whose prevailing interests are scientific or mechanical.

Abundant evidence exists of the permanence of the rhetorical tradition at the very moment when all the imperial institutions were tottering to their ruin.

" Style might degenerate from the great standards " (Dill affirms [1]), " but the standards were never forgotten ; and the passion for style of some sort was as strong under Theodoric as it was in the reign of Trajan."

The persistence of the rhetorical education was the badge of Roman citizenship ; to participate in it obliterated dis-

---

[1] *Op. cit.*, p. 391.

tinctions of time, and entitled a fifth-century Gaul or North
African to rank with the heroes of the late Republic.   As has
been said :

" . . . In the work of Martianus Capella, which was to
be the textbook of the Middle Ages, rhetoric is still treated
as if the student were a contemporary of Cicero.   All
through the five centuries of the Empire, during which
oratory had almost ceased to have any practical power, the
Roman schools maintained the tradition which had produced such triumphs of practical oratory at Rome in Cicero
and Hortensius.   The old theories of the proper divisions
of a discourse, of the varieties of style adapted to the matter,
of the figures of speech, of the rhythm and prosody of the
sentence, of the management of voice and gesture, were
taught as carefully under Romulus Augustulus as they were
when rhetoric was a practical art. . . .   The audience
whom the rhetor had in view was no longer the jury or the
public assembly, but a gathering of cultivated . . . people.
. . . Rhetoric came to represent quite as much a habit of
mind as the rules of a definite art." [1]

Haarhoff, in his ' Schools of Gaul, A Study of Pagan and
Christian Education in the Last Century of the Western
Empire,' [2] has much to say to the same effect.   One practical consideration, however, he adds in maintaining the
persistence of the rhetorical tradition, namely, that—

" it survived the more easily because of the controversial
nature of Christianity at this time and the importance of
preaching.   The change from the rhetor's ' cathedra ' to
the pulpit was often merely one of place and subject : the
method was the same.   And so the ideal of the orator
persisted." [3]

Ambrose against Symmachus has already been cited [4] ;
in much the same way Haarhoff points to Hilary of Poitiers'
invective against Constantius as an example of a speech cast
in the old rhetorical moulds, so much so that the speaker

---

[1] Dill, *op. cit.*, pp. 426–7.   [3] Dill, *op. cit.*, pp. 165–6.
[2] Oxf., 1920.   [4] *Ante*, p. 52.

abandons historical veracity, " to give it the most effective utterance." " His divisions correspond perfectly to those of the schools." [1]

" In the very monasteries " (the same writer tells us) " the artifices of the rhetor's school lingered. Valerian, Bishop of Cemelium (near Nice), gives many examples of this in his Homilies. He frequently uses Parallelism and Repetition . . . or Chiasmus and Assonance . . . or Alliteration. . . ." [2]

And of Magnus Felix Ennodius, who was later to become bishop of Pavia, " born just three years before the dethronement of the last Emperor of the West," Dill relates,[3] that although living in a time of great confusion, he was yet " as complete and artificial a product of the rhetorical discipline" as the Latin writers of earlier and more settled periods ; he was incapable, even on sacred subjects, of speaking directly and simply, and, what is of great interest to us, has preserved a long series of declamations on controversial and unreal themes, such as the words of Dido when she saw Æneas departing or of Menelaus at the sight of Troy burning—the same themes, it is to be noted, as were set Juvenal or Pliny.

In the exercises of Ennodius we come very close to the heart of the rhetorical tradition. In subject-matter they go back many centuries, in form they point forward even more. They are essentially of the type which we find in the ' Progymnasmata ' of Aphthonius, a sophist of Antioch and pupil of Libanius ; and this ' Progymnasmata ' was a favourite textbook in the schools and universities of the sixteenth and seventeenth centuries. In this way the trial subjects set to Chrysostom and Aphthonius by Libanius became in turn the trial subjects prescribed by Brinsley or attempted by Jeremy Taylor. Rhetoric as " a habit of mind " could not readily be divorced from " the rules of a definite art." The full-dress presentation which had become habitual was based on long practice.

---

[1] ' Schools of Gaul,' p. 164.
[2] *Idem*, p. 165 : The blanks represent examples of those figures supplied by Haarhoff.
[3] *Op. cit.*, pp. 391–2.

" Manner of expression " (as Professor Wight Duff writes of an earlier period [1]) " came to be deeply modified by the systematic instruction in rhetoric and by the declamatory exercises (especially the *controuersia* and *suasoria*) composed by the student practising the figures of speech, exclamations, apostrophes, interrogations, and innumerable other artifices, which he had been taught by a rhetor to consider effective for the purposes of argument or display."

The *suasoriae* were monologues, the *controuersiae* were debates ; the former gave facility in expression, the latter adroitness in managing an argument. It is not the least interesting thing about these exercises that much of our information about them is derived from the collection made by the elder Seneca. In this way these imaginary addresses or debates, often far-fetched in theme, and going beyond the most poetical imagination, became linked up with the terse, pointed, antithetic style which we associate with Seneca, and the imitations of which in sixteenth-century Latin or the modern languages we refer to as ' Senecan.'

Seneca had a peculiar fascination for early Christian writers like Tertullian, Lactantius, and Jerome, as one whom they believed to have been the correspondent of St. Paul.[2] The honour accorded to him by Dante will be recalled. This interest, there can be no question, in the case of Tertullian, resulted in imitation, and, since Professor Wight Duff reminds us that Seneca

" diversifies his science with rhetorical descriptions ; . . . illuminates a point with wonderful fertility in examples ; and . . . holds the attention by his lively manner in arguing a question," [3]

the trend of the imitation will be obvious. It was a method caught from the ' rhetors,' but it endured to give force to the preaching of Donne.

To the ' Progymnasmata ' we shall return in the following section : for the moment let it suffice to note its contents. Fabula, Narratio, Chr(e)ia, Sententia, Confutatio, Confirmatio, Locus communis, Laudatio, Vituperatio, Com-

---

[1] ' A Literary History of Rome in the Silver Age,' Lon., 1927, p. 9.
[2] *Ibid.*, p. 231.　　　　　　　　　　　[3] *Ibid.*, p. 229.

paratio, Ethopœia, Descriptio, Thesis, Legislatio—these subjects are taken in turn. Each subject begins with a short description, followed by an ' exemplum,' which is worked out with elaborate attention to its component parts. In some of the sixteenth-century Latin editions these latter are clearly enumerated in the margin.[1] On the whole it may be said that Aphthonius presented his pupils with methods " profitable either to teache perspicuously, or else to moue & perswade withall," to use Ludham's rendering of Hyperius,[2] and rhetoric in his day had not yet become the mere business of *schemes* and *tropes* it was afterwards destined to be.

The narrowing of rhetorical training and interest to the more ornamental aspects of the subject was the inevitable result of the overthrow of the Western Empire by the barbarian invasions. Even although, as we have heard Dill affirm, " style of some sort " was still cultivated under Theodoric, and the textbook of Martianus Capella carried forward the classical presuppositions into the Middle Ages, the opportunities for, and impetus towards oratory as it had formerly been practised no longer existed. Never again was oratory to attract to herself as her due all the liberal arts as *Philology* is represented as doing in Capella's allegory. The very grouping of the arts into *trivium* and *quadrivium* is significant as emphasising the break-up of the ancient culture. The end, moreover, implied by this grouping was the possession of knowledge and not its expression for the ends of public service as in earlier times. Rhetoric still remained much more important than it has been among us for the last two and a half centuries, but it was no longer a term implying at once the study of the technique of effective speaking and the co-ordination of the other arts for this specific purpose. The occasions, too, for its exercise, although they remained, as they will ever remain, associated with legislation, the deliberative assemblies and important appeals to public interest, were affected by the manner in which rhetorical instruction was given, and as lawyers, statesmen, and all public speakers came to be educated under the ægis of religion, the prevailing fashions of speech

[1] E.g. in ' Aphthonii Sophistæ Progymnasmata Rodolpho Agricola Phrisio interprete,' M.D.XL, no place, 8vo, in Bodleian.
[2] *Vid. ante*, p. 52.

were naturally those which appealed to the clergy. What the earlier ecclesiastical writers had produced, as a result of their participation in the common rhetorical education of their time, later generations of monastic and clerical writers imitated more or less on the ceremonial principle, that as there were certain forms to be observed in dedicating a church or investing a boy-bishop, so there were certain *tropes* and *figures* which were to be expected in writings or speeches.

While the mediæval sermon does not at first sight bear a marked resemblance to the classical oratory as it was adapted by the Fathers to the needs of the pulpit, though it stands in no obvious relation to Isocratean or Ciceronian prose, but seems rather a detached expression of the religious consciousness of the newly formed nationalities, there is a fundamental relationship on what may be termed the more mechanistic side, and the rhythms and patterns discoverable when the longer periods of Isocrates or Cicero are subjected to analysis not only resemble but are actually identical with those employed by mediæval churchmen. No adequate discussion exists of the stages by which classical Latin became mediæval Latin ; but Professor Croll, in the introduction to his edition of Lyly's ' Euphues ' [1] (published in 1916), gives an interesting account of the *schemata* derived from Gorgias and Isocrates, their preservation in the mediæval sermon, and their influence on the modern European vernaculars, while H. O. Taylor, in a chapter on the ' Evolution of Mediæval Latin Prose ' in his work, ' The Mediæval Mind,' [2] has done something of a similar nature.

The chief legacy of mediæval preaching, in so far as it became a store for later preachers to draw from, was clearly one of spirit and content rather than style. At a later stage we shall have to note dramatic tendencies and a poetical handling of themes which are certainly traceable to this period. For the moment it is sufficient to remember that the devices of classical rhetoric survived in the monastic schools, and were employed to a greater or less extent in

[1] ' Euphues : The Anatomy of Wit. Euphues and His England, by John Lyly,' edited by M. W. Croll and H. Clemons, Lon., 1916, pp. xv-lxiv.
[2] 2 vols., Lon., 1911, vol. ii, chap. xxxi. *Vid.* also chap. viii of the same author's ' The Classical Heritage of the Middle Ages,' New York, 3rd ed., 1911.

the mediæval sermon.   Quite apart from tradition, however, rhetoric was of importance in the fourteenth and fifteenth centuries because of the public disputations which had to be undertaken by students who had completed their studies in the *trivium*.   Such disputations, often of an extremely subtle and ingenious kind, are for ever associated with Scholasticism.   They owe more to dialectic than to contemporary rhetoric, but the minute divisions and subdivisions of the Schoolmen had an important influence on the form of the sermon.   The patristic sermon had at best remained an adaptation of the classical oration.   In other words, it consisted of continuous exposition or the application of rhetoric to a great theme.   The methods of the Schoolmen gave the sermon the logical incisiveness of the *Summa*. From then on, as Dargan notes,[1] the sermon had to " include among the elements of its ideal completeness, clear distinction and logical treatment of its material."   The insistence on minute analysis and precision of arrangement became in course of time an abuse.   Curiously enough, it was associated also with certain precepts which passed for the ideals of classical oratory.   It was the woodenness and absurdity of this mixture of Cicero and Aquinas upon which Erasmus poured contempt in his ' Encomium Moriæ '[2] ; and it was to supersede manuals advocating such a form of preaching that he undertook the description of the pulpit orator as he conceived him in the ' Ecclesiastes.'[3]

The name of Erasmus is inseparably bound up with our conceptions of Renaissance humanism, and the Renaissance gave new life to rhetoric.   What the first generation of scholars derived directly from the traditional seats of Greek learning may be seen in the ' Synopsis Rhetoricæ ' of Matthew Camariotus, a Greek who was forced to flee westward on the sack of Constantinople[4] : the current exposition of rhetoric, with its deference to Ciceronian models and Aristotelian rules, remains for us in the textbooks of Rodolphus Agricola and others.[5]   While it is true that the chief

---

[1] ' History of Preaching,' 2 vols., Lon., 1905, vol. i, p. 232.
[2] *Vide* ' Praise of Folly,' John Wilson's trans., 1668, edited by Rouse, p. 91.
[3] Klein's edition, Leipzig, 1820, is the only modern edition of this work, and is very convenient for reference, being divided into short chapters, subdivided under various headings.   It is referred to throughout.
[4] Edition used : ' A Davide Hæschelis edita,' Augsburg, 1595.
[5] E.g. in the Italian translation of the ' De Inventione,' Venice, 1567.

emphasis of Renaissance scholarship was laid upon grammar, the minute attention directed to grammatical construction was itself of importance where rhetoric was concerned. The greater familiarity with excellent models—the true classical models such as Gorgias, Isocrates, and Cicero, instead of mediæval ecclesiastical writers—reacted beneficially on contemporary education.

" The teaching of Rhetoric " (Professor Foster Watson tells us [1]) " is emphasized by Wolsey in the Statutes for Ipswich School, founded in 1528. The Elizabethan schools included it, if not specifically as a separate subject, at least in the manner and spirit of reading classical authors as well as in the exercises of the theme and oration. Indeed, if there is one school subject which seems to have pre-eminently influenced the writers, statesmen and gentlemen of the 16th and 17th centuries, in their intellectual outfit in after life, probably the claim for this leading position may justly be made for Rhetoric and the Oration."

Preachers might well have been included in this list, and the influence of contemporary education on the sermon, which could be viewed variously as theme or declamation, was certainly no less than on secular literature and orations. An oration of Daniel Heinsius, for example, ' In Theophania, siue, Domini Natalem,' [2] dating from the opening decade of the seventeenth century, is distinctly akin, not only in tone, but also actually in form, to Andrewes' series of sermons on the Nativity. The exhaustiveness which Charles II noted in Barrow, playfully alleging his unfairness to later preachers who should attempt the same subjects, was similarly a relic of the scholastic disputation, which advanced step by step with pitiless logic and extreme clarity of exposition to the overthrow of all opponents.

The transition from the school theme or university disputation to the pulpit address can often be readily illustrated from the college-exercises of young preachers, and sermons delivered before clerical and university auditories

---

[1] ' The English Grammar Schools to 1660,' p. 440.
[2] Contained in ' Danielis Heinsii Orationum Editio Nova . . . Editore Nicolao Heinsio,' Amsterdam (Elzevir), 1657. The justification for the word ' Theophania ' is made apparent by Liddell and Scott's *Lexicon*.

tend to preserve the strict methods which the preachers
have been trained to observe.   To those familiar with the
rise of Arminianism in England the name of Peter Baro is
familiar, and it is interesting to note that in three sermons,
delivered in St. Mary's, Cambridge, "*ad Clerum* (*ut
vocant*),*" marginal notes supply an indication of the manner
in which the preacher expounded his subject.   In the margins of one of these,[1] we find, for example, such directions
as the following :

> *Exordium de loci amplitudine, utilitateque ;   licet a multis
> obscurati.*
> *Divisio.*
> 1. *Questionis PROPOSITIO.*
> 2. *Q. Repetitio atque illustratio.*
> 3. *Q. Explicatio & Definitio.*
> *EPILOGUS.*

A number of subdivisions occur under each main head,
Objectio and *Solutio* being noted over against each.

In the case of Baro, then, we see the renewed attention
paid to rhetoric bearing fruit.   Fisher, Colet, and the early
English humanists, naturally enough, having been educated
in the old mediæval tradition, do not present us in their
work with so clear an application of the familiar rules.
Though Fisher, bishop of Rochester, deserves to be styled
the father of the English literary sermon—for there are
few notes, whether of pathos, vivid presentation, solemn
admonition, or sober grandeur to be found afterwards among
the greater English preachers, which, however imperfectly
expressed, are not discoverable in Fisher's sermons—yet
there is a formlessness and lack of syntactical clarity about
his work which ranks him with the mediævalists and not
with the moderns.   This is partly due to the state of the
vernacular at the time when Fisher delivered his sermons,
but it is due in greater part, as the meandering tediousness
of most mediæval literature is ultimately due, to an inability
to recognise the necessary framework of a literary composition.   Men did not paint from the nude, they did not even

---

[1] The third, from the Epistle of St. John, cap. 2, vv. 14–17, pp. 311 *seq.*,
found in ' Petri Baronis . . . in Jonam Prophetam Prælectiones 39 . . .'
Lon., 1579.

paint from life in the Middle Ages, and the monkish writers and preachers had been more taken up with the pursuit of allegories and analogies, and the cultivation of schematic patterns, with the vesture, in short, rather than the body of their addresses.

Not even a close acquaintance with dialectic could give a preacher what was required. Dialectic could *prove*, but was unable to *move* and unlikely to *delight*. Dialectic, however, was useful in managing the controversies of the Reformation period, but when the reformed position had to be presented to the common people the appeal to the emotions was the one best calculated to be effective. This to some extent, to some extent his mediæval upbringing and training, accounts for Latimer's occasionally boisterous and at all times vigorous style. The Middle Ages had enjoyed anecdotes and *facetiæ*, and Latimer still catered for this taste. The need for immediate teaching, also, and the desirability of avoiding occasions for controversy, led in England to the issue of the ' Book of Homilies,' in which was achieved a form of plain consecutive statement, which, while allowing for a certain amount of rhythmical beauty in the management of individual sentences, demanded little or no attention to composition or structure as a whole. While, therefore, in the sermons of Bancroft and Jewel we find traces of wide reading, and of such reading in the Fathers and the classical authors as was afterwards to be a distinguishing feature of seventeenth-century preaching, the customary presentation of religion, which quotation and reference were designed to illustrate and enforce, was not, in the second half of the sixteenth century, of outstanding literary quality. Archbishop Grindal at moments attained a certain grave dignity [1] ; but his style was his own, he did not share it with his contemporaries. There is no trace of like effects in the work of Sandys or John Udall. Bancroft, both in reading and manner, pointed forward to the Jacobean preachers,[2] and Thomas Playfere, afterwards a Lady Margaret Professor of Divinity in Cambridge, who has already been quoted on the manner in which sermons

---

[1] E.g. in a letter to Queen Elizabeth in defence of " prophesying "— ' Remains,' edited for the Parker Society, Camb., 1843, p. 389—which is an example of his style at its best.
[2] *Vid.* ' Sermon Preached at Paul's Cross . . . 1588.'

reached the printer, may be cited as illustrating in places the transition from the mere facetiousness of the Middle Ages to the ' wit ' of the later preaching ; but it is Playfere's thought rather than his expression that is of interest. Even when we turn to bishop Jewel and Lever, although their work affords piquant examples of the survival of traditional rhetorical devices and of their appropriation by the vernacular, we are not yet dealing with the sermon as an oration or as literature as men were soon to cultivate it.

The fact that Jewel and Lever provide examples of the *schemata* beloved of the mediæval preachers is to be noted, and Professor Croll [1] has turned it to account in tracing the antecedents of the Euphuistic style, but interesting as this evidence is, we must not stress it unduly. Jewel's sermons are essentially expository in character, and their style, although better than that hitherto achieved by any English preacher, is simple, straightforward, and plain. There is a feeling for balanced phraseology, but this is very largely due to a thorough acquaintance with the English versions of the Bible, and the longer periods are clearly built up on the model of the more continuous passages of Scripture. Some of the cadences of the translations have been taken over, and have helped to modulate commentary and exposition. It will suffice, therefore, to notice how acquaintance with tropes and figures reacted on style and appealed to men of the time, but much of this, it seems clear, was due to familiarity with and imitation of ecclesiastical writers ; and familiarity with and imitation of translations of the Scriptures were destined also to have a considerable effect. [2]

It is a commonplace to speak of the sonorous periods of Hooker, more especially when referring to his work, ' Of the Laws of Ecclesiastical Polity.' A specimen of his style, from the famous sermon ' Of the Certainty and Perpetuity of Faith in the Elect '—which occasioned Travers' ' Supplication '—goes to prove that the characteristics of what he delivered in the pulpit were identical with those of his written work in the study ; yet, although Hooker is omitted

---

[1] *Op. cit.*, pp. xlix–l.
[2] This seems to me a fair account of the composite influences that went to the shaping of Jewel's style, although Professor Croll, in support of his thesis, confines himself to the prevalence of the schemes.

from Professor Croll's examples of schematic writers, it is plain that he had made a careful study of patterns and rhythms of the old familiar sort :

" The light would never be so acceptable, were it not for that usual intercourse of darkness. Too much honey doth turn to gall ; and too much joy even spiritually would make us wantons. Happier a great deal is that man's case, whose soul by inward desolation is humbled, than he whose heart is through abundance of spiritual delight lifted up and exalted above measure. Better is it sometimes to go down into the pit with him, who, beholding darkness, and bewailing the loss of inward joy and consolation, crieth from the bottom of the lowest hell, ' My God, my God, why hast thou forsaken me ? ' than continually to walk arm in arm with angels, to sit as it were in Abraham's bosom, and to have no thought, no cogitation ; but ' I thank my God it is not with me as it is with other men.' No, God will have them that shall walk in light to feel now and then what it is to sit in the shadow of death. A grieved spirit therefore is no argument of a faithless mind." [1]

The quotation is recognisably in Hooker's manner, but its relation is obvious to the carefully cultivated or assiduously imitated religious style of the millennium that preceded it. Yet, difficult as it is precisely to define the difference, there is a difference between this and the traditional hunting of ' similar closes ' and carefully balanced figures. So far as English preaching, at least, is concerned, something has been added. Over against *light*, *darkness*, against *honey*, *gall* ; over against the Saviour and His despairing cry, the Pharisee and his self-congratulatory exclamation ; but the general impression left with the reader, as must have been the case with the auditors of the sermon, is not one of mere rhetorical dexterity. There is a " breath and finer spirit " about Hooker's handling of his theme that had not been noticeable in English preaching before then, a touch of the sublimity which is " the echo of a great soul " of which Longinus speaks, and which, although it could not be handed on directly to others, yet having once found adequate expression in English, was to remain an indication of the fuller possibilities of pulpit style and challenge the future.

[1] Keble's ed., vol. iii, pp. 474-5.

5

Nowhere in Hooker is there slavish imitation. He is Isocratean by tradition, Ciceronian in the best sense of the word, but not because of deliberate imitation of a classical original. These epithets are not to be applied to him as the epithet ' Senecan ' is applicable to Bacon or bishop Hall. The fact that in reading his work we are reminded of the Classical Orators and of the Fathers proves that there is some quality which he has in common with them, a quality at once more subtle and more admirable than meticulous attention to petty rules and ingenious verbal experiment could achieve. Even if the rhetorical education which lay behind the pulpit oratory of the seventeenth century, and the appreciation and criticism which accompanied it, remained of a somewhat mechanical type, yet the fact that the English language carried with it such possibilities of felicitous expression, and that these had been so successfully demonstrated, was a factor to be reckoned with. But for Hooker we might have had no Jeremy Taylor. Yet it is beyond question that the individual factor bulked largely in Hooker's work, and that a certain equilibrium and poise of spirit, a breadth and clarity of outlook, account in part for his success. The old classical insistence, put so forcibly by Quintilian,[1] and repeated *ad nauseam* by the Renaissance critics, that the orator must be *a good man* is illustrated in his case. Neither bigot nor partisan, nor controversialist, facetious friar pandering to the tastes of a vulgar auditory, nor zealous reformer burning with lively indignation, could achieve what Hooker achieved. Intense and passionate as Donne at moments is, ironical and sarcastic as South can be, the passion that became sublime and the irony that could deal such stinging wounds derive much of their effect from the quiet excellence of these authors' customary style. Golden Age as the seventeenth century was for English preaching, it was so solely because of the spirit which in the main was to animate its clear understanding and ready knowledge of the rhetorical art ; when preaching for a certain period became polemical, its beauty, like the beauty of all ordered things, was destroyed, and when the great spirit no longer animated the utterances of its preachers their sermons became flaccid and jejune.

Three great facts, therefore, emerge from this chapter of

---

[1] ' Institutio Oratoria,' Lib. II, xv.

our study—the definite connection of the sermon from an early period with the pagan oratory based upon the rhetorical culture of the ancient world, the survival of this culture in an attenuated form in the monastic education of the Middle Ages and the persistence of rhetorical artifices in the sermons and religious writings of that period, and, finally, a renewed interest in the principles of classical rhetoric, often, it is true, of a purely external kind, due to the Renaissance. This last, in England, led to the gradual realisation that such knowledge, when applied to religious topics, might become, in the hands of men of a generous temper, a means to the eloquent, forceful, and even beautiful expression of thoughts of the greatest moment. The precise nature of the rhetorical education of the seventeenth century and its particular adaptations to preaching must in turn be considered.

THE main causes which contributed to the immense importance which was assigned to rhetorical training in the latter half of the sixteenth and throughout the seventeenth centuries have already been indicated, and need only be briefly summarised here.   Rhetoric held its place partly as a survival from the Middle Ages, partly owing to revival of interest in classical studies which came with the Renaissance, partly—and here it links itself with the former of these causes—because university education continued to be dominated by the disputation, partly—and although this also represents a survival, yet the Renaissance increased the demand for elaborate imitation of classical models— because the diplomatic address of the ambassador and the polite welcome accorded to distinguished visitors on most official occasions remained the Latin oration.   Ability to write a theme in Latin, which might afterwards be pronounced *memoriter*, was the recognised preparative for public employment or academic success.   Whether a parent hoped that his boy should one day welcome his sovereign as mayor of his town, or take his degree at Oxford or Cambridge, the initial step was that the lad should become expert in the writing of themes, the pronouncing of orations, and the handling of declamations.   Hence came it that at the period when those divines whose sermons we are about to examine and their auditors or readers were boys at school, rhetoric was regarded as a study of the greatest moment.

Professor Foster Watson, our greatest authority on the prescribed courses of the English Grammar School in past centuries, in his dissertation on ' The Curriculum and Textbooks of English Schools in the First Half of the Seventeenth Century,' [1] has made abundantly plain the preponderantly rhetorical bias of education at this period.   It is true that Watson's two main authorities are John Brinsley's ' Ludus Literarius,' first published in 1612, and Charles Hoole's ' New Discovery of the Old Art of Teaching School,' which had an only edition in 1660.   But as Brinsley took his M.A. in 1588, and became schoolmaster of the Grammar School

---

[1] Published in ' Transactions of the Bibliographical Society,' vol. vi, part ii, October 1900 to March 1902, Lon., 1903. *Cf.* chaps. xxvi–xxviii in ' The English Grammar Schools to 1660,' by the same author.

at Ashby-de-la-Zouch, we may assume with fair certainty that his book, like Hoole's, represents the conclusion and practice of the twenty preceding years, and sufficient other evidence can be cited [1] to show that the study of rhetoric was steadily growing in importance throughout the sixteenth century. This is not to be wondered at, when we remember that " the speaking of Latin was a direct aim of school instruction," [2] and that *correct* speaking was quite naturally followed by *fine* speaking. Talæus' *Rhetoric* appeared in 1547, and it is interesting to note that Ramus published an edition of this work in 1579, for the association of the latter's name with a system of rhetoric was an additional recommendation to Protestant students, and particularly to those studying at Cambridge, where Ramus' anti-Aristotelianism was received with applause.

The association of Ramus with rhetoric is also interesting from another standpoint, namely, the way in which he combined logic with rhetoric ; indeed, Bass Mullinger records that—

" Keckermann, his rival in the schools, while unable to deny his astonishing success, ascribed it, not to any inherent merit in his method, but to the meretricious art with which he had mingled logic and rhetoric . . ." ; [3]

while his ardent admirer, Gabriel Harvey, in a passage in the latter's ' Rhetor,' maintained that even in the province of rhetoric he was entitled to a foremost place.[4] Harvey's ' Rhetor ' was published in 1577, when the Trinity College Statutes of 1560 would be in force, the ninth of which, ' De Lectorum officio,' deals, among other things, with the duties of the ' sublectores '—' Primus legat *Topica* Aristotilis ; secundus exponat vel Rodolphum Agricolam *de Inventione*, vel librum *de Elenchis* Aristotelis, vel libros qui *Analytici* dicuntur. . . .' [5] The more orthodox authors are indicated in the Statute, but the original conflict with Rome and the growing conflict of Puritanism with its

---

[1] ' The English Grammar School . . .' pp. 440-1 and 448 *seq.*
[2] *Ibid.*, p. 441.
[3] ' The University of Cambridge,' vol. ii, p. 408.
[4] *Ibid.*, p. 411.
[5] *Ibid.*, Appendix. For Rodolphus Agricola's ' De Inventione, ' see *ante*, p. 60.

antagonists made a combination of dialectic and rhetoric especially attractive. But even this attraction, as Professor Watson points out, was not the greatest merit of Ramus, but rather the fact that he " introduced the liberal quotation of writers into his works," [1] and so opened up a wider field of illustration than had hitherto been customary, a fact which led directly to the *rhetoricæ sacræ* with their Scriptural examples. For, and the fact is significant, while a certain number of the citations found in sermons of the seventeenth century are traceable to the desire to provide first-hand evidence or secure conviction by an appeal to antiquity, the habit of quoting, based as it so largely was upon the keeping of commonplace-books, was a rhetorical habit, and was bound up with the education of the time.

From such works as Leach's ' Educational Charters and Documents,' and the histories of the great public schools, we are able to form a fairly clear conception of the authors studied by a schoolboy in the late sixteenth century,[2] with whose promotion to the Fifth Form came the making of themes. The moral bias behind the choice of authors is very noticeable, and is in part a legacy of the pre-Reformation Church, in part due to the moral earnestness of the Reformers. Colet, in drawing up the Statutes of St. Paul's School, decreed the use of Erasmus' *Institutum Christiani Hominis* and *Copia*, Lactantius, Prudentius, Proba, Sedulius, Juvencus, and Mantuanus, because they were Christian,[3] followed by Vergil, Sallust, Terence, and Tully for obvious reasons, and throughout the century edification remained the prime consideration, accompanied in upper forms by attention to embellishment and illustration. Such works as Alexander Ross's ' *Virgilius Evangelizans*, or a History of Jesus Christ described in the actual words of Virgil,' or Schonæus's *Terentius Christianus*, mentioned by Watson,[4] indicate the strongly religious current of sixteenth-century thought.

John Sturm of Strassburg, an ardent reformer and as

---

[1] ' The English Grammar School,' p. 449.

[2] *Vide* in this connection Lee : ' Life of Shakespeare,' 6th ed., Lon., 1916, p. 16, and Sir John Sandys' article on "Education " in ' Shakespeare's England,' vol. i, 2 vols., Oxf., 1916.

[3] ' The Life of Dr. John Colet . . .' by Samuel Knight, D.D., Oxf., 1823, p. 309.

[4] ' The Curriculum and Text-books of English Schools . . .' pp. 91 and 232, footnote.

ardent a Ciceronian, was one of the strongest influences in shaping the Protestant curriculum in so far as it endeavoured to combine sound doctrine with a genuine cultivation of the humanities, and his method of translation from and re-translation into Latin as a means of cultivating a good style, which was so heartily advocated by Ascham in ' The School-master,' was widely accepted during his own and the following century. Thus, somewhere between 1663 and 1669, during which years the nephew of Richard Baxter is traditionally said to have been at Harrow, we find his aunt writing to him the advice : " Translate and re-translate your authors." [1] Such a practice, it goes without saying, was bound to have a lasting influence on both taste and style. Whether Ciceronianism was the fashion, or later on, partly owing to the influence of Lipsius and Muretus, Seneca's became the favourite style, when men came to write in the vernacular, unconsciously or deliberately, they imitated their classical models.

Ascham, moreover, provides us with a clearer understanding of what lay behind the contemporary feeling for choice diction and care for form :

" They be not wise . . ." (he writes [2]) " that say, ' What care I for a man's words and utterance, if his matter and reasons be good.' Good and choice meats be no more requisite for healthy bodies than proper and apt words be for good matters. . . . Ye know not what hurt ye do learning that care not for words, but for matter, and so make a divorce betwixt tongue and heart. For mark all ages ; look upon the whole course of both the Greek and Latin tongue, and ye shall surely find that when apt and good words began to be neglected . . . then also began ill deedes to spring, strange manners to oppress good order, new and fond opinions to strive with old and true doctrine, first in philosophy and after in religion ; right judgment of all things to be perverted. . . ."

In other words, the *eloquent* man not only had to be the *good* man, but training of a rhetorical kind, if rightly managed, was considered likely to be also moral training.

[1] Powicke : ' Richard Baxter under the Cross,' Lon., 1927, p. 114.
[2] Giles' ed., vol. iv, pp. 211–12.

This last point is made explicit by Brinsley in the ' Ludus Literarius,' the thirteenth chapter of which is entitled, ' Of making Theames full of good matter, in a pure stile, and with judgement.' [1] " Next after Epistles," he writes, " Theames doe follow " ; and he advocates pupils commencing these exercises by mastering Aphthonius' rules. Following an example given—and this was apparently the usual method employed—boys were set to write a theme having the proper parts, *exordium, narratio, confirmatio, confutatio,* and *conclusio* ; but this they often found difficult to do, as they had no means of providing " matter " for confirmation and confutation.   This fact leads Philoponus, one of the speakers in the book, which is in the form of a dialogue, to note the difficult character of Aphthonius for boys, and to urge that schoolmasters should consider " what is the end and purpose of their making Theames."   This question he himself answers :

" The principal end of making Theams, I take to be this, to furnish schollers with all store of the choicest matter, that they may thereby learn to understand, speak or write of any ordinary Theame, Morale or Politicall, such as usually fall into discourse amongst men and in practice of life ; and especially concerning virtues and vices." [2]

The last-mentioned idea is then further elaborated, and it is made plain that the theme aimed at the moral improvement of the theme-maker.

The difficulty for boys to find suitable matter to support their arguments, especially when these were in support of mythical and allegorical subjects, as were the *suasoriæ* and *controuersiæ* of late classical times, is next faced, and we learn that scholars were expected to collect matter " by attending carefully to their first books "—the *Sententiæ,*[3] *Cato, Æsop's Fables*—and by reading over ' Tully's sentences ' or such other ' sentences ' as they found quoted in grammars. Finally, a good collection of sententious sayings, such as Reusner's ' Symbola,' should be chosen.   The theme when completed should not to begin with be " above 12 or 16 lines " ; the written copy was then given up to the master,

---

[1] Campagnac's reprint (1917) of the 1627 ed., pp. 172 *seq.*
[2] *Loc. cit.,* pp. 174-5 ; probably ' fall ' should read ' falls.'
[3] This was the ' Sententiæ Pueriles ' of Leonhard Culmann, of Krailsheim.

and the boy pronounced what he had prepared without book.[1]

Several facts already alluded to are to be found in this account, such as the traditional character of the themes revived by the Renaissance humanists, the moral trend in the textbooks studied, and the fact that grammars were used to provide apt citations. Further information follows in Brinsley with regard to the methods employed in framing the theme. After the scholars had collected matter out of Reusner or others, they should "learne to flourish and adorne their Theames" out of Aphthonius, and this apparently was done by demanding first of all Aphthonius' arguments, "as, what reasons hee hath from the Cause, Effect, Contrarie, Similitude, Example, Testemonie," and then leading the boys to apply " what reasons every one can give of his owne, to prove the same." Objections, absurdities, and inconveniences were next to be considered, and some scholars set to answer these. The matter so prepared was then to be relegated to the five parts of the theme, already noted, and here the ' Progymnasmata ' of Aphthonius was again found useful to supply " variety of Exordiums and Conclusions." [2] Finally, we find instructions for the writing of the theme, and this it is clear is the origin of the marginal references which we have already noted in Baro's sermons. In the left-hand margin the several parts of the theme were to be indicated, as *Exordium, Narratio*, and so on, and the heads of the several arguments used noted, according to Aphthonius' usage ; while in the right-hand margin the names of the various tropes or figures employed were to be shown.[3]

These directions are of great importance to our subject, for they admit us to the very workshop where seventeenth-century pulpit oratory was framed, and explain at once the outstanding rhetorical ability of the preachers and the precision, accuracy, and method of their auditors and note-takers. The fact, moreover, that Baro, preaching *ad clerum*, very probably delivered what he had previously prepared with careful marginal notation—which no doubt is the explanation of the directions printed with his sermon—proves at once the continuity of the university study of rhetoric with rhetoric as studied in the grammar schools,

[1] *Op. cit.*, pp. 176–7.   [2] *Ibid.*, pp. 179–82.   [3] *Ibid.*, p. 185.

and the close connection of the sermon with the theme.
This connection is still further emphasised by Brinsley's
recommendations with regard to the note-taking of sermons
by schoolboys, to which allusion has already been made.
In order better to imprint the sermon in their memories
the scholars were to leave spaces between the parts, and to
divide the parts clearly by means of horizontal lines.[1] This
practice is to be found taken over by the printers of early
Jacobean sermons, which indicates that either such printed
sermons were derived from the notes of an auditor, or the
preachers themselves employed the method referred to.
Brinsley, moreover, required his scholars—

" to distinguish the severall parts by letters or figures, and
setting the summe of every thing in the Margent over-
against each matter a word or two. As Text, Division,
Summe.

First Observation, or first Doctrine, Proofes, Reasons 1.
2. 3. Uses 1. 2. 3. So the second observation or Doctrine,
Proofes, Reasons, &c. so throughout. Or what method
soever the Preacher doth use, to follow the parts after the
same manner, so well as they can.

Direct them to leave good Margents for these purposes :
and so soone as ever the Preacher quotes any Scripture, as
he nameth it, to set it in the Margent against the place, lest
it slip out of memory." [2]

After sermon-time the whole was to be revised and each
scholar to set " downe the summe of every chiefe head,
faire and distinctly in the Margent over against the place."

" By this helpe " (he concludes) " they will be able to
understand, and make a repetition of the Sermon, with
a very little meditation ; yea to doe it with admiration for
children."

But that was not the end of the business, nor at nine
o'clock next morning, when the sermon so learned was to
be turned into Latin, was it finally dropped ; but, as we
have seen,[3] the following Monday, he advised—

" . . . some one of the higher formes might be appointed
in order to make a repetition of the whole Sermon without

---

[1] *Op. cit.*, p. 256.   [2] *Ibid.*, p. 256.   [3] *Ante*, p. 33.

book, according as I showed the manner of setting it down ;
rehearsing the severall parts so distinctly & briefly, as the
rest attending may the better conceive of the whole, and not
exceed the space of a quarter of an houre." [1]

This proposal is objected to by Spoudeus, Brinsley's
imaginary interlocutor, as being too difficult to be successfully managed by boys, to whom Brinsley, in the person of
Philoponus (the name is probably significant), replies that
" the schollers will do it very readily where the Preachers
keep any good order " [2] ; and, in short, if they observe
the directions just cited.   The preachers of the next generation, it is obvious, who received this training were likely to
keep " good order," and this, along with certain traditional
reasons, was to be responsible for much of the dullness of
Puritan preaching.   Not all who wrote sermons to the
pattern prescribed by the school theme remembered to
" flourish and adorne " them, nor considered it proper to
do so ; while those preachers, on the other hand, who made
more ready use of ornament, in whose work the foliage obscures the branches, having been subjected to a somewhat
similar or identical training, in spite of the greater embellishment of their style, usually advanced, if less obviously, by
recognisable stages to a closely reasoned conclusion.

Greater subtlety in management and the employment of
a more elaborate style came with the university study of
rhetoric, and was associated with the framing of orations.
This employment Brinsley considered belonged to a later
stage in education rather than to school-work, although he
remarked that at " schooles of speciall note " an oration
would occasionally be required to entertain a benefactor.[3]
For much the same reason, namely, the immaturity of the
scholars, he advised that declamations, which he describes
as " themes on controverted matters," [4] should be confined
to " Grammatical disputations . . . leaving Logicall and
strict concluding by Syllogisms, unto the Universitie." [5]

All schoolmasters, however, did not make such distinctions
nor did all agree with the postponement proposed, for in
1659 we find Hoole laying it down that boys of the Fifth
Form were to " pronounce *Orations* on Mondayes, Tues-

---

[1] *Op. cit.*, p. 257.   [2] *Ibid.*, p. 258.   [3] *Ibid.*, p. 189.
[4] *Ibid.*, p. 184.   [5] *Ibid.*, p. 207.

dayes, and Wednesdayes," while once a week they were to
be given a theme.[1] The former were to take the form of
fictitious speeches on matter derived from Livy ; the latter
was to be a speech on an original topic set for the occasion.
Hoole definitely believed in frequency and variety in the
rhetorical exercises set ; in his opinion—

" no day in the week should passe on which some Declamation, Oration, or Theme should not be pronounced . . .
that by assiduity in these exercises, the Scholars may be
emboldened to perform them with a grace before whomso-
ever, and upon occasion of any solemnity, or coming of
Friends into the Schoole." [2]

Further he gives the direction, which can refer only to
declamations :

" There should be two standing desks set opposite in the
midst of the Schoole, for boyes to stand at, when they
pronounce." [3]

The obvious inference from the two sets of quotations
given is that either Brinsley was seeking to initiate a reform
and confine boys during their entire school-days to themes
and simple declamations, and that more elaborate attempts
were common, or with the advance of the century education
was following the natural tendency to provide instruction
of an increasingly advanced character, so that the oration
and the declamation came to be more frequently cultivated
in school. The somewhat indefinite line of demarcation
between school studies and university studies which then
existed may also account for Hoole's advice, while the con-
fusions of the civil war period with the partisan character
of the two Universities and their later subjection to Presbyterian and Independent rule may quite conceivably have
led to an advanced study and practice of rhetoric in the
schools, since for many such would be the farthest point
they would reach in the subject.

What is material to our study to note is the great import-

---

[1] ' A New Discovery of the Old Art of Teaching Schoole. . . . Edited . . .
by E. T. Campagnac,' p. 189.
[2] *Ibid.*, p. 266.   [3] *Ibid.*, p. 266.

ance attached to rhetorical training and its close connection
with the attendance of scholars at church and the notes they
were required to take of sermons, which were quite frankly
regarded as the most frequently and readily accessible
exemplars of public speaking available. It is important,
too, to remember that all who received education at one
of the public schools or a grammar school received this
training, and that, consequently, the interest in rhetoric
was widespread. Aubrey relates, for example, of Edmund,
elder brother of Thomas Hobbes, who was afterwards a
glover, that—

" he had been bred at schoole with his brother ; could
make theme, and verse, and understood a little Greek to
his dyeing day " [1] ;

and the fact that from 1606 onwards the annual ' probation '
or examination with a view to promotion at the Merchant
Taylors' School took the form of a public pronouncement
of themes and declamations, which the boys of other schools
were permitted to attend,[2] and that many of those who
competed and many of those present were afterwards not
to enter the learned professions but engage in trade, must
have increased to a great extent the contemporary knowledge
of rhetorical forms and methods among those destined to
be the richer and better-educated merchants.

Moreover, it is of consequence to bear in mind that
Brinsley was a Puritan, and that the Puritan party was
interested in such rhetorical training, even if its application
was to be severely limited when it came to the composition
of sermons. All Puritans were not of a mind with those
against whom Barrow and Greenwood, the separatists,
protested that they condemned " Logick, Rhetorike [sic]
and other liberal Artes," [3] denying preachers the use of
literary embellishments on the plea that these were the
fruits of human invention, and contending that sound
doctrine ought to be delivered either in the words of Scripture or at least without rhetorical ornaments. Not until

[1] ' Brief Lives,' ed. Clark, 2 vols., Oxf., 1898, vol. i, p. 325.
[2] Watson : ' The English Grammar School,' p. 459.
[3] ' A short Reply *vnto the last printed books of* Henry Barrow *and* John *Green-wood*, the chiefe ringleaders of our Donatists in England : . . . By *George Gyffard* . . .' Lon., 1591, 4to, p. 98.

the attacks of Webster and other fanatics in the time of the
Commonwealth were the aids of secular education in the
framing of sermons to be called in question, although the
distinction between the word of God contained in the Bible
and the word of God as mediated in sermons—which arise
from the " will of man, and therefore they oftentimes
accordinglie taste too much of that overcorrupt fountaine
from which they come "[1]—was definitely recognised.
Preachers of the Calvinistic persuasion, in the main, were
ready to employ familiar methods in logic to further their
cause, as may be gathered from Culverwel's defence of the
use of the syllogism,[2] but were concerned to keep logic
free from that adulteration with rhetorical devices for which
to some extent Ramus must be held responsible.   Thus we
find Baxter complaining that Gauden's speeches at the
Savoy Conference were all rhetoric and no logic,[3] in a context implying the former's belief in the logical method as
the proper one by which to conduct an argument ; which,
as Mr. Bass Mullinger notes, was a relic of the scholastic
disputes which survived to be taken over both by the leaders
of the Established Church and by men like Cartwright.[4]

Baxter's fuller opinion on the application of learning to
preaching we shall return to in the next section ; that,
however, there was a contemporary danger of preachers
attending overmuch to the embellishing of their sermons
and neglecting sound reasoning is made explicit by a
quotation from Selden's ' Table Talk '[5] :

[1] ' A Christian Letter . . . vnto that Reverend and learned man, Mr.
R. Hoo. [(sic) i.e. Hooker] . . .' No place, 1599, 4to, p. 21.
[2] ' Discourse of the Light of Nature,' ed. Brown, Edin., 1857, p. 18, as
against Smith, whose editor, Worthington, in his prefatory remarks to the
' Select Discourses ' (pp. xxvi–xxvii), tells us that he strove " to accommodate
his expression to ordinary vulgar capacities, being studious to be understood,
and not to be ignorantly wondered at by amusing the people either with high,
unnecessary speculations, or with hard words and vain ostentations of
scholastic learning "—quoted Bass Mullinger : ' The University of Cambridge,'
vol. iii, p. 634.   For Culverwel's stern Calvinism see Powicke : ' The Cambridge Platonists,' Lon., 1926, p. 141.
[3] ' Reliquiæ,' 1696 ed., Part II, p. 363.   Cf. ' Catholick Theologie . . .
The Third Part : . . .' Lon., 1675, fol., p. 108, where Baxter gives it as his
considered opinion that " . . . (seeing all metaphorical terms are ambiguous)
he that excessively useth them befriendeth not the Truth and the hearers
intellect, but while he is too much a Rhetorician he is too little a good Logician."
[4] ' University of Cambridge,' vol. ii, p. 415.
[5] Arber's Reprints, No. 6, p. 16.   Selden's remarks on preaching are to be
found at pp. 104–9 of Sir Frederick Pollock's ed. of T.T. (Lon., 1927).

" First in your sermons use your logic, and then your rhetoric. Rhetoric without logic is like a tree with leaves and blossoms, but no root ; yet I confess more are taken with rhetoric than logic, because they are caught with a free expression, when they understand not reason. Logic must be natural, or it is worth nothing at all ; your rhetoric figures may be learned. That rhetoric is best which is most seasonable and most catching. . . ."

The fascination which logic appears to have exerted over the Puritan preachers, and which it continued to hold in the Dissenting Academies of the eighteenth century, was almost certainly due to the cause assigned to it by Professor Watson, who considers that logic in the period under discussion had come more and more " to regard material truth as of equal, if not as of superior importance to formal truth," [1] and that such was an aspect likely to appeal to the Puritans. The close connection between logic and the declamation, which had taken the place of the mediæval *disputatio*, and the fact that the declamation and oration figure so importantly in Hoole's treatise, goes far to support the contentions of Bass Mullinger and of Watson.

The great interest of Hoole does not consist so much in his evidence as to the rhetorical exercises of his day, nor in the advice he gives on the carrying out of these exercises, in which he believed that boys should pronounce the different parts of a speech first in English and then turn them into Latin [2]—a distinctly doubtful method—but in the books prescribed to assist the scholars. These were Dugard's ' Elementa Rhetorices,' Butler's ' Rhetoric,' Farnaby's ' Index Rhetoricus,' Susenbrotus, and Horne's ' Compendium Rhetorices.' The more advanced pupils were to use Vossius' ' Partitiones Oratoriæ,' the ' Orator Extemporaneus,' [3] Tesmarus' ' Exercitationes Rhetoricæ,' Cassinus, Paiot, and " the late English Rhetorik," [4] by the last of which is intended Blount's ' Academie of Eloquence.' [5]

[1] ' The English Grammar School,' p. 89.
[2] *Op. cit.*, p. 185.
[3] Of Michael Radau.
[4] *Op. cit.*, pp. 132–3 ; for annotations on these works *vid.* Campagnac's notes.
[5] So Watson, ' The English Grammar School,' p. 443 note. This work appeared in 1654, and is entitled at the head of each page ' An English Rhetorique.'

William Dugard, Hoole's contemporary, was Headmaster
of Merchant Taylors' School during the Commonwealth,
and his book was to be used by the theme-makers with a
view to learning " Tropes and Figures, according to the
definitions given by Talæus and afterwards illustrated by
Mr. Butler." [1]   Butler's close connection with Talæus had
also been stressed by Brinsley, who described his book as
" a notable abridgement of Talaeus, making it most
plaine, and farre more easie to be learned of schollers. . . . " [2]
The method of the book was the familiar one of general
statement followed by quotations from the classical authors
illustrating a particular figure, and pointed more or less
directly to the keeping of commonplace-books, which were
a means of linking up the ordinary reading of a form with
theme-making and orations. Having regard, however,
to the youth of his scholars, and the limits necessarily set
to their reading, Hoole believed that the best way to start
such commonplace-books was to make a digest of Dugard's
' Elementa,' and so, once having procured suitable headings, to note under each whatever the scholars liked from the
other rhetorical aids catalogued, " till they be better able
to peruse other Authors, that more fully treat of the Art." [3]
Farnaby's ' Index Rhetoricus ' was particularly helpful in
this respect, as it provided, in the section entitled ' De
Formularum Usu et Imitatione,' under particular heads, a
copious collection of phrases not only out of the great orators,
but also out of the Renaissance critics and scholars.   And,
in giving directions for the writing of themes by the Fifth
Form, we find Hoole requiring that the boys should " write
at least those heads which Mr. Farnabie hath set down in his
Index Rhetoricus," [4] and then proceed to collect various
words and phrases under these, which, as the ' Index
Rhetoricus ' first appeared in 1625, we may assume to have
been the usual method of theme-writing during the thirty-
five years that had elapsed since then.

As the scholars grew older, however, their tasks became more difficult.   Clark's ' Formulæ Oratoriæ ' and
Horne's ' De Usu Authoris ' are recommended as ' helps.'

---

[1] Hoole : *op. cit.*, p. 132.
[2] ' Ludus Literarius,' Campagnac's ed., p. 204.
[3] *Op. cit.*, p. 133.
[4] *Op. cit.*, p. 181.

" Likewise " (Hoole writes [1]) " to bring themselves to an habituated perfection of a good style, they should be frequent in perusing and excerpting passages that may serve for their occasions out of *Tully, Quintilian, Livie, Salust, Tacitus, Quintus Curtius,* and the like ancient Orations."

A list of " moderne Orators " follows, among whom Muretus, Heinsius, Lipsius, and Salvatius may be noted. Finally—

" *Tesmarus,* and the *Orator extemporaneus* will shew them how to dispose their matter so, as to make an Oration of any subject in Latine, *ex tempore ;* and *Aphthonius,* and *Libanius Sophista* will furnish them with patterns in Greek. . . ."

The books recommended were to be found in the school library.

The ' Partitiones ' of Vossius, to which the elder scholars were referred, was one of the standard rhetorical works of the century, and dealt in great fullness with the whole Art. It is particularly interesting as affording clear evidence of the interest in the traditional *schemata,* and goes some way towards showing how the word-play of preachers like Andrewes originated in imitation of classical models. We wonder less when we hear the latter speak of " Micha-el and Gabri-el, and if He will ' twelve legions of Angels ' " [2] when we remember that Vossius, with whom he corresponded, writing ' De Schematibus in verbis Similis Soni,' considered a good specimen of such " plurimum ad delectandum valet," and gave as an example :

" Cicero in Lælio. Sed ut tum ad senem senex de senectute : sic in hoc libro ad amicum amicissimus de amicitia scripsi . . ." [3] ;

and it is no cause for wonder that men who, as schoolboys or university students, had hunted their authors to find such assonantal phrases for their commonplace-books would be quick to appreciate their imitation in the vernacular.

[1] *Op. cit.,* pp. 200–1.
[2] ' XCVI Sermons,' 1635, IXth Nativity Sermon, p. 80.
[3] ' Rhetorices Contractæ Sive Partitionum Oratoriarum Libri V,' Oxf., 1672, pp. 329 *seq.*

6

The interest of Blount's book lies in the fact that it was, what Hoole calls it, an ' English Rhetorik,' " comprehending," as the author claimed in the epistle dedicatory, " all the most usefull Figures, exemplified out of the *Arcadia* and other choicest Authors." [1]   In other words, it gave in English, with examples drawn from English literature, what the older rhetorics had previously given in Latin and illustrated from classical or Renaissance sources.   From the same epistle dedicatory we learn that Blount considered

" diligence and pain in collecting Common-places to be of great use and certainty in studying ; as, that which aids the memory, subministers copy to invention, and contracts the sight of judgement to a strength."

The commonplaces given—the *formulæ majores*—are collections of sayings or quotations gathered under particular heads as ' Company,' ' Constancy ' and so on, which could be used whenever a theme had to be written.   There follow the *formulæ minores*, which are short sentences extracted from many sources, illustrating various figures, and suitable for inserting into speeches.   In this connection one naturally recalls the practice of revising sermons before printing and the acknowledged habit of inserting quotations. Whatever the motive, where such insertions were not mere citations of Scripture, the origin of the habit is clear ; indeed, in a century famous for the citations and allusions in its sermons, the influence of the commonplace-book is manifest, and the approval with which these quotations were received is quite plainly connected with the prevailing practice in school and college.

The general principles underlying the keeping of commonplace-books are fairly evident, but in order that the best results might be attained scientific methods were employed.   Probably the most precise advice as to how to make profitable excerpts is contained in the manual of the Jesuit, Drexilius, to whom, naturally enough, Hoole does not refer.   Jeremy Taylor, it may be noted in passing, of all English divines, shows most acquaintance with the works of Drexilius, a fact not without interest when we remember the mosaic of quotations and allusions from very varied

[1] ' The Academie of Eloquence . . .' Lon., 1654, 12mo.

sources which that preacher's works display. Drexilius'
'Aurifodina Artium et scientiarum omnium Excerpendi
Solertia . . ." [1] throws much light on the methods employed. Starting off with the contention based on a statement of Lipsius, "pæne omnia lectio perit, quæ nihil
excerpit," [2] the author, in the first part of his work, appeals
to the example of famous writers in classical and subsequent
times who have made a practice of making excerpts. In
pars altera he comes to 'Excerptorum Methodus, seu
Quomodo Excerpendum sit,' in which a chapter [3] is devoted
to how to keep a book of extracts. In this last, for example,
under the heading LACRYMÆ, is gathered together a notable
collection of passages dealing with grief taken from famous
authors and useful for incorporation into themes and orations. [4] In subsequent chapters examples are supplied of
how to make excerpts from histories and from philosophical,
mathematical, medical, legal, and theological works. In
the third part of the manual there is a considerable amount
of advice to preachers.

Drexilius' purpose in writing his little book was clearly
to enable others, particularly intending preachers, to carry
out their excerpting as profitably as possible, just as in his
'Rhetorica Cœlestis seu Attente precandi scientia,' [5] he
had addressed himself to the arrangement and presentation
of topics in prayer. The method he illustrates, we may
assume, was the customary one, as it bears a close resemblance to the treatment of *communes loci* in contemporary
rhetorics, but Cotton Mather, early in the following century,
in his 'Manuductio ad Ministerium,' [6] in advising the keeping
of a "Quotidiana or Commonplace Book," suggests that
the student should enter his excerpts as he found them
without reference to 'heads,' but with numbers attached
to each which should correspond to the number assigned
to the usual 'heads' in an index. Although he does not
expressly say so, this latter method may well have been a
traditional one among the Puritan preachers, from whom
Mather was descended and with whom he was connected.

No great difficulty is experienced in tracing the debt of
the seventeenth-century sermon to the commonplace-book.

[1] Antwerp, 1641, sm. 8vo.
[2] *Op. cit.*, p. 2 ; *cf. ibid.*, p. 11.
[3] IV.
[4] *Vid.* ed. cit., pp. 94–101.
[5] Antwerp, 1636, 12mo.
[6] Boston, 1726, p. 72.

Dr. Evelyn Simpson has drawn attention to passages occurring twice in the work of Donne which appear to illustrate this usage,[1] and in Playfere's complete works there are several reproductions of passages already used.[2] Indeed, we find Robinson, in a note to his edition of Claude's ' Essay on the Composition of a Sermon,' declaring that " many sermons of the last century are mere commonplace collections." [3] The manner in which preachers are known to have prepared their sermons is additional proof of the persistence of this rhetorical habit. Napier, after a careful study of Barrow's manuscripts, assures us that the latter's method of framing his sermons was as follows :

" The subject chosen, he seems to have drawn up a scheme of his intended argument ; this he unfolded at some length under heads, leaving spaces for new matter ; this again, after receiving the amplifications, was written out fully. . . ." [4] ;

and the same editor claimed the dissertation ' Relating to the Dissenters ' as a genuine composition by Barrow, not only on the grounds of handwriting, but because

." the very cast of the MS. vouches for its authenticity ; the arguments are arranged under several heads, and spaces are left for new matter—Barrow's mode of composing, as evinced in many instances throughout the MSS." [5]

Such evidence is important, for Barrow's works present a peculiarly happy instance of the use of a commonplace-book, though there is little doubt that the habit of embellishing rather than illustrating a sermon by passages excerpted in reading was a pernicious one, originating, as has been hinted, less from the desire to give irrefragable proofs than from the rhetorical trend of contemporary education ;

[1] ' A Study of the Prose Works of John Donne,' p. 252.
[2] In ' The Whole Sermons. . .' 1623, pp. 186–7 reproduce much of the matter of pp. 131–2, and p. 188 repeats p. 130, the former reference pointing to an entry in a commonplace-book from Philo Judæus or some source in which Philo is quoted.
[3] Quoted Williams' ' The Christian Preacher,' 2nd ed., 1809, footnote, pp. 303–4 ; cf. Claude's ' Essay,' ed. Robinson, 3rd ed., 1788, p. 34.
[4] ' The Theological Works of Isaac Barrow . . .' Camb., 1859, p. xvi.
[5] Ed. cit., p. xxix.

since, among men brought up to the framing of themes and orations on the basis of the commonplace-book, a sermon was simply a further occasion to apply a familiar method.

The application of the title 'commonplaces' to the exercises performed by fellows of colleges at daily prayers almost certainly arose from the same habit. The 'commonplace' was a brief collection of thoughts arising out of a particular passage of Scripture and serving as a kind of 'meditation' to focus the attention of the worshippers.[1] The particular text suggested the reflections that followed, and these on occasion may well have been a collection of instances or quotations connected with the leading subject. Such a method of address was naturally inclined to be disjointed, and it is therefore not to be wondered that preaching in 'a commonplace way' did not meet with the approval of the thoughtful. Where such commonplaces did not resemble a theme garishly set out with quotations, they were often mere trite exposition.

The intimate connection of the school and university declamation or oration with preaching is further exemplified by the account given of the 'trials' of a Scots probationer in Thomas Burnet's *Life*, of his father. Among other exercises set, we are told—

" the Examiners allot a head of Divinity to each, on which they are to make a *Latin* oration, and to give out theses upon it, which they undertake to defend in publick." [2]

As a probationer's 'trials' in Scotland are an ecclesiastical test, designed not so much to discover the candidate's academic attainments as his fitness to become a preacher, it is apparent that this procedure is not to be compared with the defence of theses at Oxford or Cambridge on the occasion of a preacher taking his B.D. degree. The Latin oration was regarded as a good preparative to preaching, demonstrating as it did *partition, disposition, illustration, embellishment*, and other aspects of rhetorical practice. Yet, apart from orderliness, it is questionable if such was the case, for the excellence of the oration consisted in its care-

---

[1] *Vide* Bass Mullinger's description, 'The University of Cambridge,' vol. ii, p. 472.
[2] 'Hist. of his own Time,' vol. ii (1734), p. 674.

fully employed or consciously imitative phrasing, and this was of little account or help when it came to producing a sermon in English. Eachard's contention, therefore, that the teaching of English at the universities was necessary to aid intending preachers, and that college exercises performed in Latin did not suffice, is seen to be justified, for as he aptly remarked, although " Oratory is the same in all Languages : The same Rules being observed, the same Method, the same Arguments, and Arts of Persuasion," youths could not be expected

" so to apprehend those general Laws, as to make a just and allowable Use of them in all Languages, unless exercised particularly in them." [1]

It is for a reason closely connected with Eachard's perfectly just criticism that Smith's ' Mysterie of Rhetorique Unvail'd ' is of particular interest, because in this work not only were the tropes and figures described with " lively Definitions," but it included " Variety of *Latin, English,* & *Scriptural* Examples, Pertinent to each of them apart." It is to be noted that the work is a secular one and not a *rhetorica sacra,* and that the " Scriptural Examples " are consequently a widening of the field for illustrative purposes. Smith expressly tells us that he did not aim at writing an *Art of Rhetoric,* but rather to furnish

" a Key to unlock and lay open those abstruse difficulties which the Tropes and Figures have hitherto, not only been masked with, but lock'd up under. . . ." [2]

Smith's definitions are the current ones, but the fact that they are set out briefly in English, accompanied by examples in the vernacular and from the Authorised Version, must have been of material assistance to preachers.

For Smith rhetoric had two main parts, consisting in :

" 1. Garnishing of speech, called *Elocution.*
  2. Garnishing of the manner of utterance, called *Pronunciation.* . . ."

[1] 'The *Grounds* and *Occasions* of the *Contempt* of the CLERGY . . .' Lon., 1705, p. 23.
[2] *Op. cit.,* Lon., 1657, ' To the Reader.'

The former was concerned with—

" The fine manner of words called a *Trope ;* or,
" The fine shape or frame of speech, called a *Figure.* . . .
" A *Trope* is when words are used for elegancy in a changed signification ; or when a word is drawn from its proper and genuine signification to another. . . .
" A *Figure* in the Greek σχῆμα [*schema*] (among other things) signifies principally . . . the apparel and ornament of the body ; which by a metaphor is transferred to signifie the habit and ornament of words or speech : . . .
" A *Figure* is an ornament of elocution . . . And as in a *Trope,* or the finenesse of words, words are considered asunder by themselves, so in a *Figure,* the apt and pleasant joyning together of many words is noted : . . .
" A *Figure* is twofold, *viz.*
    1. *Figura dictionis*
    2. *Figura sententiæ.*
Whereof the former belongs to the matter, and, as it were, to the body of speech ; but the latter, to the form, and as it were to the soul, that is, to the sentence." [1]

This last distinction is rendered still clearer by Richardson, the author of ' The Logicians School-Master,' with whose work of that name are bound up imperfect notes on Ramus' ' Grammar ' and Talæus' ' Rhetoric.'

" *Figura dictionis* " (we are told) " is in the outward word, but *figura sententiæ* is in the inward matter principally, yet in the outward also . . . this *figura dictionis* is either in the measure of sounds, or in the repetition of them. . . ." [2]

Such definitions are of course by no means novel ; they are as old as the recognition of rhetoric itself as a useful art. The element of novelty in their expression at the period of our study lies in the fact that principles derived from Greek and Latin constructions, and natural to those languages,

---

[1] *Op. cit.,* pp. 1-5.
[2] *Op. cit.,* Lon., 1657, pp. 67-8. Empson, in his interesting study, ' Seven Types of Ambiguity,' Lon., 1930, p. 111—citing Shakespeare as the master-craftsman of his period and that which immediately follows, writes : " But Shakespeare's interest in the sound relationships between words was in no degree detached from his interest in their total meaning "—which is just another way of expressing this rhetorical distinction.

had come to be openly regarded as applicable to English. Herein lies the difference between Blount's 'English Rhetorique' and Smith's work : Blount was still writing a manual of rhetoric for students who were to write in Latin ; his book resembled that of North and Hillard, or any standard book on Latin composition of our own times ; Smith, on the contrary, had in view the wider extension of the rhetorical field which his threefold choice of examples indicates. That the classical figures, the legacy of Gorgianic or Isocratean rhetoric, flourished in the vernacular, and, particularly in the vernacular sermon, we have seen in the previous section, and the quotation given from Hooker is an excellent example of the *figura sententiæ*, in which the 'inward matter,' the contrast of Christ's agony and the Pharisee's self-confidence, is the preacher's principal concern, but where the *figura dictionis* has not been altogether neglected. Treating of a somewhat similar theme, in a sermon at Norwich in 1645 we find Edward Willan, of Corpus Christi College, Cambridge, and vicar of Hoxne, expressing himself as follows :

" The fairest way (though it be the furthest way) into the *City* of the *Text* is thorow the Suburbs of the verse before it. And by that way wee may observe, that Christ's way to *Heaven* was by the *Gates* of *Hell*. In the verse before the Text the Prophet foretells the *Bitternesse of Christs Passion ;* In the Text it selfe hee tells the *Blessednesse of Christs Glorification*. In that wee may behold him in his *lowest Humiliation* ; In this we may behold him in his *highest Exaltation*. In that we observe him sustaining the *fullnesse of sorrow* in his Fathers absence ; In this wee may observe him regaining the *fullnesse of joy* in his Father's Presence. In that wee may see how hee felt the heavy Hand of Gods displeasure for a time ; In this wee may see how hee found the pleasure at Gods right Hand for evermore. And thus in both together wee may observe how Christ passed by the Crosse of ignominy, and the ignominy of the Crosse, unto the Crown of Glory, and the Glory of that Crown." [1]

Willan's 'Six Sermons' appeared in 1651, Smith's 'Mysterie of Rhetorique Unvail'd' in 1657, while Richard-

---

[1] 'Six Sermons,' 1651, pp. 31, 32.

son's ' Logicians School-Master ' was reissued in the latter
year. The familiar instructions and their results can therefore be compared side by side, but it is clear that Willan's
productions represent an unusually close adoption of the
traditional figures, and that, as a rule, men assimilated the
general principles underlying the study of *trope* and *figure* and
utilised their knowledge in a less artificial manner. Lever,
Jewel, Adams, and Willan illustrate the continuity of a
schematic fashion and the application of immemorial rules,
but the fact that these preachers are outstanding examples
of the fashions indicated goes to prove that their contemporaries, though educated in the same way, were less pedantic
or less artificial in the use to which they put their training.

Smith's twofold division of rhetoric into *Elocution* and
Pronunciation is of further interest, for the word elocution has
now for long been regarded as signifying a method of delivery rather than a consideration of fine speech. This was
not so in Smith's time, and what we mean by *elocution* he
considered under *pronunciation*. A considerable amount of
attention was paid to this minor branch of rhetoric. ' To
pronounce orations ' was the contemporary phrase, and
conveyed more than mere *memoriter* delivery. Lawyers
were indebted to John Bulwer for a couple of manuals on
the subject, and the *artes concionandi* are alive to its importance. Bulwer's ' Chirologia : Or the Natvrall Langvage
of the Hand. . . . *Whereunto is added* Chironomia : Or,
the Art of Manvall Rhetoricke,' [1] together form a remarkably
comprehensive account of expressive gestures both from an
historical and from a psychological point of view ; the
latter definitely professes to teach " the artificiall managing
of the Hand in Speaking." A further treatise, promised in the
epistle dedicatory to ' Chirologia,' was ' Cephalelogia '
(" the naturall language of the Head "), but this
apparently was never completed. The existence of
this interest in the management of the hands, however,
and Bulwer's attempt to methodise it, by means of a table
of gestures somewhat resembling a chart setting out the
deaf and dumb alphabet, is to be noted. That we do
not hear more of such attempts is due probably, in part to
the general directions supplied to those practising declamations or orations in the grammar schools, in part to the grow-

[1] Lon., 1644, 8vo.

ing antipathy of Englishmen, as the seventeenth century progressed, to any extravagant expression of their feelings. Bishop Burnet, his son tells us, during his sojourn in France, where he met Daillé and Morus, " thought there entered too much of the gesture of the Theatre " into the latter's delivery,[1] and precise instructions as to gestures which might readily become mannerisms would tend to be suspect.

Pronunciation in the wider sense, of which gesticulation is a subdivision, was no doubt carefully attended to, for in an age when the closely reasoned speech was the passport to scholastic success, and the complimentary oration an *open sesame* to political employment, we can be sure that this side of rhetoric was not neglected. Neither a competent knowledge of the *formulæ oratoriæ*, nor a clever use of the most elegant ' phrase-books ' could save a speaker from ruin if his delivery was at fault, and it is one of the most striking testimonies to the unbroken tradition of public speech, and the spontaneity with which it was still employed, that in the century of our study we do not meet with the modern difficulties of indistinct and affected speech.   Nasal inflections there undoubtedly were as well as ' silver-tongued' utterances, but practically all preachers, whatever their particular theological tenets, had been trained, not only in the composition of the theme or oration, but in its ' pronunciation ' in a manner likely to be acceptable to their hearers.

From the facts that have been brought together in this chapter, therefore, it is plain that the English sermon in the seventeenth century bears a direct relation to the rhetorical bias of contemporary English education, in so far as the majority of those who became the preachers of the period had received the conventional training in theme, declamation, and oration. This relation must have been definitely emphasised by the practice of note-taking of vernacular sermons enjoined by leading schoolmasters, and the close connection of the practice with the Latin exercise, so that to most seventeenth-century boys the sermon and the school-exercise must have seemed almost inextricably combined. The young preacher setting out in life, moreover, without any practice in English composition, is bound to have regarded his first sermons as set themes on slightly different

[1] " Life," in ' Hist. of his own Time,' vol. ii (1734), pp. 676 *seq.*

topics, to be treated in the customary way. Only the wider reading necessary for the divine and the exigencies of exegesis led to a modification of the familiar methods. The layman, for the most part, stopped short of this further training, though a few contemporaries, like Wotton, Howell, Evelyn, and Milton, display an extraordinary range of theological knowledge ; but the average educated man may safely be regarded as capable of judging the sermon on the purely rhetorical side rather than as a complete whole. Follow his favourite preachers he assiduously did, took notes, compared doctrines, mastered the minor arguments of each sermon, as he and they had done from their school-days up, but no longer was the range of reading in any way comparable, and he could not always find in his common-place-book the familiar quotations which appeared in the sermons of his former school-fellows. To make themes, to dispute, even to pronounce an oration—these things they had been taught in common, but with the further training of the preacher for his task there had come about a subtle change in the execution of these things ; the oratory which they had practised in common was no longer quite the same ; it had become *sacred oratory*, and was regulated and to be judged by slightly different criteria than those with which they had been familiar in their youth. What exactly these criteria were, and how they came to affect the pulpit address it will be our task to discuss in the next chapter.

It is necessary, however, to note, in conclusion, that, in spite of the importance of rhetorical training as affording an entrance to the public services throughout the seventeenth century, the study of rhetoric was closely identified with religion and religious exposition. To some this religious connection seemed its sole justification, to others its crowning glory.[1] The Puritans regarded it less as an achievement of the classical world than as a device employed by God in dictating the Holy Scriptures, and therefore worthy of grave consideration, as is evident from Perkins' treatment of the figures of speech in his ' Art of Prophecying.' [2] For the most part there was a tendency to employ rhetorical knowledge to elucidate difficult passages of the Bible, which was one of

---

[1] *Vid.*, Peter Bertius in ' De Eloquentiæ Vi Atqve Amplitvdine Oratio . . .' Paris, 1621, pp. 25–6, for expression of the latter view.
[2] 1592 ; ' The Works,' Lon., fol., 1631, vol. ii, pp. 658–9.

Smith's avowed objects in including the ' Scriptural Examples ' we have already noted.   Three years earlier, in
1654, Thomas Hall's ' Centuria Sacra ' had appeared, pro-
fessing to give " About one hundred Rules for the expounding and clearer understanding of the Holy Scriptures.   To
which are added a Synopsis or Compendium of all the most
materiall Tropes and Figures contained in the Scriptures."
Such works were religious in motive, although they were
used to teach rhetoric, and look backwards rather to
the explication of the sacred text than forwards to the
composition of the sermon.   They are important chiefly,
as has been suggested in the case of Smith's work, because
of their break with the traditional lists of Latin examples
to which the usual ' rhetorics ' had been confined, and as
opening up the application of the rules of rhetoric to the
vernacular, or showing the application of these rules in the
pages of the vernacular Scriptures.   Taking cognisance of
the literary graces of the Biblical writings on the one hand,
on the other they prepare men to defend the truths which
these writings enshrine, and although themselves leaving
' the art of preaching ' to be expounded by those others
to whose work we now turn, they carry forward the art of
rhetoric one step farther, so that we find it less strange to
hear its familiar rules applied, although with significant
modifications, to the most sacred subjects.

IV. PREACHING AS A BRANCH OF RHETORIC

" IT is the duty, then " (wrote Augustine), " of the
interpreter and teacher of Holy Scripture, the defender
of the true faith, and the opponent of error, both to teach
what is right and to refute what is wrong, and in the performance of this task to conciliate the hostile, to rouse the
careless, and to tell the ignorant both what is occurring at
present and what is probable in the future. . . . If the
hearers need teaching, the matter treated of must be fully
made known by means of narrative. On the other hand,
to clear up points that are doubtful requires reasoning, and
the exhibition of proofs. If, however, the hearers require
to be roused rather than instructed, in order that they may
be diligent to do what they already know, and to bring
their feelings into harmony with the truths they admit,
greater rigour of speech is needed. Here entreaties and
reproaches, exhortations and upbraidings, and all the other
means of rousing the emotions are necessary." [1]

Such a declaration fully justifies Dr. Oswald Dykes'
statement, quoted in a previous chapter, that " from Augustine to Melanchthon homiletics were treated almost exclusively as an application of classical rhetoric " ; for, from
the fall of the Western Empire to the break-up of the
Western Church, wherever preaching was seriously cultivated, the principles here enunciated by Augustine, with
their obvious Ciceronian and Hellenistic ancestry, were
either openly or tacitly acknowledged. Yet, as has already
been noted in passing,[2] there had always been a slight
difference in the effect which the preacher desired to
produce compared with the mere rhetorician. Desirous as
the lawyer might be to secure the acquittal of his client, or
the legislator to sway the local senate, advocate and states-
man alike could rest content with a momentary triumph
resulting from the ' proof ' that satisfied their auditors for
the time being ; the preacher desired to create a more
lasting impression, not only to " teach so as to give instruction, and please so as to keep up the attention," but to
" sway the mind so as to subdue the will," [3] and this desire

---

[1] " De Doctrina Christiana " in ' Works of Aurelius Augustine . . . A new
trans. ed. by the Rev. Marcus Dods, D.D., vol. ix '—Lib. IV, iv.
[2] *Ante*, p. 52.   [3] ' De Doct.,' Lib. IV, esp. xiii.

led to certain modifications in his procedure. Considerations of one kind or another tended to combine with the rhetorical traditions to which the preachers subscribed, and in the sixteenth century in particular, the humanistic movement first of all, and later the contentions of the Reformation, tended more and more to emphasise the distinction of preaching from ordinary oratory, and to compel the recognition of the fact, that, although it was a rhetorical study, it was a rhetorical study which was largely affected by its singular content and the peculiar aim of its professors.

The functions of the preacher, however, as outlined by Augustine, are of great importance, for the inherited formulæ of statement, refutation, conciliation, narration, and the other ends to be kept in view, and, if need be, included in the religious address, are precisely those which we find set out in the homiletical manuals of the sixteenth and seventeenth centuries. This is no doubt partly due to tradition, but in greater part it may be attributed to the religious contests of the period, whether the great cleavage between Romanism and Protestantism or the internal divergencies within the Church of England. In an earlier century Aquinas had silenced the heretics with the aid of Aristotle's logic, and for men of a later time the rhetoric of Aristotle and the classical orators, which in the hands of the Fathers had overcome the resistance of the pagan world to the Faith, was largely grasped at in order to overcome the resistance of particular bodies of Christians to what other bodies of Christians had come to regard as the Truth. The connection of Ramus with Protestantism and a system of logic, which incidentally had rhetorical leanings, has been seen, and it is significant to find Keckermann, whose name has similar associations, publishing ' Rhetoricæ Ecclesiasticæ, Siue Artis Formandi et Habendi Conciones Sacras, Libri Dvo . . .' [1] although Keckermann would have claimed vigorously that so far as logic was concerned he made no illegitimate appeal to rhetorical methods.[2] Moreover, he was emphatic that a ' church rhetoric,' or ' art of preaching,' differed fundamentally from an ordinary rhetorical manual, since the preacher ought only to use the

---

[1] Edition used ' Editio tertia,' Hanover, 1606 ; dedication to a colleague, Reuter, dated 1600.

[2] *Vid.* Bass Mullinger : ' The University of Cambridge,' vol. ii, p. 408.

artifices of rhetoric in so far as they would help him to *teach* and *move*.[1] Beauty of diction, wealth of allusion, and eloquence for its own sake and apart from religious motives, were not to be considered.

Keckermann's direct homiletical bent, as distinguished from the mere application of rhetoric to sacred subjects, is made evident when we compare his work with that of Hyperius of Marburg who still clung tenaciously to the strict classical form of the discourse. *Exordium, division* or *proposition, confirmation, confutation,* and *conclusion* follow one another in the latter's treatise as he considered they should do in a well-composed sermon. Keckermann, on the contrary, begins straight away with his text, realising that from the words themselves, or from some circumstance related to their context, a suitable introduction could be made. His work is divided into two books, of which the former deals with the *composition*, the latter with the *delivery*, of the sermon. *Composition* is concerned with *treatment* (tractatio), which is concerned in turn with *invention* (inventio) and *disposition* (dispositio) in close relationship, and *embellishment* (exornatio). *Invention* embraces *consideration of the text* (præcognitio textus quoad scopum) *division* (partitio), and *explanation of the passage* (explicatio verborum); *disposition* consists of *amplification*, which along with *explanation* would form the body of the sermon, and *application* ; the latter can be general or specific. *Embellishment* may be effected by sheer simplicity and clarity (simplici perspicuitate), by wealth of language (copia), by effective arrangement (efficacia), or by figures (figuris). The second book treats in an obvious way of voice and gesture.[2]

Fivefold division of the discourse is still found, as can be seen from the treatment indicated, but this is not simply the old parts of the Greek oration renamed. The change to the five new interests marks the break away from the old delight in imitating the striking beginnings of the Greek Fathers, which were simply adaptations of the pagan oratory of their day,[3] and which even Erasmus, it appears, considered effective.[4] The highly coloured story-opening

---

[1] Ed. cit., p. 15.
[2] *Vid.* ' Typvs Rhetoricæ Ecclesiasticæ,' at commencement of book.
[3] *Vid.* opening of Chrysostom's first homily on the Gospel of St. John, quoted *post*, p. 143, footnote [1].
[4] ' Ecclesiastes,' Book II, xxx.

fell into disuse at the Reformation, but English preachers
at the beginning of the seventeenth century still at times
indulged in *exordia*, which did not always conform to
Erasmus' further advice that these should be congruent.[1]
We hear, for example, in Manningham's *Diary* of " one
BARLOWE, a beardless man of Pembroke Hall in Cambridge,"
who " after his prayer and before he came to his text . . .
made a large exordium," in which he drew a far-fetched
resemblance between his own case on that occasion and the
case of St. Paul among the Corinthians,[2] and of another
preacher, " a young man," who " made a finicall boy-
sterius exordium "[3] ; but such procedure, it is almost
certain, was not regarded with favour, and Donne's well-
known habit of giving out a text, and immediately placing
it, which can be paralleled in slightly different, and, at times,
less obvious form by all the more outstanding divines of the
period, may be taken as the accepted method then employed.
Donne's exegesis affords a particularly good example of
Keckermann's treatment.   First comes *præcognitio textus*,
taking the place of the old exordium, with its often extraneous matter, succeeded by *partitio et propositio*—division and
enunciation of theme.   *Explicatio verborum* follows, which
occasionally resulted in intricate and ingenious attempts at
" opening the sense " of the passage selected.   *Amplification*
could cover expatiation, where the subject chosen was an
obvious one, or confirmation and confutation in the familiar
sense.   *Application* was more than a mere conclusion, for
though the word peroration still conveys the idea of a final
stirring appeal, conclusions had come to be often only artistic
endings, and the aim of the preacher was not how to conclude his address gracefully, but how to drive home his
shafts to the hearts of his hearers.

The successive consideration of these stages in the formation of a sermon gave Keckermann opportunity of giving
much valuable advice on each.   Thus in his chapter,
' De partitione textus,'[4] he advised that texts should be
divided into the fewest possible parts, and at most into
three or four—a direct repudiation of the extensive
divisions and subdivisions of the Scholastics, which were
to be only too thoroughly imitated by some of the

---

[1] ' Ecclesiastes,' Book II, xxvi.   [3] *Ibid.*, p. 132.
[2] Camden Soc., 1868, p. 111.   [4] Ed. cit., Lib. I, vi, p. 66.

Puritans.¹ Similarly, he protested against that vice beloved
of Andrewes and the Anglo-Catholic preachers, the taking
up in turn of every word in the text :

" Nec est necesse " (Keckermann wrote), " simul et
semel totius textus verba explicare, sed phrasi vna explicata
et sententia declarata, statim amplificetur et applicetur,
et sic deinceps per reliquas partes textus procedatur." ²

Quotations from Greek and Hebrew were to be avoided
' nisi cum locus est per interpretem nimis corruptus, et in
sensum alienum tractus, aut alioquin obscurus,' in other
words, only to prevent misunderstanding or dispel obscurity.³
Obscure passages as a rule were to be explained on analogy
of those not obscure, Melanchthon being quoted to the
effect that ' verba sunt intelligenda secundum subiectam
materiam,' and an interpretation based on the ' prime
intention and scope of the author ' (' ex dicentis vel scri-
bentis primaria intentione et scopo ') recommended.⁴
The ' multiple senses ' of Scripture beloved of Origen,
Ambrose and Augustine, and enunciated as a homiletical
principle by Aquinas, are dismissed with decision.⁵

Amplification led Keckermann to discuss one of the greatest
abuses of post-Reformation preaching, namely, the excessive
quoting of passages from the Bible. Neale, it is true,
considered the immense knowledge of Scripture displayed
in the sermons of the mediæval preachers to be one of the
virtues of their preaching ⁶ ; but there is a noteworthy
difference between the happy frequency of Scriptural
allusion in the sermons of St. Bernard and the tasteless
crowding of citations which destroys any sense of argument
and defaces so much of English preaching in the time of
the Commonwealth. Quotation of Scripture to be effective
Keckermann realised must not be too frequent, because
multiplicity of citations cannot be remembered (' quia nil

---

¹ Although in the section " Of the Preaching of the Word," in ' The Directory
for the Publick Worship of God Agreed upon by the Assembly of Divines at
Westminster,' preachers are warned against excessive division of texts.
² Cap. vii, p. 69, ' De verborum explicatione.'
³ *Ibid.*, p. 70.
⁴ *Ibid.*, p. 72.
⁵ *Ibid.*, pp. 73–4.
⁶ J. M. Neale, ' Mediæval Preachers,' Lon., 1865, pp. xxv–xxvii.

7

difficilius adhærescit memoriæ quam numerus ') ; the habit, moreover, savoured of ostentation, than which nothing is more odious in a sermon ('ostentatione nihil est in concione odiosius ').[1] Citations from the Fathers, he allowed, where pertinent ('ad præsentem textum congruentia '), but again warned against over-frequent quoting, and advised immediate translation into the vernacular.[2]

On the more directly rhetorical side *amplification* is shown to be materially aided by the ' loci inuentionis.' These are of eight kinds :

" 1, ex indiuiduis, seu exemplis : 2, ex causis : 3, ex effectibus : 4, ex antecedentibus, consequentibus et connexis : 5, ex partibus : 6, ex descriptione : 7, ex comparatis : 8, ex antithesi seu oppositis. . . ."[3]

The illustrations supplied are drawn from Cyprian, Basil, Bernard, and other ecclesiastical writers, but the underlying principle is that familiar to Aphthonius and the classical rhetoricians. The examples chosen may be taken, as Borromeo suggests they ought to be, from the writings of David and Solomon,[4] the circumstances considered be those of the Biblical narrative, and the ' descriptio ' used to reprove vice and inculcate morality with an earnestness unknown to the pagan world—though the less edifying and more purely literary tendencies of this device we shall find illustrated in the second division of our study in the work of Adams—but the rhetorical tradition is clear ; though it is plain also that Keckermann intended utilising it in such a way as was legitimate to his religious purpose.

Keckermann's importance lies in the fullness of his treatment, in the fact that he came at the close of a long period of homiletical experiment and theorising,[5] and at the opening of an equally long period during which the sermon was a major interest of all thoughtful men, and during which the procedure he recommended exercised a wide influence.

[1] Cap. viii, ' De amplicatione,' p. 80.
[2] *Ibid.*, p. 81.
[3] *Ibid.*, p. 82.
[4] ' De Sacris Nostrorvm Temporvm Oratoribus,' Milan, 1632, Book III, p. 141.
[5] *Vid. op. cit.*, pp. 17, 19, and 20.

Rapin and Claude, in the third quarter of the seventeenth, and Rollin at the beginning of the eighteenth, century, dealt with the same topics largely from the same standpoint. Indeed, wherever the pulpit-address was approached as an oratorical rather than an exegetical product, the considerations Keckermann advanced were bound to apply. It is always possible to regard the emergence of this interest as coincident with a fall in temperature in the religion of the period, and in England, it is true, the more literary considerations affecting the sermon had to wait till after the Restoration [1] ; but this is merely to say that the avowed combination of literary or oratorical and theological interests was then popularly accepted as legitimate, whereas, in the first half of the seventeenth century, the preacher thought more of his expository task and less of the rhetorical possibilities of his theme, though, as ever, there were notable exceptions, and the strong rhetorical tincture inseparable from all written or spoken compositions of the period must be kept in mind.

Of the older type of English preaching-manual, Perkins' ' Art of Prophecying ' is an outstanding example.[2] Its influence and vogue were enormous, owing to the extraordinary contemporary reputation of its author, whose theological works were accorded a place alongside those of Calvin and Hooker. All through the seventeenth, and among dissenters in the following, century, this short work on preaching continued to be recommended and quoted. A summary inserted towards its conclusion gives a fair idea of its scope. This is entitled, ' The Order and Svmme of the sacred and onely Method of Preaching,' and is addressed to intending preachers [3] :

" 1. To reade the Text distinctly out of the Canonicall Scriptures.

2. To give the sense and vnderstanding of it being read, by the Scripture it selfe.

3. To collect a few and profitable points of doctrine out of the natvrall sense.

4. To apply (if he have the gift) the doctrines rightly

[1] With the important exception of course of Wilkins' work in its original edition.
[2] This is contained in vol. ii of ' The Works . . .' Lon., 1631. The Epist. ded. of ' the Art ' is dated 1592.
[3] The word ' onely ' is to be noted. *Vid. post*, p. 378.

collected, to the life and manners of men in a simple and plaine speech." [1]

Perkins stated plainly his attitude to humane learning, and in so doing had a permanent influence on the Puritan sermon. His statement is important, in view of the contentions subsequently put forward by Webster and Sydrach Simpson :

"*Humane wisdome*" (Perkins believed) "must be concealed, whether it be in the matter of the Sermon or in the setting forth of the words : because the preaching of the word is the *testimony of God*. . . ."

He then proceeds to meet an obvious objection :

" If any man thinke that by this means barbarism should be brought into pulpits ; hee must understand that the Minister may, yea and must privately use at his libertie the arts, Philosophy, and variety of reading, whilest he is in framing his sermon : but he ought in publike to conceale all these from the people, and not to make the least ostentation." [2]

The standpoint is that of extreme Calvinism, which, taking its stand on the Bible as the Word of God, could not tolerate that the Holy Text should be intermingled with profane utterances of men.[3] " Humane testimonies whether of the Philosophers, or of the Fathers," were " not to be alleaged," unless they were likely to convince the conscience of the hearer.[4] Yet Brinsley, we are to remember, was also a Puritan, and a relation of bishop Hall—himself a Calvinist—and Brinsley and Hall were both conspicuously interested in style and rhetoric. But the fact is to be noted that Brinsley's book deals with the secular part of a boy's education, and Hall, although his complete works are witness to

---

[1] Ed. cit., p. 673.   [2] Ed. cit., p. 670.

[3] This position is interestingly reaffirmed in ' The Character of an old English Puritan, or Non-Conformist,' by John Geree, M.A., Lon., 1646, 4to, p. 2 : " He esteemed that preaching best wherein was most of God, least of man, when vain flourishes of wit, and words were declined . . . ; yet could he distinguish between studied plainness, & negligent rudeness. He accounted perspicuity the best grace of a Preacher : And that method best, which was most helpful to understanding, affection, and memory. To which ordinarily he esteemed none so conducible as that by doctrine, reason, and use."

[4] *Op. cit.*, p. 664.

the extraordinary range of his literary interests and attainments, in his sermons conformed more or less to the ideal
laid down by Perkins, and, acquainted as he was with all the
devices of rhetoric, produced plain and remarkably fluent
prose. Hall, however, is eloquent in a way which Perkins
hardly contemplated, and, while avoiding the ostentatious
citation which the latter deprecates, by means of the
' descriptio ' and other of the devices which we have found
Keckermann sanctioning achieved beautiful and arresting
effects. Perkins' advice, if too closely followed, could
only result, as it did result, in baldness and inelegancy of
diction. Text followed text with the slightest possible
amount of added comment, so that the pure word might
reach men unpolluted by human additions, and the application of " the doctrines rightly collected to the life and
manners of men in a simple and plaine speech," without
literary ornament, was carefully adhered to. Yet, Perkins
gave directions in his manual as to the management of voice
and gesture, and his work is really an application of rhetoric
to the pulpit, although only of such parts of rhetoric as he
considered lawful to be used.

The sense of fitness or propriety in preaching is one which
has always to be borne in mind in dealing with seventeenth-
century sermons. Absence of literary finish or rhetorical
ornament in the earlier part of the century does not imply
lack of acquaintance with the art of composition or public
speaking. Where sermons are plain they are plain by
choice and intention. Erasmus himself, in the ' concio de
puero Jesu pronunciata a puero in nova schola Johannis
Coleti, per eum instituta Londini . . . (i.e. St. Paul's),'
had written :

" Puer apud pueros verba facturus de ineffabili puero
Jesu, non optarim mihi Tullianum illam eloquentiam,
quæ brevi atque inani voluptate aures deliniat. Quantum
enim abest Christi sapientia a sapientia mundi, (abest
autem immenso intervallo,) tantum oportet Christianam
eloquentiam a mundana differre eloquentia " [1] ;

and his opinion became widely shared. Thus, for example,
in Lloyd's ' Memoires,' we are told of Dr. Samuel Collins,

[1] ' The Life of Dr. John Colet . . .' by Sam. Knight, Oxf., 1823, " Miscellanies," No. IV, pp. 285-6.

a Regius Professor of Divinity at Cambridge, considered " the most fluent Latinist of *his* age," who was devoted not only to Tully and Isocrates, but also to " the modern *Ciceronians*, as *Longolius*, *Bembus*, *Politian*. . . . Some pieces of whom he read yearly to his dying day," that—

" as his Latin was pure and elegant, making a smooth way over the *Alps* of Philosophy and School-divinity . . . so was his English plain when he came to preach, especially to a plain Auditory, . . . knotty Timber being unfit to build with, he edified his people with profitable and plain matter. His three Spurs to virtue, were *Satyr*, *Sarcasm*, or *Irony*, and *Panegyrick ;* by the two first shaming the ill-inclined, and by the last encouraging the well-disposed. . . ."[1]

Somewhat similarly we find Mather writing of Cotton :

" Mr. *Cotton* was, indeed, a most *Universal Scholar*, and a *Living System* of the Liberal Arts, and a *Walking Library*. . . . He both wrote and spoke *Latin* also with great Facility ; and with a most *Ciceronian* Elegancy. . . . Next, for his *Logic* he was compleatly furnished. . . . But although he had been Educated in the *Peripatetick* way, yet like the other Puritans of those times, he rather affected the *Ramesian* Discipline ; and chose to follow the Methods of the Excellent *Ramus* . . . rather than the more Empty, Trifling, Alter-cative Notions, to which the works of the Pagan *Aristotle* . . . have disposed his Disciples. Lastly, for his *Theologie* . . . although amongst his Readings, he had given a Special Room unto the Fathers, and unto the School-men, yet at last, he preferr'd one *Calvin* above them all. . . . Indeed, in his *Common Preaching* he did as Basil reports of *Ephrem Syrus*, Plurimum distare a Mundana Sapientia ; and though he were a great Scholar, yet he did Conscienti-ously forbear making to the *Common People* any Ostentation of it. . . . When a *Golden Key* of Oratory would not so well open a *Mystery* of Christianity, he made no stick to take an *Iron One*, that should be less Rhetorical. You should hear few *Terms of Art*, few *Latinities*, no *Exotic* or *Obsolete* Phrases, obscuring of the Truths, which he was to bring unto the People of God. Nevertheless his more Judicious and Observing Hearers, could by his most *Untrim'd Sermons*

[1] *Op. cit.*, Lon., 1668, pp. 452–5.

perceive that he was a man of more than Ordinary Abilities. . . ." [1]

Collins and Cotton in attitude and fortune represent the two strains of English Calvinism and their attitude towards preaching is significant. Collins may be taken as typical of the Calvinism which we find in Hall and Prideaux and the early Jacobean divines, and which, after its partial eclipse in the time of the Laudian ascendency, lived on to return to the Established Church by way of the Cambridge Platonists and other conformists ; Cotton's Calvinism was of the uncompromising character which produced the Pilgrim Fathers, and later still the Dissenters. Their relation to rhetoric illustrates the same divergence. Collins' use of *Satyr*, *Sarcasm*, *Irony*, and *Panegyrick* recalls instantly Keckermann's chapter ' De exornatione,' which deals with such devices as *exclamatio*, *apostrophe*, *obsecratio*, *adiuratio* and *admiratio* [2] ; Cotton, on the other hand, was clearly following where Perkins led. On the whole, the opinions of Perkins prevailed, and except for eccentrics, who for one reason or another fall outside the theory of their party, not till the time of Bates did Puritan preaching achieve literary grace.

Baxter, although ecclesiastically he cannot be claimed for any other party than the Church of England, in spite of the fact that he was continually forced into dissent from it, may be taken as the supreme example of the deliberately plain school of preaching. Not only do his printed sermons, and the treatises into which these were frequently recast, exhibit the practice of the school, but he has made more than one open avowal of his attitude. The most important of these statements is contained in ' *Gildas Salvianus*, or the Reform'd Pastor,' a work on ' the pastoral care,' which deals in part with preaching. Baxter's main argument is that the *matter* of the discourse is of more importance than the *manner* in which it is presented.

" Ministers " (he believed), " therefore, must be observant of the Case of their Flocks, that they may know what is most necessary for them, both for Matter and for Manner. And

---

[1] Cotton Mather : ' Magnalia Christi Americana . . .' Lon., 1702, Book III, p. 25.
[2] Ed. cit., Lib. I, cap. x, pp. 122–6.

usually Matter is first to be regarded, as being of more
Concernment than the Manner. . . . It is commonly
Empty Ignorant Men that want the Matter and Substance
of True Learning, that are over Curious and Sollicitous about
Words and Ornaments, when the Ancient, Experienced,
most Learned Men, abound in Substantial Verities, usually
delivered in the plainest Dress. . . . All our Teaching
must be as Plain and Evident as we can make it. . . . He
that would be understood must speak to the Capacity of
his Hearers, and make it his Business to make himself
understood. Truth loves the Light, and is most Beautiful
when most naked. It's a Sign of an envious Enemy to
hide the Truth ; and a Sign of an Hypocrite to do this
under pretence of Revealing it : And therefore painted
obscure Sermons (like the Painted Glass in the Windows that
keep out the Light) are two [sic] oft the Marks of painted
Hypocrites. If you would not teach Men, what do you in
the Pulpit ? If you would, why do you not speak so as to
be understood ? " [1]

Preachers who were troubled with auditors who fell into
contentions over small matters and were inclined to consider
that they possessed as much knowledge as their pastors
Baxter considered most likely to establish their prestige by
taking up " some higher Points " of doctrine and " not by
heaping up Citations of Fathers, and repeating Words of
Latin or Greek. . . . " [2]

The excessive introduction of quotations, especially of
quotations in the classical languages, into sermons was a
notable feature of preaching in our century, and called for
remark not only from the more puritanical divines but from
men of all schools of theology, laymen as well as divines.
Thus in 1602 Manningham noted in his *Diary* :

" Reynolds esteems it his best glorie to quote an author
for every sentence, nay almost every syllable " ;

adding—

" soe he may indeede shewe a great memory but small
judgment " [3] ;

---

[1] *Op. cit.* (1655), in ' The Practical Works . . . of Richard Baxter,' Lon.,
1707, vol. iv, p. 358. *Cf.* Croft : ' The Naked Truth,' Lon., 1675, p. 32.
[2] *Ibid.*, p. 428.
[3] Camden Soc., 1868, p. 85.

and the biographer of Mede relates that—

" in popular Discourses or Sermons " (the latter), " disliked the unnecessary quotation of Authours and the use of foreign languages and terms of Art (too much practised even among men, otherwise learned and religious) . . . " [1] ;

which, when we remember that Mede was a kind of Father of the Platonic movement at Cambridge, is a remark of great interest.   Pearson, the author of ' An Exposition of the Creed,' whose orthodoxy goes unchallenged, in his preface to that work, published in 1659, makes plain his attitude to this contemporary custom :

" . . . I have contriv'd my exposition, so that the Body of it containeth fully what can be delivered and made intelligeable in the English tongue, without inserting the least sentence or phrase of any learned language, by which he which is not acquainted with it might be disturbed in his reading, or interrupted in his understanding." [2]

The citations from Fathers and Church historians in the original languages were inserted in the margins. As the work represents an expanded version of Pearson's addresses at St. Clement's, Eastcheap, the writer's practice stands in vital relation to contemporary preaching. The partiality both of preachers and auditories for quotations in the learned tongues was, however, very general. Some 'few years before Pearson set so good an example, and while the Westminster Assembly was sitting, Herbert Palmer, President of Queens' College, Cambridge, and one of the compilers of the ' Directory for Public Worship,' had urged upon his colleagues the need for suppressing " any use of strange languages " by preachers. " To his influence," says Bass Mullinger, " we may probably attribute the clause in the recorded proceedings prohibiting not only the " speaking of Latin, Greek and Hebrew," but also all " citations from the Fathers " [3] ; but the singular story related

---

[1] From the ' View of his Life,' annexed to Mede's ' Works,' reprinted in Barksdale's ' Memorials,' 1661, p. 158.

[2] Op. cit., Lon., 1659, Preface, unpaged.

[3] ' The University of Cambridge,' vol. iii, pp. 388–9. The passage in ' The Directory '—" Of the Preaching of the Word "—reads : " Abstaining also from an unprofitable use of unknown tongues, strange phrases, and cadencies of sounds and words ; sparingly citing sentences of ecclesiastical or other human writers, ancient or modern, be they never so elegant."

in Twells' ' *Life of Dr. Edward Pocock*,' to which the same writer alludes, demonstrates the almost inconceivable folly of the period. Not only was there a craze for sermons, but there was a demand for learned quotations from quarters where it is quite clear they could not have been understood. Pococke, one of the most notable orientalists of his day, was complained of by his parishioners for insufficiency, since he did not choose to regale them with the unintelligible scraps of Greek and Latin to which they had been accustomed.[1]

This last incident affords direct proof that once a fashion is set it is very difficult to alter it, even if its continuance conduces neither to edification nor other use. Elizabeth had endeavoured to confine preaching to homilies, Charles I and Laud to catechising ; the Puritan ideal had been the bare ' Word ' simply explained. How then are we to explain the popular predilection for learned quotations ? Partly, it appears, by the example of the court and university preachers and the desire of young men to imitate in their own parishes what they had heard in their undergraduate days ; partly by a desire to be thought learned, and partly, as has already been suggested, by the habit of regarding the sermon as a kind of theme and using the contents of a commonplace-book to aid in its composition. Rhetoric here joins hands with an ecclesiastical fashion, and when certain personal extravagances are added, the results can readily be imagined. Learned preaching was decidedly the vogue at the court of James I, as is implied by Aubrey's amusing tale—supplied by Edmund Waller—of a Cambridgeshire parson who so overstudied in an endeavour to attract attention in a sermon before the King at Newmarket that he almost lost his life, and was only revived after a curious incarceration in the stomach of one of his own cows [2] ; but the effects produced by some of the aspirants for royal favour, due to their heaping together all manner of disparate material, were, according to an early Puritan, Robert Bolton, described by the King himself as resembling " a corne-field in harvest, pestered with red and blew flowers, which choake and eat up all the good graine." [3]

[1] *Vid.* Twells : *op. cit.*, ed. 1816, vol i, pp. 92–5.
[2] ' Brief Lives,' ed. Clark, vol i, p. 138.
[3] ' Sermon Preached at Lent Assises,' bound up with ' Foure Last Things,' 1632, p. 183.

In spite, however, of the Puritan attempt to confine preachers to strictly Scriptural material, Wilkins, later one of the founders of the Royal Society, in his ' Ecclesiastes,' an *ars concionandi* first published in 1646, recommended the use of those " Heathen Writers " whose works served to confirm doctrine.[1] Of Seneca and Plutarch he remarks, quoting Erasmus :

" Seneca in traducendis vitiis salsus est et elegans, ac vehemens etiam.   De moribus nemo felicius scripsit quam Plutarchus, cujus libelli digni sunt, . . . e quibus Basilius et Chrysostomus multa videntur hausisse." [2]

This is important, as Wilkins' attitude points forward to the practice of Barrow and Tillotson, who appealed frequently to the consent of the great Pagan moralists to the main precepts of Christianity ; but it is clear that Wilkins intended rather to remind men of the substance of the classical works than to urge such wholesale quotation and allusion as the Cambridge Platonists indulged in, for he adds :

" To stuff a Sermon with citations of Authors, and the witty sayings of others, is to make a feast of vinegar and pepper ; which are healthful and delightful being used moderately as *sauces*, but must needs be very improper and offensive to be fed upon as diet." [3]

This also was the point of view expressed by Claude in his ' Essay on the Composition of a Sermon,' which Robinson assigns to the year 1676.[4] " Apothegms of illustrious men should seldom appear in a sermon," [5] is one of Claude's *dicta*, and elsewhere he protested against the array of " passages from *Pagane Authors* or *Rabbies*, or *Fathers*," which

[1] ' Ecclesiastes : or, A Discourse Concerning the Gift of Preaching, as it falls under the Rules of Art,' 8th ed., 1704, p. 20.   The ' Heathen Moralists ' whom he especially commends (pp. 116–17) are Plato, Aristotle, Antoninus, Arrianus *in Epictetum*, Cicero, Epictetus, Hierodes, Maximius Tyrius, Theophrastus, Plotinus, Plutarch, Sallust, Seneca, Simplicius *in Epictetum*, and Xenophon.

[2] ' Ecclesiastes,' Book II, xv.

[3] Ed. cit., p. 20.

[4] *Vid.* Third ed., Lon., 1788, vol. i, p. 457, footnote.

[5] *Ibid.*, vol. ii, p. 482.

preachers loved to assemble, but which he considered " only a vain ostentation of learning." [1]

Wilkins' quotation from Erasmus is of further interest, when we remember that those English preachers who prided themselves least on their catholicity and the continuity of the English Church with the Church of the Fathers and the Middle Ages had a particular affection for Seneca. Erasmus' interest was still largely the rhetorical one, summed up in the question which we found Antonius asking in the ' De Oratore '—What force can refute evil and promote virtue like that of oratory ? and Seneca's was simply a very effective type of oratory—but the praise of Seneca, which Cotton Mather records as coming from " the wise Bullinger," is much more concerned with content than with form of expression.[2]   The two, however, are closely connected, and those preachers who were more interested in inculcating moral precepts than in promoting particular ecclesiastical usages, not only tended to point to the content of the ancient moralists, and especially of Seneca, but also to imitate the latter's style.   Professor Croll has shown, in a series of studies in what he calls ' Attic ' or ' Senecan Prose,' [3] that, following the first exuberant admiration for Cicero which possessed the great sixteenth-century humanists, there came a reaction which took the form of devotion to the crisp, antithetical manner of Seneca. This was in part a contemporary vogue, which passed from Latin to the vernaculars, but it was also in part a tradition derived, as we have seen, by way of some of the early Church writers, notably Tertullian, from Seneca himself.   In consequence, although on the whole the ' Senecan ' movement is identified with the Calvinistic episcopalians and the moderate Puritans, such a preacher as Donne reveals many of the traits associated with this style of writing ; on the other hand, an orator of so luscious a style as Jeremy

---

[1] *Op. cit.*, vol. i, p. 35.

[2] ' Magnalia,' 1702, Book III, p. 144 : " Unus Seneca plus sinceriora Theologiæ posteritate reliquit, quam omnes fere omnium Scholasticorum Libri."

[3] ' " Attic Prose " in the Seventeenth Century' (reprinted from ' Studies in Philology,' vol. xviii, No. 2, April 1921) ; " Attic Prose : Lipsius, Montaigne, Bacon," in ' Schelling Anniversary Papers,' New York, 1923 ; ' Muret and the History of " Attic " Prose,' (reprinted from the ' Publications of the Modern Language Association of America,' vol. xxxix, No. 2,) 1924.

Taylor draws upon Seneca from the side of 'content.'
In short, Seneca appealed to Protestants at once for his lofty
morals and plain style, but the style in turn became a con-
vention and attracted, largely on account of its past
traditions, preachers other than Puritan ; and, as the
seventeenth century progressed, the moral note began to
be borrowed by Anglicans and to distinguish the work of
the less violent Puritans who conformed, when the actual
form in which the precepts had been embodied had given
place to a smoother and more fluid medium.

Another cause for interest in Wilkins' manual lies in the
fact of the long term of popularity and the numerous
editions which it enjoyed. The men for whom Wilkins
wrote in 1646 were very different from those for whom
John Moore, bishop of Norwich, and Dr. John Williams,
prebendary of Canterbury, re-edited the 'Ecclesiastes'
for the seventh time in 1694. Wilkins himself in his lifetime
travelled far from the theological loyalties of his youth, and
his book is bound to have appealed to preachers of very
dissimilar ideals at various periods in his career. To divines
coming fresh from the Westminster Assembly his admittance
of Pagan writers to enforce sacred doctrines was almost
certainly distasteful,[1] and to his later confederates on the
episcopal bench certain of the older Puritan writers whom
he held up as examples of sound preaching must have been
equally so. It is in the lists of preachers whose sermons
Wilkins considered suitable for confirming doctrine that the
changes in the later editions occur, fresh names being added
in order to bring the roll up to date. But at no period did
Wilkins swerve from his original contention that " the
Gift of Preaching and sacred Oratory " was " a distinct Art
in it self," [2] and that " the principal Scope of a Divine
Orator " being " to teach clearly, convince strongly, and
persuade powerfully," the chief parts of a sermon were
consequently " these three : *Explication, Confirmation, Application.*" [3] This is directly in the vein of Perkins, and marks
the divergence of ' sacred oratory ' from the secular.

One of the authors of an earlier work on preaching to
whom Wilkins referred was Richard Bernard, a Puritan
divine, whose ' Isle of Man ' is a possible prototype of the

---

[1] *Vid. ante*, p. 105, footnote [3].   [2] 1704 ed., p. 2.
[3] *Ibid.*, pp. 4 and 20.

' Pilgrim's Progress,' and who in ' The Faithfull Shepheard,'
published in 1607, gave much sensible advice to fellow-
ministers and divinity-students with regard to the framing
of sermons.   Puritan as he was, he censured the " mere
upstart quoting of Scripture . . . Chapter and Verse for
euery word " :   as " an irreuerent abuse, without profit
to the hearers ;   whose vnderstanding can neither conceiue
them, nor memorie beare them away.   Pride the inventor
to publish the excellencie of memorie. . . ." [1]   He gives,
however, minute directions for finding the ' intendment '
of a text—*Quis, quid, vbi, quibus auxilijs, cur, quomodo, quando*—
and for its division.   This is a method which is employed
effectively by Donne, but which was badly abused in the
hands of the Parliamentary preachers, although Herle's
' Tripus,' [2] which the compilers of the ' Scotch Presbyterian
Eloquence ' [3] cite as a typical example of minute division
and subdivision, is far from being the worst specimen of its
class.   The table outlining the treatment of his theme
which Herle prefixed to the published form of his discourses,
it is true, is somewhat alarming to the modern mind, and
by 1692, when the first edition of the ' Scotch Presbyterian
Eloquence ' appeared, such a treatment had passed into
discredit in favour of the essay-like sermon on one main
topic preferred by Stillingfleet and his contemporaries ;
but it was a method familiar to an earlier generation, and
no doubt expected by the note-takers who followed the
preachers in the intricate ramifications in which they indulged.   Of all English *artes concionandi* William Chappell's
is probably the most conspicuous illustration of this tendency
in homiletics.

Chappell, who was Milton's tutor at Christ's College,
Cambridge, and is reputed on doubtful evidence to have
whipped the future poet, was patronised by Laud, becoming
provost of Trinity College, Dublin, and bishop of Cork.
His ' Methodus Concionandi ' was published anonymously
in Latin in 1648, two years after Wilkins' ' Ecclesiastes.'
An English version, giving the author's name, appeared in
1656.[4]   In the interval was issued ' The Use of Holy Scrip-

[1] *Op. cit.*, chap. viii, p. 58.
[2] Three treatises, published in 1655 by Herle, prolocutor (1646) of the
Westminster Assembly.
[3] Third ed. (1719), p. 53, margin.
[4] Entitled, ' The Preacher, or the Art and Method of Preaching.'

ture Gravely and Methodically Discoursed . . .' [1] which
not only traced Chappell's ' method ' back to its source in
2 Timothy iii. 16, but expounded the passage indicated
according to that method.

" Partes Methodi," (we learn) " sunt de $\begin{cases} \text{Doctrina} \\ \text{Usu.} \end{cases}$

In Doctrina consideranda sunt $\begin{cases} \text{Præparatio ad eam} \\ \text{Tractatio ejus.} \end{cases}$

In præparatione $\begin{cases} \text{Aditus ad locum ubi est.} \\ \text{Constitutio ipsius Doctrinæ." [2]} \end{cases}$

Treatment (tractatio) consists in *explication, confirmation,* and
vindications from objections. Uses are to be applied to the
mind as *instruction* or *refutation,* to the heart, with reference
to the present time, as *reprehension* or *consolation,* and with
respect to the future as *exhortation to good,* and *dissuasion from
evil.* [3]

The governing idea of Chappell's work is well expressed
in his opening sentence :

" Methodus concionandi est discursus super textu aliquo
Scripturæ varias ejus partes secundum ordinem naturæ
disponens : unde omnium inter se convenientia judicetur
memoriâque comprehendatur."

" In their natural order " (*secundum ordinem naturæ*), as
interpreted by Chappell, gives at first sight reason for
astonishment, but when we remember the background of
scholastic theology and the contemporary methods in philosophy and logic there is less cause for surprise. [4]   If Keckermann represents the application of rhetoric in a particular
direction, and Perkins the views of a theological party
destined to influence the course of preaching in a manner
inimical to such an application, Chappell may be regarded
as effecting a kind of compromise ; his book is a highly
technicalised ' method,' scholastical and learned in its
bases, but directed strictly to religious and moral ends to the

[1] ' By William Chappell, bishop of *Corke* . . .' Lon., 1653, 8vo.
[2] ' Methodus,' cap ii.
[3] *Vid.* ' table ' inserted in front of the manual.
[4] In the " Life " of Juxon, published in Lloyd's ' Memoires,' Chappell is mentioned (p. 60) as " a man of a very strict method, being an incomparable
logician. . . ."

exclusion of art.   As such, it appealed to men in his own period ; but its appeal could not be more extensive.   Only Wilkins, of those whose manuals we have glanced at, with his fine recognition of preaching as an art as well as a species of divine ordinance, has left a book, which, while in no way neglecting the essential purpose of the sermon, brings the work of the preacher into clear relationship with the cultured interest of men, and in so doing links it to the best traditions of preceding times, and to the highest ideals of those writers in his own time with whose comments on the sermon we shall have occasion to deal further either by way of criticism or illustration.

The title of Chappell's book, moreover, recalls the extraordinary attention paid to ' method ' by preachers, particularly Puritan preachers, in the first half of the seventeenth century.   A man's ' method ' was a recognised property which was commented upon by his hearers, who were often ready to analyse it and compare it with the ' methods ' of others.   It was a kind of personal application of those hermeneutic principles we have found discussed by the writers on preaching.   At times this was a decidedly elaborate affair, as we find in the case of a celebrated Puritan, John Dod, known widely to contemporaries as ' Decalogue Dod,' from his exposition of the Ten Commandments published in 1604.   His eminence as a preacher was in part due to his having assisted three celebrated and extreme Calvinists, Fulke, Whitaker, and Chadderton, " in an Analysis and Exposition of the Epistle to the *Hebrews*, and other the hardest portions of Scripture ; and after a nonplus in his first sermon at St. Maries [Oxon], by tying himself to Words and Phrases " he was careful to proceed by the following method [1] :

" I. Analysing his Text, and observing 1. The Author. 2. The Occasion.   3. The Coherence.   4. The Scope, Design and Circumstances ; which he said was a great help to avoid confusion, to prevent impertinence, and to remedy the weakness of capacity and memory in Preachers and Hearers, provided the division of the Words were according to his direction.   1. Agreeable to the main drift of the words. 2. Into but three or four parts at the most.   3. Yet taking

[1] Lloyd's ' Memoires,' 1668, p. 131.

in the whole Text. 4. And that so, that each part may depend upon, be linked to another. 5. Avoiding subdivisions. And 6. Expressing the parts more or less in clear and popular terms.

II. Opening with these rules. 1. That there is but one literal sence of the Scripture. 2. That if there were no peculiarity in the phrase, a short Paraphrase was best. 3. That the Text is to be first accurately divided, and then clearly explicated. 4. That the Doctrine should be raised from each head as it was explained. And that either, 1. Grammatically by either having recourse to the Originals, or observing the Synonimous expressions : Or, 2. Rhetorical, by reducing improper expressions to a proper signification [1] : Or, 3. Logical, by distinguishing doubtful expressions, and defining the obscure. . . .

III. Drawing out the several Doctrines of the Text, either directly from the express words of the Text, or indirectly, 1. From the Coherence. 2. The Occasion. 3. The Principle Scope. 4. The Form. 5. The Order. 6. The Connexion. 7. The Variety of the words signification. 8. The Matter, whether Ecclesiastical, Æconomical, or Political. 9. The Similitude, *Gal.* 4. 12. 10. From Allegorical Proportions which are to be used : (1) Soberly and sparingly ; (2) Not far fetched, but proper ; (3) Briefly; (4) Rather for the reforming of the life, than the proving of any Article of Faith ; (5) And after the genuine sence of the words be first sincerely given. 11. From the Circumstance of Time, Person, Place. 12. From Examples. . . .

IV. Handling the Doctrine so drawn out. 1. By way of probation ; and that,

1. By testimonies of Scripture and other Authors ; in reference to which he practised these Rules :

   1. Each Doctrine was grounded on two Scripture testimonies at least which he opened and applied.
   2. Each quotation was well studied.
   3. And produced in the Scripture phrase . . .
   4. Choice and clear.
   5. One out of the Old Testament, another out of the New, seldom out of the Apocrypha, unless for institution of manners.

[1] Compare purpose of Smith's ' Mysterie of Rhetorique,' as outlined *ante*, pp. 86 and 92, and of the *rhetoricæ sacræ* generally.

8

6. With a Preface, shewing the end of each Quotation.

7. The Quotation of Fathers, Philosophers, Schoolmen, Historians, was choice and sparing, only when there might be such an Emphasis in the place, as might touch and work upon the conscience. . . .' [1]

Preaching according to Dod's ' method,' it is evident, could not be expected to show literary grace. It was severely practical, directed to the great ends of convincing men of sin and instructing them in virtue. Where it was imitated, as when others adopted ' methods ' of a similar type, the sermon became a kind of manual of spiritual technology divorced alike from literature and oratory. The quotation is therefore of value from a more or less negative standpoint. Preaching which followed this fashion simply has no interest for the student of literature, but modifications of such a style, and at times curious reversions to the once popular manner, in the sermons of later and more eloquent preachers are explained by it. There must have been many like John Wilson, who

" in his Younger Time . . . had been used unto a more *Methodical* way of *Preaching*, and was therefore admired above many, by no less Auditors than Dr. *Goodwin*, Mr. *Burroughs*, and Mr. *Bridge*,"

who in later life gave themselves

" Liberty to *Preach* more after the *Primitive* Manner ; without any distinct *Propositions*, but chiefly in *Exhortations* and *Admonitions*, and good wholesome *Councils*. . . ." [2]

The hortatory or admonitory manner of preaching, however, was seldom more literary than the older way of divisions and subdivisions. The rhapsodist is seldom an orator ; and many of the sermons in the field or before the Houses of Parliament during the Civil Wars show little attention paid either to exposition of doctrine or rhetorical effect. Only after 1688 with the establishment of the ser-

[1] *Op. cit.*, pp. 131–2.
[2] Mather : ' Magnalia Christi Americana,' Book III, p. 46.

mon on a ' topic,' owing to the influence of Burnet and
Sharp,[1] do genuinely literary considerations apply to the
sermon as a whole as distinct from the work of such sacred
orators as Barrow, Tillotson, and South.   Yet style was not
lost sight of ; rather it was coloured to a greater or less
extent by the immediate purpose of the preacher or the
prevailing fashion of a theological party.   Men did not
neglect style because they were ignorant of its value, or
indifferent to it, but because the exigencies of the moment
focused attention on other aspects of the sermon.   Baxter
makes this abundantly clear in his introductory epistle to
' A Saint or a Brute ' (1662), where he is speaking of his
writings ; but similar considerations are bound to have
affected his preaching.

"When I first intended writing . . ." (he says), " being
of that mind that thought nothing should be made public
but what a man had first laid out his choicest art upon I
thought to have acquainted the world with nothing but what
was the work of *Time* and *Diligence*.   But my conscience
soon told me that there was too much of Pride and selfish-
ness in this ; and that Humility and Self denial required
me to lay by the affectation of that style, and spare that
industry which tended but to advance my name with man,
when it hindered the main work, and crost my end.   And
Providence drawing forth some popular unpolished discourses, and giving them success beyond my expectation,
did thereby rebuke my selfish thoughts, and satisfy me that
the Truths of God do perform their work more by their
Divine Authority and *proper Evidence* and *material Excellency*,
than by any *ornaments* of *fleshly* wisdom ; and (as Seneca
saith) though I will not despise an *Elegant Physician*, yet will
I not think myself much the happier for his adding eloquence
to his healing art."

The conclusion arrived at by Baxter had been paralleled
earlier in the century by Cotton, who after coming under
the influence of Perkins at Cambridge had been torn
between what appeared to him conflicting aims—the
pursuit of learning and a strict conformity to godliness.

[1] Though Burnet preferred exposition of a text to " a general discourse "
still he advocated one sermon one theme.   *Vid.* ' A Discourse of the Pastoral
Care,' Third ed., 1713, p. 194.

Finally, a sermon of Sibs determined him. Its effect on his life is described as follows in ' Cottonus Redevivus ' [1] :

" Some time after this Change upon the Soul of Mr. *Cotton*, it came unto his turn again to preach at St. *Maries* ; and because *he* was to preach, an High Expectation was raised, through the *whole University*, that they should have a Sermon, flourishing indeed, with all the *Learning* of the *whole University*. Many difficulties had Mr. *Cotton* in his own mind now, what Course to steer. On the one side he considered, That if he should preach with a Scriptural and Christian *Plainness*, he should not only wound his own *Fame* exceedingly, but also tempt Carnal Men to revive an Old Cavil, *That Religion made Scholars turn Dunces*, whereby the Name of God might suffer not a little. On the other side, he considered, That it was his Duty to preach with such a Plainness, as became the Oracles of God, which are intended for the Conduct of Men in the *Paths of Life*, and not for *Theatrical* Ostentations and Entertainments, and the Lord needed not any *Sin* of ours to maintain his own Glory. Hereupon Mr. *Cotton* resolved, that he would preach a plain Sermon. . . ." [2]

What Cotton's subsequent preaching was like we have already heard. The chief thing to be borne in mind, however, is that such preaching was due to deliberate choice on the part of the preacher. Just as they felt obliged to discard the surplice and forgo ' the ceremonies,' the Puritans felt it necessary to abandon extraneous ornament in their sermons. Of Richard Capel, an Oxford Puritan, and chaplain to the notorious Somerset, it is related that—

" he kept Close to the footsteps of our choicest Worthies : as famous Master *Dod* (who used to say, that so much Latine was so much flesh in a Sermon [3]), Master *Cleaver*, Master *Hildersham*, and such other holy men . . ."

—all of them outstandingly ' plain ' preachers—and that he considered :

[1] Reprinted in ' Magnalia Christi Americana,' pp. 13–16.
[2] This ' plain ' sermon on repentance converted Preston, afterwards Master of Emmanuel, who " came to hear Mr. *Cotton* with the same itching Ears, as others were then led withal."
[3] A remark frequently quoted in accounts of Puritan preachers.

" Whereas, now adayes,[1] whilest some of our great Divines, seem to be too much taken up with quaint, and *Historicall* flourishes, there is a sensible decay of the power of God amongst us.   An *Exotick* or strange tongue in the publick Congregation (whatever men think of it) is set out as a sign of Gods displeasure, 1. Cor. 14, 21, 22.   It feeds such humours as should rather be purged out . . . The Sword of Gods Spirit can never wound so deep, as when it's plucked out of these gaudy Scabbards. . . . This curious age is too much given to the affectation of words, and phrases, and cadencies : and holy Doctor *Sibs* was wont to say, that great affectation, and good affections seldome go together . . ." [2]

On the other hand, we find so celebrated and eloquent a Puritan as Henry Smith in ' The true trial of the Spirits,' warning men, as Chrysostom had done in the ' De Sacerdotio,' that mere baldness is not to be mistaken for the Pauline aversion to the " enticing words of man's wisdom." [3]

" There is a kind of Preachers risen up of late " (Smith asserted) " which shroud and cover every rustical, and unsavoury, and childish, and absurd Sermon, under the name of the simple kind of teaching . . . but indeed to preach simply, is not to preach rudely, nor unlearnedly, nor confusedly, but to preach plainly, that the simplest man may understand what is taught. . . ." [4]

This is precisely what Erasmus states to be the object of the rhetorical training which preachers were to undergo, namely, that when they came to preach " what was obscure [will be] made clear, what was involved explained, and what was troublesome made easy " [5] ; and in the case of those Puritans who were less fanatically devoted to particular ' methods,' whether of Perkins, Dod, or others, there was a genuine attempt to keep this ideal in view. Scholastical precision and scriptural literalism might serve

[1] I.e. in the first thirty years of the century ; Capel resigned his living in 1633 on declining to read ' The Book of Sports.'
[2] Clarke's ' Lives,' 3rd (1677) ed., p. 305.
[3] Lib. IV, vi.
[4] Ser. cit., in ' The Sermons . . . 1592,' p. 120.
[5] ' Ecclesiastes,' Book II, iv.

to stimulate the academically and the theologically learned, but they must have been of little help to the ordinary man. It is pleasant, therefore, to hear of Richard Stock, another Puritan, that he was able

" not to expresse only, but to urge and presse too ; not to confirm alone, but to commend also that that he delivered with clear method, sound proof, choice words, fit phrases, pregnant similitudes, plentifull illustrations, pretty persuasions, sweet insinuations, powerful enforcements, allegations of antiquity, and variety of good literature ; that both the learnedest might receive satisfaction from him, and the very meanest and dullest might also reap benefit by him. . . ." [1]

Among the earlier Puritans such a reasonable application of rhetoric to their task as is here described was still frequently practised, and Smith and Adams, for example, except that they quote other authors and cite other examples, have a good deal in common with their Anglican contemporaries, in their fondness for allusion and love of picturesque incidents.   Even at a later period, one writer states of Harris, who was during the greater part of the Commonwealth period President of Trinity College, Oxford—

" the particular excellencies of *Nazianzen, Basil, Chrysostome, Austin, Ambrose, Bernard,* seemed all to concenter in him. He taught *Rhetorick* to speak in our Mother-tongue, and . . . may be stiled, The English Orator." [2]

On the whole, however, as the century advanced, the position adopted by Baxter came to be the prevailing one among those who wished for reforms in preaching in the Established Church.   Within that Church down to the period of the Civil Wars the ideals in preaching which Hacket ascribes to archbishop Williams may be taken as fairly representative of the dominant section of the clergy. Williams habitually—

" deliver'd that which was Oraculous, well Studied, premeditated with Care, able to draw the Conscience of his

---

[1] Clarke's ' Lives,' ed. cit., p. 64.   [2] *Ibid.*, p. 33.

Hearers into his Drag-Net, yet not with *the enticing words of Man's Wisdom, but in the demonstration of the Spirit, and of Power*, 1 Cor. 2. 4 . . . always he laid his Principles out of the Doctrine of Christ, yet he burnish'd them brighter with all art of comely Literature, as well what the Doctors of the Church afforded, as those that are without. For Human Literature is more Sacred, when it is well inoculated with Divinity ; which is willing to entertain the Assistance of every Art, not as a Corrival, but as a Handmaid. It was his Judgment, that rude unordain'd Dunces would in the Licentiousness of some Tumults thrust into our Pulpits, (and is it not come to pass to the very pricking of our Hearts ?) if the true Possessors did teach them by their Negligence, to fill up the Time with Babling and vacuity of Matter. . . ." [1]

But Williams was an archbishop, and like Andrewes, Buckeridge, Cosins, and Hacket preached to the learned and influential, to men like William Austin or Evelyn,[2] whose private meditations and correspondence reveal the same fashions in phrasing and the same wealth of patristic or scholastic allusion habitual to men in holy orders. Such sermons of Williams as exist are intricate mosaics of patristic quotation ; equally with the more extremely scriptural or intricately methodical of the Puritan sermons they were unsuited for popular auditories. Thomas Fuller, with all his *quaintness*, by employing the "plain but effectual manner" of preaching by *Doctrines* and *Uses*, which had been popularised by the German Musculus, and the formal *Reasons*, which he considered " the strength and sinews of a Sermon," [3] was able to avoid both extremes and appeal to the average intelligent listener. But the old fantastic sermon with its learned quotations held its ground among Episcopalians, and as late as 1668 South, in a sermon preached at Christ Church, Oxford, animadverted on the particular type of folly which had possessed Pococke's

[1] ' Scrinia Reserata,' 1693, Lon., fol., Part I, pp. 34, 35, but written in 1650.
[2] *Vid.* Austin's ' Devotionis Augustinianæ Flamma, or Certaine Devout, Godly, and Learned Meditations,' Lon. (sixes), sm. fol., issued posthumously in 1635, and a letter of Evelyn to Thurland printed at pp. 602–5 of the 1870 reprint of Bray's edition of the *Diary* and a selection of Evelyn's correspondence.
[3] " The Life and Work of Thomas Fuller, D.D.," prefixed to vol. i of ' The Collected Sermons . . .' ed. by Bailey and Axon, 1891, pp. xxvii *seq.*

parishioners at an earlier period. South recognised that
ridiculous as

" fustian bombast from the pulpit is, none are so transported
and pleased with it as those who least understand it.   For
still the greatest admirers of it are the grossest, the most
ignorant, and illiterate country people, who, of all men,
are the fondest of high-flown metaphors and allegories,
attended and set off with scraps of Greek and Latin. . . ." [1]

He continued with an eloquent plea for plainness in pulpit
style.

South's observations belong really to criticism, and we
shall have cause to return to them later, but they show in
what direction theory was beginning to set in influential
quarters.   It was no longer the Puritans who were clamour-
ing for a purified and restrained type of preaching, but the
clergy of the restored church, and the fact that South
attacked the outstanding faults of both parties with equal
vehemence was significant.[2]   Men of the Restoration period
had become tired of all the various ' methods' of preaching,
and were seeking to adapt their theory of preaching in a
way more suited to the needs and tastes of their time.
Nelson, in his ' Life ' of bishop Bull, describes the latter's
sermons as " a very proper Model," for young preachers,
" both as to Style and Method," adding :

" His Style is strong and manly, but yet plain and intelligible ; he abhorred all Affectations of pompous Rhetorick . . . ; his words seem chiefly chosen to cloath his
masterly Sense with Clearness and Propriety [3] ;

and Lupton, formerly Bull's curate, writes in the same
strain :

" He abhorred Affectations of Wit, Trains of fulsom
Metaphors, and nice Words wrought up with tuneful,
pointed Sentences, without any substantial Meaning at
the Bottom of them.   He looked upon Sermons consisting
of these Ingredients . . . as inconsistent with the Dignity

---

[1] ' The Works,' Oxf., 1823, vol. iv, Ser. lix, p. 151.
[2] *Vid. ibid.*, vol. iii, Ser. xxxvii, pp. 33–6, and *post*, p. 315.
[3] ' The Life of Dr. George Bull . . .' 1713, p. 488.

of serious and sacred Things, and as an Indication of a weak Judgment. . . ." [1]

Nelson and Lupton were corresponding in 1712 and were looking back to the reform in preaching which had been accomplished. The actual theory which lay behind that reformation it is more difficult precisely to determine. The later editions of Wilkins' ' Ecclesiastes ' and the chapter in Burnet's ' Pastoral Care '—the latter published in 1692—afford some light, but the good sense of Charles II and the court in this particular, the ideals of the Royal Society, the influence of the French preachers into close contact with whom many influential Englishmen of the period had been thrown, and the general desire of the nation which wished to escape from extremes and extravagances of all kinds, combined in shaping a theory, which, if much less definitely articulated than some of the older *artes concionandi*, yet was representative of the literary beliefs of the day.

In view of the third of these considerations contemporary French works on preaching are of particular importance in considering English preaching after the Restoration. Two of these, Rapin's ' Reflexions sur l'Eloquence de la Chaire,' part of his larger work on Eloquence, issued in 1672, and Claude's ' Essay ' already noted, reveal from very different angles the French attitude to our subject.

Rapin is emphatic that the Holy Scriptures rather than the classical rhetoricians are the most suitable study for divines.[2] In his opinion the preacher should *move* in order to speak of useful matters (' A dire des choses utiles '), but it is not the function of preaching to *delight* (' La Chaire ne doit pas plaisir ').[3] The most proper subjects for a discourse are not the most sublime or the most startling ; and Rapin deplores the fashion, beloved of women (' À qui les dames donnoient si fort leur approbation '), which led preachers to choose outstanding topics or divide their sermons in an ingenious manner.[4] His own ideal of pulpit oratory he expresses thus :

" L'Eloquence de la Chaire ayme la pureté, sans rechercher l'élegance : elle veut estre forte, sans se soucier d'estre

---

[1] Quoted in ' The Life of Dr. George Bull . . .' 1713, p. 490.
[2] *Op. cit.*, in ' Les Œuvres,' Tome Second, Amsterdam, 1709, p. 74.
[3] *Ibid.*, p. 86.   [4] *Ibid.*, p. 93.

agreable : elle n'a rien de grossier ny rien d'affetté : &
elle prend toûjours plus de soin de ce qu'elle pense que de
ce qu'elle dit.   Tout ce qui est étudié & brillant luy paroist
faux, elle ne peut s'en accommoder : & tout cette vaine
affectation de langage qui corrompt la pureté & la sainteté
de la parole de Dieu luy paroist profane : elle n'ayme dans
le discours que ce qui est droit, simple naturel."

After noting that familiarity with Italian and Spanish
preachers had led to the cultivation of a style unsuited to the
subject, he continues :

" On cherche les Modernes à qui l'on s'amuse : parce
que l'on ne connoist pas les Anciens, & l'on se fait une fausse
idée de cette Eloquence, dont le caractere est fort opposé
à tout ce qui est recherché, brillant, & ingenieux. La
veritable Eloquence de la Chaire ne doit rechercher à se
soûtenir, que par la grandeur des subjets qu'elle traite, par
sa simplicité, & par le bon sens. C'est l'affoiblir que de
pretendre l'orner par les richesses des Payens : on doit
bannir de la Chaire ces citations d'Auteurs profanes, &
toutes ces reflexions sur leurs maximes . . . L'Ecriture
sainte est assez riche pour fournir de son fonds les ornemens,
qui peuvent estre d'usage à cette Eloquence : quand on l'a
bien meditée, l'on sçait y trouver les raisons & les exemples,
pour établir les choses dont on parle. Toute autre autorité
ne doit point avoir lieu dans la Chaire, comme estant
étrangere & peu conforme à la sainteté de son caractere." [1]

Rapin's viewpoint is that of a cultured Frenchman of
his period. His disapproval of preachers who descend to
particulars [2] is not only conditioned by the desire to avoid
personalities, but is part of the then current insistence on
the abstract as against the concrete. For Rapin the sermon
had to conform to the accepted canons of taste which
governed lierature or oratory ; only, as with other writers
whose comments we have noted, his application of rhetorical
standards to pulpit oratory is everywhere coloured by the
nature of the subjects with which the latter deals.   Claude,
a Protestant, on the other hand, discusses the composition
of a sermon in a decidedly old-fashioned way. His treatment is largely that of the older writers from Hyperius to

[1] *Op. cit.*, pp. 98, 99.   [2] *Ibid.*, p. 100.

Keckermann. As far as English interests are concerned, his work takes a new value from the amazing wealth of annotation supplied by Robinson his translator, who caps most of Claude's observations by actual citation from English sermons from the opening of the seventeenth century down to the middle of Charles II's reign, when the ' Essay ' was composed. Most of these illustrate excesses of one kind or another and belong properly to criticism, but the fact that Claude comments adversely on such fashions as had been general among French Protestants of an earlier generation goes far to show that the desire for a less expository type of preaching had come to persist among the Huguenots as among the English Dissenters ; and it is important to remember, as may be gathered from Thomas Burnet's reference to his father's stay in France, that not only the Catholic preachers of the period, but the Protestant also, attracted and interested English travellers.

The main direction of the French sermon in the second half of the seventeenth century was towards the sustained development of a theme. The theory underlying this tendency did not so much influence English preaching as synchronised with a similar tendency in England. But the fact that French taste had declared itself in that particular way added force to the English inclination to pursue a similar course. Claude believed that sermons—

" ought to be restrained to a small number of parts, they should never exceed four or five at the most : the most admired sermons," he adds, " have only two or three parts." [1]

Such an attitude naturally opens up fresh possibilities for the sermon as an oration or as literature. In France Massillon, Fléchier, Bossuet, and Bourdaloue fixed their attention on the former possibility ; in England, Burnet, Stillingfleet, and the Latitudinarians developed the latter. In the hands of Tillotson the sermon became an essay, impressive when delivered in the pulpit, but almost certainly most fully appreciated when subsequently printed and read at leisure.

French sermons, however, whether Protestant or Catholic,

[1] *Op. cit.*, Robinson's trans., 3rd (1788) ed., vol. i, p. 43.

tended to a declamatory style foreign to the majority of English preachers, and in spite of, or rather alongside of, the professed ideal of a few clear divisions, still adhered fairly definitely to the form of the classical oration.   Catholic preachers were accustomed to pronounce a formal exordium, and then after the repetition of the *Ave* to proceed to their threefold treatment [1] ; and Claude we find did not approve of

" the custom of the *English preachers*, who enter immediately into the literal explication of the text, and make it serve for an exordium, after which they divide their discourses into several parts, which they discuss as they go on." [2]

Frenchmen, Catholic and Protestant alike, therefore, were agreed in regarding the sermon from a more rhetorical standpoint than was usual in England.   Once the custom of the French Catholics had prevailed in England.   Manningham, in describing Andrewes' sermon on Whit-Sunday, 1602, gives a kind of preamble, then adds :

" And here he made his prayer, which being ended with the Lord's Prayer, he proceeded with his text." [3]

This habit is not made obvious in the reprint of Andrewes' sermons in the Library of Anglo-Catholic Theology, but in the folio editions of the sermons, a band of ornament marks the conclusion of the *exordium* where the prayer occurred.
    South, too, after the Restoration, apparently employed this method, for in Wood's ill-natured account of the latter's mischance at court (13th April, 1662), we are told :

" Then, after a witty Preamble, he proceeded to the division of the Words ; and having performed that with great Dexterity, he lays by the Text for the present, and . . . addressed himself to the *Bid-Prayer* ; which being ended, he resumed his Text. . . ." [4]

But the custom was then rather a survival, ostentatiously cultivated perhaps to stress the restoration of old usages

[1] *Vid.* works of Massillon and Bourdaloue.
[2] *Op. cit.*, vol. ii, p. 456.
[3] ' Diary,' Camden Soc., 1868, p. 31.
[4] ' Athenæ,' 1721 ed., vol. ii, p. 1044.

in the Church, than an ideal. The whole paraphernalia of ' divisions ' was soon to be swept aside alike in England as in France. Bossuet boldly disregarded them. Of this Villemain writes :

" Sans doute ce grand orateur se fait toujours un plan régulier ; mais il ne l'annonce pas ; il avance à travers son sujet, sans indiquer sa route ; . . . pour mettre dans ses discours l'ordre véritable, c'est à dire l'unité, il se fait une idée dominante d'où il part, et à laquelle il vient, renfermant toute son éloquence dans le cercle d'une grande vérité réligieuse." [1]

Villemain's remarks are confined to a discussion of the *oraison funèbre*, but they are applicable to Bossuet's sermons in general, and to the sermons of his English contemporaries. The *idée dominante*, and the combining together of a few clear ideas forcefully expressed *within the circle of a great religious truth*, became in the last decades of the seventeenth century the aim of English preachers. In making this their ideal they were actually joining forces across the centuries with the Greek and Latin Fathers, and while avoiding the florid imagery of the former and the mystical exegesis of the latter, like them they addressed themselves to the men of their time in a manner easy to be understood and in keeping with the taste of the period. The achievement of Massillon, Bossuet, and Bourdaloue was largely determined by the courtly and educated circle in which they moved and their influence confined to that circle ; but the English sermon, representing the accepted application of rhetoric to religious topics—a restrained, highly sensitive, and often almost imperceptible application—was of more vital and far-reaching importance. After, in the hands of Tillotson, effecting an unprecedented change in English style, it remained throughout the whole of the eighteenth century, even in its most decadent form, a norm of dignified, sustained, and beautifully modulated prose, employed by Episcopalians and Dissenters alike, till upset by the irruption of a new spirit in the Wesleyan revival and of new interests under the influence of the Oxford Movement and the spread of scientific knowledge.

[1] " L'Essai sur l'Oraison Funèbre," prefixed to ' Oraisons Funèbres ' of Massillon, Fléchier, and Mascaron, Paris, no date.

Obviously the main trend of the theory underlying the composition of English sermons in the seventeenth century implies a vindication of art as against the exigencies of exposition or the influence of peculiar inspirational conceptions. The devices of rhetoric were employed, but in such a way as made less for a display of these devices than for the better management of the subject in hand. The contentions of Sydrach Simpson, Dell, and Webster, to which more than once allusion has been made, although they had place between 1653 and 1655, had indicated clearly in what direction normal English opinion lay. Simpson's imprudent contention put forth in a sermon before the University of Cambridge—

" That Humane Learning is not a preparation appointed by *Christ*, either for the right understanding or right teaching the Gospel "

was taken up by Dell, before the same auditory, in his ' Tryal of Spirits.' [1]   Dell, however, though opposed to Simpson's views, put forth in turn in the ' Stumbling-Stone '—a further sermon against a learned ministry—views only slightly less drastic. To this we have Joseph Sedgwick's reply, ' A Sermon Preached at St. Maries' in the University of *Cambridge* . . . Or, An Essay to the discovery of the Spirit of Enthusiasme and pretended Inspiration. . . .' [2]   The same year, 1653, Sedgwick issued 'Ἐπίσκοπος Διδακτικός, Learning's Necessity to an Able Minister of the Gospel.'

The positions taken up in sermon and treatise are virtually identical. Pointing in the latter to the instance of Cicero, Sedgwick shows how that great writer was profoundly learned, but concealed his art so that " the greatest part of the Auditory understood no more than that he spoke their language handsomely, and very persuasively." [3]   Learning to be of value, he stressed, must be thorough—

" smattering in Learning is altogether uselesse, and good for nothing but to fill up the period with a frivolous sentence in Latine, that is too simple to be spoke in plain English. None ever said that the conning by heart a few Logicall

terms and Philosophicall distinctions, without any conception correspondent in the minde, was any benefit to sacred
study . . . He must have fast hold of Learning and have it
perfectly at command, that intends to make any use of it
in Divinity or Humanity." [1]

In short, learning was to be regarded as a preparation to
preaching, and, as Erasmus advised in the ' Ecclesiastes,'
rhetoric and dialectic were to be learned and then passed
by.[2] All might be of help, but it was no part of the preacher's
business to display his acquaintance with his past studies.
This, as Professor Foster Watson has remarked, was the usual
conception held by Calvinistic Puritans who regarded
classicism " not as an end in itself, but as subservient and
helpful to religion." [3]   The attitude is well explained by
Mather in his ' Manuductio ad Ministerium,' [4] when
addressing his son, he says :

" When you are upon seeking an Acquaintance with any
Languages ; Let your *Aims* be these. *I Desire to* come at
those Treasures which these Tongues may be Keys unto ;
And this, that so I may be the better furnished for that
SERVICE OF GOD, which I may be called unto." [5]

Such too, throughout their existence, was the dominating
motive of the Dissenting Academies.
  On the other side, John Webster, a former Army chaplain,
at times confused with the dramatist,[6] in his ' Saints Guide '
and ' Academiarum Examen,' both published in 1654,
would tolerate no preaching which owed anything to a
learned education ; for him direct inspiration was the sole
and necessary provision the preacher must have. " Acquired
learning," in his opinion, " by itself, and of its own nature
is nothing else but sin," [7] and he attacked violently the
education of preachers and the resources of contemporary

[1] *Op. cit.,* p. 49.
[2] ' Ecclesiastes,' Book II, ii.
[3] ' The English Grammar School,' p. 539.
[4] ' Directions For a Candidate of the Ministry . . .' Boston [Mass.], 1726.
[5] *Op. cit.,* p. 26.
[6] E.g. on the title-page of ' Histrio-Mastix. A Whip for Webster (as 'tis
conceived) the Quon-dam Player : Or, The examination of one John Websters
delusive Examen of Academies.'
[7] ' The Saints Guide . . .' Lon., 1654, p. 3.

preaching.[1] The ' Examen ' is a sweeping denunciation of school and University education of the period, Oratory coming in for a fair share of the attack.[2]

Seth Ward and Thomas Hall became Webster's most noted antagonists. Hall's work is entitled—

' Vindiciæ Literarum, The Schools Guarded, Or, The Excellency and Vsefulnesse of Humane Learning in Subordination to Divinity, and preparation to the Ministry : As Also, Rules for the expounding of the Holy Scriptures. . . . '

The latter part of the book is actually the ' Centuria Sacra ' which we have already noticed. In the epistle prefixed to the polemical part, Hall declares that he is writing against all who assert—

" that Arts, Sciences, Languages, Ec are Idols, Antichristian, the Smock (sic) of the bottomlesse Pit . . ." " The Scripture also," he points out,[3] " is ful of Rhetorick, many Tropes and Figures are there, what abundance of Metonymies, Ironies, Hyperboles, Hypalliges ? "—" Logick is necessary for analysing, defining, dividing, and more orderly resolution of a Text ; . . ." [4] But " Rhetorick is abused when men coin figures, and change the literall into an Allegoricall sense, as Origen did. . . ." [5]

The general conclusion of the context is fairly clear. Learning, and rhetoric in particular, continued to be valued as preparatives or aids to preaching. Neither churchman nor dissenter defended any longer the illegitimate parade of the one or the over-formal application of the other. It is the voice of Burnet which sums up the situation for the century :

" Preaching has past through very different Forms among us, since the Reformation. But without flattering the present age,[6] or any Persons now alive, too much, it must be confessed, that it is brought of late to a much greater Perfection than it was ever before in among us. . . .

---

[1] Op. cit., p. 13.   [2] Ibid., pp. 88-9.
[3] Op. cit., p. 6.   [4] Ibid., p. 6.
[5] Ibid., pp. 82-3.   [6] Written 1692.

Our language is much refined and we have returned to the plain Notions of simple and genuine Rhetorick.

. . . The impertinent Way of dividing Texts is laid aside, the needless setting out of the Originals, and the vulgar Version, is worn out. The trifling Shews of Learning in many Quotations of Passages, that very few could understand, do no more flat the Auditory. *Pert Wit* and *luscious Eloquence* have lost their Relish. So that Sermons are reduced to the plain opening the meaning of the Text, in a few short illustrations of its Coherence with what goes before and after, and of the Parts of which it is composed ; to that is joined the clear Stating of such Propositions as arise out of it, in their Nature, Truth, and Reasonableness ; by which, the Hearers may form clear Notions of the several Parts of Religion, such as are best suited to their Capacities and Apprehensions : In all which Applications are added, tending to the Reproving, Directing, Encouraging, or Comforting the Hearers, according to the several Occasions that are offered.

This is indeed all that can truly be intended in Preaching, to make some Portions of Scripture to be rightly understood ; to make those Truths contained in them to be more fully apprehended ; and then to lay the Matter home to the Consciences of the Hearers, so directing all to some good and practical End." [1]

Burnet's summary is coloured partly by personal, partly by current taste ; it reveals at once his theological outlook, which determined for him the purpose of preaching, and his attitude to preaching as a particular species of oratory. Neither multiplication of divisions nor multiplication of quotations was to be tolerated ; the chief function of the sermon was to be borne in mind, and the manner in which the preacher proceeded was to be governed by " the plain Notions of simple and genuine Rhetorick." In recalling these essential facts connected with the sermon at the end of the seventeenth century we are brought face to face with the diversity of influences which lay behind the production of sermons in our period—the preacher's temperament, his religious outlook, and the rhetorical training he received. No one influence can account exclusively for the form of a

[1] 'A Discourse of the Pastoral Care,' 3rd ed., Lon., 1713, pp. 192–3.

9

preacher's work, though in the case of the more literary preachers the temperamental element bulks large, and in the case of those who followed the prevailing fashion of a ' school ' of theology the prepossessions of their party meant much. Below all lay the rhetorical education of the day with all that it implied for men of particular dispositions or beliefs in the way of experiment and application. The theory was there, or rather, alternating, and at times parallel bands of theory were there, which tended to combine into a kind of rainbow span which ran across the century. At times there was close correspondence between particular aspects of theory and practice, at times remarkable divergence between the theories held and their resultant practice. Always, however, unless in the case of enthusiasts and fanatics, there was the feeling for Theory in one aspect or another and a genuine attempt to approximate somehow to what men believed to be the ideal. It is this that makes important the theoretical preconceptions of the seventeenth-century preachers, because however much the caprice of genius or considerations of ecclesiastical or doctrinal moment may have affected, and did affect, their sermons, and though in the best specimens of their work we cannot see the application of theory as clearly followed as one pricks out a design from a pattern, yet, from first to last, with an almost Platonic insistence, men laboured at the shaping of their sermons in the belief that, by so doing, they were more nearly approximating to the form of the ideal discourse which their Theory tried to adumbrate.[1]

What the Practice of preaching implied in the seventeenth century it is now our duty to examine.

[1] Several of the topics discussed in the foregoing chapters are also to be found in ' English Preachers and Preaching, 1640–1670, A Secular Study,' by Caroline F. Richardson, Lon., S.P.C.K., 1928, a book which I had not the advantage of seeing until my own was completely set up in type. In several instances Miss Richardson has used the same sources in slightly different ways, but the general conclusions which we have arrived at separately will be found in most instances closely to correspond.

PART II
PRACTICE

V. General Considerations: the Anglo-Catholic Preachers, including Donne

(i) The Prolegomena; (ii) Andrewes, the 'witty' preachers, and Donne

THE practice of the English pulpiteers of the seventeenth century was no mere application of the rules and theories which we have passed in review. While the importance of the rhetorical foundations of their work must be kept in mind, the consideration of the personal factor and the influence of the theological party to which particular preachers belonged are of still greater importance. Seldom, although such examples are to be met with, was the sermon purely a *theme* on a religious topic, and for the most part the florescence of individual genius, or the century-old luxuriance of a traditional treatment, at one and the same time obscures the bare structure underlying the whole, and imparts beauty and dignity which no meticulous attention to rhetorical rules could have given. If, on the one hand, the advice of Hyperius, that the preacher should be skilled in all manner of rhetorical devices, was followed,[1] on the other hand the advice of Erasmus was heeded, and those devices once learned were laid aside [2]; so that the sermons to be discussed resemble less the performance of a swordsman in the fencing-school than the vigorous action of a man compelled suddenly to defend his life with his weapon, but one who in his hour of greatest peril is not wholly devoid of the grace which wins the fencer praise.

The general impression made on a reader of seventeenth-century sermons is the result of subject and treatment rather than of structure. The topics selected by the preacher and the way in which his thoughts " eddy about " those—to use De Quincey's striking phrase [3]—are of supreme moment. To the contemporary auditor, as has been stressed in an earlier chapter, form was quite definitely of considerable interest; but the fact remains that the reasonableness of the positions advanced, and the emotional appeal of the illustrations or embellishments employed, were the mainstay

[1] Quoted *ante*, p. 52.
[2] 'Ecclesiastes,' Book II, ii.
[3] 'Essay on Rhetoric,' Masson's ed., Lon., 1897, vol. x, p. 121, quoted in full, *ante*, pp. 49–50.

of the sermon, whether in its spoken or printed presentation. Of the latter factor we can still form a comparatively fair judgment, allowing for changes in fashions of thought and expression due to the passage of time, if we remember, that though sometimes both subject and treatment are of a traditional sort, suggested by acquaintance with patristic and mediæval preaching, the matter and manner of the sermons are most readily explained by reference either to temperament, or to the school of religious thought to which the preachers belonged. These two factors, moreover, combine subtly, as the Spaniard Huarte suggests in his curious ' Examen de Ingenios,' where—

" it is proved that the Theoricke of Diuinitie appertaineth to the understanding, and preaching (which is his practise) to the imagination," [1]—

an opinion which goes far towards explaining why among men of all types of theological conviction, unexpected, and at times decidedly puzzling, literary achievements are to be found. Calvinism did not prevent Henry Smith and Thomas Adams from introducing a pictorial element into their sermons, comparable in many places to the work of the Elizabethan pamphleteers, and the sudden strange breaking away of Donne into passages of imaginative grandeur cannot be explained with reference to the ordinary rules of exegesis which often govern the opening up of his subject. Divinity clearly required to be infused by a " breath and finer spirit," more directly akin to poetry, before great literary preaching could result. Passed through the alembic of personality, dogmatic theology issued in forms of unprecedented beauty, and, on occasion, as with a man of Baxter's calibre, austerity itself became almost sublime, like organ-music played in a wainscoted room by a woman in a Puritan habit. On the whole, however, it was the school of theology to which a preacher belonged which determined the main features of his preaching, though, among preachers of practically all ' schools,' the contribution of individual genius renders conspicuous the pulpit oratory of a few.

[1] English translation from the Italian of Camillo Camilli by ' R.C. *Esquire*,' Lon., 1616, chap. x. This entertaining work is concerned with the agelong attempt to determine, " What is intelligence and how is it produced ? " and finds a solution along the line of eugenics based on Galen's theory of Humours !

The ' school ' is of dominant importance, because, as has been shown, the ' school ' to a large measure prescribed the homiletical theory of the preacher. It determined his reading, or rather, since we know men like Bolton, Cotton, and Baxter were quite as conversant with the Fathers and Schoolmen as the bishops of the time,[1] although there is little indication of this in their sermons, the partiality displayed for a particular range of authors led to a more loving study of these, and to a more frequent quotation of their writings, than was the case among men of different outlook. Thus the influence of the Vulgate and the Fathers is obvious in the work of the Anglo-Catholic preachers, and, as is only to be expected in one who until middle life had not definitely severed his connection with the Church of Rome, quotations from the former are more numerous in Donne's sermons than in those of others. In the same way among the older generation of Puritans quotations from the Genevan version are found ; but these did not to any extent influence style, and are notable only as accounting for an expression employed now and then in order to permit the drawing of some lesson, and which falls strange on an ear familiar with the text of the Authorized Version. Upon the early Puritans, too, Calvin's works had a definite stylistic influence, and when elaborate ' methods ' of preaching, such as Hyperius, Ursinus, Musculus, or Keckermann employed, were not closely imitated, the expository lecture of Calvin was taken as a model. With the less rigid Calvinists Seneca, as we have seen, was in favour, and the classical moralists as a whole continued to gain ground as the patristic vogue ceased, or was suppressed, with the results illustrated in the work of the Cambridge Platonists, and to some extent of Jeremy Taylor. But Taylor is a man apart, and the extraordinary range of his quotations and allusions, often to the most strangely unlikely authors for a preacher to quote, is a good example of how within a particular group which sanctions certain usages an individual may develop along wholly unexpected lines. A more chastened taste for the classical moralists appears in Tillotson, but, in the majority

[1] *Vid*. Bagshawe's ' Life of Bolton,' prefixed to 1632 edition of the latter's ' Foure Last Things ' ; Mather : ' Magnalia Christi Americana,' Book III, p. 25 ; Baxter : ' Reliquiæ,' 1696 ed., p. 363—where in his tribute to Cosins the similar learning of himself and others of his sympathisers is clearly implied.

of instances, the ' reformed ' sermon at the close of the century bore testimony rather to the contemporary taste in style than to the past education or favourite studies of the preacher.

In the course of the century, it is possible to say, the sermon passed from a period in which its form and content were governed by certain rhetorical and homiletical ideals to a period when it became almost a province of literature, in so far as conformity to the prevailing literary standards was required also from the preacher. Its subject-matter underwent an equally important transformation, and the attempts early in the eighteenth century by Steele and Addison to draw men off from strife and faction in politics, by insisting on a wide range of common interests, found a counterpart in the choice of non-controversial subjects, often of a strongly ethical character, noticeable in the work of dissenters and churchmen alike in the period subsequent to the Revolution.

In order to study the prevailing fashions, whether of ' school ' or period, or rightly to evaluate the achievement of outstanding individuals, it has been found convenient to take in turn the main ' schools ' of religious thought in England during the century, and by examining each of these in some detail to note the specific excellencies or defects of each, and so arrive at some clear understanding of the composite materials out of which was formed the somewhat stereotyped sermon, of the more or less essay-type, which appealed to religious auditories in the days of Queen Anne. With this end in view the preachers of the period have been grouped in five categories, although it is obvious that any arrangement proposed is likely to prove a Procrustes' bed, and men who were bigger than any possible category can indicate will occasionally be found to have close affinities with preachers in a category other than their own. The agreed divisions have been labelled as follows : (I) the Anglo-Catholic Preachers, including Donne ; (II) the other Anglicans to 1660, including Jeremy Taylor ; (III) the non-Anglicans to 1660 ; (IV) the Cambridge Platonists and Latitudinarians ; and (V) Restoration Preachers and the Reform of Style. In each case the work of prominent preachers of a particular ' school ' has been passed in review, and the prevailing taste or ideals of their party noted ;

the work of lesser and obscure preachers has, where possible, been drawn upon for illustration, and in the case of the greater preachers the dividing-line between the merely successful preacher and the literary artist made as explicit as possible.

(i) *The Prolegomena*

Since the history of English preaching in the seventeenth century is largely concerned with ' witty ' or ' metaphysical ' preaching, the opposition offered to this fashion and the final reformation and simplification of the sermon in the period succeeding the Restoration, it is only right that first place in our study should be given to the ' metaphysical ' preachers, in order that we may form a clear idea of their work and so be able to determine as justly as possible in what respects that work was worthy of admiration and in what respects open to criticism and censure.

As is indicated clearly by Professor Spingarn (in his summary account of the subject), such ' metaphysical ' preaching had had its rise in Spain and passed into Italy marked as the *gusto espagnol*.[1] While enjoying a somewhat different career in France among the preachers described by Jacquinet in ' Des Prédicateurs Du XVIIe Siècle Avant Bossuet,'[2] the fashion gained a simultaneous hold in England. It does not seem tenable to suggest that beyond the first transportation of this style of preaching from Spain to Italy the popularity it enjoyed was due to a species of national imitation. The one definitely imitative stage in the progress of this preaching, and the moment at which and the party amid which it became a vogue in England, both tend to emphasise the same fact. What Italy learned from Spain in this connection was to draw upon certain patristic and mediæval writers who had been fond of particular devices and to imitate these devices ; and the English preachers who became the exponents of the fashion in their own country were precisely those preachers, or the disciples of those preachers, who in the later years of Elizabeth's reign were beginning to turn back to the same writers, and, naturally enough, were attracted by the same devices.

Purely ' witty ' preaching, therefore, owes much to tradition. A fondness for ' turns ' of mind comparable to their

---

[1] *Ante*, p. 4, footnote 1. [2] Paris, 1885.

fondness for ' turns ' of speech noticeable among both the Eastern and Western Fathers, and a growing fantasticalness of thought—perhaps actually provocative of, perhaps a natural reaction to the clear-cut logic of Scholasticism— typical of the Middle Ages, lie behind all subsequent preaching of this kind. The strictly ' metaphysical ' strain, if we exclude the *Physiologus* and Pliny, is a sixteenth- century feature resulting from the new worlds, geographical and scientific, which were then being opened up for man's wonder. But it is almost impossible to make a satisfactory division between the ' metaphysical ' and the ' witty,' and in the case of images and illustrations derived from such authors as Galen or Pliny, it is difficult to determine pre- cisely to what extent the learned, to what extent the pictorial element, apart from any considerations of fact, has led to individual quotations.

The attraction which the ' metaphysical ' type of preach- ing exercised on one group of English divines at the period under discussion was plainly the outcome of their theological or ecclesiastical outlook and of the reading to which that outlook led. To understand the ' reaction ' as their attitude has sometimes been called, the ' partial restoration ' or ' claim to continuity ' as they themselves regarded their position, it is necessary to consider briefly the circumstances in which these churchmen found themselves.

The ardent polemics of the Reformers of Edward VI's reign had been silenced by persecution or exile, and the Elizabethan Church, largely by will of the Queen, was in no sense a preaching Church. Elizabeth's opinion appears to have been that such persons as were likely to profit by ser- mons might have them, but that the bulk of the nation was more likely to benefit by the judicious reading of the ' Book of Homilies.' The acrimonious contentions of the exiles who had returned from Geneva, and their desire to reduce the Church of England to conformity in all points with the Discipline of Calvin, naturally strengthened the Queen's dislike of ' prophesyings.' Nor was it only the obscurer parochial clergy who desired to discuss in their pulpits such subjects as the ' divine decrees ' ; the itch for disputa- tion infected several of the leading divinity professors and university teachers. Naturally the undergraduates took sides and the mischief spread. There was move and countermove. On the one hand, Cartwright, Lady Margaret Professor of Divinity at Cambridge, was compelled to relinquish his chair and retire to Geneva. On the other hand, Mildmay founded Emmanuel College, in the same university, to be a seminary for Puritan preachers. Cartwright was deprived of his professorship in 1570, Emmanuel was founded in 1584, and by 1596 a further stage in the conflict had been reached, the stage associated with the names of Barrett and Baro. The significance of this particular controversy [1] lies in the fact that by the period in question Calvinism was no longer the unchallenged theological system of all English divines. A new spirit had begun to animate some of the younger men, and the break with Rome was seen to be not necessarily a break with the Church as it had grown up as an institution through the centuries.

By Andrewes' time, to quote the words of Canon Ottley :

" The leading principles, indeed, of the Reformation movement in the English Church were already clear : the appeal to antiquity, the retention of the ancient orders, the claim to hold what was admittedly catholic in doctrine." [2]

For, as another writer expresses it, the ideal of a reformed Church as conceived by the earlier reformers, and reasserted in the Stuart era, was—

" not the pursuit of a phantom primitive Protestantism, ever eluding the historian's grasp and finally disappearing into the dim decades of the close of the first century, but a purified Catholic Church, the old historic, visible, familiar household of faith, healed of its wounds and returning to its higher earlier self. A reformed Catholicism would be such as Chrysostom or Alfred could feel at home in, and David, Boniface, Chad or Anselm not repudiate as alien." [3]

---

[1] The circumstances of the controversy were as follows : Barrett, having been censured for attacking the prevailing doctrines of assurance and the indefectibility of faith, archbishop Whitgift was led to accept Whitaker's nine ' theses,' later known as ' the Lambeth Articles.' These in turn resulted in Baro's criticism of the positions put forward in them, followed by the latter's citation before the Heads of Houses and subsequent acquittal.

[2] ' Lancelot Andrewes ' (Leaders of Religion Series), Lon., 1894, p. 31.

[3] Macleane : ' Lancelot Andrewes and the Reaction,' Lon., 1910, p. 2.

Such an ecclesiastical position, implying as it does the acceptance of the vast depository of Catholic doctrine, places at once at the service of the preacher who accepts it, not only the resources of past centuries of theology, but the treasures of patristic and mediæval preaching into which had been poured wealth of the most diverse and unexpected sort. In aligning themselves with the Catholic Church, and insisting on the continuity of the Church of England as part of that Church, the Anglo-Catholic divines of the close of the sixteenth century were turning from the barren logic of Calvin's 'Institutes' to the beauty of classical oratory applied to religious subjects, to the tenderness and humanity of mediæval poetry, and to that pictorialism which alike in description and painting, whether the emotion it suggested was charity or terror, was characteristic of the Middle Ages. The repudiation of logic was a gain for rhetoric in the widest sense, while on the more definitely religious plane, not only was a rational assent to such doctrines as were considered of moment carefully sought after, but an intensity of loving adoration and devotion was evoked such as the religious system of Calvin was incapable of producing.

In this way the theological position of the moment led directly to a fashion in preaching ; for once English divines began to study the works of the Fathers, not primarily with a desire to furnish their bow with arrows against Rome, but as the forerunners and great teachers of the Church of which they themselves in their century were also ministers, quite different portions of the patristic writings began to attract them. Broad lines of doctrine, beautiful and effective imagery, the evidences of lively and ingenious wit employed to stimulate and delight popular auditories—these things were noted and came both to be quoted and imitated. As the study of bygone writers was no longer dictated by controversial needs there was no longer any reason why " the most primitive times " should be fixed as its limit, and the mediæval writers in turn were read and drawn upon. Moreover, that late sixteenth-century world was treading hard on the heels of earlier centuries, and its secular knowledge was still largely that which had been possessed by the theologians of the preceding millennium and in conformity with which particular theological doctrines had been evolved. Pliny, Galen, and Hippocrates were still textbooks to the Elizabethans, and the opportunity to present the material so provided in such a way as would be likely at once to astonish and to inculcate some religious truth was clearly as irresistible to bishop Andrewes and his contemporaries as it was to St. Ambrose or Antonio Vieyra.

The rhetorical continuity of the sermon has been made plain in the preceding section of this study. The strange partiality for allegorisation which infested patristic and mediæval preaching has also been glanced at and its source indicated in Jewish rabbinical exegesis. It might be supposed that, once this latter trait is accounted for, the patristic sermon would bear a fairly strong resemblance to the secular classical oration, always remembering that it was the debased oratory of the ' Second Sophistic,' rather than the true classical oratory, which the patristic orators had learned to imitate. But while the preacher's address was an oration on a religious theme it was not merely an oration. Something of the original ὁμιλία or ' sermo ' was retained ; something, too, of the awful import and unearthly sanctity of the message to be conveyed permeated the whole. Or, to speak of a very different aspect of these sermons, a curious facetiousness and almost hilarious ingeniousness were at times employed, as if the preacher were determined to compete with the comedian and to raise a laugh ere he captured a soul.

From the carefully built-up sentences of the Eastern Fathers, with their *isocola* and *antitheses*, used not merely ornately but effectively, to set out the wonder of the Divine Love, the mediæval, and after him the Anglo-Catholic, preacher, derived that appealing poetic treatment, which became the traditional manner of presenting certain themes. Thus we find Basil, in his funeral oration on the martyr Juletta, in a passage which even in translation reveals the familiar devices of classical prose, expressing for the first time in pulpit oratory in a form destined to survive, and exercise permanent influence on succeeding generations, that feeling for the contrast between the greatness of Christ and the meanness of the circumstances to which He came. Down the centuries this theme was to be re-echoed beautifully by Bernard in his ' Sermones Ad Tempora,' and to be adapted from both sources by Andrewes and the men of his school, until it passed over from preaching to poetry and was given final expression for the century by Crashaw in his Nativity Hymn. Basil's two themes—man in the *homo*centric Universe created for him and God identifying Himself with man in order to work his redemption—became a staple of all subsequent preaching :

" *What retribution* " (he enquires) " *shall we give unto the Lord, for all the gifts which He hath bestowed upon us ?* . . . From the cheerless gloom of non-existence He waked us into being ; He ennobled us with understanding ; He taught us arts to promote the means of life ; . . . He bade the animals to own us as their lords. For us the rains descend, for us the sun diffuses his creative beams ; the mountains rise, the vallies bloom, affording us a grateful habitation and a sheltering retreat. For us the rivers flow ; for us the fountains murmur ; the sea spreads wide its bosom to extend our commerce ; the earth exhausts its precious stores ; each new object presents a new enjoyment ; all nature pouring her treasures at our feet through the boundless grace of Him Who wills that all is ours !

" But why do I descant on lesser subjects, when nobler themes should grace the preacher's tongue ? For us God dwelt with man ! . . . For sinful, perishable flesh the *Word was embodied in the flesh and abode with us* . . . The benefactor tarried with the ungrateful ; the deliverer came unto the captives ; in the realms of benighted man arose the orb of righteousness . . . He, Who was exempt from suffering was stretched upon the Cross ; immortality was wedded to death ; light descended into darkness . . . He rose again for those who had fallen ; He sent forth the *spirit of adoption* ; He diffused the celestial grace . . . He accomplished all that angels can conceive, and more than man can utter."

With Chrysostom the employment of rhetoric is much more elaborate, and there is an oriental richness and profusion of epithets and images noticeable in his work which mark him off from other preachers of all ages. His remained the great name ; he was the " golden-mouthed " preacher ; and any luxuriance or excessive embroidery occurring in the sermons of later preachers must necessarily fall so far short of his that they were bound to appear to their composers rather to be unsuccessful strivings after an unobtainable ideal than to err by excess.[1] Consulted especially in

[1] A good example of Chrysostom's luxuriant style is provided by the opening of his first homily on the Gospel of St. John, which is quite clearly in the manner of the ' Second Sophistic,' and is precisely how we should expect to find Proæresius or Libanius introducing a visiting Sophist to the notice of the school or gratulating the return of a victorious emperor :

" They that are spectators of the heathen games, when they have learned that a distinguished athlete and winner of crowns is come from any quarter, run all together to view his wrestling, and all his skill and strength ; and you may see the whole theatre of many tens of thousands, all there, straining their eyes both of body and mind, that nothing of what is done may escape them. So again these same persons if any admirable musician come among them, leave all that they had in hand, which often is necessary and pressing business, and mount the steps, and sit listening very attentively to the words and the accomplishments, and criticising the agreement of the two. This is what the many do.

" Again : those who are skilled in rhetoric do just the same with respect to the sophists, for they too have their theatres, and their audience, and clapping of hands, and noise, and closest criticism of what is said. And if in the case of rhetoricians, musicians, and athletes, people sit, in the one case to look on, in the other to see at once and to listen, with such earnest attention, what zeal, what earnestness ought ye in reason to display, when it is no musician or debater who now comes forward to a trial of skill, but when a man is speaking from heaven, and utters a voice plainer than thunder ? For he has persuaded the whole earth with the sound, and occupied and filled it, not by the loudness of the cry, but by moving his tongue with the grace of God. . . . For the *son of thunder*, the beloved of Christ, the pillar of the churches throughout the world, who holds the keys of heaven, who drank the cup of Christ, and was baptised with His baptism, who lay upon his Master's bosom with much confidence,* this man comes forward to us now ; not as an actor of a play, not hiding his head with a mask, (for he hath another sort of words to speak,) nor mounting a platform, nor striking the stage with his foot, nor dressed out with apparel of gold, but he enters wearing a robe of inconceivable beauty. For he will appear before us having *put on Christ*, having his beautiful *feet shod with the preparation of the Gospel of peace ;* wearing a girdle not about his waist but about his loins, not made of scarlet leather and daubed outside with gold, but woven and composed of truth itself. Now will he appear before us, not acting a part, (for with him there is nothing counterfeit, nor fiction, nor fable), but with unmasked head he proclaims to us the truth unmasked ; not making an audience believe him other than he is, by carriage, by look, by voice, needing for the delivery of his message no instruments of music, as harp, lyre, or any other similar ; for he effects all with his tongue, uttering a voice which is sweeter and more profitable than that of any harper or any music. All heaven is his stage ; his theatre is the habitable world ; his audience, all angels, and of men as many as are angels already, or desire to become so † . . . By this Apostle stand the powers from above, marvelling at the beauty of that virtue which he drew from Christ Himself, and obtained by grace of the Spirit. For he hath made ready his soul as some well-fashioned and jewelled lyre with strings of gold, and yielded it for the utterance of something great and sublime to the Spirit."

* In this description Chrysostom is definitely adapting the advertisements of noted athletes which would give an account of their feats, just as he continues by using imagery drawn from the stage.

† This is an obvious pun in the Greek.

the controversy over transubstantiation the unrivalled wealth of his writings became a mine from which preachers might dig.   Isaac Casaubon, the friend of Andrewes, and one who declared his preference for the Anglican form of the Reformation, was so familiar with these writings that we find him saying :

" Unless my memory deceives me, Chrysostom, in his genuine works, never refers the expression ' daily bread,' in the Lord's prayer, to the eucharist " [1]—

a comment which affords an excellent illustration of how polemical considerations led to close familiarity, a familiarity almost certain to result in admiring quotation or imitation.

In Ambrose ' witty ' preachers had a great exemplar. Far less luxuriant than Chrysostom, in the sphere of allegory he permitted his imagination to run wild.   No meaning was for him too fanciful to be extracted from Scripture, and his exegesis, in places of the most unexpected sort, was undoubtedly an evil example for those striving after startling and ingenious effects.   Thus, Peter did not deny Jesus :

" Being asked, *Art thou also one of those who were with Jesus of Galilee ?* he shrank from the word of eternity ; for those who had a beginning *were* not, that is to say, He alone *was* Who *was* in the beginning.   Finally he says *I am not* ; for it belongs to Him alone *to be* Who *is* always.   Whence also Moses says, *I AM* hath sent me . . . Luke also has written that Peter when asked whether he was of them, answered at first, I know Him not.   And he spoke well ; for it were rash to say he knew Him Whom the mind of man cannot comprehend ; for no man knoweth the Son but the Father." [2]

Ambrose, moreover, attached extraordinary meanings to the letters of the Hebrew alphabet, in a way which not only proves that he did not know Hebrew, but also links him up with the Cabbalists. [3]   Pliny, too, proved a fruitful source of marvels of " unnatural natural history " of which he never

---

[1] Mark Pattison : ' Isaac Casaubon,' Oxf., 1892, p. 441.

[2] Commentary on St. Matthew xxvi. 70.

[3] Empson—*op. cit.*, p. 246—notes the " unreliable " nature of the tenses in Hebrew and " the extraordinary idioms " and " strong taste for puns " met with in that language as a fruitful source of *ambiguity*, and one which the English ' metaphysical ' poets made full use of.

tired, and the *Physiologus*—a series of descriptions of animals, probably based on stories current in Alexandria, put together in Greek early in the second century A.D., to which allusion has already been made—served him, as it was to serve generations of mediæval preachers, as a never-failing mine of illustration.

This strangely composite material, with the added psychological and philosophical interest found in Augustine, the Anglo-Catholic divines were familiar with from their habitual studies. Drilled during their school-days in the age-old rhetorical figures, they were quick to note the occurrence of these in the patristic writings.[1] What they noted they were quick to imitate in the vernacular. This they more readily attempted with the example of the mediæval preachers before them, who, as has been indicated, continued century after century to imitate the classical *schemata* in their simpler and more obvious forms.

Another characteristic element in the mediæval sermon which made a strong appeal to English preachers was the sense of drama, which, linking up with the Christmas crib and the Passiontide entombment of the Host, and similar attempts to render concrete and vivid the great facts of the ' Sacred Year,' resulted in preaching of a beautiful and moving character, such as is illustrated by the quotation given from St. Basil, and which was to find striking expression in the work of St. Bernard. Thus, for example, we find Andrewes in a Nativity sermon [2] taking over Bede's striking personification of a passage from the ' Psalms '—" Mercy and Truth are met together ; Justice and Peace have kissed each other " [3]—and the whole Anglo-Catholic school followed the work of Bernard in his devotional meditations on the birth and infancy of the Saviour.

Plants, stones, and animals, to which were attributed mythical and mystical significance, likewise passed as an interest from the mediæval to the English preachers, and in the second half of the seventeenth century, we find Bramhall

---

[1] Especially of *parison* or *paromoion*—the former being the careful balancing of adjective, noun, and verb in successive clauses, so that the clauses corresponded, the latter consisting in similarity of sound, either of an alliterative character, or *homoioteleutic*, where the similarity occurred in like endings.

[2] The XIth of the ' XCVI Sermons.'

[3] Ps. lxxxv. 10 ; for Bede's sermon *vid.* Neale's ' Mediæval Preachers and Mediæval Preaching,' pp. 9 *seq.*

10

drawing upon Pliny's tales of the overthrow of monsters by small creatures as a warning to the great Hobbes.[1] Only after the Restoration, when dissection and scientific enquiry were freely promoted by the Royal Society, did the illustrations and examples of the mediæval bestiaries fall into final disuse.

Allegory has already been touched on. Suffice it to say in this connection that what the Jewish exegetes initiated, and Origen, the Greek Fathers, and Ambrose so extensively promoted, the mediæval preachers carried to excess. Midway through the sixth century, Isidore of Seville had produced a work on the allegorical signification of scriptural passages, and in the eighth century Hrabanus Maurus compiled a dictionary of allegories, entitled 'Allegoriæ in universam sacram scripturam.' By the latter period, allegorisation, it will be seen, had become systematised, and the attitude of Aquinas, previously noted, indicates what was to be expected of a preacher.

" In the house of our soul " (Hrabanus wrote in the preface to the work just mentioned), " history lays the foundation, allegory erects the walls, anagogy puts on the roof, while tropology provides ornament." [2]

The necessity of extracting all possible types of meanings from a given passage of Scripture must have been a great drain on the resources of the mediæval preacher, and it was to meet the needs of such that Honorious of Autun, in the twelfth century, produced his collection of specimen allegories, known as the ' Speculum Ecclesiæ.' By this period the traditional allegorical renderings had become stereotyped, and Honorius was consequently able to handle his allegories more easily, and apply them more naturally than did either Isidore or Hrabanus.[3] Such stereotyped renderings, given now and then additional charm by one preacher or another, were familiar to the English divines, and at times are either alluded to or naturally employed ; but the more extravagant allegorisation of lesser men also

[1] " The Catching of Leviathan," (an appendix to ' Castigations of Mr. Hobbes . . . ' Lon., 1658,) Preface.
[2] Quoted Taylor : ' Mediæval Mind,' vol. ii, p. 48.
[3] *Vid.* Taylor : *op. cit.,* vol. ii, pp. 54–6, for Honorius' application of the parable of the Good Samaritan, which reveals the full mediæval significance given to the parable which is still current in the sermons of the Anglo-Catholic preachers.

on occasion proved attractive by reason of its ingenuity and its obvious suggestion of ' wit.'

The legendary matter contained in the Talmud, the speculations of the Cabbala, and the works which passed traditionally under the name of Hermes Trismegistus, add still further to the somewhat heterogeneous and bizarre background of this preaching ; for while the vehicle employed by outstanding preachers for over thirteen centuries, even in its most curious adaptations and often with slight recollection of its splendid originals, was that of classical rhetoric, the content of their preaching was of the most varied kind. All that was strange, unexpected, and disparate appears in close connection, and when we remember the astonishing application to study of the late Elizabethan and Jacobean divines, the habit of keeping commonplace-books, the fondness for excerpting and quoting, it is not to be wondered at that the English sermon, as it fell from the lips of the Anglo-Catholic preachers, or was carefully set out by them for the Press, was of a curiously composite and often surprising character. The sermon in the hands of these divines was seldom an original composition ; it was rather a mosaic of patristic reminiscence, scholastic allusion, and particular theological precepts sanctioned by Councils and canonists. Very seldom do references to the Classics appear, and then purely by way of illustration and without any literary appreciation of the authors cited ; and topical references, while often pertinent and vivid, have an odd habit of becoming indistinguishable from the wider context in which they occur, very much as clowns in Renaissance costume figure in *Adoration* or *Crucifixion*. In short, there is the same sense of identity and continuity about this type of sermon as there is about the theological position, and the ritualistic practices of the men who produced it. Not only was their Church, as we have heard one writer saying, the Church of Chrysostom and Alfred, of Boniface and Anselm, and their Faith the old historical Faith purified of accretions and misconceptions, but their preaching was concerned with such doctrines and their exposition followed such lines as were familiar to Basil and Augustine, to Bede and Bernard. Their sermons, apart from direct quotation, were the outcome of loving study of the works of their predecessors, and the habitual imagery which they employed, the train of ideas which the contemplation of particular circumstances aroused, and the devotion which they either personally felt or set themselves deliberately to arouse in others, were part of a great tradition. This tradition which, starting with the Greek Fathers, had descended unbroken to the Reformation, in England, in the period of our study, was to resume its influence for more than half a century, producing in the process a kind of unexpected beauty, which, except in an occasional passage of Hooker, English preaching had not hitherto known.

(ii) Andrewes, the 'Witty' Preachers, and Donne

So far as the ecclesiastical and theological attempt of a party to restore the Church of England to conformity with primitive catholicism is concerned, it is customary to speak of the process as the 'Laudian movement.' When the 'witty' or 'metaphysical' preaching of members of the party is passed in review, however, it is to Andrewes that the chief honour falls. To the men of his own time Andrewes appeared, and to men of succeeding centuries he has remained, the 'witty' preacher *par excellence*, and, as his title to this distinction is undoubted, it is therefore to his works that we naturally turn when we would discover what were the characteristics of this type of preaching, and what it was that men admired in it and were eager to imitate.

In approaching Andrewes thus it is well to recall the emphasis which Professor Grierson lays on "the more intellectual, less verbal character" of 'metaphysical' wit "compared with the conceits of the Elizabethans," [1] and to bear in mind that while Euphuism was largely a trick of expression, 'metaphysical' preaching, like 'metaphysical' poetry, revealed a habit of thought. Where a 'metaphysical' preacher (such as Willan [2]) shows apparent imitation of some of the traditional *schemata*, it will usually be found that he has a patristic or mediæval schematic passage in view, which he is actually quoting or paraphrasing at the moment, though at times, it is true, imitation occurs in the vernacular in passages not directly quoted. On the whole, however, the striving after schematic effects was not a characteristic of this preaching. Neither was the

---

[1] *Vid.* 'Metaphysical Lyrics and Poems,' pp. xiii–xvi, and *ante*, p. 7.
[2] *Vid. ante*, p. 88.

citation of fabulous natural history collected from Pliny or the *Physiologus*, nor a delight in allegory or the mystery of Hebraic words and their numerical equivalents, clear proofs of the preacher's party ; for Henry Smith and Adams showed as great fondness for " unnatural natural history " as did Andrewes and his disciples, and Smith shared to the full Donne's delight in allegory and cabbalistic speculation. Indeed, among the older generation of Puritans contemporary taste, probably shared by them, probably taken cognisance of in order to conciliate their auditories, provided, for a brief period at least, a considerable amount of common material.[1] It was not therefore so much the material as the use to which the material was put that distinguished the ' metaphysical ' preacher ; the greater ingenuity with which he adapted his examples, the more unexpected parallels which he produced, and the more subtle, psychological, and learned images which he employed—these were the characteristic traits. Not mere quotation, but quotation leading up to an unexpected ' point,' and a ' point,' which, while it was verbal, conveyed something of much greater import ; not punning and quibbling merely for their own sakes, but because amid the jingle of human phrases might be caught the accents of a divine message—these were the things that counted. To sum up, the relation of the preacher both to the learning of the past and to the active affairs of his own day was conditioned by his attitude to a theological conception of the Universe, the attitude which led to his regarding all things *sub specie æternitatis* ; from this viewpoint nothing employed could be considered merely ridiculous, for the juxtaposition that invited laughter incidentally revealed the highest truth, and the impossible itself became the credible, being, as Tertullian assured men, to be believed, *quia impossibile est.*

The earliest specimens of Andrewes' preaching which we possess are ' A Pattern of Catechistical Doctrine ' and ' The Moral Law Expounded,' not published till 1630, four years after his death, and then, obviously, derived from sermon-notes taken by some auditor, and not from a text prepared for delivery and corrected afterwards for publication.

[1] This point is very happily emphasised in Mr. Drinkwater's play ' Oliver Cromwell,' where Elizabeth Cromwell, the Protector's mother, mentions with admiration the poems of Donne and Herrick—authors whom the more fanatical Puritans of the Civil War period held in abhorrence.

These addresses, as also the sermons on the Lord's Prayer and on the Temptation (the latter of which appeared in print as early as 1592) belonged to the period when Andrewes as a young man was catechist of Pembroke Hall, his own college, in Cambridge. The two former series of addresses are unusually full of classical references and illustrations, and are typical specimens of college sermons from his day to our own ; those on the Lord's Prayer mark, as far as their imperfect and disjointed form permits us to judge, the transition from the young don, replete with classical allusion and quotation, to the young divine, even more replete with Scriptural allusion and quotation, who has made the language of the Bible his own, and is able to express what he wants to say of spiritual things in the phrases of the great spiritual leaders of Israel. The style is precisely the same as that of the sermons preached before the close of the sixteenth century at St. Giles, Cripplegate, his first cure, or before Elizabeth, and which are preserved in the canon of the ' XCVI Sermons.' Already we have traces of Andrewes' ' wit ' :

" The disciples that said, ' Shall we command that fire come down from heaven and consume them ? ' are not like God. Christ is called the ' day-star,' not the dog-star. God is said to have ' walked in the cool of the day,' not in the heat of the day." [1]

Of the " light of nature," he observed :

" The Wise Man saith, ' The soul of man is the candle of the Lord.' . . . With this light ' every one that cometh into the world is enlightened.' Howbeit this light hath caught a fall, as Mephiboseth did, and therefore it halteth ; notwithstanding, because it is of the blood royal, it is worthy to be made of." [2]

The Latin sermon preached by Andrewes at St. Paul's in 1593, at the opening of Convocation, points back to the Latin prose with which his style has affinities, and illustrates how, whether writing in Latin or in English, his mind tended to move along the same lines of wit and word-play, always

[1] ' Works ' (Library of Anglo-Catholic Theology), vol. v, p. 318, *ad init.*
[2] *Ibid.*, p. 319.

more or less directed to a moral purpose. Thus he told the assembled bishops :

" Hodie multi episcopi malunt esse morosi quam bene morati. . . . Majorem fere rationem habemus nummorum quam morum,"

or :

" At the present day, it is reported of us that we are more concerned with shearing than shepherding the sheep "— " attonsioni gregis potius quam attentioni " ;

and he recalled them to a sense of their high office as bishops by playing on the word " episcopi " :

" Episcopi estis active, id est, inspectores ; passive, id est, spectacula."

By the time of the Latin sermon Andrewes' style had been definitely formed, as we can gather from the sermon dealing with " sundry imaginations by divers erected " preached at St. Giles, Cripplegate, in the previous year, but the early emergence of ' wit ' in his college exercises and the obvious connection between his Latin and English compositions is significant. ' Witty ' preaching was clearly due to a contemporary habit of mind which found its opportunity largely through a current rhetorical fashion. The distinction drawn by Smith [1] (following older rhetoricians) between a *figura dictionis* and a *figura sententiæ*, points definitely in the same direction. Such antitheses as we noted in the quotation given from St. Basil, while belonging to the sphere of rhetoric, are used to convey the most momentous juxtapositions or apparent contradictions of thought contained in the Christian dogmata ; for Christianity is pre-eminently a religion of paradoxes. How God, eternal, invisible, and immortal, could become a child of a day old, be seen by the shepherds, be handled by Simeon, and finally die on the cross ; how a virgin might bear a son, and One Who was pronounced dead on the scrutiny of hostile executioners rise from the grave—these were facts that puzzled the minds and kindled the imaginations of the first Christians, and which were

[1] ' The Mysterie of Rhetorique Unvail'd . . .' p. 5 ; *vid. ante*, pp. 87–8.

capable of all manner of ingenious recapitulation in the centuries that followed.

Preaching on " *Unto us a Child is born, and unto us a Son is given*," we find Andrewes elaborating the twofold idea of child and son as follows :

" All along His life, you shall see these two. At His birth : a *Cratch* for the *Childe* ; a *Starre* for the *Sonne* : A company of *Shepheards* viewing the *Child* ; A *Quire* of *Angels* celebrating the *Son*. In His life : *Hungry* Himselfe, to shew the nature of the *Child* ; yet *feeding five thousand*, to show the power of the *Sonne*. At His *death* : dying on the *Crosse*, as the *Son of Adam* ; at the same time disposing of *Paradise*, as the *Sonne of God*.

" If you aske, why both these ? For that, in vaine had beene the one, without the other . . . Our nature had sinned, that therefore ought to suffer : The reason, why a *Childe*. But, that which our nature should, our nature could not beare ; not the weight of *Gods wrath* due to our sinne : But, the *Sonne* could : the reason, why a *Sonne*. The one ought, but could not : the other could, but ought not. Therefore, either alone would not serve ; they must be joyned, *Childe* and *Sonne*. But that He was a *Childe*, He could not have suffered. But that He was a *Sonne* He had sunke in His *suffering*, and not gone through with it . . . Therefore, that He might be *lyable*, He was a *Childe* ; that He might be *able* He was the Son : that He might be both, He was both."

Then follows the characteristically ' metaphysical ' part :

" This, why *God*. But why this Person, the *Sonne* ? Behold, *Adam would* have *become one of us* ; the fault : Behold, one of us will become *Adam*, is the satisfaction. Which of us would He (sic) have become ? *Sicut Dij, Scientes*, the *person* of *knowledge*. Hee therefore shall become *Adam* : a *Sonne* shall be given. *Desire* of *knowledge*, our attainder ; He, in *whom all the treasures of knowledge*, our restoring. *Flesh*, would have beene the *Word*, as wise as the *Word* ; the cause of our ruine : meet then, the *Word become flesh*, that so, our ruin repaired." [1]

---

[1] 'XCVI Sermons,' IInd Nativity sermon, p. 12. Here, and wherever reference is made to the 'XCVI Sermons,' the 3rd ed., that of 1635, is intended.

Such is the singularly happy employment of antithetic prose in order to enforce the most stupendous antitheses capable of presentation to human thought. It is to be observed, however, that this passage is no mere rhetorical *tour de force*, but conveys sound and closely reasoned theological exposition. If it goes beyond the application of the immediate text it does so only to make intelligible the *Christo*-centric system of which the text chosen for the day provides a hint. Generally speaking, this is the case with all the Anglo-Catholic preachers, and although at times their use of antithesis and other carefully cultivated devices is dictated simply by the wonder and adoration which their themes inspire, usually there is a far-reaching background of reasoned thought to be detected behind the seeming coruscations of the moment. At other times the contemplation of the paradoxes is used effectively to inspire a nobler and more truly Christian line of conduct. This we find particularly in the case of Mark Frank's sermons, which are the latest, and in some ways the finest, of all seventeenth-century Anglo-Catholic productions.[1] Dealing with Luke ii. 7 : " *She brought forth her firstborn son, and wrapped him in swaddling clothes,*" etc., Frank spoke as follows :

" . . . He that measures the Heavens with his *Span*, the waters in the *hollow* of his hand, *who* involves all things, all the treasures of Wisdom and Knowledge, in whom *all* our beings and well-beings, the decrees and fates of the world are *wrapt* from all eternity ; *he* now to come to be wrapt and made up like a *new-born* child ; who can unwind or unfold his humility ? Will our *Master* be thus dealt with as a Child ? thus handled like the *common infant* ? And shall *we* hereafter think much the *best* of us to be used like other men ? away with all our nicenesses henceforward, and be content that our *selves* and *ours* should be in all things subject to the common fate of the sons of men.

" Nor think we much, 2. to be wrapt up and bound sometimes, and denied the liberty of a *stragling* power to hurt our selves, but ever thank the *hand* that binds us up,

---

[1] Mark Frank (1613–1664), Master from 1662–4 of Pembroke College, Cambridge, obviously came very strongly under the influence of Andrewes. His ' Course of Sermons,' which appeared in 1672, is the fine flower of Anglo-Catholic preaching.

and takes care of us when we either cannot or know not how
to help our selves, would undo our selves if we were left
loose. . . . He that binds all things with his Word, makes
them up in his Wisdom, and wraps them in the Mantle of
his protection, was content to be bound up *as* a Child, when
he was a Child ; as if he had wholly laid *aside* his power,
humbled himself to be under the power and discretion of a
simple Woman, *Nurse* and *Mother*. To teach us again the
humility of a Child, to behave ourselves in every condition,
and submit to it as it requires ; if Children, to be content
with the usage of children ; if *Subjects* with the *condition* of
subjects ; if Servants, of servants, and the like." [1]

The whole sermon from which the quotation is taken is an
elaborate contemplation of the circumstances of the Nativity
in which each particular is severally considered with a view
to raising devotion and constraining men to make some
return in the way of purity or nobler moral conduct for the
amazing condescension of God. Had all Anglo-Catholic
preaching kept such ends resolutely in view little exception
could have been taken to it, and the teaching of the Faith
might have continued to be conveyed by means of an old
and decidedly charming medium. Unfortunately, however,
it was the more superficially ' metaphysical ' traits and the
more obvious turns of ' wit ' which attracted attention and
inspired imitation. As used by Andrewes, ' metaphysical '
imagery and ' witty ' handling of words or phrases never,
it is safe to say, were employed without reference to a greater
end. In the hands of the ablest preachers of his ' school,'
as Laud, Brownrig, Hacket, Cosin, or Frank, there was a
definite attempt made to imitate both form and content ;
the *figura dictionis* led on to the *figura sententiæ* ; but with
lesser men, particularly with young preachers setting out
in life and eager to be in the fashion, the inner meaning was
too often lost sight of, or was entirely lacking. The account
of the young divine digging " with much adoe . . . into
the rotten dunghills of Popish Postillers, and phantasti-
call Friars," and patching together " many gayish and gaudy
shreds of painted bables, and frothy conceipts and tricks
of wit . . .," with the result already alluded to in a quota-

---

[1] ' LI Sermons . . . Being A Course of Sermons, Beginning at *Advent*,
and so continued through the *Festivals* . . .' Lon., 1672, fol., "The Second
Sermon on Christmas Day," on *Luke* ii. 7—misprinted as *Luke* xi. 7—p. 55.

tion from Robert Bolton,[1] reveals the contemporary tendency ; and it is highly probable that the error of "one of
about four score yeares of age," mentioned by Baxter, who
" thought Christ was the Sunne that shineth in the Firmament, and the Holy Ghost the Moone," [2] had its origin in a
striking but ill-related image of a would-be 'metaphysical'
preacher.

A recurrent image in Andrewes of the 'metaphysical'
type is associated with the functioning of conduit pipes.
The erection of fountains or conduits was popular in the
early years of James I's reign [3] : probably the allusions may
be considered to some extent topical. At all events, in an
early Nativity sermon, Andrewes describes the eucharistic
bread and wine as

" the *Conduit pipes* of His *Grace* . . . *Grace* and *Truth* (now)
proceeding, not from the *Word* alone, but even from the
flesh thereto united ; the *fountaine* of the *Word* flowing into
the *cisterne* of His *flesh,* and from thence deriving downe, to
us, this *Grace* and *Truth,* to them that partake Him aright." [4]

In speaking of the coming of the Holy Ghost we get a variant
of the same image :

" The *Father,* the *Fountaine* ; the *Sonne,* the *Cisterne* ; the
HOLY GHOST the *Conduit-pipe,* or *pipes* rather (for they
are many) by and through which, they are derived downe
to us " [5] ;

while in one of the " Gunpowder sermons " there occurs
the phrase, " Through the Cisterne and Conduit of all *Thy
mercies, Iesus Christ.*" [6]

---

[1] *Vid.* 'Sermon Preached at Lent Assises' bound up with 'Foure Last
Things,' 1632, pp. 181–3, and *ante,* p. 106.
[2] Powicke : 'A Life of . . . Richard Baxter,' 1924, p. 304, Appendix 6,
" The State of His Parish in 1658," quoting Baxter's 'Confirmation & Restauration,' pp. 157–65.
[3] Mention may be made of three such—that at Carfax, Oxford, that at
Cambridge, erected by Hobson, Milton's carrier, and that which archbishop
Abbot presented to Canterbury in 1621 and which Dr. Cleland made the subject of a sermon a few years later. Cleland's sermon is entitled 'Jacob's
Well and Abbot's Conduit, Paralleled, Preached, and Applied to the Use of
the Citie of Canterbury,' and was published in London in 1626.
[4] 'XCVI Sermons,' VIth Nativity sermon, p. 52.
[5] *Ibid.,* XIVth Whit-Sunday sermon, p. 746.
[6] *Ibid.,* VIIth sermon ' Of the Gun-Powder Treason,' p. 970.

The series of sermons preached on the anniversary of the Gunpowder Plot and the somewhat similar series commemorating the conspiracy, real or supposed, of the Gowrie in Scotland are decidedly the least pleasing of all Andrewes works. One of the former, however, supplies us with an exceptionally good example of a carefully worked-out ' metaphysical ' analogy, drawn in this case from medicine. Educated men of the period, it is to be remembered, had a more encyclopædic, if often extremely unscientific, acquaintance with all kinds of learning than has for long been the case, and medical studies were not confined to intending physicians. The taste of the time, too, permitted the use of bold and vigorous metaphor, and divines, as is particularly noticeable in the case of Donne, were not likely to stickle at the more unconventional and daring metaphors, but regarded them as paralleled and justified by the outspokenness, and even unpleasant vividness, of many Old Testament figures. Accordingly Andrewes declared :

" there is not onely *fructus ventris*, there is *partus mentis* : the *minde conceives*, as well as the *wombe* : the word [conceiving] is like proper, to both. Men have their *wombe*, but it lieth higher, in them ; as high as their *hearts* ; and that which is there *conceived*, and *bred*, is a *birth*." [1]

This is only a beginning ; the elaboration follows, in which the plot is compared in ten points to the pre-natal state. The whole is worth quoting as an extreme example of this type of image :

"The more I think of it, the more points of correspondence do offer themselves to me, of a *birth* and *comming* to a *birth*, and that in every degree : 1. The *vessels* first give forth themselves, as so many *embrio's* : 2. The *vault*, as the *wombe*, wherein they lay so long : 3. They that conceived this device were the *mothers*, cleare : 4. the *fathers*, were the *fathers* (as they delight to be called) though, oft, little more than boyes ; but here, *right fathers*, in that they perswaded, it might be, why not ? might be *lawfull* ; nay, *meritorious*, then : so, it was they, that did animate, gave a *soule* (as it

---

[1] VIIIth sermon ' Of the Gun-Powder Treason,' p. 974. *Cf.* " A Sermon Preached before the Kings Maiestie at Greenwich, An. Dom. MDCVII," separately paged as IXth of ' Certaine Sermons,' p. 137.

vere) to the *treason*. 5. The *conception* was, when the *pow-der*, as the *seed* was conveighed in : 6. The *articulation*, the ouching [1] of them, in order, just as they should stand : 7. the *covering* of them, with *wood* and *fagots*, as the drawing a *skin*, over them : 8. The *Venerunt ad partum*, when all was now ready, *traine* and all : 9. The *Mid-wife*, he that was found with the *match* about him, for the purpose : 10. And *partus*, the *birth* should have bin upon the giving *fire*. If the *fire* had come to the *powder*, the *children had come to the birth.* . . ." [2]

The same type of image, based upon some particular department of knowledge, is to be met with in Laud's works. That his contemporaries regarded Laud as an imitator of Andrewes may be gathered from a letter of Chamberlain to Sir Dudley Carleton, preserved in Nichols' ' Progresses of King James,' and which refers to the first of the seven sermons as reprinted by Scott in the 1847 edition of the archbishop's works.[3]

" Herewithal " (writes Chamberlain) " I send you a Sermon of Dr. Laud's on the King's Birth-day, because it is after the manner of the Bishop of Winchester [i.e. Andrewes]'s preaching. . . ." [4]

In the sermons that have survived only one example of ' metaphysical ' wit occurs, but it is a good one, and implies an acquaintance with astronomy. Preaching in 1628 to the third Parliament of Charles I, Laud said :

" Ioyne, then, and keepe the Vnity of the Spirit, and I'le feare no danger though *Mars* were *Lord of the Ascendent*, in the very instant of this Session of *Parliament*, and in the *second house*, or *joyned* or in *aspect*, with the *Lord of the second*. . . ." [5]

Laud, however, was a distinctly ' witty ' preacher in the

[1] A printer's error for ' couching.'
[2] Sermon cit., p. 975. With this may be compared the elaborate simile derived from bone-setting, found in the XVIIIth Resurrection sermon, pp. 586-7.
[3] I.e. ' The Works of the Most Reverend Father in God, William Laud, D.D.' (Library of Anglo-Catholic Theology).
[4] Ed. cit., note to Sermon I.
[5] ' A Sermon . . . at *Westminster* : At the opening of the Parliament . . .' Lon., 1628, 4to, p. 22, reprinted ed. cit. as Sermon VI, p. 169.

more obvious sense, and Heylin, his biographer, in ' Cypri-anus Anglicus,' speaks of his " great Love to wit." [1]   More-over, his employment, on occasions of the greatest solemnity, of what at first sight appear purely ' witty ' sallies, taken along with the speeches of James I and Charles I, as reported in the various contemporary accounts of Parliamentary proceedings, is important evidence on the naturally ' witty ' trend of contemporary thought.   One is not surprised, coming straight from Andrewes, to hear Laud saying :

" The Text goes on *cheerefully*, (and so I hope doe you in hearing it :) . . ." [2]

or referring to charity as " the glue of the Spirit " [3] ; but it is arresting, when in the account of his " Troubles and Tryal," we find him, at a moment when his life hung in the balance, breaking forth into a sally which is at once ironical and *witty* in its allusions and applications.   In replying to the charges of the Scots Commissioners who had referred to him in their petition as " this great firebrand," he spoke as follows :

" In the mean time, I little deserved from them the Name of *This great Firebrand ;* for many of them have warmed themselves at me, but yet I never Fired any of them.   Nor can I make any doubt, but that God *will deliver me out of the midst of the Fire*, which he knows *I kindled not*." [4]

His speech on Tower Hill, on the 10th January, 1644, is also good evidence on this point.   Many shocking circum-stances attended his execution.   Crowds surrounded the scaffold, and men openly showed their delight that he was about to die.   A number of people had to be removed at the archbishop's request from under the boards of the scaffold to prevent blood falling on them.   It was not an hour when a man would aim at being ' witty ' to win applause, and we find him saying :

[1] 1671, fol., p. 461.
[2] ' A Sermon Preached at White-Hall, on the 24 of March, 1621 . . .' Lon., 1622, 4to, p. 22, reprinted ed. cit. as Sermon II, p. 44.
[3] ' A Sermon . . . at *Westminster* : . . .' Lon., 1628, 4to, p. 19, reprinted ed. cit. as Sermon VI, p. 167.
[4] ' The History of the Troubles and Tryal . . .' Lon., 1695, fol., p. 136.

" I am going apace, as you see, towards the Red-sea, and my feet are now upon the very brinks of it ; an Argument, I hope, that God is bringing me into the Land of Promise. . . ." [1]

Along with these examples may be taken a figure of James I in a speech to Parliament in advocacy of the Union of Scotland and England :

" I am the husband and all the whole Isle is my wife. I hope, therefore, that no man will be so unreasonable as to think that I, a Christian King under the Gospel, should be the Polygamist and husband to two wives." [2]

Such expressions go to show that the facility in discovering resemblances, often in wholly unexpected objects or events, which was the essence of ' wit,' was normal and habitual among the educated classes in the early seventeenth century. With Andrewes, and after him with other preachers, the occurrence of ' wit ' is of the most diverse and unexpected sort. It is nearly always ingenious, often far-fetched, and sometimes distinctly ludicrous, but it cannot be roundly condemned as inappropriate, because it undoubtedly recalled the wandering attention of the auditors, and had very much the same effect as the minor explosion which precedes a pyrotechnic display. Once the ' witty ' explosion is over, the ' display ' is always of an impressive and edifying nature. Often, also, the ' wit ' itself is clearly the outcome of a sanctified imagination and arises spontaneously out of the consideration of the text, and is no mere by-play judiciously introduced to enliven the exposition.

" Take not a figure," Andrewes warned his hearers,

[1] 'The Archbishop of Canterbury's SPEECH : . . . the 10 of January, 1644 . . .' Lon., 1644, 4to, p. 7.
[2] Quoted Trevelyan : " England under the Stuarts," Lon., 1916, chap. iv, p. 107 ; but Whitelock and Rushworth afford good examples of the tendency. Cf. also Todd : ' Memoirs of the Life and Writings of the Right Rev. Brian Walton . . .,' 2 vols. in one, Lon., 1821, 8vo, vol. i, p. 22, footnote, where ' Foure Speeches made by Sir Edward Dering, in the High Court of Parliament, &c., 1641,' are quoted, which go to show that Laud's adversaries were quite as ' witty ' as himself—" I hope, by the helpe of this house, before the yeare of threats be run out, his Grace will either have more grace, or no grace at all ! " (op. cit., p. 4) ; and again : " My humble motion is, that every member of the assembly, who voted their Canons, may come severally to the barre of this House, with a book of Canons in his hand, and there, unlesse he can answer the catechisme-question . . . be commanded to give fire to his own cannons ! " (ibid., pp. 11, 12).

" and make of it a plaine speech ; Seeke not to be saved by Synecdoche " [1] ; and elsewhere he speaks of serving God " by Synecdoche." [2]

Such is ' wit ' of a dignified character, closely resembling Donne's warning not to attempt to square either the circle which is the figure of God, or the circle of our own lives ; and the advice given in the figure is a sound one. The " every good gift and every perfect gift " of James i. 17, found in the Vulgate in the form " omne datum optimum, et omne donum perfectum," supplied Andrewes with a similar witty moral derived from grammar—

" He begins with the lesse, *Datum*. Weigh the word, it is but a *Participle* : they, have *tenses*, and *tenses*, *time*. So that is only *temporall*.

" But *donum* imports no *time* : . . . is fixed or permanent." [3]

On occasion the ' wit ' is of a verbal or rhetorical kind, consisting in balancing of sounds as well as in the antithesis of ideas, and so is linked up back through the centuries with schematic ecclesiastical prose. Thus we find the following :

" They cried *Crucifige*, at the time (that is) *fasten* ; *fasten* Him *to the Crosse* : but that *fastening* was His *loosing* ; for it lost Him and cost Him His life, Which was the *Solutum est* of this *Solvite* " [4] ;

or :

" *El*, the mighty GOD. As if, with that great EL [i.e. capital ' L ' as we should say] all the inferior *Els* were not attendant, *Micha-el*, and *Gabri-el* ; and (if He *will*) *twelve legions of Angels*." [5]

Andrewes was particularly fond of these assonantal effects. " If He had not *beene made*, we had beene marred," [6] occurs

---

[1] XIth sermon ' Of the Nativitie,' p. 106. *Cf.* XIIIth Whit-Sunday sermon, p. 738.

[2] XVIIIth sermon ' Of the Resurrection,' p. 587.

[3] XIVth Whit-Sunday sermon, p. 748.

[4] Xth Resurrection sermon, p. 487 ; ' lost Him and cost Him ' is of course an example of *paromoion* derived from mediæval Latin, and a popular figure at the time.

[5] IXth Nativity sermon, p. 80.

[6] IVth Nativity sermon, p. 28.

in a Nativity sermon ; and again, " this *Adoption* is the *fullnesse* of our option." [1]

The fact that *Ecce* in Scripture is a kind of alarm sounded to draw one's attention to a particular point (a patristic observation of uncertain origin), led to the remark : " The more *beholds*, the more *beholden* are we to God " [2] ; while in treating of Judas' complaint that Mary's ointment was wasted, the idea of ' perdition ' or ' loss ' is played upon— "*filius perditionis* : and this terme marreth all ; that the *childe of perdition* should finde fault with *perdition*." [3]

Some such examples, it is obvious, owe their impetus to familiarity with the Vulgate text, and demand for their full appreciation a knowledge of Latin on the part of the auditors. Others, it must be confessed, suggest to the modern mind a species of levity difficult to associate with the pulpit, and the prevalence of word-play in Andrewes' work recalls the remark of a Scots lord who heard him preach at Holyrood during the royal visit of 1617, and gave it as his opinion that " he rather plays with his text than preaches on it." [4] Any such suggestion is unfair to Andrewes and most especially so when made in connection with the celebrated " Immanu-el . . . Immanu-hell " passage which is often quoted and has suffered greatly by being taken out of its context. Actually as it occurs in one of the Nativity sermons it is extremely striking and effective, and although ' witty ' in the manner of the time, it was not undignified, and certainly not irreverent.

" This *Immanu* is a Compound againe : " (he told his hearers in explaining the text, Isaiah vii. 14) " we may take it, in sunder, into *Nobis*, and *cum* : And so then have we three pieces. 1. *El*, the mighty GOD : 2. and *Anu* wee, poore wee ; (Poore indeed, if we have all the world beside, if we have not Him to be *with us* :) 3. And *Im*, which is *Cum*, And that *cum*, in the midst betwene *nobis* and *Deus*, GOD and Vs ; to couple GOD and *us* : thereby to conveigh the things of the one, to the other." [5]

[1] IVth Nativity sermon, p. 30.
[2] VIIth sermon on Gowrie Conspiracy, p. 871.
[3] IIIrd Lent sermon, p. 289. *Cf.* VIIIth sermon on Resurrection, p. 460 : " Because it is to the *Colossians*, the *Colossus*, or capitall point of all. . . ."
[4] Whyte : ' Lancelot Andrewes and his Private Devotions . . .' Edin., 1896, p. 15.
[5] IXth Nativity sermon, p. 77.

11

Such treatment is admittedly a peculiar type of exegesis, but it was one practised by Augustine, and was due to a desire to lose no possible moral to be derived from the Scriptures. 'With' Andrewes proceeded to show might most readily be conceived by imagining the opposite state—that of lacking—and so continued :

"let *nobis* (*us*) stand by our selves, without Him, to see, what our case is, but for this *Immanuel* ; what, if this *Virgins Child* had not this day beene *borne* us : *Nobiscum* (after) will be the better esteemed. For, if this Childe be *Immanuel*, *GOD with us* ; then without this Childe, this *Immanuel*, we be without GOD. *Without Him, in this world* (saith the *Apostle* ;) And, if without him, in this, without Him, in the next : And, if without Him there, if it be not *Immanu-el*, it will be *Immanu-hel* ; and that, and no other place, will fall (I feare me) to our share. Without Him, this we are : What, with Him ? Why, if we have Him ; and GOD, by Him ; we need no more : *Immanu-el* and *Immanu-all*. All that we can desire is, for us to be *with Him*, with GOD ; and He to be *with us* : And we, from Him, or He from us, never to be parted." [1]

Taken as a whole, it must be granted of such preaching that when the flash in the pan which attracted attention was over, the preacher would be found more often than not to have hit his mark. The peacock's feathers with which he imped his dart in no way prevented the lodgment of the barb.

The endeavour, also, so patent in the Greek and Latin Fathers, particularly Augustine, to get the utmost possible meaning out of every word of Holy Writ, combined with Andrewes' personal habit of letting off words like squibs so that they break into a number of dazzling images, is well illustrated by his use of Latin words as found in the Vulgate reading of his text, not only in the more obvious way we have noted in his word-play on " the son of perdition," but in a more elaborate manner. Sometimes the Latin word begot a series of images ; sometimes the minutiæ of the text were insisted upon in order to bring home a lesson ; while occasionally, a collaboration of Latin and English words was

[1] IXth Nativity sermon, pp. 77-8.

used, as in ' the Book of Common Prayer,' to enhance and enrich the meaning.

Of the first usage, his handling of the word *Apprehendit* in his Ist Nativity sermon is a good example.   The thought of a flight and a hot pursuit—as in Francis Thompson's ' Hound of Heaven '—is insisted on :

" . . . when *Man fell*, He did all.   Made after him presently, with *Vbi es* : sought to reclaime him, *What have you done ?   Why* have you done so ? . . . gave not over His *pursuit*, though it were long and laborious, and He full weary ; though it cast Him into a *sweat*, a sweat o*f bloud* . . . followed His pursuit, through *danger*, *distresse*, yea, through *death* itselfe.   *Followed*, and so followed, as nothing made Him leave following, till He *overtooke*." [1]

Donne never did better in this vein, and had the thought been developed in a flowing period, culminating in the capture, the passage would have ranked among the great quotations habitually made from English preaching.   As it is, the jerky, graph-like progression from *apprehendit* to *apprehendit* entirely mars the effect.

This jerkiness or abruptness—the inability to achieve the λέξις εἰρομένη on which literary grace so largely depends— is not only noticeable in Andrewes' own work, but is a characteristic of all preaching which aimed at close imitation of his style.   Thus in the sermons of Ralph Brownrig (1592–1659), bishop of Exeter,[2] strict Calvinist though he was, we find the same extraordinary sketchiness, not due to slightness of treatment, but to that process which Canon Overton, in writing of these preachers, has described as " picking their texts to the very bone." [3]   In Brownrig's work there is the same employment of Latin words, or

---

[1] Ist sermon ' Of the Nativitie,' p. 4.   Quoted by Ottley, ' Lancelot Andrewes,' p. 130, who further illustrates how the sermon depends entirely on the idea of *apprehendit*, and progresses by continually recurring to the idea and renewing its examples.

[2] These consist of ' Forty Sermons ' issued in 1661, followed in 1664 by ' Twenty-Five Sermons,' both volumes being sent to the press by William Martyn, Preacher at the Rolls Chapel, to whom Brownrig's papers passed by will.   Martyn printed nothing without consulting John Gauden, Brownrig's successor in the see of Exeter, who prefixed a guarantee to each volume that the sermons as printed exactly followed the author's MSS.

[3] *Vid.* D.N.B. article on Brownrig.

groups of words—introduced always with a suggestion
of superhuman authenticity—the same division and subdivision, and the same citation at every step of Chrysostom,
Augustine, or Bernard as is found in Andrewes.   Such
sermons do not lend themselves to quotation : they contain
few or no passages which are not a mosaic of patristic
opinion, and, in Brownrig's case, there are none which reveal the charm of Andrewes' originality.   Hacket and Cosin,
while still hampered by the common procedure, much as a
heavily-armed man might be in a race, yet contrived to
impart to their performance something of the inner mood
of the master as well as traces of his outward manner.
Hacket's sermons in particular, although they bear less
external resemblance to those of Andrewes than do Brownrig's with their carefully tessellated Latin and English,
and their 'metaphysical' touches—often clearly the
attempts of a man not outstandingly gifted in noting
resemblances, wherein true 'wit' consists, yet determined
to preach in Andrewes' vein—convey more of the spirit of
their original.   They have the same vivid pictorial style,
are occasionally quaint, and more occasionally 'witty' ;
and the slow meandering exegesis, by which the words and
phrases of the text are made to give up their meanings,
enriched by patristic and rabbinical analogues or interpre-
tations, is distinctly in the manner of Andrewes.   The resemblances to the latter are numerous, and, in some cases,
consist of actual quotations,[1] which goes to show that some,
at least, of Andrewes' imitators were closely conversant with
his work.

That John Hacket (1592–1670), bishop of Coventry and
Lichfield, should have been an ardent disciple of Andrewes
is not to be wondered at, when we remember that as a boy
at Westminster School he had been among those in whose
studies Andrewes, while dean of Westminster, had taken a

---

[1] E.g. Hacket's observation : " No face can be seen in a troubled water ;
and no messenger can arrive intelligently at his ear who is perplexed with
trembling and astonishment " ('A Century of Sermons upon Several remarkable Subjects : Preached by the Right Rev. . . . John Hacket . . . Published
by Thomas Plume, D.D.' Lon., 1675, fol., ser. iv, on the Incarnation, p. 37
ad fin.) is clearly part quotation, part imitation of a passage in a Nativity
sermon of Andrewes' (Vth Nativity sermon, p. 35) which reads : " In a
troubled water, no face will well be seene, nor by a troubled minde no message
received till it be setled." The slight alterations betray the copyist whose
sentence is not so good an antithesis as the original.

personal interest.[1]   A certain colloquialism and homeliness which had given life and point to much of Andrewes' preaching reappeared also in Hacket.   The older preacher had compared the difference between the condition of Saul looking for his father's asses and Saul the king to the case of a London merchant and his " 'prentice " :

" *Saul*, Who, while he was in a poore estate, that his boy and he could not make *five pence* betweene them, *was . . . low in his owne eyes*," [2]

and had spoken of " *Thomas* with his faith in his *finger ends* " [3]—a phrase equally applicable to traffickers in grain or cloth ; and we find Hacket remarking of Satan's quotation of Scripture during the Temptation : " He [i.e. the Devil] popp'd in a place of the Psalm . . . very perversely," [4] or describing the woman who saluted Christ with the words " *Blessed is the Womb that bare thee . . .*" as—

" A good *Israelitess* she was that magnified Christ in this manner ; though she was not spoken to, yet her heart was full, and she must speak. . . ." [5]

Hacket's sermons provide several good illustrations, also, of the eagerness with which specimens of patristic ' wit ' were sought out and, at times, imitated.   Thus in a passage in a Passion sermon, in dealing with the silence of Christ before His judges, we find Hacket making use of a curious piece of exegesis akin to that on Peter's denial previously quoted from St. Ambrose [6] :

" . . . As the *Fathers* do Comment ingeniously upon this place, he dropt a word or two before *Caiaphas* and *Pilate*, but he did utterly seal up His lips before *Herod*. *Quia vocem ejus abstulerat ?* How should he speak before him who had taken away his voice ? For what was *John Baptist* but the voice of Christ ? " [7]

[1] *Vid.* ' Scrinia Reserata,' Part I, pp. 44–5.
[2] ' A Sermon preached at the Spittle,' addressed to London Merchants, p. 4.
[3] XVth sermon ' Of the Resurrection,' p. 548.
[4] XIth sermon on the ' Tentation,' p. 309.
[5] Ed. cit., p. 79.
[6] *Vid. ante*, p. 144.
[7] Ed. cit., Ist sermon upon the Passion, pp. 492 *ad fin.*

In the opening of the same sermon Hacket himself had begun in a ' conceited ' manner and continued with a ' witty ' sally of St. Jerome's :

" As Pilate sate in Judgment upon our *Saviour*, so are we met together this day to sit in judgment upon *Pilate*. The ruler marveled when his Prisoner stood before him, and said nothing for himself. But now is the time to speak. . . . When they reach'd a Reed unto our Saviour they put an Emblem into his hand, says St. *Hierom*, that their own infamy should be endited against them to after ages, *Calamum tenet in manu ut inimicorum sacrilegium scriberet*, The Reed was in his hand to pen the sacrilege of his enemies."

Another ' witty ' opening—this time apparently entirely of his own devising—occurs in one of the ' Tentation ' sermons,[1] where Hacket alludes to his preaching for the third time from the same text (Matt. iv. 1) : " Then was Jesus led up of the Spirit into the wilderness to be tempted, &c." :

" This *Text* you see, will not let me go. I have been parting from it thrice, and still it invites me to stay : As the *Levite* took his farewell at *Bethlem* sundry times, and could not get away, Judg. xix. And now I have good cause to tarry, being led by the leading of the Spirit : Whosoever shall compel thee to go a mile with him, go with him twain, says *Christ, Mat. V. 21*, and if the Spirit of *God* compel us to go with him one Sermon, we will go with him twain ; it cannot be irksome or weary to follow such contemplations."

This is true ' wit ' in the sense in which the term is applied to the work of Andrewes, where the surprising and unexpected remarks are carried on by a succession of Scriptural allusions, each more or less with a lesson or application of its own, and has no kinship with the carefully concocted cleverness of South and his admirers.

Of Corbet and King, who, partly owing to a chance reference in Scott's *Life* of Dryden, have enjoyed a kind of attenuated reputation as ' witty ' preachers, it is decidedly unfortunate that little that can entitle them to this descrip-

[1] The third of this series, p. 224.

tion remains.[1] No specimen of Corbet's vernacular preaching remains, and in a period prodigal of such exemplars King cannot be pronounced of first rank. What we do possess of Corbet is his ' Oratio Funebris Habita in Schola Theologica ab oratore Publico, in obitu Clarissimi Equitis Thomæ Bodleii,' a fluent and graceful production, distinguished by its lightness of touch from the heavy and artificial style of so many contemporary orations with their laboured imitation of Cicero. This piece has no appearance of ' wit,' and none of the ' conceited ' stylistic peculiarities which it would have been easy to introduce in Latin. It is true Sir Symonds D'Ewes records in his diary that, in 1620, when Corbet was appealing for funds for the repair of St. Paul's Cathedral, he told the clergy of his diocese—

" that although the Apostle himself did not like the stoning he got at Lystra, a good stoning was nevertheless the very thing his church in London stood most in need of " [2] ;

but this sally, like others recorded by Aubrey in his notice of the bishop,[3] has stronger affinity with the quaintness of Fuller than with true metaphysical ' wit,' and Corbet appears to have been celebrated among his contemporaries for his waggishness rather than for out-of-the-way learning ingeniously employed.

Henry King, bishop of Chichester, the other preacher mentioned by Scott, was a friend of Isaac Walton, Jonson, and Donne, and is remembered as the writer of at least one outstanding poem, the " Exequy on his Wife." Born the same year as Hacket, with the latter he was a Westminster

[1] In discussing the partiality for verbal wit of the period Scott remarks : " These outrages upon language . . . were held good arguments at the Bar, though Bacon sat on the woolsack ; and eloquence irresistible by the most hardened sinner, when King or Corbet were in the pulpit." Works, ed. Scott and Saintsbury, Edin., 1882, vol. i, p. 8. The same preachers are cited, along with the Spaniard Paravicino and the Italians Azzolini and Aresi and other continental ' metaphysicals,' as noteworthy exponents of the vogue, by Spingarn in ' Critical Essays of the Seventeenth Century,' vol. i, Introd., p. xl. With Scott's observation may be compared Boileau's, in ' L'Art Poétique,' Chant II :

" L'avocat au Palais en hérissa son style,
Et le docteur en chaire en sema l'Evangile."

[2] ' College Life in the Time of James the First, As Illustrated by An Unpublished Diary of Sir Symonds D'Ewes,' Lon., 1851, p. 91.
[3] ' Brief Lives,' Clark's ed., vol. i.

boy, and so early came under the influence of Andrewes. Writing of his poetry, Mr. Massingham has described him as " a kind of resigned, subdued and melancholy Donne, without the greater poet's fine madness on the one hand or his abstruseness on the other . . . a quietist of the deepest feeling, who knew how to express it in a grave diction . . . and a soberly rich imagery to which it is exquisitely appropriate." [1]   And what is true of King's poetry is true also of his prose.

King's resemblance to Donne is detected in the gravity of tone and richness of illustration which we find in an early printed sermon on 'David's Enlargement,' issued along with one by his brother, John King, at Oxford, in 1625 :

" A *misery* lodg'd in the heart, is like an *Exhalation* inclosed within the Earth, which shakes the foundation of Reason, and Patience ; or like a *dampe*, it overlayes the Spirites, *strangulat inclusus dolor* : but when it hath found an issue by the Eye, to weepe out at, or a vent by the tongue, straight it growes tamer. When once a window is opened to give it Aire, that fume which would have stifled us, breathes out, and cleares the roome. Such a Meteore, such a boysterous Exhalation is sinne. What strange convulsions doth it cause within the soule ? How doth it contract our hopes of Mercy ; and like as East winde dry up, and wither our comforts ? What stormes, what guilty conflicts, what blacke clouds of despaire doth it raise in the Conscience ? but so soone as a sinner recollects himselfe, is brought to a remorse, how calmely is the storme allayed, by a religious contrition ? how sweetly doth the cloud discharge itselfe, when it relents with a showre of penitent teares ? " [2]

In the same sermon we discover not only a resemblance in tone, but what seems very like direct imitation of Donne :

" Thinkest thou, by drawing a *Curtaine* about thy Bed, or by putting out a *candle* in thy *Chamber*, to hide thine *incontinence* from God, or darken his knowledge. Foole, thou canst not !   Thou bearest a *lampe* in thine own brest, *thy conscience . . . a watching Candle*, that burnes at midnight :

---

[1] 'A Treasury of Seventeenth-Century Verse,' chosen and edited by H. J. Massingham, Lon., 1920, note to p. 157.
[2] Ser. cit., pp. 6–7.

and will light the *Judge* to descry thee. Or if *that taper* burne dimmely, if it have wasted into a snuffe, so that thou hast no Conscience, or but a seared one, which lies smothering in the socket ; and can only glimmer, not shine ; why yet, God is (as Basil saith) ὁλοφθαλμός, all eye, to survey thee." [1]

That the likeness to Donne was not one of mere imitation, but resulted from a similarity of mood may be gathered from a further quotation, which reveals the passionate, almost ' physical ' note of Donne's contemplation of the Passion of Christ :

" Wilt not thou confesse thy *riots*, as well as thy *Murthers* ? the pollution of thy *thoughts*, as well as of thy *Actions* ? *Christ* thy *Saviour* suffered for both ; he bled for both. Though thy *great sinnes* opened the wide *Riuer* in his *side*, and the *currents* in his *hands* and *feete* : thy *smallest sinnes scracht* him in the *thornes*, which he wore upon his head, or at least opened a *Pore* in his *sacred Bodie*. For how knowest thou, but that, as he *bled* for thy *crimson sinnes* (as Esay calls them) through those larger wounds : so he *sweat bloud* for the sinnes of thy thoughts ; that, as he suffered for thy *great offences* upon the Crosse, so he suffered for thy *lesser crimes* in the *Garden* : that, as he did undergoe a *publique passion* for the one ; so he had an *antepassion* for the other in his *Agony* : that, as for thy foulest transgressions he became a *red sea*, a true *Jordan*, a *sanguine River* the head of which streame began at *Mount Calvary :* so before his Ascent thither, in a lower place, not farre from the Brooke Cedron, he suffered his body to become a Marish, when for thy sake the bloud wept at every Pore. . . ." [2]

Such a handling of his subject is no mere reversion on King's part to the traditional theme of the *Liber Charitatis*,

[1] Ser. cit., p. 17.   The passage in Donne which this closely imitates is to be found in the ' LXXX Sermons,' sermon lxxvi, ' Preached to the Earle of Carlile and his Company at Sion.' Dr. Evelyn Simpson, in ' A Study of the Prose Works of John Donne,' Appendix B, p. 351, notes that Viscount Doncaster was created Earl of Carlisle in September 1622, so that the sermon was probably preached after that date. King's sermon was delivered in 1625, hence conscious imitation is likely, although King's quotation from Basil points to a common original for this line of argument.

[2] *Ibid.*, pp. 19–20.

like the long passage in a Good Friday sermon by Fisher,
in which the crucified body of Christ is compared to a book
—the limbs stretched upon the cross being likened to the
parchment, the five great wounds to capital letters in red,
and the marks of the scourging to the red and blue lines
which are found in ancient ' books of hours.' [1] Nor does
it depend on St. Bernard, as do various references of a
like nature in Andrewes, who openly followed that preacher
in this type of contemplation. [2] There is an intensity of
feeling due to the strength of the preacher's imagination
about King's treatment which distinguishes him from the
other ' witty ' preachers, and brings him into the same
relationship with Donne which the others owed to Andrewes.
Unfortunately, however, King's average style falls considerably short of the distinction attained in ' David's
Enlargement,' and the majority of his sermons, while not
actually dull, are not outstanding, and derive their only
interest from occasional flashes of Andrewes-like ' wit.'
In one sermon [3] we find the burial of Christ compared to
the Trojan Horse—by being let into the earth Christ surprised the Devil !—and there is the familiar interest shown
in the precise parts of speech employed in the Scriptures,
and the lessons to be drawn from these, which had been
stressed by the Schoolmen, particularly Aquinas. [4] On the
whole, therefore, King may be regarded as a minor ' metaphysical,' and a preacher whose personal tastes and attainments rather than his participation in the common interests
and characteristics of his school entitle him to more than
passing notice. He does not, however, rank with the more
typical ' witty ' preachers, such as Brownrig, Hacket, Cosin,
or Frank.

A notable divine whose affinities with the ' metaphysical '
group are of much greater significance than the work of
either King or Corbet, was Thomas Playfere, from 1596–
1609 Lady Margaret Professor of Divinity at Cambridge,
whose collected works, issued in 1623, have at an earlier

[1] ' The English Works of John Fisher . . . Now first collected by J. E. B.
Mayor, M.A.   Published for E.E.T. Soc.,' 1876, pp. 393–6.
[2] *Vid.* Ist sermon ' Of the Passion,' p. 341 ; *ibid.*, p. 344.   *Cf.* IIIrd sermon
' Of the Passion,' pp. 363 and 364.
[3] ' A Sermon of Deliverance, Preached at the Spittle on Easter Monday,
1626,' p. 41.
[4] *Ibid.*, p. 2.   *Cf.* Andrewes' VIth sermon for Lent, p. 325.

stage in our study afforded useful evidence on the printing of sermons and the use of commonplace-books. 'The Whole Sermons' bring together various pulpit addresses delivered from 1593 onwards, and published, separately or in small collections, at subsequent times. Most interesting of these small publications is that brought out in 1603, when James I was on his way to ascend the English throne, and which consisted of 'Heart's Delight,' a Paul's Cross sermon of 1593 and 'The Power of Praier,' a sermon preached in Exeter Cathedral three years later. From the dedication of the volume it is evident that Playfere aimed at attracting the royal attention, and, although he received no further mark of favour than a chaplaincy, and, later, a Crown living, his sermons are clearly of a type which must have appealed to the sermon-loving king. Playfere's influential position at Cambridge, moreover, must have done much to popularise the vogue to which Andrewes' earliest sermons had given a distinct impetus.

Playfere's sermons are peculiarly interesting as exhibiting the great learning and the partiality for the 'conceits' beloved of the Eastern Fathers and for the more allegorical passages of Augustine, which is so noticeable a feature of the 'meta-physical' preachers. He was as 'witty' as Andrewes and suggests the somewhat sensuous flavour of Donne in his mediæval way of regarding Christ's sufferings. Yet he was an eminently practical preacher (as was Andrewes), although he delivered sound doctrine with every ingenuity of art. When he prepared his sermons for the press (as we have already seen), they teemed with allusions to and quotations from the Fathers, Schoolmen, Commentators, and classical poets carefully referred to their original sources, and from this habit we learn that very few of his illustrations and allegorisations are of his own invention. Thus we find that the description in 'Heart's Delight' of Christ as " our heavenly Vlysses," Whose cross is the mast to which we must bind ourselves for safety,[1] is a piece of wit derived from Ambrose, who most frequently of the Fathers makes allusion to the classical writers. The much-quoted remark about the triangular shape of the heart which the round world can never fill—an observation which constantly reappears in sermons by divines of various schools, and on which Eachard

[1] 'The Whole Sermons,' 1623, p. 8.

commented adversely [1]—in the same sermon is referred to Orontius, while the thought of the Triune God alone filling it is also related to a passage from the ' Soliloquies ' of Augustine. [2]

At times no direct source is given for particular ' witty ' touches, and such a remark as the following may quite well be Playfere's own :

" Saint *Peter* . . . as his faith was so great that he lept into a sea of waters, to come to Christ ; so his repentance was so great that he lept into a sea of teares when he went from Christ." [3]

On the other hand, the comparison of Christ's wounds, still visible, to a rainbow, " which assureth vs we shall neuer be drowned in the pit of everlasting perdition . . ." [4] carries with it the suggestion of an older source.

Everywhere in Playfere there is constant Scriptural allusion and quotation, and he shared to the full Andrewes' ability to refer to topical events and contemporary persons in terms of Biblical history. [5] This was a particularly common device, especially when royal personages were to be complimented, and the sermons of the period are filled *ad nauseam* with references to the British Solomon. In combining Scriptural examples with classical, Playfere, however, stood alone, and his introduction of Epaminondas and Servilius along with Moses, Ezechias, Salomon, Aaron, Noah, and other more usual figures, as types of Christ, shows affinity with the French preachers of the time who did not scruple to mingle sacred and profane history in order to achieve startling rhetorical effects. [6]

As Bloom, the editor of certain anonymous MS. sermons, published in 1831 as ' Pulpit Oratory in the Time of James the First,' rightly saw, Playfere's importance is due to his prominence as a preacher at court and to his influential position at Cambridge. This renders him peculiarly suitable to be taken as an exponent of the ' metaphysical '

---

[1] ' *Grounds* and *Occasions* of the *Contempt* of the CLERGY,' 1705 ed., pp. 51 and 52.
[2] Ed. cit., p. 40.
[3] *Ibid.*, p. 13.
[4] *Ibid.*, pp. 85–6.
[5] Ist sermon ' Of the Gun-Powder Treason,' p. 893.
[6] *Vid.* sermon of Pierre de Besse, of date 1602, quoted Jacquinet, ' Des Prédicateurs Du XVIIe Siècle,' p. 40 ; and *post*, p. 387.

style, and to be used as a touchstone in testing the quality of other and lesser preachers ; and for this reason Bloom reprinted three of Playfere's sermons along with the specimens and fragments of an anonymous court preacher. Like this anonymous preacher, Playfere, as we have seen, admits us into the workshop where ' witty ' preaching was produced, though to nothing like the same extent as the former, who shows us the sermon almost in process of composition.

In addition to complete discourses Bloom printed what he described as " desultory passages and notes upon the various heads into which the text was originally divided." From the manner in which these were put together he believed that " they were intended merely as memoranda to assist in the construction of an extemporaneous discourse, or for reference to more elaborate matter in ' another sermon-booke ' ; " and he adds :

" I have taken every possible care to give these passages exactly as they stand in the original, as they will serve to convey an idea of the method and arrangement then in use." [1]

Something as to " method and arrangement " we have examined already, and the " desultory passages " of the present preacher, who flourished about 1620, exemplify the intermediate stage in the composition of the sermon, when the outline prescribed by method is beginning to be filled in with reflections derived from the preacher's reading. [2] In one of the complete sermons—a discourse of date November 1621 which animadverts on duelling—the familiar emptying of the commonplace-book is well illustrated, and a pithy comment of Augustine's is coupled with a catalogue of unexpected deaths :

" Anacreon was choakt by the kernell of a grape ; another stifled with the yolke of an egge ; a third with a fish bone ; a fourth with a peare : Fabius the Senator with an hayre in his milke ; Catullus, the Orator with smoake ; Chrysostome with the hot Sun ; and Goodwin Earle of Kent with a crume of bread." [3]

[1] *Op. cit.*, p. 151.
[2] *Vid. op. cit.*, pp. 152–7 and 158 *seq.*
[3] *Ibid.*, p. 138.

On at least one other occasion we find mingled Biblical and classical examples of petty sins and their punishments set out in a ' connected ' manner, and almost certainly derived from an Augustinian original,[1] while the familiar divisions of the sermon into *Quando, Quis, Cui* or *ad Quem, Quid, Pro quibus, Quare,* are illustrated with great clearness and material of the most diverse sort arranged under each heading.[2]

Although Bloom's anonymous preacher does not add much to our knowledge of Anglo-Catholic preaching in his period, yet like Willan, to whom reference has already been made, he supplies evidence from a comparatively (or what may be conjecturally so described) obscure source as to the extent of the ' metaphysical ' vogue and the endeavours of preachers in every rank and before all types of auditors to preach in the manner of Andrewes. Humble as is the work of Willan and his contemporary, it brings home to us what the glamour of great names and interesting personalities in a period of stirring interest tends often to obscure, the strange obsession which this type of preaching had for the men of the time. If it shook itself free from the laboured ' methods ' of the earlier German Protestant divines, it had too often to wear a yoke derived not only from a fairly rigid rhetorical tradition, but imposed largely in servile imitation of the exegetical idiosyncrasies of the Fathers. Nor was the yoke merely exegetically burdensome, but it required to be garishly decked with ornaments of the most exotic kind, and to be worn to an accompaniment of bells and baubles in order to earn a precarious popularity. The commentaries of Calvin and the dry-as-dust exposition of the sterner Puritans were never at any time likely to prove a menace to literary style, for there could be no question of their aim and of the sphere in which they exerted an influence ; but the ' metaphysical ' preaching, taking advantage of a popular liking for ' turns ' of expression and ' turns ' also of thought, quickly created a demand for its own unusual and bizarre productions, and being of its very nature largely topical and to a great extent dependent for its success on a *viva voce* effect, the devices, whether of speech or thought, most likely to attain this end were eagerly sought after, without due regard being had to the injurious influence it

[1] *Op cit.*, p. 78.   [2] *Ibid.*, pp. 101 *seq.*

was found in time to exercise on contemporary prose style. By striving after effects which gratified the demand of the moment, ' metaphysical ' or ' witty ' preaching forfeited for practically all its leading preachers a permanent place in English literature, and the men who won the applause of their contemporaries are consequently forgotten by posterity.

More than any word-play or apparent facetiousness, or the habit of quotation in foreign tongues—which after all was common to most prose of the time—the great obstacle to the Anglo-Catholic sermon taking its place as a depart-ment of prose lay in the fact, already emphasised, that the nature of the exegesis upon which its characteristic effect depended prevented the cultivation of a fluent and orderly style. The jerkiness and brokenness of Andrewes' sermons have been commented upon, and similar tendencies noticed in those of Hacket and Brownrig. In the case of Cosin (1594–1672), bishop of Durham, another great exponent of ' metaphysical ' preaching, who persistently adhered to this method of exposition over a period of almost forty years,[1] the drawback is less pronounced, and in spite of his elaborate divisions and subdivisions, and his multitudinous citation of Fathers, Councils, and Commentators, he suc-ceeded in producing more or less connected prose. In tone Cosin strongly resembles Andrewes, and it is evident that much of his Christmas material comes largely from Chrysostom and Bernard, and is notable less for invention than setting. If at times he lacks something of the spontaneity and heart-felt devotion of Andrewes, the less interrupted flow of his exposition may be said to make good this defect.

Not to Cosin, however, but to the last and youngest of the great ' metaphysical ' divines belongs the credit of reproducing the poetical tone of the master, and by a happy fluency of style, which like a river mirrored successively the heavily fruited trees of patristic allusion and the brighter images of a fanciful ' wit,' of uniting the various components of the familiar manner in a connected and pleasing prose, which is far in advance of that of Andrewes or of any of his noted imitators. Mark Frank is the fairest star in the con-

---

[1] So his editor in a pref. note to vol. i of his ' Works,' Oxf., 1843 (Library of Anglo-Catholic Theology), p. vi. Cosin's sermons did not enjoy an edition in the seventeenth century.

stellation of the ' witty ' preachers. His ' Course of Sermons,' which appeared in 1672, is the high-water mark of Anglo-Catholic preaching.

Born in 1613, Frank became a Fellow of Pembroke College, Cambridge, in 1634, was ejected by the Parliamentary visitors ten years later, but returned at the Restoration to become Master of the College. He died in 1664. He was clearly very deeply influenced by Andrewes, especially by the finer and more imaginative side of the latter's work. The beauty of his contemplation of the swaddling of the infant Christ has already been quoted, and his quietly practical application commented upon. Much in a like vein might be quoted from Frank, who is always uniformly charming, and almost deserves to be rescued from the unkind oblivion into which he has fallen. But Frank's title to special mention is not due to the tenderness of his devotion, spontaneous and beautiful though it is, or to his Andrewes-like ' wit '—as when he told his hearers (alluding to Psalm cxlviii) :

" But sure when all things else thus come in throngs to bless him, and even Ice and Snow come hot and eager to this Feast, and willingly melt themselves into his praises, we should not, methinks, come coldly on to bless him. . . ." [1]

There is a deeper note in Frank than is heard in any other preacher of his school excepting Andrewes. King, as we have seen, is a kind of pale reflection of Donne, but Frank is no mere imitator. Imitator of Andrewes he undoubtedly was, but his merit was that, at the close of the period when ' witty ' preaching had expended itself and disgusted large numbers of Englishmen, he was able, by breaking away from the more slavish citation of authors and the persistent attempts at producing astonishing effects, to give to his sermons a new note of reflection, which recalls at times passages in the sermons of Augustine, and to his prose a gravity and dignity befitting his themes.

One of Frank's finest passages occurs in a Whit-Sunday sermon where he makes a comparison between the ' wind ' and the ' Spirit ' :

" For the *Wind* first ; They are but general notions we

[1] ' LI Sermons . . .' Lon., 1672, fol., ' The VIth Sermon On Christmas Day,' p. 106.

entertain of it.   *God brings the winds out of his treasure* says the *Psalmist. cxxxv.*7. Out of those hidden chambers they come, but where those chambers are we cannot tell. On a suddain they arise, ere we are aware, and away they go ; and who can follow them ? Who can trace their steps ? or track their way, or over-take them in their lodging at night, or tell us where it is ?

"Ask Philosophy, and let that answer you.   Whence is it that the winds arise ?   It answers you, From a thin and airy vapour drawn up out of the earth towards the middle Region of the Air, but repercust or beaten back by the gross-ness of some intervening cloud which drives it down ob-liquely with that violence we hear and feel. This, or some-thing as obscure, is all the knowledge we can get of it. For, ask now, Where that vapour rose ? It cannot tell. Which way it went ? It knows it [1] not. In what part of heaven it first became a wind ? It cannot point it out. What is become of it, now 'tis gone ? It resolves you not. Into what part of the world it is retired when all is still ? It cannot answer you.

" . . . And yet the ways of the *Spirit* are more unsearch-able : we know not anything at all of his eternal Procession, it was before any time we can imagine. We know nothing of his course or motion all that infinite while before the World began. We understand nothing distinctly of it ever since. His motions are so intricate, so various, and so infinite we cannot comprehend them. The dispositions, the gifts, the graces he works daily in us, we know not how they rise, or how they spread, or how they vanish." [2]

Such a passage recalls the sublimity of Hooker, and yet if we examine its structure we shall find that it depends for its effect on very different means from Hooker's elaborate Ciceronian sentences.   Frank's periods consist of a number of short sentences welded together without apparent effort, and he escapes the excessive ' pointedness ' of the Senecan writers and preachers largely because he is content to be brief without aiming at cleverness.   His works abound in beautiful passages, nobly conceived and unaffectedly expressed.   Perhaps the finest of all is found in a sermon for

---

[1] Folio has the misprint, " it know sit not."
[2] ' LI Sermons . . .' pp. 422-3.

St. Andrew's Day, which is in every way worthy of comparison with Donne's description of the world as a great sea [1] :

" *Regnum Dei tantum valet quantum habes*, says St. *Gregory* ; The kingdom of heaven is worth all we have, must cost us so, be it what we will, and alas ! what have we the best the richest of us, as highly as we think of our selves and ours, more than St. *Andrew* and his *brother*, a few old broken Nets.

" What are all our honours but old Nets, to catch the breath of the world, where the oldest is the best, and that which has most knots, most alliances and genealogies, the most honourable.

" What are our Estates but Nets to entangle us ? 'Tis more evident now than ever ; to entangle us in strange knots and obligations, in vexations and disquiets, in fears and dangers, to entangle silly souls besides in vanities and follies.

" What are all our ways and devices of thriving but so many several Nets to catch a little yellow sand and mud, and if you will have it in somewhat a finer Phrase, a few silver scaled fishes, in which yet, God knows, there are so many knots and difficulties, so many rents and holes for the fish to slip out of, that we may justly say they are but broken nets, and old ones too, the best of them, that will scarce hold a pull, all our new projects being but old ones new rubb'd over, and no new thing under the Sun.

" What are all these fine catching ways of eloquence, knowledge, good parts of mind and body, but so many nets and snares to take men with ? It may be finely spun, neatly woven, curiously knotted, but so full of holes, vanity and emptiness, that no net is fuller than these things we take so much pride in, so much delight in. Nay, this very body it self is but a net that entangles the soul, and the rational soul it self, too, we too often make but a net to catch flies, petty buzzing knowledges only, few solid sober thoughts ; at the best but a net for fishes of that watry and inconstant element, watry, washy, slimy notions of I know not what, of flitting worldly things ; so full of holes, too, that all good things slip out of them." [2]

The passage in its entirety is distinctly impressive, and

[1] *Vid.* Donne : ' LXXX Sermons,' sermon xii.
[2] ' LI Sermons . . .' pp. 546–7.

represents Frank at his best ; but, like Donne's, his works do not present us with a continuous series of similar felicities. Yet, the fact remains that, with the exception of King, Frank was the only imitator of Andrewes who succeeded completely in pouring the old wine of patristic allusion and fanciful ' wit ' into the new bottles of a connected literary medium, without suffering the flavour of the wine to be lost in the transference. Andrewes and his followers, Hacket, Brownrig, and even Cosin, are scarcely interesting for the form of their work. We study the former and compare the latter to discover what was the ' witty ' preaching of the seventeenth century, and to what extent the vogue prevailed, but we do not read them as we read Donne or Taylor or Barrow for the pleasure we derive from their prose style. When we have collected our specimens of ' wit,' or noted a few lively touches of contemporary reproof, we have exhausted them. To Mark Frank we return, because in his work we have all that was most delightful in the sermons of his ' witty ' contemporaries presented in a readable and fluent medium, which, although it cannot be said to mark any particular stage in the development of English prose, merits attention by its own charm and worth.

From the literary point of view Frank was the best of the Anglo-Catholic preachers, but the qualities in his work calculated to appeal to a modern critic are precisely those by reason of which he stands apart from the men of his school, the followers and imitators of Andrewes. Partly the contribution of personality, but much more the individuality of form to which he successfully attained, distinguish Frank from the other ' metaphysicals ' ; and although his attainment was much less conspicuous, and his personality of a type that left no such scarifying and unforgettable imprint on his work as did the more masculine, intensely passionate and highly intellectual nature of Donne, the excellencies of Donne and Frank alike, connected as they are with the theological and ecclesiastical party to which they belonged, are to be explained less in terms of the ' school ' than of the men.

Donne was beyond question a ' metaphysical ' preacher, just as he was a ' metaphysical ' poet, but he is hardly to be thought of as a ' witty ' preacher in the more obvious and ordinary sense in which the term is used.

He was 'Catholic' not only by conviction, as were Andrewes and Cosin or others of their ' school,' but his whole
intellectual, moral, and emotional being was saturated
with the atmosphere of Catholicism in a way which influenced his outlook and impregnated his thought as the more
purely intellectual conviction of his fellow-churchmen was
incapable of doing. To the others the problem of Anglo-
Catholicism lay in accepting and persuading others to accept
the idea of the continuity of the catholic tradition in England
in spite of the rupture occasioned by the Reformation ; to
Donne the problem lay not in growing accustomed to
consider one's self ' Catholic,' but in being reconciled to the
notion of the national church as a branch of the one true
Catholic Church. So fundamental a difference separates
Donne at once from all other divines of his time, and gives
a curious argumentativeness and air of hardly-won conviction to many of his sermons—a trait which he shares with
St. Augustine. Indeed, one cannot help feeling at times
that Donne is most earnestly persuasive where he has
doubted longest himself, or is still tempted to doubt. Only
on those topics which for him have remained largely
unchallenged, and to the elaboration of which he could
advance with the full intensity of his passionate and somewhat sensuous nature, was he able to expatiate at ease.

All Donne's doubts, however, as any close student of his
life and work is aware, were not confined to the difficulty
he experienced in accepting the position of the national
church. His subtle, self-torturing intellect, whetted on
what may be described as rapacious reading over a long
period of enforced idleness, had led him to survey problems
of a more profound order than were those usually discussed
in the schools. The author of the ' Paradoxes ' might probably have been an ordinary young man of his day ; the
author of the ' Biathanatos '—a strange and erudite discussion of suicide—was something other. Moreover, Donne
the poet, with his almost insane desire for physical sensation,
requires to be reckoned with in any estimate of Donne the
divine. The ' metaphysical ' strain, too, in Donne was
something other than it was in his contemporaries. Not
only was he more learned and so able to employ more
ingeniously erudite specimens of ' wit,' but, to quote once
more the estimate of Professor Grierson (to which allusion

has been made more than once already), he, most of all the
' metaphysicals,' illustrates " the peculiar blend of passion
and thought, feeling, and ratiocination which is their
greatest achievement." [1]   The wholesale permeation of his
work by his many-sided and peculiarly interesting personality is the secret of Donne's uniqueness.   The other preachers
of the school of Laud and Andrewes were devout, learned
and concerned about ecclesiastical politics ; Donne was
the man of the Renaissance—turned preacher—Tamerlane
confined to a pulpit, or Faustus desiring all knowledge and
avid for sensual enjoyment, but held spell-bound by the
eyes of the Crucified. Other preachers built up carefully
constructed patterns of one kind or another, but Donne
smashed all patterns, as men break ice, to recoil, as men do,
in terror from the reflections of their own faces in the waters
beneath.   He is poignant rather than sublime ; but from
first to last he is fiercely individualistic, and this, combined
with the impression he gives of having exhausted all depart-
ments of human enquiry and rung the changes on the whole
gamut of human passion, only to find intellectual satisfaction in the *dogmata* of the Christian Faith and emotional
satisfaction in the embrace of the Christian God, explains
his connection with, but superiority to, all other ' metaphysical ' divines of his time.

Space does not permit of a detailed comparison being set
out between the work of Donne and the work of Andrewes
and his immediate followers, so as to demonstrate with
precision to what extent Donne drew upon common
sources and employed common methods, and in what
respects the familiar material which we have examined was
transmuted by his greater intensity of thought and feeling
so as to achieve finer results.   Yet, although a full and careful study of all Donne's printed sermons made with reference
to his other works in prose and verse, and having in mind
constantly the characteristic traits of preachers of other
' schools,' has, so far as an intrinsic appreciation of his
work is concerned, been superseded during the years
in which this examination has been in progress by Dr.
Evelyn Simpson's ' A Study of the Prose Works of John
Donne,' nevertheless the undertaking has placed the present student of Donne and the other seventeenth-century

[1] ' Metaphysical Lyrics and Poems,' Introd., p. xvi.

divines in what is perhaps a unique position from which to determine with some exactness the relationship in which that preacher stood to his contemporaries. A briefly summarised conclusion on the matter will, therefore, it would appear, be of real service, and help to answer the initial enquiry which led to the undertaking of this piece of research.

Lives and studies of Donne and editions of particular works have been increasingly frequent since Sir Edmund Gosse led the way two years before the present century began with his ' Life and Letters of John Donne,' of which the most notable precursors to Dr. Simpson's recent study (1924) were Professor Grierson's edition of the ' Poetical Works ' in 1912, Miss M. P. Ramsay's thesis on ' Les Doctrines Médiévales chez Donne ' (1916), and Mr. Pearsall Smith's ' Selected Passages ' from the sermons (1920), to which is prefixed an interesting introductory essay. The evaluations of others and easily accessible selections from his own work have made Donne's line of thought and expression familiar to most men of literary taste, and it is not necessary to enlarge upon the distinguishing qualities of his style.

All the Anglo-Catholic divines, as do also the earlier Puritans, abound in topical references to the stirring, multi-coloured, somewhat boisterous life of their day, especially in London, and Donne's works are no exception to this characteristic, but exhibit to the full a wide acquaintance with the London of his riotous youth. This trait is one belonging to the less self-conscious life of Elizabethan times, and was to be shed afterwards, as preachers turned rather to generalisations, and abandoned particular instances in obedience to the demand for the abstract rather than the concrete which exercised the French critics and their English imitators. Yet, although the topical and contemporary enjoy a prominent place in Donne's preaching, it is evident that, if it were possible to analyse the component elements of his sermons, full-blooded and vigorous as much of his writing is, and much as it reflects his lively and adventurous commerce with the ordinary world, by far the greater part of his material is derived directly, or after undergoing a peculiar manner of distillation in the alembic of his personality, from learned sources ; and it is these which to a large extent he shared with his fellow ' metaphysicals ' but turned in many instances to such different account.

The lengthy and painstaking lists of ' authorities ' quoted in his various works, which are to be found in the appendices to Miss Ramsay's ' Les Doctrines Médiévales,' are the best possible proof of the immense range of Donne's reading—the natural result of his avowed " hydroptic immoderate desire of human learning "—while the ease with which he alludes in the sermons to one or other of the questions disputed in ' the school,' or to the various claims advanced by Roman Catholic apologists, goes to show that he had not only read over the chief works of mediæval scholarship, and the main " body of Divinity as it was then controverted betwixt the Reformed and Roman Church," [1] but had made them his own. The mediæval preoccupation of Donne was no doubt, as Dr. Evelyn Simpson points out,[2] largely due to his Roman Catholic upbringing, and to the Jesuit tutors who had charge of his education as a youth ; and, however much in later life he may have brushed aside many of the Papal claims as cobwebs obscuring the fine proportions of true apostolic Christianity, Donne's mind obviously continued to work in the syllogistic manner developed by Aquinas, and the great logical and religious conclusions of the latter remained for him the final statements upon many subjects. To some extent, also, this characteristic reacted adversely on his prose, and combined with a partiality for Tertullian and Augustine, and even for Seneca, to make him indifferent to the cultivation of a flowing style.

If we except for our present purpose Donne's interminable stores of scholastic learning, and his exposition of mediæval, quasi-philosophical, conceptions, such as has been treated fully by Miss Ramsay, we discover that his range of interests come fairly close to those of Andrewes and the Laudian divines. No enthusiasm is evident for the Classics, and Greek and Latin Fathers, or Silver Latin writers such as Seneca (whom Donne valued highly),[3] are preferred to Plato, Homer, Vergil, or Horace. In his use of patristic sources, however, one noticeable and keenly personal fact emerges, namely, the extraordinary interest he displays in

[1] Walton : ' The Life of Dr. John Donne,' Temple Classics ed., p. 11.
[2] Op. cit., chap. v. The whole chapter is an admirable account of Donne's ' mediævalism ' on both the intellectual and mystical sides.
[3] ' LXXX Sermons,' lxx, p. 713 (E) ; ibid., xxxvii, p. 362 (B).

the discrepancies and acknowledged errors of the Fathers.
Quite obviously these contradictions had been a matter of
real trouble to him, probably at the period described in the
third ' Satyre,' and it was only later that he realised, and
could point out to others, that there was never " in any
age, any Father that mistook nothing," and that it was no
" blasphemy against the Holy Ghost to note such a
mistaking." [1]

As with the other Anglo-Catholics (particularly Andrewes
who was a renowned Semitic scholar), Donne turned eagerly
to the Jewish Rabbins [2] ; the speculations of the cabbalists
also fascinated him, and his works present us with several
specimens of their interest in numbers. [3] At times he drew
unexpected and even fantastic meanings from the original
Hebrew used in a particular context, [4] to an extent not
attempted by other English ' metaphysical ' preachers,
though always, however suspect his procedure may seem to
us, with the perfectly sincere intention of extracting the
fullest possible profit from any passage of Scripture. [5] While
admitting the threefold ' sense ' of Scripture [6] he warned
against seeking too many meanings in any passage : " If
there may be danger thereby, to neglect or weaken the
literal sense it selfe " [7] ; neither, on the whole, did he tend
to allegorise, probably because for him the realisation of
religious experience transcended the wildest flights of the
allegorists. Most allegorisation which is found in his
sermons—and in this respect he again falls into line with
other ' witty ' preachers—is quoted avowedly from one or
other of the Fathers, and unacknowledged examples, [8] where
they have a strong patristic flavour, are almost certainly
in most cases reminiscent. Much the same might be said
of Donne's symbolism ; often he quotes directly, and it is

---

[1] ' LXXX Sermons,' xlix, p. 489 (C).

[2] For a most interesting account of Donne's acquaintance with rabbinical
works, see Grierson : ' Poetical Works,' vol. ii, pp. 223-4.

[3] ' Fifty Sermons,' xxix, p. 261 (D), and *ibid.* xlvii, p. 430 (B) ; *cf. ibid.*
xlix, p. 450 (B), and ' Essayes in Divinity,' pp. 98-9.

[4] ' LXXX Sermons,' xxxviii, p. 379 (E) ; *ibid.*, vii, pp. 70 (E)-71 (A) ; *ibid.*,
xxvii, pp. 268 (D, E)-269 (A).

[5] ' LXXX Sermons,' lv, p. 555 (A) and lvi, p. 564 (C, D, E).

[6] ' Fifty Sermons,' xxi, p. 176 (A).

[7] *Ibid.*, xxxvi, p. 323 (D) ; *cf.* ' LXXX Sermons,' lxx, p. 710 (A).

[8] E.g. the turning of the phrase " *without spot or wrinkle* " to mean without
the mark of original sin or the blemish of actual sins—' Fifty Sermons,' v, p.
37 (C).

difficult to judge whether he is ever original ; yet it is to be remembered that he could turn the most unlikely circumstances in his own life to symbolical uses, as is evident from more than one passage in the ' Devotions.'

Pliny was to Donne what he had been to the mediæval preachers and was to contemporary preachers of all schools,[1] and there is nothing original in the former's use of him or of those sources loosely referred to as " Naturall story." For his medical knowledge we are prepared by a letter to Sir Thomas Lucy, in which he gives an interesting account of the progress of medical knowledge from Hippocrates to Galen, and from Galen to Paracelsus,[2] whose innovations he celebrated satirically in ' Ignatius his Conclave.' On the whole, however, his medical references are less interesting than might have been expected from a man of Donne's reading.

The foregoing matter is that common to all ' metaphysical ' preachers and which Donne shared with them ; where he parted company with them was in his preoccupation with the questions debated by ' the school,' a term which he employs to embrace all the philosophic and theological doctrines which exercised the subtlety of an uninterrupted succession of thinkers stretching from St. Augustine to his own day, and which, in particular, are set out at length in the ' Summa Theologica ' of Aquinas. What these doctrines were, and how intimately they are interwoven with the texture of both Donne's prose and poetry Professor Grierson went far to illustrate in his ' Commentary ' to the latter, while Miss Ramsay, guided by the erudition of M. Picavet, has since treated the subject exhaustively. It is not necessary to discuss these beliefs in any fullness ; suffice it to note that the few main mediæval topics which occur most frequently in Donne's sermons concern the angels,[3]

[1] Some good examples of curious natural history are to be noted in the ' LXXX Sermons,' e.g. lxvi, p. 665 (B) ; *ibid.*, lxxvii, p. 788 (B) ; *ibid.*, lxi, p. 617 (B) ; ' Fifty Sermons,' xii, p. 94 (C) ; xxxvi, p. 322 (D) ; and ' XXVI Sermons,' xi, p. 156 (D) ; *ibid.*, ii, p. 24 (B).

[2] Gosse : ' Life and Letters,' 2 vols., Lon., 1899, vol. i, pp. 174-5.

[3] E.g. ' Fifty Sermons,' i, pp. 6 (E)-7 (A-E), where it is discussed : (a) how the angels know each other ; (b) whether they were created with or before this world ; (c) whether they have aged now, being created before Time began ; (d) whether they understand by *Cognitionem Matutinam* (seeing all in God) or by *Cog. Vespertinam* (a clearer manifestation of the species of things) ; and (e) what is the number of their orders. The age of the angels is discussed in ' LXXX Sermons,' iii, p. 20 (B) ; xxxiv, p. 340 (E) ; xxxviii, p. 380 (C) ; and

the creation,[1] the nature of hell-fire,[2] and the infusion or production of the soul,[3] and that (in keeping with what has already been stated to be a characteristic of all ' metaphysical ' preaching), seldom, if ever, are such topics or the theories arising from them mentioned except by way of illustrating some practical point, and usually in an easy and casual way which demonstrates that such allusion occurred spontaneously to the preacher's mind.

One differentiating characteristic of Donne, however, is the way in which he employed this strangely obscure, subtle, and erudite material. Of ' wit ' in the strict sense of a purely intellectual 'conceit' originating in some scholastic or scientific theory, although a few examples can be found in his sermons, these are not so numerous as might be expected by a reader of his poems [4] ; and, as in the case of the latter, the far-fetched example in which the ' wit ' consists is of a much less obvious, more intellectual type than was the case with Andrewes and his immediate followers.   Partly for this reason, partly because other and nobler qualities in his prose early became generally appreciated and have continued to win applause, Donne has never been regarded as a ' witty ' preacher to the same extent as others of his

lxxii, p. 729 (C) ; the precise ' moment ' of the angelic ' fall,' *ibid.*, and lxii, p. 623 (= p. 622) (C, D).   Reference to angelic knowledge occurs in the ' XXVI Sermons,' iv, p. 54 (C) : *ibid.*, xxv, pp. 393 (C)–394 (A) ; ' LXXX Sermons,' xi, p. 111 (B) ; *cf.* ' Poetical Works,' ed. Grierson, ii, pp. 34–5, where the question is referred to Aquinas' ' Summa Theol.,' I Quæst. lvii, Art. 4. Angelic progression is treated of in ' LXXX Sermons,' lxiv, pp. 644 (E)–645 (A) ; *ibid.*, lxvi, p. 666 (B)—which is not in strict accord with ' Summa Theol.,' I Quæst. liii, Art. 2 ; ' LXXX Sermons,' lv, p. 550 (D), on a kindred topic, depends directly on the ' Summa Theol.,' I Quæst. lii, Art. 2.

[1] ' LXXX Sermons,' xxx, p. 301 (B) ; lii, p. 529 (D) ; lxiv, p. 649 (B) ; lxvii, p. 675 (D) ; lxviii, p. 683 (C) ; ' Fifty Sermons,' xiiii, p. 109 (B) ; xxx, p. 266 (C, D), *et al. loc.*

[2] Discussed in the ' Summa Theol.' Supplement, Quæst. xcvii, Art. 5 ; *vid.* ' LXXX Sermons,' lxiii p. 632 (E) ; lxxvi, p. 776 (C) ; and, on a cognate topic, ' XXVI Sermons,' xix, p. 265 (C) ; ' LXXX Sermons,' xxvi, p. 353 (C).

[3] ' Fifty Sermons,' viii, p. 61 (A) ; ' LXXX Sermons,' xxxix, p. 391 (C) ; li, p. 514 (D) ; lxiv, p. 649 (B).

[4] Two of the best of these occur in a sermon at St. Paul's, and deal with problems connected with the fire of Purgatory. In the former instance Donne notes that the Fathers have erred in some places in their opinions touching that fire, but adds that this need not derogate from their holiness " because it is a fire without light " (' LXXX Sermons,' lxxvii, p. 786 (D)) ; while in the latter he answers the objections of the scientists that it is strange that the element of fire alone should produce no creatures by pointing to the Papal Indulgences produced by the fire of Purgatory, so that " no heards of Cattell upon earth can equall them. . . ." (*ibid.*, p. 787 (E)).

Anglo-Catholic contemporaries ; yet, to the men of his day, as Walton assures us, " his fancie " seemed " equalled by his great wit " ; and the crowds that hung upon his lips when he preached at St. Paul's doubtless valued his preaching more for such ' metaphysical ' touches than for the literary beauties which appeal to readers of later times. But even the conceits which occur fairly frequently in his sermons take on a graver tone than is usual in this style of preaching, and though we find much that recalls Andrewes, we find also such ideas as the following, which give evidence of a profounder reflection :

" A Crystall glasse will not show a man his face, except it be steeled, except it be darkned on the backside : Christ as he was a pure *Chrystall* glasse, as He was God, had not beene a glasse for us, to have seen our selves in, except he had been *steeled, darkened with our humane nature*." [1]

Quaintness which abounds in Andrewes is almost entirely absent from Donne, largely because he was seldom so homely in his observations or so colloquial in his speech ; nor was he especially addicted to word-play of the familiar sort. Most of the examples of the latter to be found in his work may be regarded as a legacy from mediæval prose, with its delight in *paromoion* and other *schemata*, although a few examples can be noted of the more superficially ' witty ' sort which degenerates ultimately into the pun. When he told his hearers that God " flings, and slings, and stings the soul of the sinner," [2] or spoke of " the expressing the pressing of their depressions," [3] he was making use of devices derived from remote ecclesiastical sources and carefully cultivated in England during the Euphuistic vogue of his youth ; and such a schematic pattern as is to be met with in one of The Hague sermons—" No eloquence enclined them, no terrors declined them : No dangers withdrew them, no preferment drew them " [4]—points to an affinity with Hall and Adams and the ' Senecan ' writers and preachers, as well as with his Anglo-Catholic contemporaries, and it must not be too hastily concluded that Donne made choice

[1] ' Fifty Sermons,' xxxiii, p. 292 (E).
[2] ' XXVI Sermons,' vi, p. 80 (E).
[3] ' LXXX Sermons,' xix, p. 186 (A).
[4] ' *Ibid*.,' lxxi, p. 724 (A).

of certain forms as a churchman and not rather as a literary artist.

Donne's dual rôle of preacher and man of letters is one which must not be forgotten in considering his work, especially when we bear in mind the manner in which he prepared the first folio of his sermons for the press,[1] and to this duality is due in some part the explanation of his eminence over the divines of his party. Donne was from the first, in a sense in which Andrewes and his imitators never were, a pulpit-orator. He had been an author before he became a preacher, and a poet before he had taken seriously to prose. Throughout his life he continued a ready correspondent. The gifts, therefore, which he brought to the pulpit were not only those of vast erudition and an exceptionally varied experience of life, but also a highly developed artistic sensitiveness, which led both to a fine appreciation of the stylistic qualities of others, and to the formation of the carefully elaborated and somewhat cumulative manner which he made his own. For him, as for all men of his time, the Bible was the oracle of God ; its writings were directly inspired by the Holy Spirit, and, in consequence, the style of the Bible represented a conscious act of the Divine Mind, just as really as the creation of the world. Since, therefore, Donne could say—

" the books of the Scriptures are the eloquentest books in the world ; every word in them hath his weight and value, his taste and verdure," [2] ·

it followed that the preacher, when he came to expound the Scriptures, must be careful not to derogate from the rhetorical beauty of the passage he was interpreting, by any " extemporall and irreverent, or over-homely and vulgar language " [3]—" Some degree of eloquence " was " required in the delivery of Gods Messages." [4]

The same intention which we have seen underlay the publication of Smith's ' Mysterie of Rhetorique ' led Donne to pay a scrupulous attention to the rhetorical forms of the sacred text, and to turn his study of these forms to a use far other than the ingenious comments of the schoolmen

---

[1] Vid. ante, p. 29, and p. 115.

[2] ' LXXX Sermons,' xiii, p. 133 (E).

[3] Ibid., v, p. 47 (E).

[4] Ibid. (D).

upon grammatical *minutiæ* which we have seen imitated
by King and Andrewes. Underlying his own style in
framing his sermons was Donne's belief that—

" the Holy Ghost in penning the Scriptures delights himself,
not only with a propriety, but with a delicacy, and harmony,
and melody of language ; with height of Metaphors, and
other figures, which may work great impressions upon the
Readers, and not with barbarous, or triviall, or market or
homely language . . . and they mistake it much that thinke,
that the Holy Ghost hath rather chosen a low, and barbarous, and homely style, then an eloquent, and powerful
manner of expressing himselfe." [1]

The passage may be regarded as an *apologia* for the
rhetorical preaching of the seventeenth century, and as an
explanation of its chief *raison d'être*, which seems to have been
a desire to imitate the manner of an author who was not man
but God.   For Donne and his contemporaries, as for generations of preachers before them, the vehemence and copiousness which they attributed to the Holy Ghost were things
to be imitated, and the mediæval *schemata* (or later still the
vernacular *schemata*), as they tended to give " harmony and
melody of language," were cultivated accordingly.   The
same qualities also as excited admiration in the Scriptures
were, quite naturally, eagerly noted and appreciated in the
writings of the Fathers, and we find Donne, who was at all
times keenly alive to rhetorical figures, quoting : " *Pax non
promissa sed missa*, sayes St. Bernard, in his musicall and
harmonious cadences," [2] and referring to the same Father
as one " who evermore embraced all occasions of exciting
devotion from the melodious fall of words." [3]   St. Augustine
he praised, at another time, for a striking example of
paromoion.[4]
Of all the patristic writers the one who seems most to
have influenced Donne's style was Tertullian.   In the
Table of Authors which is found at the end of the ' LXXX
Sermons,' there occur sixty-four references to Augustine,
thirty-seven to Jerome, thirty-two to Bernard, and twenty-

[1] ' LXXX Sermons,' lv, pp. 556 (E)–557 (C).
[2] *Ibid.*, i, p. 6 (B).
[3] *Ibid.*, xxviii, p. 281 (D).
[4] *Ibid.*, lxxiii, p. 747 (C).

nine to Tertullian.[1] Although the references are, strictly speaking, theological, yet the frequency of reference points to familiarity, which in turn implies influence. All the authors here mentioned tended to write tersely, in contrast to the flowing periods of the Eastern Fathers, and his manner Donne learned partly from the former, partly from his devotion to Seneca whose influence lay behind them. Allowing for the difference between seventeenth-century, rhetorical, and modern, grammatical, punctuation, Donne's style is terse and vivid. His usual sentence is brief; although in course of time he learned to combine a number of brief sentences into a vast, cumulative paragraph by means of a repeated connective, such as ' that.' The vigour and colour, however, which he imparted to his brief sentences (or sentence-clauses, as they may more properly be called in his longer sentences), point back directly to Tertullian, who was able, without any noticeable ' pointedness,' such as dogged the more deliberately antithetical ' Senecan ' sentence, to express himself always with liveliness, and often with considerable force in remarkably brief sentences.[2]

The interesting way in which Donne passed from quotation to echo, and from echo to imitation of Tertullian is well illustrated by a passage which Professor Grierson quotes in his ' Commentary ' to the poems in support of the poet's debt to that Father [3]—

" ' Canst thou choose,' says the poet in one of his later sermons,[4] ' but think God as perfect now, at least as he was at first, and can he not as easily make thee up againe of nothing, as he made thee of nothing at first? *Recognita quid fueris antequam esses.* Think over thyselfe; what wast thou before thou wast anything? *Meminisses utique, si fuisses* : if thou had'st been anything than, surely thou would'st remember it now. *Qui non eras, factus es ; cum iterum non eris, fies.* Thou that wast once nothing, wast

---

[1] The next highest number of references is twenty-eight to Gregory Magnus, twenty-seven to Chrysostom, twenty each to Ambrose and Origen, and sixteen to Gregory of Nazianzus.

[2] I am indebted to Professor Morris Croll, of Princeton University, for this valuable suggestion which might be further elaborated.

[3] ' Poetical Works,' vol. ii, p. 139.

[4] ' Fifty Sermons,' xiv, p. 169 (D).

made this that thou art now ; and when thou shalt be nothing again, thou shalt be made better then thou art yet ! ' "

Donne's quickness to note excellencies of style in others, from the epistles of St. Paul onwards, is amply proved by his own statements, and he cites several patristic sermons in illustration of effective rhetorical devices employed by earlier preachers.[1] Rhetoric he considered an important asset, in order

" to trouble the understanding, to displace, and discompose and disorder the judgement . . . or to empty it of former apprehensions, and to shake beliefe, with which it had possessed it self before, and then, when it is thus melted to poure it into new molds, when it is thus mollified, to stamp and imprint new formes, new images, new opinions in it." [2]

But it is clear that he always thought of rhetoric in the old dialectical sense, as a means of persuasion, and never in the sense of mere literary embellishment. For his preaching consisted in persuasion, and whatever conduced to that end was legitimately employed, whatever hindered or obscured that end was to be condemned.[3] His own aim in preaching is clearly expressed in the following :

" With succinctness and brevity, as may consist with clearness, and perspicuity, in such manner, and method, as may best enlighten your understandings, and least encumber your memories, I shall open unto you the meaning of the text." [4]

Yet, practical as he recognised the end of preaching to be, Donne, with his love of scriptural and patristic ' elegance,' could not fail to admire legitimate ornament in preaching. Only the question arose : When was it to be considered legitimate ? Men, he reminded one auditory,

[1] E.g. 'Fifty Sermons,' xxxix, pp. 350 (D)–351 (A) ; and cf. 'LXXX Sermons,' lxiv, p. 643 (E)—of a sermon of Damascene's in dramatic form ; ibid., lxv, p. 654 (C)—of one of Athanasius directed against heresies ; ' XXVI Sermons,' xxv, p. 377 (D)—of a conceit introduced by Ambrose.
[2] ' LXXX Sermons,' lxxi, p. 723 (E).
[3] Ibid., lxxviii, p. 794 (B, C), and lxxi, p. 721 (A).
[4] ' XXVI Sermons,' xxv, p. 364 (A).

do not plant rare and curious flowers or odoriferous herbs in a sheep-pasture :

" So if in your spirituall food, and preaching of the Word, you exact of us more secular ornament, then may serve as *Saint Augustine* says, *Ad ancillationem*, to convey, and usher the true word of life, into your *understandings*, and *affections* (for both these must necessarily be wrought upon), more then may serve *ad vehiculum*, for a chariot, for the word of God to enter, and triumph in you, this is *a treading down of the grasse*, a filling of that ground which was ordained for sheep, with things improper and impertinent to them." [1]

A gallery overcrowded with furnishings and hangings, he declared on the same occasion, becomes a wardrobe :

" So if your curiosity extort more than convenient ornament, in delivery of the word of God, you may have a good *Oration*, a good *Panegyrique*, a good *Encomiastique*, but not so good a Sermon."

The quotation of secular authors, he considered, was not to be condemned " especially in some Auditories acquainted with such learnings," [2] and he adds amusingly :

" I have heard men preach against witty preaching ; and doe it with as much wit, as they have ; and against learned preaching with as much learning as they could compasse."

Donne's great fear obviously was that men should be led away by delight in rhetorical embellishments and so miss the true end of preaching. Perhaps, also, he realised in his own case, as is so apparent in the ' Devotions,' that the line which separated the spontaneous from the conscious ' conceit' was a very thin one, and that the preacher who called in the aid of rhetoric might quite easily find himself the slave and not the master of his ally. For his own part, true to his professed aim, he sought to employ " such manner and method " as might best enlighten his hearers' under-standings and least encumber their memories, and accord-

---

[1] ' Fifty Sermons,' xxiv, pp. 202 (D)–203 (D).   [2] *Ibid.*

ingly we find him dividing up the matter of his discourses under the familiar rhetorical headings, *quando, quis, quare*, and so on, and proceeding to the division of his text into a few clearly marked sections. In this his rhetorical bent is clearly seen, which led him to avoid, on the one hand, the excessive subdivisions of the extreme Calvinists with their devotion to the syllogism, and, on the other, the elaborate word by word exegesis of Andrewes and his ' school.'

While certain personal elements give a fantastic and bizarre air to much of Donne's work, it is true to say that he possessed a breadth and sanity of outlook hardly shared by the other preachers whom we have been considering. Even in those places where Donne's personal idiosyncrasies are most apparent there is a poise and grandeur about his conceptions to which no other Anglo-Catholic preacher attained. In all the others, in Andrewes even, there is an element of opportunism—a sense of the consciously cultivated, the artificial, and the unsubstantial ; but it is otherwise with Donne. Those rhetorical ideals as they affected preaching which we have heard him give expression to, while they were many of them shared by most preachers of his day, and were the result of the common education which they received, yet in so far as they were realised more clearly by him and explicitly expressed, demonstrate Donne's greater architectonic ability, which enabled him to turn to use the curious material of the common stock in such a way as to achieve a striking and often beautiful prose.

One personal idiosyncrasy of Donne's which is responsible for a strange but characteristic note in his work is his preoccupation with the physical concomitants of death. This trait is hardly sufficiently explained by referring to the fascination which such contemplations exercised on the mediæval mind ; it is accounted for rather by the voluptuous nature of the man which sensed a fresh physical experience even in dissolution, and by the self-torturing intellect which would give him no rest, but kept thrusting into consciousness the seeming paradox of the resurrection of the body. Such recurring preoccupations serve to accentuate the strongly individual flavour of Donne's work, and this individualism, whether intellectual or emotional, is above all what distinguishes him from his contemporaries and gives him his pre-eminence. The at all times more subtle, and often highly fantastic use of far-fetched erudite information, yet employed under the direction of a strong mind acting upon clearly conceived principles, the carefully elaborated style, based upon recognisable models, yet avoiding extremes, the self-criticism closely dependent on his criticism of others—these, when brought together to the flame of a glowing and passionate personality, resulted in the production of his sermons, and go to explain how, ' metaphysical ' preacher though he was, in an age of ' metaphysical ' preachers he was a man apart.

Donne was not the last survivor of the ' metaphysical ' school, neither was he its greatest glory. It is questionable even if he may be claimed as its justification ; for, as has been already noted, the qualities for which he has long been appreciated are not especially those which he shared with his ' witty ' brethren. Like all great men, he stands apart from his age, and his achievement is rather to be gauged in terms of his many-sided personality than of a contemporary fashion ; and yet, but for an age of preaching, an age, moreover, addicted to ' witty ' and ' metaphysical ' preaching, Donne would probably have lacked the incentive which led to his success. Consequently, although he is not to be judged among the other ' metaphysical ' preachers, he is to be considered along with them, as has been done here. His work serves to emphasise the traits which we have noted in them, and combined with the outcries of their theological opponents and the more balanced criticism of those who saw in them a menace to English prose style, adds weight to the verdict of contemporaries and posterity alike, that the components of ' metaphysical ' preaching were not such as were in themselves intrinsically valuable, that the use to which they were put by the ' witty ' preachers was not consonant with the great ends of Christian oratory, and, that both the material and methods employed rendered impossible the cultivation of a prose style suited either to delivery in the pulpit or to give to religious discourses in their printed form the dignity of literature.

On two counts, therefore, both for what it was, and for what it could not become, ' witty ' preaching stands condemned.

VI. The other Anglicans to 1660, including Jeremy Taylor

TO secure a comprehensive designation which might serve to describe those Anglican divines who stood apart from the Laudian movement, whether on account of *Puritan*, or *rational*, or other considerations, or those whose main work either fell within the period directly before the triumph of Arminianism, or who, while dissociating themselves from the ecclesiastical policy which formed one of the main incentives to the Civil Wars yet remained loyal to episcopacy and to the broad traditions of Catholic doctrine, is by no means an easy task. Neither ' Church Puritans ' —meaning by the term those clergymen who desired to reform the Church of England from within, but were averse to separation in any form—nor ' Jacobean Calvinists '— a classification which tends to over-emphasise a particular aspect in the teaching of many of these preachers—is sufficiently wide a term to embrace all whom it is necessary to include. What is desired primarily is to mark the differentiation of *other Anglicans* of the period from the opening of the century down to the Restoration from those who, whether or not accepting the full doctrinal and ecclesiastical significance of Andrewes, Laud, and their party, aimed at being ' metaphysical ' or ' witty ' preachers. The fact that these *other Anglicans* differed widely among themselves and represented considerable divergence of tradition both in their theological views and in their homiletic ideals, goes without saying and is of supreme interest to our present purpose ; but the main reason for considering them as a whole, and not in separate categories (apart altogether from considerations of convenience), lies in their common, though varied, connection with the Church of England, and the definite opposition in which they stood, on the one hand, to those whom we have come to speak of as Anglo-Catholics, on the other, to those who did not scruple at separation and the formation of independent religious bodies. The divines now to be considered were, according to the light given them, loyal members of the Church of England, and that their work exhibits an undoubted variety of thought, feeling, and aim is merely an additional proof of the honoured claim of that section of the Church to be comprehensive in the fullest sense.

While, therefore, the claim of such preachers to be considered as a unity is justifiable, it is their diversity of interests and attainments which proves of greater moment. For, as might be expected from what we have learned of the theory underlying seventeenth-century preaching, such diversity was at one and the same time illustrative and influential ; it exhibited often an ideal in practice, while itself supplying a fresh incentive to the perpetuation of the ideal. Yet originality was not wanting, and this in turn served to qualify traditional modes in ways which were to prove of service beyond the bounds of party. Indeed, the great merit of much of this preaching lay in its avoidance of the two extremes—the jagged, allusive, studiously ingenious exegesis of the ' metaphysicals ' and the heavy exposition of the stricter Puritans—in the interest of freer, more fluid, and consequently more literary, addresses, which were to form to some extent the basis of the simpler post-Restoration sermon.

On one side especially is this connection remarkable— namely, that on which the earlier rationalistic preachers, Hales and Chillingworth, link up with the Cambridge Platonists and the Latitudinarians, and so point the way to what has generally been regarded as the perfection of preaching in Tillotson. But there are other links in the chain of pulpit oratory which are less obvious, and even those tendencies or experiments, made only to be abandoned, are of value to our discussion, as revealing what Englishmen, for one reason or another, determined the sermon might include, what it must necessarily reject. Leaving, therefore, Hales and Chillingworth to be considered along with those later philosopher-preachers and broad-churchmen with whom they have affinities, it will be well to pass in brief review the work of those divines, whose personal interests or the trend of whose party led to the emergence of particular traits in the sermons of the time. In order to do this as conveniently as possible, it has been found useful to focus attention in the main on several outstanding preachers of the period, while a large number of forgotten, though (in their own day) often highly valued clergymen, have been called upon to fill in the wider background. Thus Henry Smith and Thomas Adams have been considered in detail, and a large assemblage of Jacobean Calvinists has been studied in order to compare their style, thought, and reading with their Anglo-Catholic contemporaries on the one hand, and the coming Presbyterian and Independent stalwarts on the other. Names such as Ussher, Hall, and Sanderson invite particular attention, and the period under consideration will be found to embrace all but one year of the life of Fuller, and to be that which marked the publication of Jeremy Taylor's most important collection of sermons. A fourfold division has, in consequence, been made, and the uniqueness of the greater men and the relation of the less, both to them and with them to other preachers of other schools, brought out as clearly as possible.

(i) *Henry Smith, Adams, and the Earlier Calvinists*

Henry Smith and Thomas Adams were *Puritans* in the strict sense of the term. While Andrewes and Laud, and the men of their school were praying for " the restoration of the things that are wanting, the strengthening of the things that remain " [1] in the Church of England, Smith and Adams, and other preachers like-minded with them, were urging the necessity of removing much that yet remained, and were far from considering that anything was lacking so far as ritual and ceremony were concerned. Doctrinally such men were Calvinists, in their ecclesiastical outlook they were Puritans ; that is, they desired, as the Marian exiles had desired, to see the last vestiges of resemblance to the Church of Rome removed from the national church, and this the so-called " Elizabethan Settlement " appeared to them to have fallen short of doing. Such Puritanism was largely a matter of ecclesiastical outlook, although, naturally enough, men so unflinchingly determined where religious worship was concerned tended to demand a high standard of conduct in ordinary life ; but it was so far divorced from the prudery which has come to be associated with later Puritanism, that the outspokenness of the Puritan preachers, and their vivid—one might almost say lurid—imagery

---

[1] ' The Preces Privatae of Lancelot Andrewes,' trans. with introduction and notes by F. E. Brightman, M.A., Lon., 1903, p. 60.

renders them curiously distasteful to many modern palates. Moreover, Smith and Adams were both City preachers, accustomed to appeal to citizens of the type depicted in the plays of Jonson and Dekker, or to young benchers of the Inns of Court, whose experience of life (in many instances) may well have been as riotous and dissolute as that described by Donne in his early poems.

From Calvinism was derived the habit of dealing more individually and bluntly with the hearer than was customary with the more catholic preachers, while the auditory to a large extent determined the nature of the illustrative matter employed. But the fact that a man was a Calvinist must not be taken to imply that his preaching was likely to prove dull, or that he was a Puritan that his illustrations would be invariably grave and sober. The early Puritans were Elizabethans, with that full-blooded relish for a variegated life which characterised the dramatists and pamphleteers of the age, and the topical onslaughts of Puritan preachers strike at times much the same note as the more serious of the latter.[1] One of the most rigid Calvinists of the early years of James I's reign, John White (1570–1615), author of ' The Way to the True Church ' (1608), a treatise against Romanism which occasioned considerable controversy, affords an excellent example of the vigorous, colourful preachers of his type, while as yet much of the liveliness, which the pulpit then seems to have shared with the pamphlet, still lingered among the more Puritan

[1] E.g. cf. Smith's " A Preparative to Marriage," pp. 24–5 of ' The Sermons of Mr. Henry Smith . . .' Lon., 1675, with similar passages in Nashe's ' Christs Teares Ouer Ierusalem,' published in 1593. Smith died (conjecturally) in 1592, so that the contemporary nature of the invective is evident. In his sermon Smith took occasion to censure the extravagance in apparel of the City wives as follows :

" Garish Apparel hath taught many gossips to disdain their Husbands. This is the folly of some men, to lay all their pride upon their Wives ; they care not how they sloven themselves, so their Wives jet like Peacocks. But Peter I Peter, 3, 5 doth commend Sarah for her attire, and not Abraham ; shewing that Women should brave it no more than men : and God made Eves Coat of the same Cloth that he made Adam's. They covered themselves with Leaves, and God derided them not ; but now they cover themselves with pride, like Satan which is fallen down before them like lightning ; ruff upon ruff, lace upon lace, cut upon cut, four and twenty orders, until the Woman be not so precious as her Apparel ; that if any man would picture vanity, he must take a pattern of a Woman, or else he cannot draw her likeness. As Herodias was worse for her fine dancing ; so a Woman may have too many Ornaments. Frizled locks, naked breasts, painting, perfume . . . are the forerunners of Adultery. . . ."

preachers. White was a strenuous opponent of Rome, an incorrigible Calvinist and a stout champion of all that related to the Royal Prerogative. The last point is worthy of notice, especially when the apparently excessive adulation of royal personages by the Laudian divines invites criticism ; for to men of all shades of theological opinion who were unanimous in one thing only—their opposition to Rome —Elizabeth, and after her the Stuart kings, were regarded as peculiar instruments of God in preserving the nation from Popery.[1] Two sermons of White's, ' the Former Delivered at Pavls Crosse . . . March, 1615, [on] the Anniuersarie commemoration of the Kings most happy succession . . . ,' the other preached at the Spittle in 1613, reveal his lively and vivid style. In the former of these, which contains what must be one of the bluntest and most revolting statements of the Calvinistic interpretation of the Faith on record,[2] his censure of the sins of the City, especially of drunkenness, is enlivened by " a story in Athenæus of an Alehouse that came to be called, The signe of the Gally " owing to the misadventure of certain " roaring-boies," who, having drunk too deeply, mistook the house for a ship, and, believing themselves to be in danger of shipwreck, cast out all the furniture to lighten the supposed vessel. In the morning when the Magistrates came to punish them for their disturbance, being still the worse for drink, the roisterers greeted them as " Tritons,"

[1] What Puritan preachers were capable of saying about Elizabeth may be illustrated by a quotation from Robert Bolton's ' Two Sermons Preached at Northampton at Two Severall Assizes there '—one of date 1621, the other 1629—p. 12 : " The peerlesse Princesse Queene *Elizabeth*, of sweetest and dearest memory, the happiest instrument of GOD & glory of her sexe, since the most blessed Virgine." The late date is worthy of particular note.

[2] This statement which is to be found in the sermon indicated (p. 5) as printed in White's ' Workes,' published in 1624 by his brother Francis White, dean (later bishop) of Carlisle, is so extreme as to deserve quotation. After reading some hundreds of Calvinistic sermons I do not remember to have seen an equally bald and revolting statement of what is usually supposed to be the leading tenet of Calvinism. White declared :

". . . When we certainly know by the Scriptures & without controuersie believe, no small part of mankinde, in Gods decree and eternal purpose, to stand reprobate and reiected from saluation, and all the effects of election, whether in the masse of sin or otherwise, (all is one to the point of this difficultie :) when, I say, it is of all hands yeelded that there be so many reprobates, denied the grace of election, and from all eternitie, prepared, or *finished*, as the Scripture speaketh, to destruction (for what God executes in time he willes in eternity,) what shall wee say to Praier and Thanksgiuing for these ? or what benefit can either they or we receiue thereby ? . . ."

and vowed them statues and images if they should be so fortunate as to escape drowning.[1]

The tale, it will be obvious, is a curiously " merry " one for a Calvinistic preacher, and is much more likely to have been remembered for its rollicking humour than for the reproof it was intended to convey. Moreover, it is only one of many anecdotes which are scattered throughout White's sermon.

Such a tale has distinct affinities with the preaching of the friars and even with certain of the more regular mediæval clergy ; though hardly to be described as ribald, it is akin to the *facetiæ* employed by Meffreth and Raulin,[2] and which Erasmus was at pains to condemn.[3]   But it is only one of many surprising ingredients in Calvinistic and Puritan preaching.   Francis White, later bishop of Ely, and brother of the foregoing, in a Paul's Cross sermon a few years subsequent to his brother's,[4] proved almost as ' witty ' as Andrewes himself.   When his sermon was published, the following was noted as a " golden saying."

" Now if euer Church in the world had in it this ring of golden Bels,[5] it is the Church of *England* at this day. The church of *Rome* hath indeed a ring of Bels, but they be Tinne, they Latine Bels, & Latine often broken Latine too which makes the ring so much the worse " :

and Henry Smith himself is found saying :

" It was a wilde Fig-tree that *Zacchæus* climbed : but not like that unfruitful one which our Saviour cursed : for this bare most precious fruit, even such as Christ himself vouchsafed to pluck."[6]

The latter, however, is definitely reminiscent of or quoted from some Father,[7] as are almost certainly those passages

---

[1] Sermon cit. in White's ' Workes,' 1624, p. 8.
[2] *Vide* Baring-Gould : ' Post-Mediæval Preachers,' Lon., 1856, p. 98. *Cf. ibid.*, pp. 75–8.   The love of such stories, it is worth noting, was much more prevalent among English and German preachers than among French or Italian ones—Neale, ' Mediæval Preachers,' p. li.
[3] ' Ecclesiastes,' Book II, xxi.
[4] ' London's Warning. By JERVSALEM,' 1619.
[5] I.e. like those of Aaron.
[6] ' The Sermons . . .' 1675 ed.—" The Sinners Conversion "—p. 519.
[7] Samuel Price, rector of Exeter College, Oxford, in a sermon entitled ' The Spring,' published in 1609, makes the same point elaborately in a ' conceited ' manner.

in which a strong resemblance exists between Smith and Donne [1]—though direct imitation of Smith by the later preacher is always a possibility—and goes to emphasise the fact that although making a much less obtrusive use of his reading the Puritan and Calvinist shared to a large extent the reading of the 'metaphysical' and Anglo-Catholic. Smith, in particular, was probably familiar with the usual range of patristic and scholastic reading. In his 'First Sermon upon Usury,' [2] he makes use directly of the old scholastic argument against this practice : God

" never said unto Money, Encrease and multiply, because it is a dead thing which hath no seed, and therefore is not fit to engender."

In another sermon [3] Pythagoras' doctrine of the transmigration of souls is dismissed as " a fine Philosophical dream." But not so did Smith pass by the amazing natural history which he found in Pliny and the *Physiologus* and was ever ready to turn to moral account. In a sermon on the Lord's Supper the familiar parallel between Christ and the Phœnix is drawn [4] ; in 'A Preparative to Marriage' the undesirability of a wet nurse is pressed home by the argument : " Commonly the Child draweth the like infirmity from her, as the Eggs of a Hen are altered under the Hawk " [5] ; while in ' The Godly Man's Request ' occurs the common belief, challenged by Browne in the 'Pseudodoxia Epidemica,' that " the Raven and the Phœnix, and the Elephant, and the Lyon and the Hart fulfil their hundreds. . . ." [6] Adams is equally fond of such allusions, though in his case it is plain that they were at times introduced not only out

---

[1] E.g. the image of the Hat, Glove, Seamless Coat, and the references to Adam and Eve and the fig leaves, used by Smith in explaining imputative righteousness (' The Wedding Garment,' 1675 ed., pp. 129–34), are also found in Donne (' Fifty Sermons,' vii, pp. 51–3) ; and Smith notes (' The Godly Man's Request,' ed. cit., p. 232) that God clothed Adam and Eve in the skins of dead beasts as a symbol that they too should die, a thought to which Donne alludes in ' Death's Duel ' and elsewhere. Other resemblances are those to Lamech's two wives (Smith : ' A Preparative to Marriage,' p. 5 ; Donne : ' Fifty Sermons,' ii, p. 13) and to the creation of Eve from Adam's side and not from his foot, as signifying the favourable estate of a wife (Smith : ' A Preparative to Marriage,' p. 4 ; Donne : ' Fifty Sermons,' vii, p. 15). In the latter instance Donne reveals the fact that this conception originated (or, at least, is found) in St. Jerome.

[2] Ed. cit., p. 82.   [3] *Ibid.*, ' The Pilgrim's Wish,' p. 222.
[4] *Ibid.*, p. 46.   [5] Ed. cit., p. 28.   [6] *Ibid.*, p. 235.

of the desire for edification which was the ordinary motive which led Puritan preachers to employ such references, but also out of a desire to secure rhetorical parallelism. Thus, " Poyson," Adams tells us, " is life to a Serpent, death to a man : and that which is life to a man, his humidity and spettle ; they say is death to a Serpent "[1]; and the Euphuistic style, it is evident, to a large extent depended on the citation of strange examples, followed by pithy applications, as had been the case in the mediæval ecclesiastical prose on which it was so largely formed.

Smith, too, was not averse to deriving a particular lesson from the Hebrew meaning of proper names [2]—a form of exegesis taken over by the Church from the Rabbinical writers, and frequent in Donne and the other ' metaphysicals '—and the devout algebra of the Cabbalist was on occasion also turned to account by the more Puritan clergy. Robert Abbot, bishop of Salisbury, and brother of the Puritan archbishop, relates that—

" a Jewish Rabbine (Aben Ezra) giueth of the Hebrew words . . . *ish*, the *man or the husband*, and . . . *ishah*, the *woman or the wife*, that there is contained in them . . . *Iah*, which is the name of God, the letters and vowels whereof being taken out, ther remaineth nothing to be made of the rest but . . . *esh*, and . . . *esh*, that is to say, *fire*, and *fire* "[3] ;

while Adams notes (following no doubt some patristic or cabbalistic original) that—

" the *Hebrewes* well obserued, that God to those he loued, added a letter of his owne name (that *tetragrammaton*)*Iehouah*: as the letter *He* to *Abrahams* and *Sarahs* name : the letter *Iod* to *Iehosua's*, who was before called *Hoshea*." [4]

To sum up : taken as a whole, the reading of those Anglican

---

[1] " The Sovles Sicknesse " in ' The Workes,' fol., 1630 ed., p. 448.
[2] " A Preparative to Marriage " in ' The Workes ' (1675), p. 5 ; *cf.* Donne : ' Fifty Sermons,' ii, p. 13.
[3] ' A Wedding Sermon preached at the marriage of Sir John Stanhope . . . 1607,' p. 55.
[4] " The Gallants Burden," in ' The Workes,' fol., 1630, p. 3. This may be interestingly compared with Donne : ' Fifty Sermons,' xxix, p. 261.

preachers who either stood aloof from or were actively
opposed to the school of Andrewes and Laud was largely
that of their ecclesiastical opponents. During the lifetime
of James I, moreover, it is to be remembered that, however
popular ' witty ' preaching may have been, Calvinism was
still the prevailing theology favoured by the Court, and, to
a large extent, by the Universities. The *milieu* amid which
these Calvinist preachers found themselves, taking into
account the fact that a preaching *milieu* tends to be either
a composite one or sharply differentiated into University,
City, or country, and that the Court took a leading place
as a ' preaching-scene,' may be described as practically
identical with that of the Anglo-Catholics. It is, consequently, less in background or learning that the difference
between the two sets of preachers is to be looked for than in
deliberate choice, and the Puritan preachers may be said
not to have preached in the manner of the ' witty ' preachers
chiefly because they kept other aims in view, and did not
consider that the methods of the ' metaphysicals ' were
such as should be emulated. As we have seen, they
employed much of the same material as is found in Andrewes, and, if there is not the same appeal to the Fathers
as authorities in doctrinal matters, yet patristic allegorisation is retained by way of additional illustration. Nor,
although the Scriptures are usually taken alone as sources
of dogma, without the supplementary glosses of the Fathers,
and are quoted profusely, are they the only writings quoted
by the preachers ; but a tendency becomes apparent,
fostered to a considerable extent by a stylistic interest in
Seneca, but not wholly explicable on that ground, to
draw upon the classical moralists, and where the Anglo-
Catholic was ready with his phrase from the Vulgate or
some falling cadence from a Father, Adams, Hall, and
others were quick to supply an appropriate quotation from
a secular writer. The tendency was later in the hands of
the Cambridge Platonists to become as great an abuse as
the honeycomb of Biblical texts of which the sermons of the
extreme Puritans consisted, or the mosaic of patristic allusion
which we have noted in Andrewes and his imitators ; but
as found in the Jacobean Calvinists it marks the appeal to
reason, which, in spite of the apparently irrefutable dogmatism of the system, lay at the heart of the Calvinistic

theology.[1] Down to the time of Whichcote and the other
'Platonists' however, except in Hales and Chillingworth,
this appeal was largely unrecognised, and the quotations
made were designed less to convince—for what secular
writer could hope to convince if THE WORD had proved
unconvincing ?—than to embellish. Excessive quotation
of Scripture, the crying fault of the Parliamentary preachers,
is of course not wholly unexemplified, and the works of
Sebastian Benefield (1559–1630), Lady Margaret Professor
of Divinity at Oxford from 1613, and rector of Meysey-
Hampton in Gloucestershire, provide a good example
of what a learned preacher accustomed to address
University auditories thought suited also to a rural
congregation.[2]

A University sermon by Benefield, of date 1610, is a
mosaic of Scriptural quotations in Latin, Greek, and
Hebrew, and of citations from the Fathers, while a sermon
preached, presumably to an ordinary auditory, in Gloucester Cathedral in 1613, is so crammed with Latin quotations,
and hampered by citation and translation to such a degree
as to be unintelligible to an ordinary auditory, or to most
learned audiences, in delivery. In twenty-one sermons on
the first chapter of ' Amos,' which according to the prefixed
dedication to Dr. Ravis, bishop of London, were " country
Sermons," delivered at Meysey-Hampton, the same
tessellation of text and quotation is noticeable, and in this
and a second series of similar sermons, on the second chapter
of the same prophet, it is apparent that the preacher
multiplied examples out of several ancient authors rather
to illustrate his reading than to enforce his point, or inculcate

---

[1] This view is put forward and argued very convincingly by Dr. F. J.
Powicke in ' The Cambridge Platonists. A Study,' 1926, pp. 6–7.
[2] Of Benefield's sermons we possess one ' Preached in St. Maries Church
in Oxford, March xxiv MDCX . . .'; another, ' The Haven of the Afflicted,'
preached in Gloucester Cathedral in 1613 ; ' A Commentarie or Exposition
vpon the First Chapter . . . of Amos, delivered in XXI Sermons in the Parish
Church of Meisey Hampton,'1613 ; ' A Commentarie . . . vpon the second
Chapter of . . . Amos ' in a further ' XXI Sermons,' 1620 ; while in 1629
the commentaries on the first and second chapters of Amos were reprinted,
bound up with ' A Commentary . . . vpon the Third Chapter. . . . In
XVII Sermons.' Between the issue of the first and second commentaries,
there had appeared ' Eight Sermons Probably Preached in the Vniversity of
Oxford . . . Begunne in the year 1595 . . . first published . . . 1614,'
and ' The Sinne against the Holy Ghost Discovered . . .' 1615, being twelve
sermons delivered many years before " in the famous Universitie."

any fresh lesson—a feature which almost certainly betrays the commonplace-book.[1]

The discourses of Joseph Mede (1586–1638), fellow of Christ's College, Cambridge—who came to be regarded as a kind of sponsor for the Platonist divines—point in an entirely different direction from those of Benefield. Worthington, the editor of John Smith's ' Select Discourses,' performed a like service for Mede, and, writing as one in sympathy with the plainer style aimed at by Smith and his fellow-Platonists, he described Mede's style as " every where grave and proper and fitly expressive of his sense, (an argument that he was master of his Notions, and did fully comprehend them)." [2]   Book I of Mede's ' Works ' contains fifty-three ' discourses,' nine of which were published between 1624 and 1628,[3] and twelve between 1615 and 1624 [4]; the concluding six were composed in his young days, and all of them, with the exception of the last, are elaborate and point to wide reading and much study. The dating of these sermons is important as showing how at the very moment when ' witty ' or ' metaphysical ' preaching was in its most flourishing condition, a plainer and more correct style of preaching was being cultivated by a small group of thoughtful men ; but it is equally significant, and a fact to which Worthington calls attention, that there are " no needless quotations of the meaner and less significant Sentences out of Authors," and that, although loaded with Scriptural quotations, and admitting reference to Josephus fairly frequently and to one or two commentators, Mede's sermons are equally free from citations of the Fathers and of other ecclesiastical authors.

The question of the citation of authors in our period and by the divines now under discussion is one of the most interesting, affording, as it does, considerable insight into the gradual change in theological outlook which was taking place in England.   Sermons which belong to the Calvinistic period of University preaching, before the rehabilitation of the Fathers and the formulation by the Church of England

---

[1] A collection of tales of " grateful Lions " is a case in point.   This occurs in ' A Commentarie . . . vpon the second Chapter of Amos,' lecture XIIII, p. 208.

[2] General Preface to ' The Works of the Pious and Profoundly Learned Joseph Mede . . .' 3rd ed., fol., 1672.

[3] Viz. 26–37, with the exception of 30.   [4] Viz. 38–50.

of the claim to be fully ' Catholic,' tend either to be devoid of all but Scriptural quotations or to quote only the Classics or Protestant Commentators. Thus Henry Airay (1560?-1616), Provost of Queen's College, Oxford, in his ' Lectures upon the whole Epistle of St. Paul to the Philippians ' (1618) provides an example of plain, conscientious exposition, decidedly in Calvin's style, and his ideal in preaching appears to have been shared by Christopher Potter, his editor, who asserted in a foreword that—

" Gods oracles are to be faithfully expounded, not curiously minced, not loosely dallied with, and surely the plaine song of *Scripture* is the best musicke without these quavering descants of mens wit."

Thomas Sutton, a fellow of the same college, in a Paul's Cross sermon, three years previously, is found quoting the reformed theologians and the Mediæval Schoolmen rather than the Fathers ; while Plato, Aristotle, Cicero, Vergil, Lucian, and (particularly) Seneca, are freely used.[1] Almost contemporaneously,[2] Thomas Anyan, of Corpus Christi College, preaching at St. Mary's, Oxford, confined himself to the Classics and the more recent commentators, made mention of Hooker, but avoided reference to the Fathers ; whereas Richard Gardiner, of Christ Church, in a sermon ten years later in the same place,[3] added to quotations from Pliny, Plutarch, and Vergil, quotations from Hugo de S. Victor, and Aquinas, but confined his quotations from the Fathers to Jerome and Nazianzen.

Personal predilection naturally affected such citation, but, in the main, certain tendencies are clear : the stricter type of Calvinists, especially the country clergy, continued to hold by the advice given by Perkins,[4] and eschewed the intermingling of the Word with " human testimonies," though the expository sermon or " lecture " gradually gave place to the connected disquisition on a given text ; the more learned Calvinists, while adhering to their doctrinal position, displayed a fondness for quoting the classical moralists, though, as the century advanced, a Father was

[1] ' England's Second Summons,' Lon., 1615, 4to.
[2] In 1612—' A Sermon preached at S. Maries Church in Oxford. . . .'
[3] Published as ' A Sermon . . . at St. Maries,' 1622.
[4] *Vid. ante*, p. 100.

now and then cited, probably as a reminder to their auditories that the rising Arminian clergy were not the only preachers acquainted with these writers ; the most puritanically affected, moreover, were by no means the stoutest exponents of the plain scriptural sermon, but, as has been hinted in the case of Smith and Adams, the older Puritan sermon provides evidence of many unexpected interests.

Strict ' methods,' also, are less noticeable than might have been expected in the composition of sermons produced by men, some of whom have already been drawn upon as evidence of the homiletical theories of their party. Occasionally, as in the case of Robert Abbot (1588 ?–1662 ?) (who successively held the livings of Cranbrook in Kent, Southwick in Hampshire, and St. Austin's in London), ' tables ' prefixed to their sermons remind us of the clear divisions and subdivisions which the preachers had in mind,[1] and bishop Chappell's ' Sermon-Notes on II Timothie III. 16 ' as already indicated,[2] represent the application of his ' Methodus Concionandi ' to a particular text. Occasionally, too, a sermon by a Puritan divine will be found printed with carefully drawn margins, and each *doctrine* and *use* carefully marked off by printed lines ; but this, as noted in the introduction to this study, may be taken as indicating the manner in which such a sermon came to the printer's hands, rather than the method of composition of a particular preacher. Some preachers, of whom " John Barlow sometime Minister of the word at Plimmouth," who flourished between 1618 and 1632, is an instance, interspersed their exposition with *objections* and *solutions*[3] to such an extent as to earn from their theological critics the nickname of " obsollers."[4] The habit, however, is interesting as a relic

[1] Abbot's main works are ' A Hand of Fellowship . . . In Certaine Sermons . . .' 1623 ; ' Bee Thankfull London and Her Sisters ; . . .' 1626 ; ' Foure Sermons . . .' 1639 ; ' Milk For Babes : or, A Mothers Catechism . . . Whereunto also annexed, Three Sermons,' 1646, all of which are extremely rare, and fetch high prices when copies occur. The ' tables ' prefixed to the second of the above are a good example of a preaching scheme.

[2] *Ante*, pp. 110–11.

[3] *Vid.* ' The Good Mans Refuge in Affliction,' published separately in 1618, pp. 25–6.

[4] Robinson, in a *note* to his trans. of Claude's ' Essay on the Composition of a Sermon ' (3rd ed., 1788, vol. ii, pp. 225–6), by way of comment on the excessive use of " *Objections* " in Puritan sermons, says : " Butler, who knew everybody, and everything, was pleased to call a certain set of people *Obsollers* :

of their logical training, and intimately connected with the attitude of those who appealed to the Bible as an infallible book whose every statement might be made the major premiss of a syllogism. But, to an even greater degree than was the case with the Anglo-Catholic preachers, whose peculiar method of exegesis was an integral part of their style, the other Anglicans of the period, by whatever label we may be tempted to designate them, show a remarkable freedom from conformity to strict ' methods ' or preaching-schemes. Indeed, in so far as their sermons acquire literary or rhetorical interest at all, it is in proportion as they break away from the bald exposition or meticulously articulated sermon-patterns to which the more rigid Puritans persisted in adhering. It is therefore largely on grounds other than their conformity to particular homiletical ideals that these Anglican preachers invite attention, and their connection with rhetoric is of a more intricate, and often of a more surprising, sort than is indicated by the mechanical divisions of a speech or sermon.

Something of the multifarious content of Smith's work has already been glanced at ; it remains, however, to make clear his importance to a literary study of English preaching. Born in 1560, Smith probably died in 1592.[1] His inclusion in a study of seventeenth-century pulpit oratory, consequently, might seem to demand explanation. The fact, however, that a complete edition of his sermons " with other his Learned Treatises," prefaced by a life by Thomas Fuller, was issued in 1675, proves Smith's continued popularity during the intervening eighty years, and the still ready demand for his works.[2] From his own day to the

. . . these obsollers were Puritan preachers . . . so called . . . on account of their raising *objections* and then giving *solutions* in their sermons ; and also for their marking these parts of their sermon in the margins of their printed books by OB–SOL. . . ." It is interesting to note that Arthur Hildersham, a noted Puritan, and minister of Ashby-de-la-Zouche during part of the time when that other noted Puritan Brinsley was schoolmaster there, is cited by Robinson as " one of these obsollers " ; he adds : " Several of his lectures on the fourth of John are composed of *objections* and *answers*, and excellent sermons they are."

[1] Neither Fuller, who prefixed a life of Smith to the 1675 edition of ' The Sermons . . .' nor Wood discovered the exact date of his death. Wood assumed that he survived till 1593, but the title-page of the 1592 edition of the sermons reads : " Printed according to his corrected Copies in his life time," clearly implying that he was already dead by that date.

[2] In 1645 we find Edward Willan, Epist. ded., to a sermon at Norwich speaking of " Smyth," along with Pemble, Heiron, and Wheatley, as a popular Puritan preacher.

present he has been celebrated as " the silver-tongued preacher," a designation of which Fuller remarks : " and that was but one metall below St. *Chrysostom* himself." In his lifetime his popularity was great, and the reprint of his works at the date indicated proves that his posthumous popularity, and therefore the influence of his works, must have been beyond the ordinary.

Wood records that Smith took

" the Degree of Master of Arts, as a member of Hart-Hall, being then esteemed the Miracle and Wonder of his Age, for his prodigious Memory, and for his fluent, eloquent, and practical Way of Preaching. Afterwards he became Lecturer at St. *Clements Danes* without Temple Bar, near London, where being much frequented by the Puritanical Party, was by them esteemed (as he was by the generality) prime preacher of the Nation, which his Sermons, taken into the Hands of all People, did shew." [1]

Fuller informs us that, having scruples about subscription and the lawfulness of some Ceremonies [2]—

" He was loth to make a Rent either in his own Conscience or in the Church ; wherefore he resolved on this Expedient, not to undertake a Pastoral Charge but contented himself with a Lecturer's place . . ."

—a position in which several contemporary Puritans found themselves—that he enjoyed immense popularity, even among " Persons of good quality," and wielded an immense influence.[3]

[1] ' Athen. Oxon,' 1721, vol. i.

[2] A good instance of Smith's Puritan outlook occurs in a marginal note to ' A Preparative to Marriage,' 1675 ed., p. 9, where he points out the symbolical significance of the ring in weddings, but hastens to add in the margin of his sermon : " The Ceremony is not approved, but the invention declared." In ' The Trial of Vanity,' *ibid.*, p. 313, in condemning sundry sports, he gives an account very similar to Baxter (*Rel. Bax.*, 1696, p. 3) of what earned a man the title of ' Puritan ' : " If ye ask the Atheist, or Epicure, or roguish Players, what is a disturber ? You shall see that they will make Solomon *one*, because he speaketh against vanity, for this is their definition. He which will not allow men to prophane the Sabbath, but saith, that Cards, and Dice, and Stage-players, and May-games, and May-poles, and May-fools, and Morrice-dancers are *Vanity*, is a pratler, disturber, and an Arch-puritan. . . ."

[3] The practical results of Smith's preaching Fuller illustrates by relating how, on one occasion, when the former preached of Sarah's nursing of Isaac

14

" *The words of the wise . . .*" Fuller concludes, " *are like nails fastened by the Masters of the Assemblies*. And certainly this Smith had as great a dexterity as any in fastening them in the *Judgements* of his hearers, by his solid *Reasons, Fancies*, by his proper *Similitudes, Memories*, by his orderly Method, and *Consciences* by his home Applications."

Such is at once an accurate description of Smith's preaching, and like the passage already quoted from Donne,[1] a defence of the multiform appeal of seventeenth-century preaching as a whole, which, keeping in view its several aims and the varied devices necessary to attain these—such aims as from the time of the classical oratory had been recognised as incident to public speaking—sought not only to convince by sound argument but to win attention by arresting illustration. The appeal to the conscience and the desire to fix the matter of the discourse in the memory of the hearer, on the other hand, recall the change over from the Pagan to the Christian oratory. Smith has already been quoted [2] as holding that " to preach simply is not to preach rudely, nor unlearnedly, nor confusedly, but to preach plainly," and enough has been said of his participation in the learning of his day, and his occasional employment of it in ways which resemble the ' witty ' preachers, to show what he, and other Puritans, might have done had they wished. Indeed, Smith, in his moments of highest literary attainment, succeeded in developing a more reflective and continuous prose than the ' metaphysicals,' apart from Donne and Frank, ever achieved ; and, although so far as structure is concerned he may be classed with Lever and Jewel as one of those who delighted in pursuing the ancient *schemata*, yet, so far as tone is concerned, his affinities are rather with the men of letters than the preachers. The following extract, for example, on the transitoriness of human life, taken from ' The Godly Mans Request,' [3] is an interesting forerunner of the *Hydriotophia*, and while it falls far short of the superb

---

(*vid.* ' A Preparative to Marriage,' 1675 ed., pp. 28, 29) and " thereupon grounded that generall Doctrine, *that it was the duty of all Mothers to nurse their own children*," the Ladies and great Gentlewomen present were so affected that " they presently remanded their Children from the Vicinage round about *London*," where they had been put out to nurse, and " endeavoured to discharge the second moietie of a Mother."

[1] *Ante*, p. 189.   [2] *Ante*, p. 117.   [3] 1675 ed., pp. 232–3.

prose of the latter, it has little to fear from comparison with Drummond's *Cypress Grove*, an earlier and interesting expression of the same theme :

" In Paradise we might live or dye : in the world we live and must dye : in Heaven we shall live and not dye.   Before sin nothing could change us ; now every thing doth change us : for when winter comes we are cold, when age comes we are withered, when sickness comes we are weak, to shew that when death comes we shall dye.   The clothes which we wear upon our backs, the Sun which sets over our heads, the Graves which lye under our feet, the meat which goes into our mouths, cry unto us, that we shall wear, and fade and dye, like the Fishes and fowls and Beasts, which even now were living in their elements, and now are dead in our dishes.   Every thing, every day suffers some eclipse, and nothing stands in a stay, but one Creature calls to another, let us leave the World.   Our fathers summoned us, and we shall summon our children to the Grave ; first we wax old, then we wax dry, then we wax weak, then we wax sick, and so we melt away by drops ; at last as we carried others, so others carry us unto the Grave : this is the last bed which every man shall sleep in : we must return to our mother's womb."

While Smith's greatest felicities were achieved at times when he shook himself free from the necessity of continuously pressing a moral application and allowed his mind to dwell on a subject with pleasurable expatiation, in short when he became the essayist rather than the preacher, he could treat of practical things, especially spiritual conditions, with insight and vividness.   This is a typical Puritan note, and, except in the case of Donne, is almost wholly absent from Anglo-Catholic preaching.   Smith's picture of the furies congregating in the heart of the conscience-stricken sinner, found in ' The Betraying of Christ,' [1] is particularly arresting.   Opening with a further instance of contemporary schematic prose—

" There is a warning conscience, and a gnawing conscience.   The warning conscience cometh before sin : the

[1] Ed. cit., p. 340.

gnawing conscience followeth after sin. The warning conscience is often lulled asleep : but the gnawing conscience wakeneth her again "—

he proceeds to depict the condition of the man whose conscience is awakened :

" All the furies of hell leap upon his heart like a stage. Thought calleth to Fear ; Fear whistleth to Horrour ; Horrour beckoneth to Despair, and saith, Come and help to torment this sinner. One saith, that she cometh from this sin, and another saith, that she cometh from that sin : so he goeth through a thousand deaths, and cannot die. Irons are laid upon his body like a prisoner. All his lights are put out at once ; he hath no soul fit to be comforted." [1]

The passage is a curious blend of Augustine's power of depicting internal things with the Elizabethan love of lurid imagery and the terrifying accompaniments of Senecan drama. The analysis of spiritual conditions is strangely commingled with the descriptive vigour of the pamphlet, and it will be only one remove more before the sinner becomes interesting for his sin rather than interesting as a subject to be redeemed from sin. The *character*, as Mr. G. S. Gordon has shown,[2] has its origin in moral philosophy, becomes useful for illustrative purposes to rhetoric, and finally dissipates itself in witty description. While it is in its infancy it has comedy for its near neighbour : " to every Theophrastus his Menander." The history of character-writing in Greece, England, and France illustrates this contention. So far as English preaching is concerned we find the desire for the vivid presentation of spiritual conditions resulting in such dramatic portrayal of internal states as the foregoing. Before long it ceases to be the soul of man as the stage whereon the various passions play their part that is of moment, and man himself as an actor on the wider stage of the world becomes of paramount importance. Hall and Earle, our two best character-writers, were also preachers.

[1] Ed. cit., p. 340.
[2] ' English Literature and the Classics,' Oxf., 1912—" Theophrastus and his Imitators," pp. 49 *seq.*

Analysis of character, combined with familiar use of the rhetorical ' descriptio,'[1] led to the employment of the *character* in preaching, and descriptions of how certain men behave were felt to be a good way of convincing others of sin. One wonders if they were not more conducive to aiding men to detect the sins of their neighbours than effective in convincing them of their own ! Soon the *character* became interesting on its own account, and its service, as a model of virtue or to depict vice was over, and consequently it could no longer be retained as a device of the preacher. When it reappeared in the following century in the works of Law it was made to do duty as a mere lay figure to afford opportunities for moralising comments ; the living *character* by then had passed to the novel. In the early seventeenth century, however, it was vigorous and lively, and was still recognised as a rhetorical device. Smith, in spite of his feeling for vivid presentation, does not seem to have essayed this type of description ; Hall wisely detached it from his sermons, just as Theophrastus, the pioneer in character-writing, had separated his *characters* from his philosophical treatises ; but in the works of Thomas Adams, the greatest of all early Puritan Divines, the *character* remains an integral part of the sermon, and forms a most interesting feature of his art.

Of the life of Adams the meagrest details are available. Most of the information we possess of his career is derived from the prefaces to individual sermons which he published from time to time but chiefly between the years 1612 and 1625. After a period in two country charges, by 1618 he was preacher at St. Gregory's under St. Paul's Cathedral and by 1629 had settled as incumbent of St. Benet's, Paul's Wharf, to the parishioners of which, along with various patrons, was dedicated the same year the folio volume of his collected works. Such details do not help us materially to form a picture of Adams, but his outlook is probably fairly clearly indicated by the fact that the old church of St. Gregory, under the shadow of St. Paul's, was the scene, on the occasion of its redecoration in 1630-2, of the

---

[1] Keckermann : ' Rhetoricæ Ecclesiasticæ,' 1606 ed., p. 92, uses as an example of the ' descriptio ' Bernard *Super Cantica*, ser. 24, where a calumniator is depicted. *Vid.* also Wilson's ' Arte of Rhetorique ' (1553, 1560, &c.), Clarendon Press reprint, p. 187.

struggle over the placing of the communion-table at the east of the church which has survived in history because of the part played in the dispute by Laud, and that one of the principals in the controversy, Sir Henry Martin, dean of the Arches Court, Sir Henry Montague, later Earl of Manchester, and Lord Kimbolton, the latter's son, are numbered among Adams' patrons.

Adams' sermons are particularly rich in topical allusions, and, as has been already illustrated, he drew upon the contemporary deposit of strange and curious learning to secure at one and the same time an edifying moral and rhetorical effect. One feature of his work, however, calls for special remark—his great familiarity with the Classics and his almost instinctive habit of quoting from them. Not after his first college-addresses as a young don do we find allusion to the Classics in Andrewes, and even in the case of the Puritan archbishop Abbot, whose ' Exposition upon the Prophet Jonah ' [1] contains numerous quotations from the Classics,[2] it must be remembered that such quotations occur in university discourses. With Adams, on the other hand, preaching at times, it is true, before distinguished patrons but, for the most part, to a City auditory, classical allusions are constant, and classical quotations so numerous that it is difficult to open his works at random without lighting on some reference to the stories of Æsop or the *Metamorphoses*, or finding a quotation from Juvenal, Horace, or Martial, or, most frequently of all, Seneca. This feature of his work links him up closely with Joseph Hall, and together they point forward to what was to be a distinguishing characteristic of Tillotson. Adams' habit, however, of translating his quotations, when they are in verse, into doggerel couplets—a device familiar to readers of Florio's *Montaigne* and other translations of the period—was unique, and is proof of the early date of his work.

Another feature of Adams' sermons, in this case connected with their publication, which is of more than passing interest, is the strange and arresting titles under which these appeared. Burton's well-known gibe about men rushing

---

[1] In thirty sermons, published 1603.
[2] Cæsar, Plutarch, Pliny, Herodotus, Strabo, Diodorus Siculus, Tacitus, Cicero, Seneca, Lucan, Macrobius (*Somnium Scipionis*), Livy, and Ovid all come in for quotation.

into print with sermons to which they gave titles likely to
attract public attention,[1] although principally directed
against those who sought to impress by pointing to distinguished auditories before whom they had preached, might
equally well have been directed against those who endeavoured to give to their printed discourses the advantages
enjoyed at the present day by the novel but then confined
to the pamphlet and the play ; and, in an age of alluring
sermon-titles Adams', it may certainly be claimed, secured
a high place.[2] Two of his titles, moreover, ' The Sovles
Sicknesse ' and ' Mysticall Bedlam,' serve not only as striking
advertisements for printed sermons, but also usher in collections of *characters* written round a leading idea. We are
not surprised, therefore, for this and other reasons, to learn
from one of Adams' prefaces,[3] that by contemporaries he
was considered a trifle fanciful, and given to allegories and
rhetorical flourishes ; but in point of fact such sermons are
merely specimens of the " figure sermons " beloved of
Spanish preachers, some of whom, according to Claude,[4]
even laid down rules for preaching in this manner. Robinson, Claude's editor, in a note, further informs us that so
great a preacher as Cardinal Borromeo, in his Oration to
the clergy of Milan, delivered at the opening of his sixth
Provincial Council, indulged in a composition of this kind,
in which various sins are depicted in turn by their resemblance to physical diseases, very much in the manner of
Adams' earlier discourse.[5] From Robinson's note we
further learn that this fashion of strange titles and series of
religious contemplations paralleled by descriptions drawn

[1] The ' Anatomy of Melancholy,' Shilleto's ed. (Bohn Lib.), 3 vols., Lon.,
1920, vol. i, p. 34.
[2] Some of his more outstanding titles may be mentioned in passing. His
first recorded sermon was *The Gallants Burden*, followed soon after by *The
Deuills Banket*, a series of six sermons, each with a separate title: 1. ' The
Banket Propounded, Begun ' ; 2. ' The Second Service ' ; 3. ' The Breaking
Vp of the Feast ' ; 4. ' The Shot . . .' ; 5. ' The Sinners Passing-Bell ' ;
and 6. ' Physicke from Heauen.' Others are *Politicke Hunting*, *The Three
Divine Sisters*, *The White Devill* (' Or the Hypocrite Vncased : In a Sermon
Preached at Pauls Crosse, March . . . 1612,' the same year as the publication
of Webster's play ; probably this represents a topical hit), *The Cosmopolite*,
and *The Spirituall Navigator*.
[3] ' The Diuells Banket . . .' Lon., 1614, 4to, A3 verso—A4 verso, " Ad
vel in Lectorem." In the folio this appears as ' The Fatall Banket.'
[4] ' Essay on Composition of a Sermon,' Robinson's trans., 1788 ed., vol. ii,
p. 189.
[5] *Ibid.*, note,

from some variegated sphere in life flourished considerably in England in the forty years which ended about 1590.[1] Adams' productions, therefore, represent a survival rather than an innovation.

In 1615 Adams preached, on Trinity Sunday, at St. Giles Without Cripplegate, and later published his sermon with the title *The Spirituall Navigator Bound for the Holy Land*. Milton's father was at this period resident in St. Giles parish, and it is therefore possible that the future poet, then seven years of age, may have been present and heard Adams preach. The sermon was from a text from the Apocalypse —*Before the throne was a sea of glass like unto crystal* (Rev. iv. 6). After treating of the various allegorical significances of " the glassy and crystal-like sea," as expounded by Ambrose, Augustine, Brightman, Emmanuel Sa, Bullinger, and others —the authorities quoted provide a good specimen of the catholicity of Adams' reading [2]—the preacher proceeded, as Donne in his sermon at The Hague [3] four years later, to enumerate the various ways in which the world resembled a sea. Some of the parallels are extremely well drawn, and the whole sermon is not unworthy of comparison with that

[1] Robinson, who probably possessed a wider knowledge of English sermons than any subsequent writer has done, and had hoped to write a history of English preaching, in the work indicated, vol. ii, p. 189 (note), has supplied a list of such native preachers as he had been able to collect who had employed the *figure* method. These he groups as follows :

" 1. Under *medical images*—Preservative or *triacle* against the poyson of Pelagius. By Dr. Will Turner, 1551—Discovery of the English *lepers*, very noisom to the church—1. A schismatike. 2. A church-robber. 3. A simoniacke, &c. By Tho. Timme, 1592. The sick man's *salve*, &c. By Tho. Becon, 1591. A weapon-salve for the church's *sores*. Stillingfleet—The Anatomy of the Masse, 1555.

" 2. *Musical* images.—*Harmony* from Heaven—*Song* of Simeon, Luke ii. 29.— *Trumpet* of the soul, Eccl. xi. 9 by Hen. Smith, 1595—3. *Natural images* . . . 4. *Trade* images . . ."

Under the two last, as to some extent in 2, *supra*, *title* rather than series of studies attracted Robinson. The examples given under 1 are those most to our purpose. Gauden's sermon before the Lord Mayor and Aldermen of London, in St. Paul's, 1659, on Jer. viii. 11 *They have healed the hurt of the daughter of my people* (*vid.* Robinson's *Claude*, vol. i, p. 383, note), is probably a last echo of the fashion. Gauden's list of the sores from which the Church of England suffered and the remedies to be applied made his sermon, according to Robinson, " the filthiest sermon that ever *he* read."

[2] Brightman was a contemporary Puritan, who died in 1607. His commentary on the Apocalypse he claimed to have written under direct inspiration. Sa was a celebrated Jesuit commentator whose ' Notationes in totam scripturam sacram ' had the distinction of being added to the edition of the Vulgate issued by Pope Sixtus V.

[3] ' LXXX Sermons,' sermon lxxii.

of Donne, who must have been familiar with it, and may have avoided borrowing or repetition of ideas by a careful reading of the earlier discourse. After the parallels had been exhausted, Adams concluded with a description of the varied activities and innumerable follies of mankind which God, seated on His throne, beholds reflected in the mirror of the glassy sea, and so introduced his first company of *characters*.

" There runne honour and pride *æqvis ceruicibus*. There walkes fraud cheeke by iowle with a Trades-man. There stalkes *pride*, with the face of a Souldier, but habit of a Courtier ; striuing to *adde to her owne stature* : fetherd on the crowne, cork'd at the heeles, light all ouer : stretching her legges, and spreading her wings like the Ostrich, with ostentation of great flight : but *nil penna, sed usus* ; not an inch higher or better. There slugs *Idlenesse* : both hands are in the bosome, while one foote should be in the stirrop.
. . .

" Here halts *Opinion* lame not with the shortnesse, but length of his legges : one *foote* too long, that marres the *verse*. There runnes *Policie*, and moues more with an Engine, then many men can doe with their hands : . . .
" There slides by the meagre *ghost* of *malice*. . . . There flye a crew of *Oathes*, like a flight of dismall Ravens, croking the *Plague to the House*, where the *Swearer* is. . . ." [1]

The Heavenly *camera obscura* continues, presenting still fresh types of human folly, until the Divine Spectator is obviously forgotten, and the original intention of showing men their deformities and so disgusting them with their sins. Each fresh sinner is introduced out of pure love for witty description. The moral *descriptio* has become the *character*.

The publication, in the year previous (1614) to *The Spirituall Navigator*, of the collection of characters which came from the pen of Overbury and his friends had given fresh impetus to what was obviously a current fashion, and probably Adams' *characters* as depicted in his sermon were received with applause, or he may have discovered his gift for this kind of description. Certain it is, that before the

---

[1] 'The Workes,' Lon., 1630, fol., p. 411. (The 1630 ed. is quoted throughout.)

close of the year he issued a complete set of *characters* in the manner of Hall and Overbury, under the title of *Mysticall Bedlam : Or The World of Mad-Men,* dedicated to no less a person than Sir Thomas Egerton, Baron Ellesmere. After a kind of preliminary discourse based upon a piece of restrained *wit* drawn from grammar and logic, and reminiscent of Donne, with the remark, " *Stultorum plena sunt omnia,*" Adams proceeds to introduce his madmen or *characters,* presenting one and another before us that they may make us sport, just as the keepers of Bedlam in his day were accustomed to lead in their charges to provide amusement for visitors. The Epicure is chosen to " leade the ring, as the foote man of this mad Morisco," and accordingly, in the printed version is introduced, as is each *character* in turn, under a separate heading.

The Epicure

" I would faine speake (not only of him, but) with him. Can you tend it, Belly-god ? The first question of my Catechism shall be, *What is your name ? Epicure. Epicure ?* What's that ? speake not so philosophically ; but tell vs in plaine dealing what are you ? *A louer of pleasure, more then of God.* One that makes much of my selfe ; borne to liue, and liuing to take mine ease. . . . I beleeue that delicacies, iunkets, quotidian feasts, suckets and marmulads are very delectable. I beleeue that sweet wine and strong drinkes ; the best blood of the grape, or sweate of the corne is fittest for the belly. I beleeue that midnight reuels, perfumed chambers, soft beds, close curtaines, and a *Dalilah* in mine armes, are very comfortable. I beleeue that glistring silkes, and sparkling Iewels, a purse full of golden charmes, a house neatly decked, Gardens, Orchards, Fishponds, Parkes, Warrens, and whatsouer may yeeld pleasurable stuffing to the corpse, is a very heauen upon earth. I beleeue that to sleepe till dinner, and play till supper, and quaffe till midnight, and to dally till morning ; except there be some intermission to toss some paynted papers, or to whirle about squared bones . . . this is the most absolute and perfect end of man's life. . . ." [1]

The Epicure dismissed (after a decidedly fine passage

[1] ' The Workes,' 1630, pp. 498–9.

on the insecurity of all human tenures), the *Proud* is led in. First the proud man and then the proud woman is passed in review, and once more the passage is brought to an end by a reflection on human folly in the face of death. Here, as is also the case with Smith, we find the Puritan preacher joining hands with the Elizabethan pamphleteer in a highly-coloured portrayal of sin consumed by a loathsome and vividly realised mortality. Adams' words might come straight from ' Christs Tears Ouer Ierusalem ' and Nashe might be the writer :

" There is mortality in the flesh, thou so deckest : and that skin which is so bepainted with artificial complexion, shall lose the beauty and it selfe. *Detrahetur novissimum velamentum cutis.* You that sayle betwixt heauen and earth in your foure-sail'd vessels, as if the ground were not good enough to be the pavements to the soles of your feet : know that the earth shall one day set her foote on your neckes, and the slime of it shall defile your sulphured beauties : dust shall fill up the wrinckled furrowes, which age makes, and paint supplies. Your bodies were not made of the substance wherof the Angels ; nor of the nature of the starres, nor of the matter, wherof the fire, ayre, water, and inferiour creatures. Remember your Tribe, and your fathers poore house, and the pit whereout you were hewen : *Hannibal* is at the gates, death stands at your dores : be not proud, be not madde : you must die."[1]

Sufficient has been quoted to show that Adams' *characters* shared the tendency of all English *characters* to be " wits descant on any plaine song," which is precisely Overbury's definition of this kind of writing.[2] In 1616 Adams again produced a gallery of characters, this time following a traditional framework for such sermons,[3] and choosing a succession of diseases paralleled by moral distempers. Each form of illness is dealt with under ' Cause,' ' Signes and Symptoms,' and ' Curation,' and as many ' witty ' parallels as possible are drawn between the physical and the spiritual complaint. This series, entitled *The Sovles Sicknesse : A Discovrse Divine, Morall, and Physicall,* so

---

[1] 'The Workes,' p. 500.   [2] *What a Character is,* 1622 ed., Q.4.
[3] *Vid.* footnote, *ante,* p. 216.

closely resembled in plan ' A Christian Heavenly Treatise, containing Physic for the Soul,' published just then by John Abernethy, minister at Jedburgh (and afterwards bishop of Caithness), that Adams was at pains in his Epistle to the Reader to protest that his production had been "committed to the stationers hands, passed and allowed by authority ; yea . . . and, perhaps, an impression sold, before that of Mr. John Abernethy's came out." This time nineteen *characters* appeared—some of them the same types treated afresh—and a considerable advance is perceptible in the power of ' witty ' delineation. Of the vain-glorious man, whose condition is compared to 'windinesse in the stomacke' (disease 16), we are told :

" . . . When he rides his masters great horse out of ken, he vaunts of him as his owne, and brags how much he cost him. He feeds vpon others curtesie, others meat : and (whether more ?) either fats him. At his Inne he cals for chickens at spring, and such things as cannot be had ; whereat angry, he sups according to his purse with a red Herring. Farre enough from knowledge, he talkes of his castle, (which is either in the ayre or inchanted). . . . In his hall, you shall see an old rusty sword hung vp, which he sweares killed *Glendower* in the hands of his Grandsire. He fathers vpon himselfe some villanies because they are in fashion ; and so vilifies his credit to aduance it. . . . He is indeed admirations creature, and a circumstantiall Mountebank." [1]

The other *characters* are drawn with equal liveliness, and it is evident that the preacher, whatever the ostensible object of his portraits, has been carried away by his own device and become the *character-writer*. Perhaps Adams became conscious of this, or, what is more likely, he had exhausted the range of *characters* which he felt equal to presenting. In the same year as he published *The Sovles Sicknesse*, five other sermons appeared from his hand under the general title of *A Divine Herball*. In the third of these, ' The Contemplation of the Herbes,' he enumerates various herbs and compares them to corresponding virtues, very much as he had previously compared diseases and vices. But, like all

[1] ' The Workes,' pp. 470, 471.

men who have tried to portray both virtues and vices, Adams was unable to give to his virtues the life and attractiveness of his vices. Besides, he may have wished to persuade the devout, who, it seems, looked askance at his free use of *wit* and fancy, that he had not really found pleasure in the lively depicting of sinners apart from his desire to warn men from sin, and have thought that a restrained and modified use of the *character* manner of writing would best effect the transition back from the purely entertaining to the definitely edifying. *The Contemplation of the Herbes* may therefore be regarded as Adams' 'Characters of Vertues.' His effort, however, is dull after the parade of the Bedlamites or the 'witty' diagnoses of the spiritually diseased, and would not in itself have marked out Adams for mention from a number of earlier divines who essayed this kind of writing.

Apart from his *characters* Adams' prose is interesting for its variety—the blending of old and new, the conceited and the rhetorical, with the freer, grander, more poetical, and, ultimately, more beautifully handled style of Bacon and Donne and Taylor. While himself playing no definite part in discarding the old and adopting the newer manner, Adams was keenly alive to the effect to be produced by reverting from time to time to the archaic manner or experimenting with the new. His sermons, in consequence, are a kind of literary workshop of the early seventeenth century, where we may see English prose in the making. Or, perhaps, a slip-way might afford the better metaphor. Now and then we see the old rhetorical supports removed and the newly-built vessel ready to take the water ; but just then Adams remembers that he is not there to follow the completion and subsequent adventures of his ship, but to turn out as many others as possible ; and once again we are aware of the old beams—the age-old rhetorical devices— being called upon to perform their old service and support a fresh message. It was for others to choose the manner English prose should adopt ; but it remains to Adams' credit, as it gives to his work an additional importance, that he should have seen its possibilities, and amid the demands of a spiritual cure in a distracted time have experimented so interestingly with the materials he found to his hand.

All the main rhetorical forms which went to the making of

the Euphuistic style, and which Professor Croll has shown in his study of that vogue [1] to represent an attenuated but persistent survival of the Gorgianic or Isocratean figures, which descended to the Elizabethans by way of mediæval ecclesiastical prose, are profusely illustrated in Adams' work. In it it is possible to study the antitheses familiar to students of Lyly in their traditional setting of the sermon, and to note the subtle transition from the old schematic prose to the more direct style of the Jacobeans. Many passages in Adams bristle with such rhetorical comparisons as the following :

" . . . when the Sunne is hottest, the springs are coldest : and the more feruent the loue of God is to vs, the more cold is our charitie to him, and to others for him " [2] ;

or ;

" It is written of the *Thracian* flint, that it burnes with water and is quenched with oyle : fit Embleme of those wicked soules that are the worse for God's endeauour to better them. But such contrary effects hath the Gospel in contrary natures. As by the heat of the Sun waxe is softned, and yet clay is hardned : so by the preaching of the word the hearts of such as shall be saued are mollified ; but the hearts of the lost are further obdurate." [3]

Much in the same way the openings of some of Adams' sermons consist of a set of Lylyan antitheses used as a kind of definition, in the manner of Bacon in his *Essays*, each of which sets out with a kind of general statement developed in a series of brief rhetorical parallels. Thus the commencement of *Eirenopolis : The Citie of Peace* reads :

" Peace is the Daughter of Righteousnesse ; and the mother of knowledge, the nurse of Arts, and the improuement of all blessings. It is delectable to all that taste it, profitable to them that practise it ; to them that look vpon it, amiable ; to them that enioy it, a benefit inualuable. The building of Christianity knowes no other materials." [4]

[1] *Vid.* Introd. to *Euphues* (Croll and Clemons' ed.), New York, 1916.
[2] 'The Workes,' 1630, *The Forest of Thornes*, p. 1054.
[3] *Ibid.*, p. 1054.   [4] *Ibid.*, p. 995.

A careful consideration of such of his sermons as are
dated unfortunately demolishes Professor Croll's contention [1]
that Adams began in imitation of Latimer and the mediæval
preachers, as did Jewel and Lever before him, but that he
gradually shook himself free from the fascination of their
gay ornaments and rhetorical *schemata*. Taken, so far as is
possible, in chronological order, Adams' work reveals no
sign of such development, but all through his life he continued to employ the favourite *schemata* of preachers in all
ages from the time of Cyprian onwards—particularly *paromoion* [2]—with greater or less elaborateness in proportion as he
was striving after rhetorical effects. It is true that Adams
seems to us to achieve his happiest effects when he leaves the
schemata alone and takes flight on the gauzy wings which
were afterwards to bear Jeremy Taylor into the blue of
heaven in pursuit of his lark,[3] or reminds us, reminiscently
it is true, but with something of Fuller's *wit*, of our natural
swarthiness and the repeated tanning of our sins.[4] But this
is only to acknowledge that we prefer Taylor's poetical
fancy or Fuller's wit to Lyly's parallelism, and consequently
are more ready to appreciate Adams where he most resembles the later writers. The men of his own day no
doubt thought otherwise, and were ready to applaud his
balanced clauses, where adjective corresponded to adjective,
noun to noun, and a similarity of ending or resemblance in
sound was sedulously cultivated. Professor Croll's assertion

[1] *Op. cit.*, p. lv.
[2] Adams' sermons are exceptionally rich in examples of *paromoion* ; the
following are some of the many examples to be met with in his works : ed. cit.,
p. 473—" His brain is full of humour, his heart of tumour, his tongue of romour
[=rumour] " ; *ibid.*, p. 921 : " *Schola crucis, Schola lucis* : there is no such
Schoole instructing as the cross inflicting " ; *ibid.*, p. 924 : " And indeed, if
wee consider what Master we have serued, and what wages deserued, we haue
iust cause to abhorre our selves " ; *ibid.*, p. 1002 : " There is the *Diligite* of
the *Heart*, Loue your enemies. The *Benedicite* of the *Tongue*, Blesse them that
curse you. The *Benefacite* of the *Hand*, Doe good to them that hate you. . . .
Loue your enemies, there is *Affectus cordis* ; Doe them good, there is *Effectus
operis* ; . . ." The readiness with which this trait follows similar expressions
in Latin points back to its origin, or rather the immediate spring of its influence in that language.
[3] ' The Fatall Banket,' ed. cit., p. 220 : the passage opening : " As in a faire
Summers morning when the Larke hath called up the Sunne, and the Sunne
the Husbandman : when the earth hath opened her Shop of perfumes, and a
pleasant wind fannes coolenesse through the ayre ; when every creature is
reioyced at the heart ; On a suddaine, &c." is one of the finest in the whole
range of Adams' writings.
[4] *Englands Sicknesse*, ed. cit., p. 306.

that such figures—the last faint echo of classical rhetorical training—enjoyed a florescence in England among the most celebrated of the older preachers at the opening of the seventeenth century is amply justified ; but that the florescence enjoyed a sudden metamorphosis under the influence of Bacon and Donne in the actual sermons of Adams seems hardly tenable. Adams is rather to be regarded as a fellow-worker with these greater writers in breaking down the tyranny of the schematic patterns in the interests of a less pointed, more sonorous style. As early as 1614 we find him able to dispense with the wearisome second half of his antitheses, and close like Bacon with a simple statement, giving a quiet ending without the customary reverberation.[1] Space alone precludes quotation from some of the longer and more matured passages which were obviously what attracted Southey's admiration ; yet the fact remains that in sermons of late date the older, cruder use of the *schemata* recurs, which is to be explained neither as a reversion on the part of Adams, nor, as with Willan's 'Six Sermons,'[2] preached in the sixteen-forties, in terms of Dryden's gibe about stylistic abuses finding benefit of clergy, but simply points to the extraordinary experimentation that was then taking place among English writers—an experimentation in which the pulpit, as represented by Adams and men of his type, took a prominent part. The preacher, like the poet, is both moulded by his age and exerts an influence upon it, and the sermons of Adams present us with the case of a man catering at times for a popular vogue, but who in his published work was undoubtedly preparing the way among his readers for other and less jejune stylistic effects.

(ii) *Hall, Ussher, and Sanderson*

When we pass to Hall, Ussher, and Sanderson, we pass to men each of whom played a conspicuous part on the public stage, and all of whom circumstances of one kind or another rendered influential to a much wider degree than

---

[1] E.g. passage in ' The Sinners Passing-Bell,' beginning, " To all Christians : that we climb up by the stairs of these inferior creatures, &c.," ' The Workes,' 1630, p. 252.

[2] Published in 1651, *vid. ante*, p. 88.

was the case with even so celebrated a Puritan preacher as
Henry Smith.

Of the three, Joseph Hall (1574–1656), bishop successively of Exeter and Norwich, is at once the most interesting
and most important from a literary standpoint. In 1597
he claimed to lead the way as the first English satirist, and
in 1608 he definitely was first to naturalise in England
another type of classical writing—the *character*. Like Donne,
therefore, he was a man of letters before he was a divine,
and throughout his life, morose as he appears to have been
by temper and stern Calvinist as he remained by creed, his
work showed a strong literary impress. In 1837 his works
appeared at Oxford in a new edition in twelve volumes, of
which ' Volume V ' consists of forty-two sermons. These
bear a strong resemblance to Adams in tone, and in the
temperate march of the style, but point on to South by
reason of the type of *wit* which they employ. There is much
learning, often of an out-of-the-way character, reminiscent
of Burton and Ussher. Many quotations occur from, and
still more references to, the Fathers, Schoolmen, and
Rabbinical writers. Hebrew and Greek quotations are
frequently worked into the text, and, as might be expected
from a moralist, the classical satirists are extensively drawn
upon. Hall's moral pieces—such as his ' Meditations and
Vows ' (in three ' centuries '), ' Holy Observations,' ' Select
Thoughts ' or the ' Susurrium cum Deo '—helped him to a
happy knack in beginning his sermons with an aphorism,
naturally expanded, which saved him the trouble of finding
a related, or inventing a not incongruous, exordium. He
could be vivid—very much in the manner of Henry Smith
and Adams—and while his style is seldom actually terse,
it is often, when it is not encumbered by exegesis or citation,
extremely plain and easy to follow, and more nearly resembles the Restoration manner of preaching, before the
reform movement of the Royal Society preachers had
banished both allusion and quotation, than that of any
other Jacobean preacher. His sermons are carefully dated
in the edition issued at Oxford in 1837, and we are thus
able to see him pass from the lively and somewhat highly
coloured style of Adams to the soberer, more moralising
strain of the Caroline preachers, laying aside in his progress
the rather puerile ' conceits ' of the Jacobeans, in exchange

15

for the ingenious and carefully cultivated *wit* of South and his contemporaries.

Preaching in 1618 at the Spittle, Hall described the fashions of the day with a liveliness and indignation more in keeping with the satirist and the pamphleteer than the preacher :

" O God, what a world of vanity hast thou reserved us to ! . . . Imagine one of our forefathers were alive again, and should see one of these his gay daughters walk in Cheapside before him ; what do you think he would think it were ? Here is nothing to be seen but a verdingale, a yellow ruff, and a periwig with perhaps more feathers waving in the top ; three things for which he could not tell how to find a name. Sure, he could not but stand amazed to think what new creature the times had yielded since he was a man ; and if then he should run before her to see if by the foreside he might guess what it were, when his eyes should meet with a powdered frizzle, a painted hide shadowed with a fan not more painted, breasts displayed, and a loose lock erring wantonly over her shoulders, betwixt a painted cloth and skin ; how would he yet more bless himself to think, what mixture in nature could be guilty of such a monster ? " [1]

If Hall had not passed beyond this Nashe-like description he would not be distinguished from a great company of his contemporaries who employed their powers in a similar direction. By 1634, however, we find from a sermon delivered at Court during Lent, that Hall had discarded his early City manner, and was able to treat of much the same theme with dignity and restraint. His style, too, matches his mood, and is plain, orderly, and suggestive of the reflection it was designed to evoke. Yet, as a description of Adam and Eve illustrates, Hall had distinct affinities with South, and the latter's sermon depicting the condition of man before the fall,[2] if smoother in style, is in no way plainer, and is only the perfection of a manner all the characteristics of which were already present in Hall.

" How was it with the first man ? how with the next ? Could we look so far back as to see Adam and Eve, when

[1] Ed. cit., ser. vii, pp. 113–4.
[2] Delivered at St. Paul's, November 1662 ; *vid.* South's ' Works,' Oxf. ed., 1823, vol. i, ser. ii, pp. 37–8, and *post,* p. 319, footnote [3].

they were new turned out of Paradise ? . . .   Here was
Adam, delving with a jaw-bone, and harrowing with sticks
tied uncouthly together, and paring his nails with his
teeth : there was Eve, making a comb of her fingers, and
tying her raw-skinned breeches together with rinds of
trees ; or pinning them up with thorns.   Here was Adam,
tearing off some arm of a tree, to drive in those stakes, which
he hath pointed with some sharp flint ; there Eve, fetching
in her water in a shell : here Adam the first midwife to his
miserable consort ; and Eve wrapping her little one in a
skin lately borrowed from some beast, and laying it on a
pillow of leaves or grass.   Their fist was their hammer ;
their hand, their dish ; their arms and legs, their ladder ;
heaven their canopy ; and earth, their featherbed.   And
now . . . what is Adam ? " [1]

As might be expected in ' the English Seneca,' Hall's
quotations from, and references to, the classical moralists
were more frequent than those of any of his contemporaries
with the exception of Jeremy Taylor, and he alludes to sayings of Zeno, Socrates, or Seneca with an ease which bespeaks long familiarity with, and a sympathetic appreciation
of, their standpoint which would have delighted the
Cambridge Platonists.   In his final manner, if there was
none of the arresting rhetoric of his earlier work, there
was at least a straightforward plainness and directness of
expression,[2] which went far to prove that it was not necessary to be highly pictorial, or persistently allusive, or
ingeniously ' witty,' in order to escape dullness and hold the
attention of one's hearers.   Though Hall's latest manner
lacked the richness of fancy and wealth of illustration which
the prose of his middle period exhibited, yet it had a grammatical solidity and architectonic value of its own, which
augured well for the simple prose style that was to be.
As we have already seen,[3] archbishop Ussher (1581–1656)
is claimed by his biographer Parr to have introduced a

---

[1] From ' The Character of Man : *Laid forth* In a Sermon Preach'd at the
Court, . . . 1634,' Lon., 1635, 8vo, reprinted, Oxf. ed., 1837, vol. v, ser.
xxix, p. 390.
[2] Fuller tells us that Hall was commonly called " the English Seneca,
for the pureness, plainness, and fulness of his style "—Gosse : ' Life and Letters
of John Donne,' vol. i, p. 31.
[3] *Ante*, p. 8.

reform in pulpit style.   This is the more remarkable when we recall the disabilities under which he laboured, largely owing to his delight in piling up citations from the most obscure authors, a habit in which he almost equals Burton. Alluding to this Sir Edmund Chambers writes :

" Argument means for Ussher the accumulation of authorities . . . And with this is connected his renunciation of style ;   for to style the abundance of quotation must needs be fatal " [1] ;

and the same writer tells us :

" Ussher's writing is always a mosaic of quotation.   His learning is immense.   At an early age, so his biographers tell us, he sat down and read the Fathers straight through." [2]

Any of Ussher's writings, consequently, are bound to present difficulties to the student of literature, but in the case of his sermons an additional handicap exists.   Unfortunately, amid all the wealth of Ussher's collected writings, no sermons are preserved to us as they came from his pen.   Professor Elrington, who edited the complete works in 1847,[3] quotes Dr. Bernard, the archbishop's chaplain, as saying that Ussher utterly disowned any sermon-notes which might be issued in his name, and that during his lifetime he had always endeavoured to suppress such. Twenty-two sermons, however, were published in 1660 by John Crabb, William Ball, and Thomas Lye, ministers of the Gospel, who stated that " they writ them from his mouth, and compared their copies together "—an interesting footnote to a discussion of what printed sermon-texts may be said to represent.   To these Elrington added fifteen further sermons from a MS. in Balliol College Library.   The latter are quite equal in merit to the 1660 specimens, but the editor did not feel that either justified publication.

These sermons, on examination, prove to be intolerably dull.   The style is close-packed and full of incessant argu-

[1] Introd. to selections from Ussher's prose in Craik's ' English Prose Selections,' vol. ii, Lon., 1904.

[2] *Ibid.*, vol. ii, Lon., 1904.

[3] ' The Whole Works of the Most Rev. James Ussher, D.D. . . .' Dublin, 1847.

mentation, approaching in this to the manner of Baxter and other of the Commonwealth preachers. Stern and unsympathetic in tone, the message they convey is couched largely in Old Testament terms. Unlike Ussher's other writings, they are not interspersed with lavish allusion and quotation, though it is probable that quotations made during preaching were allowed to drop out by the less learned copyists who " wrote after " the preacher. This, however, seems less likely than that Ussher deliberately avoided learned citations in his sermons, as Parr relates of a noted preacher of the *floride* type, that during Ussher's stay in Oxford in 1642,[1]

" observing how plain, and yet moving they [i.e. Ussher's sermons] were, and being sufficiently satisfied that it was not for want of Wit, or Learning, that he did not do otherwise, he was soon convinced, that this was not the most ready way of gaining Souls, and therefore quitting his affected Style, and studied *Periods*, took up a more plain and profitable way of preaching. . . .[2]

The same writer also tells us of Ussher's customary practice at this period, that—

" notwithstanding the Learnedness of most of his Hearers, he rather chose a plain substantial way of Preaching, for the promoting of Piety and Vertue, than studied Eloquence, or a vain ostentation of Learning : so that he quite put out of countenance that windy, affected sort of Oratory, which was then much in use, called *floride* preaching, or strong lines." [3]

   What precisely was intended by the two last phrases may be gathered from a series of contemporary references. Thus we find Burton ' the Anatomist ' declaring that he has

" writ with so small deliberation as I do ordinarily speak, without all affectation of big words, fustian phrases, jingling

---

[1] It is interesting to Exeter men to know that Dr. Prideaux lent him his house " adjoyning Exeter College " during his stay.
[2] ' The Life of . . . James Usher . . .' 1686, p. 49.
[3] *Ibid.*, pp. 48–9.

terms, tropes, strong lines, that like *Acestes'* arrows caught
fire as they flew, strains of wit, brave heats, elogies, hyper-
bolical exornations, elegancies, &c. which many so affect." [1]

Donne, it is clear from R. B.'s lines on that preacher, was
" humm'd against " by the Puritans as " a strong-lin'd
man " [2] ; and White Kennett in his ' Register ' refers to
Donne's friend and disciple, Henry King, as " a most
admirable and florid Preacher in his younger days." The
epithet ' floride ' is used with some frequency by Wood in
the ' Athenæ,' not always, as is apparently done by Kennett,
in a complimentary sense, but tinged rather with that post-
Restoration dislike of excess with which Evelyn for example
is found employing it. [3]

In short, " floride preaching, or strong lines " were contemporary phrases for what we now describe as ' purple
patches,' especially where a writer or preacher allowed
himself to be carried away by the opportunities of elaborating a particular situation, and neglected for the time being
his main topic. The extravagances of this kind committed
by Jeremy Taylor were in course of time to be criticised by
South, and Parr, it is evident, wished to represent Ussher
as a forerunner of the ' plain ' style of preaching.

That Ussher's influence during the latter years of his life,
when, although greatly respected by men of all parties, the
system of Church government with which he was identified
had been eclipsed, should have been extensive, seems
unlikely, and the plainness of his style is in no way different
from that of hundreds of other clergymen of a Calvinistic
cast of mind who were preaching in the early seventeenth
century. It is just possible, therefore, that Parr's words
" put out of countenance " should be taken to refer to the
impression excited by a sermon of Ussher's compared with
one of Donne's or Taylor's rather than to any influence he
exerted, and may be paraphrased thus : No one who had
heard the plain and direct manner of Ussher would desire
to return to the old florid preaching. Taken thus the statement would read like personal appreciation, and no claim

---

[1] ' The Anatomy of Melancholy,' ed. cit., vol. i, p. 30.
[2] I am indebted for this reference to Professor Grierson, who also first
made clear to me the importance of Parr's remark.
[3] *Vid.* ' Diary,' 30th January, 1688, 24th March, 1695.

to a reformation of pulpit manner would seem to be advanced.

The interests that attach to the name of Robert Sanderson (1587–1663), during the greater part of his life rector of Boothby Pagnell, Regius Professor of Divinity at Oxford (1642), and finally, after the Restoration, bishop of Lincoln, are at least threefold : in his lifetime he enjoyed a great reputation as a casuist, being as one biographer states " himself for many years the *publike Reason* of the Church " [1] ; his style of writing was so highly thought of by his contemporaries that he was employed to write the new offices added to ' the Book of Common Prayer ' at the Restoration ; and he was one of five fortunate men of whose lives Isaac Walton has left delightful accounts.   From Walton we learn that—

" there was in his sermons no improper rhetoric, nor such perplexed divisions, as may be said to be like too much light, that so dazzles the eyes, that the sight becomes less perfect : but there was therein no want of useful matter, nor waste of words ; and yet such clear distinctions as dispelled all confused notions, and made his hearers depart both wiser, and more confirmed in virtuous resolutions." [2]

By another biographer we are given a description of Sanderson's immense pains in " meditating and composing his Sermons to rational and just Discourses," [3] while Walton further testifies to his inability to deliver anything unwritten and the hesitancy which caused him to write and re-write what he was to deliver—traits which probably prevented him from following his contemporaries in the production of tomes of theological learning.   As it is, we possess only thirty-six sermons from his pen.

Of these thirty-six sermons, produced over a period of twenty-nine years (1619–48), seventeen were preached AD AULAM, five AD CLERUM, six AD MAGISTRATUM, and eight AD POPULUM.   All are heavy, weighted, theological pro-

---

[1] ' Reason *and* Judgement : Or, Special Remarques Of the Life Of the *Renowned* Dr. Sanderson . . .' Lon., 1663. Signed at end D. F. (? Daniel Featley).

[2] " Life of Dr. Robert Sanderson," in Walton's ' Lives,' Temple Classics ed., 1878, vol. ii, pp. 287–8.

[3] In ' Reason and Judgement.'

ductions, and, although seven of the eight sermons AD POPULUM were delivered at Paul's Cross, these prove no exception to the general tenor of Sanderson's style. The style, which is impressive in an ecclesiastical preface (that beginning " It hath been the wisdom of the Church of England . . ." occurring in ' the Book of Common Prayer ' is from his pen), is far from being suited to the ordinary uses of preaching, nor when it appears in print can it be called literary. Yet there are certain interests in Sanderson's work. For one thing the authors from whom he quotes are noteworthy. Although fond of Tully's ' Offices,' "which he had not read over less than twenty times, and could [in later life] say without book," [1] he was equally familiar with much of Juvenal and Persius and the whole of the odes of Horace. These tastes revealed by Walton, and the number of quotations from Cicero, Seneca, Horace, and Juvenal discoverable in the thirty-six sermons, entitle Sanderson to a place among those Jacobean preachers whose interests were rather ' moral ' than ' dogmatic,' and who delighted in pointing assent to the great maxims of morality in the writings of the Pagan moralists. The tendency is most pronounced in Hall and Jeremy Taylor, and, as we have heard Andrewes saying, met with the disapproval of the less cultured Puritans who would not suffer a preacher to quote from any book but the Bible [2] ; but the tendency persisted, and when the patristic erudition of Andrewes' own school had fallen into disuse, reappeared at the end of the century in the works of Tillotson and his contemporaries.

A quotation from Lipsius' ' Epistolæ ' occurring in a sermon of 1664,[3] taken along with the general characteristics of his prose, places Sanderson, in company with Hall, among the Anti-Ciceronians, and his plainness of style and moralistic tone constitute his claims to our attention ; for, in the works of such men as Hall, Ussher, and Sanderson we recognise the existence of a parallel band of preaching extending alongside of the ' metaphysicals,' and forming the connecting link between the more highly coloured early Jacobean sermon and the quieter vogue with which the century terminated.

---

[1] *Vid.* Walton's ' Life,' ed. cit., p. 300.   [2] *Vid. ante,* p. 10.
[3] ' The Works of Robert Sanderson, D.D. . . .' Oxf., 1854, vol. iii, ser. xvi, p. 420.

(iii) Thomas Fuller

Alike in ' wit ' and outlook Thomas Fuller (1608–1661) is separated by a great gulf from those ' witty ' preachers whose work has already been examined. Not only were his political views too temperate to please the enthusiasts for Divine Right among his own party, and his ecclesiastical views not sufficiently rigid to meet with the approval of the school of Andrewes and Laud, but his ' wit ' is of an entirely different stamp. Fuller's ' wit ' depends on that genuine observation of similitudes (" such as are but rarely observed by others "), in which Hobbes considered the essence of true ' wit ' to consist,[1] is always spontaneous, and results from the turning and re-turning of a subject in the preacher's mind, so that facet after facet is exposed to the light of the glowing imagination and allowed to flash back its peculiar and often unexpectedly beautiful reflection. But always the resultant observation—the remark or the image in which the ' wit ' lies—is cognate to the original subject, either in such a way as to be readily appreciable by the hearer, or unexpectedly revealed by the adroit handling of the preacher. Fuller's " singular fertility in conjoining strange societies of thought," as Professor Saintsbury has called this process, seldom results in the ebullitions which we associate with Andrewes, and never in the impudent witticisms and ingenious conceits of South. Neither is his ' wit ' of the strict ' metaphysical ' sort, of which Donne is the great exemplar, with his amazing power of extracting from the far recesses of an erudite and idiosyncratic memory such strange correspondences in thought or fancy as surprised and delighted his auditory. Fuller's ' wit ' is something much more homely, and is due to his great familiarity with the Bible and his fine, catholic acquaintance with the every-day life of men, which continually suggested to him resemblances and applications, such as an eighteenth-century writer or a modern would either not see, or deliberately avoid employing in the interests of selection and literary self-restraint. Coleridge's oft-repeated remark that " wit was the stuff and substance of Fuller's intellect," [2] is a singularly unfortunate way of describing the working of the

[1] ' Leviathan ' (A. R. Waller's reprint of ed. of 1651—Camb. English Classics, 1904, p. 42), Part I, chap. viii.
[2] ' Notes on English Divines,' 1853, vol. i, p. 127.

latter's mind ; rather " the element, the earthen base, the
material which he worked in " (to make use of Coleridge's
metaphor), may be seen to have been a comparatively
limited range of contemporary reading, which, taken along
with his shrewd observation of men and insight into their
motives, was formative of an almost continuous series of
wise, kindly, and unexpectedly lively comparisons and
admonitions.   And it is in these, that, so far as his sermons
are concerned, Fuller's ' wit ' is comprised.

Fuller's sermons, although they appeared frequently in
print and sold readily during his life, remained uncollected
until 1891, when an edition, planned and largely carried
out by John Eglington Bailey—a Manchester business man
and admirer of Fuller—was completed and published by a
friend, W. E. A. Axon.[1] The sermons indicate the temperate
and clear-sighted outlook of the man, who was equally quick
to reprove injustice in his own party as sedition in that of
their opponents, and who, believing the function of the
Christian ministry to be one of reconciliation, endeavoured
in an age of faction to prepare the people at large for the
possibility of a settlement on a basis of generous compromise.
His moderate ecclesiastical position and fearless criticism of
all parties are made explicit by a series of utterances,[2] but this
very moderation and criticism tended to isolate him from all
parties, and must have gone far to limit the influence of his
pulpit style.   That style was itself a kind of compromise,
held together, as has previously been noticed,[3] by the
Doctrines and *Uses* dear to the Puritan, but enlivened by a
richness of fancy and allusion to secular matters foreign to
Parliamentary preaching.

[1] ' The Collected Sermons of Thomas Fuller, D.D., 1631–1659,' 2 vols.,
Lon., 1891 (Large Paper Edition limited to 100 copies).   The references are
to this edition.   Bailey was also the author of ' The Life of Thomas Fuller '
(1874), which remains the standard biography.

[2] E.g. in ' A Fast Sermon Preached on Innocents Day,' 1642, in which he
makes a strenuous appeal for peace.   He rebukes at once those who were
urging extreme reforms on the grounds that they were " necessary to salvation," and dissociates himself from the Anglo-Catholicising tendencies of Laud
and his disciples (ed. cit., vol. i, p. 249) ; yet with regard to the Ceremonies,
Fuller's attitude was precisely that of Donne : " Surely God would have the
Church, his Spouse, as not a Harlot, so not a slut. . . . (' Iosephs Party-
coloured Coat,' ser. vii ; *ibid.*, vol. i, p. 217).   His ' Triple Reconciler,'
issued in 1654 (' B. & A.,' vol. ii, p. 293 *seq.*), reveals him as one who, whatever his own preference, was desirous at all costs to keep the peace of the
Church (*vid.* especially, pp. 318 and 327).

[3] *Ante*, p. 119.

The over-eager commendation and acrimonious criticism
of contemporary preachers were very distasteful to Fuller,
and his vignette of the London Puritan at a slightly later
period of his zeal than we find him described by Andrewes
or Ben Jonson, when the prevailing topic of his conversation
had become religion, and he could quote Scripture with the
frequency of the interlocutors in the ' Friendly Debates,' is
interesting as revealing not only his personal disapproval
but also the frank demand of the contemporary auditor
that a sermon should not only be spiritually impressive but
rhetorically effective :

" Thus will they fall out about their Pastors.   The living
Minister is mine ; he that hath life, spirit, and Activity
in the manner and matter of his Delivery ; but the dead
Minister is thine [1] ; flash in his matter, confused in his
Method, dreaming in his utterance ; hee cometh not to
the quicke ; hee toucheth not the conscience ; at the most
with *Ioash*, King of Israel, 2 *Kings* 13, 18.   *He smites the
Aramites but thrice* ; leaves off reproving a vice before people
bee fully reformed.   Nay, saith the other, my Minister is
the living Minister, and thine is the dead one : Thy Pastor
is like the fire, 1 *Kings* 19, 12, flashing in the flames of ill-
tempered and undiscreete Zeale ; *but the Lord was not in the
fire* : or like the Earthquake, shaking his Auditors with ill
applyed terrors of the Law ; *but the Lord was not in the
Earthquake :* whilest my Minister is like to a *still voyce* ; *and
the Lord was in the still Voyce ;* stanching the Bleeding hearted
Penitent, and dropping the Oyle of the Gospel into the
wounded Conscience." [2]

Fuller himself believed in plain, practical preaching, and
this he regarded as in accordance with the example of the
Holy Scriptures.   Dealing with so definitive an expression
as *Bethlehem-Iudah*, he remarked :

" The *Holy Spirit* descends to our capacity, and in Scripture doth multiply words to make the matter the plainer :
let this teach the Sons of *Levi*, when they deliver one doubtful

---

[1] An allusion to 1 Kings iii. 22, where the contention of the mothers before
Solomon is related, to which Fuller has made reference.
[2] " Faction Confuted," ser. viii of ' Eight Sermons,' ' B. & A,' vol. i, p. 224.

and ambiguous Doctrine which may admit of several constructions (so that there is danger least [= lest] that people
may mistake their meaning,) to demur a while on such a
point, and not to be niggardly of their words, till they have
blotted all doubt and difficulty out of it." [1]

In other words, Fuller agreed with Hyperius that—

" the preacher doth not use amplification, to the intent to
bring to passe, that the matter might appere either greater
or lesser then it is of it selfe, or . . . in which point the
Rhetoritians doe most chiefely laboure, couetinge withall
to corrupte the iugement of the hearers . . . but to the
ende . . . to reclayme men erring from the truth, to a
prudent and sincere iudgement." [2]

Amplification, however, seldom meant for him, as it did
definitely for Jeremy Taylor, expatiation, but consisted
rather in the untold wonders of association which a phrase,
or often a single word, suggested to him, and which he
immediately shared with his hearers.

Such association with Fuller was seldom far-fetched or
drawn from sources unfamiliar to the bulk of the auditories
before whom he preached as was much of the habitual
imagery of the 'metaphysicals.' The background of
patristic allegory, rabbinical learning, and 'unnatural
natural history,' common to most early seventeenth-century
preachers, does not bulk largely in Fuller. It is seldom or
never used as a groundwork upon which to embroider quaint
or fantastic devices such as we find in Donne or Andrewes.
This, as we have noted, was not the stuff out of which Fuller
wove his ' wit ' ; he needed no such skeins ; his web was
autogenous as that of the spider. " To omit diuers Allegories," he says in one place,[3] " which Saint Augustine and
Gregorie have observed vpon this passage," and proceeds
to more practical observations. In another sermon he
remarks :

" All Metaphors in Scriptures must be tenderly toucht,

[1] ' Comment on Ruth,' ' B. & A.,' vol. i, p. 11.
[2] Ludham's trans. of Hyperius, ' The Practice of Preaching . . .' 1577,
chap. xv.
[3] ' Jacob's Vow,' ' B. & A.,' vol. i, p. 416.

lest . . . they be tortured to speake beyond and against their true intention." [1]

With him the practical application always ranked highest. When he asserts, therefore :

" Every Prick, Comma, and Accent hath his Emphasis, and must be pronounced in our practice," [2]

we can be certain that he will not lead us into any by-paths of scholastic speculation, but desires only to arrive at the plain sense of his text for our edification. Rabbinical speculations, and, in particular, those concerning numbers, he curtly dismisses.[3] Natural history of the Pliny-*Physiologus* type he turned rather more frequently to account ; but it is to be remembered that Pliny was still ' scientific ' in Fuller's day, and, in any case, the examples he employs are of a less grotesque order than those found in many of his contemporaries.[4]

Gnomic wisdom, it is obvious, attracted Fuller,[5] and so found place in his sermons [6]—probably in his case a

---

[1] ' The Grand Assizes,' ' B. & A.,' vol. ii, p. 278.

[2] ' A Christening Sermon,' ' B. & A.,' vol. i, p. 219.

[3] Twice he alludes to the " conceit " of the Rabbins " that Manna relished so to the pallats of the Jews just as the eater thereof did fancy or desire " (' Feare of losing the Old Light,' ' B. & A.,' vol. i, p. 458 ; vol. ii, p. 552 ; in the latter instance he adds : " Having the gust of flesh, fish or fowl, roast, boyl'd, or bak'd, as the eater thereof did wish or desire." If, as Axon thinks, Heycock was the founder of Heycock's Ordinary, this last touch would be distinctly appropriate to the occasion—Heycock's funeral). No other rabbinical speculations are mentioned. Of numbers he remarks : " I am no super-stitious observer, or ceremonious affecter of mystical numbers " (' VIIIth Sermon on the Temptation,' ' B. & A.,' vol. ii, p. 65) ; and he is true to his remark when dealing with the circumcision of infants on the eighth day, saying : " There I will not search with some for a secret sanctity in the Number of *eight* (as consisting of *seven*, the Embleme of *Perfection*, with the Addition of *one*, that is Intirenesse,) lest our Casuistry reap what Gods wisdom never sowed therein " (' The Infant's Advocate,' ' B. & A.,' vol. ii, p. 135).

[4] Examples of this type of natural history are a reference to the time-honoured Camomile (' Com. on 1 Cor. xi,' ' B. & A.,' vol. i, p. 138) ; to the belief that Sage was poisoned by the toad resting under its roots (' The Infant's Advocate,' ' B. & A.,' vol. ii, p. 233) ; and to " the Providence of the Pismire in biting both ends of the corn which she is about to store for the winter " (' The True Penitent,' ' B. & A.,' vol. ii, pp. 429–30.

[5] In his ' Worthies,' for example, among other introductory remarks on each county he carefully recounts such proverbs as he had noted or been able to collect.

[6] E.g. ' *The Master's eye maketh a fat Horse*,' he quotes, and continues : " And one asking, what was the best compost to Manure Land, it was answered,

characteristic substitution for an aphorism borrowed from a classical moralist, and certainly turned to similar account. This love of pithy sayings is no doubt connected with the brevity which his method of preaching entailed, but which is noticeable also in his other works. Such of his sermons as form a running commentary on a given portion of Scripture reveal his pulpit-manner at its best, but though discursive, his writings are never lacking in method.

"Marshal thy notions with a handsome method" (is his own advice). "One will carry twice more weight trussed and packed up in bundles, than when it lies untoward flapping about the shoulders. Things evenly fardled up and hanging under both heads are most portable." [1]

But the method, it is obvious, is not one which lends itself to the beauties of the cursive style. On the other hand, Fuller's diction is plain, straightforward English, hardly anywhere archaic after the lapse of two and a half centuries, in which the proportion of words of Latin and Saxon origin is mingled without any affectation or pedantry. Only one expression in the whole of his sermons arrests the attention by a conjunction of Latinate words, when he speaks of "an erratical and circumfraneous motion." [2]   Apart from this and the use of the word "comically," with the meaning "beginning happily" (derived from the mediæval definition of "comedy"), to describe the opening of one of St. Paul's voyages, [3] the sermons are entirely modern in their employment of the English language.

Another noteworthy feature of Fuller's sermons is their freedom from the old schematic features. Only one notable example of this fashion calls for remark, and that in the early 'Comment on Ruth' (1631) :

"How quickly may a *Crassus*, or *Cræsus*, be turned into a *Codrus* ; the richest, into the poorest of men. Whom

the dust of the Masters feet, meaning his presence to behold his own business " (' Com. on Ruth,' ' B. & A.,' IX, vol. i, p. 70) ; " ' *A whet is no let*,' saith the Proverb " : he recalls at another time, " Mowers lose not any time, which they spare in whetting or grinding of their Scythes " (*ibid*., p. 75).

[1] ' The Life and Wit of Thomas Fuller, D.D.'—prefixed to vol. i of ' B. & A.,' p. xxviii.
[2] ' The Best Employment,' ' B. & A.,' vol. ii, p. 397.
[3] ' B. & A.,' vol. ii, p. 329 (' The Second Reconciler ').

the Sunne-rising seeth in wealth, him the Sunne-setting may see in want." [1]

The specimen shows what Fuller might have done in this kind if he had cared to try. Fortunately his genius was too virile to expend itself constructing such trifles, and though often brief he is rarely " pointed," and then rather by accident than affectation.

Homeliness might have been expected from an author so rich in gnomic wisdom and interested in what one might almost call the folk-lore of country places. His fine sense of the sacredness of his office, however, seems to have prevented him from indulging to any great extent in homely expressions ; when he does use such it is never in the colloquial manner of Andrewes in his City sermons, but rather with a kind of unexpected naïveté, as when he says of prayer :

" Neither length nor shortness is any whit considerable to the acceptableness thereof, but the thickness of a prayer, when it is not empty nor hollow within, but well filled with Faith in the heart and middle thereof." [2]

' Conceits ' he did not much favour, although such a touch as " let us deliver our doctrine in common, and let the guilty conscience inclose it to it selfe," [3] shows what he was capable of on occasion ; but for the most part he will be found to be naturally quaint rather than deliberately striving after surprising effects. The extraordinary range and fertility of his ' wit ' are only difficult to illustrate from the multiplicity and variety of its examples. The amazing resemblances and association of ideas which occurred to Fuller cannot fail to excite in his readers (as they did in Coleridge) " the sense and emotion of the marvellous." The most unlikely sources supply him with comparisons. Thus the nefarious practices of rogues and witches yield him metaphors :

" Drunkards " (he says) " are distinguish't from the Kings sober subjects by clipping the coyn of the tongue " [4] ;

and—

[1] ' B. & A.,' vol. i, p. 62.
[2] ' The Third Reconciler,' ' B. & A.,' vol. ii, p. 365.
[3] ' A Christening Sermon,' ' B. & A.,' vol. i, p. 215.
[4] ' Eight Sermons,' ' B. & A.,' vol. i, p. 199.

" Concupiscence the witch in our souls says all the Commandments backward." [1]

At times the ' wit ' consists in a topical, or an historical, allusion, as :

" The Pope pretendeth to be the onely Successor of S. *Peter*, but in this [i.e. in denying Christ] we all have sate in his *chair*, we all have denied our Master " [2] ;

or when Latimer and Ridley are said to have borne

" the heat of the day indeed, which were burnt to ashes." [3]

Sometimes the ' wit ' results in a beautiful expression, as :

" Thanksgiving makes every creature both chew the cud, and cleave the hoofe " [4] ;

or—

" the Dove of the Spirit will not build in a Nest of [man's] [5] making, but in one of her own providing " [6] ;

always it has a liveliness and sparkle which were unknown to the ' conceit.' Many of the best examples are those which are richest in allusion to Scriptural phrasing or incident. Thus Fuller notes that Naomi, though poor, was related to the rich Boaz, and continues :

" Let this confute such as having gotten a little more thick clay than the rest of their Family, the getting of new wealth and honour makes them to lose their old eyes, so that they cannot see and distinguish their poor kindred afterwards." [7]

This is true ' wit,' and requires a familiarity with Scripture in the auditor to recall the healing of the blind man by

1 ' The Worst of Evils,' ' B. & A.,' vol. ii, p. 512.
2 ' The True Penitent,' ' B. & A.,' vol. ii, p. 434.
3 ' A Sermon of Reformation,' ' B. & A.,' vol. i, p. 307.
4 ' Com. on 1 Cor. xi,' ' B. & A.,' vol. i, p. 141.
5 Text ' this,' sense ' man's.'
6 ' The Infant's Advocate,' ' B. & A.,' vol. ii, p. 237.
7 ' Com. on Ruth,' ' B. & A.,' vol. i, p. 45.

Christ through the anointing with clay, so that the heinous-
ness of the *nouveaux riches* in inverting the process may be
apparent.   In the same manner he exclaims :

" O how glorious in Heaven will S. *Peter* appear ? who at
the preaching of one Sermon gained *Acts* 2, 4, *three thousand
souls*.   What a Constellation, what a Firmament of stars
will he alone be ? " [1]

a passage dependent for its ' wit ' on an Old Testament
allusion ? [2]

Such examples are no less creditable to the ' wit ' of the
preacher than testimony to the Scriptural knowledge of his
hearers, and illustrate the place of allusion and reminiscence
rather than startling and surprising resemblances in Fuller's
' wit ' ; but in most instances they are, as indeed Lamb
has described the characteristic sallies of Fuller's ' wit,' such
as " could never have entered into a head less entertain-
ingly constructed than that of Fuller," [3] and for this reason
may be said to place Fuller, so far as the other divines of
his period are concerned, in a category by himself.   Vivid,
plain, and earnest as Fuller's sermon-style is, the same
qualities which made him quaint and ' witty ' prevented
him from falling into line with any other group of stylists.
His ' wit,' as we have seen, was not of the ' metaphysical '
sort, yet his sermons showed him to be too spontaneous a
stylist—too rich in fancy and elegant in expression, too fond
above all of introducing an odd anecdote in the manner
almost of the Popish postillers—to make him acceptable
among the Parliamentarians.   What his influence was, if
any, it is difficult to guess.   Almost certainly he was
appreciated by a select company of moderate men in his
own time, but his manner was too individual to be imitated,
nor did circumstances favour the attempt.   During the
Commonwealth he preached on sufferance, and once the
Restoration was an accomplished fact, even had he survived
longer than merely to write his panegyric on Charles II's
return, his style was not such as was likely to have won
recognition among returning royalists.

[1] ' The Infant's Advocate,' ' B. & A.,' vol. ii, p. 243.
[2] Viz. to Daniel xii. 3.
[3] Footnote to ' Specimens from the Writings of Fuller,' reprinted in ' Collected
Works of Charles Lamb,' Lon., 1840 (Moxon).

16

(iv) Jeremy Taylor

Very different from the work of Fuller or of the ' witty ' preachers of the school of Andrewes is that of Jeremy Taylor (1613–1667), who alone of seventeenth-century divines has continued to be familiarly known from his own to the present time. While Barrow and Tillotson have long been mere names, and Donne's merits have only within recent years had full justice done them, it has been customary to couple Taylor's name with that of Sir Thomas Browne as one of the two great masters of ornate English prose in his own century. His fame, too, has been kept alive in another quarter, and Taylor's ' Holy Living ' and ' Holy Dying,' if for a time their recognition was less universal than that accorded ' The Whole Duty of Man,' have always ranked high among Anglican works of devotion, and hold a place in the affections of English churchmen equalled only by George Herbert's poems. Both as a man of letters, therefore, and as a divine Taylor has received due recognition from his countrymen, and, among other lives and studies of the man and his writings, it is interesting to record that of Willmott, who in his little book, ' Bishop Jeremy Taylor, His Predecessors, Contemporaries and Successors,' published in 1847, endeavoured for the first time to supply some definite account of the changes in pulpit oratory observable in England from the time of Fisher to that of Sherlock and Atterbury. Necessarily brief as Willmott's treatment of the subject is, it shows a generous acquaintance with the divines of the period and a sound appreciation of both their merits and their weaknesses ; and so honest an effort to ' place ' Taylor with reference to the history of English preaching from the sixteenth to the eighteenth centuries is greatly to the author's credit.

The present summary of Taylor's work must be even more brief and less adequate, but in the case of an author among whose biographers has been numbered Sir Edmund Gosse [1] no necessity for a detailed appreciation exists. It will suffice, therefore, to indicate briefly what are the chief characteristics of Taylor's sermon-style, to what extent, like Fuller's, they were personal and unique, and to what extent they bore resemblance to the work of his contemporaries.

[1] In ' English Men of Letters ' Series, 1903.

Taylor's sermons fall into two series covering a period of ten years, with eleven unconnected sermons, of which two were demonstrably preached and published before the Restoration and the other nine after that event.[1] In addition, there is a funeral sermon on Sir George Dalstone. The two main series are formed by the ' XXVIII Sermons Preached at Golden Grove ; Being for the Summer half-year,' which appeared in 1651, and consisted of a sermon for each Sunday in the year from Whit-Sunday until the twenty-fifth Sunday after Trinity, to which was added a funeral sermon on the Countess of Carbery, with the ' XXV Sermons ' of 1653, which completed this collection (known in its later and complete form as the ENIAYTOΣ), and the twenty inset ' Discourses ' judiciously interpolated in the narrative of ' The Great Exemplar,' where such ' discourses ' (as that on ' Obedience ' following the ' Considerations ' on the Circumcision) might be regarded as corresponding in some way to the incidents treated of in the previous section. ' The Great Exemplar ' was published in 1649, but, as Taylor, in one of three dedications to different parts of this work, attributed its ' first designe ' to Spencer Compton, Earl of Northampton, who was killed at Hopton Heath in 1643,[2] it may be fairly safely assumed that some at least of the material composing it, and probably all the ' discourses ' or sermons, were already in existence before the battle in which that nobleman lost his life. This dating would give us the period 1643–53 as that of Taylor's main oratorical activity. The scattered sermons add little to our knowledge or appreciation of his style, although two of his post-Restoration sermons, taken along with the sermon at Lady Carbery's funeral, entitle him to a unique place as the author of what must be considered the nearest approach in English to the *oraison funèbre*.

Dismissing the early Gunpowder sermon, which is merely an exercise set him by his patron Laud, it is noticeable that the materials that went to the making of the early sermons,

---

[1] These are the sermons appearing in the ΔΕΚΑΣ ΕΜΒΟΛΙΜΑΙΟΣ ; the two early sermons are the Gunpowder Treason one of 1638, and that at the funeral of the Countess of Carbery, 1650.

[2] ' The Great Exemplar . . . the History of the Life and Death of the ever Blessed Jesus. . . . In Three Parts,' Lon., 1649, 4to, ep. ded. of Part II, to Mary, Countess Dowager of Northampton. *Vide* also Gosse : ' Jeremy Taylor,' pp. 54–6.

now embodied in ' The Great Exemplar,' were the same as are discoverable in the ΕΝΙΑΥΤΟΣ—namely, a wealth of Biblical, patristic, and classical allusion, in almost equal ratio, a poetical fancy, and unusual felicity of language. It is true, the earlier sermons exhibit fewer sustained flights of imagination, and the tendency to expatiation independent of the general tenor of a passage is less marked, but they are nevertheless quite obviously the preludes of the nightingale. The two styles which are always found alternating in Taylor are also clearly marked, and the transition is effected easily from the rhapsodies of his more poetical manner to the plain, matter-of-fact statement of his ordinary prose.

Taylor's connection early in life with those divines who gathered about Falkland at Great Tew and prepared the way to some extent for the rationalistic divines, though themselves afterwards practically compelled to renounce the more purely philosophic standpoint from which they set out, is apparent from a statement which occurs in the ' Preface ' to ' The Great Exemplar,' in which he expresses the opinion that—

" the wisest persons, and those who know how to value and entertain the more noble faculties of their soule, and their precious houres, take more pleasure in reading the productions of those old wise spirits, who preserved naturall reason and religion in the midst of heathen darknesse (such as are *Homer*, *Euripides*, *Orpheus*, *Pindar*, and *Anacreon*, *Æschylus*, and *Menander*, and all the Greeke Poets : *Plutarch* and *Polybius*, *Xenophon* and all those other excellent persons of both faculties (whose choicest dictates are collected by *Stobæus*) *Plato* and his Schollers, *Aristotle* and after him *Porphyry*, and all his other Disciples, Pythagoras and his, especially Hierocles : all the old Academicks and Stoicks with the Roman Schooles) more pleasure I say in reading these then the trifling of many of the later Schoolemen, who promoted a petty interest of a family, or an unlearned opinion with great earnestnesse, but added nothing to Christianity, but trouble, scruple and vexation." [1]

Such a statement gives at once the clue to much of Taylor's

[1] Preface to ' Great Exemplar,' ed. cit., § 44. (The pages of the preface are unnumbered.)

work, and differentiates him from Donne and the preachers who followed and imitated Andrewes. The interest of the latter in the Fathers and Schoolmen was in their doctrinal statements, whereas Taylor draws upon these authors purely by way of enforcing a moral lesson or supplying a graceful turn of expression. The continuous flow of classical allusion, also, although closely allied to the line of thought pursued by Sheldon, Morley, and others of the Great Tew group, was used less to stimulate the appeal to reason as with Cudworth, More, and the Cambridge Platonists, or, as with men like Hall, to rebuke Christian laxity by drawing the contrast provided by the finest expressions of heathen morality, than out of a frank desire for decorative effect.

" His reading " (as Coleridge truly remarked) " had been oceanic ; but he read rather to bring out the growths of his own fertile and teeming mind than to inform himself respecting the products of those of other men." [1]

The æsthetic allusion rather than the authoritative decision was what Taylor valued, and the resultant beauty of his prose confirms the wisdom of his method. It is plain, too, that his style is an ' allusive ' one, and does not depend, as did so much of contemporary pulpit oratory, on the commonplace-book.[2] It is the choice recollection awakened in the well-stored mind by some more recent circumstance that results in the sudden allusion or the beautifully initiated train of thought. This does not mean to say that all Taylor's learning was of the recollected type, and there are instances, as Gosse pertinently remarks,[3] in which the book he happened to be reading at the moment supplied him with a continuous succession of beautiful quotations or references. But in Taylor we break with the carefully transplanted paragraph, and one touch of the lute-string suffices to reveal the melody, as the fragrance and per-fection of the rose is conjured up by its name.

[1] ' Notes on English Divines,' 1853, vol. i, p. 209.
[2] Though his acquaintance with the works of Drexilius, author of the ' Aurifodina,' already noted (ante, p. 82), is to be kept in mind.
[3] ' Jeremy Taylor,' p. 103 : " When he wrote ' Apples of Sodom ' his mind was steeped in the Hecuba of Euripides ; ' The Marriage Ring ' testifies to his deep enjoyment of the Greek Anthology ; when he sat down to meditate on ' Christian Simplicity,' he had just been reading the third book of Cicero's ' Offices.' "

Taylor's main body of sermons—those enshrined in the ΕΝΙΑΥΤΟΣ—were preached before a small and choice auditory in the private chapel of Lord Carbery's house at Golden Grove, in South Wales, and the nature of his auditory and preaching-scene is reflected in his discourses. His "special design" in his preaching, as he acknowledges in his dedication of the 1653 volume, was " to describe the greater lines of Dutie by speciall arguments " ; and he continues :

" If any witty Censurer shall say, that I tell him nothing but what he knew before ; I shall be contented with it, and rejoyce that he was so well instructed, and wish also that he needed not a Remembrancer : but if either in the first, or in the second, in the institution of some, or the reminding of others, I can doe God any service : no man ought to be offended, that Sermons are not like curious inquiries after New-nothings, but pursuances of Old truths." [1]

Taylor's aim was thus confessedly removed from the lively reprehension of the City Puritans, such as Henry Smith or Adams. In place of the topical allusion in which the latter indulged we find continual references to the classics, and the "numbering of healths by the numeral letters of Philenium's name," [2] or the immodest customs of the Persian women at feasts,[3] are substituted for the descriptions of the intemperate and the unchaste found in the earlier preachers. Neither did the allegorisation or delight in rabbinical exegesis in which the Anglo-Catholic divines revelled appeal to Taylor. Like all other learning with which he was familiar he was only interested in those branches so far as they were able to supply him with illustration or ornament. Unlike Donne he was not seriously concerned whether Adam stayed one night in Paradise or only part of the day on which he was created,

[1] All quotations are made from ' ΕΝΙΑΥΤΟΣ : A Course of Sermons for All the Sundies of the Year . . .' Lon., 1653 (sixes), sm. fol., which consists of 'XXVIII Sermons Preached at Golden Grove ; Being for the Summer half-year . . .' 1651, and 'XXV Sermons Preached at Golden-Grove ; Being for the Winter half-year . . .' 1653 (the additional sermon being that preached at the Countess of Carbery's funeral) along with the work entitled ' Clerus Domini : Or, A Discourse Of the Office Ministerial . . .' 1651. The two series of sermons retain their own numbering and pagination.
[2] ' XXV Sermons,' sermon XV, ' The House of Feasting,' p. 192.
[3] *Ibid.*, p. 200.

but he turns to account the rabbinical glosses on the early
chapters of Genesis in order to warn men of the danger of
prosperity.[1]   At another time, he tells a story which " the
old Rabbins those Poets of religion report of Moses,"[2]
merely because it adds colour to what he is relating at the
moment.   In this he was adopting the attitude of the early
Puritans rather than that of Andrewes and his school.

Curious natural history is to be met with in plenty in
Taylor, but it is never introduced ludicrously as so often in
his predecessors, and always as part of a simile.   Angels
obviously fascinated him,[3] but not so that recondite angelo-
logy which attracted Donne, and we find him employing the
Biblical reference to the angels who visited Sodom, which
later became the source of a scholastic question [4] to which
Donne alludes,[5] in a practical manner in order to arouse
men to the peril of sin.[6]

In the use of such material, however, Taylor was always
content to allude and pass on, and in spite of his fondness for
rhetorical cumulation, he never loaded any passage with a
mere list of citations, as was common with other preachers.
" I need no more authorities to this purpose," he declared
on one occasion when he had made two quotations from
St. Paul ; " these two are as certain and convincing as two
thousand." [7]

Of Taylor's debt to the Classics it is impossible to speak
adequately, so interpenetrated are all his sermons (as indeed
all his writings) with allusions to or direct quotations from
the classical poets or moralists.   Sir Edmund Gosse
notes

" his extraordinary fondness for dissolving little crystals of
such very profane writers as Martial, Catullus, and Petronius
in his holy discourse,"

---

[1] ' XXVIII Sermons,' sermon XII, ' The Mercy of the Divine Ivdgments,'
p. 154.
[2] *Ibid.*, sermon XIX, ' The Foolish Exchange,' p. 249.
[3] *Ibid.*, sermon XXI, ' Of Christian Prudence,' p. 270 ; sermon XXVI,
' The Miracles of the Divine Mercy,' p. 336, and elsewhere in all his
works.
[4] Aquinas : ' Summa Theol.,' *Pars Prima*, Quæst. lii, Art. 2.
[5] ' LXXX Sermons,' sermon lv, p. 550 (D).
[6] ' XXVIII Sermons,' sermon III, ' The Descending and Entailed Cvrse
Cut off,' p. 30.
[7] *Ibid.*, sermon VI, ' The Invalidity of a death-bed Repentance,' p. 73.

which is somewhat oddly illustrated by the way

" in which he has (in ' Of the Spirit of Grace ' [1]) built up a most brilliant summary of the mysteries of our faith on a basis so little to be anticipated as a tag from an ode of Anacreon." [2]

The spontaneity of his allusions may be gathered from the following, which is intended to illustrate that when general maxims are laid down by law there is no need to descend to particulars :

" When the Athenians forbad to transport figs from Athens, there was no need to name the gardens of Alcibiades, much lesse was it necessary to adde that Chabrias should send no plants to Sparta." [3]

Whether or not even his peculiarly select auditory followed Taylor is of little moment ; his allusions, so far as they are historical, are just, while at the same time they serve to give colour and variety to his prose.

On occasion, too, Taylor coupled Pagan and Christian allusions in a way which is reminiscent of the French preachers of the Renaissance, as where he points out that the hope of eternal life—

" will make a satyr chast, and Silenus to be sober, and Dives to be charitable, and Simon Magus to despise reputation, and Saul to turn from a Persecutor to an Apostle " [4] ;

but he never allowed his ' classicism ' to run wild, as did Pierre de Besse and his contemporaries, and, over-frequent as his allusions tend to be, there is never any danger of their becoming mere lists of instances, as in the entertaining anecdotal preaching of earlier times.

' Wit,' as understood by his contemporaries, is rare in Taylor. At times, however, he was only saved from being fantastic by the element of beauty which he usually con-

---

[1] ' XXVIII Sermons,' sermon I, p. 2.
[2] ' Jeremy Taylor ' (E.M.L.), p. 86.
[3] ' XXVIII Sermons,' sermon XVI, ' Of Growth in Sinne,' p. 200.
[4] *Ibid.*, sermon II, ' Of the Spirit of Grace,' p. 26.

trived to combine with his comparisons. Thus, prayers not made in the Spirit of Christ are described by him as

" an abominable sacrifice," (which) " send up to God no better a perfume, then if we burned *assa fœtida*, or the raw flesh of a murdered man upon the altar of incense " [1]—

a strange combination of the bizarre and the beautiful.

Although there is no mention in Taylor of the lives of the poor, there is at times a distinct homeliness in his images and expressions. The making light of sin in the young he severely censured, warning his hearers that vice should not be dismissed easily as " a trick of youth, a habit that old age will lay aside as a man pares his nails " [2] ; and of guardian angels he remarks :

" An Angell does not sit by a man, as a nurse by the babies cradle, watching every motion, and the lighting of a flie upon the childe's lip." [3]

The latter comparison, however, had a distinguished history, and on another occasion,[4] when speaking of God's care of kings, Taylor says the exact opposite, and quotes Homer (' Iliad,' iv. 130) whence the simile of the careful mother, watching " to keep gnats and flies from her dear boy sleep-ing in the cradle," is derived. From such erudite sources came, at times, the apparent homeliness of Jeremy Taylor !

Yet full of recondite and beautiful allusions as Taylor's sermons are, it is not in turning over the many-coloured shells that have been long since discarded by others, so that a hundred new and more wonderful lights and shades are made visible, that his charm lies, but in his own rich and tireless imagination. Always in him the lute-string is con-tending with the rose " for the honour of the greatest sweet-nesse," [5] and we are alternately filled with admiration by the fall of a cadence or a sudden flash of the imagination. Everywhere the poetical fancy of the preacher is evident, and everywhere his gift of language proves equal to the

[1] ' XXVIII Sermons,' sermon II, ' Of the Spirit of Grace,' p. 15.
[2] ' XXV Sermons,' sermon XXIV, ' Of Slander and Flattery,' p. 318.
[3] *Ibid.*, sermon XXIII, ' The Good and Evill Tongue,' p. 300.
[4] *Ibid.*, sermon XXI, ' Apples of Sodom,' p. 278.
[5] *Ibid.*, sermon XIII, ' Of Lukewarmnesse, and Zeal,' p. 175.

task of expression and interpretation. Many of Taylor's poetical touches are both just and beautiful. Of a sinner's broken resolutions he says :

" And his purposes untwist, as easily as the rude con-juncture of uncombining cables, in the violence of a Northern tempest " [1] ;

while of those who never discipline themselves to resist temptation, and yet hope for the reward of righteousness, he speaks thus :

" But so might an Arcadian shepherd look from the rocks, or thorow the clefts of the valley where his sheep graze, and wonder that the messenger stayes so long from comming to him to be crowned King of all the Greek Ilands, or to be adopted heir to the Macedonian Monarchy." [2]

The latter suggests once more the predominantly classical element in Taylor's work, or at least an image from one of the Greek Fathers ; but when we turn to the images in which his sermons abound, we are not met with a series of such comparisons. Instead, Taylor's images are essentially native, drawn from familiar natural objects—the birds, the seasons, the rising and setting sun, the pleasant and varied aspects of nature—to which he was accustomed. A little impersonal always, they are none the worse for that, and are delivered by being so from the " pathetic fallacies " of later and more sentimental writers.

Some of Taylor's images are both arresting and beautiful, as when he compares " cold prayers " to " the buds of roses which a cold wind hath nip'd into death," and " the discoloured *tawny face of an Indian slave*," [3] or urges his hearers to—

" desire Gods grace with great passion, and an appetite keen as a Wolf upon the cold plains of the North." [4]

[1] ' XXVIII Sermons,' sermon II, ' Of the Spirit of Grace,' p. 22.
[2] *Ibid.*, sermon XX, ' Of Christian Prudence,' p. 257.
[3] ' XXV Sermons,' sermon V, ' The Returne of Prayers,' p. 64.
[4] *Ibid.*, sermon XI, ' The Flesh and the Spirit,' p. 145.

At times, also, a whole succession of picturesque allusions
are grouped together, all tending to elucidate the same
point. This is very characteristic of Taylor, who was by
no means a profound thinker, and delighted rather to
elaborate topics about which he felt perfect certainty, than
like Donne to anatomise himself and astonish his hearers by
recounting the amazing ingenuities of his self-torturing
mind in strange cumulative periods, every fresh clause of
which corresponds to a fresh revolution of the wheels of
the rack upon which the victim is stretched. Expatiation
was his *forte*, and expatiation, while it need not imply
shallowness, does imply a limitation of theme and a tranquillity of spirit in either writer or preacher. But having
heard Taylor's own account of his purpose in preaching,
and noted his reply to his critics, we are not surprised that
the main characteristics of his preaching should be what
they are.

Closely connected with expatiation—indeed, one of his
chief methods of expatiation—is Taylor's lengthy and
elaborate type of image, which is a feature of his work too
well known to require illustration, the passage in a sermon
beginning, "For so have I seen a lark . . ." [1] or that in
' Holy Dying,' "But so have I seen a rose . . ." [2] having
become common-places of quotation from his writings.
One question, however, must be asked in passing : Are,
or are not, Taylor's images an integral part of the passages
in which they occur ? Many of them are so lengthy and
artificial that they fail to convey any sense of illustration, and
the mind has forgotten the original thread of the discourse
until it is caught up, often a little clumsily, in the second
half of the simile. The impression given by a frequent
recurrence of this type of writing is, naturally, that such
images are purely extraneous, and might be omitted without any loss to the thought of the passage. In some cases
this is true, and in all cases, when compared with the beauty
and effectiveness of Donne's, Taylor's images appear
decidedly artificial.

An examination of the main images to be noted in the
sermons, however, reveals that these are of three types.
The first type is the often elaborate, but always just and

---

[1] ' XXV Sermons,' sermon V, ' The Returne of Prayers,' p. 60.
[2] Chap. I, Sec. ii (Heber and Eden's ed. of Taylor's ' Works,' vol. iii, p. 270).

effective image, of which the comparison of the soul to the silk-worm [1] is a good instance. The second type of image, and that most frequently met with, is that which occurs after a point has already been sufficiently elaborated, and which adds nothing to the thought of the passage. Such images appear to have been added out of sheer love of their beauty and strangeness. Of this kind is the image of the Pannonian bears found at the end of a passage on the obstinacy of habitual sins.[2] The remaining type of image is that which, for reasons usually similar to the last, is found interpolated in paragraphs where its retention is quite unnecessary for the development of the theme.[3] It will be evident, therefore, from what has been said, that while Taylor's images are at times redundant or sheer interpolation, it would be unfair to dismiss all his images on these grounds, and by far the larger number, although often elaborate, contribute essentially to his line of argument in the passages with which they are connected.

Apart from his elaborate, and often gorgeous, imagery, and a certain laxity of grammatical construction, due to his partiality for cumulative clauses and the great length of many of his sentences, Taylor's style has no outstanding peculiarities. His diction, as might be expected, was highly Latinised, but his constructions, unlike those of the other great seventeenth-century writer of ornate English prose—Sir Thomas Browne—do not follow classical models. His " ideas of grammatical composition," it is true, as Gosse writes—

" were whimsical in the highest degree, and in the course of one of his long breathless sentences he will shift his tenses and link his noun to some neighbouring verb that shrinks, intimidated, from the unwelcome conjunction." [4]

[1] ' XXVIII Sermons,' sermon XI, ' The Faith and Patience of the Saints,' pp. 136–7. Other images of this type are found, *ibid.*, p. 139 ; ' XXV Sermons,' sermon VIII, p. 97 ; sermon XVI, p. 208 ; ' XXVIII Sermons,' sermon XII, p. 147 ; sermon XVI, pp. 204–5 ; sermon XVII, pp. 211–12 ; sermon XXV, pp. 314–15 ; sermon XXVII, p. 343.

[2] ' XXVIII Sermons,' sermon XVII, ' Of Growth in Sinne,' p. 221. Other such images occur in ' XXV Sermons,' sermon V, pp. 59–60 ; sermon XXV, p. 328 ; ' XXVIII Sermons,' sermon IX, pp. 112–13 ; sermon XXI, p. 266 ; sermon XXV, p. 325.

[3] Of this type the description of the ' bold trooper ' (' XXV Sermons,' sermon XIX, p. 257) is a good example ; others occur, *ibid.*, sermon IX, p. 117, and ' XXVIII Sermons,' sermon XIV, p. 180.

[4] *Op. cit.*, p. 225.

Yet such idiosyncrasies of syntax never involve difficulties of comprehension. They mark clearly, however, the individualistic note struck by Taylor's work. He was a man of no rhetorical vogue, as he was a theologian of no definitely recognisable school. Both external circumstances and his own inclinations combined to further the evolution of his prose, and cut off at Golden Grove from the constant reference to patristic sources which he had enjoyed at Oxford, (a little weary also, it would appear, of the subtle distinctions of the Schoolmen [1]), he was set free to spend on form the time other men employed in citation and polemic. His mature and well-modulated prose was the result.

Yet, in speaking of Taylor's prose we must be careful to distinguish his two manners. The continual quotation of passages of gorgeous imagery has tended to obscure the fact that Taylor was also master of an excellent plain style, comparable to that of South and other of the later preachers. Nor is this to be wondered at, when we remember his pre-occupation with moral subjects, and consider the influence which the discussion of philosophic questions was to exert on Restoration prose through the medium of the Cambridge Platonists. It was Taylor's misfortune, however, to attract such attention as he did by his more luscious style of writing, and to pass into the troubles and obscurity of his Irish exile as the exponent of the full-dress oratory of the past, rather than be accorded a place among those who, under the influence of the Royal Society, were to be the promoters of the new plain style.

Before taking leave of Taylor, one last aspect of his work falls to be noted—namely, his funeral orations. Of these we possess three—one on Lady Carbery (1650), one on Sir George Dalstone (1657), and the third on archbishop Bramhall (1663).[2] These are the only sermons in English which can in any way be compared to the great French orations of Bossuet over Condé, Père Burgoing, and Henrietta Maria.

---

[1] *Vid.* dedication of first part of ' The Great Exemplar ' to Lord Hatton of Kirby, ed. cit., a4 : ". . . I am weary and toyled with rowing up and downe in the seas of questions, which the interests of Christendome have commenced. . . ."

[2] All these are to be found in vol. viii of Heber and Eden's ed. of the ' Works,' the first and third being sermons VII and VIII respectively of the ΔΕΚΑΣ, and the Dalstone sermon appearing separately.

Donne's sermons at the funerals of Magdalen Herbert and Alderman Cokayne are much less formal, and rather turn the 'occasion' to profit (as Erasmus and Hyperius of Marburg both advised men to do [1]) than celebrate the dead at any length, although in the case of Magdalen Herbert Donne was moved to a personal tribute ; and Burnet's eulogies of Boyle and Tillotson, later in the century, it must be remembered, had the benefit of the French models. Taylor's models were almost certainly St. Basil and St. Gregory of Nazianzus, although he makes no direct allusion to the funeral addresses of these Fathers.   In each case he composed a striking and beautiful 'contemplation,' such as we find in the opening sections of ' Holy Dying,' which he followed by a separate and restrained account of the person then commemorated.   The eulogy of Bramhall is naturally more formal than either of the others, while the account of Lady Carbery is rendered extremely touching by its simplicity and the genuine sorrow of the preacher.

In both respects—that of turning the occasion to suitable account, and in celebrating the dead in a fitting manner— Taylor is to be pronounced superior to Bossuet, whose *oraisons funèbres* were mere laudatory harangues, and, however excellent they may have been as eulogies, were ill-suited alike to his sacred office and the circumstances of their delivery.   Taylor's funeral sermons, like most of his other work, are steeped in classical allusion, and introduce curious and learned topics, but they never become because of that unsuited to the occasions that produced them.   If they were not pre-eminently calculated to bring comfort to the bereaved, they were certainly the magnificent tributes of a great artist who gave freely and unsparingly of his best in order to dignify the obsequies of the departed, and when the first pang of loss had subsided were likely, on account of their very detachment, to be all the more acceptable.   In one instance, also, the pearls which were dropped lavishly into the grave were formed of the preacher's tears.[2]

[1] Erasmus : ' Ecclesiastes,' Book II, xx ; Hyperius : ' The Practise of Preaching ' (Ludham's trans., 1577), Book II, xii.
[2] For further discussion of the main features of Taylor's prose noted in this section *vid.* Introduction to ' The Golden Grove. Selections from the Sermons and Writings of Jeremy Taylor,' by Logan Pearsall Smith, Oxf., 1930, which was published too late to aid me in my analysis.

VII. The Non-Anglicans to 1660

WHILE many of those whom on account of their ecclesiastical outlook it has been customary to regard as Puritans remained within the pale of the Anglican Church and so have afforded representative preachers to the previous chapter, there remains to be considered the second generation of Puritans who flourished during the Commonwealth period, and some of whom survived to be the leading Nonconformist preachers after 1662. These divines for the most part were Presbyterians and Independents, although the greatest among them, Richard Baxter, like John Wesley in a later century, would have stoutly denied that he was anything other than a minister of the Church of England. Moreover, owing to the political complications of the times, contemporary Scots preaching falls to be glanced at, and there again will be found the paradox, that one of the ablest preachers, and one whose influence was through Burnet to be brought to bear to some extent on English preaching at a slightly later date, although for the moment a Presbyterian divine, was to live to be both a bishop and archbishop of the restored hierarchy in Scotland.

Voluminous as the output of these divines was, and prominent as were the parts played by many of them in the national affairs of their own day, amid the hundreds of printed sermons which they have left us comparatively few are of any literary importance. Indeed, no other period of seventeenth-century preaching demands so much time for its examination and yields so little in return as the Commonwealth period and the works of the non-Anglican divines. At no time probably in the world's history has preaching played so important and disproportionate a part in political and social life as it did in England during the decade 1645–55, and the preachers whom we are now considering were the demagogues as well as theologues of this time. Never before had such numbers of sermons been delivered on public or private occasions, and never before had such quantities of sermons and religious treatises come from the press. Allowing for the fact that the Westminster Assembly was a gathering of clergymen, still there is something abnormal about a day spent as Lightfoot relates

Monday, October 16th, 1643, was spent. The occasion was a solemn fast :

"First Mr. *Wilson* gave a picked psalm, or selected verses of several psalms, agreeing to the time and occasion. Then Dr. *Burgess* prayed about an hour : after he had done, Mr. Whittacre preached upon Isa. xxxvii. 3, ' This day is a day of trouble,' &c. Then, having had another chosen psalm, Mr. *Goodwin* prayed ; and after he had done, Mr. *Palmer* preached upon Psal. xxv. 12. After whose sermon we had another psalm, and Doctor *Stanton* prayed about an hour ; and with another psalm and a prayer of the prolocutor [i.e. Dr. Twisse], and a collection for the maimed soldiers . . . we adjourned till tomorrow morning." [1]

The insatiable desire for preaching was shared equally by the Parliament, and similar fasts with appropriate sermons were numerous. Victories of the Parliamentary forces in the field were celebrated in an almost identical manner. When in London as a Scots Commissioner to the Assembly of Divines we find Baillie noting with disapproval the custom of those ministers " of the best note about London " to read " four chapters [of the Bible] and expone some of them " every Sunday morning, and then, after an interlude spent in singing psalms, to preach in the usual way. Reading and ' exponing ' both on one occasion were, as he saw, unnecessary, and laid too great a strain upon the preacher,[2] although it would appear from the *Diary* of Hay of Craignethan that the Scots custom, by 1659 at least, was very similar, and that a ' lecture ' or running commentary on a passage read from the Scriptures preceded the sermon proper at each ' diet ' of worship.[3] With respect to the glut of published sermons during the Protectorate Baxter relates that at one time he was " almost faln out with " himself because he had " concurred with

---

[1] ' The Whole Works of the Rev. John Lightfoot, D.D. . . . Edited by the Rev. John Rogers Pitman . . .' 13 vols, Lon., 1825 ; vol. xiii contains ' The Journal of the Proceedings of the Assembly of Divines, from January 1, 1643, to December 31, 1644 . . .'
[2] ' Letters and Journals of Robert Baillie . . .' ed. Laing, 1841–2, vol. ii, p. 122.
[3] ' The Diary of Andrew Hay of Craignethan, 1659–1660 . . .' (Scottish Hist. Soc., 1901), p. 13.

them in over-loading the World." [1] Subsequently, when
he and his brethren had been silenced by the Conventicle
Act, he came to feel justified that while he could he had
sought to reach his fellow-countrymen.

The conditions which we glimpse behind these facts were
hardly calculated to produce pulpit oratory of a highly
finished type.   Political prejudice, religious enthusiasm and
the necessity of meeting the exigencies of the moment
influenced what was delivered.   The prevailing tone of
such sermons is one of gloomy dogma and censoriousness,
and even so gifted and lively a writer as Bunyan, if we may
judge from the solitary specimen which we possess of his
sermons, [2] and from those ' discourses ' which almost certainly embody the gist of other sermons now lost, in his
preaching and exposition of Scripture was heavy and dull.
In spite of the galaxy of great names, many of them borne
by men who played a great part in contemporary doctrinal
controversy, and in spite of the eulogies of such Puritan
historians as Calamy, Neal, and Brook, it must be stated
emphatically that the second phase of Puritan preaching
cannot be compared to the first either in wealth of literary
output or in general interest.

Cornelius Burges, Jeremiah Burroughs, William Bridge,
Edmund Calamy (the elder), Francis Cheynell, Joseph
Caryl, John Lightfoot, Stephen Marshall, Jeremiah Whitaker,
and Richard Vines—mighty men who incited armies
to battle in the name of the Lord or denounced curses
against the hesitant and the temperate—not one of them
excites the faintest interest in us at the present day ; and,
if we except Lightfoot's share in the production of Bryan
Walton's polyglot Bible, not one of them has left behind
him any work of outstanding merit.   Their sermons only
differ in degree of dullness, some of them being ' dry,'
while others may be said to be ' heavy,' most of them
suppressing all references to Fathers and Commentators,
and many of them making up amply for the avoidance of
such references in the text by crowding their margins with

[1] ' Reliquiæ Baxterianæ,' 1696, p. 106.
[2] *Vid*. Bunyan's last sermon, delivered the 19th August, 1688, immediately
before his last illness, in vol. ii of ' The Whole Works,' ed. by Offor, 3 vols.,
Glas., Edin., and Lon., 1859.   The 1692 folio of Bunyan's ' Works ' contains
several ' Discourses,' two of which are expositions of certain chapters of the
Bible.

17

interminable citations.   Nor can they be said to illustrate
a rigid adherence to the rhetorical and hermeneutic rules
laid down by the more Puritan preachers and schoolmasters.
The bigger men of any party have never adhered strictly
to the conventions favoured by their party, and these Puritan divines are no exception.   It is true that one finds
Sterry in 'The Rise, Race, and Royalty of the Kingdom
of God in the Soul of Man' proceeding by means of 'doctrine,' 'use,' 'objection,' 'answer,' and by all kinds of
divisions and subdivisions,[1] and that (at the opening of
'A Christian Directory') in explaining the difference between a treatise and a sermon Baxter more or less assumes
that a sermon will be characterised by 'explications' of
each point as it arises, "marks, contraries, counterfeits,
motives, &c.," and will have 'uses' added.[2]   But Baxter
himself, although he was always methodical, did not insist
ostentatiously on the outward evidences of his method.

The crying fault of the greater Puritans was less their
interminable divisions and subdivisions, to which it is true
as a party they were devoted, than the scrupulous plainness
of their addresses, which by their very dogmatism practically
forbade the exercise of the intellect, and their careful avoidance of arousing the whole range of emotion which the
Anglo-Catholic, and, to some extent, the older Puritan
preaching had deliberately attempted to evoke.   When
Christmas was not kept[3] the devotional feeling which had
been associated with the recurrence of the festival was
naturally lost, and the pictorialism and the poetry with all
that they revealed of the preacher's personal devotion or
inspired among his hearers came to an end.   It is no
travesty of fact to say that for the Puritan the greatest
miracle in the Universe was not the incarnation or the
passion of the Saviour, but that God should have elected
him "before all worlds" to "sit with Christ in Heavenly
places," and, as one of the 'saints,' to judge the rest of

---

[1] Published posthumously in 1683—but this book is a good example of the
practice of those Puritan divines who adhered to this method of exposition.

[2] 'Chapters from "A Christian Directory . . ."' ed. by Jeannette
Tawney, 1925, reprint of 'Advertisements,' pp. 2–3.

[3] *Vid.* in this connection Baillie's 'Journal,' ed. cit., vol. ii, p. 120, where
Baillie relates how the Scots Commissioners "prevailed with *their* friends of
the Lower House . . . that both Houses did profane this holy day [i.e.
Christmas Day] by sitting on it. . . ."

mankind. With such an outlook all the tenderness, love, and adoration of sixteen centuries was lost, and, drawing their inspiration almost wholly from Old Testament sources, it is no wonder that the morality of the preachers was a hard and inflexible one. Logic, given divine sanction because its premises were derived from the WORD, reigned supreme, and, again, as during the triumph of Scholasticism, supplanted rhetoric. What Orme writes in his biography of John Owen, moreover, is true not only of Owen, but of many of the best of this type of preacher :

" He was inexcusably indifferent to the vehicle of his thoughts. Had he written less, and paid more attention to the forming and arranging of his sentiments and language he would doubtless have been more useful. But to all ornament in theological writing he was an enemy on principle." [1]

On the other hand, we have to remember, as Orme in the same ' Memoirs ' points out,[2] that Burnet considered that the reform in preaching which took place in the course of the seventeenth century was in part due to the greater Nonconformist preachers, who as the latter observes—

" contributed more than can be well imagined to reform the way of preaching ; which, among the divines of England, before then, was overrun with pedantry, a great mixture of quotations from Fathers, and ancient writers, a long opening of a text, with the concordance of every word in it, and giving all the different expositions of it, with the grounds of them, concluding with some very short practical applications, according to the subject or the occasion." [3]

Another abuse, however, soon became prevalent—namely, the use of a peculiar vocabulary. In its Scots form the late Professor Hepburn Millar refers to this as " the vocabu-

[1] ' The Works of John Owen, D.D., Edited by Thos. Russell, M.A. With Memoirs of his Life . . . By William Orme,' 21 vols., Lon., 1826, vol. i, pp. 356–7.
[2] *Ibid.*, pp. 139–40.
[3] ' History of His Own Time,' 1724 ed., vol. i, p. 191.

lary of the Covenant"[1]; and in England we find Patrick[2] and Glanvill[3] in their criticisms of contemporary preaching glancing at the habit, which consisted largely in using novel and often unexpectedly familiar phrases to express the benefits received by the soul from God. South, also, in attacking Puritan preaching animadverted on this tendency, and objected to

" whimsical cant of *issues, products, tendencies, breathings, indwellings, rollings, recumbencies*, and Scriptures misapplied,"

adding in a footnote—

" Terms often and much used by one J.O. a great leader and oracle in these times."[4]

South, it is to be remembered, was speaking from actual knowledge of Owen's preaching, although an examination of Owen's printed sermons hardly bears out his criticism. But, the temptation to use such terms seems to have been universal among the Independent clergy, and was certainly not conducive to decorous effects. The " language of the Covenant " was in great part derived from legal phraseology, and (although the use of the latter sort of terms seems to have been greatly exaggerated by adverse critics) from phrases descriptive of the marital experience.[5] In the latter case the expressions used had decided affinities with many of the more striking passages from the Hebrew prophets ; they were not unparalleled in those series of sermons on *Canticles* which have been preserved from the Middle Ages, and indeed St. Bernard's series may be regarded as the culminating example ; but they were used by those who employed them at a moment when taste in this matter was definitely changing, and being used frequently without the consummate literary skill of a man like Donne they appeared crude and even disgusting, and

[1] ' Scottish Prose of the Seventeenth and Eighteenth Centuries,' Glas., 1912, pp. 44–6.

[2] ' A Friendly Debate Between a Conformist and a Non-Conformist,' 6th ed., 1684, p. 29.

[3] ' An Essay Concerning Preaching,' 2nd ed., 1703, p. 28.

[4] South : ' Works,' Oxf., 1823, vol. iii, ser. xxxvii, pp. 34–5. The reference is clearly to Owen.

[5] *Vid.* Hepburn Millar, passage already cited.

have been overwhelmed with disapproval. In a way, too, the use of such imagery represents the curious rebound of human nature denied the liberty of giving expression to its natural feeling of wondering adoration. Denied one outlet, the emotional side of both preacher and auditory sought eagerly for another ; the soul that might not ponder lovingly as Cosin or Frank invited it to do on the significance of the Incarnation, or Circumcision, or Candle-mas, turned eagerly to those preachers who invited it to " roll upon *Christ*, close with *Christ*, get into *Christ*." [1]

Coming to the sermons of definite preachers, we find in those of Anthony Tuckney (1599–1670), successively Master of Emmanuel and St. John's Colleges, and for a time Regius Professor of Divinity at Cambridge, a distinct breaking away from the dullness of his contemporaries and a foretaste of the manner shortly to be associated with the Cambridge Platonists. Alone of the ' Westminster ' divines his sermons can lay claim to literary finish, and in spite of the weight of learned quotation, frequently in Greek and not un-commonly in Hebrew, which renders his discourses heavy reading, he shows evident individuality of style and certain poetical qualities of a new order. Already in Tuckney we see traces of the sunlight of mind which was to be so noted a characteristic of his younger contemporaries at Cambridge, especially of " the seraphic Henry More." There is a pictorial element in his images which is distinctly Platonic, and the images are not only beautiful and arresting in themselves, but at the same time materially aid in illustrating the matter in hand. There is also a naturalness in the modulation of Tuckney's sentences that was new to English pulpit oratory. Donne and Adams and Taylor, even in their happiest moments, remain rhetoricians. The new ideal in prose was to be based upon the language of educated men in good society, and the limpid, almost Greek-like simplicity which is first met with in Tuckney was a decided advance on anything that had gone before.

A fair specimen of Tuckney's style occurs in a sermon delivered at Great St. Mary's in 1651 :

" He is a foolish Passenger, that when the Master of the Ship puts him ashore for his refreshment, or to take in

[1] *Vid.* Glanvill : ' An Essay Concerning Preaching,' ed. cit., p. 28.

something for his accommodation, stayeth so long gathering Shels [sic] on the Sand, or Flowers in the Meadow, that he loseth his Voyage : Nor is he the wisest Traveller, who for the more comfort and speed of his Journey, being by his Friend led in a plain fair way, and through pleasant Meadows, is so taken with them, that he lies down to sleep in them forgetting his Errand, and so loiters as loth to part with them, as that he is benighted and falls short of Home. A good Traveller is of another mind, and takes another course ; saith, the Coast indeed is clear and free from Theeves and Robbers, the way pleasant and Inns and other Accommodations by the way commodious ; but yet for all that (as it is in the Proverb) *utinam domi essem*, I would I were at home : And so, the fairer the way is, the more haste he makes and puts on. It is or should be so with every true Traveller Heaven-ward." [1]

Very different from Tuckney's use of images was the way in which Samuel Rutherford—from a rhetorical point of view the most interesting of the Scots Commissioners to the Westminster Assembly—employed his illustrative material. While the influence and reputation of the latter have always been far in excess of those of Tuckney, there is no comparison possible between them in their use of imagery. Rutherford's images have the forcefulness of the Hebraic images of Scripture—on which it is well to remember they were to a large extent based—which although arresting, and as passages in ' Isaiah ' show, capable of sublimity, do not coalesce easily with the subject-matter of a given passage, as does the more Greek type of image introduced by Tuckney. Both in the Vulgate and in the Authorised Version the illustration too often remains isolated owing to the sentence-stopped character of the surrounding prose. The dreams of Pharaoh or Nebuchadnezzar in their recital are stilted affairs compared with that of Er the Pamphylian, and Rutherford was often at a loss to get on with his admonitions once he had introduced his image.

The question of the scandal aroused in certain quarters by Rutherford's images has already been met. The fact is, he was overfond of images, and was inclined to forget that the homeliness of his illustrations tended at times to

---

[1] ' Forty Sermons,' Lon., 1676, ser. xxxvi, p. 622.

detract from the dignity of the subjects of which it was his
business to treat.   There is overmuch of the ploughman
lover casting in a favour to (or playing a trick upon) his
cottar-lass in the following, vivid as it is :

" Christ can come by you suddenly in a blast of a whirl-
wind, in a preaching, and cast in a coal at the window of
your soul, and leave it smoking, and slip His way.   And He
can shoot an arrow of love even to the feathers, and post
away Himself, and say, ' Pack you out.   Here is a bone for
you to gnaw on.' " [1]

" Thank God for the smell of Christ when ye cannot
get Himself," [2]

with its culinary suggestions, is typical of the inappropriate-
ness of many of Rutherford's remarks.   A fair number of
these are couched in the vernacular, which, while investing
his work with quaintness in a later age, too often serves to
emphasise his lack of decorum.
     Of Rutherford's sermons, the twenty-seven known as
' The Trial and Triumph of Faith ' [3] are most free from
peculiarities of speech or temperament, and supply the most
suitable basis for comparison with English sermons of the
period.   In these sermons Rutherford succeeded in keeping
his imagery better in hand, and he presented it in plain
straightforward language, far in advance of that employed
by the majority of English Puritans, or by his fellow-
commissioners, Henderson and Gillespie, and the Scots
preachers of the time.   What he was capable of at his best
may be gathered from a passage from this series, which
links him at once to his compatriot Leighton, then also a
minister of the Presbyterian Church, and entitles him to a
distinguished place among Puritan preachers :

" When the saints throng through the press and crowd
of the creatures (For the world is a bushy and rank wood),
thorns take hold of their garments, and retard them in their

----

[1] ' Quaint Sermons of Samuel Rutherford, Hitherto Unpublished,' edited
with a Preface by Andrew A. Bonar, D.D., Lon., 1885, ser. v, p. 102.
[2] *Ibid.*, p. 103.
[3] Dedicated to Viscountess Kenmure in 1645.

way. Faith looseth their garments, and riddeth them of
such thorny friends as are too kind to them in their journey.
Who diggeth for iron and tin in the earth with mattocks of
gold ? What wise man would make a web of cloth of gold,
a net to catch fish ? Expences should overgrow gains.
There is much of the metal of heaven in the soul. Faith
would forbid us to wear out the threads of the immortal
spirit ; such as are love, joy, fear, sorrow, upon pieces of
corruptible clay. Alas, is it faith's light that setteth men
a-work to make the soul a golden needle, and the precious
powers and perfection thereof, threads of silver, to sew
together pieces of sackcloth and old rotten rags ? What
better, I pray you, is the finest of the web in the whole
system of creation ? Certainly, the heavens must be a
thread of better wool than the clay earth ; yet, if you
should break your immortal spirit, and bend all the acts
to the highest extent of your affections, to conquer thousands
of acres of ground in the heavens, and entitle your soul to
that inheritance, as to your only patrimony without Christ,
faith's day-light should discover to you, that the finest part
of that web of creation with which you desire to clothe your
precious soul, is but base wool, and rotten thread, and
though beautiful and well dyed to the eye, yet, ' The
heavens, even all of them, shall wax old like a garment '
(Psal. cii. 26).

" And the wisdom of faith knoweth a shop, where there
is a more excellent suit of clothes for the soul, and a more
precious piece of the heaven to dwell in ; even a house
which is from heaven, with which you shall be clothed,
when life shall eat up death and mortality. (2 Cor. v.
1, 2.) " [1]

Robert Leighton (1611–1684), with whose work the
passage just quoted from Rutherford may be compared,
occupies a wholly unique niche in Scots ecclesiastical
history. A saint in an age when political and religious
partisanship ran high, he was Presbyterian minister of
Newbattle during the Commonwealth, and after the Restoration successively bishop of Dunblane and archbishop
of Glasgow. But as he had nothing in common with the
enthusiasts among the Presbyterians in his younger days,

---

[1] ' The Trial and Triumph of Faith,' Edin. ed., 1845, ser. xxi, pp. 288–9.

who desired him to " preach to the times," while he desired
only to " preach for eternity," [1] so he had nothing in
common with Sharp and Sydserff and the other " Lord-
Bishops " of the restored hierarchy in Scotland with whom
he was associated in later life. His relation to both parties
and both ecclesiastical systems was clearly that of a man
who was willing to assent rather than consent to the Powers
that were in order to be permitted freedom to exercise his
ministry in spiritual things. From 1653 to 1662 he was
Principal of Edinburgh University.

A mystic, Leighton was devoted to Thomas à Kempis,
whom in his valedictory address to the students at Edinburgh
he took occasion particularly to recommend, " ' since the
sum and substance of religion consists in imitating the
Being that is the object of your worship.' " [2]   His association with French Catholic divines during a period of travel
in France in his youth had also widened his sympathies,
and led to his extending his reading in other directions than
those usually followed by Puritan divines whether English or
Scots. Nothing either in the man or in the traditions of
contemporary Scots preaching would have led us to expect
from Rutherford the tone which is secured in such
passages as that last quoted ; Leighton's tastes and character
alike afford ample explanation of his style. An extract
from the second of the ' Eighteen Sermons ' (which, like
his ' Ten Sermons,' his ' Theological Lectures,' and his
' Commentary on the First Epistle of Peter ' all belong to
his Presbyterian period) gives a fair impression of his
manner :

" But the most of men are little within ; either they wear
out their hours in vain discourse with others, or possibly
vainer discourses with themselves ; even those that are not
of the worst sort, and possibly that have their times of
secret prayer, yet do not so delight to think of God and to
speak with him, as they do to be conversant in other affairs
and companies, and discourses, in which there is a great
deal of froth and emptiness. Men think by talking of
many things, to be refreshed, and yet when they have done,
find that it is nothing ; and that they had much better have

[1] *Vid.* " Life," prefixed to Aikman's ed. of Leighton's ' Works,' Lon., 1848.
[2] ' Works,' Aikman's ed., p. 636.

been alone, or have said nothing. Our thoughts and
speeches in most things run to waste, yea are defiled, as
water spilt on the ground, is both lost, cannot be gathered
up again, and it is polluted, mingled with dust. But no
word spoken to God, from the serious sense of a holy heart,
is lost ; he receives it, and returns it into our bosom with
advantage : a soul that delights to speak to him, will find
that he also delights to speak to it." [1]

Unfortunately, while passages of such relative excellence
are discoverable by the patient reader, Leighton's work as
a whole does not yield many passages of any length which
can be set alongside the published sermons of other and less
delightful contemporaries. His, as Sir Edmund Chambers
expresses it [2]—

" is but a lax prose, not ordered into periods and paragraphs, but ebbing and flowing comment-wise, as the
exigencies of a text require."

Such prose naturally cannot be regarded as worthy of a
prominent place in a study of English prose, yet it had a
curious influence on the subsequent form which the sermon
in England was to take. Burnet, who knew Leighton
intimately, was greatly impressed by his preaching, which
he described in his ' History of His Own Time,' as having
" a sublimity both of thought and expression in it," although
he considered " his style was rather too fine." Yet the
historian is quick to add :

" But there was a majesty and beauty in it that left so deep
an impression, that I cannot yet forget the sermons I heard
him preach thirty years ago." [3]

One of the things which attracted Burnet to Leighton's
preaching was without doubt a characteristic which Robert
Baillie (and probably the majority of his contemporaries)
disapproved of in the latter. In a letter dated the 19th

[1] ' Works,' Aikman's ed., p. 257, cols. 1–2.
[2] Craik's ' English Prose,' vol. ii, pp. 489–90—introd. to extracts from
Leighton's work.
[3] 1724 ed., vol. i, p. 135.

July, 1654, Baillie, in speaking of a young man, Andrew
Gray, and his manner of preaching, continues :

" He has the new guyse of preaching which Mr. Hew
Binning and Mr. Robert Leighton began, contemning the
ordinarie way of exponing and dividing a text, of raising
doctrines and uses ; bot runs out in a discourse on some
common head, in a high, romancing, unscriptural style,
tickling the ear for the present, and moving the affections
in some, bot leaving as he confesses, little or nought to the
memorie and understanding." [1]

Later, largely under Burnet's influence, " a discourse on
some common head " was, as we have seen in the previous
section of this study,[2] to become the ideal for the English
sermon.

At the moment Baillie's criticisms of Binning must have
seemed amply justified, for Binning is at once the most
sublime and the most unexpected of Scots Presbyterian
preachers. Along with Leighton and Henry Scougal
(author of ' The Life of God in the Soul of Man '), he stands
apart from the Scotsmen of his own day and time. There
is a considerable amount of truth in the estimate of an early
eighteenth-century biographer, when we recall the fact that
the ' wit ' of the Anglo-Catholics and the ornateness of
Taylor had ceased to please :

" Considering the Time when he lived, it might be said,
that he had carried the Orator's Prize from his contemporaries in Scotland, and was not at that Time inferior to the
best Pulpit Orators in England, the English Language
having got its greatest Embellishments and Refinings but
of late years." [3]

Binning's sermons are all of a beautiful and elevated
type, very far removed not only from Scots but also from
English Puritan preaching of his day. His style is limpid,
and flows on naturally without much obvious design. The
beginnings of his sermons are particularly good, as are also

[1] ' Letters and Journals,' ed. Laing, 3 vols., Edin., 1841–2, vol. ii, pp.
258–9.   [2] *Ante*, pp. 114–15.
[3] Patrick Gillespie's " Life " prefixed to edition of Binning's ' Works,' issued
at Edinburgh in 1735.

their conclusions in which he presses home his point with distinct effect.   Everywhere the lovable spirit of the preacher is manifest.   At a time noted for its dogmatism and prejudice his sermons sound a delightfully evangelical note.   His reading of the English preachers of all schools is obvious, and he draws upon Andrewes or other preachers of the Anglo-Catholic school and transforms some of their images into less startling and more restrained analogies. Occasionally he quotes from Latin, but immediately follows up the quotation with a translation of the phrase.   Obviously interested in rhetoric in a deeper sense than merely to have received rhetorical training, he had learned much from the preaching of his predecessors.   His prose, although less cumbered with displays of learning or philosophic reasoning, has much of the luminous charm of the Cambridge Platonists.

Binning, who died in 1653 at the age of twenty-six, had so aroused the affections of his fellow-countrymen that in 1670 the Privy Council in Scotland issued an order that none should reprint or import various collections of his sermons " for the space of 19. years to come, without the license of the Printers hereof "—so keen was the demand for copies of his works and so encouraging to piracy.   The close of the first sermon contained in ' Fellowship With God :   Or XXVIII Sermons on the I Epistle of John . . .' reveals the merits of Binning's style :

" . . . Such conjectures we have of this *Word of God*, and his eternal generation, as if Trees could take upon them to understand the nature of Beasts, or as if Beasts would presume to give an account of the spirit that acts in men : Certainly the distance is infinitly [sic] greater between God and us ;   and he must needs behold greater vanity, folly, and darknesse, in our clearest apprehensions of his Majestie, then we could find in the reasonings and conceptions of the Beasts about our nature.   When our conception in the womb, is such a mystery, as made *David* to say, *O how wonderfully am I made, and fearfully ?* he saw a curious art and wisdom in it, that he could not understand, and he believed an infinit [sic] power, he could not conceive, which surprized his soul with such unexpected matter of wonder, as made him fear and tremble at the thought of it.

I say, when the generation of a poor creature hath so much depth of wisdome in it, how canst thou think to understand that everlasting wonder of Angels, the birth and conception of *the eternal wisdom of God*? And if thou canst not understand from whence the wind comes, and whither it goes, or how thine own spirits beat in thy veins, what is the production of them, and what their motions? How can we then conceive the procession of the Holy Ghost, *which eye hath not seen, nor ear heard, nor hath it entered into the heart of man to consider it?* " [1]

Such an extract could hardly be described as in " a high, romancing, unscriptural style " except by those like Baillie devoted to " exponing and dividing a text," and adhering closely to ' doctrines ' and ' uses.' It is true, however, that there is found in Binning the same wondering adoration and delight in the paradoxes of the Nativity which is noticeable in Andrewes, Cosin, and Frank, and which was distinctly not a characteristic in Puritan preaching. [2] In dealing with these themes, moreover, he exhibits a fluidity and ease of manner all his own, and which augured well for the future of preaching once the insistence on the old heavily annotated scriptural exegesis should be discarded. Andrew Gray, also, whom Baillie named along with Leighton and Binning in his censure, although by no means comparable to either of the latter, in ' The Spiritual Warfare '—a collection of his sermons issued in 1679—illustrates interestingly the attempt to give to the sermon something of its later essay-form, which Wodrow was to describe as the " fashionable English way of preaching in harangues and without heads," [3] but which only attained its perfection of form in England in the hands of Tillotson, and in Scotland had to wait practically another century for the advent of Blair.

Reverting to the English Puritans, neither John Goodwin nor Owen has left remains of any literary value. Nor is Thomas Goodwin, another Independent giant whose voluminous theological works astonish posterity, of greater interest. The main interest in the later Puritans, who

---

[1] *Op. cit.*, Edin., 1671, pp. 11–12.
[2] *Vid.* for example, ser. ii (ed. cit.), pp. 17, 18, 20, and 23.
[3] *Vid.* Millar : ' Scottish Prose,' p. 172.

became the first Nonconformists, centres in Baxter, Howe
and Bates, and only in the case of the last-mentioned does
the literary quality of their work call for notice. Baxter's
aims in preaching have been cited in the first part of this
study,[1] and the ' Reliquiæ ' supplies us with a considerable
amount of criticism of his contemporaries. That his
plainness is directly attributable to Baxter's desire to make
his meaning clear to the most ignorant of his auditory is
beyond doubt, and that he was practical rather than
speculative is due to the same cause. Dr. Powicke has
shown that Baxter was a man of wide culture, with genuine
affinities with the Cambridge Platonists,[2] and, in the words
of one of his correspondents, the Honourable Robert Boyle,
" none of these narrow-souled divines that, by too much
suspecting Natural Philosophy, tempt many of its votaries
to suspect Theology." [3]   Glanvill, one of the most ' conceited,' though later one of the first plain preachers of the
period, admired him,[4] and Glanvill, who has been already
quoted as animadverting on the canting terms of Owen
and others, would never have been attracted by a dull
preacher or by a thinker of merely average range. It is
beyond doubt, therefore, that, as Baxter himself remarks
of the occasion of his silencing : " The arrow that wounded
us was feathered from our own wings " [5] ; and the oblivion
into which he has fallen is not due to lack of ability to set
out his materials differently but to deliberate choice.

" . . . The Plainest words " (he came to believe) " are the
profitablest Oratory in the weightiest matters.[6] Fineness
is for ornament, and delicacy for delight ; but they answer
not *Necessity*. . . . Yea when they are conjunct, it is hard
for the necessitous hearer or Reader to observe the matter
of ornament and delicacy, and not to be carried from the

---

[1] *Ante*, pp. 103–4, and p. 115.
[2] *Vid.* ' The Reverend Richard Baxter Under the Cross,' Lon., 1927, pp.
52–3, 196, 238–43, and 247–8.
[3] *Ibid.*, p. 49.
[4] *Ibid.*, p. 53, and ' Reliquiæ ' (1696), p. 378, where Baxter says that
Glanvill " had a too excessive estimation " of him.
[5] ' A Life of the Reverend Richard Baxter,' by F. J. Powicke, Ph.D., Lon.,
1924, p. 320 ; Baxter is quoting Melanchthon's ' In vulneribus nostris proprias
agnoscimus pennas,' itself an echo of Æschylus (*vid.* Loeb. ed., frag. 63).
[6] It is amusing to note the ' Senecan ' boast in this and the following
expression.

matter of Necessity ; and to hear or read a neat, concise sententious Discourse, and not to be hurt by it ; for it usually hindereth the due operation of the matter and keeps it from the heart, and stops it in the fancy, and makes it seem as light as the stile." [1]

" Wittiness " he despised as " proud foolery, which savoureth of levity," and considered to differ as much from true preaching as " a Stage-player or Morries-dancer differs from a souldier [sic] or a King " [2] ; and he affirmed as the result of his experience :

" Indeed, the more I have to do with the ignorant sort of people the more I find that we cannot possibly speak too plainly to them. If we do not speak in their own vulgar dialect, they understand us not. Nay, if we do so, yet if we compose those very words into a handsomeness of sentence, or if we speak anything briefly, they feel not what we say. Nay, I find, if we do not purposely dress out the matter into such a length of words and use some repetition of it—that they may hear it inculcated on them again—we do but over-run their understandings, and they presently lose us." [3]

Here then we have at once an implied criticism of Donne, Hall, Fuller, and Taylor [4] with their different rhetorical ideals, and an explanation of Baxter's own manner. To this end ' witty,' ' metaphysical ' preaching, ' pointed,' ' conceited ' preaching, and highly ornate preaching led, and Rhetoric, whom we have seen baptised and sent forth as the handmaid of Christ, to convince, move, and delight mankind, is thrust aside. Such a state of affairs could not be tolerated ; indeed, Baxter's own works prove that a compromise of some sort, or a reconsecration of Rhetoric, had to be attempted. That the stark plainness of the latter's work and of the other preachers of like mind served a useful purpose we have heard Burnet pointing out. The period is, as it were, a kind of dressing-room in which the sermon

[1] Powicke : ' A Life of the Reverend Richard Baxter,' pp. 282–3.
[2] Ibid., p. 283.
[3] Ibid., pp. 284–5.
[4] Andrewes and Hall are definitely mentioned ; like George Fox, Baxter did not feel that such preaching " spoke to his condition."

divested itself of the older forms of pulpit oratory before
setting out to run with applause a fresh course.   In itself,
however, this plainness too often consisted (as Baxter himself describes it) in a preacher speaking to the people " in a
familiar natural Language," and exhorting " them as if it
were for their Lives," [1] and the results are in no way literary.
Yet this very directness of approach was much to be preferred
to the stringing together of texts which is so noticeable in
Puritan preachers on the eve of and during the Civil Wars.
The opening of an Assize Sermon preached at Worcester in
1654, although slightly above the average, is sufficiently
typical of Baxter's manner to be quoted :

"Fundamentals in religion are the life of the super-
structure.   Like the vitals and naturals in the body, which
are first necessary for themselves and you also, for the
quickening and nourishing of the rest ; there being no life
or growth of the inferior parts, but what do receive from
the powers of these : it is but a dead discourse, which is
not animated by these greater truths, whatever the bulk
of the materials may consist of.   The frequent repetition,
therefore, of these is as excusable as frequent preaching :
and they that nauseate it as loathsome Cathology, do love
novelty better than verity, and playing with words to please
the fancy rather than closing with Christ [2] to save the soul.
And as it is the chief part of the cure, in most external
maladies, to corroborate the vital and natural powers, which
then will do the work themselves, so it is the most effectual
course for the cure of particular miscarriages in men's
lives to further the main work of grace upon their hearts.
. . . Could we help you to wind up the spring of faith, and
so move the first wheel of Christian love, we should find it
the readiest and surest means to move the inferior wheels
of duty.   The flaws and irregular motions without, do
show that something is amiss within, which, if we could
rectify, we might the easier mend the rest." [3]

[1] ' Reliquiæ,' 1696, p. 32.
[2] *Vid. ante*, p. 261, for Glanvill's reference to this phrase.
[3] Baxter's ' Practical Works,' ed. by Orme, 1830, vol. xvii, pp. 340–41.
The ' Works ' consist of twenty-three volumes *octavo*, of which vols. xvii and
xviii contain sermons ; but the majority of Baxter's ' treatises ' were, as has
already been shown, slightly expanded or more highly polished forms of
sermons.

Baxter's vocabulary, it will be noticed, is not a simple one, but his illustration of the wheels is good, and such as could be grasped by any intelligent auditor ; the more difficult medical imagery is very characteristic, and was doubtless designed for the better educated ; so that his style may be said to embody various elements suited to different sections of his hearers.

John Howe (1630–1705), who has been mentioned as one of the greater of the later Puritans, showed no literary genius, and Venning and Gurnall, although they have continued to appeal to those who are determined to pay to Puritanism as a movement its utmost meed of praise, provide dull reading. In William Bates (1625–1699), however, we discover a genuine stylist. A Cambridge man and a Presbyterian, he became minister of St. Dunstan's-in-the-West, London, from which he was ejected in 1662. His sermons, as published in the folio volume of his ' Works ' in 1700, are plain and easy, though inclined to bluntness, but represent an advance in fluidity on any previous Puritan preacher. He is found at his best in ' The Harmony of the Divine Attributes ' (1674), a series of ' Discourses ' which may be considered to rank as sermons, from which the following quotation is taken :

" And as by contemplating the other works of God, so especially by reflecting upon himself, *Adam* had a clear sight of the Divine *Attributes*, which concurr'd in his Creation. Whether he considered his lowest part, the Body 'twas form'd of the Earth, the most artificial and beautiful piece of the *visible* World. The contrivance of the parts, was with that proportion and exactness, as most conduc'd to Comeliness and Service. Its stature was erect and raised, becoming the Lord of the Creatures, and an observer of the Heavens. A Divine Beauty and Majesty was shed upon it. And this was no vanishing *ray*, soon *eclips'd* by a Disease, and extinguisht by Death, but shin'd in the countenance without any declination. The *Tongue* was Man's peculiar glory, being the interpreter of the mind, and capable to Dignifie all the affections of the Soul. In short, the Body was so fram'd as to make a visible discovery of the Prerogatives of his Creation. And when he reflected upon his Soul, that animated his dust, its excellent endow-

18

ments, wherein 'tis comparable to the Angels, the capacity
of enjoying God himself for ever, he had an internal and
most clear testimony of the glorious perfections of his
Creator. For Man, who alone admires the works of God,
is the most admirable of all." [1]

This style Doddridge rightly enough describes as " charming and elegant," and suggests as an influence in its formation the fact that Bates was " an admirer as well as imitator
of Cowley."[2] The latter remark by Doddridge's time was
a somewhat conventional one, and it would probably be
more accurate to say that Bates' style represents a fairly
advanced stage in the evolution of English prose to which
the popularity of Cowley gave so remarkable a fillip. But
its own direct antecedents were the plainer preachers
among the Puritans, and a few of the more Calvinistic type
of Anglican clergy. Bates' style looks backward on the
one hand to that of Hall in his less Senecan moods,[3] and forward on the other to Sherlock, in his celebrated ' A Practical
Discourse concerning Death ' (1689) ; except that it is more
speculative and less polemical, it is separated by no great
distance from that of his contemporary South. This last
point is important, as is also the general equability of tone
which distinguishes Bates' work. Where men are struggling
with involved problems, their manner of writing will either
mirror the complex of their minds or will consist of a number of blunt statements in an endeavour to represent clearly
their precise meaning. Such a style as Bates', as clearly as
does that of Tillotson, precludes any thought of struggle.
It is the result of acquiescence in a creed which the preacher
believes to be thoroughly rational. Hence the comparative
calm and modulation of the prose. But these very qualities
separate Bates from his Puritan brethren, whose soul-shatter-
ing experiences and politico-religious enthusiasms made
them indifferent to beauty of form in the midst of their
struggle with their own lower natures or with " spiritual
wickedness in high places," and link him up with the Low
Churchmen among whom in his later years he found
toleration and sympathy.

[1] *Op. cit.*, chap. [=Discourse] i, pp. 7–8.
[2] ' Lectures on Preaching . . .' in Doddridge's ' Works,' Leeds, 1804,
vol. v, Lecture ii, § 17.
[3] *Vid. ante*, p. 226, ("How was it with the first man . . .")

With Bates, therefore, Puritan preaching lost its distinctive features, and became one with the prevailing pulpit oratory of the times.   When in the eighteenth century evangelical preaching became distinguished from that of the Establishment, it was in thought rather than manner that the difference was to be observed.   Though various old features were to reappear—some of Cosin's sermons belong to his later years—and various experiments were to be tried, the trend towards simplicity became fairly well marked from the time of the Restoration, and after the Revolution of 1688 for half a century English pulpit style may be said to have been a unity.   That the Puritan stood for plainness and simplicity in style may be originally attributable to such considerations as we found Perkins outlining,[1] and at a later period to those which Baxter has made clear ; but for the later Puritans of equal if not of prior importance was the fact that they lived at a particular period, and consequently shared in a mood which was affecting the best English minds among their contemporaries.   English prose had reached a literary Breda, and only required the unanimous consent of the nation to become universally plain.   When the politicians called home the king the plain style triumphed ; but while to the Royal Society must be given the honour of definitely hall-marking the new style, to the more temperate among the Puritan preachers belongs the praise of having demonstrated to large masses of the nation, learned and unlearned, the possibilities of a simple, straightforward, unencumbered prose.   Unattractive as it often was in itself, the Puritan sermon became a kind of dam from which might be led the smooth but powerful current that was to set in motion English prose of a slightly later time.

[1] *Vid. ante*, p. 100.

SO far the divines whose work has been considered represent definite theological interests—the renewed claim to full catholicism of the Anglo-Catholics, the astonishing variety of opinion of those still within the national church, the demands of one kind or another which characterised the position of those who from the nominal establishment of Presbyterianism in 1646 definitely considered traditional Anglicanism to have been superseded. Such work has everywhere, as we have noted, a strong party flavour, though the product of particular men has naturally a certain distinction compared with the preaching of their theological confrères. For party interest (which in practically all cases was synonymous with the most sacred moral obligations recognised by the preachers in question) putting to use, with certain modifications, the rhetorical education of the time, even in the case of men of genius, may be taken as offering a full explanation of the sermons reviewed. Individual speculation, or speculation apart from the prevailing dogmas of the opposed theological parties (even in the case of Jeremy Taylor, who displayed certain eccentricities of belief), plays no part in such preaching, nor (as has been indicated) though the classical moralists were drawn upon by the more puritanically minded of the Anglicans—by men like bishop Hall or Thomas Adams—or by Taylor, do the opinions of these writers, as distinct from the illustrative value of their aphorisms, and the importance, already shown, of being able to find secular Latin tags to set against Latin tags from the Fathers, assume any importance in the thought of the divines who quote them. The chariot of Theology was borne steadily onwards by Rhetoric and Logic as yoke-fellows, although often the lustre of the lady led to the total disregard of her team ; but in no case did Philosophy as a sister attend her, whispering in her ear counsels at least as divine in their inspiration as the *dogmata* enunciated by assemblies of contending ecclesiastics. Yet alongside of those preachers whose work we have examined, and especially during the Commonwealth period, other tendencies are observable here and there in English preaching, and while the great protagonists of the religious struggle of the time were engaged in wordy, or more material, combat, another and entirely different spirit was unobtrusively contributing a new element to the sermon—an element which, although of paramount interest so far as the thought or content of the sermon is concerned, was ultimately, in spite of various ebullitions in an apparently contrary direction, to result in a permanent contribution to form and style.

It is not easy to find a comprehensive term under which to include the divines whom it is now proposed to discuss. Hunt, in his ' Religious Thought in England,' [1] remarks :

" These writers have been called Latitudinarians, Rationalists, Platonists, and some other like names, none of which are very appropriate, and all of which fail to describe the men when put into one class."

Tulloch, regarding them in the second of these aspects, has treated their work as a whole in his ' Rational Theology in England in the XVIIth Century.' Platonists, whether of Cambridge or not, they certainly were not all, and Latitudinarians, especially in the later almost political significance that attached to that word, they could not be, as two of the earliest and most interesting of their number, Hales and Chillingworth, did not live to see the Restoration. Burnet, indeed, definitely refers the term ' Latitudinarians ' to Tillotson, Stillingfleet, Patrick, and Lloyd, but while so doing gives an account of those whose teaching led to the peculiar type of opinions which these divines held,[2] thus indicating the similarity of principle underlying the attitude of the Cambridge group of thinkers with that of the party to which he himself belonged.   A further extension of those principles which the later men professed can, without much difficulty, be made to include those in whom the same temper of mind is first discernible, and Hales and Chillingworth, as well as the Cambridge Platonists, may be described as *rationalistic* Latitudinarians in distinction from the purely *political* Latitudinarians of the Restoration period.

Both Hales and Chillingworth are interesting as instances of men who discovered that the doctrinal conflicts of their day were waged less with a desire to discover the truth than

[1] Vol. i, p. 368.
[2] ' History of His Own Time,' vol. i, 1724 ed., pp. 186 *seq.*

to impose the accepted standpoint of particular theological groups. As a result of his experience as correspondent to Sir Dudley Carleton, the English Ambassador at The Hague, during the sitting of the Synod of Dort in 1618–19, Hales (as he himself quaintly phrases it) " bid John Calvin good-night," and Chillingworth, after seeking refuge for a time within the fold of the Roman Catholic Church, returned to accept ordination in the Anglican Church on the basis of his own interpretation of the Thirty-Nine Articles. Each in turn was compelled to think out anew the basis upon which religious faith might be laid and secured independent of the boasted infallibilities of Church or Book, which both alike discovered to be untenable. Both were ultimately led back to the common standpoint of human reason, illumined by the Holy Spirit, as the only certain guide to religious truth. To them, as to Hooker before them, Order alone was divine, and no particular mani-festation of it, whether prelatical or Presbyterian, might usurp the title, while the intellectual activity of men led by the Spirit of Truth, Who alone is infallible, was regarded by them as the ideal of man's spiritual and intellectual progress.

Very similar to the position arrived at in turn by Hales and Chillingworth was that more or less held in common by the Cambridge Platonists. Though their more strictly philosophic thought was stimulated by the desire to vindi-cate the immanence of spirit in the Universe against the materialism of Hobbes, and, what seemed to them, the disastrous divorce of spirit and matter in Descartes, their religious thought was obviously the outcome of a desire for a larger, more charitable, more ' rational ' faith than was envisaged on the one hand by Laudian Anglicanism with its ' ceremonies,' or on the other by Puritanism with its in-sistence on the ' eternal decrees.' The correspondence of the oldest of their number, Whichcote, with Tuckney, reveals many of the stages of their break with the old Calvinism in which they were reared, and is from first to last the record of a calmly reasoned position, devoid of any passion or vehemence. The history of the movement is that of a group of men of considerable philosophic range, at the same time deeply religious, who, themselves convinced of the " reasonableness of the Christian Faith," set themselves the task of demonstrating its rationality to others, by simplifying the number of essentials and laying stress upon the common consent of mankind to certain broad principles of morality. This latter fact led them vigorously to oppose Hobbes, who in the ' Leviathan ' had reduced morality to a matter of common agreement established by the authority of the civil magistracy. Against this contention Cudworth, in particular, urged the existence and validity of an " Eternal and Immutable Morality," while by his doctrine of a " Plastic Nature "—a reversion to the Stoic doctrine of the " Anima Mundi "—he attempted to bridge the gap left by Descartes between spirit (unextended, and consisting of pure thought) and matter (essentially extended, but incapable of thought). Such contemplations enlarged the outlook of these divines, and raised their minds above the narrow sphere where alone dogmatism and fanaticism can reign. If they too frequently preferred Plotinus to Plato, and encrusted their works with quotations from those writers and from all the classical moralists, they had yet a breadth of view and a freedom of thought unknown to their contemporaries. And such interests and such a temper as they manifested naturally were reflected in their style.

John Hales (1584–1656), the " ever-memorable," the earliest in point of date of the rationalistic divines, had little in common with the more richly variegated, almost poetical style of some members of the Cambridge school ; but his is the first voice heard in England proclaiming the ideal of toleration and comprehension which had to wait for the Revolution of 1688 to be accepted, and which even then, owing to the earlier activities of the first Restoration Parliament, was of a mutilated and less generous sort than might have been hoped for.[1] A man of wide erudition, a fellow of Merton College, Oxford, and of Eton College,

---

[1] *Vid.* his ' Tract on Schism and Schismatics,' probably written 1636, published by friends without his consent 1642 : ". . . Were liturgies and public forms of service so framed as that they admitted not of particular and private fancies, but contained only such things as in which all Christians do agree, schisms on opinion were utterly vanished. . . . Prayer, confession, thanksgiving, reading of Scripture, exposition of Scripture, administration of sacraments in the plainest and simplest manner, were matter enough to furnish out a sufficient liturgy, though nothing either of private opinion, or of Church pomp, of garments, of prescribed gestures, of imagery, of music, of matter concerning the dead, of many superfluities which creep into the churches under the name of order and decency, did interpose itself."—' Works,' Hailes' ed., 1765, vol. i, pp. 125 *seq.*

where he spent the greater part of his life, Hales stands apart from the strife of contending tongues, although reflecting deeply on the changing theology of his day. Unlike others in the century (to quote Principal Tulloch)—

" If he bade John Calvin good-night, he did not say good-morning to Arminius. . . .   When he left the narrowness of Calvinism, he did so not because he became possessed of some other narrowness, but because he saw from a higher field of vision how little dogmatic precision has to do with spiritual truth. . . ." [1]

Rather than add to the confusion of the times he restricted the circulation of his positions to " private discourses," alleging, as Clarendon reports, that

" his opinions he was sure did him no harm, but he was far from being confident that they might not do others harm who entertained them, and might entertain other results from them than he did." [2]

Whatever he wrote showed extreme clarity of thought, and this lucidity is reflected in a plain, straightforward prose, strictly dependent on the sequence of ideas which occurred to him.   The prose of his sermons, except that it is interrupted now and then to allow reference to the words of Scripture or the introduction of a quotation from the Fathers or classical authors, is essentially plain, as the following extract shows :

" If the Author of faith may alter, or if the evidence and assurance that he hath left us be not pregnant, and impossible to be defeated, there is necessarily opened an inlet to doubtfulness and wavering, which the nature of faith excludes.   That faith therefore may stand unshaken, two things are of necessity to concur.   First, that the Author of it be such an one, as can by no means be deceived, and this can be none but God.   Secondly, that the words and text of this Author upon whom we ground, must admit of no ambiguity, no uncertainty of interpretation. *If the trumpet*

[1] ' Rational Theology in England in the XVIIth Century,' 2nd ed., 2 vols., Edin. and Lon., 1874, vol. i, p. 191.
[2] ' The Life of Edward Earl of Clarendon,' Oxf., 1842, p. 929.

give an uncertain sound, who shall provide himself to battel. If the words admit a double sense, and I follow one, who can assure me that that which I follow is the truth? For infallibility either in judgment, or interpretation, or whatsoever, is annext neither to the See of any Bishop, nor to the Fathers, nor to the Councels, nor to the Church, nor to any created power whatsoever. This doctrine of the literal sense was never grievous or prejudicial to any, but onely to those who were inwardly conscious that their positions were not sufficiently grounded." [1]

' A Sermon of Duels,' preached at The Hague and consequently referable to the year 1619, being less intellectual in its reasoning but no less skilfully argumentated,[2] is valuable evidence as to the possibility of such limpidity and naturalness of style at so early a date, and may be taken, along with Parr's remark on Ussher already cited,[3] as proving that such preaching might well have been rendered acceptable but for the theological or ecclesiastical prepossessions of the Laudian and Calvinist divines.

Except for his intellectual position which dominated his style and rendered it pliable for its own purposes, William Chillingworth (1602–1644), as the godson of Laud, might easily have been numbered among the ' witty ' or ' metaphysical ' preachers. That he had something in common with the ' Senecan ' preachers is evident from part of the opening paragraph of a sermon preached before Charles I at Oxford in 1643 :

" For, as the shadows are longest when the Sun is lowest, and as Vines and other Fruit-trees bear the less fruit, when they are suffered to luxuriate and spend their Sap upon their superfluous Suckers, and abundance of Leaves : So commonly, we may observe both in Civil conversation, where there is great store of formality, there is little sincerity : and in Religion, where there is a decay of true and cordial Piety, there men entertain and please themselves, and vainly hope to please God with external formalities, and per-

---

[1] Sermon on " Abuses of Hard Places of Scripture," in ' Golden Remains,' 2nd imp., Lon., 1673, 4to, pp. 18, 19.
[2] *Vid.* ' Golden Remains,' *op. cit.,* pp. 68 *seq.*
[3] *Ante,* p. 8, and pp. 229–31.

formances, and great store of that righteousness for which Christ shall judge the World." [1]

Such images and comparisons, however, were not in Chillingworth's usual style, which is better illustrated by his further remarks on the same theme a few paragraphs later :

" And this were ill enough, were it in private, but we abuse God Almighty also with our publick and solemn formalities, we make the Church a Stage whereon to act our parts, and play our Pageantry ; there we make a profession every day of *confessing our Sins with humble, lowly, and obedient hearts*, and yet when we have talked after this manner, twenty, thirty, forty years together, our hearts for the most part continue as proud, as Impenitent, as disobedient as they were in the beginning. . . .

" If a man whom you have dealt well with, should deal so with you ; one whom you had redeemed from the *Turkish* slavery, and instated in some indifferent good inheritance, should make you fine Speeches, entertain you with Panegyricks, and have your praises always in his Mouth ; but all the while do nothing that pleases you, but upon all occasions, put all affronts and indignities upon you, Would you say, this were a thankful man ? Nay, would you not make Heaven and Earth ring of his unthankfulness, and detest him almost as much for his fair Speeches, as his foul Actions. Beloved, such is our unthankfulness to our God and Creator, to our Lord and Saviour. . . ." [2]

This is quite in the manner of ' The Religion of Protestants,' with its homely and pertinent illustrations, well-aimed arguments, and clear-sighted pressing home of every advantage. It is not a great pulpit style, and it is true, as Principal Tulloch notes, that Chillingworth's sermons as a whole " contain nothing which could have preserved his name from oblivion." [3] Yet, such as it is, Chillingworth's style represents an advance on that of Sanderson. It is flexible in a way in which Sanderson's is not, the result of

[1] ' The Works . . . Containing his Book, entitl'd The Religion of Protestants A Safe Way to Salvation ; Together with His Nine Sermons . . .' Lon., fol., 6th ed., 1704, p. 332.
[2] *Op cit.*, p. 334.
[3] ' Rational Theology . . .' vol. i, p. 306.

itself a partial freedom while continuing to rejoice in the fetters of an ecclesiastical party, as with Donne or Frank or Taylor, but with men of a larger and more generous outlook, which, though it found individual expression in ways which are interestingly various, yet in its broad outlines remained the same. For a higher synthesis than cult or dogma could supply had been discovered, and, although at the time it seemed inappropriate and unnoticed, was afterwards to bear fruit.

The work both of Mede and of Tuckney has already been noticed,[1] and their influence on the younger generation of Cambridge divines is clear. Mede may be taken as the representative of a preacher who followed the ' method ' of Perkins (like himself of Christ's College, Cambridge) ; but the fact that for theological reasons he avoided " needless Quotations " of authors earned for him the approval of Worthington, at a later period, when taste rather than theology had decided against the evil habit of much quoting. Tuckney, as we have seen, was at once plain and yet pictorial in his style, and was able to introduce images which unlike those of Taylor were not culled from Greek sources, but savoured of a Greek frame of mind. Yet, like one of his pupils, Culverwel, he was a staunch Calvinist, and the rationalistic tendencies of Whichcote caused him acute distress. In these men we see then a kind of inevitable progression : Calvinism, based on THE WORD, leading to severely Scriptural or entirely plain preaching, which in turn developed a gracious imagery of its own, and Calvinism passing beyond the explication of its own dogmatism (as Dr. Powicke rightly points out) to avail itself of that very exercise of human reason " in the strength of which Calvin himself shook off the authority of Rome." [2]

The particular topics debated between Whichcote and Tuckney as representing the newer spirit in conflict with more orthodox Calvinism are set out at length by Tulloch in his study of the Cambridge Divines.[3] They need not detain us here. Nor need a discussion of Whichcote's style, as exemplified in his ' Select Sermons ' as issued in

---

[1] For Mede, *vid. ante*, p. 205 ; for Tuckney, *ante*, pp. 261–2.
[2] ' The Cambridge Platonists,' pp. 6 and 7.
[3] ' Rational Theology . . .' vol. ii, pp. 59 *seq.*

1698 by Shaftesbury (the author of the ' Characteristics '), which, as we have already seen,[1] were put together by the editor from sermon-notes " written after him at Church." Such as they are, these sermons clearly belong to the days of Whichcote's London ministry, after the Restoration, when learned citations would no longer be acceptable, and, coming to us as they do, it is impossible to tell to what extent such quotations might have been restored or inserted had he himself published his sermons. In spite, however, of these considerations, and ignoring Shaftesbury's apologies for the

" unpolish'd style, and Phrase of our Author, who drew more from a College, than a Court ; and who was more used to School-Learning, and the Language of the University, than to the Conversation of the fashionable World,"

the sermons attain considerable excellence. Indeed, it is plain that the notes from which they were printed must have been fairly full, and that their printed form does not injuriously represent the preacher's style can be seen from the following extract :

" This I take for the certainest Matter of Experience : All things are according to the Disposition of the Receiver, One Man will interpret into a Courtesie, that which another turns into an Injury. According as Men are in Preparation and Disposition of Mind, so will things be entertain'd that are offered to Consideration, and proposed. But Truth, if it doth appear, if it be represented and fairly proposed ; it will find Entertainment in a Man's Mind ; if a Man's Mind be not by contrary Indisposition made in an Incapacity. . . . No sooner doth the Truth of God come to our Souls sight, but our Soul knows her, as her first and old Acquaintance : Which, tho' they have been by some Accident unhappily parted a great while ; yet having now, through the Divine Providence, happily met, they greet one another, and, renew their Acquaintance, as those that were first and ancient Friends." [2]

It seems almost unfair to quote Whichcote in this vein at the stage in this study at which we are arrived, for at first sight such a style seems rather that of the true-blue Latitu-

---

[1] *Vid. ante*, p. 30.   [2] ' Select Sermons,' 1698, pp. 4-5.

dinarian of the post-Restoration period.   But it is possible
to regard Whichcote's manner as uniform throughout—his
letters bear a strong resemblance to the passage just quoted—
and his plainness and directness may quite well represent
the transition from the style of Calvinists such as Tuckney
to that of the more pictorial and poetical of the ' Platonists.'

Very different in point of expression are the sermons of
Nathanael Culverwel (1618–1651),[1] whose immortal ' Discourse of the Light of Nature ' is a kind of prose dithyramb
celebrating the reconciliation of Religion and Reason.   The
latter appeared in 1652, edited by William Dillingham—
a Calvinist, who is reputed to have translated the ' Westminster Confession ' into Latin.   Culverwel's own Calvinism
was of the strictest, but his ' Discourse ' has a lofty ideality,
and an almost lyrical fervour in its advocacy and praise of
Reason, which is neither attempted nor matched by any
other member of the ' Platonic ' group.   Tempting as it is
to quote from this work, which Dillingham described as
being " weaved of Sunne-beams," the temptation must be
resisted, though the statement of a nineteenth-century
critic [2] may be noted in passing, that —

" while Culverwel, in point of philosophical genius, is
visibly allied to the other Cambridge Platonists of his day,
both in the cast of his speculation, and in the circle of his
reading, there are points of marked distinction which are
generally in his favour.   His mind is much less burdened
with the weight of his learning. . . .   His reading also
extends more impartially than theirs over the polite as well
as the philosophical literature of antiquity. . . ."

Unfortunately, the eight sermons which accompanied the
' Light of Nature ' (the seventh of which, that entitled
' Spiritual Opticks ' had appeared by itself in the previous
year, 1651,) fall far below the excellence of the ' Discourse.'
In tone and method these sermons are all very similar ;
they have good main divisions, and the treatment is straightforward ;   but, oddly enough, in view of the criticism just
quoted, they abound in learned quotations, many of these

---

[1] *Vid.* Venn's ' Alumni Cantabrigienses,' where these dates and the paternity
of Culverwel are dealt with.
[2] John (afterwards Principal) Cairns, in " A Critical Essay," prefacing ' Of
the Light of Nature A Discourse . . .' ed. by John Brown, D.D., Edin., 1857,
p. xxxi.

being in Greek and Hebrew, and there is a tendency to
illustrations rather fanciful than poetical; frequent reference occurs to the classical writers, particularly to the
moralists. The tone in some, however, in spite of these
accompaniments, resembles that of the more ordinary
Commonwealth sermon [1]—a fact which we may regard as
indicating the rock whence Culverwel was hewn, which has
already been discussed in treating of Tuckney and Whichcote. The ' Spiritual Opticks ' was probably issued by
Dillingham [2] to prepare the way for the reception of the
larger work. It resembles the ' Discourse ' both in its
arguments and its manner of exposition. A specimen may
be given to show what exactly the ' Platonic ' sermon was
like as first delivered in the chapel of Emmanuel College,
before it had been enlarged into a treatise :

" This vast volume of the creatures set out by God himself without any *errata* in it, was printed in so fair a character,
as he that ran might read it : and the least letter in it made
shew of a most divine impression. But alas ! sinne, besides
weakening of the souls eye, hath soyled and defaced the
book ; and hence we come to see in it so darkly. And yet
still the letters are visible, and carry with them the print
of a Deity. The world is, as one calls it, *Ænigma Dei*.
And it is full of looking-glasses : for God hath communicated
several resemblances of himself to the creature, as the face
sheds that image or species upon the glasse whereby it self
is represented. I need not speak of the blessed Angels,
those pure and crystal mirrours, what glorious representation they give of their Creatour : look but into your selves,
and you will find immortal souls shewing forth that image
according to that which they were made : or if you will
look up to that vast and polish'd looking-glasse, you will see
*The heavens declaring the glory of God, and the firmament shewing
his handy work*. Or cast but an eye upon the poorest and
most abject being, and even there you will find some faint
resemblance of a Deity. For as in the most glorious
creature, there is *aliquid nihili* ; so in the most contemptible
creature, as a creature, there is *aliquid Dei*." [3]

---

[1] E.g. the opening of the sermon entitled, ' The White Star ' (on ' Assurance ').
[2] It is said to be " Commended to the reader by W. D. of Emmanuel
College."
[3] ' Spiritual Opticks . . .' Cam., 1656, 4to, p. 15.

Such a style, apart from its pleasing divorce from polemics or the familiar devices of older rhetorical preachers, cannot be claimed as marking an upward stage in the evolution of the sermon.   Of the preaching of John Smith (1616–1652),[1] however, Birch, the biographer of Tillotson, remarks that it—

"contributed to raise new thoughts and a sublime style in the members of the University,"[2]

and both Worthington, who published the 'Select Discourses' in 1660, and Patrick, who preached Smith's funeral sermon, unite in their praise of the young divine. Tulloch considered that the 'Discourses' not only showed great intellectual capacity, but that "an ineffable light of spiritual genius shines in them all," that "calmly and closely reasoned, they are at the same time inspired," and that in them logical precision joined hands with imagination, so that "the result is a delightful admixture of Christian philosophy and poetry."[3]   Yet, as the same writer goes on to say :

"The poetic richness of the style seldom or never, as with Taylor, overbalances the weight of the thought. It is ornate and picturesque without being florid or tawdry. . . . The rhetorical and rational, the imaginative and spiritual, are fused and blended into a common intellectual action which enlightens while it penetrates, and touches with beauty and colour the eminences of truth which it reveals."[4]

Unfortunately, incessant quotation, especially of Plato, Plutarch, Plotinus, Tully, and Lucretius, greatly hampers Smith's style, and in several of the discourses it is almost impossible to find a straightforward piece of English.   But this difficulty of excessive quotation was common to all the Cambridge Platonists—Cudworth and More offend equally with Smith—and arose largely from a desire to prove the consent of the ancient philosophers to the positions advanced. Naturally (as Powicke indicates) these divines "used the

[1] *Vid.* Powicke, 'The Cambridge Platonists,' p. 88, for likelihood of Smith's birth occurring in 1616 and explanation of 1618, the date usually assigned to that event.
[2] Quoted Tulloch, 'Rational Theology . . .' vol. ii, p. 125.
[3] 'Rational Theology . . .' vol. ii, p. 135.
[4] *Ibid.*, pp. 135-6.

19

Platonic writers, not to establish their doctrines so much as to illustrate them," [1] for their appeal was not to the ancient philosophers as final arbiters in intellectual matters, but rather to the agreement observable between the noblest conclusions arrived at by the use of natural reason and the maxims of Christian morality. Consequently, their employment of the moralists is usually strictly illustrative, and not merely ornamental, as was the case with the earlier Calvinist preachers ; though Worthington, it must be admitted, in explaining ' To the Reader ' how the ' Select Discourses ' were prepared for the press, distinguishes between " the material Quotations " which were all carefully verified, and

" short Allusions and Expressions borrow'd out of ancient Authors, serving rather for *Ornament* than *Support* of the Matter in hand." [2]

So far as the propriety of such learned allusions is concerned, it is well to recall, as Worthington does,[3] the place and occasion of their delivery—as exercises in a college chapel. In short they were ' commonplaces ' after the customary pattern to which we have heard Sherman allude.[4]

Of the ten discourses the concluding one is said to have been

" deliver'd in publick at *Huntingdon,* where one of *Queen's* College is every year on March 25, to preach a Sermon against *Witchcraft,* Diabolical Contracts, &c." [5]

The style of this sermon, according to Worthington, is " most familiar," and the latter goes on to relate how when Smith preached to Country-Auditories—

" . . . as it was his care to preach upon arguments of most practical concernment, so was it also his Desire and Endeavour to accommodate his Expressions to ordinary vulgar

---

[1] ' The Cambridge Platonists,' p. 193. Of Smith's use of these authors Powicke remarks (*ibid.*, p. 108) : " They are used to illustrate what he is already sure of."

[2] ' Select Discourses,' 1660 ed., p. iv.

[3] *Ibid.*, p. v.

[4] *Ante,* p. 28.

[5] So Worthington's address ' To the Reader,' 1660 ed., p. xxvi.

Capacities ; being studious to be understood, and not to be
ignorantly wondred at by amuzing the People either with
high unnecessary *Speculations*, or with hard Words and vain
Ostentations of Scholastick Learning. . . ." [1]

The tenth discourse, therefore, may be taken as marking
a kind of transition between the college exercise and the
ordinary sermon, and may be profitably quoted for that
reason.

" Would wicked men dwell a little more at home, and
descend into the bottome of their own Hearts, they should
soon find *Hell* opening her mouth wide upon them, and those
secret fires of inward fury and displeasure breaking out upon
them, which might fully inform them of the estate of true
Misery, as being a short anticipation of it. But in this life
wicked men for the most part *elude* their own Misery for a
time, and seek to avoid the dreadfull sentence of their own
Consciences, by a tergiversation and flying from themselves
into a converse with other things, *Ut nemo in sese tentat
descendere* ; else they would soon find their own home too
hot for them. But while men's minds are perpetually
rambling all the world over in a pursuit of worldly designes,
they are unacquainted with the affairs of their own Souls ;
and know not how deeply a Self-converse and reflection
upon their own prodigious deformities would pierce their
Souls with anguish. . . . As *true Goodness* cannot borrow
Beauty from any external thing to recommend it self to the
Minds and Affections of Good men, seeing it self is the very
Idea and true life of all Beauty and Perfection, the source of
Bliss and Peace to all that partake of her : so neither can
Sin and Wickedness to an enlightened Soul appear more
Ugly, loathsome and hatefull, in any other shape then its
own." [2]

This passage, apart from the decidedly Platonic tincture
of the thought, might well have been written by one of the
Royal Society divines, and Barrow no doubt learned something at the feet of the Platonist preachers. Even in this
' country ' sermon, however, recourse is had to both Greek

[1] Worthington's address ' To the Reader,' 1660 ed., pp. xxvi–xxvii.
[2] ' A Christian's Conflicts and Conquests,' in ' Select Discourses,' 1660 ed.,
pp. 468–9.

and Hebrew—how employed by the preacher in delivery it
is difficult to determine. Probably in such circumstances
Smith's quotations were translated or paraphrased at the
moment, though such translations as now accompany them
appear to have been supplied by Worthington when the discourses came to be published.[1]

In his academic exercises Smith's style was of a more
exalted and poetical kind, and bears a strong resemblance
to that of More, both in form and in the emphasis laid
on the experience of the Divine Life (or Light), and the
necessity for a consequent life of practical goodness which
should make the experience manifest.[2] Although his discourses could never have become a model for public sermons
yet Smith's elevated and luminous thought served a definite
purpose among those capable of appreciating it, and
pointed the way to a nobility of treatment which the purely
dogmatic or rhetorical sermon lacked. While reading his
work one is recalled to some of the finer passages in St.
Augustine's exposition of the Scriptures, not by deliberate
echoes of the thought, but by a similarity of mind and
treatment. Many of Augustine's noblest contemplations
occur in sermons delivered " to the Commonalty," and
although Smith had for the most part an academic auditory,
still the comparative simplicity of his language (apart from
quotations) demonstrates the possibility of dealing with
profound subjects in a manner easy to be understood. This
example Tillotson in particular, Stillingfleet, and still later
men were to be quick to follow.[3]

---

[1] *Vid.* ed. cit., ' To the Reader,' pp. iv–v.

[2] *Vid.* ' The true Way or Method of attaining to Divine Knowledge,' ed.
cit., pp. 3 and 4.

[3] A good example of Augustine's extraordinary power of leading out the
thoughts of average men to the consideration of an abstract subject may be
quoted from the ' Enarrationes in Psalmos ' from an exposition delivered
" to the Commonalty." The Commentary is on Psal. lxxvi. 6. (*Vul.*) : *Of
eternal years I have been mindful :* " What are eternal years ? It is a mighty
thought. See whether the thought requireth anything but great silence. Apart
from all noise without, from all tumult of things human let him remain quite
within that would think of those eternal years. Are the years wherein we are
eternal, or those wherein our ancestors have been, or those wherein our posterity
are to be ? Far be it that they should be esteemed eternal. For what part of
these years doth remain ? Behold we speak and say *in this year* : and what have
we got of this year, save the one day wherein we are ? For the former days of
this year have already gone by, and are not to be had ; but the future days
have not yet come. In one day we are, and we say in this year : nay rather
say thou, *to-day*, if thou desirest to speak of anything present. For of the whole
year what hast thou got that is present ? Whatsoever thereof is past, is

It is interesting to note in passing that much strange natural history still finds a place among Smith's illustrations —the *Torpedo* [1] and the *Basilisk*,[2] alongside " that venomous *Solanum*, that deadly Nightshade, that drives its cold poyson into the Understandings of men " [3]—but such examples (in which the traditional mingles with the actual) merely remind us of the unscientific character of the period, before the era of experiment inaugurated by the Royal Society. They prepare us, too, in some way for the astonishing predisposition to believe in the supernatural which is met with in More and Glanvill.

Henry More (1614–1687) is in some ways the most fascinating of all the Platonist divines. " He was (as Sir Edmund Chambers reminds us [4]) the heart of the Cambridge movement . . . as Cudworth was its brain," and this, for those primarily concerned with the thought of the movement, implies a descent from the more purely philosophic world of Smith and Cudworth. Yet ' seraphic ' as men have agreed to call him,[5] More was no " beautiful and ineffectual

---

no longer ; whatsoever thereof is future, is not yet ; how then *this year* ? Amend the expression : say, *to-day*. . . . What then have we got of these years ? These years are changeable : the eternal years must be thought on, years that stand, that are not made up of days that come and depart ; years whereof in another place the Scripture saith to God, *But Thou art the Self-same, and Thy years shall not fail*." With this may be compared a passage from Smith's fifth discourse, that ' Of the Existence and Nature of God ' : " This World is indeed a great *Horologe* to it self, and is continually numbring out its own age ; but it cannot lay any sure hold upon its own past revolutions, nor can it gather up its infancy and old age and couple them up together. Whereas an *Infinitely-comprehensive Mind* hath a *Simultaneous possession of its own never-flitting life* ; and because it finds no *Succession* in its own *immutable* Understanding, therefore it cannot find any thing to measure out its own duration. And as *Time* lies in the *Basis* of all *Finite* life, whereby it is enabled by degrees to display all the virtue of its own Essence, which it cannot doe at once : so such an *Eternity* lies at the foundation of the Divinity, whereby it becomes one *without any shadow of turning*, as S. *James* speaks, without any *Variety* or *Multiplicity* within himself, which all created Beings that are carried down in the current of Time partake of. . . ." Ed. cit., p. 131.

[1] Ed. cit., p. 5.
[2] *Ibid.*, p. 28.
[3] *Ibid.*, p. 5.
[4] Introd. to extracts from More's writings in Craik's ' English Prose Selections,' vol. ii, p. 553.
[5] Whoever has seen the portrait of More in a cord-bound cassock, with a broad-brimmed hat in his hand, standing under a tree, with a stretch of meadow and the towers of Cambridge in the distance, which appeared before the Latin edition of his works (in 1675) cannot doubt of the truth of the epithet. If it be urged that the epithet can mean nothing of which we have any conception the portrait itself may well be taken as the starting-point for giving a definite content to the term.

angel, beating in the void his luminous wings in vain."
Sensitive and retiring as he was by nature, and reluctant
to enter into controversies, he was a man of strong personal
convictions arrived at from long brooding on the interpretation of life, offered not only by Plato, but almost with
equal frequency by the Neo-Platonists of Alexandria ;
and, credulous as he seems to us, he condemned with
considerable insight the more extravagant pretences of the
early Quakers.   Unfortunately, as in the case of Culverwel,
the specimens we possess of More's preaching—sixteen
' Discourses ' edited posthumously by Worthington—do not
represent his style at its finest.   Yet they have at least
this advantage, that they are less diffuse than his ordinary
style, and in them the preacher was less often distracted
by the charm of his own images, which too frequently tend
to remind one of the painted windows in old churches,
which indeed admit light, but only through an incalculable
wealth of design and tracery.   A delightful play of fancy
is, however, not wholly absent.   Thus we find him saying :

" A Nightingal may vary with her voice into a multitude
of interchangeable Notes, and various Musical falls and
risings, and yet be but a Nightingal, no Chorister : But
should she but sing one Hymn or *Hallelujah*, I should deem
her no bird but an Angel.   So the highest improvement
of Natural Knowledge, or mere Morality, will argue no
more than the Sons of Men : But to be of one will completely with God, will make us, or doth argue us to be the
Sons of God." [1]

A little later in the same discourse he describes the end of
Sanctification as follows :

" Love is the very end of it.   Shall Envy, shall Hatred,
shall Lust, Ambition, Luxury, &c., shall all these enormous
Desires and Affections be cast out of the Soul by Sanctity
and Purity, that she may be but a transparent piece of
Ice, or a spotless fleece of Snow ?   Shall she become so
pure, so pellucid, so christalline, so devoid of all stains that
nothing but still shadows and night may possess that inward
diaphanous Purity ?   Thus would she be no better than the

---

[1] ' Discourses On Several Texts of Scripture,' 1692, XIII, p. 408.

nocturnal Air, no happier than a statue of Alabaster ; it would be but a more cleanly sepulchre of a dead starved Soul. . . . No surely, there is a Resurrection to Life, Love and the Divinity, as well as a Death of the enormous Affections of this Mortal Body."

This last quotation illustrates More's particular manner at its best, when he is seeking to speak directly to an auditory, and is content with images of his own coining instead of matching these with the products of past ages. Here we see an imagination as fecund as Jeremy Taylor's, soaring less like the lark, and content to confine its personal ecstasies to ordinary plainsong for the edification of others. More's more usual ' pictorial ' manner in his longer works lacks such restraint, and suggests an unusually fertile imagination crowded with images which escape pell-mell, before their originator has had time to impose upon them any discipline of expression ; but even this marks, in one way, an advance on the carefully elaborated sentences at which Taylor aimed. The looseness of More's construction signalises the break-up of the Isocratean period as the vehicle of imagination. After the Royal Society preachers had done their work, poetic fancy, where it survived, was content to be confined, as was learned citation, to mere allusion, and, while Tillotson works sometimes in gold and porphyry, he no longer rears fantastic minarets and magnificent but useless domes, but is intent on building strongly and surely a bridge over which rational thought may pass to convince mankind.

The finest achievement of ' Platonic ' preaching must, however, be considered to belong to Ralph Cudworth (1617–1688), whose wonderful sermon, preached before the House of Commons on the 31st March, 1647, has earned a belated eulogy in Professor Grierson's recent study of religion and culture in the seventeenth century.[1]   Not only, as the latter notes, does the argument at one point recall Burke,[2] but the breadth of view and accompanying freedom of utterance have affinities with the later orator. Cudworth's *magnum opus*—' The True Intellectual System of the Universe '—offers no stylistic beauties such as can be collected in the shorter but directly philosophical works of

[1] ' Cross-Currents in English Literature of the XVIIth Century,' pp. 224 *seq.*
[2] *Ibid.*, p. 226 footnote,

Culverwel and More, nor would the posthumously published
' Treatise concerning Eternal and Immutable Morality '
call for special remark with regard to style. The sermon
before " the House," however, is not only remarkable for
the enlightenment of the positions advanced, but for the
sustained beauty and mobility of its expression. Professor
Grierson has fortunately (in the quotations chosen to illustrate Cudworth's thought) rendered readily accessible a
number of the finer passages ; having regard to style the
following may be taken as a typical passage from the
sermon :

" Indeed we seem to do something, we are always moving
and lifting at the stone of Corruption that lies upon our
hearts but yet we never stirre it notwithstanding, or at least
never roll it off from us.   We are sometimes a little troubled
with the guilt of our sinnes, and then we think we must
thrust our lusts out of our hearts, but afterwards we sprinkle
our selves over, with I know not what *Holy-water*, and so are
contented to let them still abide, quietly within us.   We do
every day truly confesse the same sinnes, and pray against
them, and yet still commit them as much as ever, and lie as
deeply under the power of them.   We have the same Water
to pump out in every Prayer, and still we let the same leake
in again upon us.   We make a great deal of noise and raise
a great deal of dust with our feet ; but we do not move
from off the ground on which we stood, we do not go forward at all : or if we do sometimes make a little progresse,
we quickly lose again the ground which we had gained :
like those upper *Planets* in the Heaven, which (as the
Astronomers tell us) sometimes move forwards, sometimes quite backwards, and sometimes perfectly stand still :
have their *Stations* and *Retrogradations*, as well as their
Direct Motions.   As if Religion were nothing else, but a
Dancing up and down, upon the same piece of ground, and
making several Motions and Friskings on it ; and not a
sober Journeying and Travelling onwards towards some
certain place." [1]

No extract unfortunately can convey the impression of
Cudworth's sermon as a whole, in which paragraph suc-

[1] ' A Sermon Preached before the Honourable House of Commons, At
Westminster, March 31, 1647,' Camb., 1647, 4to, pp. 55-7.

ceeds paragraph with the greatest possible naturalness, each
with its own quota of pertinent and happily employed
illustrations. The sermon is truly a piece of oratory, and
advances by the development of its own main thought in
place of the stereotyped divisions beloved of the older,
and the majority of those who may be called the Parliamentary, divines. It is the exposition of a great theme
rather than the explication of a text, and as such points
forward to what was later to be regarded as an ideal in
France [1] and imitated in England. It is distinguished from
the best non-Anglican preaching by its spaciousness of
treatment, which, even when the same direct means are
employed as are found in Baxter's sermons, imparts to the
simple sentences an elevation and disinterestedness to which
Puritan preaching never attained. For the same reason,
though lacking the architectonic excellence of Barrow's
prose, it may be pronounced superior in tone to much of
the latter's work. Preaching to a non-academic audience,
Cudworth was compelled to temper his philosophic speculations to suit his auditory, and so is less strictly philosophical
than Smith ; at the same time, the more lyric elements in
Culverwel and More were foreign to him, and the poetical
passages in his work depend on what eighteenth-century
writers would have described as ' imagination ' rather
than ' fancy ' ; taken altogether, the sermon represents
the fusion of the best characteristics of the ' Platonic '
preaching with the ' simplified ' sermon of the period,
whether attempted by Anglicans like Sanderson and
Ussher or Puritans like Tuckney. Deriving its impulse
from a movement of thought, such preaching rescued the
plain style from the oblivion destined to overtake all dull
preaching, by transmitting to it a new and finer spirit. In
other words, the laborious imitation and careful inlaying
of various schools was definitely set aside, and brick was
recognised as no bad material in which to build, provided
one made certain of nobility in the design.

Of less prominent members of the ' Platonic ' school it is
unnecessary to speak at length. Worthington and Dillingham, who have been mentioned as editors of Smith and
Culverwel respectively, exhibit a community of interest

---

[1] *Vid.* Fénelon, 'Dialogues Concerning Eloquence,' Stevenson's trans.,
1722, pp. 114, 115 ; *ante,* pp. 123-5.

with their greater brethren, but less ability of expression. Rust, author of ' A Discourse of Truth,' was a bigger man, but his sermons [1] show a lusciousness of style, in some ways resembling Taylor's, but hardly in the best manner of the Cambridge divines. Sterry, to whom Dr. Powicke would allot a place with the Platonists and to whom Professor Pinto has still more recently directed attention both as a mystic and a literary artist,[2] was, according to Baxter, among his contemporaries "famous for Obscurity in Preaching (being . . . too high for this World, and too low for the other) "[3] : and, although in his ' Catholick Theologie ' Baxter retracted somewhat the harshness of this criticism, the actual comments on Sterry's style, made in the latter work, will be found on examination to be strictly just :

" . . . Above all the excessive pregnancy of his wit produceth a superabundance of Metaphors or Allegories, that . . . they make up almost all his style ; so that to any ordinary Reader his matter is not so much *cloathed* in Metaphors, as *drowned, buried* or *lost*." [4]

But, although, along with the mystical, the rhetorical element in Sterry seems to have been that which attracted the notice of contemporaries, his published works show no uniform level of literary attainment. While his occasional beauties are striking, it is a fact that they are very strictly ' occasional.' Thus, while the sentences to which Professor Pinto has drawn attention [5] are discoverable in his sermons, such sentences do not occur with any frequency, and, indeed, only one of Sterry's published sermons—that en-

[1] These are : ' A sermon preached at Newtown the 29 of Octob. 1663. At the Funeral of the Rt. Honourable Hugh Earl of Mount-Alexander . . .' Dublin, 1664 ; ' A Funeral Sermon Preached at the Obsequies of the Right Reverend Father in God Jeremy Lord Bishop of Down . . . 1657,' Lon., 1668 ; and two sermons occurring in ' The Remains of that Reverend and learned Prelate, Dr George Rust. . . . Collected and Published by Henry Hallywell,' Lon., 1686, 4to.

[2] In " Peter Sterry: Puritan, Platonist, and Mystic, by V. de Sola Pinto . . . " in ' Speculum Religionis . . .' Oxf., 1929, 4to, and " Peter Sterry and his Unpublished Writings," in ' The Review of English Studies,' October 1930.

[3] ' Reliquiæ,' 1696, p. 75.

[4] ' Catholick Theologie . . . The Third Part : of God's Gracious Operations on Mans Soul . . .' p. 108.

[5] E.g. the quotation from ' England's Deliverance From the Northern Presbytery,' 1652, 4to, p. 14, quoted p. 165 ' Speculum Religionis.'

titled ' The Clouds in which Christ Comes,' delivered before
the House of Commons in 1647—taken as a whole can claim
to rank as a literary composition. This sermon, which may
be said to represent Sterry at his best, illustrates admirably
the tendency to which Baxter alludes, as can be seen from
the following quotation :

" In the midst of this Darknesse our Saviour passeth on ;
upon the backs of these Clouds he comes riding along.
Behind the visible Formes of things He hides Himselfe, and
steales in upon us ere we be aware. All Their Motions are
His Approaches. *Mat.* 24. The Disciples ask their Master,
What should be the signes of His Comming ? He relates
by way of Prophesie the whole story of the World, Publike
in Nations, Particular in Families, Private in single Persons,
From His death, to that of the whole World : And so He
answers their Question, teaching them, that as all Creatures
are the *Print* of His Feet, so their whole Conduct is the
Motion of His Feet, Their *Commotions* His *Commings on* upon
them.

" As the Whale moveth himselfe under the Waters, the
Billows rise and rowl, the Deep boyles like a Pot. Before
our Saviour's time *Lucifer* was *Leviathan*, that made the Sea
to seeth about him, like a Pot of Ointment. Now our
Lord Jesus sports Himselfe in these Waters. He makes his
way under them, and as he moves, The Deepes of Mens
Spirits, Counsailes, Common-wealths, boyle, the whole
Frame of Things reel and rowl themselves into violent
Concussions, like Waves of the Sea." [1]

Sterry's usual manner, however, is rendered dull by
strict adherence to a rigid ' method,' or consists of mere
partisan affirmation entirely foreign to the bigger men of
the Cambridge group. He is, therefore, hardly to be
reckoned of their number. [2]

[1] Ser. cit., Lon., 1648, 4to, pp. 21–2.
[2] After re-reading Sterry's sermons in the light of Professor Pinto's articles,
I have arrived at the above conclusion, in spite of the fact that the ready kindness with which Professor Pinto has discussed the matter with me personally
has been a strong inducement to join with him in setting out Sterry's claim
to a niche among English prose writers. Sterry's merits are, I feel, of too
occasional an order to entitle him to much attention as a man of letters,
and, in a sphere so rich in literary masterpieces as the seventeenth-century
pulpit, I am convinced that a more uniform level of attainment must be looked
for before a preacher can be pronounced outstanding.

Nor is the " Platonick Tincture " which Calamy ascribed to Howe [1] sufficiently outstanding to distinguish him from the better type of Puritan preachers. Baxter himself, as Powicke has shown, has decided affinities with the Platonic movement, but this was rather on the side of speculation than of thought happily expressed, and, for reasons which we have heard him reveal, did not affect his preaching.[2]

A more interesting divine whose work calls for mention in the present connection was Joseph Glanvill (1636–1680). Although of Exeter College, Oxford, certain of the positions advanced in his writings appeared to contemporaries to link him to the Platonists,[3] while Wood, in a decidedly ill-natured account in the ‘ Athenæ,’ dubs him a Latitudinarian, thus indicating the connection of rational theology and broad churchmanship. Actually, Glanvill would be more accurately described as a Cartesian, but Socratic Platonism he found useful as a philosophic progenitor of scepticism, and in scepticism he appears seriously to have believed—so far as a man of his volatile temperament was capable of believing seriously in anything—as the only possible appoach to philosophic truth. Christianity, he was careful to add, admitted of no scepticism, being founded not upon knowledge, which has constantly proved fallacious, but upon revelation which cannot deceive. Platonism, or indeed any philosophic system, it must be confessed, appealed to him primarily as good material with which to deck out his writings, whether sermons or other, and his allusions are to be regarded rather as the affectations of a man of wit desirous of posing as a philosopher than the outcome of an intellectual and emotional experience, which affected thought and style alike. The leading characteristics of the man are well portrayed in a letter written to Henry More by Worthington, in which the latter relates :

" They were smiling at St. Michael Armyn's (who was at

[1] *Memoir* before ‘ The Works of the Late Reverend and Learned John Howe, M.A.,’ 2 vols., Oxf., 1724, fol.

[2] *Vid.* ‘ Richard Baxter under the Cross,’ pp. 241 *seq.*, where Powicke is commenting on Baxter's ‘ The Reasons of the Christian Religion.’ At p. 247 we are given a list of Baxter's favourite authors, which are shown to be those of the Cambridge divines, notably Marsilio Ficino. At pp. 251–2 a fine quotaton is cited from ‘ The Reasons of the Christian Religion,’ which shows an affinity of style with Culverwel and his associates.

[3] *Vid.* Anthony Horneck's ‘ Preface ’ to ‘ Some Discourses, Sermons and Remains ’ of Glanvill, published in 1681, Lon., 4to.

Bath last summer) when they told the story of the preacher at Bath,[1] how spruce and trim he was, with his white gloves, and handkerchief, and periwig (which must now and then be pulled), and how romantic in preaching." [2]

The concluding words are arresting when we consider the date of Worthington's letter, 1668, and that three years before, Glanvill, in dedicating the ' Scepsis Scientifica ' [3] to the Royal Society, had expressed the distaste he had come to feel for " the musick and curiosity of fine Metaphors and dancing periods " of his former style, and his hearty approval of " manly sense, flowing in natural and unaffected Eloquence," which characterised the writings of the members. Yet, even in his later work, when he was definitely writing under the influence of the Royal Society, Glanvill's sentences were often excessively short, carefully balanced, and deliberately appositive, or even antithetical, and the threat was never far absent of a cast-back to the old artificial balance of ' Senecan ' prose, which is no less a threat, though the reverberation come from a silver bell. His imagination, however, became more restrained as he grew older, and his similitudes ceased to come invariably (as Greenslet happily expresses it)—

" ' trailing clouds of glory,' with a flash of poetic insight, or a setting of luminous beauty. In the later work . . . they are introduced as Bacon might have used them, to make the meaning, the content of thought, more clear and forcible." [4]

Glanvill's imagery, therefore, and much of his manner may be pronounced akin to that of Taylor and the Cambridge Platonists. He had the sunlight and pictorialism of these preachers, although his theory of preaching was directly opposed to the splendours and harmonies of their writings, and although his own sermons, in spite of their

[1] Glanvill was rector of the Abbey Church at Bath from 1666 till his death.
[2] Quoted p. 76 in ' Joseph Glanvill. A Study in English Thought and Letters of the Seventeenth Century,' by Ferris Greenslet, Ph.D., New York, 1900.   Cf. ante, p. 23, footnote [3].
[3] A revised version of ' The Vanity of Dogmatizing,' published in 1661. The former contains the story of ' The Scholar Gypsy,' which was omitted from the second form of the work.
[4] Op. cit., p. 213.

antitheses, which suggest a still older artificiality, are on the whole plain and natural. As the author of ' The Vanity of Dogmatizing ' and as a ' romantic ' preacher—although small trace of his compositions in this kind have been preserved—Glanvill may legitimately be considered with the Platonists ; in his critique of pulpit-oratory,[1] and in the greater part of his sermons he may be included among the writers of the new prose. The transition is interesting, not only in Glanvill's own work, but as illustrating to some extent the result of philosophic influence on preaching.

An example of Glanvill's ' romantic ' manner of preaching is provided in ' A Fast Sermon on the Kings Martyrdom,' 1667, in which after several pages of his plainer and more ordinary manner, the pitch is suddenly changed, and he continues :

" When fine Weather and a warm Sun, the indulgence of Heaven, and a long tranquillity, had made us fat and frolick, rich and full, our prosperity made us wanton, and our riches insolent. We began to murmur, we knew not why ; and to complain, because we had nothing to complain of. Discontents grew upon the stock of our ill Nature, and the perverseness of our humours ; and every little occasion was Fuel to the Fire that was kindling in the distempered Body. . . . Nor did things stop here. The Sparks grew into mighty Flames, and those Vapours into Thunder and Tempests : The whispers of the Corner past into the noise of a Camp ; and the murmurs of the Street into the sound of the Trumpet. The pulpit sounded as much war as the Drum ; and the Preacher spit as much flame as the Cannon. *Curse ye Meroz*[2] was the Text, and Blood and Plunder the Comment and the Use." [3]

Such a style of preaching, coming as it did in the year which saw the publication of Dryden's ' Essay of Dramatick Poesy,' is obviously a cast-back to similar strains in earlier preachers, and Dryden's remark that ' metaphysical '

[1] ' An Essay Concerning Preaching,' originally published 1678.
[2] A reference to Stephen Marshall's sermon before the House of Commons : ' Meroz Cursed . . .' Lon., 1641. The accusations levelled against Presbyterian and Independent preachers of inciting ' the Houses ' and country to war is hardly borne out by the extant remains of Parliamentary preaching.
[3] ' Some Discourses, Sermons and Remains,' 1681, pp. 164–5.

conceits [1] had found benefit of clergy might justifiably be extended to include such ' Senecan ' antitheses as are noticeable in this passage.   Yet, it is only fair to point out that while Glanvill sedulously cultivated a balanced phrasing, he avoided the similes which had formerly accompanied this manner, and chose rather to make the plain facts of science or casual observation dance to his piping.   Not till late in life did he learn to suit his style to the matter in hand, instead of compelling his matter to serve his style.   This important step he seems to have taken only after a due consideration of the ends of preaching—and possibly the growing vogue of the Royal Society prose—had forced it on his attention.   All through his life, and in all his works, however, Glanvill kept free of what he called " that silly vanity of impertinent citations," a habit which, he noted, arose from the undue respect paid to antiquity, prevented scientific research, and impeded the formation of a good style.   This attitude of mind separates him from the Cambridge writers, whose citations, although seldom " impertinent," too often hampered the progress of their prose.   It is the most " modern " note struck by Glanvill, for at no period of his career can he be said to have become quite natural, and his plainness one feels was largely due to a conformity to the fashion of those whose attention he wished to attract.   Although he was neither a great man nor a great writer, Glanvill's work is of interest as illustrating, how, avoiding dogmatism or the meticulous attention to moral duties (which could render so accomplished a writer as Taylor dull when he came to write ' Holy Living '), the plain sermon might yet be rendered agreeable and interesting both in its structure and content.

What Glanvill did not quite succeed in achieving may be studied in the work of John Norris of Bemerton (1657–1711), who may be regarded as bringing up the rear of the ' Platonic' divines.   But as Norris' happy fluidity of style, which permitted of the easy exposition of difficult intellectual ideas, and his great charm of illustration, must have been materially aided by other influences operative during his youth, which fell in the first twenty years of the Restoration period, it is hardly fair to the older divines to discuss him in

[1] " Defence of the Epilogue," in ' Essays of Dryden,' ed. W. P. Ker, vol. i, pp. 173–4.

this connection.   The fact that he dedicated his first sermon in 1685 to Henry More indicates in what direction he looked for inspiration ; but his relation to the Platonist preachers resembles somewhat Bates' connection with the Puritans. Both Bates and Norris shared with a party (or group of men) certain views which distinguished them from other divines of their time ; their style, however, is indistinguishable from that of the best preachers of all denominations, a fact which goes to show that by whatever devious roads men had arrived at this ideal—interested in it by Ussher or Hall among the Anglicans, or cultivating it as a development of the Puritan demand for plain preaching, or coming to it in an attempt to present a rational Christianity to popular auditories—the ideal of the period immediately succeeding the Restoration had come to be a plain, natural, straightforward style.   The part played by the Royal Society in setting a hall-mark to this will be shown in the following chapter.

Reverting to the sermons of those who have been most commonly regarded as the Latitudinarians, Wilkins may most conveniently be left over for discussion along with the Royal Society preachers, and Tillotson as displaying in his work the consummation of all the competing changes and experiments in preaching which we have been reviewing is best considered at the end of our study.   There remains to be noticed, Patrick, Lloyd, and Stillingfleet.

Simon Patrick (1626–1707) originally of Queens' College, Cambridge, was deeply influenced by the Platonists, and preached, as we have seen, the funeral sermon of John Smith.   His sermons are praised enthusiastically by Wilkins in later editions of the ' Ecclesiastes ' as a good model for intending preachers.   They do not, however, possess any literary grace, and adhere more closely to a rigid scheme of main sections subdivided, with ' advices ' and ' directions ' to each part, than his remarks on preaching in ' A Discourse of Profiting by Sermons,' would lead one to expect.[1]   William Lloyd (1627–1717), successively bishop of St. Asaph, of Lichfield and Coventry, and of Worcester, and one of the " seven bishops," exhibits a good plain style closely resembling that of Wilkins, but not obviously connected with the rational outlook that distinguished the

[1] *Vid. post*, p. 376.

more philosophical of his contemporaries. All Latitudinarians, however, it is clear from Fowler's account of ' The
Principles and Practices of certain Moderate Divines of
the Church of *England*,' were accused of being " moral
preachers," and caring less for sound doctrine than good
conduct.[1] Their appeal to Reason as supreme arbiter as
against the WORD, or the WORD interpreted by the " Institutes," was very distasteful to the Calvinist, while
Anglicans of the restored " High Church " party regarded
them as denying the unique authority of the Church. Their
ideal of preaching is also made plain by Fowler : they
regarded—

" no Preaching as truly *powerful*, but that which worketh
upon the *affections* by first conquering the *judgement* ; and
convinceth men of their duty by solid Reasons and Arguments. . . ."[2]

Such an ideal may be taken as finding one of its most
eloquent expressions in the sermons of the last of these men
whom it falls to consider, Edward Stillingfleet (1635–1699).
In his early ' *Irenicum*,' written when he was only twenty-
four, in an attempt to heal the breaches in the Church, he
already displayed the plain, flowing, well-modulated style
which was afterwards to characterise his great work, the
' Origines Sacræ,' published in 1662, and which we find
in his sermons at all periods of his life. Not only is his
style perspicuous and equable, but it is rendered noble by
the sublimity of the subjects which he discussed and the
propriety of the expressions he employed to elucidate his
meaning. He was careful to reject merely rhetorical aids ;
his illustrations are of a philosophical character, introduced
not for embellishment but to serve a definite purpose. The
cadence of his prose is due to the orderliness of his thoughts,
and his paragraphs mark less the convenient divisions
necessary to the orator (far less the attentive following of a
' method ' of preaching) than the rounding off of exhaustive
and self-sufficient speculations on particular subjects. Yet
his very excellence renders him more monotonous than
South, for example, whose judiciously weighed brevity and
occasional homely pithiness gave variety to his longer and

[1] *Op. cit.*, Lon., 1670, pp. 18 and 117–18.   [2] *Op. cit.*, p. 118.

20

profounder sentences. He is inferior to Tillotson, not in literary execution, but in his apparent inability to unbend, and like Atterbury afterwards, sacrifices the function of the Christian teacher to the achievement of the orator. Stillingfleet's style suggests always the lawn sleeves of the bishop or the pulpit of a university ; it conveys the impression of being in full dress, and suggests brilliant auditories and outstanding occasions, and for this reason it lacks the familiarity of manner that is acceptable to the solitary reader, or the lowering of tone that is agreeable to the closet. In consequence, therefore, of the absence of variation and lack of adaptability, it is now little known, and has come to be much less regarded than in Stillingfleet's lifetime when he was the most popular of London preachers.

The following, from a sermon delivered before Charles II on the 13th March, 1666-7, is quoted as being representative, and at the same time showing how by this period a high standard of plain yet eminently literary preaching had been attained :

" It is well for us in the Age we live in, that we have the judgment of former ages to appeal to, and of those persons in them whose reputation for Wisdom is yet unquestionable. For otherwise we might be born down by the spightful enemy to all virtue and goodness, the impudence of such, who it is hard to say, whether they shew it more in committing sin, or in defending it. Men whose manners are so bad, that scarce anything can be imagined worse, unless it be the wit they use to excuse them with. Such who take the measure of men's perfections downwards, and the nearer they approach to beasts, the more they think themselves to act like men. No wonder then, if among such as these the differences between good and evil be laughed at, and no sin be thought so unpardonable, as the thinking that there is any at all. Nay, the utmost they will allow in the description of sin is, that it is a thing that some live by declaiming against, and others cannot live without the practice of." [1]

Such preaching, except for a casual phrase here and there, might have fallen from the lips of a Victorian bishop.

[1] Sermon cit. in " Fifty Sermons Preached Upon Several Occasions . . ." Lon., 1707, being vol. i of ' The Works of . . . Dr. Edw. Stillingfleet . . . In Six Volumes,' Lon., fol., 1710.

It is the style we are accustomed to from Newman, or Mill, or Huxley, or Morley, and to say that is to acknowledge that it is modern.   Looking backwards, we see that it is due to the liberating influence of philosophy which led certain divines—those in particular whose work we have noticed in this chapter—to regard Christianity as a rational system likely to commend itself to men if clearly and plainly expounded.   While it points back to Hales and Chillingworth, it would not repudiate Hall or Sanderson, and while largely inspired by the same spirit as inspired Leighton, Baxter and Howe are separated from it by no impassable gulf.   The Cambridge Platonists fostered it in its youth, and if they at first sight seem to have cultivated the imaginative faculty at the expense of the rational, it is to be remembered that their imaginations were kindled at the fire of reason, and if for a time a certain extravagance is noticeable in their work, while it was confined to the bounds of a university, yet afterwards they laid aside the more questionable of their adornments and girded themselves to commend their message to the world.   In doing this they rendered a great service to English preaching, for from the elevation of their thoughts they supplied it with a new sublimity, and from the necessity of conveying their ideas to the many they materially aided in the fight for simplicity.

IN turning to the preachers of the Restoration period it is necessary to emphasise the object which our scrutiny has in view, for Restoration preaching, in so far as it was merely a resumption of those forms of preaching which we have already discussed, need not detain us. The fact that Cosin's sermons, as previously noted, " embrace a period of time extending from 1621–1659," [1] and display a uniformity of manner, may be taken as proof that the Anglo-Catholic type of sermon was actually continued in some quarters more or less as a party badge. Of this Evelyn affords valuable evidence, who notes in his *Diary* under date the 4th April, 1679, that Pritchard, bishop of Gloucester

" preach'd in a manner very like bishop Andrews, full of divisions, and scholastical " ;

and, as late as 1683, further records :

" A stranger, an old man, preach'd on 6 Jerem. 8 . . much after Bp. Andrews's method, full of logical divisions, in short and broken periods, and Latine sentences, now quite out of fashion in the pulpit, which is grown into a far more profitable way, of plaine and practical discourses." [2]

The " plaine and practical discourses " to which Evelyn alludes did not, however, definitely establish themselves for a few years after the Restoration, and every variety of pre Commonwealth Anglican sermon enjoyed a recrudescence although in the main the dullest, least literary type pre vailed.[3] Similarly, until 1662 Baxter and others of like ecclesiastical views continued publicly with the plain non Anglican sermon, and after that date, in private, at such licensed meeting-houses as Pinner's Hall and Salter's Hall The Cambridge Platonists, fortunately, by conforming saved their literary deposit for the Establishment.

For the first few years after the Restoration sermons repre sentative of the resumption and continuance of old vogue are found alongside of certain new adaptations. If Thomas

---

[1] *Vid.* editor's preface to Oxf. ed. of his ' Works ' in the ' Library of Anglo Catholic Theology,' 1843.

[2] *Anno* cit., 15th July.

[3] Such outstanding divines as Sheldon, Sancroft, Gunning, Morley, and Seth Ward were all remarkably dull preachers.

Pierce (1622–1691), for example, whom Pepys praises,[1] preached learned sermons, full of quotations and references to authorities often quaintly applied,[2] not far removed from Andrewes and Cosin, Adam Littleton (1627–1694), the lexicographer and successor of Busby at Westminster School, not only reverted to the old expatiation on some of the Christian paradoxes,[3] but struck in the treatment of his themes a strangely foreign note, probably considered agreeable to those acquainted with Continental Catholic preaching, and in some ways resembling the sermons of the Romanist preachers before Catherine of Braganza and (at a later period) before James II and his queen.[4] On the other hand, we find Richard Allestree (1619–1681), the supposed author of ' The Whole Duty of Man,' whose pulpit style appears to us decidedly plain,[5] described in company with John Fell (1625–1686) by White Kennett as " too quaint and elegant," [6] while the latter, a somewhat dull and heavy preacher, is stated by Evelyn to have preached before Charles II on the 24th February, 1665, " a very formal discourse, and in blank verse, according to his manner." Unfortunately, only two printed sermons of Fell's remain, but one of these, also a sermon at Court,[7] reveals what

---

[1] *Vid.* ' Diary,' 8th April, 1662–3.

[2] *Vid.* e.g. the opening of a sermon entitled ' The Primitive Rule of Reformation : Delivered . . . Before His Majesty at Whitehall, *Feb.* 1, 1662.'

[3] *Vid.* ' LXI Sermons . . .' Lon., 1680, fol., p. 54.

[4] *Vid.* ' A Select Collection of Catholick Sermons Preach'd before their Majesties King James II, Mary Queen-Consort, Catherine Queen-Dowager, &c.,' issued in 2 vols. in 1741. These sermons are said on the title-page to be ' By the Reverend Fathers : Ayray, Betham, Bix, Codrington, Ellis, Gyffard, Godden, Levison & Scarisbrike.' Sermons by a number of other preachers contemporary with these are also included. Ellis and Gyffard were the most frequent preachers. The former expressed himself in a somewhat bald but typically English manner ; the latter, on the contrary, was a highly rhetorical preacher, and along with Bix, Codrington, and Betham represents the degenerate taste of post-tridentine Catholicism as found in baroque architecture and the poems of Crashaw. It is to be remarked that the sermons delivered before Catherine of Braganza are the most extravagant.

[5] *Vid.* ' XVIII Sermons . . .' Lon., 1669, large 4to.

[6] ' A Register and Chronicle Ecclesiastical and Civil . . .' Lon., 1727, fol. The sermon referred to by Kennett as delivered at Whitehall by Allestree, 12th October, 1662, certainly makes use of the old crucifixion *motifs*, and the paradoxes of the Incarnation are elaborated in a Christmas sermon of 1665. But this was purely on the content side, and did not affect Allestree's style— a point of curious resemblance with Binning.

[7] ' The Character of the last Daies,' Oxf., 1675. The text is 2 Peter iii. 3, which proves it was not the sermon alluded to by Evelyn, and which he expressly states was from " 15 Romans 2."

Evelyn apparently intended to record.   Several paragraphs
open with decasyllabic groupings of words, and a number
of these groupings at times follow each other.   Such phrases
if read in a stilted manner, would certainly give an impression akin to blank verse.[1]

John Gauden (1605–1662), by some considered the
author of the ' Eikon Basilike,' had adapted himself to
several preaching styles in turn, before, in 1660, delivering
to the House of Commons a sermon stuck full of Greek (and
at times of Hebrew) words, and so loaded with Scriptural
quotations as to be practically unreadable, and the same
year, at the funeral of bishop Brownrig, another sermon
abounding in Greek quotations from the Fathers, and in
Latin ones from both Pagan and Christian authors, which
yet contained passages that suggest Glanvill's use of images
and something also of Glanvill's conceit.[2]   But Glanvill
enjoyed advantages which Gauden died too soon to possess,
and under the influence of the Royal Society was led to
appreciate a simpler style of preaching.   The interesting
thing about all these preachers, however, is that we see
in their work the transition from the old ' metaphysical '
preaching to the ' quaint and elegant,' with continually
less delight in the quaintness and a continually growing
insistence on the elegance, until, with the gradual change
of view as to what might be considered elegance, even the
most conservative of preaching vogues succumbed to the

---

[1] E.g. one paragraph opens : " 'Tis true the World has lasted a long time '
(sermon cit., p. 84), while the sentence, " The appearance of these scoffers in
the World / who laugh at all Religion, and despise, / a future Judgment, when
so ere it happens, / is its self / a very signal mark of its approach " (ibid., p. 15)
or that beginning : " Now whether it be reasonable for us, / to have less vener-
ation and esteem, / for the true God, then they have for the false, / . . .'
(ibid., p. 18), decidedly exemplify the tendency.   Such passages might come
straight from Massinger's ' Virgin Martyr,' or Shirley.   When prose and verse
could stand so close it is less to be wondered at that Dryden advocated the
heroic couplet for the poetical drama.

[2] E.g. " Calme and even-spun tempers of mind do not become holy men at
all times, and at all occasions ; there are *pious perturbations*, which are as if
were the *echos* of *devout souls* to the louder sound of Gods voyce " (' A Sermon
Preached in the Temple-Chappel . . .' Lon., 1660, p. 47) : or " When God
smites, it becomes us to feel his strokes, and express our sence ; *sullen* and
stupid souls argue a senseless temper, a hard heart, and a seared conscience
God that hath planted all affections and passions in us, knows how to use and
improve them, as a skilful *Lutinist* strikes on all strings, and at every stop
Though our passions are indeed grown wilde and sour naturally like *crab-
stocks* ; yet grace can graft fit cions on every one : yea and make use of men
complexions and *constitutions* to the advantage of his glory . . ." (ibid., p. 51).

prevailing taste of the Court and of the most highly educated part of society.

It is precisely in this change of taste and the consequent reform of style that the interest in Restoration preaching centres. While, on the one hand, as just indicated, the older forms of preaching gradually became transformed or definitely came to an end before the standard of prose-style set up by the Royal Society, on the other hand, it is to be remembered that the movement towards the simplification of style, away from conceits, incessant and unnecessary quotations, and phonic ingenuities imitated from ancient rhetorical practice, was not due to the sudden whim of a Court or the fiat of a Society, which for the moment was prepared to exercise some at least of the functions of an Academy. Charles II, it is clear, whatever his ultimate motives, would willingly have granted certain of the non-Anglicans toleration, but his first Parliament was hostile to the idea and prevented this ; and, in the same way, no matter what ' Directions concerning Preaching ' he might have issued or what particular tendencies in prose style he might have favoured, these would have counted for little had they not received the unanimous approval of a large and influential section of the nation.[1] Nor can it be said to have been those whose taste may be supposed to have been improved by a sojourn in France to whom the reform in style was due. It was decidedly a native product. Wilkins' ' World in the Moone '[2] had first seen light in 1638, and, though ostensibly a ' scientific ' work, falls little short in point of style of Cowley's essays two decades later. That further specimens of the plain yet fluent in secular prose are so scanty must be considered due to the pre-occupation of the times rather than to the direct opposition of other ideals. Where religious oratory is considered, however, we are able to trace the stylistic pedigree more

[1] Sir Charles Firth, in an unpublished paper on ' The Preachers of the Restoration and Revolution Period,' which he is good enough to permit my quoting, disposes as follows of the undue importance which has been attached to Charles II's personal taste in this respect : " No doubt the King's taste helped to form the public taste, but the simplification of English prose was the result of a general movement which manifested itself in every branch of literature, in the prose of Dryden and Temple as well as that of Tillotson."

[2] The full title of the work is : ' The Discovery of a New World : Or a Discourse tending to prove, that 'tis possible there may be another habitable World in the Moone.'

closely, and among Anglicans Hall, and the rationalists
Hales and Chillingworth, among the Puritans Tuckney and
Baxter, and among the Platonists More and Whichcote,
may be taken as preachers who successively, and in some
cases concurrently, maintained the tradition of a straightforward and malleable prose. Hall in some ways directly
links up with South ; similarly, Hales may be regarded as
a forerunner of Stillingfleet. The desire for a reform in a
particular direction was present during an extended period,
in some measure inspired by hermeneutic and ultimately by
theological prepossessions, but not solely attributable to
such. If the original aims of preachers of various schools
was to ensure that they should be understood, the final aim
of all was associated with a high degree of polish ; for, the
standard of style having been raised, the most direct and
least ambitious of preachers fell into line—a fact which
accounts for the decidedly monotonous suavity of much
eighteenth-century preaching.

Of the great Restoration preachers, however—and of the
six greatest English preachers, three flourished in this
period [1]—one, South, quite definitely attained excellence
without reference to the Royal Society movement—and,
indeed, in certain respects in direct hostility to it [2]—the
second, Barrow, although belonging to the Society, can
hardly be claimed as exemplifying in his pulpit oratory its
avowed ideals, while the third, Tillotson, represents rather
the summation of the best in the sermons of men of all parties
than the logical outcome of one particular mode of preaching, although on the whole his style may be claimed as an
amalgam of the Puritan and rationalist manners. In the
work of these three preachers, therefore, ample scope is
afforded to study the almost impersonal evolution of style
under contemporary influences, the distinctive contribution
of genius, and the carefully achieved perfection which was
due, not only to the taste of the moment, but to certain

[1] Outside of this period Andrewes, Donne, and Jeremy Taylor may be
considered the greatest English preachers. While the two last have received
due acknowledgment Andrewes has too long been neglected, and is certainly
entitled to a high place in this select band. Tardy recognition has been
accorded him by T. S. Eliot in the first essay of the latter's volume entitled,
' For Lancelot Andrewes,' published Lon., 1928.

[2] Evelyn relates how, at the opening of the Sheldonian Theatre at Oxford
on the 8th July, 1669, South, in his speech as Public Orator, attacked the
Royal Society. He seems to have thought scientific enquiry led to atheism.

modifications inherited from the past and largely transmitted through the personality of a particular preacher.

Oddly enough, Robert South (1634–1716), the youngest
of the three great Restoration preachers, and the survivor of
both his pulpit rivals by a considerable period, represents
a more archaic manner than the other two, but one which
may be said to have been the fine flower of Anglican preaching on its less exotic side. In considering the 'metaphysical'
vogue, influential as it was, and much favoured at Court as
it appears to have been, one cannot refrain from questioning
whether or not it was of a type which one can consider
typically English, or whether for a time familiarity with
certain rhetorical devices, allied with a returning interest
in the Fathers, did not dominate the sermon in prominent
places of delivery to the exclusion of what was more in
keeping with the spirit and temper of Englishmen in the
mass. It is true, and it deserves to be emphasised, that where
all men were 'witty,' 'witty' preaching was held in esteem,
but as the century advanced the conception of 'wit'
itself began to change, and it would probably be in no way
rash to regard Henry Hammond (1605–1660) as the most
admired type of Anglican preacher in the middle forties of
the century. His loyalty to the doctrines and constitution of
the Church was unmatched, but his style is far removed
from that of the 'metaphysicals' and more nearly resembles
that of Clarendon than does that of any other preacher.
Fell writes of this :

" . . . His style, though round and comprehensive, was
encumbred sometimes by *Parentheses*, and became difficult
to vulgar understandings " [1] ;

but the same biographer tells us that Charles I, (whom he
regarded as " the most accurate Judge and greatest Master
of English Rhetorick which the age hath given,") described
Hammond as " the most natural Orator he ever heard." [2]
The importance of these remarks lies in the inkling given
of what was admired in Court circles, and, also, in the frank

---

[1] 'The Life of the most learned, Reverend and Pious Dr. H. Hammond.
Written by John Fell, D.D. . . .' Lon., 1661, 8vo, p. 95.
[2] *Ibid.* Hammond was public orator at Oxford during the sojourn of the
Court there during the Civil War.

recognition that the plainer type of preaching had to become more malleable and responsive to the preacher's touch in order to merit critical approval. Neither Sanderson nor Hammond quite succeeded in obtaining this plasticity ; Hall, who, at his best, stood far in advance of other plain preachers of his day, had more than a little of the Puritan in his make-up ; the excellence of Hales' style belonged rather to the rationalist than to the churchman. It remained for South to turn his attention to the plain, undistinguished, often broken-backed, and practically always dull, Anglican sermon, until in his hands it became a varied and expressive medium for the conveyance of the preacher's thought.

The immediate cause of South's plainness, however, it must be confessed, was due to the period in which he commenced preaching, namely, the last years of the Commonwealth, but although he undoubtedly learned something from the Presbyterian and Independent preachers, his plainness should not be attributed to their influence. One striking thing about his work is the comparative uniformity of manner throughout. From 1679 onwards his sermons appeared in various editions, each volume containing sermons of widely different date of composition, the earlier ones being added either to make up the required number for a volume or because of their similarity of theme [1] ; but with few exceptions there is no wide difference in style to be noted within the compass of one volume—nothing that could aid in arranging the sermons in chronological order. South's distinctive manner is discernible in his earliest productions, and was due in large measure to the definiteness of his rhetorical ideals. While a considerable amount of what he had to say of preaching may best be referred to the ' critical ' part of this study, a number of observations may be noted in presenting his own work as supplying a clue to its better understanding.

As early as 1660, in ' The Scribe instructed '—a sermon

---

[1] The edition of his ' Works,' published at Oxford, 1823 (to which all references in this study are made), groups the seventy-six sermons found in six volumes in the previous editions in the first four volumes, while the posthumous works, derived from ' Two additional Volumes,' issued in 1744, along with Curll's vol. of 1717 are contained in the three last volumes. The latter were not intended for the press by the author, and so are of small value in forming an estimate of his style.

delivered at St. Mary's, Oxford [1]—South protested against two kinds of pulpit-delinquents—" such as disparage and detract from the grandeur of the gospel, by a puerile and indecent levity in the discourse of it to the people," and " such as depreciate and . . . debase the same, by a coarse, careless, rude and insipid way of preaching the great and invaluable truths of it." South's censure of the former is decidedly daring when we consider his own employment of ' wit,' often of a most unseemly kind, but the things he particularly animadverts upon are " all vain, luxurious allegories, rhyming cadencies of similar words "—in short, the *schemata* so prevalent in Adams, and, in its simple assonantal form, dear to Andrewes. The use of such devices he compares to " the plastering of marble, or the painting of gold," and their origin in imitation of Seneca is hinted at by a quotation from Quintilian, who remarked of that writer "that he did *rerum pondera minutissimis sententiis frangere*, break, and, as it were, emasculate the weight of his subject by little affected sentences." This observation South follows up with a criticism of those whose sermons were " so garnished with quibbles and trifles, as if they played with truth and immortality ; and neither believed these things themselves, nor were willing that others should."

" Is it possible" (he enquires) " that a man in his senses should be merry and jocose with eternal life and eternal death, if he really designed to strike the awful impression of either into the consciences of men ? "

And he replies :

" No, no ; this is no less a contradiction to common sense and reason, than to the strictest notions of religion. And as this can by no means be accounted divinity, so neither can it pass for wit ; . . . for true wit is a severe and a manly thing. Wit in divinity is nothing else but sacred truths suitably expressed. It is not shreds of Latin or Greek, nor a *Deus dixit*, and a *Deus benedixit*, or those little quirks, or divisions into the ὅτι, the διότι, and the καθότι, or the *egress*, *regress*, and *progress*, and other such stuff (much

---

[1] *Vid.* ' Works,' ed. cit., vol. iii, sermon xxxvii, pp. 32–9.

like the style of a lease) that can properly be called wit.
For that is not wit which consists not with wisdom." [1]

In his definition of ' wit,' South, it will be noted, was
remarkably near the ideal of the Royal Society preachers
—so many things, so many words.[2] In his practice he is
free from the faults which he enumerates—the Latin tags of
Andrewes or the divisions and subdivisions advocated by
such ' methods ' as that of Chappell—but that he was
" merry and jocose " in the most solemn contexts it is
impossible to deny, and his *jeux d'esprit* on his own showing
are indefensible.

The alternative way of preaching which South criticises
was the exhaustive Puritan one as practised by men like
Thomas Goodwin. He is unfair, however, when he describes
all such preaching as " a slight extempore business," and
indeed his own reference to the part played by " some
trusty concordance " in the preparation of such sermons is
directly self-contradictory ; but in indicating that much
of the dullness of Puritan preachers was due to a lack of a
sufficient employment of dialectic and rhetoric, so as to
render their sermons persuasive and eloquent, he was
stating no more than the truth, as we know both from
the consideration of the sermons themselves and from
Baxter's frank account of how these aids came to be
abandoned.

Eight years subsequently, in a sermon at Christ Church,
Oxford,[3] South made a strong plea for plainness in preaching, and on that occasion directly attacked the luscious
style of Jeremy Taylor,[4] with its elaborate metaphors and
poetical language. The extravagances of all parties or
persons he regarded with equal disapproval. Preaching he
considered should be " plain, natural, and familiar," and
these three qualities his own sermons possess in a high degree.
His plainness, however, is seldom dull, and he is natural
without being commonplace, and familiar without vulgarity.
Yet the fact remains that he was often unseemly, in spite of
his ideals, often almost (if not actually) scurrilous—as in
the celebrated passage on Cromwell's first entry into the

[1] Ser. cit., p. 33.   [2] *Vid. post*, pp. 331–2.
[3] Published as sermon lix in vol. iv of the ' Works,' ed. cit.
[4] *Vid.* ser. cit., p. 153.

Parliament House [1]—and while he avoided the obvious vices of the two great bodies of English preachers up to his time, his sermons are disfigured by a facetious and imprudent facility in expressing analogies, which renders them dangerously open to being considered ' witty ' in the modern sense of the term.

Among the most tolerable examples of South's ' wit,' where he is less ingenious and more spontaneously ' witty ' in the manner of Andrewes, is his remark in the sermon preached at bishop Dolben's consecration (1666) : " Where God gives a talent, the episcopal robe can be no napkin to hide it in " [2]; or the comparison of the five senses to the " cinque ports " which guard the soul, and must be secured " against the invasion of vain thoughts." [3] There is something of Fuller even in the description of St. Peter, following

" his sin close at the heels, who rose betimes to his work ; as soon as ever the cock crew, and the alarm was given." [4]

But South often allowed his ' wit ' a greater liberty, as when he attributed the nasal accents and strange delivery of the Puritans to a desire to speak " as never man spake " in imitation of Christ,[5] or in denouncing toleration and the attitude of the Broad Church party

" at a certain critical juncture of affairs not many years since, when a clergyman could hardly pass the city streets without being reviled, nay spat upon . . ."

[1] This passage is found in the viiith sermon in vol. i of the ' Works,' ed. cit., pp. 213-4, and reads : " Who, that had beheld such a bankrupt, beggarly fellow as Cromwell, first entering the Parliament house with a threadbare torn cloak, and a greasy hat (and perhaps neither of them paid for), could have suspected that in the space of a few years, he should by the murder of one king, and the banishment of another, ascend the throne, be invested in the royal robes, and want nothing of the state of a king, but the changing of his hat into a crown ? " The story that Charles II was extremely amused by this description is, as Dr. Alexander Gordon (in his article on South in the ' D.N.B.') points out, obviously fictitious when we consider that the sermon was preached on the 22nd February, 1684-5, and that Charles expired more than a fortnight previously.
[2] Ed. cit., vol. i, sermon v, p. 127.
[3] Ibid., vol. i, sermon vii, p. 195.
[4] Ibid., vol. vi, sermon xxxv, p. 265.
[5] Ibid., vol. iii, sermon xxxviii, p. 37.

concluded :

" And I hope though we churchmen had been blind before, so much dirt and spittle so bestowed might (without a miracle) have opened our eyes then." [1]

Such sallies are only too frequent in South's sermons, and lack even the questionable dignity supplied by the analogy and remote learning which characterised the ' wit ' of the older preachers. Fortunately, South did not himself set a fashion, and his ' wit ' perished with him. Apart from this tendency his prose conforms to his own standard of plainness and naturalness, and remains, after the lapse of two centuries, one of the models of English style. His remarks, if slightly rhetorical, are usually good, as the following illustrate :

" The episcopal dignity added to a good preaching faculty, is like the erecting of a stately fountain upon a spring, which still, for all that, remains as much a spring as it was before, and flows as plentifully, only it flows with the circumstance of greater state and munificence " [2] ;

or,

" It is said of Archimedes, that he would undertake to turn about the whole earth, if he could have but some place beside the earth to fix his feet upon. In like manner, as skilful an engineer as the Devil is, he will never be able to play his engines to any purpose, unless he finds something to fasten them to." [3]

While sermons known to be early in date show an inclination to imitate the older ' conceited ' and antithetic modes of the Jacobean preachers, South's style is too much of a piece throughout to permit of dividing it into periods ; but it is interesting to know that if he was alive to the dangers of Senecan pointedness it was because he had encountered them in practice.[4] Even in his reversion to

---

[1] Ed. cit., vol. iv, sermon lxi, pp. 228–9.
[2] *Ibid.*, vol. i, sermon v, p. 127.
[3] *Ibid.*, vol. iv, sermon lxviii, p. 421.
[4] *Vid.* the sermon delivered before Clarendon and later (according to Wood) before Charles II, which is especially antithetic in style (ed. cit., vol. v, sermon xiv).

this manner, however, there is a facility and brilliance which Hall at his best never attained. Thus we find him saying :

" In the alphabet of nature, it is only the first letter that is flourished. In short, there is so much difference between the present and former times, as there is between a copy and an original ; that indeed may be fair, but this only is authentic." [1]

Taken by themselves, such instances would call for small remark, but when we remember that Gauden and Glanvill, and some of the lesser preachers of the period, were showing a tendency to cultivate a similar manner of writing, it seems evident that a new danger was assailing pulpit oratory at the moment—a danger from which the efforts of the Royal Society finally delivered it. Fortunately, South had the good sense either spontaneously to abandon the cultivation of such antitheses or to fall in with the efforts of the Royal Society divines to secure a plain and straightforward style. If the much-quoted passage on Adam's philosophic endowments before the Fall [2] hardly outstrips in achievement the treatment of practically the same theme in Hall (quoted in a former chapter [3]), South's prose in its most finished passages is at once more varied, more fluent, and better modulated. His style obviously owes much to many sources—to the Calvinistic Anglicans with whose sermons, as we have seen, South's early work has affinities, to the

---

[1] Ed. cit., vol. v, sermon xiv, p. 241.
[2] Enough may be quoted of this passage to indicate its qualities : " I confess, it is difficult for us, who date our ignorance from our first being, and were still bred up with the same infirmities about us with which we were born, to raise our thoughts and imagination to those intellectual perfections that attended our nature in the time of innocence. . . . But by rating positives by their privatives and other arts of reason, by which discourse supplies the want of the reports of sense, we may collect the excellency of the understanding then, by the glorious remainders of it now, and guess at the stateliness of the building, by the magnificence of its ruins. All those arts, rarities, and inventions, which vulgar minds gaze at, the ingenious pursue, and all admire, are but the reliques of an intellect defaced with sin and time. We admire it now, only as antiquaries do a piece of old coin, for the stamp it once bore, and not for those vanishing lineaments and disappearing draughts that remain upon it at present. And certainly that must needs have been very glorious, the decays of which are so admirable. He that is comely when old and decrepid, surely was very beautiful when he was young. An Aristotle was but the rubbish of an Adam, an Athens but the rudiments of Paradise " (ed. cit., vol. i, sermon ii, pp. 37–8). [3] *Ante*, pp. 226–7.

better preachers of the Commonwealth, among whom he had appeared at the outset of his preaching career, and almost certainly, though less demonstrably, to the contemporary pulpit orators of France, Bossuet, and Bourdaloue.

A good example of his manner is supplied by a sermon delivered before the University at Oxford in 1691. The thought, it will be noticed, is more philosophic than that usually found in South, and in this respect points interestingly to the contribution of " the Cambridge divines " to the pulpit oratory of their own and succeeding times. South is speaking of the scope of natural reason :

" Let a man carefully attend to the voice of his reason, and all the dictates of natural morality, so as by no means to do any thing contrary to them. For though reason is not to be relied upon, as a guide universally sufficient to direct us what to do, yet it is generally to be relied upon and obeyed, when it tells us what we are not to do. It is indeed but a weak and diminutive light, compared to revelation ; but it ought to be no disparagement to a star, that it is not a sun. Nevertheless, as weak and small as it is, it is a light always at hand, and though enclosed, as it were, in a dark lantern, may yet be of singular use to prevent many a foul step, and to keep us from many a dangerous fall. And every man brings such a degree of this light into the world with him, that though it cannot bring him to heaven, yet if he be true to it, it will carry him a great way ; indeed so far, that if he follows it faithfully, I doubt not but he shall meet with another light, which shall carry him quite through . . ." [1]

The distinguished lineage of this last quotation—the scion of Senecan mediævalism tracing its descent through Cyprian from true classical prose, of Calvinistic as well as of non-party Anglicanism and of the Rationalists—compels us to regard South's achievement as of great importance. For, for the first time (ignoring for the moment the late date of this sermon, since many earlier sermons reveal the same characteristics) all the competing and, from different points of view, extravagant styles which had fascinated men

[1] Ed. cit., vol. ii, sermon xxiii, pp. 179 seq.

and absorbed their attention during the first sixty years of the century were successfully fused together, and the result was a plain, perspicuous and harmonious whole. In effecting this fusion South displayed remarkable common sense. A man of greater genius would have come to the task with greater bias ; but the cold almost impersonal way in which South registered the rhetorical weaknesses of his predecessors, and from time to time remodelled his own style, yet always in strict continuity, fitted him peculiarly for the task. All that a great technician could do he did ; but it remained for the finer and more sympathetic personality of Tillotson to invest with charm a manner excellently calculated to impress, but at times too truculently employed to convince or persuade.

Turning to the work of Isaac Barrow (1630–1677), mathematical scholar as well as divine, and, for five years previous to his death, Master of Trinity College, Cambridge, we are confronted, as in the earlier instance of Donne, and to some, though to a lesser, extent in that of Taylor, with the spectacle of a preacher of a highly individual and also highly intellectual type, whose mental calibre separates him from other men in his age, and imparts to the products of his pen distinctive characteristics of an unusual order. If Taylor can only be named with these others with a kind of caveat, it is not because the latter's work is not individual or remarkable in a way, but because the beautiful artificialities and serene expatiation of Taylor were undoubtedly the outcome of a less intense and also a less robust experience, which made up for what it lacked in variety by a devoted attention to elaboration and detail. Between the two remaining preachers a more equal comparison can be attempted. Both were virile, stirring men, who had seen more of actual life than usually fell to the lot of divines, even in that century of Army chaplaincies ; both were men of keen and subtle intellect, and compelled by this very fact to review the dogmas of the Christian Faith in the light of scientific knowledge ; both, as did most of their contemporaries, clearly regarded preaching as a branch of rhetoric, only they did so with a more intelligent discrimination and endeavoured to cultivate it with a backward glance to the great models of patristic oratory ; and both were endowed with unusual strength of imagination,

21

whether self-generated, or as is often the case with each, started off by the images of others, but so developed as to give a time-honoured illustration a topical effectiveness and a fresh lease of life.   While these traits belong to Donne and Barrow in common, other equally important factors serve to contrast and separate them and their work.   For one thing, as we have seen, Donne had a connection of a peculiar kind with the Anglo-Catholic divines ; but although a member of the Royal Society, Barrow cannot be classed as a " Royal Society divine," meaning by that term a clerical member of that Society whose work exemplifies the stylistic ideals set out by Sprat in his ' History of the Royal-Society.' To a greater extent even than Donne Barrow may be said to stand apart from the party with which he was associated. Donne, moreover, by training and upbringing can hardly be described as English ; there is a bizarre, foreign strain in him derived from continental Catholicism ; Barrow is English of the English all through.   This last fact accounts for much that is different in their approach to their themes. Donne, sensualist and voluptuary to the last, could find no refuge from his passionate cravings save in the arms of His God [1] ; Barrow, though his preaching throughout is characterised by strong personal devotion to the Saviour, could voice his reflections on God as follows : " ῾Ο Θεὸς γεωμετρεῖ ! Tu autem, Domine, quantus es Geometra ! "   The very rhetorical models which attracted them were significant less of their period than of themselves.   Donne, it is true, was Senecan in company with Bacon and others of his contemporaries ; but had he lived at any time in the century Augustine and Tertullian would have been bound to fascinate a man of his temperament : Barrow, at the very moment when men were out of sympathy with luxuriousness of style, turned in devoted discipleship to Chrysostom. The individualistic, self-analytical note of Augustine is clearly what interested Donne, and the style helped to elucidate the meaning ; in the same way, what appealed to Barrow in Chrysostom was apparently the practical commonsense of the preacher expressed in flowing paragraphs with wealth of lively illustration.   Other resem-

---

[1] *Vid.* "A Hymne to Christ, at the Authors last going into Germany"— ' Donne's Poetical Works,' Grierson's ed., 2 vols., Oxf., 1912, vol. i, p. 353, ll. 25–7.

blances and differences might be enumerated, but the big fact that emerges from such considerations is the sense of their dominating personalities setting a seal to the work which they undertook. Each deliberately chose to effect something different from what he saw being done around him, and in this respect Barrow stands in the greater isolation. Donne used 'metaphysical' preaching in an original way, and the results he achieved appear to us at times sublime and at others ludicrous. Barrow, while he never reached the heights attained by the earlier preacher—never quite pursued his Reason " to an *O altitudo !* "—was never entrapped by the ridiculous ; his ideas are everywhere noble and his style dignified, and it was not for nothing that the elder Pitt committed whole passages from his works to memory or recommended him as a model for the imitation of his son. The difference between Donne and Barrow may be typified by the Gothic and the Romanesque in architecture, and the preferences men express for their sermons will be largely subjective. In the evolution of English prose as exemplified by the pulpit orators neither can be considered as exercising a vital influence ; Andrewes at the beginning of the seventeenth century and Tillotson at the close provided the models to which men turned ; between lay the dull, the plain, the philosophical, and the astonishingly learned, whose varied contributions we have been considering more or less in the work of South. But the two greatest English pulpit orators, and with them the gentle and gracious Taylor, cannot be claimed as torchbearers in this race. From the first they appear invested with a kind of divinity, and stand apart.

For all his greatness and independence, however, Barrow's achievement is of considerable interest. His style represents the triumph of naturalness and plainness, yet it conveys to the reader the impression of listening to a great orator, who, however much he has thought out his positions and compelled his hearers also to think,[1] has so presented his material, with all the appropriate exposition and the most effective persuasion at his command, that his message is in danger of being overlooked in his manner, and the enjoy-

[1] Hughes, in the ' Introduction ' to his edition of Barrow's ' Works,' Lon., 1830, vol. i, p. lxxiii, notes that Warburton used to declare that " in reading Barrow, he was obliged to *think*."

ment of his artistic presentation of being substituted for the conviction it was intended to convey. Taken apart, Barrow's sentences answer well enough to the standard of simplified prose set up by the Royal Society ; but combined in paragraphs they recall the magniloquence of Isocrates or Chrysostom. The mathematician, the theologian, even the pastor, is swallowed up in the orator. Love of truth, metaphysical speculation, the commission to redeem souls —all are transformed into the noble periods of the most continuously and uniformly eloquent of English preachers. In this very excellence lay his fault and the explanation why he earned less praise from his contemporaries than he might seem to have merited. The oratory of Burke may have been sparsely regarded by a hungry ' House ' in his own day ; it is read by posterity ; but the appeal of the pulpit must be to its own day : it is of no moment what its future may be if it fails then. And Barrow's oratory was not of a kind which could ever have hoped to succeed with ordinary congregations. His themes were too exhaustively treated, and the splendour of his eloquence was dazzling, but bound soon to be fatiguing. Any imitation of it would without doubt have proved bombastic. In the circumstances, therefore, it is no wonder that among their contemporaries the less vigorous and less spectacular Tillotson should have been preferred. Barrow may be described as the English Bossuet ; but Voltaire, it is well known, preferred Bourdaloue.

Two facts connected with Barrow's sermons have already been referred to, namely, his exhaustiveness, which Charles II took occasion to rally him on, and his method of composition, by casting his matter into several main heads under which he arranged copious extracts from his commonplace-books.[1] Hughes, one of his nineteenth-century editors, has pointed out that—

" his favourite authors appear to have been Sophocles, Demosthenes, and Aristotle, among the Greek classics ; Chrysostom among the Fathers ; and Ovid among the Latin poets." [2]

At first sight the last-mentioned may appear a strange preference for such a man as Barrow, but a passage in his

[1] Vid. ante, p. 61, and p. 84.   [2] Ed. cit., p. lxxxvii.

inaugural address on his appointment to the Humanity Lecture at Cambridge gives an interesting summary of his views on the relative merits of the Roman poets, and reveals the fact that he preferred Ovid to Vergil or Horace on account of the unaffected ease, propriety and uniformity of the former's style.[1] To all his favourite authors Barrow owed much, and his great eloquence was due in large measure to his habit of transcribing the finest passages of classical and ecclesiastical writers—especially of Demosthenes and Chrysostom—by means of which he fell into their stride. His manuscripts at Trinity College are many of them largely composed of such extracts. The influence of the classical moralists on his style is pronounced, and allusion or direct quotation is responsible to a considerable extent for his tone.

Only two of Barrow's sermons were prepared for the press in his lifetime—the enormously lengthy one preached in Easter week, 1671, at the Spital, " On the Duty and Reward of Bounty to the Poor," and one delivered at the Guildhall Chapel, on Good Friday, 1677, which he did not live to see published.

" There is a tradition " (Professor Wace writes of the former) " that it occupied three hours and a half in delivery ; but since the Court of Aldermen desired the Preacher to print his sermon ' with what further he had prepared to deliver at that time ' ; and since the sermon as now printed [2] occupies not more than ninety-four octavo pages, it is thought there may be some exaggeration in this tradition. The Preacher is said to have begun to be weary with standing so long ; but it is not recorded that there was any weariness on the part of the audience." [3]

The importance of these two sermons lies in the fact that we have them in an unadulterated form, and not as in the

---

[1] *Vid.* passage quoted by Hughes, ed. cit., p. lxxxviii, from the ' Pro Human. oratio,' published in the ' Opuscula.'

[2] I.e. in Napier's ed. of Barrow's ' Works,' Camb., 1859, vol. i, pp. 7 *seq.* It occupies 39 pp. in the folio ed. of 1700.

[3] ' The Classic Preachers of the English Church ' (St. James's Lectures, 1877) Lon., 1877—" Barrow," by H. Wace, M.A., p. 29. The *locus classicus* on Barrow's exhaustiveness and the length of time he occupied in preaching occurs at pp. 146–8 of Pope's ' The Life of . . . Seth [Ward], Lord Bishop of Salisbury . . .' Lon., 1697, 8vo, though, as shown above, this account appears to be inaccurate in at least one particular.

collected edition issued by Tillotson between 1678 and 1687, from which the refined and over-scrupulous editor expunged many of the more virile expressions to be found in Barrow's MSS., erased numerous passages, and subdivided certain sermons so as to reduce them to shorter compass. During the late seventeenth and the following century Barrow's sermons as they appeared are truly described as " Tillotson's Barrow," and the early nineteenth-century editions [1] fall into line. Napier's edition of 1859,[2] however, is based upon the original MSS., and the precise nature of Tillotson's editorial attention is discussed in the introduction.[3] Inexcusable as this tampering appears, Barrow, it must be confessed, was prone to resurrect, employ or coin unusual and often uncouth words, for which Tillotson, in the interests of securing a high level of polished English, substituted simpler but often less effective expressions. The importance of the latter's rearrangements has already been noted [4] and represents the major charge against him as editor, for, apart from the omission of certain strange words, a close comparison between the text as " improved " by Tillotson and the restored text of Napier's edition does not result in two impressions being conveyed of Barrow's style. " Tillotson's Barrow " may be a little less the Barrow who not only himself stood to his gun but inspired others to defend from the attack of a corsair the ship on which he travelled to Constantinople, or was capable of overpowering a ferocious mastiff, but the general characteristics as exemplified by both texts are the same, and the alterations and omissions, though they have nothing to commend them, are the more venial, since they are less meretricious than might at first sight seem likely.

Barrow's great merits were beyond question his force, dignity, mobility, and the power to maintain or rather to reanimate attention while considering a topic from as large a number of angles as possible. This last ability he had seen exemplified in a superlative manner by Chrysostom, whose complete works he found time to read during his stay in Constantinople towards the end of the Commonwealth

[1] At the Clarendon Press, 1818, in 6 vols., 8vo, and again in 1830, 8 vols., 8vo, and Hughes' ed., Lon., 1830, 7 vols., 8vo.
[2] Pub. Camb.   [3] Ed. cit., pp. xiv seq.
[4] Ante, pp. 29-30.

period.[1] The rhetorical question followed by a reply set in a series is a well-known device of the Greek orators, and had been effectively employed by the Eastern Fathers ; and this device Barrow was fond of and used to good purpose. One of the finest examples of this in his works is found in a sermon on the Incarnation, where the advantages of Christ's birth are set forth :

" Is the birth of a Prince ever by honest Subjects entertained and celebrated with joy ? Behold a Prince born to all the World . . . Is Victory glorious and joyfull ? See the invincible warrior is issued forth into the field, *conquering and to conquer.* . . . The *captain of our salvation* appeareth, triumphing in humility ; the great blow is given ; the Devil's pride and envy are abased. . . . Is the publishing of Peace acceptable ? Behold eternal peace between heaven and earth, a general peace among men, a peace of conscience between man and himself, is now established and proclaimed : the illustrious Ambassadour, the noble hostage, the infallible pledge thereof is revealed ; *Preaching peace to them that are far off, and to them that are near. . . .*" [2]

Or, if such an instance may seem too closely modelled on patristic originals, too ' Asiatic ' in tone to be quite satisfying in an English context, the following may be quoted :

" Dost thou, fond mortal, fear to lose the favour of man, whose favour doth avail nothing to thy main interests, and cannot any-wise considerably benefit thee, (for in no respect dost thou depend on his will and providence,) but dost not fear being deprived of God's favour, upon which all thy good hangeth, wherein thy felicity consisteth, without which thou art uncapable of any prosperity, of any security, of any joy or comfort ?

" Dost thou fear the displeasure of man, of poor impotent man, a sorry frail *worm*, whose *breath is in his nostrils,* (ready to fly away in every moment) . . . whilst thou dreadest not to offend the Eternal Almighty God ? . . ." [3]

[1] *Vid.* "An Account of the Life of Dr. Isaac Barrow," by Abraham Hill, prefixed to ' The Works,' 3 vols. in two, Lon., 1700, fol., vol. i.
[2] ' Works,' 1700 ed., vol. ii, sermon xxiii, pp. 315 *seq.* References throughout are to this edition.
[3] *Ibid.*, vol. iii, sermon xxiv, pp. 328 *seq.*

Unfortunately, considerations of space forbid lengthy quotations, and to give an adequate idea of Barrow's definitely cumulative style, lengthy quotations are almost a necessity.   But enough has been quoted to show how, starting with obvious imitation of ancient models, Barrow succeeded in teaching English preaching a freer and nobler utterance.   If such rhetoric as we have glanced at first melted the heart of Theodosius and swayed the multitude of Antioch, Barrow at least succeeded in naturalising it, and learned how best to turn it to effect in moving his countrymen.

This cumulative manner, the outward expression of his many-sided reflection on any subject, is very noticeable in Barrow's work.   One of his finest passages occurs in the sermon entitled ' Of Industry in our particular Calling, as Scholars,' where the argument is sustained throughout a series of paragraphs held together by means of an unobtrusive pivotal clause—consisting of the words, " It is a calling "—which serves to introduce each fresh advantage of the scholar's lot [1] ; while an even more striking example of this usage is the solemn catalogue of consequents following upon the hypothesis of a future judgment, each introduced heavily with the word " that," which occurs in a sermon on the Creed.[2]

At times the cumulation of subordinate clauses or of sentences similarly introduced resulted in extreme brevity, and an aphoristic manner of writing ensued.   But these occasions, though characteristic, can hardly be claimed to exhibit Barrow's style at its best, and it is his more periodic manner, however simple its component parts may prove on analysis to be, that deserves attention.   A quotation from a passage on Christ as the ' Great Exemplar ' will serve to illustrate the lucidity of his style as well as his fine adherence to truth even when his theme quite obviously not only exercised his mind but kindled his emotions.

" Our Saviour's example is especially influential upon practice, in that it was, by an admirable temperament, more accommodated for imitation than any others have been.

[1] Ed. cit., vol. iii, sermon xxii, pp. 221–4.
[2] *Ibid.*, vol. ii, sermon xxxii, pp. 422–3, the " that " clauses depending on the last sentence of p. 421.   Another impressive reiteration occurs in the opening of the Passion-Sermon (delivered at the Guildhall Chapel), vol. i, sermon xxxii, p. 423.

That the perfect copie of his most holy life seems more easie
to be transcribed, than the ruder draughts of other holy
Men ; for though it were written with an incomparable
fairness, delicacy and evenness ; not slurred with any foul
blot, nor any where declining from exact straightness ;
yet were the lineaments thereof exceeding plain and simple ;
not by any gaudy flourishes, or impertinent intrigues
rendered difficult, to studious imitation ; so that even women
and children, the weakest and meanest sort of people, as
well as the most wise and ingenuous, might easily perceive
its design, and with good success write after it.   His was a
gentle and a steady light, bright indeed, but not dazling
the eye ; warm, but not scorching the face of the most
intent beholder ;   No affected singularities, no supercilious
necessities, no frivolous ostentations of seemingly high,
but really fruitless performances ; nothing that might deter
a timorous, discourage a weak, or offend a scrupulous
disciple, is observable in his practice : but on the contrary,
his conversation was full of holiness and condescension, of
meekness and sweetness, of openness and candid simplicity :
apt to envite and allure all men to approach toward it,
and with satisfaction to enjoy it." [1]

Other significant features of Barrow's prose might be
urged, as his judicious choice of language, which is
evident from the most casual quotation, and the liveliness
as well as aptness of his images. His tone, too, is worthy
of remark, depending largely, as has been already hinted,
on the note struck by the classical moralists. The passage
just quoted is not a description of Christ as Andrewes or
Donne or Taylor would have depicted Him, but something
of the rational spirit of the Cambridge Platonists has
influenced the description. He is not the Byzantine Man-
God of the earlier passage quoted with its reminiscence of
Chrysostom's own description,[2] but rather that " Word of
God " Who became incarnate in Jesus, but Whose operations fascinated all the Cambridge Platonists as offering
a reconciliation between Faith and Reason. Moreover,
the appeal to the consent of the best minds among the

---

[1] Ed. cit., vol. iii, sermon iii, p. 31 ; the complete passage ends on p. 32
with the words, " holy integrity of his life."
[2] *Vid. ante*, p. 143.

Pagan writers is as explicit in Barrow as in any of the
'Platonic' divines,[1] and certain faint glimmerings of an
interest in other religions as giving partial revelations of
the true God are found in his sermons as they may be also in
those of Tillotson.[2] Such interests are typical of a wider
outlook than was possible to men of an earlier period—to
Milton, for example, with his identification of heathen
divinities with Satan and his crew—and an enlargement of
outlook was bound to show itself ultimately in a greater
freedom of style. But, before coming to the final attainment
of a style that was outwardly polished and equable because
expressive of the inward composure and temperateness of
the author's mind, acting freely under the encouragement
of an age in which ethical interests, treated with philosophic
equanimity, had taken the place of passionate doctrinal
excitements, it is necessary to glance for a little at the part
played by the Royal Society in influencing the trend of
Restoration style, particularly so far as the sermon was
concerned.

The early emergence of a tolerably plain style in Wilkins'
'World in the Moone' has already been noticed, and it is
interesting to find Sir Edmund Gosse claiming for the
author the praise so long allotted to Tillotson, who "lived
a generation later, and learned to write English from his
study of the Bishop of Chester, whom he enthusiastically
admired."[3] That John Wilkins (1614–1672) was definitely
the first to employ a uniformly natural diction and to set
the example of a plain yet pleasingly varied style is beyond
doubt, but his efforts, as the apparently similar efforts of
Ussher (if we may trust to Parr's evidence[4]), which aimed
so severe a blow at 'florid' preaching, were rendered largely
negligible by the commotions of the times. It is not Tillotson's achievement which is of supreme importance, but
rather the influence that Tillotson was able to exert, not that
he wrote excellent prose, but that he succeeded in persuading his contemporaries that such prose was excellent, and,
being such, to be imitated. The particular standard of
preaching maintained by Wilkins during the Civil Wars

---

[1] *Vid.* ed. cit., vol. ii, sermon viii, pp. 108–12.
[2] *Ibid.*, vol. ii, sermon xi, p. 141 ; *ibid.*, vol. ii, sermon xii, p. 164.
[3] 'A History of Eighteenth-Century Literature,' Lon., 1922, p. 76.
[4] *Vid. ante,* pp. 229–31.

and Commonwealth, when he enjoyed the favour of the Parliamentary party, cannot now be judged, as no sermons of his remain from that period, but his declaration (previously quoted [1]) in the ' Ecclesiastes ' (1646) that " the principal Scope of a Divine Orator is to teach clearly, convince strongly, and persuade powerfully," which he follows up by dividing a sermon into three chief parts— " *Explication, Confirmation, Application* "—suggests a point of view nearly akin to Baxter's, and if his own sermons proved more fluent and better modulated, this must be attributed to chance rather than to design. What is important is that when Wilkins re-emerges in a position of influence, so far as style is concerned, it is in association with a group of men who were able to create a very stong bias in the direction of simplicity.

From 1645 onwards a group of distinguished scientists, including men like Wallis and Seth Ward, Savilian Professors at Oxford of Geometry and Astronomy respectively, largely owing to Wilkins' enthusiasm for scientific discussion and research, began to meet at Wadham College. [2] Afterwards the meetings were continued at Gresham College, London, and finally, in 1662, a charter was obtained from the King for the formation of the Royal Society. Thomas Sprat (1635–1713), in the second part of his ' History of the Royal-Society,' published in 1667, gives what he calls ' A Model of their Whole design,' [3] or ' an account of their aims ' as the modern phrase is. As might be expected, these aims were principally concerned with scientific research, but, as the members desired " to separate the knowledge of *Nature*, from the colours of *Rhetorick*, the devices of *Fancy*, or the delightful deceit of *Fables*," it was found necessary to draw up rules concerning, " their Manner of Discourse." Under this last heading Sprat tells us :

" They [i.e. the Members of the Royal Society] have therefore been most vigorous in putting in execution the

---

[1] *Ante*, p. 109.
[2] Sprat, ' The History of the Royal-Society of London, For the Improving of Natural Knowledge,' Lon., 1667, 4to, Part II, p. 55, gives the names of those who first met at Wadham : Dr. Seth Ward, Mr. Boyle, Dr. Wilkins, Sir Wm. Petty (the economist), Mr. Matthew Wren (later Secretary to Clarendon), Dr. Wallis, Dr. Goddard, Dr. Willis, Dr. Bathurst (President of Trinity College, Oxford), Dr. Christopher Wren, and Mr. Rook (the astronomer).
[3] *Op. cit.*, pp. 61–2.

only Remedy, that can be found for this *extravagance* [i.e. the use of the old figures of speech], and that has been, a constant Resolution to reject all amplifications, digressions, and swellings of style ; to return back to the primitive purity and shortness, when men deliver'd so many *things* almost in an equal number of *words*. They have exacted from all their members a close, naked, natural way of speaking, positive expressions, clear senses, a native easiness, bringing all things as near the Mathematical plainness as they can, and preferring the language of Artizans, Countrymen, and Merchants, before that, of Wits or Scholars." [1]

The immediate cause of this new simplification of style was the exigencies of scientific report, but the fact that between Sprat's ' History of the Royal-Society ' and his ' Account of the Life and Writings of Abraham Cowley,' which he prefixed to the latter's collected works a year later, there is a nice distinction of manner, and that the latter is smooth and easy in a way which the more *naked* ' History ' is not, suggests that within this particular group of scientists and divines there existed a high standard of fluent and facile English, and, that they were not so much originating a movement as seeking to emphasise a possibility already achieved, and to lead other men to accept their standard of style. Before the Restoration with the more illiterate Puritans denouncing humane learning and the better educated largely renouncing rhetorical aids, the prospects of an improved pulpit-style had been remote. With the return of the monarchy, and while several strange varieties of preaching styles were endeavouring to attract notice, there had come the opportunity to make a plea for a style which would be acceptable to the majority of the nation. This was precisely what the Royal Society did, and, being backed by Charles II in its efforts, the plain sermon, which aimed primarily at perspicuity but at the same time did not neglect grace and flexibility, became an accomplished fact.

Of the Royal Society divines Wilkins himself affords the most pleasing example as a preacher.[2] A quotation from

[1] *Op. cit.*, Part II, § xx.
[2] Two collections of his sermons exist : ' Sermons Preach'd Upon Several Occasions Before the King at Whitehall,' published in 1677, containing three

a sermon preached at Whitehall in 1670 provides a fair
specimen of his ordinary manner :

" I do not say, that a man's thoughts are always to be
taken up about the immediate Acts of Religion, any more
than a Traveller is always to have his mind actually fixed
upon the thought of his Journey's end. This would be inconsistent with the infirmities of our natures, and the
necessity of our condition in this World. But yet as he that
is upon a Journey, doth so order all his *Particular* Motions,
as may be most conducible to his *General* End : so should
men *habitually*, though they cannot *actually*, in every affair
have respect to their chief End, so as to observe all the duties
of Religion and never to allow themselves in any thing
against the rules of it. And he that hath this care continually upon his mind, (though he be but a Secular Person)
may properly be said to make Religion his *Business.*" [1]

Sprat himself, while smooth and pleasing, like Bates
among the Nonconformists, carried the seeds of decay in
his manner, for a little more polish and a little less conviction
would result in the fluent, platitudinous discourse of the
eighteenth century. Even the plain style, it is obvious,
required strength of personality behind it to prevent its
becoming insipid. It was Tillotson's good fortune, however, to appear at the right moment, ere the victory of the
plain style was fully assured and before reiterated practice
had rendered men adroit in contriving effects which had in
their turn become a vogue. It was his good fortune, also,
to come dowered with several gifts, and to represent in his
person as well as his style the fusion of many divergent
strains in the theological life of the century.

John Tillotson (1630–1694), who died archbishop of
Canterbury, was bred a Presbyterian. He received the
rudiments of his education from his maternal grandfather,
a strict Puritan, so that it is reasonable to suppose that it
followed pretty much the course prescribed by Brinsley.
At Clare Hall, Cambridge, his tutor, Clarkson, had strong

sermons (one preached in 1669, the two others in 1670), and (fifteen) ' Sermons Preached upon Several Occasions. . . . Never before Published,'
which appeared in 1682, Lon., 8vo.
[1] ' Sermons . . .' Lon., 1677, 8vo, pp. 57–8.

Puritan leanings, and he was a hearer of Thomas Hill, the Parliamentary Master of Trinity, and a reader of Twisse, the first prolocutor of the Westminster Assembly, and by these, and like men, became impressed by the intellectual keenness of the Calvinistic theologians. Oddly enough, he was never a hard student, and, unlike the majority of his contemporaries, kept no commonplace-book—a fact which probably saved him later from the temptation of emptying its contents into his sermons ; but he made a study of Cicero, and was familiar with the Greek Testament. Chillingworth's ' Religion of Protestants,' we learn from Burnet's sermon at his funeral, was one of the earliest influences that affected his style.[1] Dissatisfied with the pulpit oratory of his own time and the immediate past, Tillotson, to use Burnet's quaint phrase, " set a Pattern to himself, and such an one it was, that 'tis to be hoped it will be long and much followed."[2] In preparation for his task, the same writer tells us,

" he begun with a deep and close study of the Scriptures, upon which he spent four or five Years, till he had arrived at a true understanding of them. He studied next all the ancient Philosophers and Books of Morality : Among the Fathers St. *Basil* and St. *Chrysostom* were those he chiefly read. . . . His joining with Bishop *Wilkins* in pursuing the Scheme for an Universal Character,[3] led him to consider exactly the Truth of Language and Stile, in which no man was happier, and knew better the Art of preserving the Majesty of things under a Simplicity of Words ; tempering these so equally together, that neither did his Thoughts

[1] ' A Sermon Preached at the Funeral of the Most Reverend . . . John . . . Lord Archbishop of Canterbury . . . at St. Lawrence Jewry in London, on the 30th [November] . . . 1694,' Lon., 4to.

[2] *Ibid.*, p. 12.

[3] This refers to the scheme outlined in Wilkins' ' Essay Towards a Real Character, And a Philosophical Language,' a discourse presented to the Royal Society on the 13th April, 1668, and ordered by them to be printed, which it was the same year. By ' Real Character ' was meant a self-evident method of expressing ideas in writing, Wilkins holding that " it was exceedingly desirable that the *Names* of things might consist of such *Sounds*, as should bear in them some Analogy to their *Natures*, and the Figure and Character of these Names should bear some proper resemblance to these Sounds . . ." (*op. cit.*, Part IV, opening). A kind of pictorial language is suggested, specimens given and a glossary supplied. Any association with the working out of this " system " would be bound to make a man exact in the choice of words.

sink, nor his Stile swell : keeping always the due Mean between a low Flatness and the Dresses of false Rhetorick. Together with the Pomp of Words he did also cut off all Superfluities and needless Enlargements : He said what was just necessary to give clear Ideas of things, and no more : He laid aside all long and affected Periods : His sentences were short and clear : and the whole Thread was of a piece, plain, and distinct. No affectation of Learning, no squeezing of Texts, no superficial Strains, no false Thoughts nor bold Flights, all was solid and yet lively, and grave as well as Fine. . . .

" Whether he explained Points of Divinity, Matter of Controversy, or the Rules of Morality, on which he dwelt most copiously, there was something peculiar in him on them all, that conquered the Minds, as well as it commanded the Attention of his Hearers : who felt all the while that they were learning somewhat, and were never tired by him ; for he cut off both the Luxuriance of Stile, and the Length of Sermons ; and he concluded them with some Thoughts of such Gravity and Use, that he generally dismissed his Hearers with somewhat that stuck to them." [1]

The comprehensiveness of this account is only equalled by the truth of the particular observations, and it is no wonder that we find Birch in his life of Tillotson taking over the passage practically *verbatim*.[2] Birch, however, supplies an interesting summary of English preaching from the time of Fisher and Colet onwards,[3] in the course of which he ascribes " the great corruption of the oratory of the pulpit " to " Dr. Andrews," and notes that—

" the pedantry of King James I's court completed the degeneracy of all true eloquence, so that the most applauded preachers of the time are now insupportable ; and all the wit and learning of Dr. Donne cannot secure his sermons from universal neglect."

This, though strictly a piece of criticism, illustrates contemporary opinion, and the fact that Birch dismisses Hales

[1] Ser. cit., pp. 12–14.
[2] Though without acknowledgment, at pp. 21–2 of ' The Life of the Most Reverend Dr. John Tillotson . . .' Lon., 1752, 8vo.
[3] *Op. cit.*, pp. 18–20.

of Eton, Hall, and Sanderson with brief notices, and praises Chillingworth and Jeremy Taylor, is significant. Eloquence, it is obvious, was valued, but it was to be eloquence expressive of reason and which had shed pedantry and the ingenious quibbling of the ' metaphysical ' preachers.

From what has been said previously of Wilkins and others, whose attempts at reformation failed either to carry conviction or win popular assent, Canon Overton's contention that the change which took place in pulpit style in the last three decades of the seventeenth century was not solely due to Tillotson's example will appear less surprising [1] ; but the fact remains, that it was Tillotson whose pulpit manner first attracted universal admiration, and persuaded men that a plain, equable, yet judiciously modulated prose was not only possible but was also the most proper for the sermon. To a great extent his achievement is dependent on the nature of his unusual theological career, in the course of which he passed from Puritan to conformist, and, finally, at a moment of national crisis, as a Latitudinarian, was placed at the head of a church which he desired to see capable of a still greater comprehensiveness. The Anglo-Catholic excesses he had rejected in his youth when he had sat at the feet of the Cambridge Calvinists ; the same motives, however, which had resulted in the split between Tuckney and Whichcote [2] had gradually led him to adopt " larger thoughts," while the Restoration had brought about his conformity to the national church. Once within its walls Tillotson was faced with the question of what manner he should employ in his preaching. For the most part up to that moment the style of the Platonists had been confined to College exercises and University sermons, and it was not certain how it might be turned to more popular uses ; the restored Anglican preachers as a whole were decidedly dull ; to adapt in some way the best Puritan models so as to admit a greater play of intellect and employ rhetoric within discreet limits was the only course open. The result of all these circumstances, taken conjointly with temperamental considerations, was that Tillotson's style came to embody the earnestness of the Puritans with the rational

[1] J. H. Overton : ' Life in the English Church (1660–1714) . . .' Lon., 1885, pp. 257–8.
[2] *Vid.* Tulloch : ' Rational Theology,' vol. ii, pp. 59 *seq.*, and *ante*, p. 285.

element of the Cambridge Platonists in a form acceptable to the Anglicans of the period. Other men, both before and concurrently, it is true, played a part in the movement towards plainness—Latitudinarians, Royal Society preachers, men of individual genius like South and Barrow—but the fact remains that it was Tillotson who finally secured once and for all the triumph of the plain style in preaching, and so was largely instrumental in diffusing a taste for plainness and perspicuity in prose in general.

" He was not only the best Preacher of the age " (Burnet declared), " but seemed to have brought Preaching to perfection ; His Sermons were so well heard and liked, and so much read, that all the Nation proposed him as a Pattern, and studied to copy after him. . . ." [1]

It is frankly impossible to convey a true idea of Tillotson's achievement by the quotation of occasional passages, for his manner at its best is only to be gauged by the perusal of a complete sermon, such as the great sermon against atheism preached in 1664, entitled, ' The Wisdom of being Religious.' [2] Only so can his architectonic ability in designing a sermon, the propriety of his examples, and the uniform dignity yet simplicity of his diction be fully appreciated. The type of sermon to which he set the seal of his approval consists in the statement of a general proposition arising out of the text, treated of under three or four main aspects, which lead naturally to a conclusion corresponding with the proposition. The thought of each sermon is consequently very easy to follow, and, as the illustrations are all strictly pertinent—no extraneous ornament being added—the syntax natural, and the diction such as was ordinarily employed by educated men, the general effect is one of the greatest possible lucidity and charm.

As might be expected in one who had come into close contact with the ' Platonist ' divines, Tillotson makes much of the appeal to the best morality of all times. Especially is this so in his polemic against atheism. He was particularly fond of the classical moralists, and like Barrow pointed assent in their works to a series of great ethical standards

[1] ' History of His Own Time,' 1724 ed., vol. ii, p. 135.
[2] Printed as sermon i of the ' Fifty-four Sermons . . .' 1696.

and theological beliefs.[1]   His actual quotations from the
Classics, however, are immediately translated, but the easy
and natural introduction of the original phrase—rarely a
lengthy one—in his discourses imparts both variation and
dignity to his style.   His acquaintance with these writers,
moreover, had a subtler effect than is indicated by mere
allusion, and the loftiness and sublimity of their sentiments,
which found a ready echo in his own temperate and judicious reflections, are largely responsible for the impressive-
ness of his tone.   To quote Burnet once more : " He had
the brightest thoughts, and the most correct style of all our
divines," [2] and the brightness of his thought originated, as
did a similar luminosity in More and Culverwel, with
Plato and his followers, the propriety of his style, as did
that of Whichcote, from a life long regulated in accordance
with the truest philosophic practice.   Tillotson's was not a
profound or a subtle mind ; his was not an intense nature
that burned up everything that came within its range and
seared his own personality in the process ; yet he was no
mere logician, or placid moralist unmindful of his fellow-
countrymen's temptations ; like archbishop Leighton in
Scotland he had lived to recognise the futility of conflict
and desired to see established—

" a substantial and solid, a discreet and unaffected piety,
which makes no great noise and show, but expresses itself
in a constant and serious devotion, and is accompanied with
the fruits of goodness and kindness and righteousness
towards men. . . ." [3]

His plain, practical, yet agreeably varied manner of preaching was clearly one of his own contributions towards
effecting this great aim ; but the success which he met with

---

[1] Thus he deduced the belief in future rewards and punishments from
various classical myths (' Two Hundred Sermons and Discourses . . .' ed.
Barker, 1717, vol. i, sermon lvii, pp. 398–9) ; the immortality of the soul he
urges from a puzzled question of Lucretius (ibid., vol. ii, sermon cxxii, p. 129),
and an explicit statement of Cicero (ibid., p. 130 ; cf. sermon cxxiii, p. 133) ;
the foreknowledge of God from quotations from Juvenal, Cicero and Seneca
(ibid., vol. i, sermon lxxx, p. 605) ; acquiescence in the Divine will from
Epictetus (ibid., vol. i, sermon lxxxiv, pp. 635–6) ; while Plato, Cicero, and
Plutarch are all cited to prove that " Natural Light informs us that God is a
Spirit " (ibid., vol. i, sermon c, p. 749).
[2] ' History of His Own Time,' 1724 ed., vol. i, p. 189.
[3] ' Fifty-four Sermons . . .' sermon iv, p. 54.

was of a kind other than he had proposed to himself. For, much as his discourses may have tended towards the reformation of manners, at that period so earnestly set on foot, it is as the reformer of pulpit oratory and one of the prime movers in the creation of modern prose style that he has been destined to be remembered.

The merits of his style are evident from the most haphazard selection from his work, and are fairly represented by the following extract :

" I would by no means encourage men to be over censorious toward others, there is too much of that Spirit already in the world : but it is not amiss that Men should be strict and severe toward themselves. And I would to God Men would bring themselves to the test, and examine the truth and sincerity of their Religion not by the Leaves of an outward profession, but by the Fruits it produceth in their lives. Every Man that will take the pains to look into himself, and to observe his own actions, may by comparing the temper of his mind, and the general course of his life and practice with the Rules and Precepts of Religion, easily discern what power and efficacy Religion hath in him. A man may as certainly know himself, and make as sure a judgement of his state and condition toward God this way, *as a tree is known by its fruit.* Therefore let us not flatter our selves : for if we indulge any lust, or irregular passion in our Souls, and do not endeavour to mortify and subdue it ; if we allow our selves in any vicious practice in our lives ; we do but deceive our selves with an opinion of our Godliness, and whatever *the shew* and *appearance* we may make of Religion, we are certainly destitute of *the power* of it." [1]

After Tillotson the plain but well-modulated style could go no farther ; its problem for the future was to be how to maintain its level and not to become jejune or merely commonplace. It is therefore of no great value to pursue the fortunes of seventeenth-century preaching farther. Yet it is to be remembered that among Tillotson's contemporaries were several men who attained a high level of excellence in their sermons, and who cannot be considered imitators of the greater preacher. Their work may rather be regarded as bearing testimony to the influence of those

[1] ' Two Hundred Sermons and Discourses,' vol. ii, sermon clii, p. 336.

tendencies of the period of which Tillotson's work is to be considered so largely the product. Though the younger Sherlock undoubtedly learned from Tillotson,[1] William Sherlock (1641–1707), his father, may be considered as working independently in the creation of his own grave, dignified and equable style.[2] In the same way Thomas Tenison (1634–1715), Tillotson's successor in the primacy, whose style closely resembles the latter's,[3] is rather to be taken as a coadjutor than a disciple.

At the same time, it is to be remarked, many of the most prominent preachers of all types of churchmanship—Latitudinarians, Non-Jurors, and Nonconformists—fell far short of Tillotson and those who most closely resembled him. Thus bishop Beveridge (1637–1708), who was highly regarded by his contemporaries, proves on examination a dull preacher,[4] as do the Non-Jurors, Kettlewell (1653–1695) and Hickes (1642–1715). Neither were Edmund Calamy, the younger (1635?–1685), nor Nathaniel Taylor, whom Doddridge describes as " the Dissenting South," [5] of conspicuous merit ;   and Anthony Horneck (1641–1697), whom Wood in the ' Athenæ ' speaks of as a " frequent and florid preacher," [6] is better described in the words of Evelyn as " a most pathetic preacher," meaning by that, one calculated to move his auditory by an appeal to their emotions. But by the time of Fleetwood (1656–1723) one is conscious that the preacher is employing a settled plain style customarily used, and that he is neither like the last-mentioned

---

[1] *Vid.* ' Discourses Preached at the Temple Church . . .' 4 vols., Oxf., 1812.

[2] A good example of the elder Sherlock's preaching—he was the author of ' A Practical Discourse concerning Death ' which enjoyed great popularity in the eighteenth century—is the sermon entitled ' The Charity of Lending without Usury . . .' Lon., 1692, 4to.

[3] *Vid.* e.g. ' A Sermon Concerning the Wandering of the Mind in God's Service . . .' Lon., 1691, 4to.

[4] *Vid.* his ' Works,' 2 vols., fol., 1720, the anonymous editor of which quotes the tribute to Beveridge contained in Felton's ' Dissertation on Reading the Classics ' (1711).

[5] " Lectures on Preaching . . ." Lecture II, § 21, in ' The Works of the Rev. P. Doddridge,' Lon., 1804, vol. v.

[6] *Vid.* Evelyn : ' Diary,' 18th March, 1683. Horneck's own work is to be examined in ' Several (xxxix) Sermons upon the *Fifth* of St. *Matthew* . . .' 2 vols., Lon., 1692, 8vo, and a number of sermons printed singly. These supply less evidence of his ' pathetic flights ' than the comments of contemporaries would lead one to expect. *Vid.*, for example, letter of Charles Hatton to his brother, 26th November, [16]89, ' Correspondence of the Family of Hatton . . .' Camden Soc., vol. ii, p. 144.

preacher outside the reforming movement proper, nor yet with the older men in the thick of the struggle for reformation.[1] As the century progressed the inheritance upon which men were free to enter became more or less clear. Trimnell (1663–1723) definitely recognised the advantages of the generally applauded style [2] ; and Smalridge (1663–1719)—the ' Favonius ' of the ' Tatler ' [3]—whose sermons Dr. Johnson considered to be among the best in English, and Atterbury (1662–1732), who was regarded by Doddridge, hardly without exaggeration, as " the glory of our English orators," [4] without question attained their felicity and excellence of style by a careful apprenticeship in the school of Tillotson.

One preacher, among the actual contemporaries of Tillotson, however, for several reasons demands more than casual mention. Gilbert Burnet (1643–1715), bishop of Salisbury, author of ' A Discourse of the Pastoral Care,' the tenth chapter of which supplies one of our most important critiques of preaching, was the most celebrated *extempore* preacher of his day. While his remarks on contemporary preaching are reserved for another section, the excellence of his own style must be noted here. Like Tillotson he had begun life as a Presbyterian, being a Scotsman by birth, and nephew of the Covenanting lawyer, Sir Archibald Johnston, Lord Wariston. In early life he paid a visit to England, where he came into contact with both the Cambridge Platonists and the Royal Society Divines, and shortly afterwards to France, where he attended the preaching of certain Jesuit as well as Protestant preachers.[5] From 1675–84 he was chaplain of the Rolls Chapel and lecturer at St. Clement's, and took his place as a distinguished City preacher. Although Burnet was a Latitudinarian by principle his sermons differ from those of the Latitudinarians whom we have already discussed in being less philosophical

---

[1] *Vid.* ' A Compleat Collection of the Sermons . . . Written by . . . Dr. William Fleetwood . . .' Lon., 1737, fol.

[2] For sermons see Bibliography, ' English Sermons of the early Eighteenth Century.'

[3] *Vid.* Nos. 73 and 114.

[4] ' Lectures on Preaching,' Lecture IV, § 18, in ' Works,' ed. cit. Had Doddridge written " the glory of our English *pulpit* orators," his appraisal might well have stood.

[5] *Vid.* ' The Life of the Author,' at the end of vol. ii, ' History of His Own Time,' 1724 ed., pp. 676, 677.

in tone. Of the impression his sermons created on delivery
we have no means of judging, but in their printed form they
do not differ greatly from those of his more outstanding
contemporaries, and most probably represent the working-
up into a literary form of the address previously given, since
from the passage quoted earlier [1] it appears unlikely that the
address was a spirited adaptation of a written sermon.

As we now have them Burnet's sermons in their best
passages do not greatly differ from those of South, while
the ease and naturalness of his average manner is equal to
that of Wilkins and Sprat. One outstanding fault he had—
almost certainly incident to his *extempore* method—namely,
the unhappy habit of adding a further clause to an already
complete sentence, the result being to produce an effect
of bathos ; and he too frequently attempted to give coherence to somewhat lax sentences by the introduction of
weak and obvious connectives (frequently the words " I
say "). But when he wrote with care, his style was easy,
flexible, and always in keeping with his themes. He had
the happy knack of gaining the attention of his hearers by
the naturalness of his diction and the felicity of his illustrations, with the result that he was able to speak to them
nearly always of practical, and at times of more abstruse,
matters, with full confidence that he was being followed
intelligently. While much less polished than Tillotson he
was decidedly more virile, and his sermons have a fine ring
of personal conviction about them. A good specimen of
his manner is provided by the extract already given [2] from
his sermon at Tillotson's funeral. That delivered at the
funeral of the Hon. Robert Boyle in 1691 is not only one of
Burnet's best discourses, but must take rank among the
finest *oraisons funèbres* in English. The tone is elevated, the
style noble, and there are none of the rhetorical trappings
supposed to be appropriate to such an occasion. In each
case the sermon proper is followed by a brief account of
the deceased.

It was Burnet's misfortune to be overshadowed by both
South and Tillotson, but his work is decidedly interesting
as showing how, when the sermon—however originally prepared or actually delivered—came to be written down, the
preacher turned author endeavoured a conformity to the

[1] *Vid. ante,* p. 20.   [2] *Vid. ante,* pp. 334–5.

standard of style set for preaching by those, who, like Tillotson, delivered carefully written sermons.[1]　In this way the influence of the preacher passed to a wider public, and standards of good preaching partly inspired and partly came to be identical with the standards of good prose.

In this change from the bizarre and pedantic preaching of the early part of the seventeenth century to the genuinely ' modern ' note which we find struck at its close, not only did the Practice of preaching depend to a great extent upon rhetorical and theological ideals but, as has been indicated now and then, it was directly modified by criticism of one kind or another.　In consequence the part played by Criticism in relation to the experiments and transitions which we have reviewed now falls to be considered.

[1] *Vid. ante*, p. 17.—The polish of Sprat's printed sermons is another example of how the *extempore* sermon read on publication, *vid. ante*, p. 22.

PART III
CRITICISM

(i) The Attack on the 'Metaphysicals'; (ii) Rhetoricians, Puritans, and Rationalists.

PRACTICE, it may generally be assumed, follows upon theory, and tends to be modified by criticism. An aim once given, those who consider it worthy or desirable pursue it as closely as possible, only diverging from the course prescribed under pressure of new and apparently vital considerations. Yet at the outset aims will often be found to carry with them criticisms either implicit or explicit of competitive theories, and to be both the declaration by a party of its own ideals and a protest against those of its rivals. The working out of theory in practice, moreover, almost always invites fresh considerations ; for theory, unlike Aristotle's famous comments on tragedy, which are based upon a close examination of how the best tragedies known to him achieved their effects, is too often a purely abstract affair, and sets out to prescribe rules by no means deducible from the existing practice of acknowledged masters in a particular art, but framed with a view to logical consistency and completeness. Should the rules be slavishly adhered to, the pattern-maker will be satisfied, but the resultant piece of work is not likely to appeal to anyone else ; and it is precisely from the necessity of readjusting the practical outcome of individual theories to meet the comments of others that criticism derives its value and importance. Nor is this less true of preaching than of drama or poetry in general. There, as elsewhere, theory, practice, and criticism stand in an indivisible relationship, practice being explicit theory and criticism of practice leading circlewise to the formation of still newer theories. This we have already seen illustrated at various points in our study ; for, starting with a common rhetorical background, and, in the majority of instances, a similarity of rhetorical training as conveyed by contemporary education, we found a large measure of divergence in the extent to which different preachers made use of the traditional methods. The change from rhetoric to sacred rhetoric was coloured by theological prepossessions, and that being so, a difference in theological outlook naturally led to a difference in style. The Anglo-Catholic and the Puritan, as we have learned from a survey of their works, employed a large amount of the same learning, but in quite distinct ways, while fashions in syntactical patterns—such as the Senecan vogue—led to fashions in quotations, which in turn resulted in the introduction of new and at first sight apparently untheological matter. Thus Theology may be held primarily responsible for what is included in or omitted from the early seventeenth-century sermon, but omissions of one kind were sometimes responsible for inclusions of another, and Rhetoric, compelled to frame her speech to suit the 'methods' of Perkins or Chappell or the practice of Baxter, and avoiding "the tongues of men" as heard from the 'metaphysicals,' as the century advanced, learned with the Cambridge Platonists not only "the tongues of angels," but also how to impart to the sermon something of that Charity or breadth of outlook lacking which Christian oratory is bound to fail.

The reciprocation, therefore, between theological and rhetorical ideals is manifest, and what was begun at the instance of a 'school' of theological thought was in some instances continued as a badge of ecclesiastical partisanship —as the later work of Cosin marks a recrudescence of 'metaphysical' preaching—after the rhetorical fashion of which it was part had been superseded. On the other hand, stylistic ideals originating in one party are sometimes found taken over by another, and for quite different reasons ; thus the sermon which Perkins decreed should be plain " because the preaching of the word is the *testimony of God*," [1] and which in the hands of Ussher was no doubt kept plain for the same reason, comes plain from South, not because he was incapable of being 'florid' or 'schematic,' [2] but because contemporary taste—if the term may be used in a wide sense—desired the sermon to be plain. Such changes were not effected suddenly ; even Tillotson, influential as he was, achieved no sudden and incalculable dictatorship. He came, as has been shown, at the close of a period of experiment and readjustment, and his influence was due to the fact that, like Addison afterwards in the essay and Tennyson still later in poetry, he gave his contemporaries precisely what they wanted in a form of superlative excellence.

[1] *Vid. ante*, p. 100.   [2] *Vid. ante*, pp. 318–19.

The history of the English sermon in the seventeenth century, as made evident in the preceding section, represents an evolutionary process ; indeed, it is for this very reason that it was chosen as a medium in which to study the changing taste of the period, as providing a complete cross-section of contemporary prose.[1] That the sermon passed through the stages that it did was due partly to the ecclesiastical and political history of the time, partly, especially in its final stages, to the demands of a popular taste which it had itself largely cultivated. The mention of taste implies criticism, and recalls the fact that not only was the sermon the outcome of definite hermeneutic theory, but it was modified and influenced by direct criticism. The motivation of the criticism varied with the critics. Where it lacked any strong party bias it may be considered as a continuation of theory devoted less to a laying down of axioms than a discussion of the desirability or undesirability of certain practices. But theory was peculiarly liable to be influenced by theological considerations, and criticism likewise became to a large extent a series of attacks of party on party. Had it been nothing more, however, it would have been of little interest to the student of literature. But the immense influence of the sermon and its close relationship to current prose style give it a great and far-reaching importance, and the criticism of those who like Glanvill saw the sermon in relation to its wider setting, so that he demands of it what should be demanded of good prose, links up almost imperceptibly with the criticism of men like Hughes, who numbers the printed discourses of Sprat and Tillotson among the models of correct style.[2] In this way the purely hermeneutic and the literary converge, and the sermon, which in earlier times had been an oration, came to be regarded almost as an essay.

The theological and rhetorical aspects of this criticism are best taken together, and the contentions of men of various schools of thought examined, and their abiding contribution (such as it was) to a non-sectarian view of the sermon noted. In this way the more negative type of criticism is eliminated and the positive results carried for-

[1] *Vid. ante*, p. 5.
[2] John Hughes : ' An Essay of Style,' 1698, p. 80, in " Critical Essays of the Eighteenth Century," ed. by W. H. Durham, Oxf., 1915.

ward to combine with the more literary, less theological, criticism of post-Restoration times. It has been found convenient, therefore, to consider the criticism of the sermon from two standpoints, firstly, that of the sectarian critic and theorist, and secondly, in its wider aspect.

The general standpoint of the century, which regarded preaching as a branch of rhetoric directed to a particular purpose, has been made clear in our discussion of Theory, with the reasons which led to this. The common deposit and the varying use made of it have also been dealt with, not only in setting out the aims of theorists of one or other of the great theological parties, but in recording the form which the preaching of these parties took. The diversity of expression has been illustrated, starting from such vivid contrasts as ' metaphysical ' and early Puritan preaching, and presenting such opposites as the typical sermons before the House of Commons in the time of the Commonwealth and that preached to the same auditory, by a kind of irony almost, by Cudworth, and representative of the detached, philosophical, non-party sermon of the Cambridge Platonists. Finally, the gradual collapse of all the earlier modes has been noted, and the appropriation of what was most desirable and possible of combination in one structure exhibited in the achievement of Tillotson. The alleged importance of sectarian criticism, therefore, can arouse no surprise, for, when the form given to the sermon was more often than not to be accounted for by reference to the ecclesiastical convictions of the preacher, it was only to be expected that in attacking the latter's theology men should also animadvert on the vehicle of his thought. The Sedan chair had occasioned less indignation on its introduction into England but for the fact that it was first used by the hated Buckingham,[1] and to some extent the criticisms levelled at particular preaching fashions are less concerned with the fashion than with the party which affected it. On the whole, however, this is not so, but what is a very outstanding feature of the criticism of the sermon is the tendency of each party to fix on the chief weaknesses or abuses of its opponents, and to attack these relentlessly without in any

---

[1] *Vid.* Hume : ' Hist. of England,' Lon., 1818, vol. vi, pp. 168-9.

way realising the grosser faults of its own preachers. Indeed, the whole of this type of criticism was too uniformly destructive, and the great ends of the sermon as set out by Erasmus or Hyperius or Keckermann came to be forgotten. The influence of the German Protestant divines, backed by the English Calvinists, unfortunately diverted sacred rhetoric into sectarian channels, from which the Anglo-Catholic preachers, equally unfortunately, sought a means of escape, not by an appeal to the best *artes concionandi* of the past, but by an imitation of the less defensible devices found in patristic and mediæval sermons. From positions so diametrically opposite serious antagonism in ideal and practice could not but result.

(i) *The Attack on the ' Metaphysicals '*

The importance for our study of understanding clearly what ' metaphysical ' or ' witty ' preaching actually was has already been stressed. Its emergence early in the century as the most highly favoured type of preaching in influential quarters and the whole extent of its influence has been commented upon, and its leading characteristics shown. It follows naturally that a very large proportion of sermon-criticism of the period is concerned with this type of preaching, and it is not to be wondered at that in preaching manuals of a much later date its excesses of one kind or another continued to be held up as examples of all that must most be avoided. Curiously enough, no direct defence of ' metaphysical ' preaching exists. Donne's incidental defence of employing rhetoric [1] or Hacket's approval of burnishing doctrines " brighter with all art of comely Literature," [2] though no doubt intended to meet the case of their ' witty ' *confrères* might equally well be quoted in support of Jeremy Taylor or the Cambridge divines. For the Anglo-Catholic the real *apologia* lay in the appeal to the practice of past centuries ; he could point to the fact, noted later by Féne- lon, that St. Augustine, although " the most jingling Quibbler that ever wrote," " has a moving Way, even when he quibbles," [3] and it was probably his opinion that

[1] *Vid. ante*, p. 189.
[2] *Vid. ante*, p. 119.
[3] ' Dialogues Concerning Eloquence . . . Translated . . . By William Stevenson,' Lon., 1722, Dial. III, p. 181, and p. 182.

that Father was the more moving the more he quibbled. To him the "*Deus dixit . . . Deus benedixit*," of which we have heard South complaining[1] was no mere verbal *homoioteleuton*, for the one had issued in the creation of the world and the other in the promise of the Redeemer. This being so, he could hardly be expected to show that either his doctrine or manner of expounding it was contrary to traditional belief and usage. But it was precisely traditional belief and usage to which his opponents objected, and the very grounds of his defence appeared to them only an aggravation of his guilt.

What many of these opponents advocated was equally inimical to the highest end to be served by the sermon, but the fact remains that, impossible as their own methods of exegesis were as substitutes for the 'witty' sermon, their attacks were of great importance in rousing men to a realisation that such elaboration and artificiality of construction could not hope to claim the attention of men of varied interests and varied intellectual endowments as a means whereby to convey a message of vital importance. Hence, coupled with the example of moderate men within all parties (such as Hales, Ussher, Hammond, and Baxter), the adverse criticism of the 'metaphysical' vogue resulted in the demand for a simpler and more direct manner of pulpit address ; and, since the sermon, whether in its spoken or printed form, was the prime literary influence of the day, in the wholesale cultivation of a less pedantic and more fluent prose style.

The five main counts against 'metaphysical' preaching, which occur singly or collectively in contemporary criticism, or in that of a slightly later period, and with a frequency which is amply justified, were its partiality for strange and unexpected figures, its 'wit,' its passion for quotations, particularly in Latin and Greek, the exaggerated importance it attached to particular words or expressions, and its illogical and unnecessary divisions and subdivisions.

The far-fetched similitude, especially of a learned sort, calculated to surprise when employed as a religious analogy, was, as we saw at the outset of our study, a main characteristic of this preaching,[2] and examples from various 'meta-

---

[1] *Ante*, p. 315.   [2] *Ante*, pp. 6–7.

physical ' preachers have been quoted in the examination of their work. Eachard very rightly describes one large class of these as "frightful Metaphors," and their originators as " Metaphor-Mongers," who

" rake Heaven and Earth, down to the bottom of the Sea, then tumble over all Arts and Sciences, ransack all Shops and Ware-houses, spare neither Camp nor City,"

until by the indiscretion of their resemblances " the *Almighty* himself is often in danger of being dishonoured." Such preachers, he added—

" when they thus blaspheme the God of Heaven, by such unhallowed Expressions, to make amends, they'll put you in, an *As it were* forsooth, or *As I may so say.* . . ." [1]

Collections of similitudes calculated to assist beginners were procurable, and similitudes in general were defended on the ground that Christ taught by this method. But, as Eachard notes, Christ's parables recall the most familiar occupations or circumstances of those who heard them, whereas with the ' metaphysicals '—

" there is little on this side the Moon that will content them : Up presently to the *Primum-mobile*, and the Trepidation of the Firmament : Dive into the Bowels and hid Treasures of the Earth : Dispatch forthwith for *Peru* or *Jamaica* ; a Town-bred or Country-bred Similitude, it is worth nothing ! " [2]

The examples given by this critic while extravagant are by no means unparalleled,[3] and whatever the purpose of his criticism, whether pure raillery or a genuine desire to stamp out the last ebullitions of a vogue, which by the time he wrote (assuming the composition of his work to have

[1] ' The *Grounds* and *Occasions* of the *Contempt* of the CLERGY . . .' by John Eachard, D.D., 11th ed., Lon., 1705, 8vo, pp. 38, 39.
[2] *Op. cit.*, pp. 42–4.
[3] E.g. *cf.* Eachard's summary, *op. cit.*, pp. 45–6, of a sermon on Christ's passage through the signs of the Zodiac with a sermon of Jacques Marchant, a twelfth-century Benedictine, given in Baring-Gould's ' Post-Mediæval Preachers,' Introd., pp. 41–2.

23

nearly preceded its publication in 1678) still lingered (and probably to a considerable extent) in country districts, the justice of his remarks is beyond question. That the fashion as he suggests was chargeable to some extent to the exigencies of the school-theme,[1] and fostered by the commonplace-book,[2] seems hardly less true, but it is doubtful if the remedy proposed (which has already been alluded to in discussing contemporary education),[3] namely, to secure intending preachers practice in English composition, would have been likely to have had beneficial results, if the effects aimed at in the vernacular had continued to be modelled on debased classical practice.

Glanvill, whose ' Essay concerning Preaching ' appeared in the same year as Eachard's work, attacked not only ' metaphors ' but ' cadencies ' also, which as we have learned were even more directly connected with the rhetoric of the ancient world. Nor are these attacks to be regarded as due to the changed taste of the post-Restoration period, for as early as the time of Sidney, whose ' Apology for Poetry,' although not printed until twelve years later, was written in 1583, we find the latter lamenting the " painted affectation " of poets who kept commonplace-books from which they drew weird figures, and noting (with an interesting attention to schematic pattern) that this fault had

" as large possession among Prose-printers, and (which is to meruailled) among Schollers, and (which is to be pittied) among some Preachers." [4]

Similitudes as he saw were of small value—

" for the force of a similitude not being to proove anything to a contrary Disputer but onely to explane to a willing hearer, when that is done the rest is a most tedious pratling . . . " ;

yet—

" in certaine printed discourses . . . all Herbarists, all

[1] *Op. cit.*, p. 23.   [2] *Ibid.*, p. 54.   [3] *Ante*, p. 86.
[4] Sir Philip Sidney : "An Apology for Poetry," reprinted in ' Elizabethan Critical Essays,' ed. Gregory Smith, vol. i, p. 202.

stories of Beasts, Foules, and Fishes are rifled vp, that they come in multitudes to waite vpon any of our conceits." [1]

Similarly, we find Sidney's friend Fulke Greville, in a poem ' Of Humane Learning,' of almost the same date,[2] reflecting on the abuse of metaphors and declaring in lines which sound almost like a prophecy of Sprat—

" Whereas those words in euery tongue are best,
    Which doe most properly expresse the thought. . . ."

So that, whatever Sidney may himself have been guilty of in the way of ' Arcadianism,' and however much he may have approved of his contemporaries Lever and Jewel, by thoughtful men of the penultimate decade of Elizabeth's reign the change from the more purely formal ingenuities to ingenuities of a more subtle and intellectual type, such as we find in the works of Playfere, was viewed with disapproval. Thus the type of preaching which Baxter described as " proud foolery, which savoureth of levity, and tendeth to evaporate weighty Truths and turn them all into very fancies, and keep them from the heart," [3] and to which at the opening of the eighteenth century Edwards took exception[4] largely on the same grounds, was objected to at its outset, less from practical than from literary considerations, and by those in no sense led to oppose it in the interests of an ecclesiastical party. Later, when an opportunity was found for adverse criticism to be levelled at it, it was the literary interest that

---

[1] *Op. cit.*, p. 203. That Sidney himself had done something towards freeing English from this abuse was recognised by his contemporaries. Thus we find Drayton writing in his elegy, ' To my most dearely-loued friend, Henery Reynolds, Esquire, of *Poets & Poesie* ' :

" The noble *Sidney* . . .
            . . . did first reduce
    Our tongue from *Lillies* writing then in vse ;
    Talking of Stones, Stars, Plants, of fishes, Flyes,
    Playing with words, and idle Similes . . ."

' Minor Poems of Michael Drayton,' ed. by Cyril Brett, Oxf., 1907, 8vo, p. 110.
[2] This is shown by the title of Greville's volume : ' Certaine Learned And Elegant Workes of . . . Fulke, Lord Brooke, Written in his Youth, and familiar Exercise with Sir Philip Sidney,' Lon., 1633, 4to. The stanzas to which reference is made are 107–9 of the poem cited.
[3] *Vid.* Powicke's : ' A Life of the Reverend Richard Baxter,' p. 283.
[4] *Vid.* John Edwards : ' The Preacher . . .' 2nd ed., 3 vols., Lon., 1705–9, 8vo, vol. i, pp. 201–3.

predominated again, though Baxter's statement is good evidence of the line taken by the earnest, religiously minded critic in the day of the 'metaphysical' ascendency. The metaphors were of course only one element in the composition of the 'metaphysical' sermon—the element that made it peculiarly 'metaphysical.' But 'witty' preaching in general, with its puns and quibbles, its jingles and rhetorical *tours de force*, its topical references and calculated drollery, presented a wider range of attack. What was considered ' witte ' in Jacobean times is well illustrated by a passage in the *Diary* of John Rous relating to Thomas Lushington, the tutor of Sir Thomas Browne. Under the date, " October 6, 1629," Rous records :

" I was at Mondeford Courte, where asking Mr. Tayler what newes, he tould me that Mr. Barret had there showen a sermon unprinted, lately preached at Whitehall before the King, upon Mat. 28, 13, saying ' Say ye his disciples came by night,' &c. by Dr. Lushington, Oxfordiens. I asked the drifte of it ; he tould me ' witte.' I asked him what was remarkeable ; he said, first the beginning. ' What newes ? Every man askes what newes ? Every man's religion is knowne by his newes ; the Puritan talkes of Bethlehem Gabor, &c.' Besides this, the doctor fell belike to personate the chiefe priests and elders, in a flourishing description of our Saviour and his apostles, as impostors, &c. (a wicked witte), and then comes to demande, Why the soldiers should say it &c. . . . In those times, (said he) the soldiers did depose and chuse emperors, yet the time had been when the priests did this. But now peasants will doe all, by prerogative of parliament, &c." [1]

The sermon alluded to was never printed, but is typical of hundreds which were, and the sketch of its main positions preserved by Rous is an interesting commentary on Brownrig and Hacket and even on Andrewes himself. It was precisely thus that these preachers hinted obliquely at current practices, and the " wicked " *prosopopœa* is both an interesting sidelight on their manner of delivery, and a

[1] ' Diary of John Rous, Incumbent of Santon Downham, Suffolk, From 1625–1642. Edited by Mary Anne Everett Green . . . For Camden Soc.,' 1860, *loc. cit.*

reminder that the *controuersia* had been carefully transmitted across the centuries. The "resemblances" noted, instead of being conveyed by far-fetched erudite analogies, are of a homelier yet none the less surprising character.

On the punning and quibbling usually associated with 'witty' preaching Eachard is again found making a vigorous attack. In no other profession, as he pointed out, was it "imagined that blending now and then a piece of a dry Verse, and wresting here and there an old Latin Saying with a Dismal Jingle "[1] could serve any purpose; nor could it be expected to do so when used in the pulpit. Such wit, he declared, if examined, would " be found to depend upon some such Fooleries " as the chance " Ambiguity of some Word or Sentence,"[2] and, as he noted at a later stage in his treatise,[3] to the 'witty' preacher it was

" the Joy of Joys when the parts *jingle*, or begin with the same *Letter*; and especially if in *Latin*."

The explanation which he offers for the value put upon such performances closely resembles that which he supplies for the prevalence of strange metaphors, and is further evidence of the influence exercised by the contemporary rhetorical training which we examined under Theory.

In attributing to " Academick Exercises "[4] an over-great fondness for such absurdities Eachard was not alone, and we find Barrow, in a speech delivered as Moderator at Cambridge in 1651, protesting against the undue facetiousness which disfigured university speeches in his day.[5] It is true Barrow's main objection was to the licentiousness of the speeches, but the fact that eight years later, in a *Pro Lectore Humanitatis Oratio* addressed to his students, he spoke as follows :

" As to your themes, what I particularly request is, that you will attend to the argument, and make that your polestar . . ."[6]

---

[1] '*Grounds* and *Occasions*,' ed. cit., p. 28.
[2] *Ibid.*, p. 29.   [3] *Ibid.*, p. 57.   [4] *Ibid.*, p. 27.
[5] *Vid.* 'Opuscula,' quoted in " Life," prefixed to Hughes ed. of 'The Works,' p. xxi.
[6] 'Opuscula,' Napier's ed., pp. 133-4.

goes to show, as might be expected from his sermons, that he was seriously concerned about the tendency to neglect matter for the sake of cultivating the supposed ornaments of expression. In his sermon, ' Against Foolish Talking and Jesting,' [1] Barrow further animadverted on the excessive demands of the period—" this pleasant and jocular Age " as he called it—for continuous displays of wit ; but he did not descend to particular instances, choosing rather, as was characteristic of the man, to reprove the faults he detested by the cultivation of a totally different style.

It is true that Barrow's sermon, though not his speeches, and Eachard's book belong to post-Restoration criticism, [2] and that the ' wit ' they principally aim at was of the impudent disagreeable kind which we have noted in South ; but Eachard's examples tend on the whole to be of an antiquated type, and reflect directly on the works of the older ' witty ' preachers and their rustic imitators. That these writers deal with wit at a later period than falls at present to be discussed, and after the term had undergone a distinct change of meaning, is of no great importance, for the observation of Hearne at a still later time, [3] when discussing Atterbury's style, that " the study of witty expressions is to be looked upon as levity, and more proper for juvenile essays " than for the pulpit discourse, might be applied equally well to the ' metaphysicals ' or the post-Restoration ' wits.' It tends to re-emphasise, moreover, the reason for ' witty ' attempts of one kind or another as intimately associated with academic or scholastic training, and we are less surprised to hear the writer of an eighteenth-century preface at some date after 1737 referring to those who " speak continually in wretched Pun and Quibble " with no suggestion of great remoteness from his own day. [4]

---

[1] ' Works,' 1700 ed., sermon xiv, p. 176.

[2] A MS. note in a contemporary hand in my copy of the folio of 1700 written at the top of this sermon reads : " Preach'd at Court before King Charles ye Second, & particularly levelled at ye Duke of Buckingham who had affronted ye Author in ye drawing room, & was enjoin'd by ye King to attend " ; and Eachard, *op. cit.*, p. 30, writes : " It is as very a piece of Wit, as any has pass'd in Town since the *King* came in."

[3] The 16th January, 1710-11 : ' Reliquiæ Hearnianæ . . .' ed. Bliss (Lib. of Old Authors), 1869, vol. i, p. 215.

[4] In ' The Occasional Miscellany in Prose and Verse . . . With a Specimen of Sacred Poetry and Sermons . . . By John Wallis . . .' 2 vols., Newcastle-upon-Tyne, 1748. The date ' after 1737 ' is fixed by Wallis' quotations from Glover's ' Leonidas,' which appeared in that year.

Another of the main characteristics, however, of ' metaphysical ' preaching to which a more definite time-limit can be assigned was its tendency to employ learned quotations, especially quotations in the original tongues. While the Cambridge Platonists showed an equal proneness to quote, there is at least this distinction observable between the two types of quotation—those of the rationalist divines are used by way of illustration and to support particular arguments, whereas the patristic quotations embedded in the ' metaphysical ' sermon only too often were inserted for purely decorative effect. Baxter's warning against seeking to increase one's prestige by " citations of Fathers, and repeating words of Latin or Greek " has already been quoted,[1] and his analysis of the motive which led to much learned rhetorical preaching is probably a true one :

" Pride " (he wrote) " stands by and contradicteth all ; and sometimes it puts in Toys and Trifles, and Polluteth rather than Polisheth, and under pretence of laudable Ornaments, it dishonoureth our Sermons with Childish Gaudes. . . ."[2]

Baxter, however, was far from singular in his dislike of this particular habit. Keckermann, as we have seen,[3] definitely condemned it, and in England it was by no means the Puritan alone who protested against it. If we are not surprised to learn of Mede that

" in popular Discourses and Sermons, he disliked the unnecessary quotation of Authors and the use of foreign languages,"[4]

it was certainly no sympathy for Puritan preaching of any period that led Eachard to pour derision upon those who, not content to sprinkle their sermons " with plenty of *Greek* and *Latin*," " must swagger also over their poor Parishioners with the dreadful *Hebrew* it self."[5] Evelyn,

---

[1] *Ante*, pp. 103–4.
[2] ' Gildas Salvianus, or the Reform'd Pastor,' in vol. iv of ' The Practical Works,' Lon., 1707, fol., p. 368.
[3] *Ante*, p. 97.
[4] ' Memorials of Worthy Persons . . .' by Cl. Barksdale, Lon., 1661, p. 158 ; *vid. ante*, p. 105.
[5] *Op. cit.*, pp. 33 and 34.

moreover, almost certainly disapproved of this type of preaching, except to learned auditories, for he noted in his *Diary*, on the 28th December, 1656, that a stranger preached in his parish church, and

" made a confused discourse, with a great deale of Greeke and ostentation of learning to but little purpose."

Rural auditories, however, as is shown by the charge preferred against Pococke,[1] and as South distinctly tells us,[2] were the most prone to demand what they least understood, believing that a sermon was to be highly thought of in proportion to the number of quotations it contained.   This desire was partly fostered no doubt by the belief that texts quoted in the classical languages represented the actual words spoken by characters in the sacred story or by God Himself[3]; and the fact that university and court preachers, as well as young country parsons who aspired to preach at Court, quoted with astonishing frequency in preaching before country congregations led to an increase of the abuse. There was complete neglect of such advice as that given by Cardinal Borromeo to the intending preacher, " verba *antiqua* et *peregrina* fugiat," [4] advice in course of time to be re-echoed by the Protestant Claude, who described the customary array of " passages from Profane *Authors*, or *Rabbies*, or *Fathers*," as a "farrago," [5] and " a vain ostentation of learning." [6]

Clearly in its origin the citation of authorities formed part of the polemic against Rome, and it was an evil day for the Church of England when not only this custom of citation

[1] *Vid. ante*, p. 106.
[2] *Vid. ante*, pp. 119–20.
[3] Boyle was distinctly in advance of his age when he wrote : " For we must not look upon the Bible as an Oration of God to men, or as a Body of Lawes, like our English Statute-Book . . . but as a Collection of compositions of very differing sorts, and written at very distant times."—' Some Considerations Touching the Style of the H. Scriptures,' Lon., 1661, 8vo, but " writ " in Boyle's youth.   Boyle was born in 1627.
[4] Quoted in a footnote by Robinson to Claude's ' Essay,' as found in Williams : ' The Christian Preacher,' 2nd ed., 1809, p. 385. *Cf.* Borromeo's chapter, " De forma Episcopalis concionis," Book II, chap. xv, of ' De Concionante Episcopo,' Milan, 1632.
[5] Explained by ' Petit Larousse ' as " mélange de différentes espèces de grains."
[6] ' Essay on the Composition of a Sermon,' Robinson's trans., 1788, vol. i, p. 34.

but the knowledge of the works which men had previously cited began to decay. Evidence of this latter fact is supplied by a letter, of date 1680, from Evelyn to Fell, bishop of Oxford, in which the former remarks—

" the men of this curious & nicer age do not consider what has ben said or written formerly, but expect something fresh. . . ." [1]

But legitimate quoting for polemical purposes soon gave way to quoting of an entirely different kind. As we have seen, men who turned to the Fathers for arguments to support their doctrinal positions found in the patristic writers rhetorical devices of a sort with which they were familiar from their own rhetorical education, but employed with a brilliancy and verve which gave a decided impetus to their imitation. The results were, on the one hand, a reinforcement of the Senecan vogue, which for other reasons was appealing to men of the late sixteenth century both on the Continent and in England, on the other, the delight in toying with words and phrases typical of the Anglo-Catholic sermon. In its initial stages the latter habit was undoubtedly due to the rhetorical bent of the preachers and their desire to prove themselves successors of Chrysostom and Augustine. Later, as White Kennett informs us, quaintness and elegance were affected by the clergy of the Established Church as a kind of offset to " the low and coarse Language of the Enemies of the Church."[2] The abuse was certainly perpetuated by the use of the commonplace-book, and Glanvill was doing a real service in censuring

" Collectors that make Nosegays, and pick a piece out of one Author, and a piece out of another ; so that the whole is a medley of different things all mingled." [3]

But for a time the abuse continued, and far from appearing a fault was considered a virtue. In particular it took

---

[1] ' Memoirs Illustrative of The Life and Writings of John Evelyn . . .' including ' A Selection of His Familiar Letters,' ed. Bray, 1819. Reprint of 2nd ed., 1870, p. 679.
[2] ' A Register and Chronicle Ecclesiastical and Civil . . .' Lon., 1727, p. 793, left margin.
[3] ' An Essay Concerning Preaching ' (1st ed., 1678), 2nd ed., 1703, p. 66.

the form of quoting single words of Latin and Greek, often
with the express purpose of securing a jingle, and probably
at times to emphasise the ability of the preacher to produce
similar effects in the vernacular. But the attraction of
particular words had a more profound *raison d'être* connected
with the contemporary belief in the *verbatim* nature of
Scriptural utterances, and, where the preachers themselves
and the more learned of their auditories were concerned,
with the Rabbinical speculations on the inner significance
of letters and numbers.[1] Minute attendance to cases or
parts of speech provided valuable exegetical material, as
may be gathered from the work of Andrewes and Donne,[2]
and the statement of Dr. Richard Stuart, a dean of St.
Paul's, that " when the Text is pleased to expatiate, each
word must needs be Doctrinall," [3] would certainly have
been accepted by the ' metaphysicals ' as a whole. The
result of this practice was what we have already seen in
our extracts from the ' metaphysical ' sermon—the total
break up of anything approaching a connected prose style
and the multiplying of endless divisions, due not to the
careful working out of a sound rhetorical plan, but to the
caprice and ingenuity of the preachers. The connection
between words and divisions is alluded to by Edwards, who
adds that it need not have survived so long " if *Mr. Herbert*
had been attended to." [4] The reference is an interesting one,
as it brings us back to the year 1630, when Herbert was
presented to the living of Bemerton, Wiltshire, and (in the
words of Walton) " set down his rules then resolved upon "
with relation to the various duties of a country parson.[5]
Two years later these were embodied in ' A Priest to the
Temple,' in the seventh chapter of which (that entitled
' The Parson Preaching ') we find the author giving it as
his opinion that the

" way of crumbling a text into small parts, as the person
speaking or spoken to, the subject and object, and the like,

---

[1] E.g. Bishop Senhouse declared : " The very letters in Jehovah are all
quiescent," ' Four Sermons,' 1627, quoted Southey : ' Commonplace-Book,'
ed. Warter, Third Series, p. 676, col. 2.

[2] *Ante*, p. 160 and p. 184.

[3] ' Three Sermons . . .' Lon., 1656, 12mo, p. 61.

[4] ' The Preacher,' ed. cit., vol. i, p. 202.

[5] Walton's ' Life,' pp. 24 and 28–9, prefixed to Chandos' Classics ed. of
Herbert's ' Works.'

hath neither in it sweetness, nor gravity, nor variety, since the words apart are not Scripture, but a dictionary. . . ." [1]

The delight in Latin words and in multiple divisions was combined when the latter were introduced by such familiar rhetorical terms as those suggested by Bernard—*Quis, quid, vbi, quibus auxilijs, cur, quomodo, quando.*[2] Bernard it is true was a Puritan, and the Puritan, although finding the 'intendment' of his text by this method, did not ostentatiously parade the terms, which Donne and the other 'metaphysicals' did. Of this peculiarity of exegesis bishop Croft of Hereford, in 'The Naked Truth,' published in 1675, wrote :

" they divide and subdivide into generals and particulars, the *quid*, the *quale*, the *quantum*, and such-like quaksalving forms ; then they study how to hook in this or that quaint sentence of Philosopher or Father, this or that nice speculation, endeavouring to couch all this in most elegant language ; in short, their main end is to show their Wit. . . . I know full well this unapostolick way of preaching was used by some of the Ancient Fathers, especially the *Greeks*, [who], always fond of niceties and curiosities, and being now become Christians . . . transplanted their beloved Rhetorical flowers of humane Learning into Christian Gardens. . . . But when did ever any Learned, Witty, Rhetorical harangue, or cunning Syllogistical discourse convert the tythe of St. *Peter's* or St. *Paul's* foolish Preaching, as he terms it, *but the wisdom of God to those that are perfect*, and sound in the faith." [3]

That this last characteristic of the 'metaphysical' sermon was not purely a clerical affectation, but must be referred to the theological and rhetorical interests of the period, is made evident by William Austin's 'Devotionis Augustinianæ Flamma,' issued by his widow in 1635. Austin, a barrister of Lincoln's Inn, and a friend of Howell, Selden, Edward Alleyn, and other distinguished men of the period, represents

[1] Ed. cit., p. 282 ; 'Works,' edited by Robert Aris Willmott, Lon., 1854, pp. 230–1.
[2] *Ante*, p. 110 ; *cf.* Bloom : 'Pulpit Oratory in the Time of James the First,' p. 101.
[3] Chapter 'Concerning Preaching,' p. 25.

that type of theologically learned and devout layman of
which Wotton and Evelyn were also examples. The
relation of his book to Donne is striking ; he toyed with
words—often the Latin word from the Vulgate—in the same
way : he possessed a minute and accurate knowledge of the
Fathers and Schoolmen, and he delighted in the elaborate
exposition of particular phrases. His meditations, moreover, show the same clear divisions into leading topics
introduced by *Qui*, *Quando*, *Quo modo*, *Quare*, and like expressions. The meditation for Good Friday was written
somewhere about 1620, and that for Lady-Day in 1627 ;
the latter repeats the familiar paradoxes of the Incarnation so beloved of the more Catholic type of preacher.

It is possible, of course, to argue that Austin was a specially
close imitator of his favourite preachers, but his work does
not suggest mere *pastiche* ; rather it suggests a man whose
reading and education had closely resembled that of
contemporary divines, and whose devotional expression
flowed spontaneously along similar channels. If this be so
it adds confirmation to what has gradually been becoming
clearer as the different counts against ' metaphysical '
preaching are examined, namely, that such preaching was
quite definitely the product of a period when existing rhetorical training became freshly stimulated by theological
writings which themselves displayed rhetorical characteristics of a related order. The adverse criticism of this
preaching comes from those who for one reason or another,
whether on account of practical considerations like Herbert
or Baxter, or on account of a changed rhetorical or hermeneutic outlook which they accepted, like Eachard and
Glanvill, felt obliged to record their disapproval of a vogue
which could not hope to effect the main aims with which
the sermon is concerned, and was directly responsible for
perpetuating a pedantic and disjointed prose-style.

The change in point of view which came about as the
century advanced is well summarised by Glanvill in ' A
Seasonable Defence of Preaching : And the Plain Way of
it ' :

" A man doth not shew his Wit or Learning, by rolling
in Metaphors, and scattering his Sentences of Greek and
Latin, by abounding in high expressions, and talking in

the Clouds, but he is then learned, when his learning has clear'd his Understanding, and furnish'd it with full and distinct apprehensions of things ; when it enables him to make *hard* things *plain* ; and conceptions, that were *con-fused, distinct,* and *orderly* ; and he shews his learning by speaking good strong and plain Sense." [1]

Glanvill here joins hands with Erasmus, who in his 'Ecclesiastes' had given precisely the same advice [2] ; but, as we have learned from our study of Practice, many strange and competitive types of pulpit oratory were to be tried out in turn, before by general consent men of all parties were led to accept the plain, unadorned, but carefully modulated, sermon as a pulpit ideal.

(ii) Rhetoricians, Puritans, and Rationalists

Apart from ' metaphysical ' preaching, the sermon in our period may be conveniently grouped under one or other of the following heads—the rhetorical or schematic sermon of men like Adams and Hall, whose theology was of a different cast from that of their Laudian brethren, the plain sermon as advocated by Wilkins and practised by Ussher 'in the forties of the century,[3] the scriptural sermon of the Presbyterians, and, when many of these had been absorbed by the Establishment, the strange canting sermon of the Nonconformists which had grown up alongside of the former, and, finally, the rationalistic or Latitudinarian sermon. In a way, Abraham Wright, in his curious volume issued in 1656, except that he offers no specimen of the rationalists, gave the *imprimatur* to this method of distinguishing types of sermons. Wright's volume is entitled—

'Five Sermons, In Five several Styles; Or Waies of Preaching. The First in *Bp*. ANDREWS his *Way* . . . Second in *Bp*. HALL'S *Way* . . . Third in *Dr*. MAINE'S and *Mr*. CARTWRIGHT'S *Way* . . . Fourth in the PRESBYTERIAN *Way* . . . Fifth in the INDEPENDENT *Way* . . . With an *Epistle* rendring an Account of the

---

[1] *Op. cit.*, 1703 ed., p. 108 ; the ' Seasonable Defence ' first appeared in 1678.

[2] *Vid. op. cit.*, Book II, iv.

[3] The original edition of Wilkins' ' Ecclesiastes ' appeared in 1646; for references to Ussher's practice, *cir.* 1642, see *ante*, p. 8 and pp. 227-9.

Authors Designe in Printing these his Sermons, as also of the Sermons themselves.'

From the ' Epistle ' we learn that Wright's intention in issuing these sermons, of which the two by Andrewes and Hall are actual sermons by these bishops, and the remaining three almost certainly interesting " parodies " and correctly described by Wright in his title-page as " these his Sermons," was to demonstrate that while an uneducated preacher could only preach in his own vein, " a Scholar is able to preach any way to the capacitie and content of any Auditorie." Recognising that " all men will not be brought by the same way of preaching to heaven," that—

" some are well satisfied with the plain easie way of Doctrine and Use ; others are not taken with any Sermon, but what is fill'd with depth of Matter, height of Fancie, and good Language," [1]

and, obviously having in mind the attacks of such men as Dell and Webster on a learned ministry,[2] Wright urges that if all preachers were scholars it would be possible for them to adapt themselves to the tastes of varied auditories. In particular he defends the use of secular learning, declaring that " Plato, and Socrates, and Seneca were not of such a reprobate sence, as to stand wholly Excommunicate," and that

" Seneca's Positions may become Saint Paul's text ; Aristotle's Metaphysicks convince an Atheist of God, and his Demonstrations prove Shiloes Advent to a Jew. The great Apostle of the Gentiles had never converted the Nations without the help of their own Learning. It was the Gentiles Oratorie yet not without the Holy Ghost's Rhetorick, that did almost perswade Agrippa to be a Christian ; and it was the Gentiles Poetrie, but not without a Dietie in the Verse, that taught the Athenians to know an unknown God." [3]

Wright's remarks on the use of secular learning and philosophy might well have been written with the Cambridge Platonists in mind, while his reference to Aristotle

[1] A 2 ver.–A 3.   [2] *Vid. ante*, pp. 126–7.   [3] A 7 ver.–A 8.

recalls the devotion to logic of the older Puritans. What is more interesting, however, is the fact that it was possible to select five sermons, produced, or supposed to be produced, by divines of different parties, so as to render clear the distinctive feature of the party sermon.[1]

In taking leave of the ' metaphysicals ' one is by no means taking leave of the rhetorical sermon. Indeed, the rhetorical sermon proper may be regarded as surviving rather in the work of those Calvinists who were not so puritanically affected as to adhere to the precepts of strict Scriptural exposition laid down by Perkins. The schematic sermon with its figures, conceits, and antitheses was a direct heritage of the Middle Ages, and was passed on by men like Jewel and Lever (by Hooker even as we have seen [2]) to the Jacobean divines. The ' Senecan ' preachers had certainly more claim to the title rhetorical than the ' metaphysicals,' and were quite as open as the latter to Puritan attack. Thus we find Doddridge, although describing Hall as " the most elegant and polite writer of his age," noting that " He abounds rather too much with antitheses and witty turns," and blaming him for his imitation of Seneca and Augustine.[3] Baxter, too, in a passage already quoted,[4] while acknowledging Hall's charm, is candid in his confession that he considered the latter's style too elaborate to be effective.

Apart from style the content of the rhetorical sermon offended, for it drew freely upon " heathen writers," which as we know from Andrewes was bound to arouse Puritan hostility,[5] and its lively comparisons and illustrations were a further ground for complaint. It was in vain that Adams urged in defence of himself and his fellows that—

" A good Christian, that like the Bee works honey from euery flower, suffers no action, demonstration, euent, to slip

[1] That the styles of preaching affected by the different sects were clearly distinguished by contemporaries is plain from a letter of Evelyn to William Wotton, dated 12th September, 1703, in which the diarist relates how Sir William Petty had been able to divert his friends by holding forth " in tone and action ; passing from the Court pulpit to the Presbyterian and then the Independent, Anabaptist, Quaker, Fanatic, Friar, and Jesuit," and how he was prevailed upon to give a demonstration of his ability before Charles II to the latter's great amusement. " *Cf.* also Pepys : ' Diary,' 14th May, 1669.

[2] *Ante*, pp. 64–5.

[3] ' Lectures on Preaching . . .' Lecture II, § 8, in ' The Works,' 1804, vol. v.

[4] *Ante*, p. 271.   [5] *Ante*, p. 10.

by him without a question. All Obiects to a meditating
Solomon are like wings to reare and mount vp his thoughts
to Heauen." [1]

The vividness of portraiture of these divines proved their
undoing, as we have seen in the case of White's ' roaring-
boies,' [2] or Adams' Characters [3] or Hall's portrait of Adam and
Eve, [4] and just as the *controuersia* survived to be a bane to the
' metaphysical,' so the *descriptio* tended to get out of control
with full-blooded preachers who desired to reprehend sinners.
    All ' Senecan ' sermons naturally were far from being as
lively as those of Hall and Adams, and there were other
sermons that aimed at vividness without any connection with
the *schemata* ; but so far as a sermon is not mere point to point
exegesis, such as was fashionable in the time of the Parliamentary ascendency, it may be claimed as rhetorical. The
lasting contribution of those interested in Seneca was one
of thought rather than of form, and only of form in the
somewhat paradoxical sense that all preachers who were
not excessively addicted to quotation, whether of Fathers
or Scripture, were pointing the way to a plainer prose.
The vividness of the City preachers also survived to later
times in a degenerate form as the anecdotes of the sectaries.
    Against the plain Anglican sermon no criticism could be
levelled, and consequently we hear nothing of it ; yet the
fact remains that a far larger percentage of dull, straightforward pulpit addresses were delivered down to and during
the period of the Civil Wars than at first sight appears. It
is the abuses of a period that attract attention and invite
criticism ; what is unexceptional passes without notice.
The author of the ordinary plain sermon had no cause to
rush into print, and at the present day, when we light upon
sermons of this type, we lay them aside quickly because
they provide nothing that seems of moment. Yet the fact
that a very large mass of such sermons have survived is not
unimportant, and goes to show that, although the attraction of ' witty ' preachers both of the early and later sort is
undoubted, Wilkins' ' Ecclesiastes ' was written for men
who could appreciate it, and, although the result was for
long unapparent, did bear fruit.

    [1] " The Sinners Passing-Bell," a sermon of 1614 : ' Workes,' fol., 1630, p. 252.
    [2] *Ante*, pp. 199–200.   [3] *Ante*, pp. 217–20.   [4] *Ante*, pp. 226–7.

The Scriptural sermon, while quite as unliterary as the foregoing, calls for remark if only to illustrate the contrary excess to ' metaphysical ' quotation and subdivision. Taking their stand with Perkins on the grounds already outlined,[1] the Puritan divines naturally confined themselves to the Sacred Text itself. For them " the right dividing of the word " consisted of " resolution " and " application." " Resolution," Perkins had said, might be one of two things. Either it was " notation," " when as the doctrine is expressed in the place propounded," or it was " collection "—

" when the doctrine not expressed is soundly gathered out of the text. This is done by the helpe of the nine arguments, that is of the causes, effects, subjects, adjuncts, dissentanies, comparisons, names, distribution, and definition."[2]

" Application," on the other hand, suffered a fourfold division : first came mental application concerned with " doctrine " (whereby teaching was " used for the information of the mind to a right judgement,") and " redargution " (whereby teaching was " used for the reformation of the minde from error ") ; this was followed by " practicall application," whose two parts were " instruction " and ' correction."[3]

Such a method of exegesis depended partly, as we saw Wright hinting, on the application of logic, partly on the well-worn rules laid down by Aphthonius for the composition of a theme.[4] It was partly too, as Bass Mullinger notes, a survival of Scholasticism,[5] and at a period when Christianity was in peculiar danger of becoming the ' religion of a book," there was ample opportunity for its exercise. Differences of opinion arose as to the proportion of a sermon to be devoted to " doctrines " and " uses " respectively,[6] and as theological controversy and divergence of opinion continued to grow more and more acute, doctrine came more and more to predominate. In 1655 Evelyn recorded in his *Diary* that the bulk of the people—

[1] *Ante*, p. 100.
[2] ' The Art of Prophecying,' in ' The Works,' 1631, vol. ii, p. 663.
[3] *Ibid.*, p. 668.   [4] *Ante*, p. 72.   [5] *Ante*, p. 78.
[6] Clarke's ' Lives,' 1677 ed. (Life of Robt. Harris), p. 332.

24

" had no principles, and grew very ignorant of even the
common points of Christianity ; all devotion being now
plac'd in hearing sermons and discourses of speculative and
notional things " [1] ;

while the following year he wrote :

" There was now nothing practicall preached or that
pressed for reformation of life, but high and speculative
points, and straines that few understood. . . ." [2]

The legitimate Puritan complaint that—

" this curious age is too much given to the affectation of
words, and phrases, and cadencies," [3]

evokes less sympathy when we are brought face to face with
the machinery of these discourses and their increasing
abstruseness of theme.   Robinson, in a note to his translation of Claude's ' Essay,' remarks that a sermon of Owen's
(on Habakkuk iii. i), after commencing with a fourfold
division, branches into " almost one hundred and fifty
observations, uses, reasons, &c." [4]   Naturally such sermons,
however much they conformed to highly technical rhetorical
patterns which stagger the modern mind by their intricacy,
could not hope to be literary, and consequently no specimens of them are given under Practice.   Puritanically
affected though Baxter was, his sermons present us with no
examples of such excesses, in which on the other hand the
works of Thomas Goodwin abound ; but Baxter himself
as we have learned from the " Advertisements " to ' A
Christian Directory,' drew a sharp distinction between the
treatise concerned merely with " the *Directing part* " of
theology and the sermon which, he agreed, required explications, reasons, various uses, " marks," " motives, &c."
His restraint in this matter is therefore all the more
remarkable.

[1] *Anno* cit., 19th September.
[2] The 2nd November, 1656.
[3] Clarke's ' Lives,' ed. cit. (Life of Rich. Capel), p. 305.
[4] *Op. cit.*, vol. ii, p. 458.
[5] *Vid. ante*, p. 258.   The "marks" consisted of small hands with the index
finger pointing to passages of special concern.

The fact is, however, that in Baxter two distinct strains
of preaching are found combining, and it is precisely
through this combination which transformed Puritan
preaching that the latter is able to claim a place in the
reformation of pulpit style. The Scriptural sermon, with
its multiplicity of texts and interminable divisions, was
strictly a Presbyterian offset to the learned Anglo-Catholic
sermon. When the Independents came into prominence
during the Protectorate, although Goodwin and others of
their party were experts in its composition, it was no longer
regarded with the favour it had previously enjoyed, for
among preachers, large numbers of whom had not passed
through a regular course of education, the production of
such addresses would have been impossible. There had,
besides, as Baxter tells us, always been a tendency for the
masses to be

" greatly taken with a Preacher that speaketh to them in
a familiar natural Language, and exhorteth them as if it
were for their Lives ; " [1]

and such preachers the Independents and Anabaptists provided. Baxter's work represents on the one hand the definite
simplification of the elaborate Puritan sermon, on the other
the attempt to speak to his auditors with the directness which
rendered the sectaries popular. In other words, the reform
of preaching, so far as non-Anglican preaching is concerned,
came about when, in the interests of a more direct appeal,
Biblical learning and constructional technique alike ceased
to be ostentatiously paraded.

Yet this later Puritan sermon—the sermon of the type
which survived among the Nonconformists of Post-Restoration times—presented peculiar features of its own, two at
least of which offered continual targets for criticism. It
was homely and vivid in a way which the City Puritans of a
more rhetorical period hardly had been, for the men who
produced it were in a good many instances of limited if not
slight education, and their pulpit addresses were frequently
in more than doubtful taste. But along with this homeliness
of language and illustration went the flair for speculative
divinity noted by Evelyn as characteristic of the period and

[1] ' Reliquiæ,' 1696, p. 32.

due in part to the peculiar circumstances of the men who indulged in it.

The former of these new abuses is touched on by Eachard, who in illustration of the old 'figure' sermons gives a quotation from one of these on " the Sacrament and Faith " in which Christ is represented as a shopkeeper offering for sale such spiritual commodities as Balm of Gilead, Eyesalve, a Robe of Righteousness, or a Helmet of Salvation.[1] Such preaching, as the critic indicates, had been largely indulged in " for an hundred years last past ; "[2] but worse things were to come, and preachers " of somewhat too mean and dirty Imaginations " employed analogies of a sort unsuited to the reverence and dignity of their subjects.[3] This latter fault has been glanced at in describing Rutherford's preaching and forms the main theme of ' the Scotch Presbyterian Eloquence ' ; among the Nonconformists themselves it naturally met with no approval from the more learned and temperate of their number, and early in the following century we find Watts advising his pupils that—

" as your style must not affect the pomp and magnificence of the theatre, so neither should you borrow your expressions, or your metaphors, from the coarsest occupations, or any of the mean and uncleanly occurrences in life."[4]

Further evidence on this tendency is afforded by the first of the ' Friendly Debates ' where Bridge, one of the writers of the ' Apologetical Narration,' is spoken of as a typical offender.[5] This ' Debate,' of which Simon Patrick was author,[6] also points the connection between over-homely or

---

[1] ' *Grounds* and *Occasions*,' ed. cit., p. 49. Phillips, Milton's nephew, in the second part of his ' Speculum Crape-Gownorum,' 1682 (to which Sir Charles Firth has called my attention), satirises justly the preachers of sermons before the Artillery Company, the Inns of Court, or at Assizes, for attempting to use too large a number of metaphors drawn from the profession of their hearers.—*Op. cit.*, pp. 29–32.

[2] *Vid. ante*, p. 216, footnote [1].

[3] Eachard, *op. cit.*, p. 48.

[4] " Rules for the Preacher's Conduct," Discourse V, reprinted in Williams, ' The Christian Preacher,' 2nd ed., p. 154.

[5] ' A Friendly Debate Between a Conformist and a Non-Conformist,' 1684 ed., p. 149 (1st ed., 1668).

[6] The ' Debate ' here quoted, which enjoyed five editions in the course of a year, was followed in 1669 by ' A Continuation of the Friendly Debate ' also issued anonymously. Patrick, in his ' Auto-Biography ' (sole ed., Oxf., 1839, p. 59), states that he wrote the first ' Debate ' in the latter end of 1668.

actually uncouth expressions, and the exposition of odd and novel ideas. When Episcopacy was suppressed—

" if any Fellow did but light upon some new and pretty Fancy in Religion, or some odd unusual Expression, or perhaps some swelling words of Vanity ; presently he set up for a Preacher. . . . And such was the confidence of these men, both in inventing strange Language, and proclaiming their great Discoveries every where, that the poor people were perswaded, the Nation never knew what Communion with God meant till this time. . . . For one man comes and tells them of the *streamings of* Christ's *Bloud freely to* sinners : another bids them *put themselves upon the stream of Free grace*, without having any foot on their own bottom : A third tells them how they must *apply Promises*, absolute Promises." [1]

These were the men who, the same writer tells us, used such expressions as being " Godded with God, and Christed with Christ," [2] and whose hearers South describes as—

" amusing their consciences with a set of fantastical new-coined phrases, such as *laying hold on Christ, getting into Christ*, and *rolling themselves upon Christ*, and the like " ;

of whom the latter remarks :

" By which, if they mean any thing else but obeying the precepts of Christ, and a rational hope of salvation thereupon . . . it is all but a jargon of empty, senseless metaphors. . . ." [3]

But, as we learn from Glanvill's ' Essay concerning Preaching,' among the sectaries it was held that to

" tell the people that they must roll upon *Christ*, close with *Christ*, get into *Christ*, get a saving interest in the Lord *Christ*, O, this is savoury, this precious, this is spiritual teaching indeed." [4]

---

[1] *Op. cit.*, p. 29.　　　　　　　　　　　[2] *Ibid.*, p. 31.
[3] ' Works,' ed. cit., vol. ii, sermon xxviii, p. 346.
[4] 2nd ed., 1703, p. 28.

The ' pretious ' and ' powerful ' preacher was (to quote Eachard)—

" he that thunders out *Christ* a Thousand Times in a *Sermon*." [1]

Even some of the greater Puritans did not escape this pitfall, for Owen, as we have heard South stating,[2] indulged in the

" whimsical cant of *issues, products, tendencies, breathings, indwellings, rollings, recumbencies,* and scriptures misapplied." [3]

Not only were the expressions offensive in themselves, but the conceptions they were intended to convey belonged to a region of erratic speculative religion entirely divorced from sound teaching. Oddly enough, an excessive devotion to doctrine had resulted directly in the wildest species of speculation and the suppression of practical admonitions. By the " spiritually minded " man of the period the preaching of ordinary duties was regarded as " mere morality."

Jeremy Taylor's " Rules and Advices " to the Clergy of his diocese not to " spend " their

" sermons in general and indefinite things, as in exhortations to the people to get Christ, to be united to Christ, and things of the like unlimited signification,"

but to descend to particular instances of right conduct,[4] is a good example of the measures taken by Anglican preachers to combat these evils. The sermons of Cudworth and More are directly concerned with recalling men from disputings about doctrine to the living of a good life, and the ideal of the rationalist preacher is well expressed by Fowler who declared—

" the grand designe of the Gospel is to make men good ; not to intoxicate their brains with notions, or furnish their

---

[1] ' Some Observations upon the Answer to . . . the Grounds and Occasions . . .' 7th ed., 1705, p. 105.
[2] *Ante*, p. 260.
[3] ' Works,' ed. cit., vol. iii, sermon xxvii, pp. 34–5.
[4] ' Works,' ed. Eden-Heber, vol. i, p. 107.

heads with a systeme of opinions [1] ; but to reform mens
lives, and purifie their natures." [2]

A just reply to those who laid stress upon a " sanctified "
vocabulary was furnished by Whichcote (in his correspondence with Tuckney) : " Men (he said) may preach Christ
' though they do not name Christ in every sentence and
period of words.' " [3]   But to do so was to risk the oppro-
brium of being a ' moral ' preacher, and this even a cultured
Nonconformist like Jennings, head of the dissenting academy
at Kibworth, and Doddridge's tutor, considered no light
matter. The prevailing preaching mode of the later seventeenth century seemed to him to lack the distinctive note of
Christianity. Hence we find him saying :

" Suppose the ghosts of PAUL and SENECA to come, mere
strangers, into an assembly where one is haranguing the
people in this abstracted manner ; I am apt to think
SENECA would claim him as a philosopher of his own sect
and religion." [4]

That there was an element of truth in this complaint must
be admitted, for although Wright's approval (previously
quoted) of employing philosophy to support religion was
justified, yet many of the later Latitudinarian sermons are
little better than essays in moral philosophy. The rationalistic sermon, like its rivals, was not exempt from abuses
and evoked in its turn a full share of criticism.

This last type of sermon was assailable on two grounds—
those of form and content. The fact is, the two were really,
as they always are, indissoluble. Both the ' metaphysical '
and the ' doctrinal ' or ' scriptural ' sermon failed to achieve
the λέξις εἱρομένη because of the disjointed nature of the
material they presented. The rationalistic sermon, on the
contrary, for the very reason that it was rationalistic, had
unusual possibilities of fluency and coherence. To those
who held by " methods " or looked for " the vocabulary of
the Covenant " or its equivalent such a style of preaching

[1] A direct hit at both ' speculative ' and ' doctrinal ' preaching.
[2] ' The Principles and Practices Of certain Moderate Divines . . .' Lon.,
1670, 8vo, p. 18.
[3] Powicke : ' The Cambridge Platonists,' p. 63.
[4] Williams : ' Christian Preacher,' ed. cit., p. 63.

was naturally anathema. We have already noted Baillie's attack on " the new guyse of preaching " which Binning and Leighton apparently were the first to introduce in Scotland,[1] and Patrick's ' Discourse of Profiting by Sermons ' [2] reveals the fact that the same objection was raised in England to the post-Restoration Anglican sermon.

" Some indeed," (Patrick wrote) " I have heard, found fault with our Sermons for not keeping the old method (as they call it) of *Doctrine, Reason*, and *Use :* which is altogether unjust as well as frivolous." [3]

Patrick then proceeded to show that the only purpose of method was convenience and to ensure effect, adding that—

" the ancient Doctors of Religion . . . spake to the Business before them, without observing any constant Rule at all in their Discourses . . . without making particular Observations, or concluding all with distinct Uses . . . but only with a general Application."

Of this last procedure St. Chrysostom furnished a good example.[4]

The point at issue was one which was being canvassed contemporaneously in France, where, as we have learned from Villemain,[5] Bossuet discarded meticulous attention to division in favour of the unity supplied by " une idée dominante d'où il part, et à laquelle il vient," and where Fénelon was to express the conclusion arrived at by men of his time, that

" for the most part, Divisions give only a *seeming* Order ; while they really mangle and clog a Discourse. . . . There remains no true Unity after such Divisions." [6]

In both countries, therefore, the sermon was able to shake itself free of that close attention to rhetorical rules to which the older type of *rhetorica sacra* had been devoted, and became, more particularly in its printed form (which is our

---

[1] *Ante*, pp. 266–7.   [2] Lon., 1684.   [3] *Op. cit.*, p. 5.
        [4] *Op. cit.*, p. 7.   [5] *Ante*, p. 125.
    [6] ' Dialogues Concerning Eloquence,' Stevenson's trans., 1722, p. 114,
(Dialogue II).

immediate concern), a piece of polite literature to be judged by current literary standards. South's celebrated attack on the preaching of Jeremy Taylor,[1] while directed primarily against ornate and rhetorical preaching, was not merely incidental to the former's plea that sermons should be "plain, natural, and familiar," but was part of a larger national movement which was demanding that prose style in general should conform to these standards. So also there is more than a personal reorientation in things philosophical denoted by Parker's distaste for the "luscious stile" of the "Platonick Authors"; and his recognition that to discourse of "the nature of Things in Metaphors and Allegories" was "nothing else but to sport and trifle with empty words,"[2] taken along with Sprat's exposition of the stylistic aims of the Royal Society, provides the *raison d'être* of a simplified prose. The Latitudinarians, as Fowler pointed out—

"affect not Bumbastic words, trifling Strains of Wit, foolish Quibbling, and making pretty sport with Letters and Syllables in their Preaching; but despise those doings as pedantick and unmanly. But on the contrary, they use a Style that is very *grave*, and no less significant,"[3]

On its content side, also, Fowler is to be heard defending the Latitudinarian sermon, for its handling of "those subjects that are of weightiest and most necessary importance," setting out clearly

"the excellency of the Christian Religion, the Reasonableness of its precepts, the nobleness and generosity of its designe, and its admirable fitness for the accomplishment of it."[4]

The charge against the 'moral' preachers (which he describes as "vetus hæc calumnia") is answered by Nicholls in the following passage which forms an interesting comment on various outworn fashions :

"Siqui vero sunt inter nos de gente Theologica beatuli & delicati ; (ut pauci admodum sunt) quibus Paganorum

---

[1] 'Works,' ed. cit., vol. iv, sermon lix, p. 153.
[2] 'A Free and Impartial Censure of the Platonick Philosophie,' 1666, p. 74.
[3] 'The Principles and Practices Of certain Moderate Divines . . .' p. 104.
[4] *Ibid.*, pp. 41–2.

Argumenta maximè arrident ;   aut qui nimis Rationi
Humanæ indulgent, neglecta Scripturarum Authoritate,
vel ad puriorem styli elegantiam ostentandam, vel ad
orationum Ethnicarum venustates consequendas : aut
denique qui receptæ jam apud nos eloquentiæ vim nervos-
que, accersitis flosculis & fucis, infringere conantur : hos
nolumus defendere, sed Adversariorum sannis & ludibrio
excipiendos ultrò tradimus." [1]

The reference to the " recepta jam apud nos eloquentia "
is of special interest as emphasising how for men at the end
of the seventeenth century a standard had been set and a
level of attainment reached, particularly as we know in the
sermons of Tillotson, by which for a long time to come the
compositions of the preacher were to be judged.   Sectarianism no longer persisted in a struggle to maintain a particular
mode of preaching as being the only allowable manner in
which the preacher could address his fellows.[2]   The fact that
Bates, Benjamin Calamy, Whichcote, Stillingfleet, and later
men like Atterbury and Smalridge, so closely resemble one
another is significant.   The summary quoted from Burnet
at the close of our study of Theory,[3] which sketches at once
the phases through which preaching passed during the
century and the ideal with which the century concluded,
may be paralleled by a letter of Lupton's quoted in Nelson's
' Life ' of bishop Bull.   After remarking that Bull

" abhorred Affectation of Wit, Trains of fulsome Metaphors,
and nice Words wrought into tuneful, pointed Sentences,
without any substantial Meaning at the Bottom of them " ;

and

" looked upon Sermons consisting of these Ingredients,
. . . as inconsistent with the Dignity of serious and sacred
Things, and as an Indication of a weak Judgment . . ."

Lupton continued with a discussion of ' wit ' in the later
sense of that term.   " True Wit," he believed, " justly
applied, doth deserve the utmost Praise, in Sermons as well

---

[1] ' Defensio Ecclesiæ Anglicanæ,' Lon., 1707 (sixes), p. 334.
[2] *Ante*, p. 99.   [3] *Ante*, pp. 128–9.

as in other Discourses." [1]   Ignoring for the moment the point he is making, the naturalness with which Lupton coupled " sermons " with " other Discourses " marks a change in men's attitude to the sermon.   It had ceased to be regarded as a unique and awful promulgation of a Divine message to be conveyed by methods, which, although we have seen their intimate dependence both on traditional rhetorical modes and current rhetorical practice, yet carried with them a fairly definite suggestion of almost superhuman authority ; instead, it was recognised to be intimately related to the literary practice of the day, and as such laid itself open to the criticism to which all literary products must submit.

In coming to this conclusion the post-Restoration critics and their successors were simply acknowledging the undoubted fact that for their century the sermon was the foremost literary influence.   Whether in its oral or printed form it reached and made an impression on thousands. If what it set before men represented a debased form of oratory, born of imitative pedantry or theological prejudice, then the taste of the period as well as the theology would be tainted and tend to applaud what was least admirable.   If, on the other hand, a simple and straightforward type of sermon could be popularised the taste of those who either read or heard it would be to a corresponding extent improved.   To effect this end, however, both Practice and Criticism had to combine, and mere sectarian criticism— the criticism of party by party usually from purely theological or ecclesiastical considerations—had to be superseded by criticism of the sermon in a wider context and with regard to its place in the literary life of the time.

To this more liberal criticism it is now our duty to turn.

[1] ' The Life of Dr. George Bull ' (completed December 1712), Lon., 1713, 8vo, p. 490.

THAT the sermon, when considered apart from mere theological or sectarian prejudice, should not only have assumed literary importance, but also come to be regarded as a norm of prose style, will occasion no surprise to anyone conversant with seventeenth-century English literature, and, in particular, with the literary criticism of the period. Prose was not then, as it has come to be since, cultivated for its own sake. It was the means whereby the historian, the philosopher, or the student of manners and morals—if one may apply such a general title to include writers so diverse as Hoby, Ascham, Peacham, and the pamphleteers—conveyed accounts of past events, rational speculation, educational ideals or disapproval of contemporary tendencies to those to whom they wished to appeal with these topics. Diaries, biographies, and letters naturally employed the same vehicle, but not, apparently, until the time of Howell was the letter to an imaginary correspondent thought on as a literary device. Lyly and Sidney may at first sight appear exceptions to this condition of things, but even with these writers the desire to instruct took precedence of the delight in writing, and the elaboration of their style, while deliberate, was largely incidental. The essay as it came at length from the hands of Cowley and Temple was as yet a novelty, and, as men knew it in the writings of Montaigne, must have appeared to them, as it did to Ben Jonson, likely to be the result of " undigested " reading and over-hasty writing.[1] Prose as an end in itself did not exist. The great questions for Criticism raged around Wit, whether morality alone or morality combined with pleasure should be the aim of imaginative compositions, the manner in which learning should be employed in these, and to what extent artificiality and elaborateness of expression should be encouraged or abandoned. And in all cases these considerations were discussed with reference to the drama or the long poem (whether in its epic or ' heroic ' form), or to translation as affecting one or the other. It was the wit to be employed by poet or dramatist that was debated, whether or not either should ' delight ' as well as

[1] 'Discoveries,' G. B. Harrison's reprint, Bodley Head Quartos, p. 31.

'instruct,' and to what standard of diction each should conform. There was small need to reflect on these considerations as connected with prose, for the historian or educationist, setting out with a useful task to perform, had no occasion to defend himself; it was not his business primarily to be 'witty,' nor, until the prevailing vices largely connected with current rhetorical practice had attracted attention by their conspicuous exercise in another sphere, was his pedantry or his syntactical ingenuity seriously questioned. Criticism confined itself to the creative, and prose was regarded as being mere reproduction of patterns and was slighted accordingly.

It was, however, when this reproductive element in prose began to assume illegitimate proportions, so that particular modes, originally of oratorical expression, were in danger of exercising a unique dominance, that the attention of criticism was necessarily turned to prose. The accepted definition of Wit and canons of Taste, and the possibility of securing for both drama and poetry a simple but elegant form of expression was threatened, while the most frequent non-poetical declamations (namely, those of the pulpit), and the most ordinarily and widely read prose (the sermon), continued to broadcast and encourage antiquated rhetorical fashions of one kind or another. If the newer attitude to prose—that discernible in the 'essays' or 'attempts' of Cowley to express not in a poetical medium thoughts for their own sake apart from a secondary utilitarian reason—sprang up independently of the attack on rhetorical extravagance, so that the attack must not be regarded as initiating English literary prose as an independent *genre*, yet the fact remains that the adverse criticisms of the sermon on literary grounds, which followed on the Restoration, did stress emphatically the separation of oratory from written or printed prose, though both, it is obvious, depend for their effects on the application of many common rules. The recognition of prose synchronised with the decline of the sermon as an oration, and did so because the sermon from the last two decades of Elizabeth's reign to the time of the Civil Wars had been the prevailing prose type, and had tended in consequence to set the fashion in one direction or another. Over against Lever and Jewel may be set Lyly; against Smith and Adams, Nashe and the pamphleteers;

over against Donne, Bacon ; while the Latitudinarian
sermon had a near neighbour in the prose of Halifax " the
Trimmer."

Nor is this merely to say that in any given decade the
sermon and contemporary prose will show a close correspondence ; for the fact must be faced, that, although the
causes that led to preacher and author presenting a similarity
of style are alike traceable to the educational system and the
theory of taste of their period, yet for a few hundreds (if
so many) who read the work of a particular author,
thousands undoubtedly heard (or read) either the preacher
in question or the work of other preachers of a similar
rhetorical bent.　There is only one ' Devotionis
Augustinianæ Flamma ' [1] but hundreds of ' metaphysical '
sermons ; and where two men show similar tendencies in
their work, the existence of a group or party behind one of
them is sufficient to suggest their respective importance.
It is impossible to argue that men read ' Euphues ' in such
numbers that a demand for schematic preachings ensued,
or that they developed a taste for ' metaphysical ' conceits
to which Andrewes and his disciples found it necessary to
pander.　In the first instance, there was a considerable
proportion of Englishmen who appreciated schematic
patterns in both Lyly and the preachers, but the fact that a
widespread delight in such sprang up must be attributed
directly to the latter.　In the same way the ' metaphysicals ' were the corrupters of contemporary taste and not
themselves its victims.

The sermon, therefore, may be regarded not only as
itself providing a species of prose, but as a kind of index
of what men were likely to attempt or applaud in contemporary literature.　The theory of prose style, as we
noted at the outset, if it is to be understood properly,
demands an examination of the taste and influence of the
pulpit.[2]　To supply the latter has been the main aim of our
study.　Knowing both the theory from which the preachers
started and the different modifications which theory underwent in practice, knowing also the extent to which criticism
of a non-literary sort played a part in determining the form
and content of the sermon, it is possible for us to relate the

---

[1] *Vid. ante*, p. 119, and pp. 363–4.
[2] *Vid. ante*, p. 4.

general principles which emerge in this connection to the wider literary criticism of the period. While it is true that those who wrote of preaching naturally did so with reference to the function which it set out ostensibly to perform, in so far as they were returning to consider the sermon as a whole, as it had been considered by Augustine, Erasmus, or Kecker-mann, and not in its party significance, the particular features which they suggested, or of which they disapproved, bore direct relationship to the ordinary critical canons of their day.

Taking in turn, therefore, the leading topics of the critics in the wider sphere, and comparing them with the pronouncements of those who wrote on preaching, the correspondence between the two aspects of criticism becomes evident. South, Glanvill, and Lupton have each been quoted on Wit,[1] and there is sufficient diversity in the quotations to indicate the different shades of meaning which the term bore for different writers in the course of the century. The noting of resemblances, with its consequent " rolling in metaphors " of which Glanvill spoke, was a direct allusion to the early ' metaphysical ' form of Wit, whereas South's statement that " Wit in divinity is nothing else, but sacred truths suitably expressed," taken along with Lupton's reference to " true Wit," calls to mind those features which earned applause at a later date. For Wit, we must not be led to forget, was not itself a manner of expression—although sometimes the word is used loosely to denote typical effects achieved by the exercise of Wit—but in its correct and primary meaning described a mental faculty. Hobbes, for example, distinguishes as follows between Wit and Judgment :

" Those that observe their similitudes, in case they be such as are but rarely observed by others, are sayd to have a *Good Wit* ; by which . . . is meant a *Good Fancy*. But they that observe their differences, and dissimilitudes ; which is called *Distinguishing*, and *Discerning* and *Judging* . . . in case such discerning be not easie, are said to have a *good Judgement*." [2]

---

[1] *Ante*, p. 315, p. 6 and pp. 378–9, respectively.
[2] ' Leviathan,' ed. A. R. Waller, Cambridge English Classics, 1904, Part I, chap. viii, p. 42.

He continues, however, by noting the secondary meaning of Wit as a product :

" Judgement . . . without Fancy is Wit, but Fancy without Judgement not " ;

and gives as an example of Fancy lacking Discretion the playing

" with sounds, and æquivocall significations of words ; and that many times with encounters of extraordinary Fancy ; "

which he follows up by saying :

" But in a Sermon . . . there is no Gingling of words that will not be accounted folly." [1]

Locke makes precisely the same distinction, namely, that Wit lies

" most in the assemblage of ideas, and putting those together with quickness and variety wherein can be found any resemblance or congruity, thereby to make up pleasant pictures . . . ; judgement . . . lies quite on the other side, in separating . . . ideas wherein can be found the least difference. . . ." [2]

The fact that Locke mentions " congruity " is important, for " rarely observed " similitudes, consisting largely of what Jonson described as " *Metaphors* farfet," [3] were the accepted evidence of Wit in the time of the ' metaphysical ' poets and preachers ; but by 1677, when Dryden prefixed to ' The State of Innocence ' his " Apology for Heroic Poetry and Poetic License," the idea of congruity or propriety had become incorporated with the term. For Dryden, as for his contemporaries both French and English, Wit was " a propriety of thoughts and words, or, in other

[1] ' Leviathan,' ed. cit., p. 44.
[2] ' Essay on the Human Understanding,' Book II, chap. xi (edition used 13th London, 1846, p. 91).
[3] ' Discoveries,' ed. cit., p. 73.

terms, thoughts and words elegantly adapted to the subject "[1]—a definition remarkably akin to South's,[2] which, it is to be noted, was given seventeen years earlier.

Here, then, we have a clear case of the pulpit, contrary to what might be expected, leading in the van of reform, and the instance is worth remarking. In spite of the inset definition the evidence afforded by the sermon in question is of the corrupting effects of clerical taste and not of the reverse ; for South would never have been led to advance a statement as to the nature of true Wit had he not felt moved, as we have already heard,[3] to attack both the absurdity of the ' metaphysicals ' and the cant of the Independents. Both types of preachers, however, and all types of preachers who indulged in particular preaching vogues, had, or had had, ample opportunity to exercise an extensive and disastrous influence, for as Davenant pointed out in his Preface to ' Gondibert ' :

" Divines . . . are Tetrarchs of Time, of which they command the fourth Division, for to no less the Sabbaths and Daies of Saints amount ; and during those daies of spiritual triumph Pulpits are Thrones, and the people oblig'd to open their Eares. . . ."[4]

What the auditors were likely to hear, so far as Wit was concerned, Davenant had already outlined—from the young, " the Musick of words " and the refining of speech " above the vulgar Dialect " ; from the old, " agnominations " and " a kinde of an alike tinkling of words " ; from still others bitter reprehension of faults.[5]

It is true that Davenant collected his examples of what

[1] Loc. cit., ' Essays of John Dryden,' ed. W. P. Ker, vol. i, p. 190. Cf. La Bruyère : ' Des Ouvrages de l'esprit '—" Tout l'esprit d'un auteur consiste à bien définir et à bien peindre," (' Les Caractères ou les Mœurs de ce siècle,' first published in 1688), ' Œuvres . . . Nouvelle Edition . . . Par M. G. Servois,' Tome Premier, Paris, 1865, p. 116.

[2] Ante, p. 315.

[3] Ante, p. 260 and pp. 315–6.

[4] Loc. cit., reprinted in Spingarn : ' Critical Essays of the Seventeenth Century,' vol. ii, p. 34. Davenant was writing in 1649 or 1650, but in 1687, the anonymous pamphlet, ' Good Advice to the Pulpits '—an unexpectedly cogent plea for religious toleration—alluded to the enormous influence of the Pulpit (' To the Reader,' A2–A3). Phillips, also, in the second part of ' Speculum Crape-Gownorum,' 1682, informs us that sermons and plays were of about equal frequency in booksellers' shops.—Op. cit., p. 17.

[5] Ibid., quoted Spingarn, op. cit., pp. 21–2.

25

the people mistook for Wit from poetry, and that he admitted that the influence of the pulpit was quite disproportionate to the time the preachers commanded,[1] but the false Wit which disfigured poetry disfigured no less the sermon and extended the influence of an objectionable vogue by the frequency of the preaching by which it was perpetuated. The faults which Davenant criticises are those with which we have become familiar from our study of the sermon, and were due to a mistaken conception of how Wit should manifest itself. Davenant's preface belongs to the year 1650, and in 1678, when Glanvill came to write his 'Essay Concerning Preaching,' there were still those who (among other reasons) condemned sermons if " the words be not chosen, and the periods even, and the matter witty and diverting." [2] Preachers who attended to these details appeared to Glanvill to display

" a vain endeavour to entertain, and please conceited Hearers, without design either to inform the Judgment, to ingage the Will, or to stir up any devout Affections." [3]

Obviously Glanvill felt about the matter very much as did his contemporary La Bruyère, who wrote ironically :

" C'est avoir de l'esprit que de plaire au peuple dans un sermon par un style fleuri, une moral enjouée, des figures réiterées, des traits brillants et de vives descriptions . . ."

but was quick to add—

" . . . mais ce n'est point en avoir assez. Un meilleur esprit néglige ces ornements étrangers indignes de servir à l'Évangile : il prêche simplement, fortement, chrétiennement." [4]

Portions of Glanvill's discussion on Wit have already been noted,[5] and the general conclusions he arrived at are well summarised in these words :

[1] Loc. cit., p. 34.
[2] Op. cit., 2nd ed., 1703, p. 5.
[3] Ibid., p. 59.
[4] " De la Chaire " in ' Les Caractères ou les Mœurs de ce Siècle,' ed. cit., Tome Second, p. 225.
[5] Ante, p. 6.

" The Preacher should endeavour to speak sharp, and quick thoughts, and to set them in lively colours ; this is proper, grave, and manly Wit. . . ." [1]

Such Wit, it is apparent, could be employed upon whatever kind of composition was in request, whether long poem, play, or sermon, and the close resemblance between Glanvill's definition and that quoted earlier from Dryden goes to emphasise the united front that had come to be presented by the man of letters and the preacher. Wit could no longer be accused of finding " benefit of clergy," [2] but a common conception of Wit adaptable to all literary purposes had been agreed upon.

Another malady in spreading which the pulpit played a conspicuous part was the plague of pedantic quotations which infected both poetry and preaching in the first half of the seventeenth century. Professor Grierson's ' Commentary ' to the Oxford edition of Donne's poems [3] affords a striking illustration of how learned the poetry of the time could be ; and, to quote a contemporary example, Jonson's notes to his tragedy of ' Sejanus ' open up a similar prospect for the drama. What the English ' metaphysical ' preachers were capable of we have seen, and, if they avoided one of the worst features of late sixteenth-century preaching in France, in which (in the words of La Bruyère)—

" Le sacré et le profane ne se quittoient point . . . saint Cyrille, Horace, saint Cyprien, Lucrèce, parloient alternativement," [4]

rabbis, Fathers, and allegorists, along with Pliny and the mediæval bestiaries were freely drawn upon, and Latin, Greek, and even Hebrew phrases inserted into their discourses. The demand created by such " Shews of Learning," as Burnet called them,[5] has already been discussed,

---

[1] ' Essay Concerning Preaching,' ed. cit., p. 71.
[2] ' Essays of John Dryden,' ed. W. P. Ker, vol. i, p. 173, " Defence of the Epilogue."
[3] ' Poetical Works,' 2 vols., 1912, vol. ii.
[4] " De la Chaire " in ' Les Caractères,' ed. cit., Tome Second, p. 224; cf. Jacquinet : " Des Predicateurs de dix-septième siècle avant Bossuet,' pp. 34–5 and p. 50, where the common heritage of Pierre de Besse and du Bartas is discussed.
[5] ' A Discourse of the Pastoral Care,' 3rd ed., 1713, chap. ix, p. 192 ; the first edition appeared in 1692.

and we are therefore not surprised to learn from Glanvill that " quotations from Fathers and Philosophers, Authorities and Citations in Latin and Greek " were at one time eagerly looked for.[1]

What this type of pedantry resulted in outside of the sermon may be seen in Burton's ' Anatomy ' or the now long unread works of Ussher. In a less unpalatable form it appears as an ingredient in Bacon's essays and, though more or less confined to the margins, in so charming a book as Taylor's ' Holy Dying.' The fact is, that in the period in question, the evidences of learning were expected from all who wrote, and their style was regarded with approval or disapproval according as it imitated successfully some age-old traditional mode or failed in the attempt. From this attitude of mind the pulpit address was not exempt, though the restraint of the plainer preachers must have struck a warning note, and Wilkins' declaration (in 1646) that " the greatest learning is to be seen in the greatest plainness " [2] was an indication of what might be expected in the future. In France, as Spingarn reminds us, in discussing the French critics of the time—

" the grave and academic style of their treatises was being superseded by the cultivated and well-bred manner of gentlemen ; the control of criticism was passing from *savants* to *beaux esprits*." [3]

In England, though on a minor scale, and sadly hampered by contemporary political and theological upheaval, a similar course is observable, and the sermon, which became plain on sectarian grounds, in its less bald and uncompromising forms contributed largely to the possibility of a plain and straightforward prose.

The simplification of prose style in our century, for which Sprat's declaration of the Royal Society ideal is a kind of charter, was directly concerned with the shedding of inadvisable mannerisms whether of imagery, vocabulary, or syntax, so that a " natural way of speaking," " a native easiness," might be possible. For those faults, which he

[1] ' Essay Concerning Preaching,' p. 11.
[2] ' Ecclesiastes,' 8th ed., 1704, p. 251.
[3] ' Critical Essays of the Seventeenth Century,' Introd., p. xxvi.

described as " this vicious abundance of Phrase, this trick of Metaphors," [1] Sprat saw clearly that contemporary education was to blame.

" We all value one another " (he declared) " so much upon this beautiful deceipt, and labour so long after it in the years of our education, that we cannot but ever after think kinder of it than it deserves." [2]

Other abuses had come about during the Civil Wars when the language had

" received many fantastical terms, which were introduc'd by our *Religious Sects*, and many outlandish phrases, which several *Writers* and *Translators* in that great hurry brought in and made free as they pleas'd." [3]

As a remedy for these varied abuses thoughtful men proposed setting up an Acadamy such as had been established in France, and the Royal Society, so far as its own writings were concerned, determined on " bringing all things as near the Mathematical plainness " as possible, " and preferring the language of Artizans, Countrymen, and Merchants, before that of Wits or Scholars." [4]

Chamberlayne, who in his ' Angliæ Notitia ' followed up another of Sprat's suggestions by supplying a short account of England in his own day, in his address " To the Reader," states explicitly that the object of writing being to inform the Reader's understanding, " therefore the Author hath industriously avoided all curious *Flowers of Rhetorick*." [5] But the distinction between a " florid " style and " the language of Artizans, Countrymen and Merchants " was great, and while the latter, with certain reservations, might serve very well for scientific reports, it is obvious that it could not become an ideal for writing in general. It is not surprising, therefore, to learn that the essentials of good

[1] ' The History of the Royal-Society of London . . .' Lon., 1667, 4to, Part II, § xx.
[2] *Ibid.*   [3] *Ibid.*   [4] *Ibid.*
[5] *Op. cit.*, ' The Second Part,' Lon., 1671, 12mo. The first part of the work appeared in 1669. Edward Chamberlayne, the author, was tutor to George, Prince of Denmark, afterwards husband of Queen Anne.

prose came to be referred to the standard of speech employed at Court or among gentlemen in ordinary conversation. Dryden, it is well known, did not hesitate to claim for his age a greater refinement of language than had been attained by any previous generation,[1] and declared that he

" must freely and without flattery, ascribe it to the court ; and, in it, particularly to the King, whose example gives a law to it." [2]

But, while it is beyond dispute that the taste of the Restoration Court exercised a decided influence in the simplification and refinement of style, whether, as Dryden had in mind, in the drama, or in prose, it must not be overlooked that where gentlemen, as distinct from scholars or divines, were concerned, an unaffected manner of writing had from a much earlier period been favourably regarded. Of this the address to the reader before Boyle's ' Considerations Touching the Style of the H. Scriptures ' affords interesting evidence ; for, although Boyle's work did not appear till 1661, it is expressly stated to have been written in his youth, which, as he was born in 1627, gives a conjectural date shortly after Ussher's influence had been felt at Oxford, and round about the period of Wilkins' ' Ecclesiastes.' In the passage in question Boyle expressed the hope that

" Severer Divines may safely Pardon some Smoothnesse in a Discourse Written Chiefly for Gentlemen, who would scarce be fond of Truth in every Dresse, by a Gentleman who fear'd it might misbecome a Person of his Youth and Quality Studiously to Decline a fashionable Style."

Boyle's statement is an important one for various reasons. In the first place, it emphasises the point made by Sir Edmund Gosse that Wilkins and not Tillotson was the real initiator of the reform in style,[3] and it more than suggests

---

[1] " Defence of the Epilogue," in ' The Essays . . .' ed. Ker, vol. i, p. 164.
[2] *Ibid.*, p. 176. *Cf.* Burnet : ' History of His Own Time,' 1724, vol. i, p. 191, who wrote of Charles II : " The King had little or no literature, but true and good sense ; and had got a right notion of style ; for he was in *France* at a time when they were much set on reforming their language. It soon appeared that he had a true taste." This last, according to Burnet, was shown by his approving of the style of the discourses of the Latitudinarians, " which was clear, plain, and short." But *vid. ante*, p. 311, footnote[1].
[3] *Ante*, p. 330.

that among well-bred and well-educated men on the eve of
the Civil Wars the pulpit style of Sanderson and Hammond
was had in most estimation. Further, it goes a good way
towards showing that but for vitiated taste or sectarian
prejudice of one kind or another the sermon might at a
much earlier period than it did have become a model of
plainness and lucidity. The sermon, however, as we have
seen, remained ' metaphysical ' or became fantastic, until
saved by an amalgamation of the rationalists with the more
sober of the Nonconformist preachers.

When Glanvill wrote his ' Essay Concerning Preaching '
he was addressing, as was natural, the clergy of the Established Church, but his comments on the method and style of
preaching were applicable to the sermon as a whole, no
matter by what sect or body of churchmen it was to be
delivered, and directly corresponded with the literary ideals
of the day. For Glanvill preaching had to be " PLAIN,
PRACTICAL, METHODICAL, AFFECTIONATE," [1] and, excluding
the last as not always suitable to the business in hand, these
were precisely the conditions which men expected Restoration prose to fulfil. A style that should be natural, " such
as the matter, and the Capacities, and the wants of the
Auditors " required, that " should be obvious and plainly
laid down," not " Cryptick to surprise, not designed to take
the phancy with the unexpectedness and strangeness " of
what was said but " to inlighten the mind," and which
avoided the vice (so particularly hated by French critics)
of abounding " with too many Particulars " [2]—such a
style was not only admirably suited to the sermon, but was
naturally that aimed at by prose writers in general.

What Glanvill meant by PLAIN he is careful to tell us.
" Hard words," curious terms, the " affected use of scraps
of *Greek* and *Latin*," and that " bastard kind of eloquence
. . . which consists in affectations of wit and finery, flourishes,
metaphors, and cadencies," were obstructions to plainness upon which he and his lay contemporaries were
definitely agreed, if " mysterious notions " and " phantas-
tical phrases " were bugbears peculiar to the pulpit." [3] To
break from this whole series of encumbrances for good and

[1] *Op. cit.*, 2nd ed., 1703, p. 11.
[2] *Ibid.*, p. 39.
[3] *Ibid.*, pp. 12 *seq.*

all was the task of poet, prose-writer, and preacher alike. This could only be effected by dealing with each of the abuses in turn, and by attending to purity of diction, simplicity of construction, appropriateness of imagery, and the orderly arrangements of the topics to be discussed.

Dryden, with a fine combination of literary discrimination and patriotism, declared roundly :

" Our language is noble, full, and significant ; and I know not why he who is master of it may not clothe ordinary things in it as decently as the Latin, if he use the same diligence in his choice of words " [1]—

a statement which renders inexcusable the continuous introduction of classical words or phrases, as if to plead excuse for personal poverty by a reference to a rich relative. Sprat's statement with respect to the introduction of new and strange words has already been given,[2] and is more or less supported by a letter of Evelyn to Sir Peter Wyche, the chairman of a committee appointed by the Royal Society to consider the improvement of the English tongue. In this, written in June 1665, Evelyn declared :

" I conceive the reason both of additions to, and the corruption of the English Language . . . has proceeded . . . from Victories, Plantations, Frontiers, Staples of Com'erce, pedantry of Scholes, Affectations of Travellers, Translations, Fancy and style of Court, Vernility & mincing of Citizens, Pulpits, Political Remonstrances, Theaters, Shopps, &c." [3]

Evelyn's inclusion of the pulpit is significant, and when we recall the quotations given from his *Diary* to illustrate different preaching vogues, the justice of the inclusion is evident.   But the sermon as Burnet depicted it in a notable passage of his ' Discourse of the Pastoral Care ' [4] was a sermon which had shaken itself free of the incubus of ' wit ' and pedantry, and was become a model for contemporary prose.

[1] " An Essay of Dramatic Poesy," in ' The Essays . . .' ed. Ker, vol. i, p. 104.
[2] *Ante*, p. 389.
[3] ' Memoirs . . . And A Selection of His Familiar Letters . . . Edited by William Bray . . .'   Reprint 1870 of 2nd (1819) ed., pp. 628–9.
[4] *Ante*, p. 129.

In the sermon as Burnet conceived of it :

" Things must be put in a clear light, and brought out in as short Periods, and in as plain Words as may be . . . the Figures must be easy, not mean, but noble, and brought in upon Design to make the Matter better understood. The Words . . . must be simple, and in common Use ; not savouring of the Schools, nor above the Understanding of the People. All long *Periods*, such as carry two or three different Thoughts in them, must be avoided ; for few Hearers can follow or apprehend these." [1]

For the last reason, although Burnet preferred the exposition of a text to " a general Discourse," such as was fashionable in France, he was careful to stress that each sermon should be concerned with one " point," or theme, and no more. [2]

But such a sermon, it is obvious, prepared or preserved in writing would be an excellent piece of prose, and the fact that men became accustomed to sermons of such a character was bound to act as a safeguard in the interests of future prose. What was looked for and appreciated in a sermon of the post-Restoration period is made plain by the elder Sherlock's tribute to Benjamin Calamy, uttered in 1636 :

". . . His constant preaching, though without any vain affectation of learning, which serves only to amuse not to instruct, did sufficiently discover both his natural and acquired abilities. He had a clear and distinct apprehension of things, an easy and manly rhetoric, strong sense conveyed to the mind in familiar words, good reasons inspired with a decent passion, which did not only teach, but move and transport the hearers, and at the same time gave light and heat." [3]

By 1692 Burnet could write :

" The Nation has got into so good a Taste of *Sermons*, from

[1] ' A Discourse of the Pastoral Care,' 3rd (1713) ed., combining p. 195 with pp. 198–9.
[2] *Ibid.*, p. 194.
[3] Funeral sermon by Dr. William Sherlock, Dean of St. Paul's, quoted vol. i, p. 58, of ' An Historical Account of My Own Life . . . By Edward Calamy, D.D.', ed. John Towill Rutt, 2nd ed., 1830.

the vast Number of those excellent ones that are in Print, that a mean Composition will be ill heard. . . ." [1]

Such a taste, it goes without saying, was not created of a sudden. It had its origin, partly, as Burnet himself suggests, in the better type of Nonconformist preaching,[2] and partly in that tendency towards plainness and good sense which, though often unnoticed, had always been a factor in English preaching. Even if there were an ingredient of flattery in Arderne's statement, made about twenty years before Burnet wrote, that no country had

" ever shewed better Preachers then ours, and ours never so good ones as now, especially for the vertues of Stile and vigorous management of real arguments," [3]

there was also an ingredient of truth. The gradual convergence of the discourses of all theological parties which we have studied under Practice resulted in a type of sermon for which no one party had alone prepared the way, but which could claim as sponsors Hall, Hales, Hammond, Baxter, and Whichcote. The fact that Benjamin Calamy, a Conformist, and Bates, a Nonconformist, resemble each other does not mean that men had exhausted themselves in the theological disputes of the times, but that a uniformity of ideal had been accepted by the nation at large. That this was so was due to no one cause, but that it was due to both the negative and positive influence of the preaching of the period immediately preceding is largely true ; the ' metaphysicals,' the Scriptural and doctrinal preachers, and the fanatics had demonstrated *ad nauseam* what could no longer be tolerated, and the plain preachers came into their own.

The triumph of style which was thus effected, although it may best be described as the triumph of a movement or of a number of tendencies, remains associated with the name of one man—Tillotson. For the men of his own day and their immediate successors, Tillotson's style not only

---

[1] ' Pastoral Care,' ed. cit., p. 202.
[2] *Ante*, p. 259.
[3] ' Directions Concerning the Matter and Stile of Sermons, Written . . . by J. A., D.D.,' Lon., 1671, 12mo, p. 68.

appeared excellent in itself but a model for what English style should be. Thus we find Hughes, in his essay ' Of Style,' published in 1698, advising his readers to study the most correct writers in the language, and naming Temple, Sprat, and Tillotson as those to whose works they should pay particular attention.[1] Hughes reduced " the Qualifications of a good Style " to Propriety, Perspicuity, Elegance, and Cadence,[2] and it is obvious, although he refers particularly to Tillotson under the head of Propriety, that he regarded the latter's prose as possessing all four qualities in a high degree. His description of Elegance illustrates not only what such prose as Temple's essays might be expected to reveal, but what the first generation of Restoration church-goers heard from the lips of Tillotson and Stillingfleet :

" Elegance of Thought is what we commonly call Wit, which adds to Propriety, Beauty, and pleases our Fancy, while Propriety entertains our Judgment. This depends so much on Genius that 'tis impossible to teach it by Rules. . . . Elegance consists very much in a genteel Ease and Freedom of expression ; it is like a coy Mistress, of so nice a Humour, that to court her too much, is the surest way to loose her. . . ."[3]

To this then had preaching come. The *extempore* addresses of the Apostles with their vivid reminiscence and eagerly inserted ' proofs ' had been succeeded by the orations of the Greek and Latin Fathers trained in all the intricacies of contemporary rhetoric ; the triumphs of the latter had been followed in turn by the formal and theological ingenuities of the mediæval preachers and the earnestness and polemics of the Reformers ; until, at length, in England, there had come about that abnormal interest in preaching with its extravagances of one kind or another which had played so large a part in shaping English prose style. The connection between the criticism of the sermon and the purely literary criticism of the period has now been examined, and

[1] Quoted from reprint in ' Critical Essays of the Eighteenth Century,' edited by W. H. Durham, Oxf., 1915, p. 80.
[2] *Ibid.*, p. 80.
[3] *Ibid.*, p. 82.

the coincidence of view in several particulars displayed.
If the evidences of agreement are few, they are at least
positive, and show either an anticipation of views
subsequently adopted by literary critics or an agreement
with current literary theory, while the paucity of the
examples is readily explained by the slight attention which
up till then had been given to prose. That in the end
preaching and prose could be judged by the same standards
is itself evidence of the closeness of their connection, for taste
in so large measure depends on what is most widely dissemi-
nated, that but for the reformation and simplification of
the pulpit-address it is almost certain there would have
been no simplification of English prose ; or, at least, such
simplification as might have resulted from the influence of
the Court, and the growth of scientific enquiry, would never
have been universally accepted and applauded as that
which the example and influence of the preachers brought
about. If Elegance of Style, according to Hughes' quaint
simile, is " like a coy Mistress," in England, it may be said,
she was first wooed by the divines and given a place in the
Temple, where men at rare intervals learned to revere her,
and heard from her lips the musical and luminous utterance
towards which in their best literary efforts they laboured
ever afterwards to approach.

The threefold survey of English preaching in the seventeenth century which it was proposed to make has now
been concluded. It remains briefly to summarise the facts
that have been learned from the different aspects of this
study.

In the first place, it has been made clear that the sermon
of the period was no mere expository discourse, inspired
solely by the desire to commend religious truth to its
hearers, but a highly finished rhetorical product standing in
direct relationship to wider rhetorical aims. It was so for
two reasons—partly because of its descent at several removes
from a late and debased form of classical oratory, partly
because contemporary education was still largely rhetorical,
and the sermon, like the forensic and deliberative speech,
depended in large measure on the school theme, and the
orations and declamations of the University. Ample proof

of these facts is afforded by the prescriptions of educationists of the day, by traits found in the sermons themselves, and by particular references of critics. Rhetoric, received into the Church, for thirteen centuries almost completely dominated its public utterances, and the *rhetoricæ sacræ*, though at times concerned rather with the elucidation and appreciation of Scripture than with the composition of sermons, were not far removed from the *artes concionandi* with their manifest intention of instructing men how to preach effectively.

If anything, however, the *artes concionandi* represent a second element discernible in the seventeenth-century sermon, namely, the influence of theological outlook. The sermon was not only an oration adapted to suit religious purposes, the successor, in other words, of classical epideictic oratory ; but its form as well as its content, and its form often largely owing to its content, was determined by particular doctrinal or ecclesiastical considerations. The great examples for our period of party aims affecting the form of the sermon are of course supplied by the ' metaphysicals,' the doctrinal Puritans, and the more fantastic of the Independents. As it was, had the matter ended there, it might have been allowed to rest, but in an age when those who read at all read mainly sermons, or other devotional works written by preachers, the influence of current preaching fashions was immense, and largely determined the literary taste of the period. The corruptions of clerical taste were therefore of consequence from two separate points of view. They were undesirable in themselves as diverting attention from the main end of preaching, and they exercised a disastrous influence on contemporary style. Hence it comes about that the sermon in its main idiosyncrasies during the course of the century supplies a direct and many-sided commentary on literary fashions ; for it was itself, though not always of a literary character, the prevailing type of prose, and while undoubtedly reflecting the taste of its auditors, equally undoubtedly, and to a far greater extent, helped to determine that taste.

The theological or sectarian influence played a much more important part in preaching than might at first sight be supposed, for its main function was a selective one— the determining of what should be preached and in what

manner—so that it was ultimately responsible for particular
vogues or fashions.   Schools of theological thought not only
wished to give utterance to particular dogmas, but they
tended to do so by traditional means or to create for themselves means adequate to their intention.   Consequently,
while accepting the necessary rhetorical basis of the sermon,
they either deliberately made use of or rejected particular
rhetorical devices.   And by these choices or rejections the
course of prose style was largely influenced, any accepted
mode being able not only to make a wide appeal but
inspiring in practically all cases a lively criticism.

A further type of selection within the bounds of the
party sermon resulted from the temperament of particular
preachers.   Not only were certain topics customary for
certain schools of thought and certain modes of expression
carefully cultivated by preachers of these schools ; but men
whose sermons conform in the main to the standards set
by their party yet supply instances of curious and highly
interesting divergence from the general practice.   Certain
only of the party topics are selected, and their style conforms
less strictly to the accepted standards.   It is in these things
that the contribution of genius to the sermon becomes
evident.

The contribution of genius so far as the sermon is concerned consisted hardly at all in anything novel.   The
great seventeenth-century preachers were not men who
opened up new aspects of doctrine or introduced surprising
variations in style.   Their greatness was not emphasised
by any marked break with the belief or practice of the
theological parties to which they belonged.   It was demonstrated not by their choice of different preaching
material, but by their different handling of the common
deposit.   Andrewes was the greatest of the ' metaphysicals,'
South the greatest of the Restoration preachers, while Tillotson may be said to have been great because of his combination of the finest elements in several distinct types of pulpit
oratory.   In the same way Donne, Jeremy Taylor, and
Barrow all three towered above and yet were intimately
connected with their fellows.   Donne, as has been shown,
was a ' metaphysical ' preacher, yet his ' Senecanism '—
largely due to his devotion to Tertullian—was not the
customary manner in which ' metaphysical ' preachers

expressed themselves ; whether regarded with the associates of his early days as a rationalist or taken with the rather dull bishops of his later years, the instinct for ornate periodic prose exhibited by Taylor strikes a decidedly personal note ; Barrow, a mathematician and fellow of the Royal Society, sent forth his sermons freed of the trammels to which as a Society Sprat and his fellow-members objected, but reinforced by a *copia verborum* that made them eloquent as it had made eloquent those of Chrysostom centuries before. In each case party and preacher stood in close relationship, but in each case the inoculation of the type with strongly individual traits led to the production of oratory of a superior kind, which, as it happened, in two of the three instances, was destined not only to be effective in its spoken form, but to enjoy a justifiable longevity and reputation as English prose.

What has just been said answers to some extent the question of Donne's relative position among English pulpiteers whose works have taken their place as literature. He was a man of a party and of a period, and both facts bulked prominently in the formation of his style ; for had he accepted any other theological position or been born at any other time, the range of his interests and his manner of expressing himself would certainly have been vastly different. That, however, he had not always belonged to the national church and had come to his theological position only after a titanic struggle, complicated by a coeval struggle of the higher over the lower in his own nature, and that his range of reading as well as experience of life had been far wider than that of his ' metaphysical ' contemporaries, imparted to his thought, and, consequently, to the expression of his thought, a range and an intensity which give his work its distinctive tone and make it even at its crudest and most fantastic singularly impressive. His is not a greatness measurable by conformity to some accepted standard of taste and practice, and hence such as can be compared with the achievements or shortcomings of other men. Almost he might be claimed as the last great man produced by the Renaissance, and though " born out of due time " and obliged to utter his meaning to men in such language as they could understand, the atmosphere which that utterance creates and leaves with us is that of a richer,

freer, more many-sided life than that participated in by
contemporary divines. There can be no question that he was
the greatest of the Jacobean divines, but it is impossible to
calculate the degree in which he excelled the others ; for
they, interesting and attractive as many of them were, wrote
to known rules and conformed to recognised patterns, and
did so either more or less successfully than one another ;
but the distinguishing feature of Donne's prose was contributed by the peculiar constitution of the man—at once
ardently passionate and ardently intellectual—and accurately to assess this or to bring it within the range of comparison is clearly impossible.

Taylor's excellencies were of another order, and though
his work owes its charm to undoubted manifestations of
genius, yet it is genius brooding gently over the chaos of
contemporary erudition and rhetoric, and inducing to
suit peculiar ends a particular kind of order. Like his own
lark he rose singing, and, having ascended, continued to sing
with no diminution in the quality of his notes ; but the
notes, however skilfully he produced them, were those
familiar to rhetorical education, and the themes which
induced in him raptures were the commonplaces of contemporary preaching. He cannot therefore justly be
compared with Donne, but remains a first-rate example of
how a man of taste and discernment might improve upon
and render attractive what from the hands of others had
come unnoticed.

Barrow, on the other hand, more than any preacher in
the century, stands apart from it, and yet but for the
century could not possibly have produced his sermons.
Only an age immeasurably devoted to sermons could have
tolerated Barrow's exhaustiveness, and Barrow confined to
a shorter discourse would have been like an eagle in a cage.
His style was one which demanded unrestricted liberty
to develop and is directly referable to the habit of thought
of the man. The length of his addresses is not due to love
of expatiation, but resulted from the desire to speak of
momentous matters in a manner at once adequate, dignified, and persuasive, Before Burke he is the one great
orator produced by England. Nothing in the preaching
amid which he had grown up or in that which surrounded
him in his manhood can account for his eloquence ; yet his

theological position is that asserted (in spite of all coteries and attacks) by the Anglican Church from Elizabethan days to his own, and his style, when minutely analysed, conforms readily to the reforming ideals of his time. His work, therefore, may be regarded as standing in direct relationship to both his predecessors and his contemporaries, while his style represents the application of good sense to the rhetorical presentation of moral and religious considerations.

Greater man and greater preacher than Tillotson as Barrow was, the fact must be faced that his style, although splendidly adapted for the oration or formal speech, could never have become a model for prose. Successfully wielded as it doubtless was in the hands of its creator, such a style, when imitated by lesser men, would have become either bombastic or tedious. It remained, therefore, to influence some of the greatest parliamentary orators of the next century, while Tillotson rose into eminence with his carefully phrased and beautifully modulated sermons, which became not only a model for preaching but were themselves prose compositions of remarkable excellence.

The praise accorded Tillotson was due largely to the attacks of the critics on other types of preaching, and the general agreement arrived at by those who discussed sermons and those who discussed style in a wider context. The earlier critics had been content to attack their theological rivals and to denounce their style as out of keeping with what they believed to be the sacred aim of pulpit-oratory. But the later critics of the post-Restoration period were concerned not only with the abuses which had taken possession of the sermon, but desired a reform of pulpit style as a step towards the simplification of style in general. Perverted and ill-applied rhetoric came to be condemned, not because particular preachers or their parties did not approve of its use, but as being inherently unsuitable to the sermon and offensive to cultivated taste. In this way the two strains of criticism—what may be described as hermeneutic criticism and literary criticism—combined, and the dramatists, the poets, and the essayists found an ally in the preacher, who had come to desire, quite as much as they, an elegance and unaffected ease of manner. The pulpit, consequently, which for long had been the last refuge of

26

antiquated modes of rhetorical expression, and a prime corrupter of style, not only assented to a reform too frequently attributed solely to the Court acting under French influence and the growing exigencies of natural science, but was itself a pioneer in the movement for a simplification of style.

Thus prose, which too long had been neglected by the " Courts of Apollo " and the Muses, was at length rendered plain and serviceable, yet not without beauty or elegance, and suited to any task which Englishmen might in the future impose, being first perfected in the hands of Tillotson and other divines as might best tend AD MAJOREM DEI GLORIAM.

SELECT BIBLIOGRAPHY

A. BIBLIOGRAPHICAL SOURCES

BROOK, Benjamin : The Lives of the Puritans . . . From the Reformation under Queen Elizabeth, To the Act of Uniformity in 1662. 3 vols.   Lon., 1813, 8vo.

CALAMY, Edmund : The Nonconformist's Memorial ; Being an Account of the Lives, Sufferings, and Printed Works of the Two Thousand Ministers Ejected from the Church of England, chiefly by the Act of Uniformity, Aug. 24, 1666 . . . Abridged . . . with . . . Several New Lives . . . By Sam. Palmer. 2nd ed., 3 vols.   Lon., 1802–3, 8vo.

CAMB. HIST. OF ENGLISH LIT. : vol. vii, chap. vi, bib. to the Ven. W. H. Hutton's ' Caroline Divines ' ; vol. viii, chap. xii, bib. to the Ven. W. H. Hutton's ' Divines of the Church of England ' ; vol. viii, chap. xi, bib. to ' Platonists and Latitudinarians,' by J. Bass Mullinger.

CONCISE DICTIONARY OF NATIONAL BIOGRAPHY.

COOPER, Chas. H. & Thompson : Athenæ Cantabrigienses. Vol. ii, 1586–1609.   Camb., 1861. Vol. iii, 1609–1611, with additions by Bradshaw, Mayor *et al.*   Camb., 1913.

NEAL, Daniel : The History of the Puritans . . . Vols. iv and v.   Lon., 1822, 8vo.

OVERTON, J. H. : Life in the English Church (1660–1714). Lon., 1885, 8vo.

STATIONERS' REGISTERS : A Transcript of the Registers of the Company of the Stationers of London, 1554–1640, ed. by Edward Arber, vol. iii, 1601–20, vol. iv, 1620–40 ; A Transcript of the Registers, etc., 1640–1708, by G. E. Briscoe Eyre, vols. i, ii, and iii.

VENN, John & J. A. : Alumni Cantabrigienses, Part I,—1751. Camb., 1922–7.

WOOD, Anthony à : Athenæ Oxonienses . . . 2 vols. Lon., 1721, folio.

B. THEORY : RHETORICAL AND HOMILETICAL

(*a*) RECENT AND CONTEMPORARY WORKS ON RHETORIC AND PREACHING

(1) *Rhetorics*

(i) *Continental :*

BERTIUS, Peter : De Eloqventiæ Vi Atqve Amplitvdine Oratio . . .   Paris, 1621, 8vo.

CAMARIOTUS, Matthew : Synopsis Rhetoricæ . . . Augsburg, 1595, 4to.

HEINSIUS, Daniel : Danielis Heinsii Orationum Editio Nova
. . . Accedunt Dissertationes aliquot, cum nonnullis Præ-
fationibus, Editore Nicolao Heinsio. . .
Amsterdam 1657, 8vo.
MELANCHTHON, Philip : Elementorum Rhetorices Libri Dvo,
in ' Opera . . . Omnia,' ed. by C. G. Bretschneider,
vol. xiii. Halle, 1846, 8vo.
RAMUS, Peter : P. Rami Scholæ in Liberales Artes. [For
' Scholarum Rhetoricarum in Ciceronis Oratorem.']
Basil, 1569, sixes.
RAPIN, Paul de : Les Œuvres . . . Qui contiennent Les
Reflexions sur L'Eloquence . . . (Tome Second)
Amsterdam, 1709, 8vo.
VETERUM ALIQVOT De arte Rhetorica traditiones, . . .
[This contains, among other rhetorical works, Rutilius
Lupus : ' de figuris sententiarum . . .' ; Aquilus : ' de
nominibus figurarum . . .' ; and ' Aphthonij præexercitamenta,
Joanne Maria Catanæo interprete.'] Basil, 1521, 4to.
VOSSIUS, Gerard J. : Elementa Rhetorica Oratoriis ejusdem
Partitionibus accommodata . . . Amsterdam, 1666, 8vo.
VOSSIUS, Gerard J. : Gerardi Johannis Vossii Rhetorices Con-
tractæ Sive Partitionem Oratoriarum. Libri V . . .
Oxf., 1672, 8vo.

(ii) English :
BLOUNT, Thos. : The Academie of Eloquence Containing a
Compleat English Rhetorique, Exemplified, With Common-
Places, and Formes, digested into an easie and Methodical
way to speak and write fluently, according to the mode of
the present times . . . Lon., 1654, 12mo.
BULWER, John : Chirologia : Or the Natvrall Langvage of the
Hand. Composed by the speaking Motions, and Discours-
ing Gestures thereof. Whereunto is added Chironomia : Or,
the Art of Manvall Rhetoricke. Lon., 1644, 8vo.
FARNABY, Thos. : Index Rhetoricus Et Oratorius . . . Cui
adjiciuntur Formulæ Oratoriæ. Et Index Poeticus. . . .
Edita Novissima . . . [' Index Rhet.,' 1st ed., 1625.]
Lon., 1713, 4to.
HALL, Thos. : Vindiciæ Literarum, The Schools Guarded : Or,
The Excellency and Vsefulnesse of Humane Learning in
Subordination to Divinity, and preparation to the Ministry :
As Also, Rules for the expounding of the Holy Scriptures :
With a Synopsis of the most materiall Tropes and Figures
contained in the Sacred Scriptures . . . Lon., 1655, 8vo.
[The last portion of this work is sometimes referred to as
Hall's ' Rhetorica Sacra,' and is so named on a separate
title-page, date 1654.]

RICHARDSON, Alex. : The Logicians School-Master : Or, A Comment Upon Ramus Logick. By Mr. *Alexander Richardson* . . . Whereunto is added, His Prelections on *Ramus* his *Grammer ; Taleus* his *Rhetorick* ; . . . Never before Published. Lon., 1657, 8vo.

SMITH, John : The Mysterie of Rhetorique Unvail'd Wherein above 130 The Tropes *and* Figures are severally derived from the Greek into English, together with lively Definitions and Variety of $\begin{cases} Latin \\ English \\ Scriptural \end{cases}$ examples Pertinent to each of them apart. . . . Lon., 1657, 8vo.

(2) *English School-books treating of Rhetoric*

BRINSLEY, John : Ludus Literarius or the Grammar Schoole . . . Edited with Introduction and Bibliographical notes By E. T. Campagnac. [Contemp. eds. 1612, 1627.] Liverpool Univ. Press, 1917, 8vo.

BUTLER, Chas : Rhetoricæ Libri Dvo. Qvorum *Prior de Tropis & Figuris, Posterior de Voce & Gestu* Præcipit : In Vsum Scholarum . . . Qvibus Recens Accesservnt *de* Oratoria Libri duo. Lon., 1629, 4to.
Oratoriæ Libri Dvo : Qvorum *Alter ejus Definitionem, Alter Partitionem* Explicit : In Vsum Scholarum. . . Oxf., 1633, 4to.

CLARKE, John : Transitionvm Formulæ, in usum Scholarum concinnatæ. Secunda Editio, cum Additione . . . Lon., 1628, 8vo.

HOOLE, Chas : A New Discovery Of the old Art of Teaching Schoole, In four small Treatises. . . . Edited with Bibliographical Index by E. T. Campagnac. [Reprint of 1660 ed.] Liverpool Univ. Press, 1913, 8vo.

SHORTHAND MANUALS in conjunction with the foregoing :

BALES, Peter : The Writing Schoolmaster : . . . The first Booke, Entituled : The Arte of Brachygraphie : that is, to write as fast as a man speaketh treatably . . . Lon., 1590, 4to.
[' The Arte of Brachygraphie,' alone, Lon., 1597, 12mo.]

EVERHARDT, Job : An Epitome of Stenography . . . Lon., 1658, 8vo.

SHELTON, Thos. : Zeilographia, or A New Art of Short-writing never before published. Lon., 1650, 8vo.[1]

(3) ' *Artes Concionandi* '

AMES, Wm. : Puritanismus Anglicanus, sive Præcipua Dogmata eorum, qui inter vulgo dictos Puritanos in Anglia, rigidiores habentur. Amsterdam, 1658, 12mo.

ARDERNE, James : Directions Concerning the Matter and Stile of Sermons . . . Lon., 1671, 12mo.

BERNARD, Richard : The Faithfull Shepheard . . . Lon., 1607, 4to.[2]

BORROMEO, Federigo (Cardinal) : Federici Borromæi Cardinalis, et Archiepiscopi Mediolani De Concionante Episcopo Libri Tres. Milan, 1632-3, sm. fol.

De Sacris Nostrorvm Temporvm Oratoribvs Libri Quinqve. [Bound up with foregoing.] Milan, 1632, sm. fol.

BOWLES, Oliver : De Pastore Evangelico Tractatvs . . . Lon., 1649, 4to.

CHAPPELL, William : Methodus concionandi . . . Lon., 1648, 8vo.

The Use of Holy Scripture Gravely and Methodically Discoursed . . . Lon., 1653, 8vo.
[This consists of ' Sermon Notes on II Timothie III. 16. Being the Theologicall Ground of another Treatise of the Author extant under the title of METHODUS CONCIONANDI, Containing a learned and brief exemplification of the same Method. Translated (a great part) out of his Latine Copie.']

DREXILIUS, Jerome : Rhetorica Cœlestis . . . Antwerp, 1635, 12mo.

EGGELING, Francis : ΣΥΝΘΕΩ ! De Veterum Concionibvs Dissertatio . . . Helmstadt, 1661.

ERASMUS, Desiderius : Ecclesiastæ, sive de ratione concionandi, Libri Quatuor . . . ed. Fred. Augustus Klein. Leipzig, 1820, 8vo.

FERRARIVS, Francis Bernard : . . . De Ritv Sacrarum Ecclesiẹ Catholicẹ Concionum, Libri Dvo. Milan, 1620, 4to.

HYPERIUS, Andrew : The Practice of preaching . . . Conteyning an excellent Method how to frame Divine Sermons

---

[1] *Noah Bridge's* ' Stenographie and Crytographie,' Lon., 1659, 8vo ; *Jeremiah Rich's* ' The Penns Dexterity,' 1659, or ' The Pens Dexterity Compleated . . .' Lon., 1659, 8vo ; and *John Willis'* ' The Art of Stenography . . .' 9th ed., Lon., 1628, 12mo, have no religious reference or intention, although Rich's became the favourite Puritan method.

[2] Gives contemporary conception of preaching among other advice intended for young ministers.

. . . First written in Latin . . . Englissed [sic] by John
Ludham . . . Lon., 1577, 8vo.
KECKERMANN, Bartholomew : Rhetoricæ Ecclesiasticæ, *Siue*
Artis Formandi et Habendi Conciones Sacras, Libri Dvo :
Methodice Adornati *per Præcepta & Explicationes* . . .
Editio tertia. Hanoviæ, 1606, 8vo.
LUCY, Wm., bp. of St. Davids : A Treatise of the Nature of a
Minister In all its Offices . . . Lon., 1678, 4to.
PERKINS, Wm. : The Works of that Famovs and Worthy
Minister of Christ . . . The Second Volume.

Lon., 1631, fol.
[For : ' The Art of Prophecying. Or, A Treatise Concerning the Sacred and Onely Trve Manner and Methode
of Preaching. First written in Latine by Mr. William
Perkins : and now faithfully translated into English (for
that it containeth many worthy things fit for knowledge of
men of all degrees). By Thomas Tvke, Lon., 1631.']
WILKINS, John, bp. of Chester : Ecclesiastes, Or, A Discourse
concerning the Gift of Preaching as it falls under the rules
of Art. Lon., 1646, 4to.
A Discourse Concerning the Gift of Prayer . . . Whereunto
is added, Ecclesiastes . . . 8th ed. ' corrected and much
Enlarged.' Lon., 1704, 8vo.

(*b*) LATER WORKS ON PREACHING USED IN ILLUSTRATION

CLAUDE, John : An Essay on the Composition of a Sermon
Translated from the original French of the Rev^d. John
Claude, Minister of the French Reformed Church at
Charenton. With Notes. By Robert Robinson . . . The
3rd ed., 2 vols. Lon., 1788, 8vo.
[French original, *ante* 1674.]
EDWARDS, John : The Preacher. A Discourse, Shewing,
what are the Particular Offices *and* Employments Of those
of that Character . . . To which is added, A Catalogue
of some Authors who may be beneficial to young Preachers
and Students in Divinity. 3 vols. Lon., 1705–9, 8vo.
MATHER, Cotton : Manuductio ad Ministerium. Directions
For A Candidate of the Ministry Wherein, First, a Right
Foundation is laid for his Future Improvement ; And,
Then, Rules are offered for such a Management of his
Academical and Preparatory Studies : And thereupon, For
such a Conduct after his Appearance in the World ; as
may Render him a Skilful and Useful Minister of the
Gospel. Boston, 1726, 4to.
OWEN, Henry : Directions for Young Students in Divinity,

with regard to those Attainments, which are necessary to qualify them for Holy Orders . . . London, 1766, 4to.

WILLIAMS, Edward : The Christian Preacher, or, Discourses on Preaching, By Several Eminent Divines, English and Foreign, Revised and Abridged ; With an Appendix on The Choice of Books . . . Second ed., Lon., 1809, sm. 8vo.

C. THE PRACTICAL BACKGROUND : ENGLISH PREACHING FROM FISHER TO HOOKER

BANCROFT, Rich, archbp. of Canterbury : A sermon preached at Paul's Cross the 9th of February . . . 1588.
Lon., 1588, 4to.

BRADFORD, John (Martyr) : Two notable Sermons . . . the one of Repentance 1553, and the other of the Lorde's supper. Lon., 1574, 4to.

BULLINGER, Henry : A Sermon of the true confessinge of Christe . . . made in the convocation of the clergie at Zurich . . . 1555 . . . [Trans. and published in Elizabeth's reign.]

COLET, John, dean of St. Paul's : The sermo[n] of doctore Colete made to the Convocation at Paulis.
No. pl. or date, 4to.

FISHER, John, bp. of Rochester : The English Works . . . Now first collected by John E. B. Mayor, M.A. Published for E.E.T S. . . . Lon., 1876, 8vo.

GILPIN, Bernard : The Life of Bernard Gilpin . . . by . . . Geo. Carleton, Ld. bp. of Chichester . . . With his [Gilpin's] Sermon preached before King Edward the Sixth, Anno 1552 . . . Lon., 1636, 4to.

GRINDAL, Edmund, archbp. of Canterbury : A ser. at the funeral solemnitie of the most high and mighty Prince Ferdinandus, the late Emperor of most famous memorye . . . Lon., 1554, 4to.

The Remains . . . Edited for the Parker Society by the Rev. Wm. Nicholson . . . Camb., 1843, 8vo.

HAWEIS, John Oliver, M.A. : Sketches of the Reformation and Elizabethan Age, Taken from the Contemporary Pulpit.
Lon., 1844, 8vo.

HOOKER, Rich. : The Works. Edited by the Rev. John Keble . . . 3rd ed., 3 vols. Oxf., 1845, 8vo.

HOOPER, John, bp. of Gloucester (martyr) : A funerall Oratyon made the xiiij day of January . . . . Lon., 1649, 4to.

An oversight and deliberacion Vpon the holy Prophete Jonas . . . in seven sermons. Anno. M.D.L. . . .
Lon., 1550, 4to.

An Homelye to be read in the tyme of pestylence . . . [at top of sermon, 1553]. No pl. or date, 4to.

JEWEL, John, bp. of Salisbury : Certaine Sermons Preached
   before the Queenes Majestie, and at Paules Crosse . . .
   Whereunto is added a short Treatise of the Sacraments
   . . .   Lon., 1603, 4to.
LATIMER, Hugh, bp. of Worcester (martyr) : Sermons . . .
   Edited for the Parker Society by the Rev. Geo. Elwes
   Corrie, B.D. . . . 2 vols.   Camb., 1844, 8vo.
SANDYS, Edwin, archbp. of York : [22] Sermons. Lon., 1585, 4to.
SERMONS, or Homilies Appointed to be read in Churches.
   [Being a reprint of the ed. of 1563.]   Lon., 1833, 4to.
TAVERNER, Rich. : Postils on the Epistles and Gospels. Com-
   piled and Published . . . in the year 1540. And now
   edited by Edward Cardwell, D.D. . . .   Oxf., 1841, 8vo.
UDALL, John : Obedience to the Gospell. Two Sermons.
                                      Lon., 1588, 4to.

D. REPRESENTATIVE ENGLISH SERMONS OF THE SEVENTEENTH CENTURY[1]

ABBOT, Geo., archbp. of Canterbury : An Exposition upon the
   Prophet Jonah : Contained in certain [30] Sermons . . .
                                      Lon., 1600, 4to.
   A Sermon Preached . . . At the Funerall . . . of Thomas
   Earle of Dorset . . .   Lon., 1608, 4to.
ABBOT, Robt., bp. of Salisbury : The Exaltation of the kingdome
   and Priesthood of Christ. In certain Sermons . . . 1596.
                                      Lon., 1601, 4to.
   A Wedding Sermon preached at the marriage of Sir John
   Standhope . . . 1607.   Lon., 1608, sm. 8vo.
   The Old Waye : A Sermon Preached at Oxford . . . the Act
   Sunday, 1610.   Lon., 1610, 4to.
ABBOT, Robt. (of Cranbrook) : A Hand of Fellowship . . . In
   certain sermons . . .   Lon., 1623, 4to.
   Bee Thankfull London and Her Sisters . . . Lon., 1626, 4to.
   Foure Sermons . . .   Lon., 1639, sm. 12mo.
   Milke For Babes . . . Whereunto also annexed, Three
   Sermons.   Lon., 1646, 8vo.
ADAMS, Thomas : The Workes . . . Being the Summe of his
   Sermons, Meditations, and other Divine and Morall Dis-
   courses.   Lon., 1630, folio.
   Reprint : ed. by the Rev. Joseph Angus, D.D., Nichol's
   Standard Divines. 3 vols.   Edin., 1861.

[1] This term has been used to cover ' commonplaces,' ' discourses,' ' treatises,' and ' commentaries ' of a homiletic nature, often originally prepared
as sermons. Except where the complete title of a sermon is given, the profuse
use of capitals and italics has been dispensed with as not being material to
the purpose. A certain number of recurring contractions have also been
introduced, as ' bp.' = bishop, ' ser.' = sermon, etc.

AIRAY, Henry : Lectures upon the Whole Epistle of St. Paul to
the Philippians . . .　　　　　　Lon., 1618, 4to

ALLESTREE, Rich. : A Sermon Preached in St. Peter's Westminster . . . 1660 at the Consecration of [several bishops]
Lon., 1660, 4to

Eighteen Sermons whereof Fifteen Preached before the King.
Lon., 1669, large 4to

AMBROSE, Isaac : Prima, Media, & Ultima . . . In Three
Treatises to which is annexed a Sermon . . .
Lon., 1659, 4to.

Redeeming the Time . . .　　　　　　Lon., 1658, 4to.

Looking unto Jesus : A View of the Everlasting Gospel
Glasg., 1758, 4to

ANDREWES, Lancelot, bp. of Winchester : XCVI Sermons . . .
The 3rd ed., Lon., 1635, folio.

The Works.—Library of Anglo-Catholic Theology. 11 Vols.
[Vols. i–v contain Sermons.]　　　　Oxf. 1841–54, 8vo

ANGIER, John : An helpe to better hearts . . . in several
sermons . . .　　　　　　Lon., 1647, sm. 12mo.

ANNELEY, Sam. : A Sermon preached in the Hble. House of
Commons.　　　　　　Lon., 1648, 4to.

ANYAN, Thomas : A Sermon preached at St. Maries Church in
Oxford . . . 1612　　　　　　Lon., 1612, 4to.

ARCHBOLD, John : The Beauty of Holiness, a Sermon preached
at Court.　　　　　　Lon., 1621, 4to.

ARMITAGE, Timothy : Sermons . . .　　　Lon., 1678, 8vo.

ARROWSMITH, John : The Covenant—Avenging Sword [Before
H. of Commons.[1]]　　　　　　Lon., 1643, 4to.

Englands Eben-Ezer . . . [Before both Houses].
Lon., 1645, 4to.

ASHE, Simeon : A Support for the sinking Heart.
Lon., 1642, 4to.

The Best Refvge For the Most Oppressed. Before H. of C.
Lon., 1642, 4to.

The Church Sinking　. . Before H. of L.　1644.
Lon., 1645, 4to.

Religious Covenanting Directed . . .　　Lon., 1646, 4to.

ATKINS, John : The Christian race : A Sermon . . .
Lon., 1624, 4to.

ATTERBURY, Francis, bp. of Rochester : Sermons and Discourses On Several Subjects. 3rd ed., 2 vols.
Lon., 1730, 8vo.

Sermons on Several Occasions . . .　2 vols. Lon., 1734, 8vo.

---

[1] From here onwards ' H. of C.' = ' House of Commons,' ' H. of L.' =
' House of Lords.' Where no separate date of delivery is given the year of
publication coincides with the year when the sermon was preached.

ATTERBURY, Lewis : Ten Sermons Preach'd before Her Royal
    Highness the Princess Ann . . .   Lon., 1699, 8vo.
  A Second Volume of [12] Sermons . . .   Lon., 1703, 8vo.
ATTERSOLL, William : A Commentarie Vpon the Epistle of
    Saint Paule to Philemon.   Lon., 1612, folio.
  The New Covenant, or A Treatise of the Sacraments. 2nd ed.
                                          Lon., 1614, sm. 4to.
  A Commentarie upon the Fourth Booke of Moses . . .
                                          Lon., 1618, folio.
  Three Treatises . . .   Lon., 1632, 4to.
  The Principles of Christian Religion.   Lon., 1635, 8vo.
AUSTIN, Robt. : Allegiance not Impeached : viz. By the Parlia-
    ments taking up of Arms . . .   Lon., 1644, 4to.
BABINGTON, Gervase, bp. of Worcester : The Workes . . .
    Containing three Sermons.   Lon., 1615, folio.
BAILLIE, Robt. : Satan the Leader in chief to all who resist the
    Reparation of Sion . . . in a Sermon to the Hble. H. of
    C. . . .   Lon., 1643, 4to.
  Errours And Induration . . . in a Sermon Before the Rt.
    Hble. H. of Peers . . .   Lon., 1645, 4to.
BARKER, Matthew : A Christian Standing . . . Upon the true
    Foundation . . . [Before H. of C.]   Lon., 1648, 4to.
  The Faithful and Wise Servant.   Lon., 1657, 4to.
BARLOW, John : A Christians Last Day, Is His Best Day.
                                          Lon., 1618, 4to.
  The Good Mans Refuge in Affliction.   Lon., 1618, 4to.
  Hierons Last Fare-well, A Sermon . . . at the Funerall of
    . . . Samuel Hieron . . . The Good Mans Priviledge.
                                          Lon., 1618, 4to.
  The Joy of the Upright Man.   Lon., 1618, sm. 4to.
  A Sermon . . . .   Lon., 1618, 4to.
  The Trve Gvide to Glory.   Lon., 1619, 4to.
  An Exposition of the Second Epistle of . . . Paul to Timothy,
    the first Chapter.   Lon., 1625, 4to.
  An Exposition of the First and Second Chapters of the Latter
    Episte [sic] of the Apostle Paul to Timothie. Lon., 1632, folio.
BARLOW, Thomas, bp. of Lincoln : The Genuine Remains
    . . . Containing divers Discourses . . .   Lon., 1693, 8vo.
BARLOW, William, bp. of Lincoln : A Sermon preached at
    Paules Crosse . . . 1600. With a short discourse of the
    late Earle of Essex his confession, and penitence . . .
                                          Lon., 1601, 8vo.
  The Sermon Preached at Paules Crosse, the tenth day of
    November, being the next Sunday after the Discoverie of
    the late Horrible Treason [i.e. the Gunpowder Plot].
                                          Lon., 1606, 4to.

A Brand, *Titio Erepta*. On the fifth day of November last . . .
    Lon., 1607, 4to.
The Eagle and the Body . . . [a] Sermon preached before
    Queene Elizabeth . . . in Lent Anno 1601.
    Lon., 1609, 4to.
A Treatise of Fornication . . . Also, A Penitentiary
    Sermon . . .   Lon., 1609, 8vo.
BARO, Peter : Petri Baronis . . . in Jonam Prophetam Præ-
    lectiones 39 . . .   Lon., 1579, folio.
    [The vol. also contains three sers., delivered at Cambridge
    ad Clerum.]
BARROW, Isaac : The Works . . . In Three Volumes. Published
    by His Grace, Dr. John Tillotson . . . Lon., 1700, folio.
    The Theological Works . . . In Nine Volumes. Edited . . .
    By The Rev. Alex. Napier . . .   Camb., 1859, 8vo.
    [Napier's ed. restores the reading of Barrow's MSS.
    which had been tampered with by Tillotson.]
BASTARD, Thos. : Twelve Sermons . . . Lon., 1615, sm. 4to.
BATES, William : The Works . . . [Containing sermons.]
    Lon., 1700, folio.
BAXTER, Rich. : The Practical Works . . . With a Life of the
    Author, and a Critical Examination of his Writings, by the
    Rev. William Orme. 23 vols.   Lon., 1830, 8vo.
    [Vols. xvii and xviii contain sermons.]
BAYLY, John : Two Sermons . . . [' The Angell guardian,' and
    ' The Light enlightening.']   Oxf., 1630, 4to.
BAYNE[s], Paul : Commentarie upon the first chap. of the
    Epistle of St. Paul to the Ephesians . . .   Lon., 1618, 4to.
    The Christians garment ; a sermon . . .   Lon., 1618, 4to.
    The Trial of a Christians estate . . . a sermon . . .
    Lon., 1618, 4to.
    A Counterbane against earthly carefulness ; a sermon.
    Lon., 1619, 4to.
    The mirrour or Miracle of Gods love . . . a sermon.
    Lon., 1619, 4to.
BEDELL, William, bp. of Kilmore : A Sermon Preached at
    Christ-Church Dublin . . . 1634.   Lon., 1659, 4to.
BENBRIGGE, John : Christ Above All Exalted. Lon., 1645, 4to.
BENEFIELD, Sebastian, Lady Margaret Professor of Divinity,
    Oxford, 1613 : A Sermon Preached in St. Maries Church
    in Oxford . . . MDCX . . .   Oxf., 1611, 4to.
    The Haven of the Afflicted. A Sermon . . . in the Cathedral
    Church of Gloucester . . .   Oxf., 1613, 4to.
    A Commentarie . . . vpon the First Chapter . . . of Amos,
    deliuered in xxi Sermons . . . Herevnto is added a Sermon
    vpon I Cor. 9, 19 . . .   Oxf., 1613, 4to.

[The foregoing were reprinted with]

A Commentary . . . vpon the Third Chapter . . . of Amos Delivered in xvii Sermons . . .   Lon., 1629, 4to.

Eight Sermons Publikely Preached in Vniversity of Oxford . . . Begunne in . . . 1595 . . . Now first published . . .   Oxf., 1614, 4to.

The Sinne against the Holy Ghost Discovered . . . in Twelve Sermons . . .   Oxf., 1615, 4to.

BENSON, George : A Sermon Preached at Pavles Crosse . . .   Lon., 1609, 4to.

BERNARD, Rich. : Ruths Recompense : Or a Commentarie Vpon the Booke of Rvth . . . Deliuered in severall Sermons.   Lon., 1628, 4to.

BEVERIDGE, William, bp. of St. Asaph : The Works . . . 2 vols.   Lon., 1720, folio.

BEWICK, John : Confiding England Vnder Conflicts . . .   Lon., 1644, 4to.

BILSON, Thos., bp. of Winchester : The effect of certaine Sermons Touching the Full Redemption of mankind . . . *Preached at Paules Crosse and else where in London* . . . Lond., 1599, 4to.

A Sermon preached at [the Coronation of James I] . . . the xxv of July, 1603.   Lon., 1604, 8vo.

BINNING, Hugh : Fellowship with God : Or, xxviii Sermons on the I Epistle of *John, Chaps.* 1, and 2. Edin., 1671, sm. 8vo.

The Works . . . [Being sermons on the Catechism and 86 others.]   Edin., 1735, 4to.

BLACKALL, Ofspring, bp. of Exeter : The Works . . . Consisting of Eighty Seven Practical Discourses Upon Our Saviour's Sermon on the Mount : Together with his Sermons preach'd at Boyle's Lecture . . . in . . . 1700 . . . 2 vols.   Lon., 1723, folio.

BLACKWELL, Elidad : A Caveat for Magistrates. Lon., 1645, 4to.

BLAGUE, Thomas : A Sermon preached at the Charterhouse before the king, on Ps. I, 1, 2.   Lon., 1602, 8vo.

BODEN, Joseph : An Alarme Beat Vp in Sion. Lon., 1644, 4to.

BOLTON, Robt. : A Discourse About the State of Trve Happinesse : Delivered in Certaine Sermons in Oxford, and at Pauls Crosse . . .   Lon., 1611, 4to.

Some Generall Directions for a Comfortable Walking with God : Delivered in the Lectvre at Kettering . . .   Lon., 1625, 4to.

Helpes to Hvmiliation . . .   Oxf., 1631, 12mo.

Instrvctions for a Right Comforting Afflicted Consciences . . . Delivered . . . in the Lectvre at Kettering . . .   Lon., 1631, 4to.

Mr. Boltons Last and Learned Worke of the Foure last
Things . . . With an Assize Sermon . . .
> Lon., 1632 (eights), sm. 4to.

Two Sermons Preached at Northampton at Two Seuerall
Assises there. Lon., 1635, 4to.

The Workes . . . 5 vols. Lon., 1641, 4to.

BOLTON, Sam. : A Tossed Ship making safe to Harbor . . .
> Lon., 1644, 4to.

The Trve Bovnds of Christian Freedome . . . Lon., 1644, sm. 8vo.

. . . The Sinfulnes of Sin : held forth in a Sermon . . .
[to H. of C.] Lon., 1646, 4to.

The Arraignment of Errovr Lon., 1646, 4to.

Deliverance in the Birth : Or, A Sermon preached before
the . . . H. of Peeres . . . 1646. Lon., 1647, 4to.

The Guard of the Tree of Life, or, a Sacramental Discourse . . . Lon., 1647, 4to.

The Dead Saint Speaking . . . in severall Treatises.
> Lon., 1657, folio.

BOND, John, Master of the Savoy : A Dove of Hope, Also Holy
and Loyall Activity. Two Treatises delivered in severall
Sermons . . . Lon., 1641, 4to.

Salvation in a Mystery . . . a Sermon . . . before the
Hble. H. of C. . . . Lon., 1646, 4to.

Occasus Occidentalis . . . laid forth in two severall
Sermons . . . Lon., 1645, 4to.

Eshcol, Or Grapes (among) Thorns . . . A Thanksgiving
Sermon, to the Hble. H. of C. Lon., 1648, 4to.

BOND, Sampson : A Sermon Preached before the Reverend
Committee of Divines . . . Lon., 1646, 4to.

BOUGHEN, Edward : A Sermon of Confirmation . . . 1619.
> Lon., 1620, 4to.

Two Sermons : The First Preached at Canterbury . . .
1635. The Second . . . at Saint Pauls Crosse . . .
> Lon., 1635, 4to.

A Sermon Concerning Decencie and Order . . . 1637.
> Lon., 1638, 4to.

BOURNE, Immanuel : The rainebow or a sermon on Gen. ix, 13.
> Lon., 1617, 4to.

The godly mans gvide a sermon on Jas. iv, 13.
> Lon., 1620, 4to.

The true way of a Christian . . . preached at Paules Crosse,
1617. Lon., 1622, 4to.

BOWLES, Edward : Good counsell for evil times. Lon., 1648, 4to.

BOWLE, John, bp. of Rochester : A Sermon Preached . . . at
the Funerall of . . . Henrie Earle of Kent . . . 1614.
> Lon., 1615, sm. 4to.

A Sermon Preached at Mapple-Durham in Oxfordshire . . .
                              Lon., 1616, sm. 4to.
*Concio ad . . . Patres et Presbyteros totius Provinciæ Cantuar. in
Synodo Londini Congregatos, habita . . . 1620.*
                              Lon., 1621, 4to.
BOWLES, Oliver : Zeale for Gods House Quickened. [Before
    Lords, Commons and Divines.]   Lon., 1643, 4to.
BOYS, John, dean of Canterbury : The Workes . . .
                              Lon., 1622, folio.
    Remaines . . . Containing Sundry Sermons . . .
                              Lon., 1631, 4to.
BRADSHAW, John : Anastasis : Britannica et Hibernica.
    [2 sers., one May 24, 1660, the other June 28, 1660—on
    Charles II's proposed and actual return.]
                              Lon., 1660, 4to.
BRADSHAW, William : Two marriage sermons : the former . . .
    by Thos. Gataker . . . the latter . . . by . . . William
    Bradshaw.   Lon., 1620, sm. 4to.
BRAMHALL, John, archbp. of Armagh : The Works . . . Col-
    lected into One Volume.   Dublin, 1677, folio.
BRAY, William : A Sermon of the sacrament of the Lords
    Supper.   Lon., 1641, 4to.
BRIDGE, William, (a writer of the ' Apologetical Narration ') :
    Two Sermons . . .   Lon., 1642, 4to.
    A Sermon Preached unto the Voluntiers of the City of
    Norwich . . .   Lon., 1642, 4to.
    Jacobs Covnsell, And King Davids Seasonable Hearing It
    . . . a Sermon before the Hble. H. of C.   Lon., 1643, 4to.
    A Sermon Preached before the Hble. H. of C.
                              Lon., 1643, 4to.
    England Saved With a Notwithstanding . . . a Sermon to
    the Hble. H. of C. . . . 1647.   Lon., 1648, 4to.
    The Freeness of the Grace and Love of God . . . in 7 sers.
                              Lon., 1671, 8vo.
    Bridges Remaines, being VIII Sermons . . .
                              Lon., 1673, sm. 8vo.
BRINSLEY, John : The Preachers Charged . . . Lon., 1631, 4to.
    The Healing of Israel's Breaches . . . delivered in six Sermons
    in the Church of Great Yarmouth.   Lon., 1641, 4to.
    A Parlie with the Sword . . .   Lon., 1643, 4to.
    A Looking-Glasse for Good Women . . .   Lon., 1645, 4to.
BROOKS, Thomas : The Glorious Day of the Saints Appearance.
                              Lon., 1648, 4to.
BROWNE, Thomas : The copie of the Sermon preached before
    the Universitie at St. Maries in Oxford on Ps. cxxx.
                              Oxf., 1634, 4to.

27

BROWNING, John : Concerning publike prayer . . . six ser-
mons . . .   Lon., 1636, 4to.
BROWNRIG, Ralph, bp. of Exeter : Fourty Sermons . . .
                                    Lon., 1661 (fours), folio.
Twenty Five Sermons . . .   Lon., 1664, sm. folio.
BRUCE, Robert : [5] Sermons vpon the Sacrament of the Lords
Supper : Preached in the Kirk of Edinburgh . . .
                                        Edin., no date, 8vo.
[11] Sermons Preached in the Kirk of Edinburgh . . .
                                          Edin., 1591, 8vo.
[These 16 sermons appeared in English as ' The Way to
true peace and rest . . . ' Lon., 1617, 4to.]
Sermons by the Rev. Robert Bruce . . . Reprinted from the
Original Edition of M.D.XC. and M.D.XCI . . . by the
Rev. Robt. Wodrow . . .   Edin., 1843, 8vo.
BUCKERIDGE, John, bishop of Ely : A Sermon Preached before
the Kings Maiestie, on Tuesday the 23, of September, 1606.
                  [No title-page, merely sermon-top.]
A Sermon Preached before His Maiestie . . . March 22, 1607.
                                          Lon., 1618, 4to.
BULKELEY, Peter : The gospel-covenant . . . preached in
Concord in New-England.   Lon., 1651, sm. 4to.
BULL, George, bishop of St. David's : Some Important Points of
Primitive Christianity Maintained and Defended ; In
Several Sermons. Ed. with a Life by Robt. Nelson. 3 vols.
                                          Lon., 1713, 8vo.
BUNYAN, John : The Works . . . The First Volume . . . [All
that ever was published.]   Lon., 1692, folio.
The Whole Works . . . With Editorial Prefaces, Notes and
Life . . . by George Offor . . . 3 vols.
                        Glas., Edin. & Lon., 1859, 4to.
BURGES(s), Anthony : Spiritual Refining : Or a Treatise of
Grace and Assurance . . . Being cxx Sermons.
                                          Lon., 1652, folio.
BURGES, Cornelius : A Sermon preached to the Hble. H. of C.
. . . Novemb. 17, 1640.   Lon., 1641, 4to.
Another Sermon preached to the Hble. H. of C. . . .
November the fifth, 1641.   Lon., 1641, 4to.
Two Sermons preached to the Hble. H. of C. at two Publike
Fasts . . . March 30, 1642 [and] . . . April 30, 1645.
                                          Lon., 1645, 4to.
The Necessity of Agreement with God . . . a Sermon
preached to the Rt. Hble. the Noble H. of Peers . . .
                                          Lon., 1645, 4to.
BURGESS, Dan. : The Church's Triumph over Death. A
Funeral-Sermon . . .   Lon., 1694, 8vo.

The Craftsman : A Sermon Or Paraphrase upon several Verses of the 19th Chapter of the *Acts* . . . *Composed by the late Daniel Burgess, and intended to be Preached by him in the High Times, but prevented by the burning of his Meeting-House.* 3rd ed. Lon., 1720, 8vo.

BURNET, Gilbert, bp. of Salisbury : Subjection for Conscience sake Asserted in a Sermon preached . . . 1674.
Lon., 1675, 4to.

A sermon preached at . . . the Funeral of Mrs. Anne Seile . . . Lon., 1678, 4to.

A sermon preached before the Lord Mayor . . . of London.
Lon., 1681, 4to.

A sermon preached on the Fast-Day, Decemb. 22, 1680 . . . before the Hble. H. of C. Lon., 1681, 4to.

A Sermon preached before the Aldermen of the City of London . . . Jan. 30, 1680/1 . . . Lon., 1681, 4to.

An Exhortation to Peace and Union. A Sermon . . . at the Election of the Lord-Mayor. Lon., 1681, 4to.

A Sermon preached at the Funeral of Mr. James Houblon.
Lon., 1682, 4to.

A sermon preached at the Chappel of the Rolls, on the fifth of November, 1684. Lon., 1684, 4to.

A sermon . . . before His Highness the Prince of Orange, the 23d. of December, 1688. Lon., 1689, 4to.

A sermon preached before the H. of C. . . . January 1688 Being the Thanksgiving-Day for the Deliverance of the Kingdom from Popery and Arbitrary Power. Lon., 1689, 4to.

A sermon preached at the Coronation of William III and Mary II . . . April 11, 1689. Lon., 1689, 4to.

A sermon preached before the H. of Peers . . . the 5th of November, 1689 . . . Lon., 1689, 4to.

A sermon preached before the King & Queen . . . on Christmas-Day, 1689. Lon., 1690, 4to.

A sermon preached before the Queen. Lon., 1690, 4to.

A ser. preached before the King and Queen at White-Hall . . . 1690, Being the Day of Thanksgiving for His Majesties Preservation and Success in Ireland. Lon., 1690, 4to.

A ser. preached before the Court of Aldermen . . . March 12, 1689/90. Lon., 1690, 4to.

A sermon preached before the King and Queen . . .
Lon., 1691, 4to.

A sermon preached . . . 1691. Being the Thanksgiving-Day for the Preservation of the King, and the Reduction of Ireland. Lon., 1691, 4to.

A sermon preached at the Funeral of the Hon. Robert Boyle . . . January 7, 1691/2. Lon., 1692, 4to.

A sermon preached before the Queen . . . in Lent.
           Lon., 1694, 4to.

A sermon preached before the Queen . . . on the 29th of May, 1694, Being the Anniversary of King Charles II his Birth and Restauration.   Lon., 1694, 4to.

A sermon preached at the Funeral of the Most Reverend Father in God John [Tillotson] . . . Ld.-Archbp. of Canterbury . . . 1694.   Lon., 1694, 4to.

A sermon preached before the King . . . 1694/5.
           Lon., 1695, 4to.

A sermon preached before the King . . . December, 1697. Being the Day of Thanksgiving for the Peace.
           Lon., 1698, 4to.

Charitable Reproof. A Sermon preached . . . to the Societies for Reformation of Manners . . . 1700.
           Lon., 1700, 4to.

Of the Propagation of the Gospel in Foreign Parts. A Ser. preached . . . 1703/4. Before the Society incorporated for that purpose.   Lon., 1704, 4to.

A sermon preached at the Cathedral Church of Salisbury on the xxviith Day of June MDCCVI. Being the Day of Thanksgiving for the Great Successes God has given to the Arms of Her Majesty and Her Allies in Flanders and Spain.
           Lon., 1706, 4to.

A sermon preached in Lent . . . 1705/6.   Lon., 1706, 4to.

BURROUGHS, Jeremiah : The excellency of a gracious spirit, in a treatise upon Numbers xiv, 24.   Lon., 1639, 8vo.

Sions Joy. A sermon preached to the Hble. H. of C. . . . For the Peace concluded between England and Scotland.
           Lon., 1641, 4to.

Moses his self-denyall . . .   Lon., 1641, sm. 8vo.

Moses his choice . . .   Lon., 1641, 4to

The Glorious Name of God . . . Opened in two Sermons . . .   Lon., 1643, 4to

An exposition of the prophesie of Hosea. 4 vols.
           Lon., 1643–61, 4to

A sermon preached before the Rt. Hble. the H. of Peeres
           Lon., 1646, 4to

A sermon preached before the H. of C. . . .   Lon., 1646, 4to

BURTON, Henry, (fellow-sufferer with Prynne and Bastwick)
Israels fast ; or a meditation upon Josh. vii, 8.
           Lon. 1628, 4to

The seven vials . . .   Lon., 1628, 4to

For God, and the King. The summe of Two Sermons . .
           No pl., 1636, 4to

A most godly sermon on Luke ix, 23.   Lon., 1641, 4to

England's Bondage . . . A sermon preached before the
Hble. H. of P. . . .   Lon., 1641, 4to.

BURTON, William : The rousing of the sluggard, delivered in
seven sermons.   Lon., 1634, 8vo.

BYAM, Henry : A Retvrne from Argier. A sermon preached at
Minehead in the Country of Somerset . . . at the read-
mission of a relapsed Christian into our Church.
                                        Lon., 1628, 4to.

xiii Sermons : Most of them Preached before His Majesty
King Charles II in His Exile.   Lon., 1675, 8vo.

BYFIELD, Nicholas : The signes ; or an essay concerning the
assurance of Gods Loue and mans saluation.
                                        Lon., 1614, 8vo.

The cure of the feare of death.   Lon., 1618, 8vo.

A commentary or sermons upon 1 Peter chap. ii.
                                        Lon., 1623, 4to.

Sermons upon Peter III, 1-10.   Lon., 1626, 4to.

BYFIELD, Richard : Zion's answer to the nations ambassadors
. . . a fast sermon on Isa. xiv, 32.   Lon., 1645, 4to.

CALAMY, Benjamin : A Sermon preached before the . . . Lord
Mayor . . .   Lon., 1673, 4to.

A sermon preached at St. Lawrence-Jury . . . [After the Rye
House Plot].   Lon., 1683, 4to.

A ser. prd. before the . . . Lord Mayor . . . on the Anniversary Fast for the Dreadful Fire in the year 1666.
                                        Lon., 1685, 4to.

CALAMY, Edmund (the elder) : The Noble-Mans Patterne
. . . in a sermon preached before the Rt. Hble. H. of L.
                                        Lon., 1643, 4to.

An Indictment Against England . . . a sermon preached
before the Rt. Hble. H. of L. . . . 1644.   Lon., 1645, 4to.

Englands Antidote . . . a sermon before the Hble. H. of C.
                                        Lon., 1645, 4to.

CALAMY, Edmund (the younger) : A Funeral Sermon Preach'd
at the Interment of Mr. Samuel Stephens . . .
                                        Lon., 1694, 4to.

CALDERWOOD, David, (the historian) : The Pastor and the
Prelate, or Reformation and Conformitie shortly compared . . .   No pl., 1628, sm. 4to.

CARDELL, John : Gods Sovereign Power over Nations.
                                        Lon., 1648, 4to.

CARPENTER, Nathanael : Chorazin & Bethsaidas woe . . .
                                        Lon., 1633, 8vo.

CARPENTER, Richard : The Sovls Sentinel . . . A sermon
preached at the funerall Solemnities of the Rt. Worshipfull
Sir Arthur Ackland Knight . . .   Lon., 1612, 8vo.

A Pastoral Charge . . . at the Trienniall Visitation of the
  Ld. Bp. of Exon. . . .   Lon., 1616, 8vo.
Christs Larvmbell of Love Resovnded.   Lon., 1616, 8vo.
The Conscionable Christian . . .Three Assize Sermons.
                                           Lon., 1623, 4to.
CARTER, John : The Nail hit on the head . . .
                                    No pl., or date, 4to.
The Wheel turned by a voice from the throne of Glory,
  Described in a sermon . . .   Lon., 1647, 4to.
A Rare Sight, Or, the Lyon : Sent from a farr Country, and
  presented to the City of Norwich, in a sermon . . . 1650.
                                           Lon., 1653, 4to.
The Tomb-Stone, or a broken and imperfect Monument, of
  that Worthy Man, Mr. John Carter . . . By his un-
  worthy son John Carter, Preacher of the Gospell . . . in
  . . . Norwich.   Lon., 1653, 8vo.
CARTER, Thomas : Prayers Prevalencie . . . [before H. of C.]
                                           Lon., 1643, 4to.
CARTER, William : Israels peace with God . . . before H. of C.
                                           Lon., 1647, 4to.
Light in Darkness : Described in a ser. prd. before the Hble.
  H. of C., November 24, 1647.   Lon., 1648, 4to.
CARYL, Joseph : The Workes of Ephesus Explained in a Sermon
  before the Hble. H. of C. . . .   Lon., 1642, 4to.
The Nature, Solemnity . . . of a Sacred Covenant . . . in
  a Sermon at Westminster . . . A Sermon preached at the
  late Solemne Assembly, for the taking of the Covenant,
  upon Friday the sixt of this instant October, 1643.
                                           Lon., 1643, 4to.
Davids Prayer for Solomon . . .   Lon., 1643, 4to.
The Arraignment of Unbelief . . . in a sermon to the Hble.
  H. of C. . . .   Lon., 1645, 4to.
The Present Duty and Endeavour of the Saints . . . 1645.
                                           Lon., 1646, 4to.
Heaven and Earth Embracing . . . In a sermon preached
  before the Hble. H. of C. . . . 1645.   Lon., 1646, 4to.
Englands Plus ultra . . . [before H. of C.] . . . 1646.
                                           Lon., 1646, 4to.
The Oppressor Destroyed . . . A Sermon at Pauls . . . 1651.
                                           Lon., no date, 4to.
A Sermon prd. to, and Directing in, the Great Duty of
  Praising God. Preached to the Parliament . . . 1656.
                                           Lon., 1657, 4to.
CASE, Thomas : Gods Waiting to be Gracious . . . Delivered
  in certaine Sermons . . .   Lon., 1642, 4to.
A sermon preached before the Hble. H. of C. Lon., 1645, 4to.

A Model of True Spiritual Thankfulnesse . . . [before
H. of C.] . . . 1645.   Lon., 1646, 4to.
Deliverance-Obstruction . . . [before H. of Peers.] . . .
1646.   Lon., 1646, 4to.
CAWDRY, Daniel : Hvmilitie, The Saints Liverie . . . in two
Sermons at Blacke-Fryers in London . . . 1624.
                                         Lon., 1624, 4to.
Three Sermons . . .   Lon., 1641, 4to.
The Good Man a Publick Good . . . in a ser. prd. to the
Hble. H. of C.   Lon., 1643, 4to.
CHAMBER, Humphrey : A Divine Ballance to weigh Religious
Fasts in . . . [before H. of C.]   Lon., 1643, 4to.
Pauls Sad Farewel . . .   Lon., 1655, 4to.
CHARNOCK, Stephen : Several Discourses Upon the Existence
and Attributes of God . . .   Lon., 1682, folio.
The Works . . . Being Several Discourses Upon Various
Divine Subjects. Vol. ii.   Lon., 1684, folio.
CHESHIRE, Thomas : A sermon preached at . . . Westminster
. . . [before the Lords and Judges].   Lon., 1642, 4to.
CHEYNELL, Francis : Sions Memento, and Gods Alarum . . .
before the Hble. H. of C.   Lon., 1643, 4to.
A sermon preached before the Hble. H. of C. . . .
                                         Lon., 1645, 4to.
The Man of Honour described in a ser. prd. before the
Lords of Parliament . . .   Lon., 1645, 4to.
A ser. prd. to the Hble. H. of C. . . . 1646.
        [Title-page wanting in Bodleian copy.]   — 4to.
CHILLINGWORTH, William : The Works . . . Containing his
Book Entitl'd The Religion of Protestants A Safe Way to
Salvation : Together with His Nine Sermons preached
before the King, or vpon eminent Occasions . . . with
Nine Additional Discourses.   Lon., 1704, folio.
CLAGETT, William : Seventeen Sermons . . . 2nd ed.
                                         Lon., 1704, 8vo.
Eleven Sermons . . . 3rd ed.   Lon., 1704, 8vo.
CLARKE, John : Leaven, corrupting the Childrens Bread . . .
in two sermons . . . 1645.   Lon., 1646, 4to.
CLARKE, Samuel : The Works . . . in four Volumes [Vols.
i and ii contain sermons.]   Lon., 1738, folio.
CLEAVER. Robt. : Foure Sermons. The two first Of Godly
Feare . . . by Robt. Cleaver. The two last . . . by
Rich. Webb. [*Vid. infra* Dod.]   Lon., 1613, 4to.
CLELAND, James : Jacobs Well and Abbots Conduit Paralleled,
Preached and Applied to the Use of the Citie of Canterbury.
                                         Lon., 1626, 4to.

CLERKE, Rich. : Sermons . . . [Edited posthumously by Chas. White.] Lon., 1637, folio.

COKAYN, Geo. : Flesh Expiring . . . Lon., 1648, 4to.

COLEMAN, Thomas : The Hearts Ingagement : a Sermon Preached at St. Margarets Westminster . . . 1643 [At the taking of the Covenant.] Lon., 1643.

The Christians Covrse and Complaint . . . a ser. prd. to the Hble. H. of C. Lon., 1643, 4to.

Hopes Deferred . . . before H. of. C. Lon., 1645, 4to.

COLLIER, Giles : The taking Away of Righteous & Merciful Persons . . . Oxf., 1661, 4to.

COLLIER, Jeremy : The Difference between the Present and Future State of our Bodies Considered in a Sermon . . . Lon., 1686, 4to.

Several Discourses Upon Practical Subjects. Lon., 1725, 8vo.

COLLINGES, John : Elisha's Lamentation for Elijah . . . 1655. Lon., 1657, 4to.

CONANT, John (Rector of Exeter College 1649–62) : The Woe and Weale of Gods People. Displayed in a ser. prd. before the Hble. H. of C. . . . 1643. Lon., 1643, 4to.

Sermons Preach'd on Several Occasions. [Published by John Williams, bp. of Chichester.] Vols. i & ii, 2nd ed., Lon., 1699, 8vo ; Vols. iii–iv, Lon., 1698–1722, 8vo.

COOPER, John : The Foolish Prophets Displayed . . . Lon., 1636, 4to.

COOPER, Thomas : The Worldlings Aduenture Discovering the feareful estate of all Earth-wormes, and men of this World . . . Deliuered in two Sermons . . . at Ovendell . . . Lon., 1619, 4to.

CORBETT, Edward : Gods Providence, a ser. prd. before the Hble. H. of C. . . . 1642. Lon., 1642, 4to.

CORBETT, Rich., bp. of Oxford : *Oratio Funebris Habita in Schola Theologica . . . in obitu Clarissimi Equitis Thomæ Bodleii* [Part of 'Ivsta Fvnebria Ptolomæi Oxoniensis T—. B—. . . .' Oxford, 1613. It is included in ' Trecentale Bodleianum,' 1913.]

COSIN, John, bp. of Durham : The Works . . . First Collected. [Library of Anglo-Catholic Theol.] Oxf., 1843–1855, 8vo. [Vol. i contains sermons.]

COTTON, John (of Boston, New England) : Gods Mercie Mixed With His Iustice . . . edited by Matt. Swallowe. Lon., 1641, 4to. [' Gods Mercie Manifest in His Iustice ' and ' The Wicked Craft to insnare Gods People ' follow in same volume.]

The Covenant of Gods Free Grace. Lon., 1646, 4to.

COOPER [or COUPER], Wm., bp. of Galloway : Two Sermons

preached in Scotland before the Kings Maiesty : The one, in his Chappell Royal of Holy-Roode house at his Highnesse comming in : The other, in the Church of Dumfries at His Highnesse going out . . . Lon., 1618, 4to.

The Triumph of a Christian Containing three excellent and heauenly Treatises . . . Lon., 1633, 4to.

CRADOCK, Walter : The Saints Fulnesse of Joy . . . before the H. of C. Lon., 1646, 4to.

CROOKE, Samuel : The Ministerial Husbandry and Building . . . 1612. Lon., 1615, 4to.

The Discovery of the Heart . . . a sermon preached . . . at Bath . . . 1613. Lon., 1615, 4to.

[A second ser., ' The Waking Sleeper,' is bound up with this.]

CUDWORTH, Ralph : A Sermon Preached before the Hble. H. of C. . . . March 31, 1647. Camb., 1647, 4to.

A Sermon Preached to the Honourable Society of Lincolnes-Inne . . . Lon., 1664, 4to.

CULVERWEL, Nathanael : Spiritual Opticks . . . a sermon . . . Camb., 1651, 4to.

An Elegant and General Discourse of the Light of Nature, With severall other Treatises . . . Lon., 1654, 4to.

CUSHMAN, Robt. : A sermon preached at Plimmoth [sic] in New England, December 9, 1621 . . . Wherein is shewed the danger of selfe-loue . . . Together with a preface, Shewing the state of the country, and condition of the savages.
Lon., 1622, 4to.

DELL, William : The *Building* and *Glory* of the *truely Christian and Spiritual Church* . . . Preached to *His Excellency Sir Tho. Fairfax* and the General Officers of the Army . . . at Marston . . . June 7, 1646. Lon., 1646, 4to.

Right Reformation . . . before H. of C. Lon., 1646, 4to.

DENNE, Henry : The Man of Sin Discovered. Lon., 1645, 4to.

DILLINGHAM, William : Prove all things . . . Handled in two sermons at St. Maries in Cambridge, the first on the Commencement Sabbath, July 1, 1656 . . . Camb., 1656, 4to.

A sermon at the Funeral of the Lady Elizabeth Alston . . . Septemb. 10, 1677. Lon., 1678, 4to.

DOD, John, and CLEAUER, Robt. : A Plaine and Familiar Exposition of the Ten Commandments . . .
Lon., 1609, 4to.

DOLBEN, John, archbp. of York : A sermon prd. before His Majesty on Good-Friday . . .1664/5. Lon., 1665, 4to.

A sermon preached before the King . . . June 20th, 1665. Being the Day of Solemn Thanksgiving for the late Victory at Sea. Lon., 1665, 4to.

DOMINIS, Antonio de :   Sermon De Mre Marc-Anthoine de Dominis, Archevesque de Spallato. Faict le premier Dimanche de l'Aduent, de l'année 1617 à Londres en la Chapelle des Merciers, qui est l'Eglise des Italiens à eux adressee. Traduit d'Italien en François.
                                                  Charenton, 1619, 4to.
DONNE, John, dean of St. Paul's :   LXXX Sermons . . .
                                                  Lon., 1640, folio.
Fifty Sermons . . .   Lon., 1649, folio.
XXVI Sermons . . .   Lon., 1660/1, folio.
The Works . . . 6 vols.   Lon., 1839, 8vo.
DOUGLAS, Robt. :   The Forme and Order of the Coronation of Charles the Second King of Scotland . . . as it was acted and done at Scoone . . . 1651.   Aberdeen, 1651, 4to.
     [Pp. 13–19 consist of ' Sermon preached at Scoone Jan. first 1651 At the Coronation of Charles the Second . . . by Master Robert Dowglas, Minister at Edinburgh, Moderator of the . . . Generall Assembly.']
Master Dowglasse His Sermon Preach't at the Downsitting of the last Parliament of Scotland, 1661.   Lon., 1661, 4to.
DOVE, Henry :   A ser. prd. before the Rt. Hble. the Ld. Mayor.
                                           Lon., 1682, 4to.
A ser. prd. before the King . . . 1684/5.   Lon., 1685, 4to.
DUPPA, Brian, bp. of Salisbury :   Angels Rejoicing for Sinners Repenting. Delivered in a Sermon . . . Lon., 1628, 4to.
The Soules Soliloquie . . . A Sermon before the King at Newport . . . 1648.   No pl., 1648, 4to.
DURHAM, William :   Encouragement to Charity. A Sermon preached at the Charterhouse Chapel . . . 1678.
                                            Lon., 1679, 4to.
DURYE, John :   Israels Call to March out of Babylon . . . [before H. of C.].   Lon., 1646, 4to.
DYKE, Dan. :   Six Evangelical Histories . . . opened and handled . . .   Lon., 1617, 4to.
EACHARD, John (of Darsham, Suffolk) :   Good Newes for all Christian Souldiers . . .   Lon., 1645, 4to.
The Axe against Sin and Error . . . a ser. on Matt, 3. 10.
                                            Lon., 1646, 4to.
EATON, Rich. :   A ser. preached at the Fvneralle of . . . Master Thomas Dutton . . .   Lon., 1616, 4to.
EEDES, Rich. :   Six Learned and godly Sermons : Preached some of them [3] before the Kings Maiestie, some [2] before Queene Elizabeth.   Lon., 1604, 8vo.
ELLIS, Clement :   A Ser. prd. on the 29th of May 1661.
                                               Oxf., 1661, 4to.

ELLIS, John junr. : The Sole Path to a Sound Peace . . . [before H. of C.].   Lon., 1643, 4to.
ESTWICK, Nicholas : A Learned and Godly Sermon Preached . . . MDCXXXI at the Funerall of Mr. Robert Bolton.
                                                      Lon., 1639, 4to.
EVANCE, Dan. : The Noble Order . . . [to the Lords] . . . 1645.   Lon., 1646, 4to.
FARRINGDON, Anthony : XXX Sermons.   Lon., 1657, folio.
    Forty Sermons [1] Preached at the Parish-Church of St. Mary Magdalene Milk-street, London.   Lon., 1663, folio.
    Fifty Sermons . . . [similarly prd.]   Lon., 1684, folio.
FATHERS, John : The Strife of Brethren . . . Two Sermons.
                                                      Lon., 1648, 4to.
    The Content of a Wayfaring Man . . . Two Sermons.
                                                      Lon., 1648, 4to.
FEAKE, Christopher (Fifth Monarchy man) : A Beam of Light Shining in the midst of much Darkness . . .
                                                      Lon., 1639, 4to.
FEATLEY (or FAIRCLOUGH), Dan. : Clavis Mystica. [70 sermons]
                                                      Lon., 1636, folio.
FELL, John, dean of Christ Church and bp. of Oxon : The Character of the last Daies. A sermon preached before the King.   Oxf., 1675, 4to.
    A sermon preached before the House of Peers on December 22, 1680 . . .   Oxf., 1680, 4to.
FENNER, William : The Works. [Being 14 sers. entitled ' A Treatise of the Affections : or the Souls Pulse . . . Together with Twenty Nine Choice Sers. . . .']
                                                      Lon., 1657, folio.
FENTON, Roger : A ser. preached at St. Mary Spittle . . . 1613.
                                                      Lon., 1616, 4to.
    A ser. at Mercers chapell in Lent 1614.   Lon., 1616, 4to.
    A ser. at the Funerall of Mr. John Stokile . . . 1613.
                                                      Lon., 1616, 4to.
    A sermon at the Funerall of Mr. John Newman . . .
                                                      Lon., 1616, 4to.
    [Two Sermons, one] Preached . . . 1616 in the Parish Church of S. Stephen in Walbrooke London ; the other At an anniversarie Solemnitie . . . of the Companie of Grocers of London.   Lon., 1615, 4to.
FLAVEL, John : The Whole Works . . . In Two Vols.
                                                      Lon., 1701, folio.

---

[1] The copy of the ' Forty Sermons ' in Exeter College Library was given to Rector Conant by Isaac Walton shortly before his death, and bears an inscription in Walton's handwriting : " Isaac Walton given to me by Mr, Marryot May 9, 1663."

FLEETWOOD, William, bp. of Ely : A Compleat Collection of the Sermons, Tracts, and Pieces of all Kinds.

             Lon., 1737, folio.

FORD, Simon : A Christian's Acquiescence.   Lon., 1665, 8vo.

FORSYTH, James : The Bitter Waters of Babylon.

             Lon., 1615, 4to.

FRANK, Mark : LI Sermons . . .   Lon., 1672, folio.

    [The foregoing are reprinted in two vols. in the Library of Anglo-Catholic Theol., Oxf., 1849.]

FREEMAN, John : A sermon preached without a Text at the Inner Temple . . . 1643.   Lon., 1643, 4to.

FREEMAN, Sam. : The Israelite Indeed. A ser. preached at the Funeral of Mark Cottle . . . 1681.   Lon., 1682, 4to.

FULLER, Thomas : The Collected Sermons . . . 1631–1659. Edited by the late John Eglington Bailey, F.S.A., Completed by William E. A. Axon, M.R.S.L. . . . 2 vols.

          Lon., 1891 (large paper ed.).

GAGE, Thomas : The Tyranny of Satan . . . a ser. preached in Paules Church . . . 1642.   Lon., 1642, 4to.

GALLOWAY, William : A Thanksgiving Sermon for the Peace Preach'd . . . 1697.   Lon., 1697, 4to.

GARDINER, Rich. : A ser. preached at St. Maries in Oxford . . . 1622.   Oxf., 1622, 4to.

    A sermon . . . on the day of His Maiesties Happy Inauguration . . . 1642.   Lon., 1642, 4to.

GASKARTH, John : A Description of the Unregenerate . . . in a ser. preach'd before the University of Cambridge, on Commencement Sunday . . . June 30, 1700.

          Camb., 1700, 4to.

GATAKER, Thos. : Gods Parley with Princes . . . The Svmme of two sermons . . .   Lon., 1620, 4to.

    The Christian Mans Care . . .   Lon., 1624, 4to.

    Jacobs Thankfulnesse to God . . .   Lon., 1624, 4to.

    Gods Eye on His Israel . . .   Lon., 1645, 4to.

    A Mistake or Misconstruction Removed.   Lon., 1646, 4to.

GAUDEN, John, bp. of Exeter : The Love of Trvth and Peace. A Sermon Preached before the Hble. H. of C. . . . Novemb. 29, 1640.   Lon., 1641, 4to.

    Three Sermons Preached upon Severall Publike Occasions.

          Lon., 1642, 4to.

    A ser. preached in the Temple-Chappel, at the Funeral of . . . Dr. Brounrig . . .   Lon., 1660, 8vo.

    ΜΕΓΑΛΕΙΑ ΘΕΟΥ. Gods great Demonstrations . . . a ser. prd. before the Hble. H. of C. . . . 1660. Lon., 1660, 4to.

GEE, Edward : Of the Improvement of Time. A ser. preached before the Queen . . . 1692.   Lon., 1692, 4to.

GEREE, John : The Red Horse . . . at Pauls . . . 1648.
Lon., 1648, 4to.

GIBSON, Sam. : The Ruine of the Authors and Fomentors of Civill Warres . . . [before H. of C.].　　Lon., 1648, 4to.

GILBERT, William : Architectonica Consolationis . . .
Lon., 1640, 4to.

GILLESPIE, Geo. : A ser. preached before the Hble. H. of C. . . . 1644.　　Lon., 1644, 4to.

A ser. preached before the Rt. Hble. the H. of L. Lon., 1645, 4to.

GIPPS, Geo. : A ser. preached . . . to the Hble. H. of C.
Lon., 1645, 4to.

GLANVILL, Joseph : Some Discourses, Sermons, And Remains . . . pub. by Anthony Horneck.　　Lon., 1681, 4to.

GOODWIN, John : ΘΕΟΜΑΧΙΑ ; Or the Grand Impudence of man running the hazard of Fighting Against God.
Lon., 1644, 4to.

PHILADELPHIA : Or, XL Queries on Baptism.
Lon., 1653, 4to.

ΒΑΣΑΝΙΣΤΑΙ. Or the Triers Tried.　　Lon., 1657, 4to.

πλήρωμα τὸ πνευματικόν. Or . . . the Divinity . . . of the Holy Ghost Asserted . . . in several Sermons . . .
Lon., 1670, 4to.

GOODWIN, Thomas : The Works . . . [5 vols.]
Lon., 1681–1704, folio.

GOUGE, William : The Saints Support . . . [before H. of C.].
Lon., 1642, 4to.

The Progress of Divine Providence . . . [before H. of Peers].
Lon., 1645, 4to.

The Right Way . . . before the Lords.　　Lon., 1648, 4to.

A Learned . . . Commentary on the whole Epistle to the Hebrewes . . . 2 vols.　　Lon., 1655, folio.

GRANT, John : Gods Deliverance of Man by Prayer.
Lon., 1642, 4to.

GRAY, Andrew : The Mystery of Faith . . . Or some Sermons concerning Faith . . . Whereunto are added other three Sermons, Two concerning the Great Salvation . . . and a third concerning Death.　　Edin., 1671, 12mo.

The Spiritual Warfare : Or, some Sermons concerning the Nature of Mortification . . . Whereunto are added other two Sermons concerning the Mystery of Contentment.
Lon., 1679, 8vo.

Eleven Communion Sermons . . .　　Edin., 1716, 8vo.

GREENE, John : Nehemiah's Teares . . . [before H. of C.].
Lon., 1644, 4to.

The Churches Duty for received Mercies . . . [before H. of C.] . . . 1646.　　Lon., 1647, 4to.

GREENHILL, William : The Axe at the Root . . . before H. of C.   Lon., 1643, 4to.
   The Sound-hearted Christian . . . With several other Sermons . . .   Lon., 1671, 8vo.

GREGORY, Francis : Teares and Bloud. [2 sers. at St. Mary's, Oxford.]   Oxf., 1660, 4to.

GREGORY, John : The Works . . .   Lon., 1671, 4to.

GRENVILLE, Denis : The Compleat Conformist . . . in a ser. preached . . . in Durham Cathedral . . . 1682. Lon., 1684, 4to.
   A ser. preached in the Cathedral Church of Durham, Upon the Revival of the Ancient Laudable Practice . . . in having Sermons on Wednesdays and Fridays, during Advent and Lent.   Lon., 1686, 4to.

GRIFFITH, Matt. : A Patheticall Perswasion to pray for Publick Peace . . .   Lon., 1642, 4to.

GUNNING, Peter, bp. of Ely : The Paschal or Lent-Fast . . . At first deliver'd in a ser. preached before his Majesty in Lent, and since enlarged . . .   Lon., 1662, 4to.

GURNALL, William : The Christian in Compleat Armour . . .
   The first part.   Lon., 1655, 4to.
   The second part.   Lon., 1658, 4to.
   The third and last part.   Lon., 1662, 4to.
   The Christians Labour and Reward . . . a sermon . . .
                    Lon., 1672, 8vo.

HACKET, John, bp. of Lichfield : A Century of Sermons . . . pub. by Thomas Plume, D.D.   Lon., 1675, folio.

HAKEWILL, Geo. (Rector of Exeter Coll., 1642–49) : King Davids Vow for Reformation . . . Deliuered in twelve sermons before the Prince his Highnesse vpon Psalm 101.
                    Lon., 1621, 8vo.
   A Comparison between the Dayes of Purim and that of the Powder treason . . .   Oxf., 1626, 4to.

HALES, John, provost of Eton : Golden Remains . . . The Second Impression.   Lon., 1673, 4to.

HALL, Joseph, bp. of Exeter : The Works . . . [Contains 12 sermons.]   Lon., 1625, folio.
   The Works . . . A New Ed. in 12 vols.   Oxf., 1837, 8vo.
     [Vol. v contains 42 sermons.]

HAMMOND, Henry : The Christians Obligations to Peace and Charity. Delivered In a Advent Sermon at *Carisbrooke Castle, Ann.* 1647. And Now published with ix Sermons more . . .   Lon., 1649, 4to.
   The Works . . . 4 vols. [Vol. iv contains ' A Paraphrase and Annotations upon the Psalms, As also upon the ten first chapters Proverbs [*sic*], together with xxi Sermons.']
                    Lon., 1684, folio.

Howe, John : The Works . . . 2 vols. Lon., 1724, folio.

Hughes, Geo. : The Art of Embalming Dear Saints . . .
Lon., 1642, 4to.

VAE—EVGE—TUBA. Or, the Wo—Ioy—Trumpet—[a ser.
before H. of C.]. Lon., 1647, 4to.

Jackson, Thos. (President of C.C.C., Oxford) : Nazareth to
Bethlehem. Oxf., 1617, 4to.

Diverse Sermons. Oxf., 1637, 4to.

The Works . . . 2 vols. Lon., 1673, folio.

Jackson, Thos. (Prebend. of Canterbury) : Judah must into
Captivitie : Six Sermons Lately preached in the Cathedral
Church of Christ in Canterburie . . . Lon., 1622, 4to.

The Raging Tempest stilled . . . Opened and explained in
weekly Lectures . . . in the Cathedral Church of Christ
Canterb. Lon., 1623, 8vo.

Christs Answer unto Johns Questions. Lon., 1625, 4to.

Jacobson, John : Ecclesiastes. The Worthy Churchman, Or,
The Faithfvll Minister of Jesus Christ. Described by
polishing the twelve Stones in the High-Priests Pectorall ;
as they were first glossed . . . in a Synod-Sermon ; and after
enlarged by way of discourse, to his two Brethren.
Lon., 1628, 4to.

Jenkyn, William : The Stil-Destroyer . . . [before Ld. Mayor].
Lon., 1645, 4to.

Reformation's Remora . . . [before H. of Peers].
Lon., 1646, 4to.

A Sleeping Sicknes . . . [before H. of Peers].
Lon., 1647, 4to.

Jessop, Constant : The Angel of the Church of Ephesus No
Bishop. Lon., 1644, 4to.

Jones, David : A ser. . . . at St. Mary's, Oxford, 1698.
Oxf., 1698, 4to.

Kelsey, Joseph : Christ Crucified. A ser. preached at Salisbury . . . 1691. Lon., 1691, 4to.

Ken, Thos., bp. of Bath and Wells : The Prose Works . . .
Collected by James Round, B.D. . . . [There are three
sermons in this volume.] Lon., 1838, 8vo.

Kentish, Rich. : A Sure Stay for a Sinking State . . . [before
H. of C.]. Lon., 1648, 4to.

Kettlewell, John (Nonjuror) : A Compleat Collection of the
Works . . . 2 vols. Lon., 1719, folio.
[Vol. i. contains 9 ' Discourses.']

Kiffin, William : Certain Observations Vpon Hosea.
Lon., 1642, 4to.

King, Henry, bp. of Oxford : David's Enlargement . . .
Lon., 1625, 4to.

28

A Sermon of Deliverance . . . at the Spittle on Easter
Monday, 1626.   Lon., 1626, 4to.
Two sers. preached at White-Hall in Lent . . . 1625 and
. . . 1626.   Lon., 1627, 4to.
An Exposition vpon the Lords Prayer . . . in certain sers.,
in the Cathedral Church of S. Paul.   Lon., 1628, 4to.
A ser. preached at St. Pavls March 27, 1640, Being the
Anniversary of his Majesties Happy Inauguration.
                                        Lon., 1640, 4to.
A ser. preached before the Kings Most Excellent Majesty
at Oxford.   Oxf., 1643, 4to.
KING, John, bp. of London : The Fovrth Sermon Preached at
Hampton Court . . . 1606.   Oxf., 1606, 4to.
A ser. preached in Oxon : the 5 of November 1607.
                                        Oxf., 1607, 4to.
A ser. preached in St. Maries at Oxford . . . the day of his
sacred Maiesties Inauguration . . .   Oxf., 1608, 4to.
A ser. preached at White-Hall the 5 day of November ann.
1608.   Oxf., 1608, 4to.
Vitis Palatina. A ser. appointed to be preached at Whitehall
upon the Tuesday after the mariage [sic] of the Ladie
Elizabeth . . .   Lon., 1614, 4to.
A ser. of Pvblicke Thanks-Giving for the happy recouery of
his Maiesty . . . 1619.   Lon., 1619, 4to.
A ser. at Paules Crosse . . . 1620.   Lon., 1620, 4to.
KING, John (prebend of Ch. Ch., Oxon) : Davids Strait . . .
[Printed with ' Davids Enlargement.' Vid. supra Henry
King.]   Oxf., 1625, 4to.
KNELL, Paul : The Life-Guard of a Loyall Christian . . .
                                        Lon., 1648, 4to.
LAKE, Arthur, bp. of Bath and Wells : Sermons with some
Religious and Diuine Meditations.   Lon., 1629, folio.
Ten Sermons Vpon Severall Occasions . . . Lon., 1641, 4to.
LANEY, Benjamin, bp. of Ely : A Sermon Preached before His
Majesty at Whitehall, April 5, 1663 . . . Lon., 1663, 4to.
A Sermon Preached before His Majesty at Whitehall,
March 12 166⅘ . . .   Lon., 1665, 4to.
LANGFORD, Geo. : Manassehs Miracvlous Metamorphosis . . .
a ser. preached before the thrice-famous Vniversity of
Cambridge . . . 1621.   Lon., 1621, 4to.
LAUD, William, archbp. of Canterbury : The Works . . .
[Library of Anglo-Cath. Theol.]. 7 vols. Oxf., 1847, 8vo.
[Vol. i contains seven sermons.]
LEIGHTON, Robt., archbp. of Glasgow : The Works . . . To
which is prefixed a Life of the Author by James Aikman,
Esq., Complete in One Volume.   Lon., 1848, 8vo.

Ley, Robt. : The Fvry of Warre . . . before H. of C.
Lon., 1643, 4to.
   A Monitor of Mortalitie, in two sers.   Lon., 1643, 4to.
Ley, Robt. : The Scepter of Righteousness. A ser. prd. at
   Paules Crosse . . .   Lon., 1619, 4to.
Lightfoot, John : Elias Redivivus : A ser. preached before the
   Hble. H. of C. . . .   Lon., 1643, 4to.
   A ser. preached before the Hble. H. of C. . . . Lon., 1645, 4to.
   A ser. preached before the Hble. H. of C. . . . Lon., 1647, 4to.
   The Works . . . 2 vols.   Lon., 1684, folio.
      [Vol. ii, 2nd part contains sers.]
Littleton, Adam (the Lexicographer) : Sixty One Sermons . . .
Lon., 1680, folio.
Lloyd, William, bp. of Worcester : A ser. preached at the
   Funeral of . . . John [Wilkins] late Ld. bp. of Chester. . .
   1672.   Lon., 1672, 4to.
   A Ser. at the Funeral of Sr Edmund-Bury Godfrey . . . 1678.
Lon., 1678, 4to.
Lockyer, Nicholas : A Ser. preached before the Hble. H. of C.
Lon., 1646, 4to.
Loe, William : The Kings Shoe . . . A Sermon before the King
   at Theobalds . . . 1622.   Lon., 1622, 4to.
Love, Christopher (principal in ' Love's Plot ') : Englands
   Distemper . . .   Lon., 1645, 4to.
   The Christians Directory . . .   Lon., 1653, 4to.
   The Combate between the Flesh and Spirit . . . being the
   summe . . . of xxvii Sermons.   Lon., 1654, 4to.
   Grace : The Truth and Growth . . . Thereof. The summe
   and substance of xv Sermons.   Lon., 1654, 4to.
   Hell's Terror Or a Treatise of the Torments of the Damned.
Lon., 1655, 4to.
   A Treatise of Effectual Calling and Election in xvi Sermons.
Lon., 1655, 4to.
Love, Rich. : The Watchmans Watchword.   Lon., 1642, 4to.
Lovell, Robt. : The Publican Becoming a Penitent. [2 Sers.]
Lon., 1625, 4to.
Lowde, James : The Reasonableness of the Christian Religion,
   a Sermon . . . at Stickley in Cleveland, in Yorkshire.
Lon., 1684, 4to.
Lucas, Rich. : An Enquiry after Happiness. Vol. i.
Lon., 1685, 8vo.
   Humane Life Or, A second part of the Enquiry . . . 3rd ed.
Lon., 1696, 8vo.
   Religious Perfection : Or, A third part of the Enquiry.
Lon., 1696, 8vo.
   Twelve Sermons . . .   Lon., 1699, 8vo.

LYNCH, John : Three Sermons, Two of Them Appointed for the Spittle . . . by John Squier . . . and John Lynch. [*Vid. infra* John Squire.]   Lon., 1637, 4to.

A ser. preached in S. Pauls Church in London.
          Lon., 1637, 4to.

Pasche Christianum . . .   Lon., 1637, 4to.

MANNINGHAM, Thos., bp. of Chichester : Praise and Adoration. Or, a ser. on Trinity-Sunday before the University of Oxford 1681.   Lon., 1682, 4to.

The Nature and Effects of Superstition . . . before the Hble. H. of C. . . . the fifth of November, 1692.
          Lon., 1692, 4to.

A Sermon Concerning Publick Worship . . . 1691/2.
          Lon., 1692, 4to.

A ser. preached at the Parish-Church of St. Andrews Holborn, the 30th of December 1694. On the most lamented Death of our most Gracious Sovereign Queen Mary.
          Lon., 1695, 4to.

A sermon upon the late Dreadful Storm . . . 1703.
          Lon., 1704, 4to.

MARTIN, Thos. : Englands Spirituall Languishing . . . [before H. of C.]   Lon., 1648, 4to.

The Blessed Estate of them that die in the Lord.
          Lon., 1656, 4to.

MARSHALL, Stephen : A ser. preached before the Hble. H. of C. 1640.   Lon., 1641, 4to.

A Peace Offering to God. A ser. preached to the Hble. H. of C. . . .   Lon., 1641, 4to.

Meroz Cursed Or, a ser. preached to the Hble. H. of C.
          Lon., 1641, 4to.

Reformation and Desolation : Or a ser. preached to the Hble. H. of C. . . . 1641.   Lon., 1642, 4to.

The Song of Moses . . . in a ser. preached to the Hble. H. of C.   Lon., 1643, 4to.

A Sacred Record . . . A Thanksgiving ser. preached to the two Houses of Parliament . . . June 19, 1645. Being the Day of their Publick Thanksgiving to Almighty God for the Great and Glorious Victory . . in Naseby-field.
          Lon., no date, 4to.

The Strong Helper . . . a ser. before the Hble. H. of C.
          Lon., 1645, 4to.

Gods Masterpiece. A ser. . . . preached to the Rt. Hble. the House of Peers . . .   Lon. 1645, 4to.

A Two-edged Sword out of the Movth of Babes . . .
          Lon., 1646, 4to.

A Sermon preached to the two Houses of Parliament . . .
1647.   Lon., 1647, 4to.
Emmanuel : A Thanksgiving ser. preached to the Hble.
H. of C. . . .   Lon., 1648, 4to.
A Thanksgiving ser. preached to the Rt. Hble. the Lord
Maior . . . 1648.   Lon., 1648, 4to.
The Sinne of Hardnesse of Heart . . . a ser. preached to the
Hble. H. of C. . . .   Lon., 1648, 4to.
The Power of the Civil Magistrate in matters of Religion
vindicated . . . in a ser. preached before . . . Parl.
[Pub. posthumously by Geo. Firmin.]   Lon., 1657, 4to.
MAYNARD, John : A ser. prd. to the Hble. H. of C. . . . 1644.
                                             Lon., 1645, 4to.
A Shadow of the Victory of Christ . . . before H. of C.
                                             Lon., 1646, 4to.
MAYNE, Jasper : A Sermon Concerning Unity and Agreement.
Preached at Carfax Chvrch in Oxford . . . 1646.
                                         No place, 1646, 4to.
A late Printed Sermon Against False Prophets, Vindicated
by Letter, From the causeless Aspersions of Mr. Francis
Cheynell.   No place, 1647, 4to.
A Sermon Against Schisme : . . . Preacht in the Church of
Wattlington in Oxford-shire, with some Interruptions,
September 11, 1652. At a publick dispute held there, Be-
tween Jasper Mayne, D.D.   And one——   Lon., 1652, 4to.
A Sermon Preached at the Consecration of . . . Herbert
[Croft] Lord Bishop of Hereford . . .   Lon., 1662, 4to.
MEDE, Joseph : The Works . . . 3rd ed.   Lon., 1672, folio.
MEWE, William : The Robbing and Spoiling of Jacob and
Israel . . [before the H. of C.]   Lon., 1643, 4to.
MILLER, William : A ser. preached at the Fvnerall of the
Worshipful Gilbert Davies Esquire, at Christow in Deuen.
                                             Lon., 1621, 4to.
MOCKET, Thos. : Gospell Duty and Dignity.   Lon., 1648, 4to.
MOORE, John, bp. of Norwich : A ser. preached on the 28th of
June, at St. Andrewes' Holborn . . .   Lon., 1691, 4to.
MORE, Henry : [16] Discourses on Several Texts of Scripture
. . .   Lon., 1692, 8vo.
MORLEY, Geo., bp. of Worcester : A ser. preached at the
Magnificent Coronation of . . . Charles the IId . . . the
23d of April . . . 1661.   Lon., 1661, 4to.
A ser. preached before the King . . . November 5, 1667.
                                             Lon., 1683, 4to.
MORTON, Thos., bp. of Durham : A ser. preached before the
Kings most Excellent Majestie, in the Cathedrall Church of
Dvrham . . . 1639.   Lon., 1639, 4to.

The Presentment of a Schismaticke . . . in his sermon preached at the Cathedral Church of Saint Pauls the 19. of June 1642. Lon., 1642, 4to.

MOSSOM, Robt., bp. of Derry : The King on his Throne . . . 2 sers. at York. Lon., 1642, 4to.

MYRIELL, Thos. : The Stripping of Joseph . . . Lon., 1625, 4to.

NALTON, James : Delay of Reformation provoking Gods further Indignation . . . [before H. of C.]. Lon., 1646, 4to.

NEWCOMEN, Matt. : The Craft and Crvelty of the Churches Adversaries . . . [before H. of C.]. Lon., 1643, 4to.

Jerusalems Watch-Men . . . before H. of C. Lon., 1643, 4to.

The Duty of such as would Walke Worthy of the Gospel . . . a ser. at Pauls . . . 1646. Lon., 1646, 4to.

NEWTON, Geo : Mans Wrath and Gods Praise . . . Lon., 1646, 4to.

NICHOLLS, Wm. : The Advantage of a Learned Education. Being a Sermon Preached at the *Cathedral Church of St. Paul* On St. *Paul's* Day 169⅞. Before the Gentlemen Educated at *That* School, upon the Reviving their Antient Anniversary Meeting. Lon., 169⅞, 4to.

NORRIS, John (of Bemerton) : A ser. preached before the University of Oxford . . . 1685. Oxf., 1685, 4to.

. . . Discourses Upon the Beatitudes. Lon., 1690, 8vo.

NOURSE, Peter : A ser. preached at the Publick Commencement at Cambridge . . . July 1698. Lon., 1698, 4to.

NYE, Stephen : A Discourse concerning Natural and Revealed Religion. Lon., 1696 (sixes).

OATES, Titus (figure in ' The Popish Plot ') : A ser. preached at St. Michaels Wood-street . . . Lon., 1679, 4to.

OLDISWORTH, Giles : The Father of the Faithfull Tempted . . . Oxf., 1676, 4to.

OUTRAM, William : Twenty Sermons Preached upon Several Occasions. Lon., 1682, 8vo.

OWEN, John : The Works . . . Edited by Thomas Russell, M.A. With Memoirs of his Life and Writings by William Orme. 21 vols. Lon., 1826, 8vo.

[Vols. xv, xvi, and xvii contain sers.]

PALMER, Herbert : The Dvty and Honovr of Church-Restorers . . . [before the H. of C.] Lon., 1646, 4to.

PARR, Elnathan : The Workes . . . 3rd ed. Lon., 1633, folio.

PATRICK, Simon, bp. of Chester : A ser. preached before . . . the Prince of Orange . . . January, 1688 [with a second part of same]. Lon., 1689, 4to.

Two sers. One against Murmuring, the other against Censuring, preached at St. Pauls Covent-Garden. Lon., 1689, 4to.

A ser. preached before the Queen . . . 1688/9. Lon., 1689, 4to.

A ser. prd. before the King and Queen . . .1690.
                              Lon., 1690, 4to.
A ser. preached before the Queen . . . 1692. Lon., 1692, 4to.
   [*Vid. infra* John Smith, 'Select Discourses,' to which is
   annexed a ser. preached by Patrick at Smith's funeral.]
PEARSON, John, bp. of Chester : The Minor Theological Works
   . . . Now first collected, with a Memoir of the Author
   . . . by Edward Churton, M.A.   2 vols.   Oxf., 1844, 8vo.
   [Vol. ii contains a number of sermons, Latin and
   English.]
PELLING, Edward : David and the Amalekite . . . a ser.
   preached on Jan. 30, 1682.   Lon., 1683, 4to.
A Discourse Concerning the Existence of God.
                              Lon., 1696, 8vo.
PERNE, Andrew : Gospel Courage . . . before H. of C.
                              Lon., 1643, 4to.
A ser. preached before the Hble. H. of C. 1643.
         [No title-page, only sermon-top.]   — 4to.
PETERS, Hugh : Gods Doings and Mans Duty . . . in a ser.
   preached before both Houses of Parliament . . . 1645 . . .
                              Lon., 1646, 4to.
A ser. . . . preached before his Death.   Lon., 1660, 4to.
PETERS, Thos. : A Remedie Against Ruine . . . a ser. preached
   at the Assises at Lanceston . . 1651.   Lon., 1652, 4to.
PHILIPS, Edward : Certaine Godly and Learned Sermons . . .
   Deliuered . . . in Saint Sauiours in Southwarke. And
   taken by the pen of H. Yeluerton . . .   Lon., 1605, 4to.
PIERCE, Thos. : A ser. preached at St. Margarets in Westminster
   before the Hble. H. of C. . . . the 29th Day of May.
                              Lon., 1661, 4to.
The Primitive Rule of Reformation . . . in a ser. before his
   Majesty . . . Feb. 1, 1602 . . .   Oxf., 1663, 4to.
A Collection of xi [actually x] Sermons Upon Several Occa-
   sions. [Including 'The Primitive Rule of Reformation,'
   heard by Pepys at Whitehall, Feb. 1, 1662.]   Oxf., 1671, 4to.
The Law and Equity of the Gospel . . . And other sers.
                              Lon., 1686, 4to.
PIKERING, Benjamin : A Firebrand Pluckt out of the Bvrning.
   A ser. . . . before the Hble. H. of C. . . . 1644.
                              Lon., 1645, 4to.
PLAYFERE, Thos. : The Whole Sermons of That Eloquent
   Divine. . .   Lon., 1623, 8vo.
POWELL, Walter : Newes of Newters . . . a ser. 1644.
                              Lon., 1648, 4to.
PRESTON, John : [5] Sermons preached before his Maiestie,
   and vpon other speciale occasions.   Lon., 1631, 4to.

Fovr Godly and Learned Treatises . . . 3rd ed. Lon., 1635, 4to.

PRICE, Dan. : The Spring, a ser. preached before the Prince at S. James . . .   Lon., 1609, 4to.

Spiritvall Odovrs to the Memory of Prince Henry. In Fovre of the Last Sermons preached in St. James after his Highnesse death.   Oxf., 1613, 4to.

Maries Memoriall . . .   Lon., 1617, 4to.

PRICE, Sampson : The Beavty of Holines . . . Lon., 1642, 4to.

PRICE, William : A ser. preached at St. Maries Spittle . . . 1642.   Lon., 1642, 4to.

PRIDEAUX, John (rector of Exeter Coll., Oxford, 1612–1642), bp. of Worcester : A ser. preached on the fifth of October 1624 At the Consecration of St. James Chappell in Exeter Colledge.

Christs Covnsell for ending Law Cases . . . in two sermons.

A Christians Free-Will Offering . . . in a ser. on Christmasse day at Ch. Ch. in Oxford.

Gowries Conspiracie. A ser. preached at St. Maries in Oxford.

Higgaion & Selah : For the Discouery of the Powder-Plot A ser. preached at St. Maries in Oxford.

Reverence to Rvlers. A ser. preached at the Covrt.

The Dravght of the Brooke. A ser. preached at the Covrt.

Dauids Reioycing for Christs Resvrrection.

The Christians Expectation. A ser. preached at the Covrt.

Idolatrovs Feasting. A ser. preached at the Covrt.

Ephesvs Backsliding . . . in a ser. preached at Oxford in St. Maries.

The First Frvits of the Resvrrection.

Hezekiah's sicknesse and recouery.

Perez-Vzzah . . . in a ser. before his Majesty at Woodstocke Avgvst . . . 1624.

Wisdomes Ivstification. A ser. preached at the Covrt.

Heresies Progresse . . . a ser. preached at the Covrt.

A Plot for Preferment. A ser. preached at the Covrt.

The Patronage of Angels. A ser. preached at the Covrt.

           All the above : Oxf., 1636, 4to.

[The above are collected in one volume in Exeter College Library, but with separate title-pages and pagination ; the title-page and pp. 1–4 of ' Hezekiah's sicknesse . . .' are lacking.]

PRIOR, Thos. : A ser. at the Fvnerall of the Rt. Rev. Father in God, Miles [Smith], Late Ld. bp. of Glovcester . . . 1632.
[Appended to fol. vol. of Smith's sers., *vid. infra* Miles Smith.]

RAMSEY, John : Morbus Epidemicus . . .   Lon., 1656, 4to.

READING, John : A ser. delivered at Maidston . . . Assizes
. . . 1641. Lon., 1642, 4to.

REYNER, Edward : Orders from the Lord of Hostes . . .
Lon., 1646, 4to.

REYNOLDS, Edward, bp. of Norwich : The Peace of Jerusalem.
A ser. preached in the Parliament-House . . .
Lon., 1656, 4to.

Sion's Praises Opened in a Sermon. Lon., 1657, 4to.

An Explication of the fourteenth Chapter of the Prophet
Hosea, in several sermons . . . Lon., 1658, 4to.

The Works . . . Lon., 1658, folio.

The Wall & Glory of Jerusalem . . . before . . . the Lord
Mayor . . . 1659. Lon., 1659, 4to.

Divine Efficacy without Humane Power . . . in a ser. before
the Rt. Hble. the H. of C. . . . 1660. Lon., 1660, 4to.

The Author and Subject of Healing in the Church . . . before
the Rt. Hble. the Parliament . . . 1660. Lon., 1660, 4to.

A Sermon Preached before the Peers . . . *November* 7, 1666.
Being a Day of Solemn Humiliation for the Continuing
Pestilence . . . Lon., 1666, 4to.

A Sermon Preached before the King At White-Hall, On
March 22, 1667. Lon., 1668, 4to.

ROMAN CATHOLIC SERMONS : A Select Collection of Catholic
Sermons Preach'd before their Majesties King James II,
Mary Queen-Consort, Catherine Queen-Dowager, &c.
2 vols. Lon., 1741, 4to.
    [By the Reverend Fathers : Ayray, Betham, Bix, Cod-
rington, Ellis, Giffard, Godden, Levison, Scarisbrike,
Humberstone, Cross, Hall, Persall, Jenks, and Blake.]

RUDD, Anthony, bp. of St. Davids : A ser. preached at the Court
. . . before the Kings Maiesty vpon Sunday . . . 13 of
May 1604. Lon., 1604, 8vo.

RULE, Gilbert : A Sermon Preached before His Grace the
Kings Commissioner, And the Three Estates of Parliament
[in Scotland] May the 25th, 1690. Edin., 1690, 4to.

Two Sermons Preached at the Meeting of the Council of
George Heriot's Hospital, At Edinburgh [of which the
former is by Rule]. Edin., 1695, 4to.

RUST, Geo., bp. of Dromore : A ser. preached at Newtown the
29 of Octob. 1663. At the Funeral of the Rt. Honourable
Hugh Earl of Mount-Alexander . . . Dublin, 1664, 4to.

A Funeral Sermon Preached at the Obsequies of the Right
Reverend Father in God Jeremy [Taylor] Lord Bishop of
Down . . . 1667. Lon., 1668, 4to.

RUTHERFORD, Sam. : A ser. preached before the Rt. Hble. H. of
L. at Westminster . . . 1645. Lon., 1645, 4to.

The Trial and Triumph of Faith . . .   Edin., 1845, 8vo.
Fourteen Communion Sermons . . . with a Preface and Notes
by the Rev. Andrew A. Bonar, D.D.
          Glasgow (preface signed 1876 ; 2nd ed. 1877), 8vo.
Quaint Sermons . . . Hitherto Unpublished With a preface
by the Rev. A. A. Bonar, D.D.   Lon., 1885, 8vo.

SANCROFT, William, archbp. of Canterbury : A ser. preached in
St. Peter's Westminster . . . at the consecration of seven
bishops.   Lon., 1660, 4to.
Lex Ignea . . . a ser. preached before the King Octob. 10,
1666. At the Solemn Fast appointed for the late Fire in
London . . .   Lon., 1666, 4to.
A ser. preached to the H. of Peers . . . 1678.
          Lon., 1678, 4to.
Occasional Sermons . . .   Lon., 1694, 8vo.
    [The last consists of the foregoing and no other sermons.]

SANDERSON, Robt., bp. of Lincoln : Two Sermons preached at
Pavles-Crosse, London . . .   Lon., 1628, 4to.
XXXIV Sermons . . . 6th ed.   Lon., 1674, folio.
The Works . . . Now first collected by William Jacobson,
D.D. . . . 6 vols.   Oxf., 1854, 8vo.
    [Vol. iii contains the sermons.]

SCLATER, William : The Remedie of Schisme . . .
          Lon., 1643, 4to.
The Royal Pay . . . Delivered . . . before the Honourable
Military Company . . .   Lon., 1671, 4to.

SCOTT, John : A ser. preached before the Hble. the Ld. Mayor.
          Lon., 1673, 4to.
A ser. preached before the Rt. Hble. the Ld. Mayor, 1683.
          Lon., 1684, 4to.
A ser. preached before the Rt. Hble. the Ld. Mayor . . .
          Lon., 1686, 4to.
A ser. preached at the Funeral of Sr. John Buckworth . . .
1687.   Lon., 1688, 4to.

SEAMAN, Lazarus : A Glasse for the Times . . .
          Lon., 1650, 4to.

SEDGWICK, Obadiah : England's Preservation Or a ser. . . .
preached to the Hble. H. of C. . . . 1642.
          Lon., 1642, 4to.
Hamans Vanity . . . before H. of C.   Lon., 1643, 4to.
The Best and the Worst Magistrate . . .   Lon., 1648, 4to.

SEDGWICK, William : Scripture a Perfect Rule . . .
          Lon., no date, 4to.
Zion's Deliverance . . . before H. of C. 2nd ed.
          Lon., 1643, 4to.

SERMON, Edmund : The Wisdom of Publick Piety Discoursed in a Sermon . . . before . . . the Lord Mayor . . . 1679.
Lon., 1679, 4to.

SHARP, John, archbp. of York : A ser. preached before the Lords Spiritual and Temporal . . . the fifth of November, 1691. Lon., 1691, 4to.

A ser. preached before the King & Queen . . . on Christmas Day, 1691. Lon., 1692, 4to.

A ser. preached before the Queen . . . Easter-Day . . . 1692. Lon., 1692, 4to.

SHARROCK, Robt. : De Finibus Virtutis Christianæ. Preached in Winchester Cathedral. Oxf., 1673, 4to.

SHAWL, John : A Broken Heart. Lon., 1643, 4to.

SHELDON, Gilbert, archbp. of Canterbury : Davids Deliverance and Thanksgiving. A ser. preached before the King at Whitehall . . . June 28, 1660. Being the Day of Solemn Thanksgiving for the Happy Return of His Majesty.
Lon., 1660, 4to.

SHELDON, Rich. : A ser. preached at Pavls Crosse . . . by Rich. Sheldon, a Conuert from out of Babylon . . .
Lon., 1625, 4to.

SHERLOCK, Thos., bp. of London : Discourses preached at the Temple Church, and on Several Occasions. . . . 4 vols.
Oxf., 1812, 8vo.

SHERLOCK, William, dean of St. Paul's : A ser. preached before the . . . H. of C. . . . 1691/2 . . . Lon., 1692, 4to.

A sermon preached at the Temple Church . . . 1692.
Lon, 1692, 4to.

The Charity of Lending without Usury . . . in a sermon before the . . . Ld. Mayor . . . Lon., 1692, 4to.

A ser. preached before the Queen . . . 1691/2.
Lon., 1692, 4to.

SHERMAN, John : A Greek in the Temple : Some Common-places delivered in *Trinity Colledge* Chapell in *Cambridge*, upon Acts xvii, part of the 28 verse . . . Camb., 1641, 4to.

SHUTE, Nathaniel : Corona Charitatis. . . . A Sermon Preached in Mercers Chappell, *May 10, 1625*. Lon., 1626, 4to.

SIBBS, Rich. : Light from Heaven . . . In foure Treatises.
Lon., 1638, 4to.

An Exposition of the Third Chapter of the Epistle of St. *Paul* to the Philippians : Two Sermons of Christian Watchful-nesse [and other sers.]. Lon., 1639, 4to.

Beames of Divine Light Breaking forth from severall places of holy Scripture . . . In xxi Sermons . . .
Lon., 1639, 4to.

The Beasts Dominion . . . The Rvine of Mysticall Jericho

. . . The Vnprosperous Bvilder . . . The Svccessfvll Seeker . . . [and other sermons—11 in all—issued by Arthur Jackson]. Lon., 1639, 4to.

Bowels Opened : Or, a Discovery of the Neare and Deare Love, *Union* and *Communion* betwixt Christ, and the Chvrch . . . Delivered in divers Sermons on . . . Canticles. Lon., 1641, 4to.

The Glorious Feast of the Gospel . . . in diverse Sermons. Lon., 1650, 4to.

SIBTHORPE, Robt. : A Covnter-Plea to an Apostates Pardon. A ser. preached at Paules Crosse . . . 1617. Lon., 1618, 4to.

Apostolike Obedience Showing the Duty of Subiects to pay Tribute and Taxes to their Princes . . . Lon., 1627, 4to.

SIMPSON, Sydrach : Reformations Preservation . . . [before H. of C.]. Lon., 1643, 4to.

A ser. preached . . . before sundry of the H. of C. Lon., 1643, 4to.

SMALLWOOD, Geo. : Ἔργον ψεύδους καὶ Μισθὸς ἀληθείας, Or, The Wicked Mans sad Disappointment, and the Righteous Mans Recompense ; Being a Sermon Preached . . . 1661, at the Solemn Funerals of the Right Worshipful Sir Abraham Raynardson. Lon., 1661, 4to.

SMITH, Henry : The Sermons . . . gathered into one volume. Lon., 1592.

[Contains ' A Preparative to Marriage ' and 35 sers.]

The Sermons . . . Together with other his Learned Treatises : All now gathered into one volume. Also the Life of the . . . Authour, by Tho. Fuller . . . Lon., 1675.

SMITH, John : Select Discourses . . . Lon., 1660, 4to.

SMITH, Miles, bp. of Gloucester : 16 Sermons . . . Lon., 1632, folio.

SOUTH, Robert : The Works . . . 7 vols. Oxf., 1823, 8vo.

SPALDING, John : A Sermon Preached before His Grace, George Earl of Melvil, Their Majesties High Commissioner, . . . In the Parliament House [i.e. in Edinburgh] . . . May 11, 1690. Edin., 1690, 4to.

Synaxis Sacra ; or, A Collection of Sermons preached at several Communions. Edin., 1703, 4to.

SPARROW, Anthony, bp. of Norwich : A Rationale, Or Practical Exposition of the Book of Common-Prayer . . . With his Caution to his Diocese . . . and His Famous Sermon of Confession and the Power of Absolution . . . [Ed. in 1721 by Samuel Downes]. Lon., 1722, 8vo.

SPARSTOWE, William : Englands Patterne . . . before both Houses of Parliament. Lon., 1643, 4to.

SPENCER, John (Master of C.C.C. Camb.) : The Righteous Ruler. A Sermon preached at St. *Maries* In Cambridge June 28, 1660 . . . Camb., 1660, 4to.

SPENSER, John (President of C.C.C. Oxford) : A Learned and Graciovs Sermon Preached at Pavles Crosse . . .
Lon., 1615, 4to.

SPRAT, Thos., bp. of Rochester : A Sermon preached before the King . . . 1676. Lon., 1676, 4to.

A sermon preached before the King at White-Hall, December . . . 1678. Lon., 1678, 4to.

A ser. preached before the King . . . Lon., 1678, 4to.

A ser. preached . . . at the Anniversary Meeting of the Sons of Clergy-men . . . Lon., 1678, 4to.

A ser. . . . before the Hble. H. of C. . . . January 30th, 1677/8. Lon., 1678, 4to.

A ser. preached before the Artillery Company of London.
Lon., 1682, 4to.

A ser. . . . before the King and Queen . . . 1690.
Lon., 1690, 4to.

Sermons Preached on Several Occasions. Lon., 1710, 8vo.

SQUIRE, John : A ser. preached at the Hertford Assises . . . 1616. Lon., 1617, 4to.

A ser. preached in Paules Church upon Saint Stevens day 1618. Lon., 1618, 4to.

Three Sermons Two of Them Appointed for the Spittle . . . [*Vid. supra* John Lynch.] Lon., 1637, 4to.

STAMPE, William : A ser. before his Maiestie at Ch. Ch. in Oxford . . . 1643. Lon., 1643, 4to.

STANDHOPE, Geo. : Sermons Preach'd Upon Several Occasions.
Lon., 1700, 8vo.

STAUNTON, Edmund : Phinehas zeal . . . before the H. of L. . . . 1644. Lon., 1645, 4to.

STERRY, Peter : The Spirit Convincing of Sinne . . . [before H. of C.] Lon., 1645, 4to.

The Clouds in which Christ Comes . . . [before H. of C.].
Lon., 1648, 4to.

The Teachings of Christ in the Soule . . . a sermon before the Hble. H. of Peers . . . Lon., 1648, 4to.

The Comings Forth of Christ . . . [To Parl.] 1649.
Lon., 1650, 4to.

England's Deliverance From the Northern Presbytery, . . . A Thanksgiving Sermon . . . Nov. 5, 1651 . . . Before . . . Parliament. Lon., 1652, 4to.

The Way of God with His People . . . [before the Peers].
Lon., 1657, 4to.

A Discourse of the Freedom of the Will.

Lon., 1675, large 4to.

The Rise, Race, and Royalty of the Kingdom of God in the Soul of Man. Opened in several Sermons upon *Matthew* 18. 3. As Also The Loveliness & Love of Christ Set forth In several other Sermons upon *Psal.* 45, v, 1, 2 . . .

Lon., 1683, 4to.

STILLINGFLEET, Edward, bp. of Worcester : The Works . . . 6 vols. Lon., 1710, folio.

[Vol. i contains ' Fifty Sermons . . .' Lon., 1707.]

STRATFORD, Nicholas, bp. of Chester : A Dissuasive from Revenge. Lon., 1684, 4to.

STRONG, William : A ser. preached before the Hble. H. of C. . . . 1645. [No title-page, only sermon-top.] — 4to.

The day of Revelation . . . [before H. of C.].

Lon., 1645, 4to.

The Commemoration . . . of Mercy . . . [before H. of C.].

Lon., 1646, 4to.

The Vengeance of the Temple . . . a sermon . . . 1648.

Lon., 1648, 4to.

A Voice from Heaven . . . a Sermon at Pauls . . . 1653.

Lon., 1654, 4to.

STUART, Rich. : Three Sermons Preached By the Reverend, and Learned Dr. *Richard Stuart*, Dean of St. *Pauls* . . . *To which is aded* [*sic*], A fourth Sermon, Preached by the Right Reverend . . . Samvel Harnsnett, Lord Arch-Bishop of *Yorke*. Lon., 1656, 12mo.

SUDBURY, John : A Sermon Preached At the Consecration of [Gilbert Sheldon to the Bishopric of London and of four other bishops] . . . 28. *October*, 1660.

Lon., 1660, 4to.

SUTTON, Thomas : Englands Second Summons. A Sermon preached at Paules Crosse . . . 1615 . . . Lon., 1615, 4to.

SWIFT, William : A Sermon preached at the Funerall of . . . Mr. Thomas Wilson, in his owne Church . . . in Canterbury . . . 1621. Lon., 1622.

[This ser. is alluded to by Swift, Dean of St. Patrick's in the anecdotes of his family—*Vid.* Sheridan's ' Life of Dr. Swift,' Lon., 1734, p. 546.]

TAYLOR, Francis : Gods Covenant the Churches Plea . . . [before H. of C.]. Lon., 1645, 4to.

TAYLOR, Jeremy, bp. of Down and Connor : A Sermon Preached in Saint Maries Church in Oxford. Vpon the Anniversary of the Gunpowder-Treason. Oxf., 1638, 4to.

ENIAYTOΣ. A Covrse of Sermons For All the Sundaies of the Year . . . Lon., 1653 (sixes), sm. fol.

The Whole Works . . . With a Life of the Author, and a Critical Examination of his Writings, by the Rt. Rev. Reginald Heber, D.D. . . . Revised and Corrected by the Rev. Chas. Page Eden, M.A. 10 vols. [Vols. iv and viii contain sermons.] Lon., 1847–52, 8vo.

TAYLOR, Nathaniel : Pray for the Peace of Jerusalem. A Visitation sermon preached at Gainsborough . . . 1691.
Lon., 1691, 4to.

A Funeral Sermon on the Decease of the Reverend Mr. Rich. Mayo . . . 1695. Lon., 1695, 4to.

A Funeral Sermon Occasioned by the Sudden Death of the Reverend Mr. Nath. Vincent. Lon., 1697, 4to.

A Funeral Sermon Occasioned by the Death of the Lady Lane.
Lon., 1699, 4to.

TAYLOR, Thomas : A Mappe of Rome . . . Preached in fiue Sermons on occasion of the Gunpowder Treason . . .
Lon., 1620, 4to.

TEMPLE, Thomas : Christ's Government . . . a ser. before the Hble. H. of C. . . . Lon., 1642, 4to.

TENISON, Thomas, archbp. of Canterbury : A Ser. against Self-Love . . . before the . . . H. of C. . . . 1689.
Lon., 1689, 4to.

A Sermon Concerning the Wandering of the Mind in God's Service. Preached before the Queen . . . February 15, 1690/1. . . . Lon., 1691, 4to.

A sermon preached at the Anniversary Meeting of the Clergymens Sons . . . 1691.

TERRY, Edward : ΨΕΥΔΕΛΕΥΘΕΡΙΑ ! or Lawlesse Liberty . . . [before H. of C.]. Lon., 1646, 4to.

THOMAS, William : A Vindication of Scripture and Ministry.
Lon., 1657, 4to.

THORNDIKE, Herbert : The Theological Works . . . [Library of Anglo-Catholic Theol.] 6 vols. Oxf., 1844 *et seq.*, 8vo.

THOROWGOOD, Thomas : Moderation Ivstified . . . [before H. of C.] . . . 1644. Lon., 1645, 4to.

TILLINGHAST, John (fifth monarchy man) : Demetrivs his Opposition to Reformation. Lon., 1642, 4to.

Mr. Tillinghasts Eight Last Sermons. Lon., 1655, 8vo.
[The first ser. is entitled : ' The Fifth Kingdome or King-dome of Christ . . .']

TILLOTSON, John, archbp. of Canterbury : The Works . . . containing Fifty-four Sermons and Discourses . . . Together with the Rule of Faith . . . Lon., 1696, folio.

The Works . . . Containing Two Hundred Sermons and

Discourses . . . Published from the Originals by Ralph Barker, D.D., Chaplain to his Grace.   2 vols.
Lon., 1717, folio.

TOMBES, John : Iehovah Iireh . . .   Lon., 1643, 4to.

TORSHEL, Sam. : The Palace of Justice . . . before H. of C.
Lon., 1646, 4to.

TRAHERNE, Thomas : Christian Ethicks : Or Divine Morality.
Lon., 1675, 8vo.

TRAY, Richard : The Right Way of Protestantism . . .
Lon., 1643, 4to.

TRIMNELL, Charles, bp. of Winchester : A ser. preached in the Cathedral Church of Norwich . . . 1697.   Lon., 1697, 4to.

TUCKNEY, Anthony : The Balme of Gilead . . . A ser. preached before . . . the Hble. H. of C.   Lon., 1643, 4to.
Forty Sermons . . .   Lon., 1676, 4to.

TURNER, Bryan : Testimonium Jesu . . . A ser. preached before . . . the Ld. Mayor . . .   Lon., 1681, 4to.

TURNER, Francis, bp. of Ely : A ser. preached before the King on the 30th of January 1680/1.   Lon., 1681, 4to.
A ser. preached before the King in the Cathedral Church of Winchester . . . 1683.   Lon., 1683, 4to.
A ser. preached before the King, on Easter-Day, 1684.
Lon., 1684, 4to.
A ser. preached at the Anniversary Meeting of the Sons of Clergy-Men . . . 1684.   Lon., 1685, 4to.
A ser. preached before their Majesties K. James II and Q. Mary, at their Coronation . . . April 23, 1685 . . .
Lon., 1685, 4to.

UDALL, Ephraim : The Good of Peace . . . a sermon preached in the Cathedrall Church of S. Paul . . . 1642.
Lon., 1642, 4to.

USSHER, James, archbp. of Armagh : The Whole Works . . . Edited by Charles Richard Elrington, D.D.   16 vols.
[Vol. xiii contains sermons.]   Dublin., 1847, 8vo.

VALENTINE, Thomas : A ser. preached to the Hble. H. of C. . . .
Lon., 1643, 4to.

VENNING, Ralph : A Warning to Backsliders . . . Delivered in a sermon at Paules, before the . . . Ld. Mayor . . .
Lon., 1654, 4to.
Mercies Memorial . . . in a sermon before the . . . Ld. Mayor . . . the 5th of November, 1656.   Lon., 1657, 4to.
Things Worth thinking on . . . Together with a sermon entituled the Beauty of Holiness.   2nd ed.   Lon., 1665, sm. 8vo.
The Dead Instructing the Living : Or, Mr. Ralph Venning's Sick-bed Studies.   In III Sermons.
Lon., 1675, 12mo.

(Reprints) : The Saddest Thing in the World. (Howe's Reprints, No. 1.) Lon., no date (paper), 8vo.
Light from Heathen Lamps. (Howe's Reprints, No. 3.)
Lon., no date (paper), 8vo.
VINES, Richard : Sermons Preached upon several Publike and Eminent Occasions . . . Collected into one Volume.
Lon., 1656, 4to.
[Includes 'Calebs Integrity,' 1642, 'Magnalia Dei ab Aquilone,' 1646, 'The Authors, Nature, and Danger of Heresie,' 1646, and other sers. preached before H. of C., and separately published shortly after their 'occasion.']
WAGSTAFFE, Thos. the elder (Nonjuror) : A sermon preached at Stowe . . . 1683. Lon., 1683, 4to.
A ser. preach'd before the Rt. Hble. the Ld. Mayor . . . 1684. Lon., 1685, 4to.
A sermon . . . 1685. Lon., 1685, 4to.
A sermon . . . in St. Mary le Bow . . . 1687.
Lon., 1688, 4to.
WAKE, William, archbp. of Canterbury : An exhortation to Mutual Charity and Union Among Protestants . . .
Lon., 1689, 4to.
A sermon preached before the Hon. H. of C. . . .
Lon., 1689, 4to.
Sermons and discourses on Several Occasions.
Lon., 1690, 8vo.
A sermon preached before the Queen at Whitehall . . . M.D.C. XCI. Lon., 1691, 4to.
. . . A sermon . . . Upon the . . . Death of . . . Queen Mary . . . Lon., 1695, 4to.
WALKER, Anthony : The True Interest of Nations a sermon . . . at the Lent Assizes at Chelmsford . . . 1690/1.
Lon., 1691, 4to.
WALKER, Geo. : A sermon preached before the Hon. H. of C. . . . 1644. Lon., 1645, 4to.
WALLIS, John (Savilian Professor of Geometry, Oxford) : Theological discourses . . . And III Sermons Concerning the Blessed Trinity . . . [with other sermons].
Lon., 1695, 4to.
WARD, John : A sermon preached before the Hon. H. of C. . . .
Lon., 1645, 4to.
WARD, Sam. : A Coal from the Altar . . . a sermon preached at a general Visitation at Ipswich. Lon., 1615.
WARD, Seth, bp. of Salisbury : A Discourse of Toleration.
Lon., 1668, 4to.
The Christians Victory over Death. A sermon at the

29

Funeral of the most Honourable George [Monck] Duke of Albemarle . . . 1670.   Lon., 1670, 4to.

A Sermon Against the Anti-Scripturists. Also Another concerning the *Sinfulness, Danger,* and *Remedies* of Infidelity. Preached at White-Hall.   Lon., 1670, 8vo.

An Apology for the Mysteries of the Gospel . . . a sermon . . . 1672/3.   Lon., 1673, 4to.

WARREN, John : Mans Fury Subservient to God's Glory . . . [before Parl.] 1656.   Lon., 1657, 4to.

WATSON, Rich. : A sermon Touching Schisme . . . at St. Maries in Cambridge.   Camb., 1642, 4to.

WATSON, Thos. : God's Anatomy Upon Man's Heart. Or a sermon preached by Order of the Hon. H. of C. . . .
                    Lon., 1649, 4to.

The Saint's Delight. To which is annexed a Treatise of Meditation.   Lon., 1657, 8vo.
    [The vol. containing the foregoing also contains ' An Appendix to the Former Discourses,' and ' Christs Loveliness, Or, A Discourse setting forth the Rare Beauties of the Lord Jesus . . .']

The Godly Man's Picture . . .   Lon., 1660, 8vo.

WEBB, Rich. : Foure Sermons. The two first . . . by Robert Cleaver. The two last of Christs Love and Life . . . by Richard Webb.   Lon., 1613, 4to.

WHICHCOTE, Benjamin : Select Sermons . . . [Pref. by Lord Shaftesbury, author of the ' Characteristics.']
                    Lon., 1698, 8vo.

WHINCOP, John : Israels Tears for Distressed Zion . . . [before H. of L.].   Lon., 1645, 4to.

Gods Call to Weeping and Mourning . . . [before H. of C.] . . . 1644.   Lon., 1646, 4to.

WHITAKER, Jeremiah : Eirenopolis, Christ the Settlement of Unsettled Times . . . [before H. of C.].   Lon., 1642, 4to.

The Christians Hope Triumphing . . . [before H. of L.].
                    Lon., 1645, 4to.

The Christians great design on earth . . .   Lon., 1645, 4to.

The Danger of Greatnesse . . . [before Lords and Commons] . . . 1645.   Lon., 1646, 4to.

WHITBY, Dan. : Three Sermons preached at Salisbury.
                    Lon., 1683, 4to.

Sermons on the Attributes of God.   2 vols.   Lon., 1710, 8vo.

XII Sermons Preach'd at the Cathedral Church of Sarum.
                    Lon., 1726, 8vo.

WHITE, Francis, bp. of Ely : Londons Warning by Jerusalem. A sermon preached at Pauls Crosse on Mid-Lent Sunday last.   Lon., 1619, 4to.

The Workes of . . . John White . . . Together with a Defence of the Way to the True Church, in answer to a Popish Treatise written by T.W.P. entituled White Died Blacke. By Francis White . . .   Lon., 1624, folio.

WHITE, John : *Vid*. foregoing.
[There are two sermons—one at the Spittle, Easter 1613, the other on the anniversary of the King's accession, 1615.]

WHITE, John (' the patriarch of Dorchester ') : The Troubles of Jerusalem's Restauration . . . 1645.   Lon., 1646, 4to.

WHITE, Nath. : The Pastors Charge and Care . . .
                                        Lon., 1645, 4to.

WILDE, Geo., bp. of Derry : A Sermon preached . . . in St. Maries Oxford, before the Great Assembly of the Members of the Hon. H. of Commons . . .
                                        Oxf., 1643, 4to.

WILKINS, John, bp. of Chester : A sermon preached before the King . . . March, 1668/9.   Lon., 1669, 4to.
A sermon preached before the King . . . February 1669/70.
                                        Lon., 1670, 4to.
[XV] Sermons Preached Upon Several Occasions.
                                        Lon., 1682, 8vo.
[These are 15 additional sers. to ' Sermons preached upon several occasions before the King at Whitehall,' Lon., 1677, 8vo, which contains those noted above, and one other.]

WILKINSON, Henry : A Sermon Against Lukewarmnesse in Religion . . . 1640.   Lon., 1641, 4to.
Miranda, Stupenda . . .
[A Thanksgiving sermon to the H. of C. 1646, for the surrender of Oxford.]   Lon., 1646, 4to.

WILLAN, Edward : Six Sermons . . .   Lon., 1651, 4to.

WILLIAMS, Griffith, bp. of Ossory : Several Sermons on Solemn Occasions . . .   Lon., 1665, 4to.

WILLIAMS, John, archbp. of York : A Sermon of Apparell, Preached before the King's Maiestie . . . 1619.
                                        Lon., 1620, 4to.
Great Britains Solomon. A Sermon preached at the Magnificent Funerall, of the most high and mighty King James . . . 1625.   Lon., 1625, 4to.
A sermon preached in the Collegiate Church of S. Peter in Westminster . . . 1625 [before H. of L.].   Lon., 1628, 4to.
Perseuerantia Sanctorum. A Sermon . . . Preached before the Lords of the Parliament . . . 1628.   Lon., 1628, 4to.

WILSON, Thomas : Jerichoes Down-Fall . . . [before H. of C.] . . . 1642.   Lon., 1643, 4to.

WILSON, Thomas, bp. of Sodor and Man : The Works . . . ed.
 by John Keble.   Oxf., 1847–63, 8vo.
   [Vols. ii and iii contain 99 sermons ; vol. v contains the
 ' Sacra Privata.']
WOODCOCKE, Francis : The Two Witnesses . . . in several
 sermons.   Lon., 1643, 4to.
 Joseph Paralleled by the present Parliament . . . [before H.
 of C.] . . . 1645.   Lon., 1646, 4to.
 Lex Talionis . . . [before H. of C.] . . . 1645.
                                           Lon., 1646, 4to.
WORSHIP, William : Earth raining upon Heaven. A Sermon
 . . . at the Assises . . . at Nottingham . . . 1614.
                                           Lon., 1614, 4to.
 The Patterne of an Invincible Faith. A Sermon preached at
 Paules Crosse . . . 1616.   Lon., 1616, 4to.
WORTHINGTON, John : Select Discourses . . . With the Author's
 Character by Archbishop Tillotson.   Lon., 1725, 8vo.
WRIGHT, Abraham : Five Sermons, In Five several Styles ; Or
 Waies of Preaching.   Lon., 1656, 8vo.
   [Being actual sermons of bishop Andrewes and bishop
 Hall, with three others—" the 3rd in Dr. Maine and Mr.
 Cartwrights' way, the 4th in the Presbyterian, and the last
 in the Independent way "—parodies by Wright.]

E. CRITICISM : WORKS (MAINLY CONTEMPORARY)
CONTAINING REFLECTIONS ON THE SEVEN-
TEENTH-CENTURY SERMON

BAKER, Thos. : Reflections Upon Learning, Wherein is shewn
 the Insufficiency Thereof, in severall Particulars. In order
 to evince the Usefulness and Necessity of Revelation.
 [Pub. anonymously.]   Lon., 1700, 8vo.
BAXTER, Rich. : *Gildas Salvianus*, or the Reformed Pastor, 1st ed.
 1655, in ' The Practical Works . . . In Four Volumes
 . . .'   Lon., 1707, folio.
BLACKWALL, Anthony : The Sacred Classics Defended and
 Illustrated : Or, An Essay Humbly Offer'd towards Proving
 the Purity, Propriety, *and* True Eloquence of the Writers
 of the New Testament. . . . 2 vols.   Lon., 1737, 8vo.
BOLOE, Thos. : Rhetorick Restrained, Or, Dr. *John Gauden*
 . . . His Considerations of the Liturgy of the Church of
 England considered and clouded.   Lon., 1660, 4to.
BOYLE, Robt. (the Hon.) : Some Considerations Touching the
 Style of the H. Scriptures . . .   Lon., 1661, 8vo.

BURNET, Gilbert, bp. of Salisbury: A Discourse of the Pastoral Care . . . The Third Edition, with a new Preface suited to the present Time . . .   Lon., 1713, 8vo.

CERTAINE CONSIDERATIONS touching the better pacification and *Edification of the Church* of England : *Dedicated to* his most Excellent Majestie.   Lon., 1640, 4to.

DELL, Wm. : The Tryal of Spirits. Testified from the Word of God to the University-Congregation in *Cambridge* . . . Whereunto is added A plain and necessary confutation of divers Errors Delivered by Mr. Sydrach Simpson In a Sermon preached to the same Congregation the last Commencement there, *Anno* 1653. Wherein (among other things) is declared . . . That Humane Learning is not a preparation appointed by *Christ*, either for the right understanding or right teaching the *Gospel*.   Lon., 1653, 4to.

A Plain and Necessary Confvtation of divers gross and Antichristian Errors, Delivered To the *Vniversity*, Anno 1653. By Mr. *Sydrach Simpson*.   Lon., 1654, 4to.

EACHARD, John : Works. Viz. I. The *Grounds* and *Occasions* of the *Contempt* of the CLERGY . . . 11th ed.
                                        Lon., 1705, 8vo.

? A Free and Impartial Enquiry . . .   Lon., 1673, 12mo.[1]

FENELON, F. de la M. : Dialogues Concerning Eloquence . . . Translated from the French, and illustrated with Notes and Quotations ; by William Stevenson, M.A. . . .
                                        Lon., 1722, 8vo.

FORDYCE, David : Theodorus : A Dialogue Concerning the Art of Preaching. By Mr. David Fordyce, Late Professor of Philosophy in the Marischal College of *Aberdeen*. . . . The Second Edition. To which is added, A Sermon on the Eloquence of the Pulpit.   Lon., 1753, 8vo.

FOWLER, Edward, bp. of Gloucester : The Principles and Practices Of certain Moderate Divines of the Church of *England*, (greatly mis-understood), Truly Represented and Defended . . . In A Free Discourse between two Intimate Friends. In two parts.   Lon., 1670, 8vo.

FRIENDLY DEBATES : A Friendly Debate between a Conformist and a Non-Conformist. 5th ed.   Lon., 1669, 8vo.

A Continuation of the Friendly Debate.   Lon., 1669, 8vo.
[Both by Simon Patrick, bp. of Ely.]

GEREE, John : The Character of an old English Puritan, or Non-Conformist.   Lon., 1646, 4to.

GLANVILL, Joseph : An Essay Concerning Preaching . . . 2nd ed.   Lon., 1703, 8vo.

[1] Attributed to Eachard by Brit. Museum Catalogue.

A Seasonable Defence of Preaching. And the Plain Way of it. 2nd. ed. Lon., 1703, 8vo.

GOOD ADVICE to the Pulpits . . . Lon., 1687, 4to.

MARTIN, Edward : Doctor Martin, Late Dean of Ely, His Opinion [Concerning various theological & ecclesiastical controversies.] Together, With his Character of divers English Travellers, in the time of the Late Troubles. Communicated by five pious and learned Letters in the time of his Exile. Lon., 1662, 12mo.

NICHOLLS, Wm. : Gulielmi Nicholsii Presbyteri Defensio Ecclesiæ Anglicanæ . . . Lon., 1707 (sixes).

A Defence of the Doctrine and Discipline of the Church of England . . . 3rd ed. Lon., 1720, 8vo.

PARKER, Sam., bp. of Oxford : A Brief Account of the New Sect of Latitudinarians : Together with some Reflections upon the New Philosophy. Lon., 1669, 4to.

PATRICK, Simon, bp. of Ely : A Discourse of Profiting By Sermons. Lon., 1684, 4to.

PHILLIPS, John : A Satyr Against Hypocrites. [1st ed. 1655.] Lon., 1677, 4to.

Speculum Crape-Gownorum . . . new Foyl'd with Reflections On some of the late High-Flown Sermons . . . Lon., 1682, 4to.

Speculum Crape-Gownorum, The Second Part . . . Lon., 1682, 4to.

ROLLIN, Charles : The Method of Teaching and Studying The Belles Lettres . . . With Reflections on Taste ; and Instructions with regard to the Eloquence of the Pulpit, the Bar, and the Stage . . . Translated from the French. Lon., 4 vols. (4th ed.), 1749, 8vo.

SCOTCH PRESBYTERIAN ELOQUENCE, The : Or the Foolishness of their Teaching Discovered from their Books, Sermons, and Prayers . . . 3rd ed. with additions. Lon., 1719, 8vo.

SEDGWICK, Joseph : Ἐπίσκοπος Διδακτικός Learning's Necessity to an Able Minister of the Gospel. Lon., 1653, 4to.

SEPPENS, Robt. : Rex Theologus The Preachers Guard and Guide In the Didactical Part of his Duty. Or, A Vindication, shewing that the King's Majesty's Letter to the late L. Archbishop of Canterbury [i.e. Chas. II's " Directions concerning Preachers," 1662] is most Conformable to the judgment and Practice of Antiquity. Lon., 1664, 4to.

TRAVERS, Walter : Ecclesiasticæ Disciplinæ, Et Anglicanæ Ecclesiæ Ab Illa Aberrationes, Plena è verbo Dei, & dilucida explicatio. Excvdebat Adamvs de Monte. 1574.

A Fvl And Plaine Declaration of Ecclesiastical Discipline ovt of the VVord of God, and of the declining of the Chvrch of England from the same. Geneva, 1580.

[Englished by Cartwright at Geneva ; First ed. published in England, 1574.]

WALLIS, John : The Occasional Miscellany, in Prose and Verse. Consisting of A Variety of Letters, Written originally to a Young Gentleman Who Design'd to go into Holy Orders : With a Specimen of . . . Sermons . . . 2 vols.
Newcastle-upon-Tyne, 1748, 4to.

WARD, Seth, bp. of Salisbury : Vindiciæ Academiarum Containing, Some briefe Animadversions upon Mr. Websters Book, Stiled, The Examination of Academies. [Pub. anonymously.] Oxf., 1654, 4to.

WEBSTER, John : The Saints Guide, Or, Christ the Rule, and Ruler of Saints. Lon., 1654, 4to.
Academiarum Examen, Or the Examination of Academies.
Lon., 1654, 4to.

F. LIVES, DIARIES AND MEMOIRS (CONTEMPORARY)

AUBREY, John : ' Brief Lives,' chiefly of Contemporaries, set down . . . between the years 1669 and 1696. Edited from the Authors MSS. By Andrew Clark. 2 vols.
Oxf., 1898, 8vo.

BAILLIE, Robt. : Letters and Journals of Robert Baillie, A.M. Principal of the University of Glasgow. M.DC.XXXVII–M.DC.LXII. Edited . . . By David Laing, Esq. 3 vols.
Edin., 1841–42, 8vo.

BARKSDALE, Clement : Memorials of Witty Persons.
Lon., 1661, 12mo.

A Remembrancer of Excellent Men. Lon., 1670, 8vo.
[Both being mainly ' lives ' of leading seventeenth-century divines, e.g. Walton's ' Hooker,' &c.]

BARLOW, William, bp. of Lincoln : The Svmme and Svbstance of the Conference . . . at *Hampton Court* January 14, 1603. Lon., 1604, 4to.

BARWICK, John : ʼIEPONIKHΣ Or The Fight, Victory, and Triumph of S. Paul. Accommodated To the Right Reverend . . . Thomas [Morton] Late L. Bishop of Duresme, In a Sermon Preached at his Funeral . . . 1659. Together With the Life of the said Bishop. Lon., 1660, 4to.

BARWICK, Peter : Vita *Johannis Barwick*, S.T.P. . . . A Petro Barwick, M.D. . . . Conscripta . . . Lon., 1721, 8vo.

BAXTER, Rich. : Reliquiæ Baxterianæ : or, Mr. Richard Baxter's Narrative of The Most Memorable Passages of his

Life And Times Faithfully Publish'd from his own Original
Manuscript, By Matthew Sylvester. Lon., 1696, folio.

BEDELL, William, bp. of Kilmore, [Lives of] : A Character of
Bishop Bedell [By Nicholas Bernard, dean of Kilmore].
Lon., 1659, 4to.

The Life of William Bedell, D.D. . . . By bp. Burnet.
Lon., 1685, 4to.

Speculum Episcoporum : or the Apostolique Bishop, being
Memoir of the Life and Episcopate of Dr. William Bedell
. . . By his son-in-law, the Rev. Alex. Clogy, M.A. . . .
Printed for the first time . . . from the original MS. . . .
Ed. by W. Walter Wilkins. Lon., 1862, 8vo.

Two Biographies . . . With a Selection of his Letters and
An Unpublished Treatise. Edited With Notes and Index
By E. S. Shuckburgh . . . Camb. Univ. Press, 1902.
[Being ' Life' by Wm. Bedell and ' Life' by Clogie.]

BIRCH, Thos. : The Life of the Most Rev. Dr. John Tillotson
. . . Compiled chiefly from his Original Papers and Letters.
Lon., 1752, 8vo.

BRAMSTON, John (Sir) : The Autobiography . . . Now First
Printed from the Original MS. [Camden Soc.]
Lon., 1845.

BURNET, Gilbert, bp. of Salisbury : History of His Own Time.
2 vols. Lon., 1724–34, folio.

BURTON, Thos. : Diary of . . . Member in the Parliaments of
Oliver and Richard Cromwell, from 1656 to 1659 . . .
Edited and Illustrated by John Towill Rutt. 4 vols.
Lon., 1828, 8vo.

CALAMY, Edmund : An Historical Account of My Own Life,
With Some Reflections On The Times I Have Lived In.
(1671–1731) . . . Edited and Illustrated With Notes,
Historical and Biographical. By John Towill Rutt.
2nd ed., 2 vols. Lon., 1830, 8vo.

CARTWRIGHT, Thos., bp. of Chester : The Diary of . . .[from
Aug. 1686 to Oct. 1687] Now First Printed from the
Original MS. [Camden Soc.] Lon., 1843, 4to.

CAVENDISH, Margaret (Duchess of Newcastle) : CCXI Sociable
Letters. Written by . . . The Lady Marchioness of Newcastle. Lon., 1664, folio.

CHAMBERLAYNE, Edward : Angliæ Notitia, Or the Present
State of England . . . Lon., 1669, 12mo.

The Second Part . . . Lon., 1671, 12mo.

CLARENDON, Edward, Earl of : The History of the Rebellion
and Civil Wars in England . . . Also his Life Written by
Himself . . . A New Edition. 1 vol.
Oxf. Univ. Press, 1843, 8vo.

CLARKE, Sam. : A General Martyrologie . . . Whereunto is added The Lives of Thirty-Two English Divines . . . [3rd ed.]   Lon., 1677, folio.
    [1st ed., 1659. The thirty-two 'lives' in this ed. are said to be " Corrected and Enlarged."]

CONWAY LETTERS : The Correspondence of *Anne, Viscountess Conway, Henry More*, and their Friends, 1642–1684, Collected . . . *&* Edited with a Biographical Account, by Marjorie Hope Nicolson.   Lon., 1930, 8vo.

DAVIES, Rowland, LL.D. (Very Rev.) : Journal . . . From March 8, 1688–9. To September 29, 1690. Edited . . . by Rich. Caulfield . . . For Camden Society.
                                                    Lon., 1857.

D'EWES, Simonds (Sir) : The Autobiography and Correspondence . . . ed. by James Orchard Halliwell, Esqr. . . . 2 vols.   Lon., 1845, 8vo.
    College Life in the Time of James the First, as Illustrated by an Unpublished Diary of Sir Symonds D'Ewes . . .
                                                    Lon., 1851, 8vo.
    The Journal of . . . Edited by Wallace Notestein.
                                      Yale Univ. Press, 1923.

ELLIS, Henry (Sir) : Original Letters of Eminent Literary Men of the Sixteenth, Seventeenth, and Eighteenth Centuries : With Notes and Illustrations . . . [Camden Soc.]
                                                    Lon., 1843.

EVELYN, John : Memoirs Illustrative of The Life and Writings of John Evelyn, Esq., F.R.S. . . . Comprising His Diary, From the Year 1641 to 1705–6. And a Selection of His Familiar Letters . . . Edited by William Bray, Esq. . . . [Reprint of 2nd ed.]   Lon., 1870, 8vo.

FEATLY, Daniel : Reason *and* Judgement : Or, Special Remarques Of the Life of the *Renowned* Dr. Sanderson, Late Lord Bishop of *Lincoln*.   Lon., 1663, 4to.

FELL, John, bp. of Oxford : The Life of The most Learned, Reverend and Pious Dr. H. Hammond. Lon., 1661, 8vo.

FOX, George : The Journal . . . Edited . . . by Norman Penney, F.S.A. 2 vols.   Camb., 1911, 8vo.

FRAMPTON, Robert, bp. of Gloucester : The Life of . . . Edited by T. Simpson Evans, M.A.   Lon., 1876, 8vo.

FULIGATIUS, Jacob : Vita Roberti Bellarminis Politiani . . . A Jacobo Fvligatio Soc. Jesv Italicè primum scripta : A Silvestro Petra Sancta eiusdem Soc Latinè reddita . . .
                                      Antwerp, 1631, 8vo.

GUMBLE, Thos. : The Life of General Monck . . .
                                                    Lon., 1671, 8vo.

HACKET, John, bp. of Lichfield : Scrinia Reserata : A Memorial

Offer'd to the Great Deservings of John Williams . . . Ld.
Archbishop of York.   Lon., 1693, folio.
HARRIS, William, D.D. : A Historical and Critical Account [of]
Hugh Peters.   After the Manner of Mr. Boyle.
                                        Lon., 1751, 4to.
HATTON : Correspondence of The Family . . . A.D. 1601–1704.
Edited by Edward Maunde Thompson.   2 vols.   [Camden
Soc.]   1878.
HAY, Andrew : The Diary of Andrew Hay of Craignethan
1659–1660.   Edited with Introduction and Notes, by
Alex. Geo. Reid, F.S.A.Scot.   [Scottish Hist. Soc.]
                                        Edin., 1901, 8vo.
HERBERT, Edward, Ld. of Cherbury : The Life . . . Written
by Himself.   Edited by Henry Morley, LL.D. . . .
                                        Lon., 1893, 8vo.
HEYLIN, Peter : Aerius Redivivus : Or, The History of the
Presbyterians . . . From the Year 1536, to the Year 1647.
                                        Oxf., 1670, folio.
Cyprianus Anglicus : Or, The History of the Life and Death
of . . . William [Laud] . . . Lord Archbishop of Canter-
bury.   Lon., 1671, folio.
HOLLES, Denzil, Lord : Memoirs . . . From the Year 1641
to 1648.   Lon., 1699, 8vo.
HOWELL, James : Epistolæ Ho-Elianæ . . . Edited by Joseph
Jacobs.   Lon., 1890, 8vo.
HOWIE, John : The Scots Worthies.   [Pref. to First Ed. signed
1775, but consists of ' lives ' collected from earlier sources.]
                                        Glasgow, no date, 8vo.
HUTCHINSON, Lucy : Memoirs of the Life of Colonel Hutchinson
. . . with Additional Notes by C. H. Firth . . .
                                        Lon., 1906, 8vo.
JOHNSTON, Arch. : Diary of Sir Archibald Johnston of Wariston
1632–1639.   Edited from the Original Manuscript, with
Notes and Introd., by Geo. Morison Paul, LL.D.
                                        Edin., 1911, 8vo.
KENNET, White, bp. of Peterborough : A Register and Chronicle
Ecclesiastical and Civil . . . From the Restauration of
King Charles II.   Lon., 1727, folio.
KIRKTON, James : The Secret and True History of the Church
of Scotland.   From the Restoration to the Year 1678.   By
the Rev. Mr. James Kirkton . . . Edited from the MSS.
by Chas. Kirkpatrick Sharpe, Esq.   Edin., 1817, sm. folio.
LAUD, William, Archbishop : The History of the Troubles and
Tryal . . .   Lon., 1695, folio.
LLOYD, David : Memoirs of the Lives, Actions, Sufferings &
Deaths of those Noble, Reverend, And Excellent Person-

ages, That Suffered . . . for the Protestant Religion . . . In our late Intestine Wars. From the Year 1637, to the Year 1660. And from thence continued to 1666 . . .
Lon., 1668, folio.

MANNINGHAM, John : Diary . . . 1602–1603. Edited from the Original Manuscript by John Bruce, Esq., And presented to the Camden Society by William Tite. [Camden Soc.]
Lon., 1868.

MATHER, Cotton : Magnalia Christi Americana : Or, The Ecclesiastical History of New-England, From . . . 1620 unto . . . 1698. Lon., 1702, folio.

NALSON, John : An Impartial Collection of the Great Affairs of State, From the Beginning of the Scotch Rebellion In the Year MDCXXXIX. To the Murther of King Charles I. . . . 2 vols. Lon., 1682–3, folio.

NELSON, Robert : The Life of Dr. George Bull, Late Lord Bishop of St. Davids. Lon., 1713, 8vo.

ORTON, Job : Memoirs of the Life, Character, and Writings, of the late Rev. Philip Doddridge . . . A New Edition.
Lon. 1819, 8vo.

PARR, Richard : The Life Of the Most Reverend Father in God, James Usher . . . Lon., 1686, folio.

PATRICK, Symon : The Auto-Biography . . . Now First Printed from the Original Manuscript. Oxf. 1839, 8vo.

PEPYS, Sam. : The Diary (1659–1669). Ed. by Lord Bray-brooke. Lon., 1889, 8vo.

POPE, Walter : The Life of the Right Reverend Father in God Seth [Ward] . . . With a Brief Account of Bishop Wilkins, Mr. Lawrence Rooke, Dr. Isaac Barrow, Dr. Tubervile, and others. Lon., 1697, 8vo.

PRIDEAUX, Humphrey : Letters of . . . to John Ellis . . . Edited by Edward Maunde Thompson. For Camden Society. Lon., 1875.

ROUS, John : Diary of John Rous, Incumbent of Santon Downham, Suffolk, From 1625 to 1642. Edited by Mary Anne Everett Green . . . [Camden Soc.] 1856.

RUSHWORTH, John : Historical Collections . . . Beginning The Sixteenth Year of King JAMES, Anno 1618. And ending the Fifth Year of King CHARLES, Anno 1629.
Lon., 1659, folio.
Historical Collections Abridg'd and Improv'd. 6 vols.
Lon., 1703–8, 8vo.

RUTHERFORD, Sam. : Letters . . . With a sketch of his Life . . . by the Rev. Andrew Bonar, D.D. 3rd. ed.
Edin., 1894, 8vo.

THORESBY, Ralph : The Diary . . . (1677-1724). Now first published from the original Manuscript by the Rev. Joseph Hunter, F.S.A. 2 vols. Lon., 1830, 8vo.

TONG, Wm. : Some Memoirs of the Life and Death of the Reverend Mr. John Shower, Late Minister of the Gospel in *London* . . . Together with his Funeral Sermon Preach'd at Old-Jury, July 10, 1715. Lon., 1716, 8vo.

VERNEY, F. P. & M. M. : Memoirs of the Verney Family During the Seventeenth Century Compiled from the Papers . . . at Claydon House . . . 2nd ed., 2 vols.
Lon., 1904, 8vo.

WALKER, John : An Attempt Towards Recovering an Account of the Numbers and Sufferings of the Clergy of the Church of England . . . Sequester'd, Harrass'd, Ec. in the late Times of the Grand Rebellion : Occasion'd by the Ninth Chapter (now the Second Volume) of Dr. *Calamy's Abridgment* of the Life of Mr. Baxter. Lon., 1714, folio.

WALTON, Isaac : The Lives of Dr. John Donne, Sir Henry Wotton, Mr. Rich. Hooker, Mr. Geo. Herbert [with the life of Dr. Robt. Sanderson.] Lon., 1898, 8vo.

WARD, Rich. : The Life of the Learned and Pious Dr. Henry More. Lon., 1710, 8vo.

WARTON, Thos. : The Life And Literary Remains of Ralph Bathurst, M.D., Dean of Wells and President of Trinity College in Oxford. Oxf., 1761, 8vo.

WHITELOCK, Bulstrode : Memorials of the English Affairs From the Beginning of the Reign of Charles the First To the Happy Restoration of King Charles the Second . . . A New Edition in Five Volumes. Oxf., 1853, 8vo.

WHITELOCK, James, Kt. : Liber Famelicus . . . Edited by John Bruce, Esq., V.P.S.A. [Camden Soc.] Lon., 1858.

WINSTANLEY, Wm. : The Loyall Martyrology, or Brief Catalogues and Characters of the most Eminent Persons who Suffered for their Conscience during the late times of Rebellion . . . As Also Dregs of Treachery : With its Catalogue and Characters of those Regicides . . . with others of that Gang most eminent for Villainy.
Lon., 1665, 8vo.

WOOD, Anthony : The Life and Times of . . . 1632–1695, described by Himself. Collected from His Diaries and Other Papers. By Andrew Clark, M.A. 4 vols.
Oxf. Historical Soc., 1891–95, 8vo.

WORTHINGTON, John : The Diary and Correspondence . . . Edited by James Crossley. 3 vols. 1847, 1855, 1886, 8vo.
[Being vols. xxii, xxxvi and cxiv of the Chetham Soc. Publications.]

YONGE, Walter : Diary . . . Written at Colyton and Axminster, Co. Devon. From 1604 to 1628. Edited by George Roberts . . . [Camden Soc.]   Lon., 1848.

G. MODERN LIVES AND STUDIES OF THE SEVEN-TEENTH-CENTURY CHURCH AND DIVINES

BAILEY, John Eglinton : The Life of Thomas Fuller.
                                                    Lon., 1874, 8vo.
BARCLAY, Robert : The Inner Life of the Religious Societies of the Commonwealth . . .   Lon., 1876, 8vo.
BLOOM, J. H. : Pulpit Oratory in the Time of James the First, Considered, And Principally Illustrated by Original Examples.   Lon., 1831, 8vo.
CLARKE, T. E. S., and FOXCROFT, H. C. : A Life of Gilbert Burnet :
   I. Scotland 1643–1674. By T. E. S. Clarke, B.D.
   II. England 1674–1715. By H. C. Foxcroft.
                                                    Camb., 1907, 8vo.
CLASSIC PREACHERS, The, of the English Church : Lectures delivered at St. James's Church in 1877. With an Introduction by John Edward Kempe. [Being studies of Donne, Barrow, South, Beveridge, Wilson and Butler.]
                                                    Lon., 1877, 8vo.
COLERIDGE, S. T. : Notes on English Divines . . . ed. by the Rev. Derwent Coleridge, M.A. . . . 2 vols.
                                                    Lon., 1853, 8vo.
ELIOT, T. S. : For Lancelot Andrewes . . .   Lon., 1928, 8vo.
FAUSSET, Hugh I'Anson : John Donne. A Study in Discord.
                                                    Lon., 1924, 8vo.
FRERE, W. H. : A History of the English Church . . . Vol. v. In the Reigns of Elizabeth and James I. (1558–1625).
                                                    Lon., 1904, 8vo.
GOSSE, Edmund : The Life and Letters of John Donne . . . 2 vols.   Lon., 1899, 8vo.
   Jeremy Taylor (E.M.L. Series).   Lon., 1903, 8vo.
HUTTON, W. H. : A History of the English Church . . . Vol. vi. From the Accession of Charles I to the Death of Anne (1625–1714) . . .   Lon., 1903, 8vo.
JACQUINET, P. : Des Prédicateurs Du XVIIᵉ Siècle. Avant Bossuet . . .   Paris, 1885, 8vo.
KNIGHT, Sam. : The Life of Dr. John Colet . . . (New ed.)
                                                    Oxf., 1823, 8vo.
MACLEANE, Douglas : Lancelot Andrewes and the Re-action. (New ed.)   Lon., 1910, 8vo.
MACNICOL, D. C. : Master Robert Bruce.   Edin., 1907, 8vo.
MASSON, David : The Life of John Milton : narrated in con-

nexion with the Political, Ecclesiastical and Literary History of His Time. Camb., 1859, 8vo.

OTTLEY, R. L. : Lancelot Andrewes. [Leaders of Religion Series] Lon., 1894, 8vo.

OVERTON, J. H. : Life in the English Church (1660–1714) . . . Lon., 1885, 8vo.

The Nonjurors. Their Lives, Principles and Writings. Lon., 1902, 8vo.

PARKER, Irene : Dissenting Academies in England. Camb., 1914, 8vo.

PATTISON, Mark : Isaac Casaubon (1559–1614). 2nd ed. Oxf., 1892, 8vo.

POWICKE, Fred. J. : A Life of the Reverend Richard Baxter, 1615–1691. Lon., 1924, 8vo.

The Reverend Richard Baxter Under the Cross 1662–1691. Lon., 1927, 8vo.

The Cambridge Platonists. A Study. Lon., 1926, 8vo.

' SCOTTISH DIVINES, 1505–1872 ' : St. Giles Lectures, 3rd Series. [For Lectures on *Archbp. Leighton* by Principal John Tulloch and *Sam. Rutherford* by the Rev. Pearson McAdam Muir, D.D.] Edin., 1883, 8vo.

STEPHEN, James (Sir), K.C.B. : Essays in Ecclesiastical Biography. [1st ed. 1849.] New ed., Lon., 1872, 8vo.

TODD, Henry John : Memoirs of the Life and Writings of the Rt. Rev. Brian Walton, D.D. . . . Editor of the London Polyglot Bible. With Notices of his Coadjutors in that Illustrious Work ; of the Cultivation of Oriental Learning in this Country, Preceding and during their Time. 2 vols. in one. Lon., 1821, 8vo.

TULLOCH, John : Rational Theology and Christian Philosophy in England in the Seventeenth Century. 2 vols. Edin., 1872, 8vo.

WHITING, C. E., D.D., B.C.L. : Studies in English Puritanism from the Restoration to the Revolution 1660–1688. S.P.C.K., 1931, 8vo.

WHYTE, Alex. : Lancelot Andrewes and his Private Devotions, A Biography, a Transcript, and an Interpretation. Lon., 1896, 8vo.

WILLMOTT, Robt. Aris : Bishop Jeremy Taylor, His Predecessors, Contemporaries and Successors. Lon., 1847, 8vo.

WORDSWORTH, Christopher : Ecclesiastical Biography : Or Lives of Eminent Men, Connected with the History of Religion in England . . . 6 vols., 2nd ed. Lon., 1818, 8vo.

[Consists of reprints of celebrated ' Lives ' such as Cavendish's ' Life of Wolsey,' Walton's ' Lives,' &c., with annotations.]

H. WORKS OTHER THAN SERMONS, LIVES OR 'ARTES CONCIONANDI,' BY SEVENTEENTH-CENTURY DIVINES, WITH A BEARING UPON THIS STUDY

? ALLESTREE, Rich. : The Practice of Christian graces, or the Whole Duty of Man . . . 1st ed. Lon., 1658, 8vo.
The Works of the Learned and Pious Author of the Whole Duty of Man. Oxf., 1684, folio.
AMES, William : The Marrow of Sacred Divinity . . .
Lon., 1642, 12mo.
ANDREWES, Lancelot, bp. of Winchester : Preces Privatae, edited by the Rev. F. E. Brightman. Lon., 1903, 8vo.
BATES, William : The Harmony of the Divine Attributes . . .
Lon., 1674, 4to.
Considerations of the Existence of God . . . 2nd ed.
Lon., 1677, 8vo.
The Divinity of the Christian Religion Proved by the Evidence of Reason, and Divine Revelation.
Lon., 1677, 8vo.
BAXTER, Rich. : One Sheet against the Quakers.
Lon., 1657, 8vo.
A Second Sheet for the Ministry Iustifying our Calling Against Quakers, Seekers, and Papists. Lon., 1657, 8vo.
Catholick Theologie : . . . In Three Parts . . .
Lon., 1675, fol.
BAYLY, Lewis, bp. of Bangor : The Practice of Piety.
Lon., 1842, 8vo.
BERNARD, Rich. : The Isle of Man, or The Legal Proceeding in Man-shire against Sinne . . . 1st ed. 1627.
Lon., 1668, 12mo.
BROUGHTON, Hugh : The Works of the Great Albionean Divine [ed. by John Lightfoot]. Lon., 1662, folio.
CAMBRIDGE PLATONISTS, THE : Being Selections from the Writings of Benjamin Whichcote, John Smith, and Nathanael Culverwel With [an] Introduction by E. T. Campagnac.
Oxf., 1901, 8vo.
CHEYNELL, Francis : Chillingworthi Novissima, Or, The Sicknesse, Heresy, Death and Buriall of William Chillingworth. Lon., 1644, 4to.
CUDWORTH, Ralph : The True Intellectual System of the Universe : The First Part . . . Lon., 1678, folio.
CULVERWEL, Nathanael : Of the Light of Nature. A Discourse . . . Edited by John Brown, D.D., Edinburgh. With a critical Essay on the Discourse by John Cairns, M.A., Berwick-on-Tweed. Edin., 1857, 8vo.

DONNE, John : Pseudo-Martyr Lon., 1610, 4to.
BIAΘANATOΣ . . . Lon., 1644, 4to.
Essayes in Divinity . . . Lon., 1651, 12mo.
Paradoxes & Problems . . . Lon., 1652, 12mo.
The Poems . . . Edited with Introductions and Commentary,
by Herbert J. C. Grierson. 2 vols. Oxf., 1912, 8vo.
Donne's Sermons. Selected Passages with an Essay by
Logan Pearsall Smith. Oxf., 1920, 8vo.
Devotions Upon Emergent Occasions . . . Edited by John
Sparrow. Camb., 1923, 8vo.
EDWARDS, Thos. : The First and Second Part of Gangræna :
Or a Catalogue and Discovery of many of the Errors,
Heresies, Blasphemies and pernicious Practices of the
Sectaries. . . . The third Edition, corrected and much
Enlarged. Lon., 1646, 4to.
The third Part of Gangræna. Or, a new and higher
Discovery of the Errors, Heresies, Blasphemies . . . of the
Sectaries of these times. . . . Lon., 1646, 4to.
GLANVILL, Joseph : Scepsis Scientifica . . . an Essay of the
Vanity of Dogmatizing . . . Lon., 1665, 4to.
ΛΟΓΟΥΘΡΗΣΚΕΙΑ : Or A Seasonable Recommendation, and
Defence of Reason in the Affairs of Religion . . .
Lon., 1670, 4to.
LIGHTFOOT, John : The Whole Works . . . Edited by the Rev.
John Rogers Pitman . . . 13 vols. Lon., 1825, 8vo.
[Vol. xiii contains ' The Journal of the Proceedings of
the Assembly of Divines From January 1, 1643, to December
31, 1644.']
MORE, Henry : An Explanation of the Grand Mystery of
Godliness . . . Lon., 1660 (sixes), large 8vo.
A Collection of Several Philosophical Writings . . .
(' Antidote against Atheism,' ' Enthusiasmus Triumphatus,'
' Letters to Des-Cartes,' ' Conjectura Cabbalistica,' &c.)
Lon., 1662 (sixes), large 8vo.
A Modest Enquiry into the Mystery of Iniquity, the First
Part . . . Lon., 1664 (sixes), large 8vo.
Divine Dialogues . . . Lon., 1668, 8vo.
NORRIS, John (of Bemerton) : An Idea of Happiness in a Letter
to a Friend . . . Lon., 1683, 8vo.
The Theory and Regulation of Love . . . 2nd ed.
Lon., 1694, 8vo.
Treatises upon Several Subjects. Lon., 1697, 8vo.
An Essay Towards the Theory of the Ideal or Intelligible
World. Part I. Lon., 1701, 8vo.
Part II. Lon., 1704, 8vo.
A Practical Treatise Concerning Humility. Lon., 1707, 8vo.

A Treatise Concerning Christian Prudence . . .
Lon., 1710, 8vo.

A Collection of Miscellanies : Consisting of Poems, Essays . . .
Lon., 1710, 8vo.

PARKER, Sam., bp. of Oxford : A Free and Impartial Censure of the Platonick Philosophie . . . 2nd ed. Oxf., 1667, 8vo.

A Discourse of Ecclesiastical Politie . . . Lon., 1670, 8vo.

A Demonstration of the Divine Authority of the Law of Nature . . . Lon., 1681, 4to.

PEARSON, John, D.D. : An Exposition of the Creed.
Lon., 1659, 4to.

RUST, Geo., bp. of Dromore : A Discourse of the Use of Reason in Matters of Religon . . . Translated into English, with Annotations upon it, by Hen. Hallywell. Lon., 1683, 4to.

The Remains . . . collected and published by Henry Hallywell. Lon., 1686, 4to.

SCOUGAL, Henry : The Life of God in the Soul of Man . . . With a preface by Gilbert Burnet . . . 11th ed.
Lon., 1775, 12mo.

A New Ed. [Edited by Jas. Cooper, D.D.]
Aberdeen, 1892, 8vo.

SPRAT, Thomas, bp. of Rochester : The History of the Royal-Society of London . . . Lon., 1667, 4to.

TRAHERNE, Thos. : Centuries of Meditations . . . Edited by Bertram Dobell. Lon., 1908, 8vo.

WILKINS, John, bp of. Chester : The discovery of a New World : Or A Discourse tending to prove, that . . . there may be another habitable World in the Moone . . . 3rd impression. Lon., 1640, 8vo.

A Discourse concerning a New Planet . . . Lon., 1640, 8vo.

An Essay Towards a Real Character, and a Philosophical Language. . . . Lon., 1668, 4to.

Of the Principles and Duties of Natural Religion. Two Books. Lon., 1678, 8vo.

Mathematical Magick . . . Lon., 1680, 12mo.

K. OTHER SEVENTEENTH-CENTURY BOOKS AND WRITINGS CONSULTED

AUSTIN, William : Devotionis Augustinianæ Flamma, or Certaine Devout, Godly, and Learned Meditations . . .
Lon., 1635 (sixes), sm. folio.

BIBLIOTHECA HEINSIANA Sive Catalogus Librorum, Quos . . . collegit Vir Illustris Nicolaus Heinsius, Dan. Fil.
Leyden, 1682, 12mo.

30

CRAIK, Henry : English Prose Selections, Vol. ii. Sixteenth
Century to the Restoration. Lon., 1904, 8vo.
Vol. iii. Seventeenth Century . . . Lon., 1906, 8vo.
CROFT, Herbert, bp. of Hereford : The Naked Truth . . . [For
chapter ' Concerning Preaching.'] Lon., 1675, 4to.
DREXILIUS, Jerome : Aurifodina Artium et scientiarum omnium
Excerpendi Solertia, *Omnibus litterarum amantibus monstrata.*
Antwerp, 1641, sm. 8vo.
EVERARD, Robt. (Capt.) : An Epistle to the General Congrega-
tions Of the Non-Conformists . . . The Second Edition,
containing . . . Additions and Enlargement.
No place, 1664, 8vo.
FELTHAM, Owen : Resolves Divine Morall and Politicall.
[Temple Classics ed.] [§ XX ' Of Preaching.']
Lon., 1904, 8vo.
GALES, Theophilus : The Covrt of the Gentiles : Or A Discourse
touching the *Original* of Human Literature, both *Philologie*
and *Philosophie*, from the Scriptures and Jewish Church
. . . 3 vols. Oxf., 1669–77, 4to.
GREVILLE, Fulke : Certaine Learned And Elegant Workes . . .
Written in his Youth . . . Lon., 1633, 4to.
The Remains . . . Being Poems of Monarchy and Religion.
Lon., 1670, 8vo.
HARVEY, Gabriel : Marginalia Collected and Edited by G. C.
Moore Smith.
Shakr. Head Press : Stratford-on-Avon, 1913, 8vo.
HERBERT, Geo. : The Works . . . in Prose and Verse.
Edited by Robert Aris Willmott. [For ' A Priest to the
Temple,' chap. vii, " The Parson Preaching."]
Lon., 1854, 8vo.
HUARTE, John : Examen de Ingenios. The Examination of
mens Wits. . . . Translated out of the Spanish tongue by
Mr. Camillo Camilli. Englished out of his Italian by R. C.
Esquire. Lon., 1616, 4to.
L'ESTRANGE, Roger : The Dissenter's Sayings . . . Published in
their own Words . . . The second ed. . . . Lon., 1681, 4to.
MARVEL, Andrew : Mr. Smirke : Or, The Divine in Mode . . .
No place, 1676, 4to.
PEACHAM, Henry : The Compleat Gentleman 1634 With an
Introduction by G. S. Gordon. [Tudor & Stuart Lib.]
Oxf., 1906, 8vo.
SELDEN, John : Table Talk . . . Newly Edited for the Selden
Society by the Rt. Hon. Sir Frederick Pollock, Bt., K.C.,
D.C.L. Lon., 1927, 8vo
WOTTON, Henry (Sir) : Reliquiæ . . . The second *Edition.*
with large *Additions.* Lon., 1654, 4to.

L. MISCELLANEOUS

I. BACKGROUND

(a) Classical Rhetoric

DE QUINCEY, Thos. : The Collected Writings . . . by David Masson. Vol. x. [Contains ' Rhetoric ' : ' A Brief Appraisal of the Greek Literature . . . Pt. II. The Greek Orators.'] . . . Lon., 1897, 8vo.

DILL, Samuel : Roman Society in the Last Century of the Western Empire. 2nd. ed. Lon., 1905, 8vo.

DUFF, J. Wright : A Literary History of Rome in the Silver Age From Tiberius to Hadrian. Lon., 1927, 8vo.

HAARHOFF, Theodore : Schools of Gaul : A Study of Pagan and Christian Education In the Last Century of the Western Empire. Oxf. Univ. Press, 1920, 8vo.

HATCH, Edwin : The Influence of Greek Ideas and Usages Upon the Christian Church. (Hibert Lectures, 1888 : Lecture IV, ' Greek & Christian Rhetoric.') Lon., 1890, 8vo.

JEBB, R. C. : Attic Orators . . . 2 vols. Lon., 1886, 8vo.

(b) Mediæval Thought and Preaching

BARING-GOULD, Sabine : Post-Mediæval Preachers. Lon., 1865, 8vo.

NEALE, J. M. : Mediæval Preachers and Mediæval Preaching, A Series of Extracts translated from the Sermons of the Middle Ages . . . Lon., 1856, 8vo.

OWST, G. R. : Preaching in Mediæval England. Camb., 1926, 8vo.

TAYLOR, Henry Osborne : The Mediæval Mind. A History of the Development of Thought and Emotion in the Middle Ages. 2 vols. Lon., 1911, 8vo.
The Classical Heritage of the Middle Ages. 3rd ed. New York, 1911, 8vo.

(c) Contemporary Education

MALLET, Charles E. (Sir) : A History of the University of Oxford ; Vol. ii. The Sixteenth and Seventeenth Centuries . . . Oxf., 1924, 8vo.

MULLINGER, J. Bass : Cambridge Characteristics in the Seventeenth Century : or the Studies of the University and their Influence on the Character and Writings of the Most Distinguished Graduates during that Period . . . Lon. and Camb., 1867, 8vo.
The University of Cambridge. 3 vols. Camb. Univ. Press, 1873–1911, 8vo.

SHAKESPEARE'S ENGLAND : An Account of the Life and Manners
of his Age.   2 vols.   Oxf., 1917, 8vo.
[Vol. i, chap. viii : ' Education,' by Sir John E. Sandys,
Litt.D.   Chap. ix : ' Scholarship,' by the same writer.]
SHAKESPEARE'S ENGLAND, Life in : A Book of Elizabethan
Prose.   Compiled by John Dover Wilson, M.A.
Camb., 1920, 8vo.
[Chap. iv : ' Education,' § 2 The Grammar School ;
§ 3 The University.]
WATSON, Foster : ' The Curriculum and Text-books of English
Schools in the First Half of the Seventeenth Century,' in
Transactions of the Bibliographical Society.   Vol. vi, Part II,
Oct. 1900–March 1902.   Lon., 1903.
The English Grammar Schools to 1660 : their Curriculum
and Practice.   Camb. Univ. Press, 1908, 8vo.

II. PREACHING : MODERN STUDIES

BLAIKIE, W. Garden, D.D. : . . . For the Work of the Ministry.
Lon., 1873, 8vo.
[Chap. iv gives a short sketch of ' the History of the
Christian Pulpit ' ; chap. viii treats of ' Pulpit Style.']
The Preachers of Scotland from the Sixth to the Nineteenth
Century.   Twelfth Series of Cunningham Lectures . . .
Edin., 1888, 8vo.
[Useful for historical information about Knox, Bruce and
seventeenth-century preachers.]
BROADUS, J. A., D.D. : A Treatise on the Preparation and
Delivery of Sermons . . .   Lon., 1898, 8vo.
BROWN, John, D.D. : Puritan Preaching in England . . .
[Being the Lyman-Beecher Lectures on Preaching at Yale
University, 1899.]   Lon., 1900, 8vo.
DARGAN, E. C., D.D. : A History of Preaching . . . 2 vols.
Vol. i. : ' From the Apostolic Fathers to the Great Re-
formers ' ;   Vol. ii : ' From the Close of the Reformation
Period to the End of the Nineteenth Century . . .'
Lon., 1905, 8vo.
DODDRIDGE, Philip, D.D. : The Works . . . Vol. v.   [Lectures
on Preaching . . .]   Lon., 1804, 4to.
[Gives interesting comments on the style of various
Puritans and C. of E. preachers of ' the last age,' and after
1700.]
DYKES, J. Oswald, D.D. : The Christian Minister and his
Duties . . .   Edin., 1908, 8vo.
[Pt. III : ' The Minister as Preacher ' deals interestingly
with Hyperius of Marburg and the application of Classical
Rhetoric to Christian Preaching.]

FAIRBAIRN, Patrick, D.D. : Pastoral Theology : A Treatise on the Official Duties of the Christian Pastor.
Edin., 1875, 8vo.
[Chaps. iv. and v. deal with preaching.]
PHELPS, Austen, D.D. : The Theory of Preaching.
Lon., 1882, 8vo.
SMITH, David, D.D. : The Art of Preaching.
Lon., no date, 8vo.
VINET, Alexander : Homiletics ; or, The Theory of Preaching. Translated from the French by the Rev. A. R. Fausset, M.A. 2nd ed. Edin., 1858, 8vo.

III. CONTEMPORARY CRITICISM [1]

DRYDEN, John : Essays . . . Selected and Edited by W. P. Ker, M.A. . . . 2 vols. Oxf., 1900, 8vo.
SMITH, G. Gregory : Elizabethan Critical Essays. 2 vols.
Oxf., 1904.
SPINGARN, J. E. : Critical Essays of the Seventeenth Century. 3 vols. Oxf., 1908, 8vo.

IV. CHARACTER-WRITERS

CHARACTERS from the Histories and Memoirs of the Seventeenth Century. With an Essay on the Character . . . by David Nichol Smith . . . Oxf., 1918, 8vo.
CHARACTER WRITINGS of the Seventeenth Century. Ed. by Henry Morley, LL.D. . . . Lon., 1891, 8vo.
[Includes Overbury, Hall, Earle, Breton, Butler and others.]
EARLE, John, bp. of Salisbury : Microcosmography : or A Piece of the World Discovered ; in Essays and Characters . . . A new ed. . . . by Philip Bliss . . . Lon., 1811, 8vo.
HALL, Joseph, bp. of Exeter : Characters of Vertues and Vices. In two Bookes. Lon., 1608.
LA BRUYÈRE, Jean de : Œuvres de . . . Nouvelle Edition. . . . Par M. G. Servois. [Tome Premier and Tome Second, for ' Les Caractères . . .'] Paris, 1865, 8vo.
LAW, William : Characters and Characteristics Selected and Arranged with an Introd., by Alexander Whyte, D.D. 2nd ed. Lon., 1893, 8vo.
OVERBURY, Thos., Kt. : The Miscellaneous Works . . . Now first collected . . . by Edward F. Rimbault, LL.D.
Lon. (Lib. of old Authors), 1890, 8vo.

---

[1] Works more directly concerned with criticism of the sermon are listed in Section E, *supra*.

THEOPHRASTUS : The Characters, Greek Text with English trans. by R. C. Jebb. Lon. and Camb., 1870, 8vo.
English Literature and the Classics. [For ' Theophrastus and his Imitators,' by G. S. Gordon.] Oxf., 1912, 8vo.

V. FRENCH SERMONS CONSULTED

BOSSUET, Jacques : Oraisons Funèbres . . . Avec une Introduction . . . par Alfred Rebellian . . . Onzième edition . . . Paris, 1920, 8vo.
Sermons Choisis . . . Notices, Annotations par Henri Clouard. Paris, no date, 8vo.
BOURDALOUE, Louis : Sermons du Père Bourdaloue, de la Compagnie de Jesus . . . 13 vols. Paris, 1750, 8vo.
DAILLÉ, Jean : Melange De Sermons, Prononcés . . . à Charenton pres de Paris. [Première Partie.] Amsterdam, 1658, 8vo.
DRELINCOURT, Charles : Sermon Svr La Paix . . . Charenton, 1649, 4to.
Sermon Svr Le Delvge. Charenton, 1651, 4to.
Le Pastevr Fidele, Ov Sermon Svr Les Actes Des Apôtres . . . Prononcé . . . Octobre 1658. [Pref. signed, Nov. 1658.] Charenton ?, 1658, 4to.
DU MOULIN, Pierre : Premiere Decade de Sermons . . . Geneva, 1643, 8vo.
Decade de Sermons. Avec Traité de Melchisedec. Sedan, 1653, 8vo.
MASSILLON, Jean Baptiste : Sermons et Morceaux Choisis . . . Paris, 1844, 8vo.
VILLEMAIN, François : Massillon, Fléchier, Mascaron : Oraisons Funèbres, Précédées de L'Essai sur L'Oraison Funèbre. Paris, no date, 8vo.

VI. ENGLISH SERMONS OF THE EARLY EIGHTEENTH CENTURY [1]

BRADBURY, Thos : God's Empire over the Wind, Consider'd in a Sermon . . . Lon., 1704, 8vo.
Five Anniversary Sermons Upon the Fifth of *November* ; the Day of our Happy Revolution. Lon., 1705, 8vo.
The Son of Tabeal. A Sermon Occasion'd by the French Invasion In Favour of the Pretender . . . Lon., 1708, 8vo.
BUTLER, Joseph, bp. of Durham : Fifteen Sermons Preached

---

[1] In some cases these are by preachers whose ' period ' fell at the very close of the seventeenth century, and whose earlier work is included in Section D, *supra*. In other cases early eighteenth-century sermons have been used for comparison. Where a preacher was well established by the end of the seventeenth century his later publications have been added to the earlier list.

at the Rolls Chapel . . . Edited by the Rt. Rev. J. H.
Bernard, D.D. . . .   Lon., 1913, 8vo.
HOADLY, Benjamin, bp. of Salisbury : A ser. preached on the
Eight of March, 1704/5 being the Anniversary Day of
Thanksgiving for the Queen's Accession to the Crown.
                                       Lon., 1705, 4to.
A ser. preached before the . . . Ld. Mayor . . .
[Origin of the Bangorian controversy.] Lon., 1705, 4to.
The Works . . . 3 vols.   Lon., 1773, folio.
HOLE, Matt. (Rector of Exeter Coll. 1716–30) : Practical
Discourses on All the Parts and Offices of the Liturgy.
                                       Lon., 1716, 8vo.
Practical Discourses upon All the Collects, Epistles, &c . . .
                                       Lon., 1716, 8vo.
Practical Discourses on the *Nature, Properties* and *Excellencies* of Charity . . . To which is prefix'd a Visitation
Sermon.   Oxf., 1725, 8vo.
HOUGH, John, bp. of Lichfield and Coventry : A ser. preached
before the Societies for Reformation of Manners . . . 1704.
                                       Lon., 1705, 4to.
Sermons and Charges . . . With a Memoir of his life by
Wm. Russell, B.D.   Oxf., 1821, 8vo.
SMALRIDGE, Geo. : Sixty Sermons . . .   Oxf., 1724, folio.
TRIMNELL, Chas., bp. of Winchester : A ser. preached in the
Cathedral-church of Norwich, September the 7th, 1704.
Being the Day of Thanksgiving . . . for the late Glorious
Victory . . . at Blenheim.   Norwich, 1704, 4to.
Episcopal Authority . . . [A ser. preached at Leicester 1707.]
                                       Lon., 1708, 4to.
A ser. preached at the Cathedral Church of St. Paul. Before
the Sons of the Clergy . . . 1707.   Lon., 1708, 4to.
A ser. preached at the Parish-Church of St. James's, Westminster . . . 1708.   Lon., 1708, 4to.
A ser. preached at St. Peter's Mancroft in Norwich . . .
1708.   Norwich, 1708, 8vo.
A ser. preached at the Parish-Church of St. James's, Westminster . . . 1708.   Lon., 1709, 4to.
WATTS, Isaac : The Works . . . Compiled by the Rev. Geo.
Burden. 6 vols.   Lon., 1810, 4to.

VII. STUDIES IN LIFE, THOUGHT AND LITERARY FORMS OF
THE SEVENTEENTH CENTURY

BUCHAN, John : Montrose.   Lon. (1928 ed.), 8vo.
CARTWRIGHT, Julia (Mrs. Henry Ady) : Madame. A Life of
Henrietta, Daughter of Charles I, And Duchess of Orleans.
                                       Lon., 1894, 8vo.

CROLL, Morris, W. : Euphues : The Anatomy of Wit. Euphues and His England. By John Lyly. Ed. by Morris W. Croll, Ph.D., and Henry Clemons, A.M.   Lon., 1916, 8vo.
' Attic Prose ' in the Seventeenth Century.   [Reprinted from ' Studies in Philology,' Vol. xviii, 2 April, 1921.]
Muret and the History of ' Attic ' Prose.
    [Reprinted from the ' Publications of the Modern Language Association of America,' Vol. xxxix, No. 2.]   1924.
Schelling Anniversary Papers.   New York, 1923, 8vo.
    [For ' Attic Prose : Lipsius, Montaigne, Bacon.']
GOSSE, Edmund : A History of Eighteenth Century Literature (1660–1780) . . .   Lon., 1922, 8vo.
GREENSLET, Ferris : Joseph Glanvill. A Study in English Thought and Letters of the Seventeenth Century.
                    Now York, 1900, 8vo.
GRIERSON, H. J. C. : Cross Currents in English Literature of the XVIIth Century. . . .   Lon., 1929, 8vo.
HUNT, John : Religious Thought in England from the Reformation to the End of Last Century . . . 3 vols.
                    Lon., 1873, 8vo.
MILLAR, John Hepburn : Scottish Prose of the Seventeenth and Eighteenth Centuries.   Glasgow, 1912, 4to.
NICHOLS, John : The Progresses, Processions, and Magnificent Festivities of King James the First . . . 4 vols.
                    Lon., 1828, 8vo.
RAMSAY, Mary P. : Les Doctrines Médiévales chez Donne. . .
                    Oxf., 1917, 8vo. (paper covers).
SIMPSON, Evelyn M. : A Study of the Prose Works of John Donne.   Oxf., 1924, 8vo.
SPECULUM RELIGIONIS : [for Study of Peter Sterry by V. de S. Pinto] . . .   Oxf., 1929, 4to.
WILLETT, Gladys E. : Traherne (An Essay).
                    Camb., 1919 (Boards).

VIII.   OTHER BOOKS USED

APHTHONIUS, Progymnasmata Rodolpho Agricola Phrisio interprete . . .   No place, 1540, 8vo.
BLAIR, Hugh : Sermons . . . 5 vols.   Lon., 1807–8, 8vo.
A CHRISTIAN Letter of certaine English Protestants . . . vnto that Reverend and learned man, Mr. R. Hoo (sic) requiring resolution in certaine matters of doctrine (which seeme to overthrow the foundation of Christian Religion, and of the church among vs) expreslie contained in his fiue bookes of Ecclesiasticall Pollicie [sic].   No place, 1599, 4to.
DRAYTON, Michael : Minor Poems, ed. by Cyril Brett.
                    Oxf., 1907, 8vo.

EMPSON, William : Seven Types of Ambiguity. Lon., 1930, 8vo.

GILLIES, John : Historical Collections Relating to Remarkable Periods of the Success of the Gospel, and Eminent instruments Employed in Promoting it. In Two Volumes. . . . Compiled by John Gillies One of the Ministers of Glasgow. Glasgow, 1754, 8vo.

GRIERSON, H. J. C. : Metaphysical Lyrics and Poems of the Seventeenth Century. Donne to Butler. Selected and ed. with an Essay . . . Oxf., 1921, 8vo.

GYFFORD, Geo. : A short Reply vnto the *last printed books of* Henry Barrow *and* John *Greenwood*, the chiefe ringleaders of our Donatists in England. Lon., 1591, 4to.

HEARNE, Thos. : Reliquiæ Hearnianæ : . . . Being Extracts from his MS. Diaries, Collected, With a few notes, By Philip Bliss. 3 vols. [Lib. of Old Authors.]
Lon., 1869, 8vo.

LETSOME, Sampson : The Preacher's Assistant, In Two Parts. A Series of the Texts of all the Sermons and Discourses Preached upon, and published Since the Restoration, to the Present Time. Part II. An Historical Register Of all the Authors in the Series, containing, A succinct View of their several Works . . . [Pref. dated Feb. 8, 1753.]
Lon., no date, 8vo.
[Unfortunately not always the earliest or best edition, but the most readily obtainable is cited.]

MURALT, Beat Ludwig : Letters sur Les Anglois et les François. . . . [No author's name or place of publication.] 1725, 8vo.

NASHE, Thos. : Christs Teares Over *Jersualem* [reprint of 1593 ed.] in the Works . . . Edited from the Original Texts By Ronald B. McKerrow. Text : vol. ii. Lon., 1904, 8vo.

SAINTSBURY, Geo. : A History of English Prose Rhythm.
Lon., 1912, 8vo.

SIMPSON, Percy : Shakespearean Punctuation.
Oxf., 1911, 8vo.

SKEAT, Walter : A Glossary of Tudor and Stuart Words . . . Collected by Walter W. Skeat. Edited with Additions by A. L. Mayhew. Oxf., 1914, 8vo.

SOUTHEY, Robt. : Common-Place Book . . . Edited by his son-in-law, John Wood Warter, B.D. Lon., 1849–51.

STEPHEN, Leslie : History of English Thought in the Eighteenth Century. 2 vols. Lon., 1875, 8vo.

STRONG, S. Arthur : A Catalogue of Letters And Other Historical Documents Exhibited in the Library at Welbeck. [For ' Advices ' of Duke of Newcastle to Charles II.]
Lon., 1903, 4to.

INDEX

[1] Wherever in this index *Taylor* occurs alone, *Jeremy Taylor* is intended.

31

32*

Stillingfleet's style to that of, 307 ; lack of plasticity in style of, 313 ; Birch on, 336 ; contemporary esteem for, 391

Sandys, Edwin, style of, 63

Savoy Conference, Baxter on Gauden's rhetorical speeches at, 78

schemata, 17th-cent. preoccupation with, 41 ; of Scholastics, resemblance to classical oratory, 42 ; derivation of, from Gorgias and Isocrates, and preservation in mediæval sermon, 59 ; interest in, in Vossius, 81 ; classical, imitation of, by mediæval and Anglo-Cath. preachers, 145 ; 145 *n.* ; imitation of mediæval, in vernacular preachers, 148 ; interest of Donne in, 187 ; 189 ; use of, by H. Smith, 210–11 ; effect of, on Adams' style, 223 ; South's censure of, 315 ; not invariable accompaniment of vivid preaching, 368

schematic, patterns, mediæval pursuit of, 63 ; writers, Hooker one of the, 65 ; fashion, Lever, Jewel, Adams, and Willan exemplars of, 89 ; effects, not characteristic of Anglo-Cath. preaching, 148 ; pattern, in Donne, 187 ; prose, transition from, to Jacobean directness, 222 ; features, freedom of Fuller from, 238–9 ; South's ability to be, 348 ; sermons of Adams and Hall, 365 ; sermon, the, among Calvinists, 367 ; preaching, and *Euphues*, 382

schemes, Hyperius on, 52 ; as sole end of rhetoric, 58

Scholastic[s], *schemata* of, and classical oratory, 42 ; disputations of, influence of, on sermon form, 60 ; Barrow's exhaustiveness as survival of their methods, 61 ; their method of disputation borrowed by later divines, 78 ; repudiation by Keckermann of multiple divisions of, 96 ; reading, Puritans and Anglo-Catholics equally familiar with ; argument against usury, H. Smith's use of, 201 ; speculation, Fuller's avoidance of, 237 ; question, a, how used by Donne and Taylor, 247 ; learning, J. Smith's avoidance of, in ordinary sermons, 291 ; *scholastical* sermon, by Pritchard, 308 ; *Scholasticism*, tyranny of logic in Commonwealth preaching similar to that under, 259 ; Puritan exegesis a survival of, 369 ; *the School*, Donne's familiarity with questions of, 183 ; 185–6 ; *Schoolmen*, familiarity of Puritan preachers with, 135 ; 135 *n.* ; H. King and parts of speech as stressed by, 170 ; allusions to, Playfere's additions of, to printed sermons, 171 ; Hall's many quotations from, 225 ; Taylor's preference for classical moralists to, 244 ; different use of, by Taylor and Andrewes, 245 ; Taylor's attitude to subtleties of, 253 ; Austin's knowledge of, 304

school[s], public, at Ashby-de-la-Zouch, Brinsley Master of, 32 ; Ipswich, Wolsey's Statutes for, 61 ; Merchant Taylors', annual themes at, 77 ; Dugard as Headmaster of, 80 ; St. Paul's, Erasmus' *concio* for, 101 ; Westminster, Hacket, protégé of Andrewes at, 164 ; Littleton, as successor of Busby at, 309

-books, Colet's list for St. Paul's, 70 ; Brinsley on those helpful in making themes, 72 ; Hoole on those helpful for themes, 79

of Theology, importance of, for style, 9 ; 130 ; 134 ; 135 ; preachers divided according to, in order to assess debt to, 136 ; attempt among preachers of Andrewes', to relate form and content, 154 ; excellent prose of Donne and Frank due to personality rather than to, 179 ; of Andrewes and Laud, difference of Donne from other preachers of, 181 ; attempts of, to govern preaching abandoned, 297 ; connection of, with rhetorical fashions, 348 ; influence of, on sermon forms ; relation of individual genius to, 398

Scotch Presbyterian Eloquence, examples in, due to *extempore* preaching, 17 ; on Herle's 'Tripus' as example of subdividing in sermons, 110 ; on unseemly metaphors, 372

Scougal, Henry, difference of, from contemporary Scots preachers, 267

Sedgwick, Joseph, defence by, of learned ministry against Dell and Simpson, 126–7

Selden, John, on logic and rhetoric in sermons, 78–9 ; Austin a friend of, 363

Claude on, 122–3 ; English, literary influence of, 125 ; importance of diversity of influences behind, 129–30 ; seldom purely a theme ; as result of subject and treatment rather than structure, 133 ; matter and manner of, due to temperament or school of thought, 134 ; *reformed*, of late 17th cent., due to taste of period ; as a literary rather than homiletical product, 136 ; facetiousness in, 141 ; mediæval, dramatic element in, and Anglo-Cath. preaching, 145 ; Anglo-Cath., composite character of, 147 ; *witty*, in course of construction, Playfere and Bloom and, 173 ; divisions of, illustrated by Bloom, 174 ; Anglo-Cath. reason for failure as prose, 175 ; simple post-Restoration, normal Anglican preaching basis of, 196 ; older Puritan, unexpected interests of ; Puritan habit in composition of, 207 ; Puritan, literary interest of, due to neglect of *methods*, 208 ; *characters* integral part of, in Adams, 213 ; *figure*, account of, 215–16 ; 216 *n.* ; *antithesis* in traditional setting of, 222 ; Gray's contribution to essay-form of, 269 ; Commonwealth period a kind of tiring-house for, 271–2 ; Puritan, as starting-point of plain prose, 276 ; rationalist contribution to, 276–7 ; *Platonic*, Culverwel's sermon as specimen of, 288 ; ordinary, J. Smith's country sermon as transition from college-exercise to, 291 ; simplified, Cudworth's sermon before Parliament as fusion of *Platonic* and, 297 ; plain Anglican, as used by Baxter till 1662, 308 ; plain Anglican, South's transformation of, 314 ; 17th-cent. Theology as determining factor in ; contribution of Camb. Platonists to ; plain, contemporary taste and, 348 ; evolutionary nature of, in 17th cent. ; as reflex of taste of period ; influence of theory and criticism on ; relation of, to contemporary prose style ; as an essay, 349 ; sectarian and literary criticism of, 349–50 ; tendency to neglect main ends of, 351 ; Anglo-Cath., un-literary criticism of ; *witty*, impossible substitutes proposed for, 352 ; *metaphysical*, decorative use of quotations in, 359 ; *metaphysical*, stylistic poverty of, 362 ; *metaphysical*, Eachard's and Glanvill's censure of, 364 ; plain, stages leading to, 365 ; varieties of, in 17th cent., 365 ; plain Anglican, difficulty of criticising ; few printed specimens of, 368 ; Baxter on requisite parts of, 370 ; Scriptural, and the Independents' plain sermon, 371 ; rationalistic, weakness of ; *metaphysical*, failure of *doctrinal* and, to attain flowing style ; rationalistic, dangerous fluency of, 375 ; post-Restoration, attack on lack of *doctrines* in, 376 ; emergence of, as literature in early 18th cent., 376–7 ; Latitudinarian, defence of, 377 ; as literature, early 18th-cent. tendency to regard as ; as chief literary influence of 17th cent. ; necessity for secular criticism of, 379 ; as norm of prose style, reason for, 380 ; as impetus to antiquated rhetorical fashions ; as main prose type, 381 ; paramount influence of, on style ; as index of contemporary taste, 382 ; great influence of, Davenant on, 385–6 ; influence of, Phillipps on, 385 *n.* ; sectarian plainness of, and reform of prose, 388 ; sectarianism as vicious influence on style of ; Glanvill's ideal for, applicable to all sects, 391 ; contribution of criticism of, to contemporary literary criticism, 395–6 ; doctrinal implications of, 397 ; post-Restoration condemnation of rhetoric unsuited to, 401

extempore, vogue of, 15 ; as an ideal ; Friars and, 17 ; Nairn on ; as a Restoration fashion, 20 ; as usual Anglican form in late 17th cent., 25 ; variation of published version from, 36–7

memoriter, use of, in Scotland ; vogue of, among Puritans ; remarks of Edwards on, 20 ; insistence of Puritans on, 21 ; Palmer's defence of ; French influence in favour of, 23 ; Nonconformists' use of, 25 ; Puritan partiality for, 26

written and read, advantage of, 15 ; 26 ; Andrewes ' XCVI Sermons ' as examples of, 16 ; Tillotson and, 17 ; importance of, in Reformation period, 17–18 ; 18 *n.* ; use of, by Sanderson and Hall, 18 ; divergence from, in publication, Bilson's evidence to, 19 ; Restoration attitude to ; censured by Monmouth at Cambridge, 23 ; influence of Puritan upbring-

*Made and Printed in Great Britain
by Hazell, Watson & Viney Ltd.
London and Aylesbury*